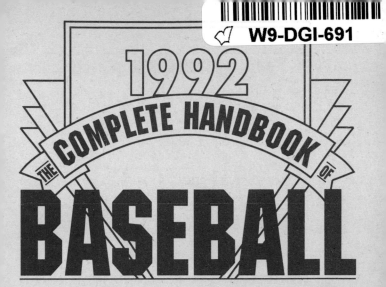

1992

THE COMPLETE HANDBOOK OF

BASEBALL

FOR THE SPORTS FAN . . .

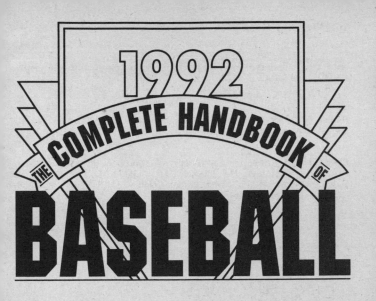

1992
THE COMPLETE HANDBOOK OF
BASEBALL

EDITED BY
ZANDER HOLLANDER

AN ASSOCIATED FEATURES BOOK

A SIGNET BOOK

ACKNOWLEDGMENTS

Courtesy of the free-agent circus, this 22nd edition of *The Complete Handbook of Baseball* needed jugglers extraordinaire and couldn't have been done without the high-wire performances of contributing editor Howard Blatt, stats whiz Lee Stowbridge, DH Eric Compton and the writers listed on the contents page. We also thank Fred Cantey, Linda Spain, Kevin Mulroy, Richie Sherwin, Phyllis Merhige, Katy Feeney, Susan Aglietti, the team publicity directors, Seymour Siwoff, the Elias Sports Bureau, MLB-IBM Information System, Dot Gordineer of Libra Graphics and Westchester Book Composition.

Zander Hollander

PHOTO CREDITS: Cover—Focus on Sports. Inside photos—Marc Blanchette, Ira Golden, Bob Haskell, David Liam Kyle, Jack Maley, Vic Milton, Rosemary Rahn, Mitch Reibel, Wide World, UPI and the major-league team photographers.

SIGNET
Published by the Penguin Group
Penguin Books USA Inc., 375 Hudson Street,
New York, New York 10014, U.S.A.
Penguin Books Ltd, 27 Wrights Lane,
London W8 5TZ, England
Penguin Books Australia Ltd, Ringwood,
Victoria, Australia
Penguin Books Canada Ltd, 10 Alcorn Ave.,
Toronto, Ontario, Canada M4V 3B2
Penguin Books (N.Z.) Ltd, 182-190 Wairau Road,
Auckland 10, New Zealand

Penguin Books Ltd, Registered Offices:
Harmondsworth, Middlesex, England

First Signet Printing, March, 1992
10 9 8 7 6 5 4 3 2 1

CONTENTS

Editor's Note: The material herein includes trades and rosters up to the final printing deadline.

STEPHEN KING'S FIELD OF DREAMS

By BOB HASKELL

"In 1958 the diamond shape of the infield had been defined not by limed basepaths but in ruts made by running feet. They had no actual bases, those boys who had played baseball here . . . but four pieces of dirty canvas were always kept under the loading bay behind the long brick building, to be ceremonially taken out when enough kids had drifted into the back lot to play ball, and just as ceremonially returned when the shades of evening had fallen thickly enough to end further play."

Stephen King, IT

Stephen Edwin King had settled into a black, overstuffed chair in a corner of his office in Bangor, Me. Stacked on his lap were a half-dozen books that people believed needed his autograph to be complete, just one of the routine tasks attendant to being a famous author known for his horror books and movies.

The other matter at hand on that pleasant afternoon last October was a labor of love—the baseball field that was King's brainchild and that was being built with $1 million of his money about a mile up Union Street from where he sat.

The beard that he grows for most winters, which he starts with the World Series, showed larger growths of white than it had in the past. The signing of the books, an interview with a book reviewer later in the afternoon and the next day's trip to New York were unavoidable demands on this workaholic writer who is 44 and at the peak of his game.

Bob Haskell, editor of the Midweek section for the Bangor Daily News *in Maine, was a sportswriter for the newspaper for 13 years. He has known Stephen King for more than 20 years.*

Stephen King prizes the Georgia clay in his infield.

But, it is baseball that keeps him young.

It has been his oasis and his escape for more than 30 years—since marveling over Don Larsen's perfect game during the 1956 World Series that he watched on a tiny black-and-white television when he was nine and living with his mother in Stratford, Conn.

Okay. It is no longer such a big secret that King is a baseball junkie; that he loved the Dodgers until they abandoned Flatbush; that he hates everything about the Yankees except for Larsen's perfect game; and that his feelings for the Red Sox fall somewhere into his emotional mix alongside family, marriage and sex.

King joins Seattle's Ken Griffey Jr. in Red Sox dugout.

So it should not be a surprise that King wanted to build a baseball field—as fine a baseball field as his money and considerable influence could build—in his adopted mid-Maine city.

Nor should it be a surprise that the field in Bangor is being compared to the field in Iowa that Ray Kinsella, a.k.a. Kevin Costner, fashioned on his farm in the movie *Field of Dreams*.

Some of the Maine natives have nicknamed King's enterprise the "Field of Screams." He does, after all, write better horror stories than he turns a double play.

"We need something on the West Side. Baseball is so important to the community. Adults will always come to see kids play as long as it's a little better than a sandbox," said King.

It all began with a conversation between King and his baseball companion Dave Mansfield, with whom he coaches a Senior League team in Bangor.

"I called him and asked him to come on over and help work on the field," said Mansfield, who was coaching a Little League team that included King's youngest son, Owen, in 1989. That team won the state championship.

"A lot of friendships have been developed by baseball," added Mansfield of the bond that has grown stronger as he and King have coached young teenagers.

"Baseball is like chess," Mansfield said. "You have to know what the next move will be. And you have to be able to execute it. Steve is pretty good at that. Our kids are taught to look ahead. He loves the kids who play and he understands what each is able to do or should be able to do."

King also understands that young people need a decent place to play. Therefore, the new field will be much better than a sandlot. That was obvious as it was being built of Georgia clay and Kentucky bluegrass last fall—a far cry from the rutted basepaths and dirty canvas bases of which King had written in *IT*.

The red and gold maple leaves surrounding Hayford Park were seasonal reminders of the World Series being played in distant stadiums and of a long winter before baseball would again be played in Bangor and at the University of Maine 15 miles north in Orono.

"Bangor is a Little League town," King said. "It has always been a Little League town and it will always be a Little League town. But when people get to junior high school, they start playing on fields that are just as big as the one in Atlanta. And those bigger fields around here are the pits.

"Dave Mansfield and I were raking up the field one day, trying to get ready for a Senior League game. We were out there in the mud. It was an impossible job. So I said, 'Let's build a Cadillac field that everybody can play on above Little League.' This field will be able to accommodate everybody up to college-level games."

That was the field that took shape last summer and during the fall—while the Red Sox were giving chase to the Blue Jays before settling for second in the American League East, while Butch Hobson was summoning up his resources for the 1992 season as the successor to Joe Morgan and while the Twins and the Braves were engaged in what could truly be called a Fall Classic.

King's field is being fashioned on a section of public park which separates one of the city's outdoor swimming pools, a covered hockey arena and a creative playground of swings, slides and wooden spires.

The field will be defined by:

• Dimensions of 330 feet down the foul lines, 375 feet in the power alleys, and 400 feet to straightaway center.

• Two hundred tons of porous Georgia clay, which dries quickly and grooms easily, as the top layer of the diamond.

• 115,000 square feet of durable Kentucky bluegrass sod covering the infield and the outfield.

• A grandstand for 1,500 fans that angles around the back of home plate.

• A 15-foot-wide warning track of pink stone dust from Maine's renowned Mt. Desert Island.

• A mile of four-inch drainage pipe beneath the soil so the field will dry quickly after a rain.

• A computer-driven, three-section sprinkler system featuring 41 sprinkler heads able to pop up and water the grass in the middle of the night during a late-summer dry spell.

• A lighting system meeting National Collegiate Athletic Association standards that will give the impression that this Little League city has acquired a minor-league team.

"Steve told me last May that he wanted a state-of-the-art baseball field," said sandy-haired Gary Crowell, a carpenter and contractor from Stoneham, Me., who has worked on King's homes since 1978.

"This field has been designed around a million-dollar budget," added Crowell, who was overseeing the construction. "We'll come in within five percent of that, one way or the other."

But a million dollars does not buy as much as it did when young Stephen King watched *The Millionaire* on his mom's tiny black-and-white television. It is not buying as much of a baseball field as he had originally hoped it would.

There is the matter of the press box. The original blueprints included a press box with a spired roof and three broadcast booths sitting above the center section of the seats, directly behind home plate, offering a panoramic view of the field.

But something had to give. According to Crowell, the priorities were quickly decided and simply stated. Put the money into the field—the diamond, the sprinklers and drain piping, the Georgia clay and Kentucky bluegrass.

The field comes first. The press box comes last. This field was being built for the players, not the greater glory of Stephen King.

King leaves no doubt about what he believes, of where he stands. His pronouncements are punctuated by his imposing, 6-4 stature and a Mr. Hyde appearance which makes him the most easily recognized author since Mark Twain.

You see him. You hear him. You listen.

"The two things that have surprised me the most this fall is that so many people believed Clarence Thomas over Anita Hill and that the Red Sox fired Joe Morgan. I don't think there was any need for it.

"Baseball giveth and baseball taketh away. The year 1986 was the worst of my life after the World Series," said King of the autumn the Red Sox came within one out of losing the American League championship and within one out of winning the World Series.

Earlier that season, King had been riled by a Bangor sportswriter's prediction that the Red Sox would be out of the running by Flag Day.

King was so sure his team was so much better than that prediction that he made a bizarre bet with the writer. The loser would eat crow, in the form of a chicken dinner, in his underwear in public on or around June 14. The winner would serve the crow.

By June 14, Flag Day, the Red Sox were leading their division by four games. On July 1, on the gazebo behind Bangor's statue of Paul Bunyan, King delighted in making the sportswriter "eat crow" before a couple of hundred spectators and several television cameras. King wore a tuxedo. The sportswriter wore his underwear. I will remember this story for a long time. I was the sportswriter.

"Baseball is my barometer. I reached the age of maturity when [the Red Sox] hired Morgan," said King. "That's when I felt I knew what I wanted to do with the rest of my life."

That's why his life was thrown a little off center when Morgan was fired following a solid, second-place finish in 1991. King is not a fan of Hobson, Morgan's replacement.

"Butch Hobson looks like he should be the second lead on a soap opera—'The Line Drives of Our Lives,'" said King. "He has the Vegas hairdo and the gold chain and everything."

There is no question that the field in Bangor is a monument to King's deep and abiding love for the game.

"Baseball has saved my life," said King. "Every time I needed

Tuxedo-clad King makes newsman Bob Haskell "eat crow."

a lifeline, baseball was it. I grew up alone. My mother worked. I was a latch-key kid before anyone knew what a latch-key kid was. I would watch baseball when I got home from school. I listened to the games on the radio before that.

"I loved Brooklyn, you know, before they moved to the West Coast. I haven't cared very much for the Dodgers since they made that move."

The field is an extension of his backyard in Bangor. You can't see the Kings' home from the field through the treeline. But anyone who knows Bangor knows the home is there, that the red Victorian house is as distinctive as the author.

It is logical to compare King to Ray Kinsella, of *Field of Dreams*.

After all, Kinsella was a baseball junkie who had also cheered for Brooklyn. He was a man of intellect who had the fortitude to idolize Shoeless Joe Jackson, despite the fact that Jackson was baseball's most famous outcast before Pete Rose.

But the figure in the movie most like King is Terence Mann, played by James Earl Jones.

Go beneath the surface differences—that Mann was an overweight black man who became a recluse in Boston; that Stephen King looks like a long-retired small basketball forward by comparison.

Mann had written the best books of his generation and had been a pioneer in the civil rights and anti-war movement during the Sixties. King likewise became an outspoken opponent of the Vietnam War.

Mann's enduring dream was to play at Ebbets Field with Jackie Robinson and the Brooklyn Dodgers. King's one great regret was that he did not play high-school baseball because he lived seven miles from his school, Lisbon Falls in western Maine, and there were always chores waiting for him at home.

Mann became a proponent of the Field of Dreams as a monument to the grand game. He believed with his heart that Kinsella, who was facing bankruptcy, should not sell the farm because all people needed the field.

"The one constant is baseball," Mann reasoned. "Baseball has marked the time. This field, this game, is a part of our past, Ray. It reminds us of all that once was good and it could be again. Oh, people will come, Ray, people will most definitely come."

And one fine day this spring, Stephen King will put aside his word processor and throw out the first ball at *his* Field of Dreams— and people will come.

The Fire That Rages In Jack Morris' Belly

By PATRICK REUSSE

Following the 1986 season, Jack Morris and his agent, Dick Moss, went on a mission to prove collusion by baseball owners. They traveled from city to city, offering the services of Morris to teams, to see if a club was willing to come through with more than a three-year contract.

One of Morris' stops was in Minneapolis, where the pitcher and Moss held a negotiating session with Twins' general manager Andy MacPhail and owner Carl Pohlad. MacPhail considered the entire situation to be a Moss-orchestrated sham.

At one point, MacPhail expressed his disgust, telling Moss and Morris that all they were doing was trying to embarrass the Twins. Morris put that evil smirk on his face and said to MacPhail: "What's the matter? Can't you take the heat?"

MacPhail recalled: "There was a lot of pressure—a lot of tension—and I could remember thinking, 'That SOB, Morris, he is enjoying this.' He was telling me, 'I can take the heat.'"

Four years later, MacPhail was desperate for a pitcher capable of taking the heat. The Twins had won the World Series—without Morris—in 1987. By the middle of 1989, they were fading, fading to the point that MacPhail sent the ace of the pitching staff, Frank Viola, to the Mets for five pitchers.

Without a workhorse starter, the Twins had tumbled to last place in the AL West in 1990. They had lost third baseman Gary Gaetti as a new-look free agent to California and reliever Juan Berenguer as a new-look free agent to Atlanta. They had been unsuccessful in attempts to sign left-handed hitters Kirk Gibson

Patrick Reusse, a sports columnist for the Minneapolis Star Tribune, *is a lifelong resident of Minnesota. Like Jack Morris, he has fond memories of Killebrew, Oliva, Allison and Met Stadium.*

Jack Morris lets go after DP in Game 7 of '91 Series.

and Franklin Stubbs, and pitcher Mike Boddicker.

"I made an offer to Morris where the better he pitched, the more money he could make," MacPhail said. "There was a challenge in the contract. From what I saw when we negotiated four years earlier and from what I saw when I had watched him pitch, Morris was a guy who liked to be challenged."

Morris took the deal from the Twins. It was loaded with incentives. It offered him an opportunity to declare himself a free agent after the first, second and third seasons of a four-year contract.

When Morris signed, he did so with that evil smirk well in place. "I'm going to pitch up a storm," he said. "I'm going to haul the Twins off the bottom and make them contenders. Then, you're going to have to pay me $5 million a year, and like it."

And that is what happened: Jack Morris, villified by the media and the fans during his final season in Detroit, came to Minnesota, grabbed the Twins by the scruffs of their last-place necks and carried them to a second World Series victory in five years. Morris earned $3.8 million in that incentive-laden contract and another $119,579 as a winner's share for the Series, and then he declared himself a free agent, a situation where they had to pay up or face the wrath of the Minnesota fans.

But it was on the morning of Oct. 27, 1991, months before his desertion to the Toronto Blue Jays with a two-year, $10.85-million contract and a third-year option for $5.15 million, when Morris became a hero of enormous proportions with the Minnesota fans—a hero in ranking only behind the center fielder, Kirby Puckett.

Puckett's marvelous performance in Game 6 had just allowed the Twins to even the Series at three victories apiece. And now, with the Twins still alive, the starter for Game 7, the starter for the third time in the Series and for the fifth time in the postseason— Mr. Morris—came into an interview room in the basement of the Metrodome.

Morris looked at the room full of reporters—focused into the television cameras with a heroic sneer—and said: "In the immortal words of the late, great Marvin Gaye, 'Let's get it on.'"

The Minnesota fans loved it. When Morris went to the Metrodome's mound for Game 7, "Let's Get It On" came blaring over the sound system, and the crowd let out a cheer that caused witnesses to shiver in anticipation.

"Goosebumps," Morris said. "It gave me goosebumps."

And he gave the Atlanta Braves goose eggs.

The willingness to accept and to offer a challenge is always close to the surface with Jack Morris. No one ever took on a challenge with more determination than did Morris in the seventh game. It was scoreless for nine innings, when manager Tom Kelly told Morris that he was out of the game.

"Nine scoreless innings . . . his third start in nine nights," Kelly said. "What more can you ask of a guy? I told him, 'You were unbelievable. That's enough.'"

Morris said it was not enough. It was not enough, because the Twins were not yet World Series champions. He insisted on going out for the 10th—a scoreless 10th—and then the Twins won it in the bottom of the inning. Morris had enough energy left to run from the dugout and escort home Dan Gladden with the winning run.

Morris is a man of contradictions.

He is capable of tears of sentiment when talking about the opportunity to pitch Game 1 of the Series for his hometown team in front of the hometown fans. He is capable of crude remarks to a woman reporter who happened by his locker two years ago in Detroit.

He is capable of a pitching performance as relentless and historic as the 10-inning shutout of the Braves. And, now 36 and a veteran of 216 big-league victories and 3,290 innings, he remains capable of acts of petulance on the mound that are worthy of a Little Leaguer.

There are nights when he glares at umpires on every borderline pitch, when he stops and kicks the mound on any ball that eludes a fielder. Even in Game 7, he was glaring down at plate umpire Don Denkinger from the start.

"One pitch," Tom Kelly said. "One pitch and Jack is mad at the umpire. I thought, 'Boy, this is going to be beautiful.' "

It was beautiful. Morris' behavior on the mound is as befuddling to teammates as it is, on occasion, to Kelly.

Greg Gagne, the Twins' magnificent defensive shortstop, felt the sear of Morris' gaze a few times last summer. "You know he's trying to win, but you try to keep your emotions under control as much as possible," Gagne said. "Sometimes a ball goes through and he starts kicking the dirt and shaking his head. You think he's mad at you. You don't know what he's thinking. That's Jack. It's the way he gets going, I guess."

No one had to put up with the Morris temper more often than Brian Harper, the Twins' catcher. Morris was capable of bouncing one of those nasty forkballs on the plate, then putting his hands on his hips in disgust if Harper let it dive away from him.

"I don't know whether the way he behaves out there takes the edge off the fielders, but I think it can take the edge off Jack," Harper said. "When he gets so upset on a call or a play in the field, it takes him a few pitches to get back into a groove. You can't always afford that . . . I'll go to the mound and try to calm him down. Sometimes I can tell he's just not listening."

There was an occasion during the World Series when pitching coach Dick Such was sent to the mound to talk to Morris. When Jack saw him coming, he turned his back, faced the outfield and acted like a man waiting for a bus, ignoring Such completely.

"A lot of times out there, I'm angry at myself, not anyone else," Morris said. "I never mean to show anyone up. I just hope no one expects me to start acting like I like to lose. I care, I guess. That's the bottom line: I care. I've made a lot of mistakes, but I keep trying to do better. I guess that's what you're supposed to do in this crazy world we live in."

Morris' world took a crazy turn last year. He was raised in St. Paul, Minn. At the same time he was coming back home to pitch for the Twins, the team he cheered for as a kid, his marriage to Carolyn Morris was coming apart. Those dual emotions might be the reason Morris was forced to wipe away the tears the day he signed with the Twins, again when talking about starting the World Series for the Twins, and yet again when he talked of his sons—Austin and Erik—being there to watch him pitch that enormous seventh game.

"They were too young when we won it in Detroit in 1984," Morris said. "They were just little babies then. They were at the ballpark a couple years ago when I threw a one-hitter against Kansas City in Detroit, and that was a great day for them. But I think they really understand now."

What his sons understood, Morris said, is their father was put on this earth to pitch seventh games of the World Series—to pitch in baseball's most important moment. Morris is 4-0 in two winning World Series and 7-1 in the postseason, the only loss for Detroit—against the Twins—in the 1987 playoffs.

"He's the man," Kelly said. "We got him to pitch the big games. He can make me look very smart. He's gifted. He's different than the rest of us in that respect. He's in amazing shape and just bounces back."

The most amazing example of Morris' resiliency came at midseason, when he was drilled on the right forearm by a line drive hit by Detroit's Milt Cuyler. You could hear the crack on Morris' bone high above Tiger Stadium in the press box. There was a contusion and a horrendous bruise.

The Twins' starting pitching was in bad shape at that moment. Scott Erickson was floundering. Allan Anderson had been sent to the minors. And, it looked as though Morris would be gone for 2-3 weeks.

Morris looked at that ugly bruise, felt the pain in his forearm and said: "I'll take my regular turn."

It sounded preposterous. Morris pitched five days later.

"I think a lot of it is just mind over matter," Morris said. "Pain is something we all have to deal with. Some guys are mentally tougher than others. I'm not saying I am, but I just try

Morris won Series MVP award with spectacular performance.

to turn it into a positive thing. I hate being injured or being sick so much that when it happens, I just get upset and it makes me want to come back and do well.''

Morris hates it when he has to go a few days without competing in something. During the summer, he uses the competitive fire on baseball. During the offseason, it is an arduous workout program that allows him to report to training camp, to throw that hard-on-the-arm forkball inning after inning, 240-plus innings per year.

Morris can't explain the intensity and the need to compete. He just knows that they are there.

"I have no idea why, but you can ask my high school basketball coach, Ron Causton," Morris said. "Mondays were always the worst day for me. He kicked me out of practice several times on Mondays. I think it was because we didn't play until Tuesday night and we just had the weekend off. I had some steam to let off.

"I also know that I never have played well against poor teams in any sport. I always enjoyed playing the best. It was like, 'I might get beat, but I just want to show them I can play at their level.' As a young kid, that's the way I thought, and I guess that's the way I still am.

"I'm going to live until I'm 112 because I have no ulcers and no worries inside. I let everybody see what's inside me, and what you see is what you get."

Morris left St. Paul 18 years ago, to attend Brigham Young University. He left with a dream of some day playing for the hometown Twins.

"I remember when I was seven, I told my mom some day I'd play in old Met Stadium," he said. "Well, they moved the stadium on me. But at least I got the opportunity to see my dream become reality. I guess that makes me one of the luckiest people in the world."

When Morris returned as a Minnesota resident 18 years later, it was as an aging biker, riding to the Metrodome on his monster Harley, wearing a Harley-Davidson jacket, wearing his hair in a greased-up pompadour. No helmet. On that Harley, Black Jack is not a helmet-wearing type.

Assuming Morris makes it through spring training in his usual fit condition, he might be in line to establish a record by starting a season opener for the 13th consecutive year. He now shares that distinction with Hall of Famers Robin Roberts and Tom Seaver.

"Those are two very big names," Morris said. "I guess that means I've been around a long time—so long, I probably pitched against Roberts. I know I pitched against Seaver."

For 10 seasons, from 1979 through '88, Morris' record was a spectacular 173-112. Then he hit the wall. In 1989, Morris suffered a chip fracture in his right elbow, went on the disabled list for the first time and finished 6-14. In 1990, he started off miserably after the shortened spring training and went 15-18. Then, he came back to go 18-12, with 247 innings pitched, for the Twins.

Morris has pitched more than 235 innings 10 times. He reached 293⅔ innings during the 1983 season. "I felt it at the end of that year," he said. "I found out that 290 is a whole lot of innings. Most of the time, how you feel at the end of the season depends on how you pitched in your last game."

So Morris felt like the king of the world after the 10 scoreless innings that beat the Braves.

"I can't put into words how much respect I have for that man," Atlanta's David Justice said.

How does he keep going—through all of those years, through all of those innings? How does a pitcher become a pitching machine?

"My mechanics have to be good, and I keep my legs as strong as I can. Look at Seaver. Jim Palmer. Nolan Ryan. The guys who have pitched for 20 years delivered their pitches from the right place. They weren't flopping all around in their delivery. I know myself so well by now that I can tell when my arm is dropping down. I have telepathy between my muscles and my brain.

"Old pitchers tell you that the legs are the first thing to go. They also say the legs are 50 percent of pitching. As long as you're getting a strong push off the mound, you can be effective.

"Maybe I don't have that couple extra inches on my fastball that I had when I was younger. I hope my mental approach and gut feeling of what pitch to throw makes up for that lack of velocity. I know only one way to pitch, and that's hard. If I back off and get cutesy, my stuff just gets worse."

Three hundred victories? "I've thought about it," said Morris, 84 away from 300. "It would be pushing my ability, but I always have pushed myself. The biggest waste in the world is a waste of talent."

No one would suggest that Morris has wasted an ounce of his ability. The unforgiving fire that burns inside of him has seen to that. Years later, Morris returned home and celebrated, with MacPhail, a World Series victory. Yet, the tour he was forced to take with Moss to help prove the owners' collusion—still brings a flash of anger from Morris.

"I was mad at the baseball world at the time," Morris said. "I felt that I played long enough and deserved that thing called free agency, and there was no free agency.

"Basically, what we were talking about is collusion. I had something to do with that little word . . . a little word that cost the owners $280 million to settle. They were found guilty of it, and now they are paying for it."

When you toss a challenge at Jack Morris—whether he is pitching or negotiating or riding a Harley—you will see the evil smirk, and you will find out that he can take the heat.

How to Hit the Jackpot! Meet the $1.55-Million Yankee Bonus Baby

By TOM VERDUCCI

Behind a rusted trailer on a bumpy, dirt road in Beaufort, N.C., just past abandoned cars dead in the tall marsh grass, stands a new, 2,500-square foot contemporary home. It is the house that Brien Taylor built.

Taylor, who turned 20 in December, built it not with his bare hands but with his left arm, his pitching arm. Taylor has the gift of being able to throw a baseball 98 mph. As a high-school senior, his pitching talents brought major-league scouts to his remote coastal Carolina hometown. That led to his selection by the Yankees as the No. 1 pick in the amateur draft last June, which led to a record $1.55-million signing bonus, which led to all sorts of goodies that he never before enjoyed—such as his first suit, a sporty car, his picture on a bubble-gum card and, of course, a fully-equipped modern home for his family.

"It's very, very joyous living quarters," said Scott Boras, Taylor's agent. "It's a nice, new home. It's not an estate. It's American middle class. It's part of a great story.

"Society likes the underdog. Everyone likes Brien's story. I know when I think about Brien Taylor, I'll always remember it as one of the most rewarding experiences in what I do, just because of the impact you can have on a family.

"You see a young man go from a frown to a smile, his family go from a trailer to a nice home, and it's nice to know it's because he's doing something that he really, really enjoys and is very

Tom Verducci tours the bigs and Beaufort as Newsday's *national baseball columnist.*

Brien Taylor didn't have to earn it the old-fashioned way.

successful at. It's a heart-warming and fulfilling story, to see him come from a very rough past."

Does it sound like a made-for-television movie? You bet. A major Hollywood production company contacted Boras and the Taylor family about buying the rights to their story. The company especially was interested in Bettie Taylor, who sorts crabs at a Beaufort (pronounced BO-furt) seafood company. Bettie, with advice from Boras, conducted tough negotiations with the Yankees in which she persuaded them to raise their original offer of $350,000 more than four times over. The "60 Minutes" team also produced a segment on the Taylors' story.

Not everyone is going giddy about Brien's instant fame and fortune. Many baseball executives wondered about the wisdom of giving a high-school pitcher $1.55 million. Taylor comes without a warranty or guarantee. Only 10 percent of all players who sign professional contracts ever make it to the big league. Less than 60 percent of first-round picks ever play in a major-league game.

The last high-school pitcher to be drafted No. 1 was Houston schoolboy David Clyde, whom Texas took with the first pick of the 1973 draft. Clyde won only 18 games in his major-league career, lost 33 and compiled a 4.63 ERA.

"It's not like the NFL or the NBA," Padres' general manager Joe McIlvaine said. "Baseball is a much more inexact science. I was shocked by what the Yankees did."

The Yankees, though, believe Taylor is an exceptional talent who they could not afford to lose. He is a lanky 6-3 and 195 pounds. Taylor is such a good athlete that his friends call him "Smooth" because of his moves on the basketball court. He has run the 100-meter dash in 10.7 seconds.

Given the swampy surroundings in Beaufort and the conditions of the trailer in which he grew up, Taylor is their diamond in the rough. He is expected to begin this season at Class A Greensboro and could make it to Yankee Stadium for the 1994 season, if not the end of the 1993 season.

"The last time we scouted him before the draft he really turned it up a notch," said Yankee general manager Gene Michael. "We got him at 98 on our radar gun. In the Instructional League, after not pitching all summer, his first five pitches in his first inning all were 95 or better. He threw his change-up about 88 mph. That's the speed of an average major-league *fastball*.

"We think once he refines his mechanics he can consistently throw at 100 mph. There are only one or two players in the big leagues right now who can do that. Maybe Rob Dibble and maybe one other guy. Brien is something special."

Opposing batters can expect a blur at close to 100 mph.

Said Taylor, "I think I can make it to New York in two years. I expect to do well. But I'm looking forward to the better competition. I'm looking forward to getting hit. That's how you get better."

Taylor was born the day after Christmas, 1971. Bettie had decided months before on the name for what would be the second of her four children. While pregnant, she saw *Brian's Song*, the stirring movie about former Bears' running back Brian Piccolo. She was so touched by the story that she decided, "I'm going to name this child Brian." But she spelled Brien with a "e" on the birth certificate.

"Brian Keith, the actor, I thought he had an 'e,' " Bettie said. "I guess I made a mistake."

It wasn't long before people began to notice Brien's arm.

"One day when he was about three, he picked up a bottle and threw it clear across the room," Bettie said. "One of his uncles said, 'Whatever you do, get that boy on a pitcher's mound.' "

He grew up throwing rocks at birds, at street signs and at bottles in ditches. By the time he was ready for Little League, "Everybody knew about his arm," said Gary Chadwick, who would be Brien's coach at East Carteret High School.

"I umpired one of his games when he was 10 or 11," Chadwick said. "I think he walked 10 guys before striking somebody out. By high school, you could see he was going to be a good pitcher. The best part is that he's never let any of the attention change him."

N.C. Williams, an assistant principal at East Carteret, said Brien is "a lot like this dad," Willie, a brick mason.

"He's very laid-back and easy-going," Williams said. "He is a quiet, unassuming type of kid. And he comes from a very close-knit family."

Brien grew up in that trailer, a narrow, lopsided box of about 800 square feet. A sheer piece of fabric was used as a door between the kitchen and rear bedrooms. A naked light bulb illuminated the kitchen, where the backpiece to the stove was burned and the back to one of the wooden chairs was missing from its spindles.

"I know this community might not be a whole lot to look at," Bettie said. "But if you have a problem, all the neighbors have to do is know about it and you've got help."

The Taylors live in North River, a section seven miles inland from the touristy waterfront area of Beaufort. Most of the town's 908 blacks in a population of 3,808 live in the North River area, which is named for the body of water in which Bettie and her two daughters often fish for flounder for dinner.

The 1980 Census found the median household income in Beaufort to be $12,040 or 11 percent below the state average. And 16.2 percent of the families, or nine percent above the state average, live below the poverty level.

"I would say we're poor," Bettie said, "but not dirt poor. The kids had everything they needed, even some luxuries."

The Taylors had an encyclopedia set, a *National Geographic* subscription, but no telephone. Brien turned out to be such a sought-after player, though, that Bettie finally relented and installed a telephone last year.

"Worst mistake I ever made," she said with a laugh, after the phone rang constantly all summer.

"It's pretty hard to believe," Brien said. "I always thought I'd make the draft, but this isn't where you see a lot of baseball players, like California or Florida. I didn't know if I'd ever get noticed."

As a senior, Taylor was 8-2 with an 0.85 ERA. He allowed only 18 hits while striking out 203 batters in 84 innings. Battalions of scouts ventured to Beaufort to watch him pitch, though by the end of his season it was so obvious that he would be picked first or second that only the Yankees and Braves sent representatives to his games.

The Yankees, holding the first pick after finishing with the most losses in the American League in 1990, debated right up until the night before the draft whether to take Taylor or Mike Kelly, an outfielder from Arizona State University.

"They were so close in all our evaluations," Michael said. "It could have gone either way. But I'd say the determining factors were Taylor being left-handed for Yankee Stadium and the fact that one of our strengths is right-handed-hitting outfielders."

Soon after the Yankees took Taylor, Bettie told Michael she would accept nothing less than the $1.2 million that Oakland gave Todd Van Poppel, the Athletics' first-round pick in the 1990 draft. Van Poppel's money was payable over three years and included a $500,000 signing bonus.

The Yankees offer started at $350,000. When Atlanta signed Kelly to a $575,000 bonus, the Yankees improved their offer to $650,000, with another $50,000 to cover college expenses. Bettie, under Boras' advice, held firm. She once even questioned whether the Yankees were exploiting their cultural and economic conditions.

"As things go along, I'm beginning to wonder," Bettie said. "Is it because we're back here, we're poor and we're black? I'm not saying that is the case, but if it is I can live with that, too."

Michael replied, "Anyone who knows me knows I'm not that way. I think they have been misled some."

On August 25, with the two sides still apart, Brien left home to register for classes at Louisburg Junior College in North Carolina. Once Brien attended his first class the next day—a tennis class—the Yankees would not have been able to negotiate with him until after the conclusion of the Louisburg baseball season. Then, if they did not sign him at least 24 hours before the June draft, they would lose the rights to him.

Finally, just hours before Taylor's first class, the Yankees reached agreement with Bettie and Boras on the $1.55-million signing bonus, the largest bonus in sports history for a high-school athlete. The bonus was payable in two checks of $775,000—one almost immediately after the signing and the other on Jan. 10.

The Yankees brought the Taylors to New York for a news conference and a whirlwind tour of city. It was only the third time Brien had been away from home. He once attended a baseball camp at a North Carolina college and another time he visited an aunt in Maryland. Those trips were nothing like this, though, especially when the Taylors ordered a big room-service breakfast at a midtown hotel.

"I couldn't believe how expensive it was," Bettie said.

The signing reverberated throughout baseball like the aftershocks of an earthquake. Baseball executives, particularly those in small-market cities, worried about how they would be able to sign future No. 1 picks after this record-setting precedent by the Yankees.

"The draft was created to allow for equity," Reds' general manager Bob Quinn said. "But equity is being destroyed by this [signing]. When you have to draft in terms of signability rather than pure ability, than you can't compete. Some people better wake up and wake up fast. This has gotten out of hand."

Boras coldly responded to such charges by saying, "You don't play the game in a city. You play the game in a market. And if you can't afford it, maybe you're in the wrong market."

Baseball owners, at their next quarterly meeting, immediately went about drafting a proposal that would allow teams to control the rights to a drafted player for as many as three years, rather than one. That would allow teams more leverage in negotiating with high-school players. The proposal, which baseball people were calling "The Boras Clause," still is being studied.

Meanwhile, Taylor took a look at the first of his bonus checks and decided, "There are a lot of digits." Boras also secured "a lucrative deal" for Brien with one baseball-card company and began negotiations with at least two others. The agent quickly put Brien on a modest allowance.

"The one thing he did say to me was, 'I want my family to live in a nice home,' " Boras said.

Construction began immediately. Brien did have one request for himself: his first car.

"I told him he could have a moderately priced car," Boras said. "An expensive car and the minor leagues don't go hand-in-hand, not when you're parking on gravel roads and leaving your car unattended for 10-day road trips. I told Brien, 'You buy an expensive car with major-league money. This is for the security of your family.' "

Taylor bought a $15,000 black Mustang GT from Parker Ford in Morehead City, N.C. According to a salesman there, "Everything that you can get on it, it's got it." Taylor's brother washes cars for that dealership.

"I got a deal on it," Taylor said with a smile.

Taylor also bought six pairs of jeans, four pairs of slacks, a set of suitcases and the first suit he's ever owned. "Bought it in Morehead City," Boras said. "It's gray, Yankee gray."

Taylor's professional career unofficially began Sept. 12, when he reported to the Yankees' Instructional League team in Tampa for the seven-week season. He received no salary there. He was paid $15 a day in meal money with another $7 per day for incidentals.

"He was very, very comfortable with the whole process," Boras said. "His mother and father came down to see him after three weeks. They brought down his car, which he was real happy about. He had to hoof it around there for three weeks.

"He formed very close relationships with the other players. They watched a lot football together, ate at smorgasbords and they might even have looked at a few girls, though that's the one thing he doesn't talk to me about. He really enjoyed himself."

Likewise, the Yankees were impressed with Taylor. Kiki Hernandez, Taylor's first catcher, remarked that Taylor's fastball moved "eight to 12 inches." Pitching coach Tony Cloninger needed to see Taylor warm up only once before he exclaimed, "I can't believe how live his arm is!"

Taylor's left arm is long, thin and limber. When he throws, it is like a rubber garden hose snapped to life when the water is suddenly turned on full blast. His velocity comes so naturally that Taylor finds it almost impossible to simply lob a baseball.

"It's real tough for me," he said. "Even when I'm throwing soft, it's hard. It caused some errors in high school, because I'd

Father Willie and mother Bettie celebrate Brien's contract.

throw to a base and the ball would move so much, or the other guy was afraid of getting hit, that sometimes he couldn't catch it.''

While everyone was drooling over his fastball, the Yankees saw potential in his sweeping curveball, too.

''He's going to have a John Candelaria-type breaking ball,'' said Brian Sabean, the Yankees' vice president of player development. ''He can be downright nasty, especially on left-handers.

''We know we have something very valuable here. Obviously, it's a big responsibility. This is not a race to get him to the big leagues. We want to bring him along slowly so that when he does get to the big leagues, he's there to stay.''

Said Brien, ''If you just throw 95, by the seventh inning you've given up five runs. The secret is changing speeds and moving the ball around. That's what I try to do."

Boras compared Taylor to another of his clients, Steve Avery of Atlanta, another young left-handed pitcher. Avery made it to the big leagues at age 20, but struggled to a 3-11 record in 1990. He bounced back with a breakthrough season last year, going 18-8 before winning two games by 1-0 scores in the National League Championship Series against Pittsburgh. He didn't get a decision in the World Series, but was a formidable foe for the Twins.

"When I watch Steve pitch I really think about Brien a great deal," Boras said. "Like Steve, Brien's velocity really went up between ages 18 and 19. And Brien is a ferocious competitor like Steve. Their external appearances may not show it. They both have such a calm nature. But they are fierce on the mound."

Taylor comes from a town of legends. Beaufort was established in 1713, seized by the Spanish in 1747, taken by the British in 1782 and then claimed by those other Yankees in 1862 during the Civil War. Pirates, including the infamous Blackbeard, once cruised its coast. One pirate was said to have buried his girlfriend in a keg of rum there, for preservation purposes. And another local story has it that a British soldier was granted his request to be buried standing up, facing England and saluting the Queen.

Now Beaufort has the legend of Brien Taylor, who grew up in a dilapidated trailer at the end of dirt road, who made the baseball world flock to his tiny town because of his mighty fastball and who earned $1.55 million shortly after graduating high school and before throwing his first pitch as a professional.

"I don't know what it was before," said Chadwick, his high-school coach, "but Brien's the biggest thing to hit this town now."

Lemke to Larsen to Rhodes: From Unsung To World Series Heroes

By JOE GERGEN

According to Mark Lemke's calculations, it's a 45-minute ride from his home in Utica, N.Y., to Cooperstown. He's driven through the hamlet many times, but not until the conclusion of the 1991 season had he thought to tour the National Baseball Hall of Fame. That he now has reason to stop is one of the more heartwarming stories in World Series annals.

Shortly after Lemke's Atlanta Braves lost an ennervating seven-game classic to the Minnesota Twins last October, the second baseman was asked for his bat by a museum official. The man said he wanted to display it among the memorabilia in the Hall's World Series exhibit. "That'll be real nice," said Lemke, reduced to understatement by the tension of the final two games and the fact the Twins won both by a single run in extra innings.

Neither Lemke nor anyone else could have imagined such a development at the start of the Series, let alone the start of a season. That the Twins and Braves each qualified for the Fall Classic after finishing last in their respective divisions the previous year should have been surprise enough for baseball. Under the circumstances, perhaps it was fitting that the leading batter over the seven games that built to as taut a climax as the sport can muster would be a light-hitting infielder who expected to be used as a defensive specialist.

Lemke would have been thrilled just to make an appearance in such a grand setting. After all, this is a man who was a 27th-round draft choice, a man who labored five years in Class

Joe Gergen's columns traverse the sports spectrum for Newsday *and* The Sporting News.

Mark Lemke scores winning run in Game 3 of '91 Series.

A ball before experiencing a taste of the major leagues, a man whose security was as tenuous as the next ground ball. Certainly, he wasn't going to become a star on the strength of a .225 career average.

"I learned when I was coming up there's an inevitable point for each player when they're not going to want you around any-more," he said. "You play each game as if it's your last because one day you're going to be right."

And he did play each game of the World Series as if there would never be another. He played with such grit and determi-nation, mixed with a dash of magic, that the fans in Atlanta-Fulton County Stadium chanted "MVP!" in his honor when he ap-proached the plate in Game 5 as the Braves were en route to a 3-2 lead. Had they managed to score just one more run in either Game 6 or 7 at the Metrodome, it's likely that little Mark Lemke, who stands 5-9 in spikes, would have been recognized as the Most Valuable Player.

As it was, he had to settle for the glory of a .417 average, the memory that he had driven in the winning run and scored the winning run in games completed on the same day (Oct. 23) and a permanent place on the list of unlikely heroes in World Series history. Even in defeat, he had distinguished himself in the manner of Dusty Rhodes, Gene Tenace and Mickey Hatcher, largely anonymous players who achieved celebrity status on the basis of a stunning performance in the Series.

Not that they were his role models when he was growing up in Utica. When it came to October, he imagined himself to be Johnny Bench or Pete Rose, a switch-hitter like himself. A few years later, he liked to pretend he was Reggie Jackson.

"You couldn't grow up in the New York at that time and not know all about Reggie Jackson, Mr. October, and what he did in the World Series," Lemke said. "I loved being Reggie. I never did hit them quite as far as Reggie, though."

Nor did he step out of character in his first World Series. The man didn't hit a home run, although his three triples matched his career total. What he did, however, recalled the feats of Billy Martin, Al Weis and Brian Doyle, skilled glove men who demonstrated unexpected muscle in baseball's showcase event.

It also brought to mind the legend of Hank Gowdy and the "Miracle Braves" of 1914, when the franchise was anchored in Boston. Those Braves also had come from last place to win a National League pennant, but they had been in the basement as late as mid-July. In qualifying for their first World Series, they were huge underdogs against the famed Philadelphia Athletics, world champions in three of the four previous seasons.

Remarkably, Boston registered the first sweep in Series history, prodding Philadelphia owner-manager Connie Mack to break up his famed $100,000 infield and the most effective pitching staff in the major leagues. The hero was Gowdy, a catcher whom the Braves had acquired from the New York Giants three years earlier and a .243 hitter during the regular season. He announced his intentions in the first game when he singled, doubled and tripled in a 7-1 victory.

Gowdy, who later would become the first major leaguer to enlist in the service following the outbreak of World War I, never stopped hitting. He had a homer, triple and three doubles in the four games and his average of .545 marked the first time a regular had batted over .500 in a Series.

He also drew five walks. "My regret," Mack said later, "is that I didn't walk him oftener." Gowdy and pitcher Ken Rudolph, who was credited with the victories in the first and fourth games, received such instant acclaim that they were recruited to perform a nightclub comedy act in the offseason for $1,500 a week, considerably more than the wages they earned in baseball.

It was in the 1920 World Series that an obscure second baseman gained immortality without even swinging a bat. Indeed, Bill Wambsganss hit only .154 as the Cleveland Indians overcame the Brooklyn Dodgers, five games to two, in what was then a best-of-nine affair. The play that would never be forgotten occurred in the fifth game with the Tribe leading, 7-0.

Singles by Pete Kilduff and Otto Miller in the fifth inning threatened the Cleveland cushion. With Clarence Mitchell at the plate, Brooklyn manager Wilbert Robinson ordered a hit-and-run play. At the sight of the base-runners breaking, Wambsganss ran to cover second base, placing himself directly in the path of Mitchell's line drive.

Wambsganss caught the ball in stride and stepped on second to double up Kilduff. When he turned to throw to first, he got the surprise of his life. Miller was standing a few feet away, frozen in his tracks. All the second baseman had to do was take a few steps and tag Miller for the first and only unassisted triple play in a World Series game. The Dodgers never recovered, losing that game, 8-1, and the next two contests by scores of 1-0 and 3-0.

"Many don't even remember the team I was on, or the position I played, or anything else," Wambsganss said many years later. "They just remember Wambsganss, triple play."

Three years later, a bandy-legged outfielder whom many considered a clown took his place in the World Series pantheon. He would be back many times in the distant future, as manager of the mighty New York Yankees, but he made his first splash against the Yankees as a member of the Giants. The occasion was the initial Series staged in Yankee Stadium.

Although the ballpark was built specifically with Babe Ruth in mind, the light-hitting Stengel took advantage of the dimensions by hitting a game-winning, inside-the-park homer to left-center field in one game and a line drive into the right-field stands for the only run in another. The man mugged for the crowd on the first occasion and thumbed his nose at the Yankee dugout on the second. Ruth and the Yankees triumphed in six games for their first in a long line of championships, yet no one had a better time than the journeyman who once had doffed his cap to let loose a sparrow.

His enjoyment was short-lived. In spite of Stengel's .417 Series average, he was traded by John McGraw to the lowly Braves. "Maybe I'm lucky," Stengel decided. "If I'd hit three homers,

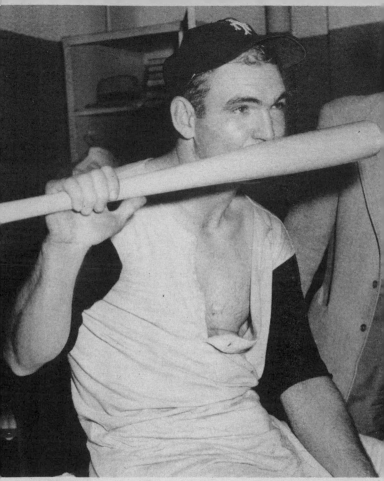

Dusty Rhodes pinch-hit N.Y. Giants to championship in 1954.

McGraw might have sent me out of the country.''

It was another Subway Series that raised not one nor two but three undistinguished players to prominence. None of their names would be found in a major-league boxscore the following season, but Floyd (Bill) Bevens, Cookie Lavagetto and Al Gionfriddo helped make the 1947 Fall Classic between the Yankees and Dodgers among the more memorable. The three all played significant roles in Game 4.

The Yankees were leading, two games to one, when first-year manager Bucky Harris sent Bevens, a 7-13 pitcher during the regular season, to the mound. He surprised everyone, including himself, by holding the Dodgers hitless through eight innings. Although he had yielded eight base on balls and a run, his team led, 2-1, in the ninth when he walked Carl Furillo with one out.

Bevens then retired Johnny Jorgensen for the second out before Gionfriddo, pinch-running for Carl Furillo, stole second. Harris ordered an intentional walk to the dangerous Pete Reiser. With Eddie Stanky due next, Brooklyn manager Burt Shotton sent up Lavagetto, a part-time outfielder who planned to retire at the conclusion of the season, as a pinch-hitter. On the second pitch from Bevens, Lavagetto sliced a line drive off the convoluted right-field wall in Ebbets Field and both runners scored, saddling the Yankee pitcher with a one-hit defeat.

Gionfriddo would have a final moment of glory in Game 6 when, as a defensive replacement, he ran back, back, back to the warning track in distant left field and leaped to rob Joe DiMaggio with two on and the Yankees trailing, 8-5. The Dodgers' 8-6 triumph forced a seventh game in which the Yankees rallied from a 2-0 deficit to win, 5-2, with the help of airtight relief pitching by Bevens and Joe Page. For Bevens, who came down with a sore arm, it would be his last major-league appearance.

Stengel was in the manager's seat when the Yankees returned to the World Series in 1949. They would win five consecutive championships under his direction. The fourth and fifth titles they owed in large measure to the play of Martin, a scrappy rookie who had caught Stengel's eye while the old man was managing Oakland in the Pacific Coast League.

Martin made the key defensive play of the 1952 Series, racing from the back of the infield to make a shoetop grab of Jackie Robinson's popup with the bases loaded and the Yankees leading the Dodgers, 4-2, in Game 7. In 1953, against the same opponent, he drew attention for his bat. The skinny second baseman hit .500 with two homers and drove in eight runs, including the game-winner in the deciding contest. "We wuz beat by a .257 hitter," moaned Brooklyn manager Charlie Dressen.

But perhaps no one ever made the transition from nonentity to World Series hero in as dramatic a fashion as Dusty Rhodes. The man was a spare outfielder whose defensive liabilities kept him on the bench as the Giants rolled to the National League pennant in 1954. Still, he could swing a bat, as the Cleveland Indians soon discovered.

The Tribe had won a record 111 games in coasting to the

American League flag. They had a brilliant pitching staff and a powerful lineup and were heavy favorites to win the Series. But in Game 1, after Willie Mays had preserved a 2-2 tie with an astonishing catch of Vic Wertz' drive to deepest center field, Rhodes exploited the peculiar dimensions of the Polo Grounds. Appearing as a pinch-hitter in the 10th inning, he lofted a soft fly that landed in the first row of the right-field seats, barely 260 feet away, for a three-run homer.

It was only the beginning. In Game 2, his pinch-single in the fifth inning tied the score at 1-1 and he later homered in a 3-1 victory. His bases-loaded pinch-single in the third inning was the key hit in the Giants' 6-2 rout in Game 3. Although he wasn't needed as New York completed a startling sweep with a 7-4 triumph in Game 4, there wasn't much doubt about the identity of the star of stars. Rhodes finished his part-time duties with a .667 average, two homers and seven runs batted in.

Pitchers dominated the next two Series, which again matched the Yankees and Dodgers. The 1955 event featured Johnny Podres, a 23-year-old left-hander who had lost more games than he won during the regular season. But he beat the Yankees twice, including a 2-0 shutout in Game 7, with a combination of fastballs, change-ups and moxie. "I was lucky," he said after he had accounted for Brooklyn's first [and last] world championship, "but I was damn good, too."

Whereas Podres went on to a long career and other successful World Series appearances a decade later in Los Angeles, Don Larsen staked his reputation on one day during the 1956 Fall Classic. On that day, he retired all 27 Dodger batters he faced. Larsen had been a big loser earlier in his career while with Baltimore and he was renowned for his big thirst. But on Oct. 8, 1956, he struck out pinch-hitter Dale Mitchell to complete a 2-0 victory and make history.

"The imperfect man pitched the perfect game," wrote Joe Trimble in the *New York Daily News*. It was the first perfecto at the major-league level since 1922 and remains one of a kind in World Series annals.

In capping a remarkable ascension from ninth in the National League the previous year to a championship in 1969, the Miracle Mets had many improbable heroes. If Al Weis wasn't the most formidable, that's because the utility infielder was the weak, silent type. The veteran spoke softly but carried a small stick, batting .215 during the season.

Still, the oft-traded, 31-year-old with the crew cut provided a young team with stability. Manager Gil Hodges used him to spell

Perfect Game: Yanks' Don Larsen delivers final pitch in 1956.

both shortstop Bud Harrelson and second baseman Ken Boswell and he responded with exceptional defense and a minimum of chatter. "I don't say much," he explained, "but I play the game hard in my own way."

Platooning with Boswell in the Series, he played superbly. And he stunned the favored Baltimore Orioles and his teammates alike. He drove in the winning run in New York's victory in Game 2 and his homer evened the score in Game 5, which the Mets went on to win, completing their stunning rise to the top. Weis finished with five hits, four walks, a sacrifice fly and a .455 average.

That a catcher emerged as the star of the 1972 Series surprised no one. That the catcher turned out to be Fury Gene Tenace of the Oakland A's startled everyone, including the man himself. "You can't predict anything in this game," he explained.

The Cincinnati Reds had proclaimed themselves the best team in baseball after defeating the defending champion Pittsburgh Pirates in the National League playoffs. They certainly had the best catcher in the game, future Hall of Famer Johnny Bench. But Tenace, who had grown up in Lucasville, Ohio, 100 miles from

Cincinnati, stole the spotlight in the first game when he hit a two-run homer in the second inning and followed with a solo shot in the fifth, providing all the runs in a 3-2 victory. Never before in baseball history had a man homered in his first two Series at-bats.

Tenace, who played several positions with varying degrees of effectiveness, also starred in the seventh game, won by the same team and by an identical score. In all, he hit four homers (one fewer than he had all season), equaling a Series record shared by Babe Ruth and Lou Gehrig among others, and drove in nine of the A's 16 runs while batting .348. "He was the biggest factor," said Bench, limited to a .261 average and one home run.

An injury to All-Star second baseman Willie Randolph on the final weekend of the 1978 season appeared to weaken the Yankees for their one-game playoff against Boston for the American League East title. But they rallied to win that memorable contest, defeated the Kansas City Royals in the championship series and then defused the Los Angeles Dodgers in the World Series with the help of a youngster whose big-league experience consisted of 52 at-bats. His name was Brian Doyle.

The younger brother of Denny Doyle, the starting second baseman for Boston in the 1975 Series, not only performed brilliantly at the position against the Dodgers but he led regulars from both teams in batting with a .438 average. "The guy they sent out to replace one of the best ballplayers in the American League played as well as Willie Randolph does," Los Angeles outfielder Bill North said in tribute. "He put the final nails in our coffin."

Even Doyle was amazed by his success, which included five hits in succession in the fifth and sixth games. "This is unbelievable," he said when it was over. "I feel like Cinderella. I've been to the ball."

It was no awestruck kid who started the 1988 Series in left field for the Dodgers, but the fact that Mickey Hatcher was a veteran didn't make him any less eager. A veteran utilityman who played with the exuberance of a large puppy, Hatcher homered in his first Series at-bat—earning a place in baseball lore among the likes of Rhodes and Tenace—and raced around the bases so quickly he couldn't recall the experience an hour later. "He ran so fast," noted third-base coach Joey Amalfitano, "it was as if he thought they would suddenly change their minds and take it back."

The former Oklahoma wide receiver was the spiritual leader of the Dodger subs, who called themselves the Stuntmen in deference to their Hollywood neighborhood. Injuries to several regulars, including National League MVP Kirk Gibson, pushed

Hatcher to the forefront and he responded with two homers, five RBI and a .368 average in a five-game defeat of the heavily-favored Athletics. "Can you believe it?" Hatcher said.

For that matter, how believable was the Braves' Lemke? This was a a kid who learned to switch-hit because the field at the Mohawk Valley Psychiatric Center, where he played hardball as a youngster, was not your standard diamond.

"You could only hit the ball to one side of the field," he recalled. "There was no left field. There was nothing but trees in left field, so if you hit it over there you were out. No one liked going into the trees to get the ball out. It was a great field. It was a mental institution but we didn't mind. The patients would walk by every once in a while, but it didn't bother us."

So Lemke turned around and batted left-handed. It was a skill that served him well against the Twins and a pitching staff dominated by right-handers. Jeff Treadway was the Braves' nominal starter at second base during the season but he suffered several injuries, among them a sore right hand that troubled him down the stretch. Lemke filled in admirably in the last two weeks and during the NL Championship Series, but he positively blossomed in the World Series.

In a 24-hour period, the man singled across David Justice with the winning run in the 12th inning of Game 3, then started the winning rally in the ninth inning of Game 4 that same night with a leadoff triple. He added to his burgeoning legend with two more triples in the Game 5 rout. After 794 minor-league games and years of working for recognition, Lemke was an overnight star.

That doesn't guarantee him a future in the sport. Brian Doyle, displaced by Randolph in 1979, appeared in only 71 additional major-league games after the October of his dreams. For over-achievers like Lemke, the struggle is never ending. But as long as the World Series retains its place in American culture, his fame will be everlasting.

INSIDE THE

AMERICAN LEAGUE

By TONY DeMARCO and TOM PEDULLA
Ft. Worth   *Gannett Newspapers*
Star Telegram

PREDICTED ORDER OF FINISH	*East*	*West*
	Boston Red Sox	Texas Rangers
	Toronto Blue Jays	Oakland Athletics
	Detroit Tigers	Seattle Mariners
	Baltimore Orioles	Minnesota Twins
	New York Yankees	Kansas City Royals
	Milwaukee Brewers	California Angels
	Cleveland Indians	Chicago White Sox

Playoff Winner: Boston

EAST DIVISION		Owner		Morning Line Manager
1	**RED SOX** New jockey helps	Jean Yawkey Red, white & blue	1991 W 84 L 78	5-2 Butch Hobson
2	**BLUE JAYS** Keen contender	W.R.R. Ferguson Blue & white	1991 W 91 L 71	3-1 Cito Gaston
3	**TIGERS** Bear watching	Tom Monaghan Navy, orange & white	1991 W 84 L 78	6-1 Sparky Anderson
4	**ORIOLES** Best of rest	Lawrence Lucchino Black & orange	1991 W 67 L 95	15-1 John Oates
5	**YANKEES** Still a way to go	George Steinbrenner III Navy blue pinstripes	1991 W 71 L 91	20-1 Bucky Showalter
6	**BREWERS** Used up early	Bud Selig Blue, gold & white	1991 W 83 L 79	30-1 Phil Garner
7	**INDIANS** Can see 'em all	Richard & David Jacobs Black & orange	1991 W 57 L 105	50-1 Mike Hargrove

Fenway Classic

92nd Running. American League Race. Distance: 162 games plus playoff. Payoff (based on '91): $119,579.66 per winning player, World Series; $73,323.41 per losing player, World Series. A field of 14 entered in two divisions.

Track Record: 111 wins—Cleveland, 1954

	WEST DIVISION	Owner		Morning Line	Manager
1	**RANGERS** Patience pays off	G. Bush/E. Rose Red, white & blue	1991 W 85 L 77	4-1	Bobby Valen-tine
2	**ATHLETICS** Not quite enough	Walter A. Haas Jr. Forest green, gold & white	1991 W 84 L 78	6-1	Tony La Russa
3	**MARINERS** Final run in Seattle	Jeff Smulyan Blue, gold & white	1991 W 83 L 79	8-1	Bill Plummer
4	**TWINS** Not this time	Carl Pohlad Scarlet, white & blue	1991 W 95 L 67	10-1	Tom Kelly
5	**ROYALS** Still short	Ewing Kaufmann Royal blue & white	1991 W 82 L 80	12-1	Hal McRae
6	**ANGELS** More changes needed	Gene Autry Red, white & navy	1991 W 81 L 81	14-1	Buck Rodgers
7	**WHITE SOX** No go, even with Bo	J. Reinsdorf/E. Einhorn Navy, white & scarlet	1991 W 87 L 75	15-1	Gene Lamont

In wide-open race, **RANGERS** finally click on all hooves to win by a nose over **ATHLETICS**. **MARINERS** and defending champion **TWINS** show early foot but lose stride midway in the course. **ROYALS**, **ANGELS** and **WHITE SOX** can't stay with the pack.

RED SOX hold off defending champion **BLUE JAYS** in neck-and-neck finish. **TIGERS** make strong strides before stumbling in the stretch. **ORIOLES** and **YANKEES** drop back after fast start. **BREWERS** are outclassed and **INDIANS** barely get a call.

CALIFORNIA ANGELS

TEAM DIRECTORY: Chairman: Gene Autry; Pres./CEO: Richard Brown; Exec. VP: Jackie Autry; Sr. VP-Dir. Player Pers.: Whitey Herzog; Sr. VP-Baseball Oper.: Daniel O'Brien; Dir. Minor League Oper.: Bill Bavasi; VP-Pub. Rel. and Broadcasting: Tom Seeberg; Dir. Media Rel.: Tim Mead; Trav. Sec.: Frank Sims; Mgr. Buck Rodgers. Home: Anaheim Stadium (65,158). Field distances: 333, l.f. line; 386, l.c.; 404, c.f.; 386, r.c.; 333, r.f. line. Spring training: Mesa, Ariz., and Palm Springs, Cal.

SCOUTING REPORT

HITTING: GM Whitey Herzog had envisioned a juiced-up lineup containing free agents Bobby Bonilla, Danny Tartabull and Wally Joyner, but he came away from the winter meetings counting on ex-Phillie Von Hayes (.225, 0, 21), ex-Met Hubie Brooks (.238, 16, 50) and the unproven Lee Stevens (.314, 19, 96 for AAA Edmonton) instead. Talk about comedowns.

Instead of power, the Angels will try to win with speed. Luis Polonia (.296, 48 steals) and Junior Felix (.283, 7 steals) will hit at the top of the lineup, but only because free agent Otis Nixon decided to spurn the Angels and return to Atlanta. Fading veterans Lance Parrish (.216, 19, 51) and Gary Gaetti (.246, 18, 66) are back after the Angels could find no takers last winter. On the other hand, Dave Winfield left as a free agent and figures to be missed. The Angels may not finish 13th in runs (653), homers (115) and on-base percentage (.314) again, as manager Buck Rodgers has promised. But they don't figure to rise much higher than that, either.

PITCHING: At least the Angels held on to their three excellent left-handers—Jim Abbott (18-11, 2.89), Chuck Finley (18-9, 3.80) and Mark Langston (19-8, 3.00)—the chief forces behind the second-best ERA in the AL at 3.69. Joe Grahe (3-7, 4.81) will fill another rotation spot, along with Scott Lewis (3-5, 6.27). The Angels added Giant free agent Don Robinson (5-9, 4.38), but free agent Kirk McCaskill (10-19, 4.26) opted for the White Sox.

No AL closer is more overpowering than Bryan Harvey (2-4, 1.60 ERA, 46 Sv), whose fastball-forkball repertoire led to 101 strikeouts and only 17 walks in 78⅔ innings. The Angels got him help in ex-Brewer Chuck Crim (8-5, 4.63), who will set up along with Mark Eichhorn (3-3, 1.98) and Scott Bailes (1-2, 4.18). But, other than Harvey, this is hardly a fearsome bunch.

Jim Abbott has gone from curiosity to 18-game winner.

FIELDING: The Angels finished third in the AL in fielding percentage at .984, but don't expect them to wind up there again this season. Parrish's skills eroded dramatically last season, when he committed a league-leading 19 passed balls. Gaetti is solid, but not the third baseman he used to be. Felix isn't a front-line defensive center fielder, though he does have a strong arm. Polonia has made strides to reach the average level in left. Hayes will stay mostly in right field, but could spell Stevens at first base against some left-handers. However, they're going to miss Joyner at first. Dick Schofield Jr. is a reliable glove man at short.

OUTLOOK: Herzog is expected to build a winner for owner Gene Autry, but the free hand Whitey thought he would get surprisingly wasn't there during the winter meetings. Herzog was undermined in his effort to re-sign Joyner by Autry's wife, Jackie. That hurt on the field, at the plate and at the box office. Herzog scrambled best he could to turn last year's last-place, 81-81 team into a contender, but he also lost out in the bidding for Bonilla, another of his targets. What's left doesn't appear to be enough even for the canny Rodgers to mold into a contender.

CALIFORNIA ANGELS 1992 ROSTER

MANAGER Buck Rodgers
Coaches—Rod Carew, Deron Johnson, Bobby Knoop, Marcel Lachemann,
Ken Macha, Jimmie Reese

PITCHERS

No.	Name	1991 Club	W-L	IP	SO	ERA	B-T	Ht.	Wt.	Born
25	Abbott, Jim	California	18-11	243	158	2.89	L-L	6-3	210	9/19/67 Flint, MI
43	Bailes, Scott	California	1-2	52	41	4.18	L-L	6-2	171	12/18/62 Chillicothe, OH
36	Beasley, Chris	Edmonton	3-5	89	51	5.26	R-R	6-2	190	6/23/62 Jackson, TN
		California	0-1	27	14	3.38				
—	Butcher, Michael	Midland	9-6	88	70	5.22	R-R	6-1	200	5/10/65 Davenport, IA
—	Crim, Chuck	Milwaukee	8-5	91	39	4.63	R-R	6-0	185	7/23/61 Van Nuys, CA
45	Eichhorn, Mark	California	3-3	82	49	1.98	R-R	6-3	210	11/21/60 San Jose, CA
42	Erb, Michael	Edmonton	1-0	41	26	3.76	R-R	6-4	210	3/19/66 San Diego, CA
31	Finley, Chuck	California	18-9	227	171	3.80	L-L	6-6	215	11/26/62 Monroe, LA
20	Grahe, Joe	Edmonton	9-3	94	55	4.01	R-R	6-0	200	8/14/67 West Palm Beach, FL
		California	3-7	73	40	4.81				
34	Harvey, Bryan	California	2-4	79	101	1.60	R-R	6-2	220	6/2/63 Chattanooga, TN
—	Johnson, Dave	Baltimore	4-8	84	38	7.07	R-R	5-11	183	10/24/59 Baltimore, MD
12	Langston, Mark	California	19-8	246	183	3.00	R-L	6-2	185	8/20/60 San Diego, CA
46	Lewis, Scott	California	3-5	60	37	6.27	R-R	6-3	178	12/5/65 Grants Pass, OR
		Edmonton	3-9	110	87	4.50				
—	Robinson, Don	San Francisco	5-9	121	78	4.38	R-R	6-4	240	6/8/57 Ashland, KY
—	Swingle, Paul	Palm Springs	3-4	57	63	4.42	R-R	6-0	185	12/21/66 Inglewood, CA
35	Young, Cliff	Edmonton	4-8	72	39	4.90	L-L	6-4	210	8/2/64 Willis, TX
		California	1-0	13	6	4.26				
—	Zappelli, Mark	Midland	2-2	33	31	2.48	R-R	6-0	160	7/21/66 Santa Rosa, CA
		Edmonton	2-1	24	16	4.44				

CATCHERS

No.	Name	1991 Club	H	HR	RBI	Pct.	B-T	Ht.	Wt.	Born
14	Orton, John	Edmonton	55	5	32	.224	R-R	6-1	192	12/8/65 Santa Cruz, CA
		California	14	0	3	.203				
13	Parrish, Lance	California	87	19	51	.216	R-R	6-3	225	6/15/56 Clairton, PA
24	Tingley, Ron	California	23	1	13	.200	R-R	6-2	194	5/27/59 Presque Isle, ME
		Edmonton	16	3	15	.291				

INFIELDERS

No.	Name	1991 Club	H	HR	RBI	Pct.	B-T	Ht.	Wt.	Born
11	DiSarcina, Gary	Edmonton	121	4	58	.310	R-R	6-1	180	11/19/67 Malden, MA
		California	12	0	3	.211				
38	Flora, Kevin	Midland	138	12	67	.285	R-R	6-0	180	6/10/69 Fontana, CA
		California	1	0	0	.125				
3	Gaetti, Gary	California	144	18	66	.246	R-R	6-0	200	8/19/58 Centralia, IL
8	Hayes, Von	Philadelphia	64	0	21	.225	L-R	6-5	185	8/31/58 Stockton, CA
		Scranton	2	0	0	.250				
—	Phillips, J.R.	Palm Springs	117	20	70	.248	L-L	6-1	185	4/29/70 West Covina, CA
6	Rose, Bobby	Edmonton	72	6	56	.298	R-R	5-11	185	3/15/67 West Covina, CA
		California	18	1	8	.277				
17	Schofield, Dick	California	96	0	31	.225	R-R	5-10	179	11/21/62 Springfield, IL
10	Sojo, Luis	California	94	3	20	.258	R-R	5-11	174	1/3/66 Venezuela
9	Stevens, Lee	Edmonton	151	19	96	.314	L-L	6-4	220	7/10/67 Kansas City, MO
		California	17	0	9	.293				

OUTFIELDERS

No.	Name	1991 Club	H	HR	RBI	Pct.	B-T	Ht.	Wt.	Born
16	Abner, Shawn	San Diego	19	1	5	.165	R-R	6-1	194	6/17/66 Hamilton, OH
		California	23	2	9	.228				
7	Brooks, Hubie	New York (NL)	85	16	50	.238	R-R	6-0	190	9/24/56 Los Angeles, CA
—	Curtis, Chad	Edmonton	136	9	61	.316	R-R	5-10	175	11/6/88 Marion, IN
40	Davis, Chili	Edmonton	117	13	56	.278	R-R	6-3	170	11/25/64 Lemon Grove, CA
		California	0	0	0	.000				
—	Edmonds, James	Palm Springs	55	2	27	.294	L-L	6-1	190	6/27/70 Fullerton, CA
47	Felix, Junior	California	65	2	26	.283	S-R	5-11	165	10/3/67 Dominican Republic
		Palm Springs	23	2	10	.359				
22	Polonia, Luis	California	179	2	50	.296	L-L	5-8	150	10/12/64 Dominican Republic
—	Salmon, Tim	Midland	114	23	94	.245	R-R	6-5	200	8/24/68 Long Beach, CA

ANGEL PROFILES

LUIS POLONIA 27 5-8 150   Bats L Throws L

Outfielder emerged as one of AL's best leadoff hitters and top base-stealing threats in first full season as regular player... His 48 steals were fourth in AL behind Rickey Henderson, Roberto Alomar and Tim Raines... Hit .296, but that represented a 39-point drop from 1990 mark... Made dramatic improvement defensively, but still remains a DH candidate... Acquired in steal from Yankees, April 29, 1990, he cost Angels only Claudell Washington and Rich Monteleone... Earned $770,000 in 1991... Spent time in jail between 1990 and 1991 seasons after arrest in Milwaukee for having sex with a 15-year-old girl... Born Oct. 12, 1964, in Santiago City, D.R.... Signed as undrafted free agent by A's in January 1984.

Year	Club	Pos.	G	AB	R	H	2B	3B	HR	RBI	SB	Avg.
1987	Oakland	OF	125	435	78	125	16	10	4	49	29	.287
1988	Oakland	OF	84	288	51	84	11	4	2	27	24	.292
1989	Oak.-NY (AL)	OF	125	433	70	130	17	6	3	46	22	.300
1990	NY (AL)-Cal.	OF	120	403	52	135	7	9	2	35	21	.335
1991	California	OF	150	604	92	179	28	8	2	50	48	.296
	Totals		604	2163	343	653	79	37	13	207	144	.302

VON HAYES 33 6-5 185   Bats L Throws R

Angels acquired veteran outfielder from Phillies in December for Kyle Abbott and Ruben Amaro Jr.... Is coming off worst pro season... Missed 73 games with broken right forearm after being hit by Tom Browning pitch as he was on the disabled list from June 15 until Sept. 3... Injury probably derailed trade since Phillies had been talking to Reds, White Sox and Twins... Twelve of first 23 hits were for extra bases, but he went from April 10 until May 9 without a run-scoring hit... Went homerless for first time in pro career... Batted just .191 in April... Selected by Indians in seventh round of 1979 draft... Traded to Phillies for five players, including Julio Franco, before 1983 season... Enjoyed his best season in 1986, leading NL in doubles and runs while ranking among leaders in hits, average, RBI, slugging percentage (.480), on-base percentage (.381) and walks

(74) . . . Born Aug. 31, 1958, in Stockton, Cal. . . . Most overpaid Phillie, earning $2.2 million in 1991.

Year	Club	Pos.	G	AB	R	H	2B	3B	HR	RBI	SB	Avg.
1981	Cleveland	OF-3B	43	109	21	28	8	2	1	17	8	.257
1982	Cleveland	OF-3B-1B	150	527	65	132	25	3	14	82	32	.250
1983	Philadelphia . . .	OF	124	351	45	93	9	5	6	32	20	.265
1984	Philadelphia . . .	OF	152	561	85	164	27	6	16	67	48	.292
1985	Philadelphia . . .	OF	152	570	76	150	30	4	13	70	21	.263
1986	Philadelphia . . .	1B-OF	158	610	107	186	46	2	19	98	24	.305
1987	Philadelphia . . .	1B-OF	158	556	84	154	36	5	21	84	16	.277
1988	Philadelphia . . .	1B-OF-3B	104	367	43	100	28	2	6	45	20	.272
1989	Philadelphia . . .	OF-1B-3B	154	540	93	140	27	2	26	78	28	.259
1990	Philadelphia . . .	OF	129	467	70	122	14	3	17	73	16	.261
1991	Philadelphia . . .	OF	77	284	43	64	15	1	0	21	9	.225
	Totals		1401	4942	732	1333	265	35	139	667	242	.270

HUBIE BROOKS 35 6-0 190   Bats R Throws R

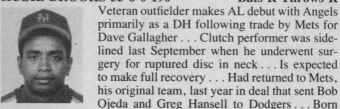

Veteran outfielder makes AL debut with Angels primarily as a DH following trade by Mets for Dave Gallagher . . . Clutch performer was sidelined last September when he underwent surgery for ruptured disc in neck . . . Is expected to make full recovery . . . Had returned to Mets, his original team, last year in deal that sent Bob Ojeda and Greg Hansell to Dodgers . . . Born Sept. 24, 1956, in Los Angeles . . . Drafted third overall by Mets in 1978, he came to majors as third baseman and played infield positions until Expos moved him to outfield in 1988 . . . Expos had acquired him and four others from Mets in Gary Carter deal after '84 season . . . Starred at Arizona State . . . Earned $2,316,667 last year.

Year	Club	Pos.	G	AB	R	H	2B	3B	HR	RBI	SB	Avg.
1980	New York (NL)	3B	24	81	8	25	2	1	1	10	1	.309
1981	New York (NL)	3B-OF-SS	98	358	34	110	21	2	4	38	9	.307
1982	New York (NL)	3B	126	457	40	114	21	2	2	40	6	.249
1983	New York (NL)	3B-2B	150	586	53	147	18	4	5	58	6	.251
1984	New York (NL)	3B-SS	153	561	61	159	23	2	16	73	6	.283
1985	Montreal	SS	156	605	67	163	34	7	13	100	6	.269
1986	Montreal	SS	80	306	50	104	18	5	14	58	4	.340
1987	Montreal	SS	112	430	57	113	22	3	14	72	4	.263
1988	Montreal	OF	151	588	61	164	35	2	20	90	7	.279
1989	Montreal	OF	148	542	56	145	30	1	14	70	6	.268
1990	Los Angeles . . .	OF	153	568	74	151	28	1	20	91	2	.266
1991	New York (NL)	OF	103	357	48	85	11	1	16	50	3	.238
	Totals		1454	5439	609	1480	263	31	139	750	60	.272

LANCE PARRISH 35 6-3 225   Bats R Throws R

Another aging Angel whose performance slipped... Batting average of .216 was 41 points below career mark prior to 1991... Hit 19 homers, pushing his career total to 304... Drove in only 51 runs, second-lowest total in 14-year career, excluding 1981 strike season ... Struck out an alarming 117 times in 402 at-bats... Defensive skills behind the plate also eroding... Career turned downward day he left Detroit for Philadelphia in 1987... Has been an All-Star eight times, including five years in a row, from 1982-86... Signed by Angels as free agent prior to 1989 season... Born June 15, 1956, in Clairton, Pa.... Earned $2,416,667 last season... Tigers drafted him 16th overall in 1974.

Year	Club	Pos.	G	AB	R	H	2B	3B	HR	RBI	SB	Avg.
1977	Detroit	C	12	46	10	9	2	0	3	7	0	.196
1978	Detroit	C	85	288	37	63	11	3	14	41	0	.219
1979	Detroit	C	143	493	65	136	26	3	19	65	6	.276
1980	Detroit	C-1B-OF	144	553	79	158	34	6	24	82	6	.286
1981	Detroit	C	96	348	39	85	18	2	10	46	2	.244
1982	Detroit	C-OF	133	486	75	138	19	2	32	87	3	.284
1983	Detroit	C	155	605	80	163	42	3	27	114	1	.269
1984	Detroit	C	147	578	75	137	16	2	33	98	2	.237
1985	Detroit	C	140	549	64	150	27	1	28	98	2	.273
1986	Detroit	C	91	327	53	84	6	1	22	62	0	.257
1987	Philadelphia	C	130	466	42	114	21	0	17	67	0	.245
1988	Philadelphia	C-1B	123	424	44	91	17	2	15	60	0	.215
1989	California	C	124	433	48	103	12	1	17	50	1	.238
1990	California	C-1B	133	470	54	126	14	0	24	70	2	.268
1991	California	C-1B	119	402	38	87	12	0	19	51	0	.216
	Totals		1775	6468	803	1644	277	26	304	998	25	.254

GARY GAETTI 33 6-0 200   Bats R Throws R

First year as Angel was one of his worst in 10-year career... His .246 average and 66 RBI were his lowest totals since 1985... Hit two more homers than in 1990, but had only 18... His All-Star Game appearance in 1990 may be his last... Has averaged 18 homers and 75 RBI over last three seasons... From 1986-88, those averages were 31 homers and 102 RBI... Third baseman's error total rose to 17, rather high for a four-time Gold Glove winner... Signed four-year deal with Angels as new-look free agent prior to last season... Earned $2.7 million in 1991 ... Twins' first-round pick in 1978 left Minnesota in part because of clubhouse problems resulting from his conversion from hellraiser into born-again Christian . . . Born Aug. 19, 1958, in Centralia, Ill.

Year	Club	Pos.	G	AB	R	H	2B	3B	HR	RBI	SB	Avg.
1981	Minnesota	3B	9	26	4	5	0	0	2	3	0	.192
1982	Minnesota	3B-SS	145	508	59	117	25	4	25	84	0	.230
1983	Minnesota	3B-SS	157	584	81	143	30	3	21	78	7	.245
1984	Minnesota	3B-OF-SS	162	588	55	154	29	4	5	65	11	.262
1985	Minnesota	3B-OF-1B	160	560	71	138	31	0	20	63	13	.246
1986	Minnesota	3B-SS-OF-2B	157	596	91	171	34	1	34	108	14	.287
1987	Minnesota	3B	154	584	95	150	36	2	31	109	10	.257
1988	Minnesota	3B-SS	133	468	66	141	29	2	28	88	7	.301
1989	Minnesota	3B-1B	130	498	63	125	11	4	19	75	6	.251
1990	Minnesota	3B-1B-SS-OF	154	577	61	132	27	5	16	85	6	.229
1991	California	3B	152	586	58	144	22	1	18	66	5	.246
	Totals		1513	5575	704	1420	274	26	219	824	79	.255

JUNIOR FELIX 24 5-11 165   Bats S Throws R

Injuries limited outfielder to 230 at-bats—not quite what Angels expected when they got him from Toronto with Luis Sojo for Devon White and Willie Fraser prior to 1991 season . . . Hit career-best .283, but his two homers, 26 RBI and seven steals were career lows by far . . . Production of two years ago—15 homers, 65 RBI, 13 steals—is more indicative of his potential . . . Earned $310,000 in 1991 . . . Still a raw talent . . . Was discovered at a track meet six years ago by Blue Jays scout Epy Guerrero . . . Hadn't played baseball since youth days . . . Born Oct. 3, 1967, in Laguna Sabada, D.R.

Year	Club	Pos.	G	AB	R	H	2B	3B	HR	RBI	SB	Avg.
1989	Toronto	OF	110	415	62	107	14	8	9	46	18	.258
1990	Toronto	OF	127	463	73	122	23	7	15	65	13	.263
1991	California	OF	66	230	32	65	10	2	2	26	7	.283
	Totals		303	1108	167	294	47	17	26	137	38	.265

JIM ABBOTT 24 6-3 210   Bats L Throws L

Put it all together in third season and victory total could have been higher than 18 with more support . . . Bullpen blew a handful of leads that he left them . . . Strong second half put him among AL leaders in several catergories . . . Was 11-5 and lowered his ERA from 3.45 to 2.89 after All-Star break . . . Now, he is known for something more than just overcoming lack of right arm . . . Has 40 victories in three seasons . . . Set career highs in starts (35), innings (243) and strikeouts (158) . . . Eighth choice overall in 1988 draft after storybook amateur career that was capped by Sullivan Award and a gold medal in 1988 Olympics ... Born Sept. 19, 1957, in Flint, Mich.... Earned $312,500 in 1991.

Year	Club	G	IP	W	L	Pct.	SO	BB	H	ERA
1989	California	29	181⅓	12	12	.500	115	74	190	3.92
1990	California	33	211⅔	10	14	.417	105	72	246	4.51
1991	California	34	243	18	11	.621	158	73	222	2.89
	Totals	96	636	40	37	.519	378	219	658	3.72

BRYAN HARVEY 28 6-2 220   Bats R Throws R

Named Rolaids Reliever of the Year after saving 46 games and posting 1.60 ERA ... Save total tied him for third-highest in history, behind Bobby Thigpen (57 in 1990) and Dennis Eckersley (48 in 1990) ... Allowed only 51 hits and 17 walks in 78⅔ innings ... Struck out 101 while walking just 17 ... Blew only three save opportunities ... Fastball and forkball combination is all he needs ... Saved 25 games in each of two previous seasons and has 113 in his career ... Earned $1.04 million in 1991, not bad for someone who was signed by Angels out of a tryout camp in 1984 ... Was playing softball with his father on nationally ranked Howard's Furniture team at the time ... Born June 2, 1963, in Chattanooga, Tenn.... Signed as undrafted free agent in August 1984.

Year	Club	G	IP	W	L	Pct.	SO	BB	H	ERA
1987	California	3	5	0	0	.000	3	2	6	0.00
1988	California	50	76	7	5	.583	67	20	59	2.13
1989	California	51	55	3	3	.500	78	41	36	3.44
1990	California	54	64⅓	4	4	.500	82	35	45	3.22
1991	California	67	78⅔	2	4	.333	101	17	51	1.60
	Totals	225	279	16	16	.500	331	115	197	2.45

CHUCK FINLEY 29 6-6 215   Bats L Throws L

Slipped to third-best left-hander in rotation after holding staff ace status previous two seasons ... Went 18-9, but ERA rose by 1.40 from 1990 ... Main problem was lack of control ... Walked 101 in 227⅓ innings, fourth-highest total of passes in AL ... Served up 23 home runs ... Narrowly missed third consecutive All-Star Game selection ... One of game's winningest pitchers over last three years at 52-27 ... Earned $2.5

million in 1991 and signed four-year, $18.5-million contract in December...First-round pick in January 1985 draft...Born Nov. 16, 1962, in Monroe, La.

Year	Club	G	IP	W	L	Pct.	SO	BB	H	ERA
1986	California	25	46⅓	3	1	.750	37	23	40	3.30
1987	California	35	90⅔	2	7	.222	63	43	102	4.67
1988	California	31	194⅓	9	15	.375	111	82	191	4.17
1989	California	29	199⅔	16	9	.640	156	82	171	2.57
1990	California	32	236	18	9	.667	177	81	210	2.40
1991	California	34	227⅓	18	9	.667	171	101	205	3.80
	Totals	186	994⅓	66	50	.569	715	412	919	3.35

MARK LANGSTON 31 6-2 185   Bats R Throws L

Reversed miserable 1990 season, as pressure of signing $16-million, free-agent contract faded...Led Angels' quality trio of left-handers with 19 victories, seven complete games, 246⅓ innings and 183 strikeouts...Earned second trip to All-Star Game with 12-3 record...Actually pitched better in second half, lowering ERA from 3.84 to 3.00 despite 7-5 mark...Victory total matched career high, previously reached in 1987...Season helped him shed .500-pitcher label as his career mark improved to 115-101...Combined with Mike Witt for a no-hitter against Seattle, April 11, 1990...Earned $3.55 million in 1991...Born Aug. 20, 1960, in San Diego...Mariners' third-round pick in 1981...Won Gold Glove in 1991.

Year	Club	G	IP	W	L	Pct.	SO	BB	H	ERA
1984	Seattle	35	225	17	10	.630	204	118	188	3.40
1985	Seattle	24	126⅔	7	14	.333	72	91	122	5.47
1986	Seattle	37	239⅓	12	14	.462	245	123	234	4.85
1987	Seattle	35	272	19	13	.594	262	114	242	3.84
1988	Seattle	35	261⅓	15	11	.577	235	110	222	3.34
1989	Seattle	10	73⅓	4	5	.444	60	19	60	3.56
1989	Montreal	24	176⅔	12	9	.571	175	93	138	2.39
1990	California	33	223	10	17	.370	195	104	215	4.40
1991	California	34	246⅓	19	8	.704	183	96	190	3.00
	Totals	267	1843⅔	115	101	.532	1631	868	1611	3.76

TOP PROSPECTS

LEE STEVENS 24 6-4 220   Bats L Throws L

His time has come after three years with Edmonton (AAA)...Hit

.314 with 19 homers and 96 RBI there in 1991 . . . Also hit .293 in 58 at-bats for Angels . . . First baseman-outfielder batted .214 with seven homers and 32 RBI for Angels in 1990, replacing injured Wally Joyner . . . Born July 10, 1967, in Kansas City . . . Angels drafted him 22nd overall in 1986.

GARY DiSARCINA 24 6-1 180   **Bats R Throws R**
Slick-fielding shortstop may get a chance this spring . . . Hit .310 with 58 RBI and 16 steals for Edmonton (AAA) in 1991 . . . In 18 late-season games, he hit .211 for Angels . . . Sixth-round pick in 1988 draft . . . Born Nov. 19, 1967, in Malden, Mass.

Angel of mercury Luis Polonia stole 48 bases.

MANAGER BUCK RODGERS: Bounced by Montreal in mid-season, he landed back where he spent his entire nine-year playing career as a catcher... Replaced Doug Rader Aug. 26, when Angels were 61-64 and finished 20-17... His job, along with GM Whitey Herzog's, is to inject youth and speed into aging, pitching-deep team... Said of last year's team: "This isn't a very good team, but it just happens to have some very good players." ... Highly regarded among managers for his handling of pitchers and getting the most out of what he's given... Was NL Manager of the Year in 1987, when he led Expos to 91-71 record and third-place finish... Best job may have been in 1990, when Expos finished 85-77 after massive free-agent exodus ... His teams have never finished higher than third, never lower than fifth... Fired by Brewers after 23-24 start in 1982, when club went on to win pennant under Harvey Kuenn... Three-time minor-league Manager of the Year... First name is Robert... Was a lifetime .232 hitter after being selected by Angels from Detroit in expansion draft... Born Aug. 16, 1938, in Delaware, Ohio... Owns lifetime managerial record of 664-611.

ALL-TIME ANGEL SEASON RECORDS

BATTING: Rod Carew, .339, 1983
HRs: Reggie Jackson, 39, 1982
RBI: Don Baylor, 139, 1979
STEALS: Mickey Rivers, 70, 1975
WINS: Clyde Wright, 22, 1970
      Nolan Ryan, 22, 1974
STRIKEOUTS: Nolan Ryan, 383, 1973

CHICAGO WHITE SOX

TEAM DIRECTORY: Chairman: Jerry Reinsdorf; Vice Chairman: Eddie Einhorn; Exec. VP: Howard Pizer; VP-Baseball Adm.: Jack Gould; Sr. VP-Major League Oper.: Ron Schueler; VP-Scouting and Minor League Oper.: Larry Monroe; Dir. Baseball Adm.: Dan Evans; Dir. Pub. Rel./Community Affairs: Doug Abel; Publicity Mgr.: Dana Noel; Trav. Sec.: Glen Rosenbaum; Mgr.: Gene Lamont. Home: Comiskey Park (43,000). Field distances: 347, l.f. line; 382, l.c.; 400, c.f.; 383, r.c., 347, r.f. line. Spring training: Sarasota, Fla.

SCOUTING REPORT

HITTING: Built on speed and defense, the White Sox suddenly found themselves in a new ballpark where the ball carries unexpectedly well and they weren't quite prepared. That made the quick development of Frank Thomas (.318, 32, 109) and Robin Ventura (.284, 23, 100) even more important.

Bo Jackson (.225, 3, 14) could provide needed punch as a fulltime DH, but who knows about his hip? Carlton Fisk (.241, 18, 74) was re-signed, a wise move, and Steve Sax, who came in the Melido Perez trade, carries the bat that led the Yankees in batting average (.304), hits (198), multi-hit games (58), doubles (38) and runs (85) last year. Dan Pasqua (.259, 18, 66) is dangerous against right-handed pitching. And the prediction here is that Tim Raines (.269, 5, 50) gets back to the .280-.290 range in

Patience and power make Frank Thomas a huge Sox-cess.

his second AL season.

With Lance Johnson (.274, 0, 49, 26 steals), Ozzie Guillen (.273, 3, 49, 21 steals), Raines (51 steals) and Sammy Sosa (.203, 10, 33, 13 steals), the White Sox' running game is as good as any in the AL. However, they must improve on their 10th-place ranking in runs (681) to get anywhere.

PITCHING: Part-time rock-'n-roller Jack McDowell (17-10, 3.41, 15 complete games) developed into a full-fledged ace. Now the White Sox are hoping 22-year-old Alex Fernandez (9-13, 4.51) does the same to further bolster a staff that tied for fourth in the AL in ERA at 3.69. Greg Hibbard (11-11, 4.31) and Wilson Alvarez (3-2, 3.51) need to improve and 44-year-old Charlie Hough (9-10, 4.02) has to knuckle down one more year. Kirk McCaskill (10-19, 4.26) figures as a key free agent signee from the Angels. Bobby Thigpen (7-5, 3.49, 30 Sv) is allowing far too many runners to be an elite closer. Scott Radinsky (5-5, 2.02, 8 Sv) could step up to a co-closer role. New manager Gene Lamont has plenty of options in Donn Pall, Ken Patterson, Wayne Edwards plus youngsters Ramon Garcia, Roberto Hernandez and Jeff Carter.

FIELDING: Johnson is one of the most underrated defensive center fielders in the AL. With Johnson flanked by Raines and Sosa, there is no faster outfield alignment in the game. Guillen's error total rose to 21 in 1991, but he remains an elite shortstop, now teamed with Sax at second. Ventura is very good at third. Fisk is catching less and DHing more, but Ron Karkovice is one of the game's best receivers.

Thomas' shoulder injury makes him somewhat questionable at first. Craig Grebeck isn't as sure-handed at second base as Scott Fletcher, whom he has replaced.

OUTLOOK: The team built by Larry Himes according to Jeff Torborg's pitching and defense philosophy no longer has Himes or Torborg to lead it. Instead, owner Jerry Reinsdorf's meddling has left Ron Schueler and Lamont in charge.

Thomas and Ventura will be hard-pressed to match their break-through seasons of '91. Sax comes off a big year, but the aging Fisk and Hough figure to play more limited roles. And there's something else to consider: the White Sox won 26 games in their last-at-bat en route to an 87-75, second-place finish a year ago. That isn't likely to happen again. The White Sox could win the West, but the feeling here is that they're headed in the other direction.

CHICAGO WHITE SOX 1992 ROSTER

MANAGER Gene Lamont
Coaches—Jackie Brown, Terry Bevington, Walt Hriniak, Doug Mansolino,
Joe Nossek, Mike Squires

PITCHERS

No.	Name	1991 Club	W-L	IP	SO	ERA	B-T	Ht.	Wt.	Born
40	Alvarez, Wilson	Birmingham	10-6	152	165	1.83	L-L	6-1	175	3/24/70 Venezuela
		Chicago (AL)	3-2	56	32	3.51				
41	Carter, Jeff	Vancouver	3-7	80	40	3.05	R-R	6-3	195	12/3/64 Tampa, FL
		Chicago (AL)	0-1	12	2	5.25				
50	Drahman, Brian	Chicago (AL)	3-2	31	18	3.23	R-R	6-3	205	11/7/66 Kenton, KY
		Vancouver	2-3	24	17	4.44				
45	Edwards, Wayne	Chicago (AL)	0-2	23	12	3.86	L-L	6-5	185	3/7/64 Burbank, CA
		Vancouver	3-9	65	35	6.26				
32	Fernandez, Alex	Chicago (AL)	9-13	192	145	4.51	R-R	6-1	205	8/13/69 Miami, FL
53	Garcia, Ramon	Birmingham	4-0	39	38	0.93	R-R	6-2	200	12/9/69 Venezuela
		Vancouver	2-2	27	17	4.05				
		Chicago (AL)	4-4	78	40	5.40				
39	Hernandez, Roberto	Vancouver	4-1	45	40	3.22	R-R	6-4	225	11/11/64 Puerto Rico
		Birmingham	2-1	23	25	1.99				
		Chicago (AL)	1-0	15	6	7.80				
27	Hibbard, Greg	Chicago (AL)	11-11	194	71	4.31	L-L	6-0	190	9/13/64 New Orleans, LA
		Vancouver	0-0	5	3	3.38				
49	Hough, Charlie	Chicago (AL)	9-10	199	107	4.02	R-R	6-2	190	1/5/48 Honolulu, HI
52	Howard, Chris	Birmingham	6-1	53	52	2.04	R-L	6-0	185	11/18/65 Lynn, MA
15	McCaskill, Kirk	California	10-19	178	71	4.26	R-R	6-1	205	4/9/61 Canada
29	McDowell, Jack	Chicago (AL)	17-10	154	191	3.41	R-R	6-5	180	1/16/66 Van Nuys, CA
22	Pall, Donn	Chicago (AL)	7-2	71	40	2.41	R-R	6-1	183	1/11/62 Chicago, IL
34	Patterson, Ken	Chicago (AL)	3-0	64	32	2.83	L-L	6-4	210	7/8/64 Costa Mesa, CA
42	Perschke, Greg	Vancouver	7-12	176	98	4.65	R-R	6-3	180	8/3/67 LaPorte, IN
31	Radinsky, Scott	Chicago (AL)	5-5	71	49	2.02	L-L	6-3	190	3/3/68 Glendale, CA
47	Ruffin, Johnny	Sarasota	11-4	159	117	3.23	R-R	6-3	172	7/29/71 Butler, AL
48	Scheid, Rich	Vancouver	6-7	67	57	6.08	L-L	6-3	185	2/3/65 Staten Island, NY
37	Thigpen, Bobby	Chicago (AL)	7-5	70	47	3.49	R-R	6-3	195	7/17/63 Tallahassee, FL
51	Wapnick, Steve	Syracuse	6-3	72	58	2.76	R-R	6-2	200	9/25/65 Panorama City, CA
		Chicago (AL)	0-1	5	1	1.80				

CATCHERS

No.	Name	1991 Club	H	HR	RBI	Pct.	B-T	Ht.	Wt.	Born
72	Fisk, Carlton	Chicago (AL)	111	18	74	.241	R-R	6-2	225	12/26/47 Bellows Falls, VT
20	Karkovice, Ron	Chicago (AL)	41	5	22	.246	R-R	6-1	215	8/8/63 Union, NJ
5	Merullo, Matt	Chicago (AL)	32	5	21	.229	L-R	6-2	200	8/4/65 Ridgefield, CT
		Birmingham	6	2	3	.214				

INFIELDERS

No.	Name	1991 Club	H	HR	RBI	Pct.	B-T	Ht.	Wt.	Born
28	Beltre, Esteban	Denver	13	0	8	.171	R-R	5-10	155	12/26/67 Dominican Republic
		Vancouver	94	0	30	.271				
		Chicago (AL)	1	0	0	.167				
21	Cora, Joey	Chicago (AL)	55	0	18	.241	S-R	5-8	152	5/14/65 Puerto Rico
		South Bend	1	0	0	.200				
14	Grebeck, Craig	Chicago (AL)	63	6	31	.281	R-R	5-7	160	12/29/64 Johnstown, PA
13	Guillen, Ozzie	Chicago (AL)	143	3	49	.273	L-R	5-11	155	1/20/64 Venezuela
54	Martin, Norberto	Vancouver	94	0	20	.278	S-R	5-10	164	12/10/66 Dominican Republic
6	Sax, Steve	New York (AL)	198	10	56	.304	R-R	6-0	183	1/29/60 Sacramento, CA
35	Thomas, Frank	Chicago (AL)	178	32	100	.318	R-R	6-5	240	5/27/68 Columbus, GA
23	Ventura, Robin	Chicago (AL)	172	23	100	.284	L-R	6-1	192	7/14/67 Santa Maria, CA

OUTFIELDERS

No.	Name	1991 Club	H	HR	RBI	Pct.	B-T	Ht.	Wt.	Born
12	Huff, Mike	Clev.-Chi.(AL)	61	3	25	.251	R-R	6-1	180	8/11/63 Honolulu, HI
8	Jackson, Bo	Sarasota	2	0	2	.333	R-R	6-1	225	11/30/62 Bessemer, AL
		Birmingham	4	0	0	.308				
		Chicago (AL)	16	3	14	.225				
1	Johnson, Lance	Chicago (AL)	161	0	49	.274	L-L	5-11	155	7/6/63 Cincinnati, OH
56	Lee, Derek	Birmingham	50	5	16	.325	L-R	6-0	195	7/28/66 Chicago, IL
		Vancouver	94	6	44	.295				
24	Newson, Warren	Vancouver	41	2	19	.369	L-L	5-7	190	7/3/64 Newnan, GA
		Chicago (AL)	39	4	25	.295				
44	Pasqua, Dan	Chicago (AL)	108	18	66	.259	L-L	6-0	205	10/17/61 Yonkers, NY
30	Raines, Tim	Chicago (AL)	163	5	50	.268	S-R	5-8	185	9/16/59 Sanford, FL
25	Sosa, Sammy	Chicago (AL)	64	10	33	.203	R-R	6-0	175	11/12/68 Dominican Republic
		Vancouver	31	3	19	.267				

WHITE SOX PROFILES

FRANK THOMAS 23 6-5 240   Bats R Throws R

"Big Frank" in more ways than one . . . Drew AL MVP consideration after leading club in hitting (.318), homers (32) and RBI (109) . . . First baseman-DH led majors with eye-popping total of 138 walks, 30 more than NL leader Brett Butler . . . On-base percentage of .453 also led majors by wide margin . . . Former Auburn football teammate of Bo Jackson, he caught three passes as a freshman tight end . . . Eighth pick overall in 1989 draft . . . Named Minor League Player of the Year by *Baseball America* in 1990 . . . Was promoted in August 1990 and hit .330 in 191 major-league at-bats . . . Born May 27, 1968, in Columbus, Ga. . . . Earned only $120,000 in 1991, but his big-dollar days are coming.

Year	Club	Pos.	G	AB	R	H	2B	3B	HR	RBI	SB	Avg.
1990	Chicago (AL) . .	1B	60	191	39	63	11	3	7	31	0	.330
1991	Chicago (AL) . .	1B	158	559	104	178	31	2	32	109	1	.318
	Totals		218	750	143	241	42	5	39	140	1	.321

BO JACKSON 29 6-1 225   Bats R Throws R

Released in spring training by Kansas City because of what was supposed to be a career-threatening hip injury, he was back Sept. 2 as DH against those same Royals. Who else but Bo? . . . Outfielder got more attention when he was not playing than he did after his return . . . Was less than impressive in final month, finishing at .225 with three homers and 14 RBI in 68 at-bats . . . Earned $700,000 guaranteed in 1991 and picked up $310,000 in incentive money for being available in the final 31 games . . . Royals grew tired of circus surrounding fourth-round pick in 1986 . . . Signing by White Sox angered some of younger, underpaid players . . . His football days apparently are over after hip failed physical by Los Angeles Raiders . . . Born Nov. 30, 1962, in Bessemer, Ala.

Year	Club	Pos.	G	AB	R	H	2B	3B	HR	RBI	SB	Avg.
1986	Kansas City . . .	OF	25	82	9	17	2	1	2	9	3	.207
1987	Kansas City . . .	OF	116	396	46	93	17	2	22	53	10	.235
1988	Kansas City . . .	OF	124	439	63	108	16	4	25	68	27	.246
1989	Kansas City . . .	OF	135	515	86	132	15	6	32	105	26	.256
1990	Kansas City . . .	OF	111	405	74	110	16	1	28	78	15	.272
1991	Chicago (AL) . .	DH	23	71	8	16	4	0	3	14	0	.225
	Totals		534	1908	286	476	70	14	112	327	81	.249

OZZIE GUILLEN 28 5-11 155   Bats L Throws R

Slick-fielding shortstop topped .270 mark for fourth time in seven seasons . . . Hit two homers in span of seven at-bats after totalling seven in first six-plus seasons . . . Finished year with career-high three homers . . . Gold Glove Award winner in 1990, but he committed 21 errors last year . . . AL Rookie of the Year in 1985 . . . Came up up in Padres' system . . . Acquired in deal for Lamarr Hoyt after the 1984 season and Hoyt's career faded soon after . . . Earned $1.6 million in 1991 . . . Follows Chico Carrasquel and Luis Aparicio in long line of quality White Sox shortstops from Venezuela . . . Born Jan. 20, 1964, in Ocumare del Tuy, Venezuela.

Year Club	Pos.	G	AB	R	H	2B	3B	HR	RBI	SB	Avg.
1985 Chicago (AL) . .	SS	150	491	71	134	21	9	1	33	7	.273
1986 Chicago (AL) . .	SS	159	547	58-	137	19	4	2	47	8	.250
1987 Chicago (AL) . .	SS	149	560	64	156	22	7	2	51	25	.279
1988 Chicago (AL) . .	SS	156	566	58	148	16	7	0	39	25	.261
1989 Chicago (AL) . .	SS	155	597	63	151	20	8	1	54	36	.253
1990 Chicago (AL) . .	SS	160	516	61	144	21	4	1	58	13	.279
1991 Chicago (AL) . .	SS	154	524	52	143	20	3	3	49	21	.273
Totals		1083	3801	427	1013	139	42	10	331	135	.267

ROBIN VENTURA 24 6-1 192   Bats L Throws R

Blossomed into league's most productive third baseman in second full season . . . Improved from five homers and 54 RBI in 1990 to 23 homers and 100 RBI . . . This is the same guy who suffered through an 0-for-41 slump two years ago . . . Also developed into one of AL's best defensive third basemen . . . Committed 18 errors, but also made numerous standout plays and was rewarded with a Gold Glove . . . Member of 1988 U.S. Olympic team . . . First-round pick and 10th player taken overall in 1988, out of Oklahoma State . . . Earned $150,000 in 1991, making him another big bargain . . . Born July 14, 1967, in Santa Maria, Cal.

Year Club	Pos.	G	AB	R	H	2B	3B	HR	RBI	SB	Avg.
1989 Chicago (AL) . .	3B	16	45	5	8	3	0	0	7	0	.178
1990 Chicago (AL) . .	3B-1B	150	493	48	123	17	1	5	54	1	.249
1991 Chicago (AL) . .	3B-1B	157	606	92	172	25	1	23	100	2	.284
Totals		323	1144	145	303	45	2	28	161	3	.265

TIM RAINES 32 5-8 185   Bats S Throws R

Didn't quite live up to expectations of $3.5-million salary in 1991, his first season in Chicago after dozen in Montreal . . . Finished at .268 after dreadful start . . . Announced in spring training he wanted to be known by nickname "Rock" . . . After a month or so, mired in a slump, he decided to go back to Tim . . . Finished third in AL with 51 steals, his highest total in five years . . . Ranks eighth all-time with 685 steals . . . Acquired with Jeff Carter for Ivan Calderon and Barry Jones prior to 1991 season . . . Named son after close friend and former teammate, Andre Dawson . . . Born Sept. 16, 1959, in Sanford, Fla.

Year	Club	Pos.	G	AB	R	H	2B	3B	HR	RBI	SB	Avg.
1979	Montreal	PR	6	0	3	0	0	0	0	0	2	.000
1980	Montreal	2B-OF	15	20	5	1	0	0	0	0	5	.050
1981	Montreal	OF-2B	88	313	61	95	13	7	5	37	71	.304
1982	Montreal	OF-2B	156	647	90	179	32	8	4	43	78	.277
1983	Montreal	OF-2B	156	615	133	183	32	8	11	71	90	.298
1984	Montreal	OF-2B	160	622	106	192	38	9	8	60	75	.309
1985	Montreal	OF	150	575	115	184	30	13	11	41	70	.320
1986	Montreal	OF	151	580	91	194	35	10	9	62	70	.334
1987	Montreal	OF	139	530	123	175	34	8	18	68	50	.330
1988	Montreal	OF	109	429	66	116	19	7	12	48	33	.270
1989	Montreal	OF	145	517	76	148	29	6	9	60	41	.286
1990	Montreal	OF	130	457	65	131	11	5	9	62	49	.287
1991	Chicago (AL)	OF	155	609	102	163	20	6	5	50	51	.268
	Totals		1560	5914	1036	1761	293	87	101	602	685	.298

CARLTON FISK 44 6-2 225   Bats R Throws R

Despite signs that age is catching up, White Sox re-signed free agent for one year at $1 million . . . Slipped to .241 batting average, his lowest in five years . . . But added 18 more homers to his major-league record for catchers, which stands at 351 . . . Spent more time as DH, giving way to defensive whiz Ron Karkovice behind the plate . . . Still sticking to rigid weight-lifting regimen . . . It's difficult to believe, but has played more games with White Sox (1,253) than with Red Sox (1,078) . . . Career hit total is 2,303, including 372 homers . . . Earned $1.25 million in 1991, his 20th full season in a probable

Hall of Fame career . . . Born Dec. 26, 1947, in Bellows Falls, Vt. . . . Red Sox drafted him fourth overall in 1967.

Year	Club	Pos.	G	AB	R	H	2B	3B	HR	RBI	SB	Avg.
1969	Boston	C	2	5	0	0	0	0	0	0	0	.000
1971	Boston	C	14	48	7	15	2	1	2	6	0	.313
1972	Boston	C	131	457	74	134	28	9	22	61	5	.293
1973	Boston	C	135	508	65	125	21	0	26	71	7	.246
1974	Boston	C	52	187	36	56	12	1	11	26	5	.299
1975	Boston	C	79	263	47	87	14	4	10	52	4	.331
1976	Boston	C	134	487	76	124	17	5	17	58	12	.255
1977	Boston	C	152	536	106	169	26	3	26	102	7	.315
1978	Boston	C-OF	157	571	94	162	39	5	20	88	7	.284
1979	Boston	C-OF	91	320	49	87	23	2	10	42	3	.272
1980	Boston	C-OF-1B-3B	131	478	73	138	25	3	18	62	11	.289
1981	Chicago (AL)	C-1B-3B-OF	96	338	44	89	12	0	7	45	3	.263
1982	Chicago (AL)	C-1B	135	476	66	127	17	3	14	65	17	.267
1983	Chicago (AL)	C	138	488	85	141	26	4	26	86	9	.289
1984	Chicago (AL)	C	102	359	54	83	20	1	21	43	6	.231
1985	Chicago (AL)	C	153	543	85	129	23	1	37	107	17	.238
1986	Chicago (AL)	OF-C	125	457	42	101	11	0	14	63	2	.221
1987	Chicago (AL)	C-1B-OF	135	454	68	116	22	1	23	71	1	.256
1988	Chicago (AL)	C	76	253	37	70	8	1	19	50	0	.277
1989	Chicago (AL)	C	103	375	47	110	25	2	13	68	1	.293
1990	Chicago (AL)	C	137	452	65	129	21	0	18	65	7	.285
1991	Chicago (AL)	C-1B	134	460	42	111	25	0	18	74	1	.241
	Totals		2412	8515	1262	2303	417	46	372	1305	125	.270

LANCE JOHNSON 28 5-11 155   Bats L Throws L

Speedster turned in typical season . . . Hit .274, four points above career average entering 1991 . . . Didn't hit a homer for second time in three years and has only one in major-league career . . . Drove in 49 runs, two less than in his first full season in 1990 . . . Stole 26 bases, matching his career average . . . Slap hitter who exemplifies hitting coach Walt Hriniak's philosophy . . . Outstanding defensive center fielder . . . Committed only two errors . . . Acquired from St. Louis for Jose DeLeon and Ricky Horton prior to 1988 season . . . Drafted three times before he signed with St. Louis as sixth-rounder in 1984, out of the University of South Alabama . . . Earned $320,000 in 1991 . . . Born July 6, 1963, in Cincinnati.

Year	Club	Pos.	G	AB	R	H	2B	3B	HR	RBI	SB	Avg.
1987	St. Louis	OF	33	59	4	13	2	1	0	7	6	.220
1988	Chicago (AL)	OF	33	124	11	23	4	1	0	6	6	.185
1989	Chicago (AL)	OF	50	180	28	54	8	2	0	16	16	.300
1990	Chicago (AL)	OF	151	541	76	154	18	9	1	51	36	.285
1991	Chicago (AL)	OF	159	588	72	161	14	13	0	49	26	.274
	Totals		426	1492	191	405	46	26	1	129	90	.271

STEVE SAX 32 6-0 183   Bats R Throws R

Traded by Yankees for Melido Perez in January ... Reasserted himself as quality offensive player, boosting average to .304, 44 points above previous season ... Led Yankees in batting average (.304), hits (198), multi-hit games (58), doubles (38), runs (85) and at-bats (652) ... Cracked career-high 10 home runs, most by Yankee second baseman since Gil McDougald's 12 in 1958 ... Was hitting .231 through May 27, but hit .330 rest of the way ... Dodgers' ninth-round pick in 1978 became NL Rookie of the Year with Los Angeles in 1982 ... Contributed to Dodgers' world championship in 1988 with .300 batting average during upset of Oakland ... Born Jan. 29, 1960, in West Sacramento, Cal. ... Signed initially as a free agent before 1989 season, he earned $1,633,334 in 1991.

Year	Club	Pos.	G	AB	R	H	2B	3B	HR	RBI	SB	Avg.
1981	Los Angeles ...	2B	31	119	15	33	2	0	2	9	5	.277
1982	Los Angeles ...	2B	150	638	88	180	23	7	4	47	49	.282
1983	Los Angeles ...	2B	155	623	94	175	18	5	5	41	56	.281
1984	Los Angeles ...	2B	145	569	70	138	24	4	1	35	34	.243
1985	Los Angeles ...	2B-3B	136	488	62	136	8	4	1	42	27	.279
1986	Los Angeles ...	2B	157	633	91	210	43	4	6	56	40	.332
1987	Los Angeles ...	2B-OF-3B	157	610	84	171	22	7	6	46	37	.280
1988	Los Angeles ...	2B	160	632	70	175	19	4	5	57	42	.277
1989	New York (AL)	2B	158	651	88	205	26	3	5	63	43	.315
1990	New York (AL)	2B	155	615	70	160	24	2	4	42	43	.260
1991	New York (AL)	2B-3B	158	652	85	198	38	2	10	56	31	.304
	Totals		1562	6230	817	1781	247	42	49	494	407	.286

JACK McDOWELL 26 6-5 180   Bats R Throws R

Earned serious Cy Young Award consideration with 17-10 record, 3.41 ERA and second-highest innings pitched total in AL (253⅔) ... Reed-thin right-hander showed remarkable durability, completing 15 games. That's more than the total amassed by six AL teams ... "Black Jack" also is lead singer, guitarist and song writer for modern rock group, V.I.E.W. ... White Sox reliever Wayne Edwards is the band's drummer ... Earned $175,000 in 1991 and wasn't happy about it ... When Bo Jackson was signed, he threatened walkout along with Greg Hibbard before being talked out of it ... Born Jan. 16,

1966, in Van Nuys, Cal. . . . White Sox drafted him fifth overall in 1987.

Year	Club	G	IP	W	L	Pct.	SO	BB	H	ERA
1987	Chicago (AL)	4	28	3	0	1.000	15	6	16	1.93
1988	Chicago (AL)	26	158⅔	5	10	.333	84	68	147	3.97
1990	Chicago (AL)	33	205	14	9	.609	165	77	189	3.82
1991	Chicago (AL)	35	253⅔	17	10	.630	191	82	212	3.41
	Totals.	98	645⅓	39	29	.574	455	233	564	3.61

DAN PASQUA 30 6-0 205   Bats L Throws L

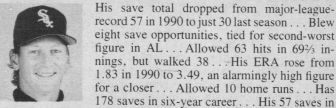

Established career high with 66 RBI . . . Provided left-handed power with 18 homers, his second-highest total . . . Shuffled between left field, first base and designated hitter, amassing second-highest total of at-bats in career with 417 . . . Didn't steal a base in 1991 and has only five in six-plus seasons . . . Won't win any Gold Gloves, but does have strong arm in left . . . Earned $800,000 in 1991 . . . Acquired from Yankees before 1988 season in five-player deal involving Richard Dotson . . . Born Oct. 17, 1961, in Yonkers, N.Y. . . . Yanks' third-round pick in 1982 . . . As free agent, he re-signed for $6 million over three years.

Year	Club	Pos.	G	AB	R	H	2B	3B	HR	RBI	SB	Avg.
1985	New York (AL)	OF	60	148	17	31	3	1	9	25	0	.209
1986	New York (AL)	OF-1B	102	280	44	82	17	0	16	45	2	.293
1987	New York (AL)	OF-1B	113	318	42	74	7	1	17	42	0	.233
1988	Chicago (AL) . .	OF-1B	129	422	48	96	16	2	20	50	1	.227
1989	Chicago (AL) . .	OF	73	246	26	61	9	1	11	47	1	.248
1990	Chicago (AL) . .	OF	112	325	43	89	27	3	13	58	1	.274
1991	Chicago (AL) . .	1B-OF	134	417	71	108	22	5	18	66	0	.259
	Totals		723	2156	291	541	101	13	104	333	5	.251

BOBBY THIGPEN 28 6-3 195   Bats R Throws R

His save total dropped from major-league-record 57 in 1990 to just 30 last season . . . Blew eight save opportunities, tied for second-worst figure in AL . . . Allowed 63 hits in 69⅔ innings, but walked 38 . . . His ERA rose from 1.83 in 1990 to 3.49, an alarmingly high figure for a closer . . . Allowed 10 home runs . . . Has 178 saves in six-year career . . . His 57 saves in 1990 were 11 more than previous record and he amassed them in a record 65 opportunities . . . Earned $2,416,667 in 1991 . . . Born July 17, 1963, in Tallahassee, Fla. . . . Played mostly outfield at

Mississippi State, where he out-hit Rafael Palmeiro one season . . . White Sox' fourth-round pick in 1985.

Year	Club	G	IP	W	L	Pct.	SO	BB	H	ERA
1986	Chicago (AL)	20	35⅔	2	0	1.000	20	12	26	1.77
1987	Chicago (AL)	51	89	7	5	.583	52	24	86	2.73
1988	Chicago (AL)	68	90	5	8	.385	62	33	96	3.30
1989	Chicago (AL)	61	79	2	6	.250	47	40	62	3.76
1990	Chicago (AL)	77	88⅔	4	6	.400	70	32	60	1.83
1991	Chicago (AL)	67	69⅔	7	5	.583	47	38	63	3.49
	Totals	344	452	27	30	.474	298	179	393	2.89

KIRK McCASKILL 30 6-1 205   Bats R Throws R

Had worst season, dropping to 10-19 after posting winning records in three previous full seasons . . . But Angel free agent wound up with three-year, $6-7-million White Sox contract . . . Made 29 starts through Sept. 4 without missing a turn, but made only one more start in final month . . . Fourth-round pick by Angels in 1982, one year after he was first collegian picked in NHL draft, by Winnipeg . . . Didn't give up hockey until 1984 . . . Earned $2.1 million in 1991 . . . Born April 9, 1961, in Kapuskasing, Ontario.

Year	Club	G	IP	W	L	Pct.	SO	BB	H	ERA
1985	California	30	189⅔	12	12	.500	102	64	189	4.70
1986	California	34	246⅓	17	10	.630	202	92	207	3.36
1987	California	14	74⅔	4	6	.400	56	34	84	5.67
1988	California	23	146⅓	8	6	.571	98	61	155	4.31
1989	California	32	212	15	10	.600	107	59	202	2.93
1990	California	29	174⅓	12	11	.522	78	72	161	3.25
1991	California	30	177⅔	10	19	.345	71	66	193	4.26
	Totals	192	1221	78	74	.513	714	448	1191	3.86

ALEX FERNANDEZ 22 6-1 205   Bats R Throws R

Finished strong, spawning optimism that he may be ready to step up and join Jack McDowell as top-flight starter . . . Was 2-7 with a 6.46 ERA June 6 . . . Finished 9-13 with 4.51 ERA . . . Allowed 186 hits in 191⅔ innings and struck out 145 . . . Has to cut down total of 88 walks . . . Already has pitched 1½ major-league seasons at age 22 . . . Born Aug. 13, 1969, in Miami . . . First-round pick of Brewers in 1988, but turned them down to attend University of Miami . . . Later enrolled in Miami-Dade South Junior College to be eligible for draft again . . . Picked fourth overall in 1990 by White Sox, who paid him a $350,000 signing bonus . . . Earned $120,000 in 1991.

Year	Club	G	IP	W	L	Pct.	SO	BB	H	ERA
1990	Chicago (AL)	13	87⅔	5	5	.500	61	34	89	3.80
1991	Chicago (AL)	34	191⅔	9	13	.409	145	88	186	4.51
	Totals	47	279⅓	14	18	.438	206	122	275	4.29

CHARLIE HOUGH 44 6-2 190   Bats R Throws R

Veteran knuckleballer did it again ... Won nine games, posted 4.02 ERA and gobbled up 199⅓ innings to ease strain on an otherwise youthful rotation ... Let go by Rangers after 1990, he proved them wrong ... Didn't join rotation to stay until May 11 ... Rangers' all-time leader in virtually every pitching category ... Spent 10½ seasons there, winning 139 games ... Has 195 victories and 61 saves in three decades ... Earned $800,000 in 1991 ... Born Jan. 5, 1948, in Honolulu ... Began career as undrafted free agent with Dodgers in 1966.

Year	Club	G	IP	W	L	Pct.	SO	BB	H	ERA
1970	Los Angeles	8	17	0	0	.000	8	11	18	5.29
1971	Los Angeles	4	4	0	0	.000	4	3	3	4.50
1972	Los Angeles	2	3	0	0	.000	4	2	2	3.00
1973	Los Angeles	37	72	4	2	.667	70	45	52	2.75
1974	Los Angeles	49	96	9	4	.692	63	40	65	3.75
1975	Los Angeles	38	61	3	7	.300	34	34	43	2.95
1976	Los Angeles	77	143	12	8	.600	81	77	102	2.20
1977	Los Angeles	70	127	6	12	.333	105	70	98	3.33
1978	Los Angeles	55	93	5	5	.500	66	48	69	3.29
1979	Los Angeles	42	151	7	5	.583	76	66	152	4.77
1980	Los Angeles	19	32	1	3	.250	25	21	37	5.63
1980	Texas	16	61	2	2	.500	47	37	54	3.98
1981	Texas	21	82	4	1	.800	69	31	61	2.96
1982	Texas	34	228	16	13	.552	128	72	217	3.95
1983	Texas	34	252	15	13	.536	152	95	219	3.18
1984	Texas	36	266	16	14	.533	164	94	260	3.76
1985	Texas	34	250⅓	14	16	.467	141	83	198	3.31
1986	Texas	33	230⅓	17	10	.630	146	89	188	3.79
1987	Texas	40	285⅓	18	13	.581	223	124	238	3.79
1988	Texas	34	252	15	16	.484	174	126	202	3.32
1989	Texas	30	182	10	13	.435	94	95	168	4.35
1990	Texas	32	218⅔	12	12	.500	114	119	190	4.07
1991	Chicago (AL)	31	199⅓	9	10	.474	107	94	167	4.02
	Totals	776	3306	195	179	.521	2095	1476	2803	3.66

TOP PROSPECTS

JEFF CARTER 27 6-3 195   Bats R Throws R

Yo-yoed between Chicago and Vancouver (AAA) ... With White Sox, he finished 0-1 with 5.25 ERA in five games, including two starts ... Allowed eight hits and walked five in 12 innings ... Went 3-7 with 3.05 ERA for Vancouver ... Acquired from Montreal with Tim Raines for Ivan Calderon and Barry Jones prior to last season . . . Never had ERA above 2.77 in Montreal system . . . Expos' 19th-round pick in 1987 . . . Born Dec. 3, 1964, in Tampa.

ROBERTO HERNANDEZ 27 6-4 225   Bats R Throws R
How's this for a major-league debut: he carried no-hitter into seventh inning against Kansas City Sept. 2 . . . That was two months after undergoing a 10½-hour procedure to remove a blood clot from his forearm . . . Operation also included ligament transplant from leg to forearm . . . Wound up 1-0 with 7.80 ERA for White Sox . . . Was 4-1 with 3.22 ERA for Vancouver (AAA) . . . Was 2-1 with 1.99 ERA for Birmingham (AA) . . . No. 1 pick of Larry Himes' Angels in 1986 . . . As White Sox GM, Himes traded outfielder Mark Davis for him, Aug. 3, 1989 . . . Born Nov. 11, 1964, in Santurce, P.R., but grew up in New York City.

MANAGER GENE LAMONT: Gets first chance as a major-league manager, succeeding Jeff Torborg . . . Comes highly recommended by mentor Jim Leyland, whom the White Sox first pursued . . . Joined Pirates one day after Leyland became manager in 1985 and was Bucs' third-base coach for six seasons . . . Also handled club's defensive alignment and outfield instruction . . . Managed eight years in Royals' system (1978-85) and reached Southern League (AA) championship series with Jacksonville in 1982 and '83 . . . Ten players on Kansas City's 1985 championship team played for him in the minors . . . A former catcher, he hit .223 in 159 major-league at-bats spread over five seasons with Detroit . . . Had only one full season in the majors (1974) . . . Tigers' first-round pick (11th overall) in 1965 draft . . . Born Christmas Day, 1946, in Rockford, Ill.

ALL-TIME WHITE SOX SEASON RECORDS

BATTING: Luke Appling, .388, 1936
HRs: Dick Allen, 37, 1972
       Carlton Fisk, 37, 1985
RBI: Zeke Bonura, 138, 1936
STEALS: Rudy Law, 77, 1983
WINS: Ed Walsh, 40, 1908
STRIKEOUTS: Ed Walsh, 269, 1908

KANSAS CITY ROYALS

TEAM DIRECTORY: Chairman: Ewing Kauffman; Pres.: Joe Burke; Exec. VP/GM: Herk Robinson; VP-Adm.: Dennis Cryder; VP-Player Pers.: Joe Klein; Dir. Scouting: Art Stewart; Dir. Minor League Oper.: Steve Schryver; VP-Pub. Rel.: Dean Vogelaar; Trav. Sec.: Dave Witty; Mgr.: Hal McRae. Home: Royals Stadium (40,625). Field distances: 330, l.f. line; 385, l.c.; 410, c.f.; 385, r.c.; 330, r.f. line. Spring training: Baseball City Stadium, Orlando, Fla.

SCOUTING REPORT

HITTING: The Royals had to do something after losing free agent Danny Tartabull from an already punchless attack and they acted in a big way. Former Angel Wally Joyner (.301, 21, 96), a free-agent import, will fit in the No. 3 spot, in front of former Met Kevin McReynolds (.259, 16, 74). The other two Mets acquired in the Bret Saberhagen deal, Keith Miller (.280, 4, 23) and Gregg Jefferies (.272, 9, 62), will hit at the top of the order,

Talented Brian McRae is chip off old manager.

allowing manager Hal McRae to drop his son Brian (.261, 8, 64) lower down.

There's still a spot for George Brett (.255, 10, 61) and Jim Eisenreich (.301, 2, 47), but the same can't be said for Kirk Gibson (.236, 16, 55). Mike Macfarlane (.277, 13, 41) is one of the AL's better offensive catchers. Kevin Seitzer (.265, 1, 25) will get one more chance to resurrect his fading career. Shortstop David Howard (.216, 1, 17) will have to improve to keep his job.

PITCHING: The Royals shopped Kevin Appier (13-10, 3.42) and Tom Gordon (9-14, 3.87), but found that it cost them their two-time Cy Young Award winner Saberhagen to get the offensive help they needed. Now they can only hope Appier and Gordon step up.

Mark Gubicza (9-12, 5.68) isn't the same pitcher after arm problems. Mike Boddicker (12-12, 4.08) is durable if not overpowering and don't overlook Luis Aquino (8-4, 3.44). The Royals would like to overlook the $13-million contract they gave to bust Mark Davis (6-3, 4.45), who may be in the rotation. If so, he would be the only left-hander. Closer Jeff Montgomery (4-4, 2.90, 33 Sv) could use help. It looks as if youngsters Mike Magnante (0-1, 2.45) and Joel Johnston (1-0, 0.40) will have to play major setup roles.

FIELDING: Those who watch the younger McRae every day say it's hard to imagine someone playing center field any better. McReynolds will be a solid right fielder, jittery former infield liability Jefferies will try left field, and if that doesn't work, move back to third. But the Royals do want to find one spot for him and leave him there. Few are better than Joyner around first base and strong-armed ex-Oriole Bob Melvin will support Macfarlane behind the plate. Miller is much like departed second baseman Bill Pecota—a career utility man who is solid wherever you put him, but spectacular nowhere.

OUTLOOK: General manager Herk Robinson put it this way: The Royals finished sixth two years in a row with Saberhagen, so why not try something different? This is a changed team from the Royals club that went 82-80 in 1991, but it still can't match the Royals' championship teams that were led by Hal McRae, the player, in the 1970s. How the malcontent McReynolds and the bratty Jefferies fit into the low-key Royals atmosphere will be a key determinant in just where the team finishes. But the middle of the pack looks like a solid bet.

KANSAS CITY ROYALS 1992 ROSTER

MANAGER Hal McRae
Coaches—Glenn Ezell, Adrian Garrett, Guy Hansen, Lynn Jones, Bruce Kison, Lee May

PITCHERS

No.	Name	1991 Club	W-L	IP	SO	ERA	B-T	Ht.	Wt.	Born
55	Appier, Kevin	Kansas City	13-10	208	158	3.42	R-R	6-2	200	12/6/67 Lancaster, CA
27	Aquino, Luis	Kansas City	8-4	157	80	3.44	R-R	6-1	195	5/19/65 Puerto Rico
52	Boddicker, Mike	Kansas City	12-12	181	79	4.08	R-R	5-11	185	8/23/57 Cedar Rapids, IA
—	Clark, Dera	Omaha	6-9	130	106	4.51	R-R	6-1	205	4/14/65 Monahans, TX
50	Corbin, Archie	Memphis	8-8	156	166	4.66	R-R	6-4	190	12/20/67 Beaumont, TX
		Kansas City	0-0	2	1	3.86				
48	Davis, Mark	Kansas City	6-3	63	47	4.45	L-L	6-4	210	10/19/60 Livermore, CA
16	Gordon, Tom	Kansas City	9-14	158	167	3.87	R-R	5-9	180	11/18/67 Sebring, FL
23	Gubicza, Mark	Kansas City	9-12	133	89	5.68	R-R	6-5	225	8/14/62 Philadelphia, PA
58	Johnston, Joel	Omaha	4-7	74	63	5.21	R-R	6-4	220	3/8/67 West Chester, PA
		Kansas City	1-0	22	21	0.40				
57	Magnante, Mike	Omaha	6-1	66	50	3.02	L-L	6-1	180	6/17/65 Glendale, CA
		Kansas City	0-1	55	42	2.45				
59	Maldonado, Carlos	Omaha	1-1	61	46	4.28	R-R	6-1	215	10/18/66 Panama
		Kansas City	0-0	8	1	8.22				
—	Meacham, Rusty	Toledo	3-1	125	70	3.09	R-R	6-2	165	1/27/68 Stuart, FL
		Detroit	2-1	28	14	5.20				
—	Moeller, Dennis	Memphis	4-5	53	54	2.55	R-L	6-2	195	9/15/67 Tarzana, CA
		Omaha	7-3	78	51	3.22				
21	Montgomery, Jeff	Kansas City	4-4	90	77	2.90	R-R	5-11	180	1/7/62 Wellston, OH
—	Richardo, Hipolito	Memphis	3-11	99	75	4.27	R-R	6-1	160	8/22/69 Dominican Republic
—	Pierce, Ed	Memphis	5-11	136	90	3.84	L-L	6-1	185	10/6/68 Arcadia, CA
34	Wagner, Hector	Omaha	5-6	86	36	3.44	R-R	6-3	200	11/26/68 Dominican Republic
		Kansas City	1-1	10	5	7.20				

CATCHERS

No.	Name	1991 Club	H	HR	RBI	Pct.	B-T	Ht.	Wt.	Born
15	Macfarlane, Mike	Kansas City	74	13	41	.277	R-R	6-1	205	4/12/64 Stockton, CA
24	Mayne, Brent	Kansas City	58	3	31	.251	L-R	6-1	190	4/19/68 Loma Linda, CA
2	Melvin, Bob	Baltimore	57	1	23	.250	R-R	6-4	207	10/28/61 Palo Alto, CA
7	Spehr, Tim	Omaha	59	6	26	.274	R-R	6-2	205	7/2/66 Excelsior Springs, MO
		Kansas City	14	3	14	.189				

INFIELDERS

No.	Name	1991 Club	H	HR	RBI	Pct.	B-T	Ht.	Wt.	Born
47	Berry, Sean	Omaha	97	11	54	.264	R-R	5-11	210	3/22/66 Santa Monica, CA
		Kansas City	8	0	1	.133				
5	Brett, George	Kansas City	129	10	61	.255	L-R	6-0	205	5/15/53 Glendale, WV
39	Cole, Stu	Omaha	115	3	39	.261	R-R	6-1	175	2/7/66 Charlotte, NC
		Kansas City	1	0	0	.143				
19	Conine, Jeff	Omaha	44	3	15	.257	R-R	6-1	220	6/27/66 Tacoma, WA
46	Hamelin, Bob	Omaha	24	4	19	.189	L-L	6-0	230	11/29/67 Elizabeth, NJ
31	Howard, David	Kansas City	51	1	17	.216	S-R	6-0	165	2/26/67 Sarasota, FL
		Omaha	5	0	2	.122				
9	Jefferies, Gregg	New York (NL)	132	9	62	.272	S-R	5-10	185	8/1/67 Burlingame, CA
—	Joyner, Wally	California	166	21	96	.301	L-L	6-2	203	6/16/62 Atlanta, GA
—	Miller, Keith	New York (NL)	77	4	23	.280	R-R	5-11	185	6/12/63 Midland, MI
33	Seitzer, Kevin	Kansas City	62	1	25	.265	R-R	5-11	190	3/26/62 Springfield, IL
3	Shumpert, Terry	Kansas City	80	5	34	.217	R-R	5-11	190	8/16/66 Paducah, KY

OUTFIELDERS

No.	Name	1991 Club	H	HR	RBI	Pct.	B-T	Ht.	Wt.	Born
22	Eisenreich, Jim	Kansas City	113	2	47	.301	L-L	5-11	195	4/18/59 St. Cloud, MN
30	Gibson, Kirk	Kansas City	109	16	55	.236	L-L	6-3	225	5/28/57 Pontiac, MI
—	Gwynn, Chris	Los Angeles	35	5	22	.252	L-L	6-0	210	10/13/64 Los Angeles, CA
—	Koslofski, Kevin	Memphis	93	7	39	.324	L-R	5-8	165	9/24/66 Decatur, IL
		Omaha	28	2	19	.298				
56	McRae, Brian	Kansas City	164	8	64	.261	S-R	6-0	185	8/27/67 Bradenton, FL
—	McReynolds, Kevin	New York (NL)	135	16	74	.259	R-R	6-1	215	10/16/59 Little Rock, AR
—	Moore, Kerwin	Baseball City	102	1	23	.210	R-R	6-1	190	11/29/70 Detroit, MI
51	Pulliam, Harvey	Omaha	89	6	39	.257	R-R	6-0	210	10/20/67 San Francisco, CA
		Kansas City	9	3	4	.273				
25	Thurman, Gary	Kansas City	51	2	13	.277	R-R	5-10	175	11/12/64 Indianapolis, IN

ROYAL PROFILES

WALLY JOYNER 29 6-2 203   Bats L Throws L

Picked right time for best season since 1987 ... Hit career-high .301 with 21 homers and 96 RBI and made tearful farewell to Angels when he opted for a one-year, $4.2-million pact with Royals in December ... Hadn't hit more than 16 homers or driven in more than 85 runs in previous three seasons ... Bounced back from injury-shortened 1990, when a stress fracture of his right knee limited him to 83 games ... Was hitting .326 with 57 RBI at All-Star break ... Slick-fielding first baseman committed eight errors ... Set career highs in 1987 with 34 homers and 117 RBI ... Earned $2.1 million in 1991 ... Third-round pick by Angels in 1983 draft, after playing three years at Brigham Young ... Born June 16, 1962, in Atlanta.

Year	Club	Pos.	G	AB	R	H	2B	3B	HR	RBI	SB	Avg.
1986	California	1B	154	593	82	172	27	3	22	100	5	.290
1987	California	1B	149	564	100	161	33	1	34	117	8	.285
1988	California	1B	158	597	81	176	31	2	13	85	8	.295
1989	California	1B	159	593	78	167	30	2	16	79	3	.282
1990	California	1B	83	310	35	83	15	0	8	41	2	.268
1991	California	1B	143	551	79	166	34	3	21	96	2	.301
	Totals		846	3208	455	925	170	11	114	518	28	.288

BRIAN McRAE 24 6-0 185   Bats S Throws R

The manager's son ... But this exciting center fielder earned his way into lineup before Papa Hal arrived ... Gold Glove-caliber talent ... Those who watch him every day say it's hard to imagine somebody being better defensively ... Offense isn't bad either ... His 64 RBI from leadoff spot were second on club ... Stole 20 bases in 31 tries ... Should improve that total with experience ... Made major-league debut Aug. 7, 1990, when he jumped from Double-A ... Earned $124,000 in 1991 ... Royals' first-round pick in 1985 draft ... Born Aug. 27, 1967, in Bradenton, Fla.

Year	Club	Pos.	G	AB	R	H	2B	3B	HR	RBI	SB	Avg.
1990	Kansas City	OF	46	168	21	48	8	3	2	23	4	.286
1991	Kansas City	OF	152	629	86	164	28	9	8	64	20	.261
	Totals		198	797	107	212	36	12	10	87	24	.266

GEORGE BRETT 38 6-0 205   Bats L Throws R

Couldn't follow up on unexpected batting title in 1990, dropping 74 points to .255 . . . Previous lowest batting average in 18 full seasons was .282 . . . Ten homers were his lowest total since 1978, excluding strike year of 1981 . . . Has hit .300 or better 11 times, including .390 mark in 1980 . . . Won batting titles in three decades (1976, 1980 and 1990) . . . Moved to first base in 1987 after 12 years at third . . . Likely to become only the eighth third baseman elected to Hall of Fame . . . Only 164 hits shy of 3,000 . . . Second-round pick in 1971 draft . . . Salary in 1991 was $1,838,661 . . . Born May 15, 1953, in Glendale, W. Va.

Year	Club	Pos.	G	AB	R	H	2B	3B	HR	RBI	SB	Avg.
1973	Kansas City . . .	3B	13	40	2	5	2	0	0	0	0	.125
1974	Kansas City . . .	3B-SS	133	457	49	129	21	5	2	47	8	.282
1975	Kansas City . . .	3B-SS	159	634	84	195	35	13	11	89	13	.308
1976	Kansas City . . .	3B-SS	159	645	94	215	34	14	7	67	21	.333
1977	Kansas City . . .	3B-SS	139	564	105	176	32	13	22	88	14	.312
1978	Kansas City . . .	3B-SS	128	510	79	150	45	8	9	62	23	.294
1979	Kansas City . . .	3B-1B	154	645	119	212	42	20	23	107	17	.329
1980	Kansas City . . .	3B-1B	117	449	87	175	33	9	24	118	15	.390
1981	Kansas City . . .	3B	89	347	42	109	27	7	6	43	14	.314
1982	Kansas City . . .	3B-OF	144	552	101	166	32	9	21	82	6	.301
1983	Kansas City . . .	3B-1B-OF	123	464	90	144	38	2	25	93	0	.310
1984	Kansas City . . .	3B	104	377	42	107	21	3	13	69	0	.284
1985	Kansas City . . .	3B	155	550	108	184	38	5	30	112	9	.335
1986	Kansas City . . .	3B-SS	124	441	70	128	28	4	16	73	1	.290
1987	Kansas City . . .	1B-3B	115	427	71	124	18	2	22	78	6	.290
1988	Kansas City . . .	1B-SS	157	589	90	180	42	3	24	103	14	.306
1989	Kansas City . . .	1B-OF	124	457	67	129	26	3	12	80	14	.282
1990	Kansas City . . .	1B-OF-3B	142	544	82	179	45	7	14	87	9	.329
1991	Kansas City . . .	1B	131	505	77	129	40	2	10	61	2	.255
	Totals		2410	9197	1459	2836	599	129	291	1459	186	.308

GREGG JEFFERIES 24 5-10 185   Bats S Throws R

A victim of too much advance publicity as a minor leaguer, he has not yet lived up to expectations . . . Joined Royals with Kevin McReynolds and Keith Miller in December trade that sent Bret Saberhagen and Bill Pecota to Mets . . . Set career-high in stolen bases with 26 in 1991, but most of other numbers were down . . . Below average defensively, he has been hurt by frequent shifts between second and third base . . . Stole home for first time in career Sept. 4 against Astros . . .

Struggled through 0-for-23 slump in early September . . . Was homerless from right side for 13 months before connecting against Reds' Randy Myers Aug. 25 . . . Had at least one hit in 14 straight starts in early July . . . Landed on disabled list in May with pulled muscle in rib cage . . . Selected by Mets in first round of 1985 draft . . . Named Minor League Player of the Decade for the 1980s by *Baseball America* . . . Led NL in doubles in 1990 . . . Born Aug. 1, 1967, in Burlingame, Cal. . . . Earned $425,000 in 1991.

Year Club	Pos.	G	AB	R	H	2B	3B	HR	RBI	SB	Avg.
1987 New York (NL)	PH	6	6	0	3	1	0	0	2	0	.500
1988 New York (NL)	3B-2B	29	109	19	35	8	2	6	17	5	.321
1989 New York (NL)	2B-3B	141	508	72	131	28	2	12	56	21	.258
1990 New York (NL)	2B-3B	153	604	96	171	40	3	15	68	11	.283
1991 New York (NL)	2B-3B	136	486	59	132	19	2	9	62	26	.272
Totals		465	1713	246	472	96	9	42	205	63	.276

KEVIN McREYNOLDS 32 6-1 215   Bats R Throws R

"K-Mac" was part of Mets' general offensive lethargy in 1991 and he was traded to Royals in December with Gregg Jefferies and Keith Miller for Bret Saberhagen and Bill Pecota . . . . . . Except for tying career high in doubles with 32, he had his least productive season in five years as a Met . . . One of smoothest left fielders in baseball, he frequently filled in as center fielder after Vince Coleman was sidelined . . . Hampered by back spasms at times, he hit just four homers from July 29-Oct. 2 . . . Missed time in April after injuring knee on Opening Day and started season 1-for-27 . . . Selected by Padres in first round of 1981 draft . . . Traded to Mets in eight-player deal that cost them Kevin Mitchell following 1986 season . . . Finished third in 1988 MVP voting . . . Born Oct. 16, 1969, in Little Rock, Ark. . . . Earned $2,266,667 in 1991.

Year Club	Pos.	G	AB	R	H	2B	3B	HR	RBI	SB	Avg.
1983 San Diego	OF	39	140	15	31	3	1	4	14	2	.221
1984 San Diego	OF	147	525	68	146	26	6	20	75	3	.278
1985 San Diego	OF	152	564	61	132	24	4	15	75	4	.234
1986 San Diego	OF	158	560	89	161	31	6	26	96	8	.288
1987 New York (NL)	OF	151	590	86	163	32	5	29	95	14	.276
1988 New York (NL)	OF	147	552	82	159	30	2	27	99	21	.288
1989 New York (NL)	OF	148	545	74	148	25	3	22	85	15	.272
1990 New York (NL)	OF	147	521	75	140	23	1	24	82	9	.269
1991 New York (NL)	OF	143	522	65	135	32	1	16	74	6	.259
Totals		1232	4519	615	1215	226	29	183	695	82	.269

JIM EISENREICH 32 5-11 200   Bats L Throws L

Topped .300 mark for first time in five seasons . . . But hit only two homers, drove in 47 runs and stole five bases as his playing time decreased . . . Reached career highs in 1989 with nine homers, 59 RBI and 27 steals . . . Versatile performer can play all three outfield positions and first base . . . Won much-chronicled battle with Tourette's Syndrome with help of medication . . . Twins' 16th-round pick in 1980 was claimed on waivers by Royals in 1986, on recommendation of scout who watched him in semipro games . . . Missed most of 1982, 1983 and 1984 and virtually all of 1985 and 1986 because of his condition . . . Earned $950,000 in 1991 . . . Born April 18, 1959, in St. Cloud, Minn. . . . Accepted arbitration in December.

Year	Club	Pos.	G	AB	R	H	2B	3B	HR	RBI	SB	Avg.
1982	Minnesota	OF	34	99	10	30	6	0	2	9	0	.303
1983	Minnesota	OF	2	7	1	2	1	0	0	0	0	.286
1984	Minnesota	OF	12	32	1	7	1	0	0	3	2	.219
1987	Kansas City . . .	DH	44	105	10	25	8	2	4	21	1	.238
1988	Kansas City . . .	OF	82	202	26	44	8	1	1	19	9	.218
1989	Kansas City . . .	OF	134	475	64	139	33	7	9	59	27	.293
1990	Kansas City . . .	OF	142	496	61	139	29	7	5	51	12	.280
1991	Kansas City . . .	OF-1B	135	375	47	113	22	3	2	47	5	.301
	Totals		585	1791	220	499	108	20	23	209	56	.279

MIKE MACFARLANE 27 6-1 205   Bats R Throws R

Knee injury cut season in half, just when he was blossoming . . . Still finished with career-high 13 homers, one more than career total before 1991 . . . Hit 12th and 13th homers on July 14 and went under the knife two days later . . . Returned to action Sept. 18 . . . Catcher improved throwing percentage considerably with help of pitching staff that paid more attention to holding runners closer . . . Hit .255 with 58 RBI in 1990, his first as a regular . . . Fourth-round pick of Royals in 1985 draft . . . Salary was $260,000 in 1991 . . . Born April 12, 1964, in Stockton, Cal.

Year	Club	Pos.	G	AB	R	H	2B	3B	HR	RBI	SB	Avg.
1987	Kansas City . . .	C	8	19	0	4	1	0	0	3	0	.211
1988	Kansas City . . .	C	70	211	25	56	15	0	4	26	0	.265
1989	Kansas City . . .	C	69	157	13	35	6	0	2	19	0	.223
1990	Kansas City . . .	C	124	400	37	102	24	4	6	58	1	.255
1991	Kansas City . . .	C	84	267	34	74	18	2	13	41	1	.277
	Totals		355	1054	109	271	64	6	25	147	2	.257

KEVIN APPIER 24 6-2 200   Bats R Throws R

Developed into front-line starter in second full season . . . Tied Bret Saberhagen for staff lead in victories with 13 . . . Led staff in shutouts (three), starts (31) and innings pitched (207⅔) . . . Was 3-7 on June 7 before finishing 10-3 . . . Won seven consecutive decisions over 11 starts from June 18-Aug. 13 . . . Pitched back-to-back shutouts over Boston and New York in August . . . Is 25-18 with a 3.10 ERA over last two years . . . AL Rookie Pitcher of the Year in 1990, when he also finished third in AL Rookie of the Year balloting behind Indians' Sandy Alomar Jr. and Yanks' Kevin Maas . . . First-round pick by Royals in 1987 draft . . . Salary was $215,000 in 1991 . . . Born Dec. 6, 1967, in Lancaster, Cal.

Year	Club	G	IP	W	L	Pct.	SO	BB	H	ERA
1989	Kansas City	6	21⅔	1	4	.200	10	12	34	9.14
1990	Kansas City	32	185⅔	12	8	.600	127	54	179	2.76
1991	Kansas City	34	207⅔	13	10	.565	158	61	205	3.42
	Totals	72	415	26	22	.542	295	127	418	3.43

MIKE BODDICKER 34 5-11 185   Bats R Throws R

Wasn't free-agent savior Royals hoped he would be, but wasn't a Mark Davis-type flop, either . . . Consistent, if not spectacular . . . Was 7-7 at All-Star break and finished 12-12 . . . Earned $3,166,667 in 1991, first year of a three-year contract . . . Orioles' sixth-round pick in 1978 . . . Reached double figures in wins for ninth consecutive year . . . AL Rookie of the Year in 1983, when he was 16-8 for Baltimore . . . Led AL with 20 victories and 2.79 ERA in 1984, when he was named an All-Star for only time . . . Born Aug. 23, 1957, in Cedar Rapids, Iowa.

Year	Club	G	IP	W	L	Pct.	SO	BB	H	ERA
1980	Baltimore	1	7	0	1	.000	4	5	6	6.43
1981	Baltimore	2	6	0	0	.000	2	2	6	4.50
1982	Baltimore	7	25⅔	1	0	1.000	20	12	25	3.51
1983	Baltimore	27	179	16	8	.667	120	52	141	2.77
1984	Baltimore	34	261⅓	20	11	.645	128	81	218	2.79
1985	Baltimore	32	203⅓	12	17	.414	135	89	227	4.07
1986	Baltimore	33	218⅓	14	12	.538	175	74	214	4.70
1987	Baltimore	33	226	10	12	.455	152	78	212	4.18
1988	Balt.-Bos.	36	236	13	15	.464	156	77	234	3.39
1989	Boston	34	211⅔	15	11	.577	145	71	217	4.00
1990	Boston	34	228	17	8	.680	143	69	225	3.36
1991	Kansas City	30	180⅔	12	12	.500	79	59	188	4.08
	Totals	303	1983	130	107	.549	1259	669	1913	3.70

TOM GORDON 24 5-9 180   Bats R Throws R

Still searching for niche, but has youth and devastating curve on his side... Took turn in rotation until just after All-Star break, then moved to bullpen, where he is expected to stay as setup man... Numbers were remarkably similar in the two roles... Was 5-8 as starter, 4-6 as reliever... A power pitcher, despite small frame... Struck out 167, walked 87 and allowed 129 hits in 158 innings... Allowed club-high 16 homers ... Was AL Rookie Pitcher of the Year in 1989, when he was 17-9... Sixth-round pick in 1986 draft... Earned $325,000 in 1991... Born Nov. 18, 1967, in Sebring, Fla.

Year	Club	G	IP	W	L	Pct.	SO	BB	H	ERA
1988	Kansas City	5	15⅔	0	2	.000	18	7	16	5.17
1989	Kansas City	49	163	17	9	.654	153	86	122	3.64
1990	Kansas City	32	195⅓	12	11	.522	175	99	192	3.73
1991	Kansas City	45	158	9	14	.391	167	87	129	3.87
	Totals	131	532	38	36	.514	513	279	459	3.79

JEFF MONTGOMERY 30 5-11 180   Bats R Throws R

Grabbed firm hold on closer's role, finishing with 33 saves in 39 opportunities... Had total of 42 saves in 1989 and 1990 after starting each of those years as setup man before assuming closer's role... Had five saves and a win in April, when Royals were 8-11... Blew two saves in three tries just before John Wathan was fired May 22... ERA was hurt when he allowed seven runs in 2⅔ innings June 23. Wipe that away and his ERA drops from 2.90 to 2.27... Saved seven games in 11 days from July 23-Aug. 2, including three in a row against Milwaukee July 23-25... Reds' ninth-round pick in 1983 was acquired for outfielder Van Snider prior to 1988 season... Earned $1,085,000 in 1991... Born Jan. 7, 1962, in Wellston, Ohio.

Year	Club	G	IP	W	L	Pct.	SO	BB	H	ERA
1987	Cincinnati	14	19⅓	2	2	.500	13	9	25	6.52
1988	Kansas City	45	62⅔	7	2	.778	47	30	54	3.45
1989	Kansas City	63	92	7	3	.700	94	25	66	1.37
1990	Kansas City	73	94⅓	6	5	.545	94	34	81	2.39
1991	Kansas City	67	90	4	4	.500	77	28	83	2.90
	Totals	262	358⅓	26	16	.619	325	126	309	2.66

Kevin Appier finished Royally, winning 10 of last 13.

TOP PROSPECTS

TIM SPEHR 25 6-2 205   **Bats R Throws R**
Catcher got chance when Mike Macfarlane had knee surgery . . .
Hit only .189 in 74 at-bats, but did belt three homers and drive
in 14 runs for Royals . . . Also had five doubles among his 14 hits
. . . Hit .274 with six homers and 26 RBI for Omaha (AAA)
. . . Fifth-round choice in 1988 draft . . . Helped Arizona State to
College World Series that year . . . Born July 2, 1966, in Excelsior
Springs, Mo.

JEFF CONINE 25 6-1 220   **Bats R Throws R**
Good-hitting first baseman had season destroyed by injury . . .
Batted .257 with only three homers in 171 at-bats for Omaha
(AAA) . . . More indicative of his potential is 1990 season for
Memphis (AA), when he hit .320 with 15 homers, 95 RBI and
21 steals . . . Went 5-for-20 for Royals in September that year . . .
Picked in 58th round of 1987 draft . . . Born June 27, 1966, in
Tacoma, Wash.

JOEL JOHNSTON 25 6-4 220 **Bats R Throws R**
Hard thrower who found himself after promotion in September
. . . In 13 relief appearances with Royals, he had microscopic 0.40
ERA and allowed only nine hits . . . Struck out 21 while walking
only nine in 22⅓ innings . . . Was 4-7 with 5.21 ERA and eight
saves for Omaha (AAA) . . . Third-round pick in 1988 . . . Born
March 8, 1967, in West Chester, Pa.

HARVEY PULLIAM 24 6-0 210 **Bats R Throws R**
Outfielder hit .257 with six homers and 39 RBI for Omaha (AAA)
before solid showing in 18-game callup . . . With Royals, he hit
.273 with three homers in 33 at-bats . . . Four of nine hits were
for extra bases . . . Hit 16 homers for Omaha in 1990 . . . Third-
round pick in 1986 draft . . . Born Oct. 20, 1967, in San Francisco.

MANAGER HAL McRAE: Back in organization where he
made his mark as a player . . . Replaced former
teammate John Wathan May 24 . . . Team was
six games under .500 when he took over and
finished four games over . . . Royals were 66-56
under him . . . Has rare opportunity to manage
his son, Brian . . . Only fifth black manager in
major-league history, following Frank Robinson, Larry Doby, Maury Wills and Cito Gaston
. . . Left job as Expos' hitting instructor to manage . . . Was minor-
league hitting instructor for Pirates in 1988 and 1989 and remains
one of game's foremost hitting authorities . . . Brought back aggressive style that characterized Royals of his era . . . Hit .290 in
18 major-league seasons, the last 15 with Kansas City . . . Hit .300
or better six times, including career-high .332 in 1976 . . . Drove
in major-league-high 132 runs in 1982 . . . Played in eight League
Championship Series and four World Series . . . Born July 10,
1945, in Avon Park, Fla.

ALL-TIME ROYAL SEASON RECORDS

BATTING: George Brett, .390, 1980
HRs: Steve Balboni, 36, 1985
RBI: Hal McRae, 133, 1982
STEALS: Willie Wilson, 83, 1979
WINS: Bret Saberhagen, 23, 1989
STRIKEOUTS: Dennis Leonard, 244, 1977

MINNESOTA TWINS

TEAM DIRECTORY: Owner: Carl Pohlad; Pres.: Jerry Bell; Exec. VP/GM: Andy MacPhail; VP-Player Pers.: Terry Ryan; Dir. Media Rel.: Rob Antony; Trav. Sec.: Remzi Kiratli; Mgr.: Tom Kelly. Home: Hubert H. Humphrey Metrodome (55,883). Field distances: 343, l.f. line; 408, c.f.; 327, r.f. line. Spring training: Fort Myers, Fla.

SCOUTING REPORT

HITTING: They don't have overwhelming power or speed, but what the defending world champion Twins do have is a group of patient contact hitters who aren't afraid to take a walk and are willing to give themselves up to score runs. The Twins led the majors with a .281 team average and were fourth in the AL in runs with 776 in 1991.

Kirby Puckett (.319, 15, 89) topped .300 for the fifth time in six years, while late bloomer Shane Mack (.310, 18, 74) did so for the second time. And now the Twins will have Pedro Munoz, a .300 hitter in the minors, in left in place of Dan Gladden.

No catcher has put up an average to match that of Brian Harper (.311, 10, 69) over the last three years. Chili Davis (.277, 29, 93) and Kent Hrbek (.284, 20, 89) provide the power and the double-play combination of AL Rookie of the Year Chuck Knoblauch (.281, 1, 50) and Greg Gagne (.265, 8, 42) can hit, too.

PITCHING: For a team that boasted four pitchers who received Cy Young Award consideration last year, the Twins aren't in the best shape here.

Jack Morris' departure creates a huge void in an otherwise youthful rotation. Kevin Tapani (16-9, 2.99) inherits the No. 1 starter's role and the enigmatic Scott Erickson (20-8, 3.18) has to prove himself again after a second-half collapse. The rest of the rotation is a question mark, although the best bets to fill it out are Mark Guthrie (7-5, 4.32), David West (4-4, 4.54), Paul Abbott (3-1, 4.75), Danny Neagle (0-1, 4.05) and rookie Willie Banks (1-1, 5.71).

Carl Willis (8-3, 2.63) had a career year as a setup man. Veterans Steve Bedrosian and Terry Leach weren't re-signed, so free agent addition Bob Kipper (2-2, 4.65 for the Pirates) was imported for middle relief. At least Rick Aguilera (4-5, 2.35, 42 Sv) is around to protect late-inning leads.

Twins' mighty mite Kirby Puckett is at .320 lifetime.

FIELDING: If there is a constant with Tom Kelly's teams, it's that they play outstanding defense. The Twins, second to the Orioles in fielding percentage at .985 in 1991, annually are at or near the top of the team fielding list. Puckett won another Gold Glove in center, but club officials thought Mack had a better defensive year in right.

The infield is uniformly excellent with Hrbek, Knoblauch, Gagne and Mike Pagliarulo. Knoblauch's error total was high (18), but he has excellent hands and range. Gagne is a superb shortstop with a very strong arm. Hrbek is more nimble than he appears. The only weak spot is behind the plate with Harper.

OUTLOOK: The Twins, with their 95-67 turnaround in 1991, taught us nobody can be counted out. They went from last to first and then won their second world championship in five years. But, repeating in the game's toughest division is a little too much to ask after losing your staff ace—particularly when you can't depend on another career year from a handful of players who were magical in 1991.

MINNESOTA TWINS 1992 ROSTER

MANAGER Tom Kelly
Coaches—Terry Crowley, Ron Gardenhire, Rick Stelmaszek, Dick Such, Wayne Terwilliger

PITCHERS

No.	Name	1991 Club	W-L	IP	SO	ERA	B-T	Ht.	Wt.	Born
37	Abbott, Paul	Portland	2-3	44	40	3.89	R-R	6-3	193	9/15/67 Van Nuys, CA
		Minnesota	3-1	47	43	4.75				
38	Aguilera, Rick	Minnesota	4-5	69	61	2.35	R-R	6-5	205	12/31/61 San Gabriel, CA
23	Banks, Willie	Portland	9-8	146	63	4.55	R-R	6-1	190	2/27/69 Jersey City, NJ
		Minnesota	1-1	17	16	5.71				
19	Casian, Larry	Minnesota	0-0	18	6	7.36	R-L	6-0	170	10/28/65 Lynwood, CA
		Portland	3-2	52	24	3.46				
59	Edens, Tom	Portland	10-7	161	100	3.01	L-R	6-2	185	6/9/61 Ontario, OR
		Minnesota	2-2	33	19	4.09				
19	Erickson, Scott	Minnesota	20-8	204	108	3.18	R-R	6-4	225	2/2/68 Long Beach, CA
—	Garces, Richard	Portland	0-1	13	13	4.85	R-R	6-0	215	5/18/71 Venezuela
		Orlando	2-1	16	17	3.31				
53	Guthrie, Mark	Minnesota	7-5	98	72	4.32	S-L	6-4	196	9/22/65 Buffalo, NY
—	Kipper, Bob	Pittsburgh	2-2	60	38	4.65	R-L	6-2	180	7/8/64 Aurora, IL
—	Mahomes, Pat	Orlando	8-5	116	136	1.78	R-R	6-1	175	8/9/70 Bryan, TX
		Portland	3-5	55	41	3.44				
58	Neagle, Denny	Portland	9-4	105	94	3.27	L-L	6-4	209	9/13/68 Prince Georges, MD
		Minnesota	0-1	20	14	4.05				
—	Newman, Alan	Visalia	6-5	92	79	3.51	L-L	6-6	212	10/2/69 La Habra, CA
		Orlando	5-4	67	53	2.69				
36	Tapani, Kevin	Minnesota	16-9	244	135	2.99	R-R	6-0	187	2/18/64 Des Moines, IA
—	Trombley, Mike	Orlando	12-7	191	175	2.54	R-R	6-2	200	4/14/67 Springfield, MA
—	Tsamis, George	Orlando	0-0	7	5	0.00	R-L	6-2	175	6/14/67 Campbell, CA
		Portland	10-8	168	75	3.27				
—	Wassenaar, Rob	Portland	2-2	25	21	1.44	R-R	6-2	200	4/28/65 Denver, CO
		Portland	4-4	77	62	3.26				
48	Wayne, Gary	Portland	4-5	68	66	2.79	L-L	6-3	200	11/30/62 Dearborn, MI
		Minnesota	1-0	12	7	5.11				
39	West, David	Orlando	0-0	1	0	0.00	L-L	6-6	231	9/1/64 Memphis, TN
		Portland	1-1	16	15	6.32				
		Minnesota	4-4	71	52	4.54				
51	Willis, Carl	Portland	1-1	11	0	1.64	L-R	6-4	212	12/28/60 Danville, VA
		Minnesota	8-3	89	53	2.63				

CATCHERS

No.	Name	1991 Club	H	HR	RBI	Pct.	B-T	Ht.	Wt.	Born
12	Harper, Brian	Minnesota	137	10	69	.311	R-R	6-2	205	10/16/59 Los Angeles, CA
16	Parks, Derek	Orlando	55	6	31	.215	R-R	6-0	205	9/29/68 Covina, CA
15	Webster, Lenny	Portland	82	7	34	.252	R-R	5-9	192	2/10/65 New Orleans, LA
		Minnesota	10	3	8	.294				

INFIELDERS

No.	Name	1991 Club	H	HR	RBI	Pct.	B-T	Ht.	Wt.	Born
7	Gagne, Greg	Minnesota	108	8	42	.265	R-R	5-11	172	11/12/61 Fall River, MA
—	Garcia, Cheo	Orlando	140	9	75	.282	S-R	5-11	165	4/27/68 Venezuela
—	Gilbert, Shawn	Orlando	135	3	38	.255	R-R	5-9	170	3/12/65 Camden, NJ
4	Hrbek, Kent	Minnesota	131	20	89	.284	L-R	6-4	253	5/21/60 Minneapolis, MN
27	Jorgensen, Terry	Portland	136	11	59	.298	R-R	6-4	213	9/2/66 Kewaunee, WI
11	Knoblauch, Chuck	Minnesota	159	1	50	.281	R-R	5-9	175	7/7/68 Houston, TX
9	Larkin, Gene	Minnesota	73	2	19	.286	S-R	6-3	199	10/24/62 Astoria, NY
31	Leius, Scott	Minnesota	57	5	20	.286	R-R	6-3	207	9/24/65 Yonkers, NY
13	Pagliarulo, Mike	Minnesota	102	6	36	.279	L-R	6-2	195	3/15/60 Medford, MA
18	Sorrento, Paul	Portland	126	13	79	.308	L-R	6-2	217	11/17/65 Somerville, MA
		Minnesota	12	4	13	.255				

OUTFIELDERS

No.	Name	1991 Club	H	HR	RBI	Pct.	B-T	Ht.	Wt.	Born
1	Brown, Jarvis	Portland	126	3	37	.289	R-R	5-7	177	3/26/67 Waukegan, IL
		Minnesota	8	0	0	.216				
—	Bruett, J.T.	Portland	98	6	35	.284	L-L	5-11	175	10/8/67 Milwaukee, WI
25	Bush, Randy	Minnesota	50	6	23	.303	L-L	6-1	190	10/5/58 Dover, DE
44	Davis, Chili	Minnesota	148	29	93	.277	S-R	6-3	210	1/17/60 Jamaica
24	Mack, Shane	Minnesota	137	18	74	.310	R-R	6-0	190	12/7/63 Los Angeles, CA
5	Munoz, Pedro	Portland	67	5	28	.316	R-R	5-10	200	9/19/68 Puerto Rico
		Minnesota	39	7	26	.283				
34	Puckett, Kirby	Minnesota	195	15	89	.319	R-R	5-8	216	3/14/61 Chicago, IL

TWIN PROFILES

KIRBY PUCKETT 31 5-8 216   Bats R Throws R

What's not to like? Hit above .300 for the fifth time in six years at .319 . . . Raised power numbers to 15 homers and 89 RBI, but probably never will reach totals of 1986-88 again . . . Had career-high six-hit game against Texas May 23 . . . Doubled off White Sox' Greg Hibbard for 1,500th career hit June 29 . . . Has made six consecutive AL All-Star teams . . . Hit an incredible .406 against left-handed pitching . . . Hit .372 in his first at-bats . . . Center fielder has won four Gold Gloves . . . Almost never stops smiling . . . Earned $3,166,667 and Gold Glove in 1991 . . . Twins' first-round pick in January 1982 draft . . . Born March 14, 1961, in Chicago . . . Hit 12th-inning homer in World Series Game 6 to keep Twins alive.

Year	Club	Pos.	G	AB	R	H	2B	3B	HR	RBI	SB	Avg.
1984	Minnesota	OF	128	557	63	165	12	5	0	31	14	.296
1985	Minnesota	OF	161	691	80	199	29	13	4	74	21	.288
1986	Minnesota	OF	161	680	119	223	37	6	31	96	20	.328
1987	Minnesota	OF	157	624	96	207	32	5	28	99	12	.332
1988	Minnesota	OF	158	657	109	234	42	5	24	121	6	.356
1989	Minnesota	OF	159	635	75	215	45	4	9	85	11	.339
1990	Minnesota	OF-2B-SS-3B	146	551	82	164	40	3	12	80	5	.298
1991	Minnesota	OF	152	611	92	195	29	6	15	89	11	.319
	Totals		1222	5006	716	1602	266	47	123	675	100	.320

KENT HRBEK 31 6-4 253   Bats L Throws R

Another year of respectable, but slightly underachieving power numbers for the hometown hero . . . Has averaged 23 homers and 82 RBI over last four seasons . . . Struggled more than ever against left-handed pitching in 1991 . . . For someone who aspires to wrestle under the pseudonym "Tyrannasaurus Rex" after he retires, he is quite nimble around first base . . . Just don't tell that to Braves' Ron Gant, whom he separated from first base in controversial World Series play . . . Earned $2.6 million in 1991 . . . Hit only .115 with one homer and two RBI in World Series . . . Twins' seventh-round pick in 1978 draft . . . Born

May 21, 1960, in Bloomington, Minn. and grew up in shadow of old Metropolitan Stadium.

Year	Club	Pos.	G	AB	R	H	2B	3B	HR	RBI	SB	Avg.
1981	Minnesota	1B	24	67	5	16	5	0	1	7	0	.239
1982	Minnesota	1B	140	532	82	160	21	4	23	92	3	.301
1983	Minnesota	1B	141	515	75	153	41	5	16	84	4	.297
1984	Minnesota	1B	149	559	80	174	31	3	27	107	1	.311
1985	Minnesota	1B	158	593	78	165	31	2	21	93	1	.278
1986	Minnesota	1B	149	550	85	147	27	1	29	91	2	.267
1987	Minnesota	1B	143	477	85	136	20	1	34	90	5	.285
1988	Minnesota	1B	143	510	75	159	31	0	25	76	0	.312
1989	Minnesota	1B	109	375	59	102	17	0	25	84	3	.272
1990	Minnesota	1B-3B	143	492	61	141	26	0	22	79	5	.287
1991	Minnesota	1B	132	462	72	131	20	1	20	89	4	.284
	Totals		1431	5132	757	1484	270	17	243	892	28	.289

SHANE MACK 28 6-0 190   Bats R Throws R

Right fielder started hitting in second half of 1990 and didn't stop—until the 1991 World Series, when he batted .130 . . . Reached career highs in virtually every offensive category in 1991, when he established himself as one of AL's better right fielders . . . Hit .356 after the All-Star break . . . Earned $270,000 in 1991 . . . Picked by Twins from Padres in December 1989 minor-league draft and San Diego is still looking for a center fielder . . . Was 11th pick overall in 1984 draft . . . Member of U.S. Olympic Team that summer . . . Born Dec. 7, 1963, in Los Angeles . . . Re-signed one-year, $1.07-million contract in January.

Year	Club	Pos.	G	AB	R	H	2B	3B	HR	RBI	SB	Avg.
1987	San Diego	OF	105	238	28	57	11	3	4	25	4	.239
1988	San Diego	OF	56	119	13	29	3	0	0	12	5	.244
1990	Minnesota	OF	125	313	50	102	10	4	8	44	13	.326
1991	Minnesota	OF	143	442	79	137	27	8	18	74	13	.310
	Totals		429	1112	170	325	51	15	30	155	35	.292

CHILI DAVIS 32 6-3 210   Bats S Throws R

Enjoyed renaissance upon emerging from Doug Rader's doghouse in California . . . Chronic back problems eased . . . Set career highs in homers (29) and RBI (93) as fulltime DH . . . Plays field only in emergencies, such as Game 5 of the World Series . . . Had 19 homers and 52 RBI in big first half . . . Salary was $1.7 million in 1991, first year of deal signed as new-look free agent . . . Giants' 11th-round pick in 1977 slipped to 12 homers and 58 RBI in 1990, one year after Angels' team MVP season in 1989 . . . Real name is Charles Theodore Davis . . . Born Jan. 17, 1960, in Kingston, Jamaica . . . Hit .222 with two homers and four RBI in World Series after enjoying big ALCS vs. Blue Jays.

Year	Club	Pos.	G	AB	R	H	2B	3B	HR	RBI	SB	Avg.
1981	San Francisco	OF	8	15	1	2	0	0	0	0	2	.133
1982	San Francisco	OF	154	641	86	167	27	6	19	76	24	.261
1983	San Francisco	OF	137	486	54	113	21	2	11	59	10	.233
1984	San Francisco	OF	137	499	87	157	21	6	21	81	12	.315
1985	San Francisco	OF	136	481	53	130	25	2	13	56	15	.270
1986	San Francisco	OF	153	526	71	146	28	3	13	70	16	.278
1987	San Francisco	OF	149	500	80	125	22	1	24	76	16	.250
1988	California . . .	OF	158	600	81	161	29	3	21	93	9	.268
1989	California	OF	154	560	81	152	24	1	22	90	3	.271
1990	California	OF	113	412	58	109	17	1	12	58	1	.265
1991	Minnesota	OF	153	534	84	148	34	1	29	93	5	.277
	Totals		1452	5254	736	1410	248	26	185	752	113	.268

CHUCK KNOBLAUCH 23 5-9 175   Bats R Throws R

Capped AL Rookie of the Year season with 15 postseason hits, a record for first-year players . . . Hit .308 with two RBI in World Series . . . Capably filled No. 2 spot in Twins' order, helped by uncanny ability to hit to right field . . . Struck out only 40 times in 565 at-bats . . . Made high total of 18 errors, but has all the defensive tools at second base . . . Stole 25 bases in 30 tries . . . Hit only major-league homer July 31 and it was a game-winner . . . Earned the minimum $100,000 in 1991 . . . Twins' first pick in 1989 draft, after All-American season at Texas A&M . . . Born July 7, 1968, in Houston.

Year	Club	Pos.	G	AB	R	H	2B	3B	HR	RBI	SB	Avg.
1991	Minnesota	2B-SS	151	565	78	159	24	6	1	50	25	.281

GREG GAGNE 30 5-11 172   Bats R Throws R

Your basic steady shortstop . . . Committed just nine errors and finished behind only Cal Ripken in fielding percentage among AL shortstops (.984) . . . Went 76 games from May 2-Aug. 12 (319 total chances) without an error . . . Has excellent range and strong throwing arm . . . Hit game-winning homer in Game 2 of World Series . . . Yanks' fourth-round pick in 1979 raised average 30 points from 1990 . . . Salary was $1,733,333 in

1991 . . . Acquired from Yankees in deal involving Roy Smalley, April 10, 1982 . . . Born Nov. 12, 1961, in Fall River, Mass.

Year	Club	Pos.	G	AB	R	H	2B	3B	HR	RBI	SB	Avg.
1983	Minnesota	SS	10	27	2	3	1	0	0	3	0	.111
1984	Minnesota	PR-PH	2	1	0	0	0	0	0	0	0	.000
1985	Minnesota	SS	114	293	37	66	15	3	2	23	10	.225
1986	Minnesota	SS-2B	156	472	63	118	22	6	12	54	12	.250
1987	Minnesota	SS-OF-2B	137	437	68	116	28	7	10	40	6	.265
1988	Minnesota	SS-OF-2B-3B	149	461	70	109	20	6	14	48	15	.236
1989	Minnesota	SS-OF	149	460	69	125	29	7	9	48	11	.272
1990	Minnesota	SS-OF	138	388	38	91	22	3	7	38	8	.235
1991	Minnesota	SS	139	408	52	108	23	3	8	42	11	.265
	Totals		994	2947	399	736	160	35	62	296	73	.250

BRIAN HARPER 32 6-2 205   Bats R Throws R

Few catchers can match his offense . . . Has averaged .309 with eight homers and 62 RBI over last three seasons . . . Hit .435 in 12-game streak from April 30-May 18 . . . Also had 13-game hitting streak in June . . . Was hitting .332 at All-Star break . . . Hit .381 vs. Braves in World Series . . . Defense is another matter . . . Threw out only 18 percent of would-be base-stealers . . . Earned $737,500 in 1991 . . . Signed by Twins as free agent prior to 1988 season . . . Angels' fourth-round pick in 1977 first appeared in majors with California in 1979, but didn't log more than 131 big-league at-bats in any year until 1988 . . . Born Oct. 16, 1959, in Los Angeles . . . Accepted arbitration in December.

Year	Club	Pos.	G	AB	R	H	2B	3B	HR	RBI	SB	Avg.
1979	California	DH	1	2	0	0	0	0	0	0	0	.000
1981	California	OF	4	11	1	3	0	0	0	1	1	.273
1982	Pittsburgh	OF	20	29	4	8	1	0	2	4	0	.276
1983	Pittsburgh	OF-1B	61	131	16	29	4	1	7	20	0	.221
1984	Pittsburgh	OF-C	46	112	4	29	4	0	2	11	0	.259
1985	St. Louis	OF-3B-C-1B	43	52	5	13	4	0	0	8	0	.250
1986	Detroit........	OF-1B-C	19	36	2	5	1	0	0	3	0	.139
1987	Oakland	OF	11	17	1	4	1	0	0	3	0	.235
1988	Minnesota	C-3B	60	166	15	49	11	1	3	20	0	.295
1989	Minnesota	C-OF-1B-3B	126	385	43	125	24	0	8	57	2	.325
1990	Minnesota	C-3B-1B	134	479	61	141	42	3	6	54	3	.294
1991	Minnesota	C-1B-OF	123	441	54	137	28	1	10	69	1	.311
	Totals		648	1861	206	543	120	6	38	250	7	.292

Chuck Knoblauch was AL Rookie of the Year.

MIKE PAGLIARULO 32 6-2 195   Bats L Throws R

Left-handed half of third-base platoon (with Scott Leius) that adequately replaced departed free agent Gary Gaetti in 1991 . . . Tireless work ethic fits in with blue-collar team and so does his strong defense . . . Had 30-game errorless streak from June 11-July 31 . . . Nowhere near the power hitter he was with Yanks in 1986 and 1987, when he averaged 30 homers and 79 RBI . . . But did hit a career-high .279 in 1991, a full 43 points above his career average . . . Hit game-winning homer in ALCS Game 3, starting him on a 5-for-8 streak in final three games, and batted .273 with one homer in World Series . . . Yanks' sixth-round pick in 1981 signed with Twins as free agent prior to 1991 season . . . Re-signed as free agent for $1.2 million in January . . . Born March 15, 1960, in Medford, Mass.

Year	Club	Pos.	G	AB	R	H	2B	3B	HR	RBI	SB	Avg.
1984	New York (AL)	3B	67	201	24	48	15	3	7	34	0	.239
1985	New York (AL)	3B	138	380	55	91	16	2	19	62	0	.239
1986	New York (AL)	3B-SS	149	504	71	120	24	3	28	71	4	.238
1987	New York (AL)	3B-1B	150	522	76	122	26	3	32	87	1	.234
1988	New York (AL)	3B	125	444	46	96	20	1	15	67	1	.216
1989	New York (AL)	3B	74	223	19	44	10	0	4	16	1	.197
1989	San Diego	3B	50	148	12	29	7	0	3	14	2	.196
1990	San Diego	3B	128	398	29	101	23	2	7	38	1	.254
1991	Minnesota	3B	121	365	38	102	20	0	6	36	1	.279
	Totals		1002	3185	370	753	161	14	121	425	11	.236

Scott Erickson must relocate form of 12-3 first half.

SCOTT ERICKSON 24 6-4 225   **Bats R Throws R**

Enigmatic righty was AL's best pitcher at All-Star break—and nowhere near that in the second half . . . Was AL Pitcher of Month in May, when he was 5-0 with 1.36 ERA . . . Before elbow strain cut into velocity, he was 12-3 and put together a 30⅓-inning scoreless streak . . . Spent from June 30-July 15 on disabled list . . . Was only 8-5 after that and had two more dismal postseason starts, prompting manager Tom Kelly to question him . . . Did rebound for seven strong innings in World Series Game 6, but wound up with 5.06 ERA vs. Braves . . . Earned just

$143,500 in 1991 . . . Twins' fourth-round pick in 1989 draft, out of University of Arizona . . . Born Feb. 2, 1968, in Long Beach, Cal.

Year	Club	G	IP	W	L	Pct.	SO	BB	H	ERA
1990	Minnesota.........	19	113	8	4	.667	53	51	108	2.87
1991	Minnesota.........	32	204	20	8	.714	108	71	189	3.18
	Totals............	51	317	28	12	.700	161	122	297	3.07

KEVIN TAPANI 28 6-0 187　　　　Bats R Throws R

Most consistent of Twins' top three starters . . . Was AL Pitcher of the Month in August, when he was 5-0 . . . Went 11-2 after All-Star break . . . Allowed more than four earned runs in only one of 34 starts . . . Walked none or one in 21 starts . . . Has never walked more than three in any of his 67 major-league starts . . . Lost six consecutive decisions in May, when he received only 10 runs of support . . . Lost ALCS Game 2 and was roughed up in Game 5, allowing five runs in four innings . . . Went 1-1 with 4.50 ERA in World Series, including 3-2 victory in Game 2 . . . Salary was $197,500 in 1991 . . . Part of big payoff from Mets in Frank Viola deal, July 31, 1989 . . . Born Feb. 18, 1964, in Des Moines, Iowa . . . Athletics' second-round pick in 1986.

Year	Club	G	IP	W	L	Pct.	SO	BB	H	ERA
1989	New York (NL)......	3	7⅓	0	0	.000	2	4	5	3.68
1989	Minnesota.........	5	32⅔	2	2	.500	21	8	34	3.86
1990	Minnesota.........	28	159⅓	12	8	.600	101	29	164	4.07
1991	Minnesota.........	34	244	16	9	.640	135	40	225	2.99
	Totals............	70	443⅓	30	19	.612	259	81	428	3.45

RICK AGUILERA 30 6-5 205　　　　Bats R Throws R

Emerged as one of league's best closers . . . Saved 42 in 51 opportunities, including 20 of 22 after the All-Star break . . . Tied major-league record with 10 saves in June . . . Was 9-for-9 in August . . . Posted 1-1 record, two saves and 1.80 ERA in four World Series outings . . . Converted all five postseason opportunities . . . Surrendered just one earned run from July 19-Sept. 25, a stretch of 22⅔ innings in 23 appearances . . . Tied Jeff Reardon's club single-season save record . . . Has 74 saves in two years . . . Earned $1,533,333 in 1991 . . . Another of the trio of pitchers remaining on Twins' staff from Frank Viola trade of July 31, 1989 . . . Born Dec. 31, 1961 in San Gabriel, Cal. . . . Mets' third-round pick in 1983.

Year	Club	G	IP	W	L	Pct.	SO	BB	H	ERA
1985	New York (NL)	21	122⅓	10	7	.588	74	37	118	3.24
1986	New York (NL)	28	141⅔	10	7	.588	104	36	145	3.88
1987	New York (NL)	18	115	11	3	.786	77	33	124	3.60
1988	New York (NL)	11	24⅔	0	4	.000	16	10	29	6.93
1989	New York (NL)	36	69⅓	6	6	.500	80	21	59	2.34
1989	Minnesota	11	75⅔	3	5	.375	57	17	71	3.21
1990	Minnesota	56	65⅓	5	3	.625	61	19	55	2.76
1991	Minnesota	63	69	4	5	.444	61	30	44	2.35
	Totals	244	683	49	40	.551	530	203	645	3.33

TOP PROSPECTS

PEDRO MUNOZ 23 5-10 200   **Bats R Throws R**
Hit .316 with five homers and 28 RBI for Portland (AAA) in 1991 . . . With Twins, he batted .283 with seven homers and 26 RBI in 183 at-bats . . . Outfielder might step in for Dan Gladden . . . Many questioned Twins leaving him off postseason roster . . . Acquired from Blue Jays, July 27, 1990 . . . Signed by Toronto as free agent at age 16 . . . Won club MVP for Florence (A) in 1987 at age 17 . . . Born Sept. 19, 1968, in Ponce, P.R.

LENNY WEBSTER 27 5-9 192   **Bats R Throws R**
Twins didn't lose a game during his two-week stay with them last May . . . Catcher hit .294 and smacked three homers in only 34 at-bats for Twins . . . Batted .252 with seven homers and 34 RBI for Portland (AAA) . . . Twins' 21st-round pick in 1985 draft . . . Born Feb. 10, 1965, in New Orleans.

WILLIE BANKS 23 6-1 190   **Bats R Throws R**
Numbers never have equalled potential for this hard thrower, but he could emerge . . . Earned first major-league victory Aug. 6 vs. Oakland . . . Was 1-1 with 5.71 for Twins in five appearances . . . Finished 9-8 with 4.55 ERA for Portland (AAA) . . . Twins' No. 1 pick and third player taken overall in 1987 draft . . . Born Feb. 27, 1969, in Jersey City, N.J.

PAUL SORRENTO 26 6-2 217   **Bats L Throws R**
Good-hitting first baseman needs opportunity . . . Twins thought enough of him to include him on postseason roster . . . Batted .308 with 13 homers and 79 RBI for Portland (AAA) and .255 with

four homers and 13 RBI in 47 at-bats for Twins . . . Angels' fourth-round pick in 1986 was acquired in Bert Blyleven deal prior to 1989 season . . . Born Nov. 17, 1965, in Somerville, Mass.

MANAGER TOM KELLY: Entered 1991 season with questions surrounding his longevity and ended it with 95-67 record, his second world championship and AL Manager of the Year honors . . . Also pulled quite a reversal in his media relations. With help of a club-hired consultant, the dour disposition was replaced by a cooperative nature . . . What really matters is that his players swear by him and love to play for him . . . Excellent handler of pitching staff and he usually presses right buttons with platoon system . . . After six seasons with Twins, his career record is 437-396 . . . Replaced Ray Miller, Sept. 12, 1986 . . . After 1987 world championship, Twins dropped to second, then fifth, then seventh at 74-88 in 1990 . . . Was Twins' third-base coach from 1983 until taking over for Miller . . . Three-time minor-league Manager of Year from 1979-81 . . . Spent all but 49 games of 11-year playing career in minors . . . An outfielder, he hit .181 in 127 at-bats for Twins at end of 1975 season and never got another chance . . . Born Aug. 15, 1950, in Graceville, Minn.

ALL-TIME TWIN SEASON RECORDS

BATTING: Rod Carew, .388, 1977
HRs: Harmon Killebrew, 49, 1964, 1969
RBI: Harmon Killebrew, 140, 1969
STEALS: Rod Carew, 49, 1976
WINS: Jim Kaat, 25, 1966
STRIKEOUTS: Bert Blyleven, 258, 1973

OAKLAND ATHLETICS

TEAM DIRECTORY: Owner/Managing Partner: Walter A. Haas Jr.; COO: Wally Haas; VP-Baseball Oper.: Sandy Alderson; Dir. Player Dev.: Karl Kuehl; Dir. Scouting: Dick Bogard; Dir. Media Rel.: Kathy Jacobson; Dir. Baseball Inf.: Jay Alves; Trav. Sec.: Mickey Morabito; Mgr.: Tony La Russa. Home: Oakland Coliseum (47,313). Field distances: 330, l.f. line; 375, l.c.; 400, c.f.; 375, r.c.; 330, r.l. line. Spring training: Phoenix, Ariz.

SCOUTING REPORT

HITTING: Jose Canseco (.266, 44, 122) may never be a 40-40 man again, but he remains one of the league's most dangerous sluggers. What the Athletics need to get back on top are more characteristic seasons from Rickey Henderson (.268, 18, 57) and Mark McGwire (.201, 22, 75) plus healthy returns by Carney Lansford and Walt Weiss, whose seasons were ruined by injury.

Never a team that hits for a high average, the Athletics slipped to .248, 13th in the AL, in 1991. Designated hitter Harold Baines led the club with a .295 mark, so the Athletics did not have a .300 hitter. But they were fifth in runs with 760, thanks to their 159 home runs. All the pieces are still there, including the usually overlooked Dave Henderson (.276, 25, 85).

PITCHING: The Athletics have no choice but to hope for a return to form by both longtime ace Dave Stewart (11-11, 5.18) and 1990 Cy Young Award winner Bob Welch (12-13, 4.58). Mike Moore (17-8, 2.96) emerged as the team's best starter last year, but beyond that, the rotation looks hazy. It will be filled by Ron Darling (3-7, 4.08 with Athletics) and young arms such as Joe Slusarski (5-7, 5.27) and Reggie Harris, who was plagued by arm injuries in 1991.

Only Dennis Eckersley could save 43 games and log a 2.96 ERA and have it considered a down year. Rick Honeycutt (2-4, 3.58) bounced back from surgery, while Gene Nelson (1-5, 6.84) will get another chance after a lost 1991 season. Steve Chitren (1-4, 4.33) is thought to be Eckersley's heir apparent. Joe Klink's 4.35 ERA was more indicative of his season than his 10 relief wins. The arrivals of heralded prospects Todd Van Poppel, David Zancanaro and Don Peters could be as soon as late this season.

Jose did you see Canseco's career-high 44 homers?

FIELDING: Defense has always been an overlooked part of the Athletics' success and the expected returns of Weiss and Lansford should make things better. But 5-8 Mike Gallego, a whiz around second base, opted as a free agent to sign with the Yankees. Left fielder Rickey Henderson has been a Gold Glove winner, Dave Henderson is a very reliable center fielder, and Canseco, when properly focused, is solid in right. First baseman McGwire's soft hands belie his bulk. Terry Steinbach is merely average behind the plate.

OUTLOOK: Watch the Athletics this year and you will see one of two things—a stirring return to division title contention for the game's best team from 1988-90 or the end of a great run under manager Tony La Russa to be followed by rebuilding. With several key veterans in the final year of their contracts, it is now or never. The same could be said of McGwire's career, which spiraled dangerously downward last year. The sentiment here is that too many cracks have developed for the Athletics, 84-78 in 1991, to get all the way back on top. But they could come close.

OAKLAND ATHLETICS 1992 ROSTER

MANAGER Tony La Russa
Coaches—Dave Duncan, Reggie Jackson, Art Kusnyer, Rene Lachemann, Dave McKay, Tommie Reynolds

PITCHERS

No.	Name	1991 Club	W-L	IP	SO	ERA	B-T	Ht.	Wt.	Born
53	Briscoe, John	Huntsville	2-0	4	6	0.00	R-R	6-3	185	9/22/67 La Grange, IL
		Tacoma	3-5	76	66	3.66				
		Oakland	0-0	14	9	7.07				
55	Campbell, Kevin	Tacoma	9-2	75	56	1.80	R-R	6-2	225	12/6/64 Marianna, AK
		Oakland	1-0	23	16	2.74				
49	Chitren, Steve	Oakland	1-4	60	47	4.33	R-R	6-0	180	6/8/67 Japan
—	Darling, Ron	NY (NL)-Mont.	5-8	119	69	4.37	R-R	6-3	195	8/19/60 Honolulu, HI
		Oakland	3-7	75	60	4.08				
22	Dressendorfer, Kirk	Tacoma	1-3	24	19	10.88	R-R	5-11	190	4/8/69 Houston, TX
		Oakland	3-3	35	17	5.45				
43	Eckersley, Dennis	Oakland	5-4	76	87	2.96	R-R	6-2	195	10/3/54 Oakland, CA
—	Erwin, Scott	Modesto	1-0	13	22	2.70	R-L	6-2	210	8/21/67 Tampa, FL
		Huntsville	1-4	22	30	3.63				
45	Guzman, Johnny	Huntsville	2-1	44	23	3.48	R-L	5-10	155	1/21/71 Dominican Republic
		Tacoma	2-5	80	40	6.78				
		Oakland	1-0	5	3	9.00				
32	Harris, Reggie	Tacoma	5-4	83	72	4.99	R-R	6-1	190	8/12/68 Waynesboro, VA
		Oakland	0-0	3	2	12.00				
40	Honeycutt, Rick	Madison	0-1	1	1	18.00	L-L	6-1	191	6/29/54 Chattanooga, TN
		Modesto	0-0	5	5	0.00				
		Oakland	2-4	38	26	3.58				
58	Klink, Joe	Modesto	0-0	5	1	3.60	L-L	5-11	175	2/3/62 Johnstown, PA
		Oakland	10-3	62	34	4.35				
21	Moore, Mike	Oakland	17-8	210	153	2.96	R-R	6-4	205	11/26/59 Eakly, OK
19	Nelson, Gene	Oakland	1-5	49	23	6.84	R-R	6-0	174	12/3/60 Tampa, FL
30	Osteen, Gavin	Huntsville	13-8	173	105	3.54	R-L	6-0	195	11/27/69 Orange City, CA
30	Show, Eric	Modesto	0-1	3	1	16.88	R-R	6-1	185	5/19/56 Riverside, CA
		Tacoma	3-2	40	27	2.68				
		Oakland	1-2	52	20	5.92				
37	Slusarski, Joe	Tacoma	4-2	46	25	2.72	R-R	6-4	195	12/19/66 Indianapolis, IN
		Oakland	5-7	109	60	5.27				
34	Stewart, Dave	Oakland	11-11	226	144	5.18	R-R	6-2	200	2/19/57 Oakland, CA
59	Van Poppel, Todd	Huntsville	6-13	132	115	3.47	R-R	6-5	200	12/9/71 Hinsdale, IL
		Oakland	0-0	5	6	9.64				
50	Walton, Bruce	Tacoma	1-1	47	49	1.35	R-R	6-2	195	12/25/62 Bakersfield, CA
		Oakland	1-0	13	10	6.23				
35	Welch, Bob	Oakland	12-13	220	101	4.58	R-R	6-3	195	11/3/56 Detroit, MI

CATCHERS

No.	Name	1991 Club	H	HR	RBI	Pct.	B-T	Ht.	Wt.	Born
—	Mercedes, Henry	Modesto	100	4	61	.258	R-R	5-11	185	7/23/69 Dominican Republic
6	Quirk, Jamie	Oakland	53	1	17	.261	L-R	6-4	200	10/22/54 Whittier, CA
36	Steinbach, Terry	Oakland	125	6	67	.274	R-R	6-1	195	3/2/62 New Ulm, MN

INFIELDERS

12	Blankenship, Lance	Oakland	46	3	21	.249	R-R	6-0	185	12/6/63 Portland, OR
		Tacoma	32	1	11	.294				
46	Bordick, Mike	Tacoma	22	2	14	.272	R-R	5-11	175	7/21/65 Marquette, MI
		Oakland	56	0	21	.238				
45	Brosius, Scott	Tacoma	70	8	31	.286	R-R	6-1	185	8/15/66 Hillsboro, OR
		Oakland	16	2	4	.235				
31	Hemond, Scott	Tacoma	89	3	31	.272	R-R	6-0	205	11/18/65 Taunton, MA
		Oakland	5	0	0	.217				
23	Howitt, Dann	Tacoma	120	14	73	.267	L-R	6-5	205	2/13/64 Battle Creek, MI
4	Lansford, Carney	Oakland	1	0	1	.063	R-R	6-2	195	2/7/57 San Jose, CA
25	McGwire, Mark	Oakland	97	22	75	.201	R-R	6-6	225	10/1/63 Pomona, CA
—	Paquette, Craig	Huntsville	99	8	60	.262	R-R	6-0	185	3/28/69 Long Beach, CA
22	Weiss, Walt	Oakland	30	0	13	.226	S-R	6-0	175	11/28/63 Tuxedo, NY
57	Witmeyer, Ron	Tacoma	113	15	80	.262	L-L	6-3	215	6/28/67 West Islip, NY
		Oakland	1	0	0	.053				

OUTFIELDERS

3	Baines, Harold	Oakland	144	20	90	.295	L-L	6-2	195	3/15/59 Easton, MD
33	Canseco, Jose	Oakland	152	44	122	.266	R-R	6-4	240	7/2/64 Cuba
42	Henderson, Dave	Oakland	158	25	85	.276	R-R	6-2	210	7/21/58 Dos Palos, CA
24	Henderson, Rickey	Oakland	126	18	57	.268	R-L	5-10	195	12/25/58 Chicago, IL
13	Jennings, Doug	Tacoma	89	3	44	.268	L-L	5-10	175	9/30/64 Atlanta, GA
		Oakland	1	0	0	.111				
16	Wilson, Willie	Oakland	70	0	28	.238	S-R	6-3	200	7/9/55 Montgomery, AL

ATHLETIC PROFILES

JOSE CANSECO 27 6-4 240   Bats R Throws R

One of few A's whose performance improved in 1991 . . . Right fielder established career high with 44 homers, tying Tigers' Cecil Fielder for league title . . . Hit 35 homers in last 100 games and has 209 in just six-plus seasons . . . Drove in 122 runs, two short of his career high . . . Topped 100 RBI for fifth time in six years . . . Also stole 26 bases and had a much-publicized rendezvous with Madonna . . . Missed only eight games as back problems that plagued him in 1990 eased . . . Still only "40-40" man in history . . . Earned $3.5 million in 1991, part of five-year, $23.5-million deal . . . One of three Cuban-born major leaguers . . . Born July 2, 1964, in Havana . . . A's made him 15th-round draft choice in 1982.

Year Club	Pos.	G	AB	R	H	2B	3B	HR	RBI	SB	Avg.
1985 Oakland	OF	29	96	16	29	3	0	5	13	1	.302
1986 Oakland	OF	157	600	85	144	29	1	33	117	15	.240
1987 Oakland	OF	159	630	81	162	35	3	31	113	15	.257
1988 Oakland	OF	158	610	120	187	34	0	42	124	40	.307
1989 Oakland	OF	65	227	40	61	9	1	17	57	6	.269
1990 Oakland	OF	131	481	83	132	14	2	37	101	19	.274
1991 Oakland	OF	154	572	115	152	32	1	44	122	26	.266
Totals		853	3216	540	867	156	8	209	647	122	.270

RICKEY HENDERSON 33 5-10 195   Bats R Throws R

Record-setting 939th stolen base was highlight in an otherwise down season . . . Spent spring sulking about club's refusal to renegotiate his contract . . . Performance looked as if he sulked through the season, too . . . Averaged dipped from career-best .325 in 1990 to .268 . . . Home-run total dropped from 28 to 18 . . . Left fielder did win his 11th stolen-base title in 12 years with 58. But that was seven fewer than in his AL MVP year of 1990 and he was caught or picked off 18 times . . . Enters this season with 994 steals . . . Topped 100-run mark for the fourth consecutive year and 10th time in 13 seasons . . . Earned $3.25 million in 1991 . . . Born Dec. 25, 1958, in Chicago, but was raised in Oakland . . . A's got him back from Yanks for Greg Cadaret,

Eric Plunk and Luis Polonia, June 20, 1989 . . . A's drafted him in fourth round in 1976.

Year	Club	Pos.	G	AB	R	H	2B	3B	HR	RBI	SB	Avg.
1979	Oakland	OF	89	351	49	96	13	3	1	26	33	.274
1980	Oakland	OF	158	591	111	179	22	4	9	53	100	.303
1981	Oakland	OF	108	423	89	135	18	7	6	35	56	.319
1982	Oakland	OF	149	536	119	143	24	4	10	51	130	.267
1983	Oakland	OF	145	513	105	150	25	7	9	48	108	.292
1984	Oakland	OF	142	502	113	147	27	4	16	58	66	.293
1985	New York (AL)	OF	143	547	146	172	28	5	24	72	80	.314
1986	New York (AL)	OF	153	608	130	160	31	5	28	74	87	.263
1987	New York (AL)	OF	95	358	78	104	17	3	17	37	41	.291
1988	New York (AL)	OF	140	554	118	169	30	2	6	50	93	.305
1989	NY (AL)-Oak. . .	OF	150	541	113	148	26	3	12	57	77	.274
1990	Oakland	OF	136	489	119	159	33	3	28	61	65	.325
1991	Oakland	OF	134	470	105	126	17	1	18	57	58	.268
	Totals		1742	6483	1395	1888	311	51	184	679	994	.291

HAROLD BAINES 33 6-2 195   Bats L Throws L

DH came off knee surgery and put together his best season since 1987 . . . Reached 20 homers for the first time in four years . . . His 90 RBI ranked second on club to Jose Canseco's 122 . . . Had only 65 RBI in 1990, when he was obtained from Texas for pitchers Scott Chiamparino and Joe Bitker Aug. 29 . . . Both of those pitchers had elbow surgery in 1991, making the deal look even worse for Texas . . . Man of few words, he used only 16 in his speech on Harold Baines Day at Comiskey Park in 1990, when White Sox retired his jersey . . . Drew a club-record 21 intentional walks . . . White Sox' first pick in 1977 draft . . . Earned $1.33 million in 1991 . . . Born March 15, 1959, in Easton, Md.

Year	Club	Pos.	G	AB	R	H	2B	3B	HR	RBI	SB	Avg.
1980	Chicago (AL) . .	OF	141	491	55	125	23	6	13	49	2	.255
1981	Chicago (AL) . .	OF	82	280	42	80	11	7	10	41	6	.286
1982	Chicago (AL) . .	OF	161	608	89	165	29	8	25	105	10	.271
1983	Chicago (AL) . .	OF	156	596	76	167	33	2	20	99	7	.280
1984	Chicago (AL) . .	OF	147	569	72	173	28	10	29	94	1	.304
1985	Chicago (AL) . .	OF	160	640	86	198	29	3	22	113	1	.309
1986	Chicago (AL) . .	OF	145	570	72	169	29	2	21	88	2	.296
1987	Chicago (AL) . .	OF	132	505	59	148	26	4	20	93	0	.293
1988	Chicago (AL) . .	OF	158	599	55	166	39	1	13	81	0	.277
1989	Chi. (AL)-Tex.	OF	146	505	73	156	29	1	16	72	0	.309
1990	Tex.-Oak.	OF	135	415	52	118	15	1	16	65	0	.284
1991	Oakland	OF	141	488	76	144	25	1	20	90	0	.295
	Totals		1704	6266	807	1809	316	46	225	990	29	.289

MARK McGWIRE 28 6-6 225   **Bats R Throws R**

Power production suffered alarming drop... Hit .201 with only 22 homers and 75 RBI, all career lows... Batting average was 34 points below his previous worst season and 52 points below his career mark prior to 1991... Failed to hit 30 homers for first time in five seasons ... Never had fewer than 95 RBI before last season... Still voted All-Star Game starter by fans, but didn't play because of an injury... At least his defense didn't suffer, as he finished second among AL first basemen with a .994 fielding percentage... Set major-league records for rookies with 49 homers and .618 slugging percentage in 1987... Earned $2.85 million in 1991... Born Oct. 1, 1963, in Pomona, Cal.... A's drafted him 10th overall in 1984.

Year	Club	Pos.	G	AB	R	H	2B	3B	HR	RBI	SB	Avg.
1986	Oakland	3B	18	53	10	10	1	0	3	9	0	.189
1987	Oakland	1B-3B-OF	151	557	97	161	28	4	49	118	1	.289
1988	Oakland	1B-OF	155	550	87	143	22	1	32	99	0	.260
1989	Oakland	1B	143	490	74	113	17	0	33	95	1	.231
1990	Oakland	1B	156	523	87	123	16	0	39	108	2	.235
1991	Oakland	1B	154	483	62	97	22	0	22	75	2	.201
	Totals		777	2656	417	647	106	5	178	504	6	.244

TERRY STEINBACH 30 6-1 195   **Bats R Throws R**

Set career highs in hits (125), doubles (31) and RBI (67), but hit fewest homers (six)... Started 106 games behind the plate... Threw out only 29 percent of would-be base-stealers and committed alarming total of 15 errors... Earned $1.05 million in 1991... Homered in his first major-league at-bat... Two-time All-Star... Was MVP in 1988 All-Star Game, when he homered and drove in two runs... Born March 2, 1962, in New Ulm, Minn.... Athletics' ninth-round pick in 1983.

Year	Club	Pos.	G	AB	R	H	2B	3B	HR	RBI	SB	Avg.
1986	Oakland	C	6	15	3	5	0	0	2	4	0	.333
1987	Oakland	C-3B-1B	122	391	66	111	16	3	16	56	1	.284
1988	Oakland	C-3B-1B-OF	104	351	42	93	19	1	9	51	3	.265
1989	Oakland	C-OF-1B-3B	130	454	37	124	13	1	7	42	1	.273
1990	Oakland	C-1B	114	379	32	95	15	2	9	57	0	.251
1991	Oakland	C-1B	129	456	50	125	31	1	6	67	2	.274
	Totals		605	2046	230	553	94	8	49	277	7	.270

DAVE HENDERSON 33 6-2 210   Bats R Throws R

Was on way to his best season until he was slowed by second-half injuries . . . Had .298 average, 18 homers and 50 RBI at the All-Star break, but finished at .276 with 25 homers and 85 RBI . . . Home-run total was a career high, one more than in 1988 . . . Had nine assists in center field . . . Has averaged .275 with 21 homers and 80 RBI in four seasons since signing with A's as a free agent . . . Last season marked first time in six years he wasn't on a division winner . . . Hit dramatic pennant-winning homer for Boston in 1986 ALCS against California . . . Earned $2.6 million in 1991 . . . Born July 21, 1958, in Dos Palos, Cal. . . . Mariners' first-round pick in 1977 signed with A's as free agent prior to 1988 season.

Year	Club	Pos.	G	AB	R	H	2B	3B	HR	RBI	SB	Avg.
1981	Seattle	OF	59	126	17	21	3	0	6	13	2	.167
1982	Seattle	OF	104	324	47	82	17	1	14	48	2	.253
1983	Seattle	OF	137	484	50	130	24	5	17	55	9	.269
1984	Seattle	OF	112	350	42	98	23	0	14	43	5	.280
1985	Seattle	OF	139	502	70	121	28	2	14	68	6	.241
1986	Sea.-Bos	OF	139	388	59	103	22	4	15	47	2	.265
1987	Boston	OF	75	184	30	43	10	0	8	25	1	.234
1987	San Francisco	OF	15	21	2	5	2	0	0	1	2	.238
1988	Oakland	OF	146	507	100	154	38	1	24	94	2	.304
1989	Oakland	OF	152	579	77	145	24	3	15	80	8	.250
1990	Oakland	OF	127	450	65	122	28	0	20	63	3	.271
1991	Oakland	OF-2B	150	572	86	158	33	0	25	85	6	.276
	Totals		1355	4487	645	1182	252	16	172	622	48	.263

DENNIS ECKERSLEY 37 6-2 195   Bats R Throws R

Biggest problem with his 1991 effort was that it paled compared to his phenomenal 1990 performance . . . Saved 43 games in 51 opportunities after failing only twice in 50 chances two years ago . . . Allowed only 60 hits and nine walks in 76 innings, as opposed to 41 hits and four walks in 73⅓ innings in 1990 . . . His ERA did rise from 0.61 to 2.96 and he surrendered 11 homers . . . He and Jeff Reardon became the first two relievers to record three 40-plus save seasons . . . Nine of his 43 saves came against California . . . One of six pitchers who have won at least 100 and saved at least 100 . . . One of five $3-million men on A's, he earned exactly that amount in 1991 . . . Born Oct. 3, 1954, in Oakland . . . Indians' third-round pick in 1982 has 188 career saves, all in last five seasons since being dealt from Cubs with

Dan Rohn for Dave Wilder, Brian Guinn and Mark Leonette,
April 3, 1987.

Year	Club	G	IP	W	L	Pct.	SO	BB	H	ERA
1975	Cleveland	34	187	13	7	.650	152	90	147	2.60
1976	Cleveland	36	199	13	12	.520	200	75	155	3.44
1977	Cleveland	33	247	14	13	.519	191	54	214	3.53
1978	Boston	35	268	20	8	.714	162	71	258	2.99
1979	Boston	33	247	17	10	.630	150	59	234	2.99
1980	Boston	30	198	12	14	.462	121	44	188	4.27
1981	Boston	23	154	9	8	.529	79	35	160	4.27
1982	Boston	33	224⅓	13	13	.500	127	43	228	3.73
1983	Boston	28	176⅓	9	13	.409	77	39	223	5.61
1984	Boston	9	64⅔	4	4	.500	33	13	71	5.01
1984	Chicago (NL)	24	160⅓	10	8	.556	81	36	152	3.03
1985	Chicago (NL)	25	169⅓	11	7	.611	117	19	145	3.08
1986	Chicago (NL)	33	201	6	11	.353	137	43	226	4.57
1987	Oakland	54	115⅔	6	8	.429	113	17	99	3.03
1988	Oakland	60	72⅔	4	2	.667	70	11	52	2.35
1989	Oakland	51	57⅔	4	0	1.000	55	3	32	1.56
1990	Oakland	63	73⅓	4	2	.667	73	4	41	0.61
1991	Oakland	67	76	5	4	.556	87	9	60	2.96
	Totals	671	2891⅓	174	144	.547	2025	668	2685	3.47

MIKE MOORE 32 6-4 205   Bats R Throws R

Emerged as club's most effective starter after
sub-par 1990, when velocity and fortitude were
questioned . . . Posted second-lowest ERA of
career (2.96) and tied his second-best win total
(17) . . . Finished strong, winning eight of 10
decisions in second half, including last five . . .
Seattle made him first player picked in 1981
draft . . . Signed with Oakland as a free agent
before 1989 season after six years with Mariners . . . Record is
49-34 in three years for A's, but he remains a sub-.500 pitcher
for his career . . . Earned $1.56 million in 1991 . . . Born Nov. 26,
1959, in Eakly, Okla.

Year	Club	G	IP	W	L	Pct.	SO	BB	H	ERA
1982	Seattle	28	144⅓	7	14	.333	73	79	159	5.36
1983	Seattle	22	128	6	8	.429	108	60	130	4.71
1984	Seattle	34	212	7	17	.292	158	85	236	4.97
1985	Seattle	35	247	17	10	.630	155	70	230	3.46
1986	Seattle	38	266	11	13	.458	146	94	279	4.30
1987	Seattle	33	231	9	19	.321	115	84	268	4.71
1988	Seattle	37	228⅔	9	15	.375	182	63	196	3.78
1989	Oakland	35	241⅔	19	11	.633	172	83	193	2.61
1990	Oakland	33	199⅓	13	15	.464	73	84	204	4.65
1991	Oakland	33	210	17	8	.680	153	105	176	2.96
	Totals	328	2108	115	130	.469	1335	807	2071	4.06

Mike Moore's second-half stuff got him 17 A's victories.

DAVE STEWART 35 6-2 200   **Bats R Throws R**

String of outstanding seasons came to crashing halt . . . Fell to 11-11 after averaging 21 victories over the past four years . . . Even more alarming was 5.18 ERA . . . Allowed 245 hits and 105 walks in 226 innings . . . Opponents hit .281 against him . . . ERA was 2.56 in 1990 and it hadn't been above 3.74 in his five seasons in Oakland . . . At least he retained his workhorse status, leading staff in innings pitched (226) once again . . . Missed chance to become first pitcher since Catfish Hunter to record five consecutive 20-win seasons . . . Started on Opening Day for fourth consecutive time . . . Had April winning streak snapped at 20 . . . Earned $3.5 million in 1991 . . . Born Feb. 19, 1957, in Oakland . . . Dodgers' 16th-round pick in 1975 came to A's after Phils released him in 1986.

Year	Club	G	IP	W	L	Pct.	SO	BB	H	ERA
1978	Los Angeles	1	2	0	0	.000	1	0	1	0.00
1981	Los Angeles	32	43	4	3	.571	29	14	40	2.51
1982	Los Angeles	45	146⅓	9	8	.529	80	49	137	3.81
1983	Los Angeles	46	76	5	2	.714	54	33	67	2.96
1983	Texas	8	59	5	2	.714	24	17	50	2.14
1984	Texas	32	192⅓	7	14	.333	119	87	193	4.73
1985	Texas	42	81⅓	0	6	.000	64	37	86	5.42
1985	Philadelphia	4	4½	0	0	.000	2	4	5	6.23
1986	Philadelphia	8	12⅓	0	0	.000	9	4	15	6.57
1986	Oakland	29	149⅓	9	5	.643	102	65	137	3.74
1987	Oakland	37	261⅓	20	13	.606	205	105	224	3.68
1988	Oakland	37	275⅔	21	12	.636	192	110	240	3.23
1989	Oakland	36	257⅔	21	9	.700	155	69	260	3.32
1990	Oakland	36	267	22	11	.667	166	83	226	2.56
1991	Oakland	35	226	11	11	.500	144	105	245	5.18
	Totals	428	2053⅔	134	96	.583	1346	782	1926	3.70

BOB WELCH 35 6-3 195   Bats R Throws R

Developed bad case of post-Cy Young Award blues, falling from 27-6 with a 2.95 ERA in 1990 to 12-13, 4.58 . . . Maybe there was something to having Ron Hassey around as his personal catcher, after all . . . Made 35 starts and logged 220 innings . . . His ERA was above 4.00 for first time in his career . . . Led staff with 25 home runs allowed, one more than Dave Stewart . . . Enters 1992 only 12 wins short of 200 . . . Was 8-5 at All-Star break, then endured 4-8 second half . . . Earned $3.45 million in 1991, the first year of a four-year, $13.8-million deal . . . Born Nov. 3, 1956, in Detroit . . . Dodgers' first-round pick in 1977 came to A's in three-team, eight-player deal prior to 1988.

Year	Club	G	IP	W	L	Pct.	SO	BB	H	ERA
1978	Los Angeles	23	111	7	4	.636	66	26	92	2.03
1979	Los Angeles	25	81	5	6	.455	64	32	82	4.00
1980	Los Angeles	32	214	14	9	.609	141	79	190	3.28
1981	Los Angeles	23	141	9	5	.643	88	41	141	3.45
1982	Los Angeles	36	235⅔	16	11	.593	176	81	199	3.36
1983	Los Angeles	31	204	15	12	.556	156	72	164	2.65
1984	Los Angeles	31	178⅔	13	13	.500	126	58	191	3.78
1985	Los Angeles	23	167⅓	14	4	.778	96	35	141	2.31
1986	Los Angeles	33	235⅔	7	13	.350	183	55	227	3.28
1987	Los Angeles	35	251⅔	15	9	.625	196	86	204	3.22
1988	Oakland	36	244⅔	17	9	.654	158	81	237	3.64
1989	Oakland	33	209⅔	17	8	.680	137	78	191	3.00
1990	Oakland	35	238	27	6	.818	127	77	214	2.95
1991	Oakland	35	220	12	13	.480	101	91	220	4.58
	Totals	431	2732⅓	188	122	.606	1815	892	2493	3.27

RON DARLING 31 6-3 195   Bats R Throws R

Bounced from Mets to Expos to A's in final year before becoming eligible for free agency ... Put up numbers that didn't do much for his market value as he finished a combined 8-15 ... Suffered second losing season in a row after posting 86-55 mark in first six-plus seasons with Mets ... Traded to Montreal for reliever Tim Burke July 15 ... Stayed there long enough to make three starts before going to A's for minor-league pitchers Russ Cormier and Matt Grott ... Earned $1.96 million for his travel-filled 1991 season ... Born Aug. 19, 1960, in Honolulu ... Rangers drafted him ninth overall in 1981, out of Yale ... Accepted arbitration in December.

Year	Club	G	IP	W	L	Pct.	SO	BB	H	ERA
1983	New York (NL)	5	35⅓	1	3	.250	23	17	31	2.80
1984	New York (NL)	33	205⅔	12	9	.571	136	104	179	3.81
1985	New York (NL)	36	248	16	6	.727	167	114	214	2.90
1986	New York (NL)	34	237	15	6	.714	184	81	203	2.81
1987	New York (NL)	32	207⅔	12	8	.600	167	96	183	4.29
1988	New York (NL)	34	240⅔	17	9	.654	161	60	218	3.25
1989	New York (NL)	33	217⅓	14	14	.500	153	70	214	3.52
1990	New York (NL)	33	126	7	9	.438	99	44	135	4.50
1991	NY (NL)-Mont.	20	119⅓	5	8	.385	69	33	121	4.37
1991	Oakland	12	75	3	7	.300	60	38	64	4.08
	Totals	272	1712	102	79	.564	1219	657	1562	3.56

TOP PROSPECTS

TODD VAN POPPEL 20 6-5 200   Bats R Throws R

Made major-league debut Sept. 11, only 14 months after he graduated from high school ... Lasted 4⅔ innings against White Sox, allowing seven hits and five runs and striking out six ... Would have been certain No. 1 overall pick in 1990 draft, but lasted until 14th overall because of his strong commitment to attend the University of Texas ... A's convinced him otherwise with a then-record, $1.2-million deal that included a major-league contract ... Was 6-13 despite a 3.47 ERA for a last-place Huntsville (AA) team ... Born Dec. 9, 1971, in Hinsdale, Ill.

SCOTT BROSIUS 25 6-1 185   Bats R Throws R

Injury to Carney Lansford gave this third baseman his first major-league chance Aug. 5 ... Hit .235 in 68 at-bats and stole three bases for Oakland ... Also played second base, left field and right field for A's ... Hit .286 with eight homers and 31 RBI for Tacoma

(AAA)... Born Aug. 15, 1966, in Hillsboro, Ore.... A's made him 20th-round pick in 1987.

DAVID ZANCANARO 23 6-1 170　　　**Bats S Throws L**
Another member of strong pitching crop... Left-hander was 5-10 with a 3.38 ERA in 28 starts for Huntsville (AA) in 1991 ... Was selected as compensation pick (34th overall) in 1990 draft ... Attended UCLA... Born Jan. 8, 1969, in Carmichael, Cal.

RON WITMEYER 24 6-3 215　　　**Bats L Throws L**
Made major-league debut in August... Only hit in 19 at-bats came Sept. 7 off Detroit's Mark Leiter... First baseman hit .262 with 15 homers and 80 RBI for Tacoma (AAA)... Seventh-round pick in 1988 draft... Played on two NCAA national champions at Stanford... Born June 28, 1967, in West Islip, N.Y.

MANAGER TONY La RUSSA: For the first time in four years, there was no postseason for the A's, but that didn't diminish his reputation... Held team together and in race until late August despite collapse of pitching staff, injuries and sub-par seasons from key regulars... Snapped June 1, the night Terry Steinbach was beaned in Chicago, and got into a postgame shouting match with a Chicago sportswriter... Winning percentage dipped slightly, but 516-373 mark in Oakland is quite impressive... Took over in mid-1986, shortly after being fired in Chicago, where he spent seven years... Career record is sparkling 1,038-883... Was an A's bonus baby in 1962, when he was drafted out of high school... Hit only .199 with no homers and seven RBI in 176 major-league at-bats spread over six seasons ... One of five lawyer-managers in baseball history... Played youth baseball with Reds' manager Lou Piniella... Born Oct. 4, 1944, in Tampa.

ALL-TIME A's SEASON RECORDS

BATTING: Napoleon Lajoie, .422, 1901
HRs: Jimmie Foxx, 58, 1932
RBI: Jimmie Foxx, 169, 1932
STEALS: Rickey Henderson, 130, 1982
WINS: John Coombs, 31, 1910
　　　　Lefty Grove, 31, 1931
STRIKEOUTS: Rube Waddell, 349, 1904

SEATTLE MARINERS

TEAM DIRECTORY: Owner: Jeff Smulyan; Pres.: Gary Kaseff; VP-Baseball Oper.: Woody Woodward; VP-Scouting and Player Dev.: Roger Jongewaard; Dir. Baseball Adm.: Lee Pelekoudas; Farm Dir.: Jim Beattie; Dir. Pub. Rel.: David Aust; Trav. Sec.: Craig Detwiler; Mgr.: Bill Plummer. Home: Kingdome (57,748). Field distances: 331, l.f. line; 376, l.c.; 405, c.f.; 352, r.c.; 314, r.f. line. Spring training: Tempe, Ariz.

SCOUTING REPORT

HITTING: Kevin Mitchell didn't arrive in time to save Jim Lefebvre's job, but he will make new manager Bill Plummer's easier—not to mention Ken Griffey Jr.'s. With the powerful ex-Giant Mitchell (.256, 27, 69) batting behind him, Griffey (.327, 22, 100) will get much better pitches to hit and that means he isn't likely to lead the AL in intentional walks again. Mitchell could be positively scary in the cozy Kingdome and his ability to hit breaking balls will serve him well in the AL.

Jay Buhner (.244, 27, 77) will provide some protection for Mitchell and left-handed-hitting Pete O'Brien (.248, 17, 88) and Tino Martinez (.326, 18, 66 for AAA Calgary) can also provide power. All of this heightens the need for leadoff hitter Harold Reynolds (.254, 3, 57) to rebound from two consecutive seasons in the .250 range and for Edgar Martinez (.307, 14, 52) to put together another .300 season in the No. 2 spot.

PITCHING: Few teams could afford to trade three pitchers like Mike Jackson, Billy Swift and Dave Burba to get an impact slugger of Mitchell's caliber and not suffer much as a result. But the Mariners are one of them—provided closer Mike Schooler (3-3, 3.67, 7 Sv) has overcome two years of shoulder problems. If not, the bullpen load could fall on late-blooming Calvin Jones (2-2, 2.53) and his nasty forkball. Russ Swan (6-3, 3.43) is an adequate setup man, but isn't closer material. Gene Harris (0-0, 4.05) also is back after a short retirement.

The Mariners feel Erik Hanson (8-8, 3.81) has recovered from elbow trouble and will assume the No. 1 starter's role with Brian Holman (13-14, 3.69) out until at least July because of rotator cuff surgery. Randy Johnson (13-10, 3.98) remains an overpowering if inconsistent force. Bill Krueger (11-8, 3.60) was a painful loss via free agency. Rich DeLucia (12-13, 5.09), who got a lot of run support in his first year, will have to improve.

Dad is retired, but Ken Griffey Jr. has just begun.

The Mariners regard Roger Salkeld and Dave Fleming as future stars and both could have an impact this season.

FIELDING: Griffey has begun what many expect to be a string of Gold Glove Award-winning years in center. Dave Valle is one of the league's better defensive catchers and right fielder Buhner possesses one of the game's strongest outfield arms. Second baseman Reynolds no longer has the Gold Glove skills of his past. Omar Vizquel is a steady and underrated shortstop.

OUTLOOK: The Mariners may not be long for Seattle, but on the field, things have never looked better for this club. They finished above .500, at 83-79, for the first time in their history in 1991 and can be considered legitimate contenders after acquiring Mitchell. Fans in St. Petersburg can only be drooling in anticipation.

SEATTLE MARINERS 1992 ROSTER

MANAGER Bill Plummer
Coaches—Gene Clines, Roger Hansen, Rusty Kuntz, Marty Martinez,
Russ Nixon, Dan Warthen

PITCHERS

No.	Name	1991 Club	W-L	IP	SO	ERA	B-T	Ht.	Wt.	Born
55	DeLucia, Rich	Seattle	12-13	182	98	5.09	R-R	6-0	180	10/7/64 Reading, PA
35	Fleming, Dave	Jacksonville	10-6	140	109	2.70	L-L	6-3	200	11/7/69 Queens, NY
		Seattle	1-0	18	11	6.62				
		Calgary	2-0	16	16	1.13				
39	Hanson, Erik	Seattle	8-8	175	143	3.81	R-R	6-6	210	5/18/65 Kinnelon, NJ
		Calgary	0-0	6	5	1.50				
47	Harris, Gene	Seattle	0-0	13	6	4.05	R-R	5-11	190	12/5/64 Sebring, FL
		Calgary	4-0	35	23	3.34				
36	Holman, Brian	Seattle	13-14	195	108	3.69	R-R	6-4	185	1/25/65 Denver, CO
51	Johnson, Randy	Seattle	13-10	201	228	3.98	R-L	6-10	225	9/10/63 Walnut Creek, CA
52	Jones, Calvin	Calgary	1-1	23	25	3.91	R-R	6-3	185	9/26/63 Compton, CA
		Seattle	2-2	46	42	2.53				
27	Knackert, Brent	San Bernardino	0-0	4	7	2.08	R-R	6-3	190	8/1/69 Los Angeles, CA
40	Nelson, Jeff	Jacksonville	4-0	28	34	1.27	R-R	6-8	225	11/17/66 Baltimore, MD
		Calgary	3-4	32	26	2.90				
33	Newlin, Jim	Jacksonville	6-5	64	48	2.25	R-R	6-2	205	9/11/66 New Orleans, LA
—	Remlinger, Mike	Phoenix	5-5	109	68	6.38	L-L	6-0	195	3/23/66 Middletown, NY
		San Francisco	2-1	35	19	4.37				
29	Schooler, Mike	Jacksonville	1-1	11	12	5.56	R-R	6-3	220	8/10/62 Anaheim, CA
		Seattle	3-3	34	31	3.67				
37	Swan, Russ	Seattle	6-2	79	33	3.43	L-L	6-4	215	1/3/64 Fremont, CA
42	Woodson, Kerry	San Bernardino	2-0	28	14	1.95	R-R	6-2	190	5/18/69 Jacksonville, FL
		Jacksonville	4-6	79	50	3.06				
41	Zavaras, Clint	San Bernardino	1-3	40	38	3.79	R-R	6-1	175	1/4/67 Denver, CO
		Jacksonville	2-2	31	21	4.60				

CATCHERS

No.	Name	1991 Club	H	HR	RBI	Pct.	B-T	Ht.	Wt.	Born
9	Bradley, Scott	Seattle	35	0	11	.203	L-R	5-11	185	3/22/60 Montclair, NJ
31	Campanis, Jim	Jacksonville	96	15	49	.248	R-R	6-1	200	8/27/67 Fullerton, CA
45	Howard, Chris	Calgary	72	8	36	.246	R-R	6-2	200	2/27/66 San Diego, CA
		Seattle	1	0	0	.167				
20	Pirki, Greg	San Bernardino	75	14	53	.314	R-R	6-5	225	8/7/70 Long Beach, CA
		Peninsula	63	6	41	.264				
10	Valle, Dave	Seattle	63	8	32	.194	R-R	6-2	200	10/30/60 Bayside, NY

INFIELDERS

No.	Name	1991 Club	H	HR	RBI	Pct.	B-T	Ht.	Wt.	Born
8	Amaral, Rich	Calgary	120	3	36	.346	R-R	6-0	175	4/1/62 Visalia, CA
		Seattle	1	0	0	.063				
43	Cochrane, Dave	Calgary	61	3	37	.321	S-R	6-2	180	1/31/63 Riverside, CA
		Seattle	44	2	22	.247				
11	Martinez, Edgar	Seattle	167	14	52	.307	R-R	5-11	175	1/2/63 New York, NY
23	Martinez, Tino	Calgary	144	18	86	.326	L-R	6-2	205	12/7/67 Tampa, FL
		Seattle	23	4	9	.205				
12	O'Brien, Pete	Seattle	139	17	88	.248	L-L	6-2	195	2/9/58 Santa Monica, CA
4	Reynolds, Harold	Seattle	160	3	57	.254	S-R	5-11	165	11/26/60 Eugene, OR
2	Schaefer, Jeff	Seattle	41	1	11	.250	R-R	5-10	170	5/31/60 Patchogue, NY
13	Vizquel, Omar	Seattle	98	1	41	.230	S-R	5-9	165	4/24/67 Venezuela

OUTFIELDERS

No.	Name	1991 Club	H	HR	RBI	Pct.	B-T	Ht.	Wt.	Born
1	Briley, Greg	Saettle	99	2	26	.260	L-R	5-8	165	5/24/65 Greenville, NC
19	Buhner, Jay	Seattle	99	27	77	.244	R-R	6-3	205	8/13/64 Louisville, KY
28	Cotto, Henry	Seattle	54	6	23	.305	R-R	6-2	180	1/5/61 Bronx, NY
24	Griffey Jr., Ken	Seattle	179	22	100	.327	L-L	6-3	200	11/21/69 Donora, PA
26	Lennon, Patrick	Calgary	137	15	74	.329	R-R	6-2	200	4/27/68 Whiteville, NC
		Seattle	1	0	1	.125				
7	Mitchell, Kevin	San Francisco	95	27	69	.256	R-R	5-11	210	1/13/62 San Diego, CA
—	Powell, Alonzo	Calgary	72	7	43	.375	R-R	6-2	190	12/12/64 San Francisco, CA

MARINER PROFILES

KEN GRIFFEY Jr. 22 6-3 200   Bats L Throws L

The Franchise—and he's only 22 . . . Led club in hitting (.327), RBI (100) and three other major offensive categories . . . Youngest player to drive in 100 since Al Kaline in 1956 and the 12th-youngest all-time . . . Gold Glove-winning center fielder is a regular on the highlight shows . . . Improved batting average 27 points in 1991 after 36-point hike in 1990 . . . Set new highs in RBI, doubles (42) and stolen bases (18) . . . Immaturity still shows on occasion . . . Enjoyed playing with dad, Ken Sr. . . . Earned $700,000 in 1991, but is on the way to multi-millionaire status . . . Was youngest player in majors in 1989 at 19 . . . First pick overall in 1987 draft, out of Moeller High in Cincinnati . . . Born Nov. 21, 1969, in Donora, Pa.

Year	Club	Pos.	G	AB	R	H	2B	3B	HR	RBI	SB	Avg.
1989	Seattle	OF	127	455	61	120	23	0	16	61	16	.264
1990	Seattle	OF	155	597	91	179	28	7	22	80	16	.300
1991	Seattle	OF	154	548	76	179	42	1	22	100	18	.327
	Totals		436	1600	228	478	93	8	60	241	50	.299

EDGAR MARTINEZ 29 5-11 175   Bats R Throws R

Among AL third basemen, only he and Wade Boggs have hit better than .300 in each of last two seasons . . . Drew 84 walks, pushing his on-base percentage to .405, the fifth-best mark in AL . . . Established career highs in homers (14), RBI (52) and doubles (35) . . . Very slow . . . Has only three career stolen bases . . . Defensive range was helped by arthroscopic surgery, but it is still below average . . . Committed 15 errors . . . Earned $350,000 in 1991 . . . Cousin of Carmelo Martinez . . . Signed as a free agent by Mariners in 1982 . . . Played six minor-league seasons before reaching majors to stay . . . Born Jan. 2, 1963, in New York, N.Y.

Year	Club	Pos.	G	AB	R	H	2B	3B	HR	RBI	SB	Avg.
1987	Seattle	3B	13	43	6	16	5	2	0	5	0	.372
1988	Seattle	3B	14	32	0	9	4	0	0	5	0	.281
1989	Seattle	3B	65	171	20	41	5	0	2	20	2	.240
1990	Seattle	3B	144	487	71	147	27	2	11	49	1	.302
1991	Seattle	3B	150	544	98	167	35	1	14	52	0	.307
	Totals		386	1277	195	380	66	5	27	131	3	.298

JAY BUHNER 27 6-3 205   Bats R Throws R

Temperamental slugger finally fulfilled power potential . . . Belted 27 homers, ranking in tie for 10th-highest total in AL . . . Blasted one of the longest homers in Yankee Stadium history, a 479-foot shot off Wade Taylor July 25 . . . Man of streaks both good and bad . . . Hit .284 with seven homers, 25 RBI in August . . . Had 24 homers by Aug. 13, then didn't hit another until Sept. 30 . . . Drove in career-high 77 runs . . . Key was staying healthy long enough to get 406 at-bats . . . Free swinger who struck out 117 times . . . Has rocket arm in right field . . . Notched 15 assists . . . Mariners got him and two minor leaguers from Yankees for Ken Phelps, July 21, 1988 . . . Made $247,500 in 1991 . . . Born Aug. 13, 1964, in Louisville, Ky. . . . Began career with Pirates organization as January 1984 secondary draft pick.

Year	Club	Pos.	G	AB	R	H	2B	3B	HR	RBI	SB	Avg.
1987	New York (AL)	OF	7	22	0	5	2	0	0	1	0	.227
1988	NY (AL)-Sea. . .	OF	85	261	36	56	13	1	13	38	1	.215
1989	Seattle.	OF	58	204	27	56	15	1	9	33	1	.275
1990	Seattle.	OF	51	163	16	45	12	0	7	33	2	.276
1991	Seattle.	OF	137	406	64	99	14	4	27	77	0	.244
	Totals		338	1056	143	261	56	6	56	182	4	.247

KEVIN MITCHELL 30 5-11 210   Bats R Throws R

Talented but troubled left fielder brings slugger's bat to Seattle following December trade that sent pitchers Billy Swift, Mike Jackson and Dave Burba to the Giants . . . Mariners also got lefty Mike Remlinger . . . He totaled just 42 at-bats in September and October and hit .190 . . . Still managed to rank ninth in NL in homers (27) . . . Blasted five homers in first five games, then season went downhill . . . Underwent arthroscopic knee surgery June 3 . . . Suffered groin injury and sore wrist over last month . . . Made only 113 appearances, his least since his rookie year . . . For that, 1989 NL MVP was paid $3,750,000 . . . His home run and RBI (69) totals and average (.256) were lowest since 1988 . . . Came to Giants from Padres with Craig Lefferts and Dave Dravecky for Mark Davis, Chris Brown, Keith Comstock and Mark Grant, July 7, 1987 . . . Mets soured on him and dealt him to Padres in 1986 as part of package for Kevin McReynolds . . .

Originally signed by Mets as free agent in November 1980 . . .
Born Jan. 13, 1962, in San Diego.

Year	Club	Pos.	G	AB	R	H	2B	3B	HR	RBI	SB	Avg.
1984	New York (NL)	3B	7	14	0	3	0	0	0	1	0	.214
1986	New York (NL)	OF-SS-3B-1B	108	328	51	91	22	2	12	43	3	.277
1987	S.D.-S.F.	3B-SS-OF	131	464	68	130	20	2	22	70	9	.280
1988	San Francisco	3B-OF	148	505	60	127	25	7	19	80	5	.251
1989	San Francisco	3B-OF	154	543	100	158	34	6	47	125	3	.291
1990	San Francisco	OF	140	524	90	152	24	2	35	93	4	.290
1991	San Francisco	OF-1B	113	371	52	95	13	1	27	69	2	.256
	Totals		801	2749	421	756	138	20	162	481	26	.275

HAROLD REYNOLDS 31 5-11 165   Bats S Throws R

Set club RBI mark for second baseman, breaking his own record . . . RBI total has increased
in each of his six full seasons . . . Three-time
Gold Glove winner led AL second basemen in
putouts, total chances and double plays . . . Did
commit 18 errors, tied for second-most among
AL second basemen . . . Hit over .300 at home,
close to .200 on road . . . Two-time All-Star is
Mariners' most popular player . . . Has spent entire 11-year pro
career in Seattle organization . . . Second pick overall in 1980 draft
. . . Earned $1,866,667 in 1991 . . . Born Nov. 26, 1960, in Eu-
gene, Ore.

Year	Club	Pos.	G	AB	R	H	2B	3B	HR	RBI	SB	Avg.
1983	Seattle.	2B	20	59	8	12	4	1	0	1	0	.203
1984	Seattle.	2B	10	10	3	3	0	0	0	0	1	.300
1985	Seattle.	2B	67	104	15	15	3	1	0	6	3	.144
1986	Seattle.	2B	126	445	46	99	19	4	1	24	30	.222
1987	Seattle.	2B	160	530	73	146	31	8	1	35	60	.275
1988	Seattle.	2B	158	598	61	169	26	11	4	41	35	.283
1989	Seattle.	2B	153	613	87	184	24	9	0	43	25	.300
1990	Seattle.	2B	160	642	100	162	36	5	5	55	31	.252
1991	Seattle.	2B	161	631	95	160	34	6	3	57	28	.254
	Totals		1015	3632	488	950	177	45	14	262	213	.262

DAVE VALLE 31 6-2 200   Bats R Throws R

A local pub used his batting average as price
of its draft beer . . . Customers got good deal
. . . Reached season-ending .194 mark by hitting close to .300 in final five weeks . . . Was
hitting .135 with four homers and nine RBI in
171 at-bats at All-Star break . . . Hit all eight of
his homers on the road . . . Catcher did gun
down 39 percent of would-be base-stealers,
drawing Gold Glove consideration . . . Hasn't hit above .237 since

1987, his rookie season . . . Has averaged .204 over last two years . . . Also injury-prone . . . Has been on DL six times since reaching majors . . . Second-round pick in 1978 draft . . . Didn't reach majors to stay until 1986 . . . Salary was $666,667 in 1991 . . . Born Oct. 30, 1960, in Bayside, N.Y.

Year	Club	Pos.	G	AB	R	H	2B	3B	HR	RBI	SB	Avg.
1984	Seattle	C	13	27	4	8	1	0	1	4	0	.296
1985	Seattle	C	31	70	2	11	1	0	0	4	0	.157
1986	Seattle	C-1B	22	53	10	18	3	0	5	15	0	.340
1987	Seattle	C-1B-OF	95	324	40	83	16	3	12	53	2	.256
1988	Seattle	C-1B	93	290	29	67	15	2	10	50	0	.231
1989	Seattle	C	94	316	32	75	10	3	7	34	0	.237
1990	Seattle	C-1B	107	308	37	66	15	0	7	33	1	.214
1991	Seattle	C-1B	132	324	38	63	8	1	8	32	0	.194
	Totals		587	1712	192	391	69	9	50	225	3	.228

PETE O'BRIEN 34 6-2 195   Bats L Throws L

Bounced back from injury-filled 1990 with respectable power numbers . . . Home run (17) and RBI (88) totals were highest since 1987, but he hit only .248 . . . Led AL first basemen with .997 fielding percentage . . . Committed only five errors . . . Made a dozen starts in left field for first time, making room for Tino Martinez at first base . . . Averaged only 11 homers and 51 RBI from 1988-90, when he went from Rangers to Indians to Mariners . . . Highest-paid Mariner in 1991 at $2,037,500 . . . Signed four-year deal with Mariners as free agent before 1990 season . . . Born Feb. 9, 1958, in Santa Monica, Cal. . . . Rangers' 15th-round draft choice in 1979.

Year	Club	Pos.	G	AB	R	H	2B	3B	HR	RBI	SB	Avg.
1982	Texas	OF-1B	20	67	13	16	4	1	4	13	1	.239
1983	Texas	1B-OF	154	524	53	124	24	5	8	53	5	.237
1984	Texas	1B-OF	142	520	57	149	26	2	18	80	3	.287
1985	Texas	1B	159	573	69	153	34	3	22	92	5	.267
1986	Texas	1B	156	551	86	160	23	3	23	90	4	.290
1987	Texas	1B-OF	159	569	84	163	26	1	23	88	0	.286
1988	Texas	1B	156	547	57	149	24	1	16	71	1	.272
1989	Cleveland	1B	155	555	75	144	24	1	12	55	3	.260
1990	Seattle	1B-OF	108	366	32	82	18	0	5	27	0	.224
1991	Seattle	1B-OF	152	560	58	139	29	3	17	88	0	.248
	Totals		1361	4831	584	1279	232	20	148	657	22	.265

OMAR VIZQUEL 24 5-9 165   Bats S Throws R

Established himself in first full season as regular shortstop . . . Hit .230 with career-high 41 RBI and only 13 errors in 142 games . . . Was Mariners' Opening Day shortstop in 1989, at age 21, and hit .220 in 143 games . . . Started 1990 on disabled list with knee injury and wasn't recalled until July 5 . . . Fits good-field, no-hit mold . . . His only 1991 homer came off Angels' Kirk McCaskill . . . Stole seven bases in nine tries . . . Tied club record with five hits July 18 at Milwaukee . . . Signed as a free agent by Seattle in 1984 . . . Earned $180,000 in 1991 . . . Born April 24, 1967, in Caracas, Venezuela.

Year	Club	Pos.	G	AB	R	H	2B	3B	HR	RBI	SB	Avg.
1989	Seattle	SS	143	387	45	85	7	3	1	20	1	.220
1990	Seattle	SS	81	255	19	63	3	2	2	18	4	.247
1991	Seattle	SS-2B	142	426	42	98	16	4	1	41	7	.230
	Totals		366	1068	106	246	26	9	4	79	12	.230

RANDY JOHNSON 28 6-10 225   Bats R Throws L

Tallest player in major-league history . . . Still searching for mechanical consistency . . . Finished second in AL with career-high 228 strikeouts in 201⅓ innings . . . But also led AL in walks with 152, one more than the number of hits he allowed . . . Took no-hitter into ninth against Oakland Aug. 14 before Mike Gallego singled . . . His 13 wins were one short of total in 1990 . . . His ERA climbed slightly from 3.65 in 1990 to 3.98 . . . Walked 10 in four innings July 17 at Milwaukee . . . Threw first no-hitter in club history, June 2, 1990 against Detroit . . . Selected to 1990 All-Star team, but didn't pitch . . . Came from Montreal along with Brian Holman and Gene Harris for Mark Langston, May 26, 1989 . . . Earned $350,000 in 1991 . . . Born Sept. 10, 1963, in Walnut Creek, Cal. . . . Expos' second-round pick in 1985.

Year	Club	G	IP	W	L	Pct.	SO	BB	H	ERA
1988	Montreal	4	26	3	0	1.000	25	7	23	2.42
1989	Montreal	7	29⅔	0	4	.000	26	26	29	6.67
1989	Seattle	22	131	7	9	.438	104	70	118	4.40
1990	Seattle	33	219⅔	14	11	.560	194	120	174	3.65
1991	Seattle	33	201⅓	13	10	.565	228	152	151	3.98
	Totals	99	607⅔	37	34	.521	577	375	495	4.01

BRIAN HOLMAN 27 6-4 185　　　　Bats R Throws R

Set career highs with 13 wins and 195⅓ innings pitched . . . Threw three shutouts and also shared two others with Billy Swift . . . Finished 13-14 despite 3.69 ERA . . . Lost four in a row from June 14-July 5, when he received only three runs of support in four outings . . . Opening Day starter in 1990, he lost that designation to Erik Hanson in 1991 . . . Came within one out of perfect game against Oakland, April 20, 1990. Ken Phelps spoiled everything with a pinch-hit homer . . . Earned $300,000 in 1991 . . . Born Jan. 25, 1965, in Denver . . . Obtained from Expos with Randy Johnson and Gene Harris for Mark Langston, May 25, 1989 . . . Expos drafted him 16th overall in 1983.

Year	Club	G	IP	W	L	Pct.	SO	BB	H	ERA
1988	Montreal	18	100⅓	4	8	.333	58	34	101	3.23
1989	Montreal	10	31⅔	1	2	.333	23	15	34	4.83
1989	Seattle	23	159⅔	8	10	.444	82	62	160	3.44
1990	Seattle	28	189⅔	11	11	.500	121	66	188	4.03
1991	Seattle	30	195⅓	13	14	.481	108	77	199	3.69
	Totals	109	676⅔	37	45	.451	392	254	682	3.71

MIKE SCHOOLER 29 6-3 220　　　　Bats R Throws R

Bullpen closer was rendered almost useless by shoulder trouble that has plagued him since final month of 1990 season . . . Pitched only 34⅓ innings and recorded only seven saves . . . Didn't pitch until July 12 . . . Didn't get first save until July 26 . . . Never fully re-established his velocity or closer status . . . His troubles followed two successful years during which he saved 30 and 33 games respectively . . . Set AL record for fastest ascent to 50 career saves, reaching the plateau 110 games. That was one game off Todd Worrell's major-league-record pace . . . Made $490,000 in 1991 . . . Second-round pick in 1985 draft . . . Born Aug. 10, 1962, in Anaheim, Cal.

Year	Club	G	IP	W	L	Pct.	SO	BB	H	ERA
1988	Seattle	40	48⅓	5	8	.385	54	24	45	3.54
1989	Seattle	67	77	1	7	.125	69	19	81	2.81
1990	Seattle	49	56	1	4	.200	45	16	47	2.25
1991	Seattle	34	34⅓	3	3	.500	31	10	25	3.67
	Totals	190	215⅔	10	22	.313	199	69	198	2.96

ERIK HANSON 26 6-6 210   **Bats R Throws R**

Elbow trouble curtailed development of one of game's best young pitchers . . . Made only one start between May 11 and June 22 . . . Went on disabled list May 31 . . . Finished 8-8 with 3.81 ERA in 27 starts . . . Hurt by lack of support, he lost five one-run games in which he allowed three runs or less . . . Allowed 182 hits in 174⅔ innings, but walked only 56 while striking out 143 . . . Went 18-9 with 3.24 ERA and 211 strikeouts in 236 innings in breakthrough 1990 season . . . Went 9-5 with 3.18 ERA in 1989 . . . Earned $400,000 in 1991 . . . Second-round pick in 1986 draft . . . Born May 18, 1965, in Kinnelon, N.J.

Year	Club	G	IP	W	L	Pct.	SO	BB	H	ERA
1988	Seattle	6	41⅔	2	3	.400	36	12	35	3.24
1989	Seattle	17	113⅓	9	5	.643	75	32	103	3.18
1990	Seattle	33	236	18	9	.667	211	68	205	3.24
1991	Seattle	27	174⅔	8	8	.500	143	56	182	3.81
	Totals	83	565⅔	37	25	.597	465	168	525	3.40

TOP PROSPECTS

ROGER SALKELD 21 6-5 215   **Bats R Throws R**
Can't-miss prospect . . . Went 8-8 with 3.05 ERA for Jacksonville (AA) in 1990 . . . Allowed only 131 hits in 154 innings . . . Struck out 159 and walked only 55 . . . Third pick overall in 1989 draft . . . Was 30-7 with 404 strikeouts in 264 innings in high school . . . Born March 6, 1971, in Burbank, Cal.

TINO MARTINEZ 24 6-2 205   **Bats L Throws R**
Should stick as first baseman after back-to-back big seasons with Calgary (AAA) . . . Hit .326 with 18 homers and 86 RBI there in 1991 before September recall . . . Has .211 average, four homers and 14 RBI in 180 major-league at-bats . . . Member of 1988 U.S. Olympic team . . . Mariners' first pick in 1988 draft . . . Born Dec. 7, 1967, in Tampa.

DAVE FLEMING 22 6-3 200   **Bats L Throws L**
Recalled in September after posting combined 12-6 mark for Jacksonville (AA) and Calgary (AAA) . . . Was 1-0 despite 6.62 ERA

in nine games in Seattle, including three starts . . . Allowed 19 hits but only three walks in 17⅔ innings . . . Led University of Georgia to 1990 NCAA College World Series championship as he saved title game against Oklahoma State with three scoreless innings . . . Third-round pick in 1990 . . . Born Nov. 7, 1969, in Queens, N.Y.

PATRICK LENNON 23 6-2 200   **Bats R Throws R**
First-round pick in 1986 finally made major-league debut in 1991 . . . Had one hit in eight at-bats . . . Outfielder hit .329 with 15 homers, 74 RBI and 12 steals for Calgary (AAA), the best of his five minor-league-seasons . . . Born April 27, 1968, in Whiteville, N.C.

MANAGER BILL PLUMMER: Players' choice to replace Jim Lefebvre, the most successful manager in Mariner history . . . Wasn't leading candidate until players were asked for their input . . . They like his no-nonsense approach . . . Religious man who will run a disciplined ship . . . In 13th season in Mariner organization, he began managerial career with San Jose of California League in 1980 . . . Won Midwest League title with Wausau in 1981 . . . Mariners' bullpen coach in 1982-83 . . . Managed four more years in minors before returning to Mariner staff in 1988 . . . Has served as bullpen coach and third-base coach . . . Finished modest seven-year career as major-league catcher with Mariners in 1978 . . . Career average only .188 . . . Hit 14 homers, drove in 88 runs in 892 career at-bats . . . Served as Johnny Bench's backup with the Reds (1972-77), never getting more than 159 at-bats, but does have two World Championship rings (1974, 1975) . . . Father, William, and uncle, Earl (Red) Baldwin, both had stints with Seattle minor-league franchises . . . Born March 21, 1947, in Oakland.

ALL-TIME MARINER SEASON RECORDS

BATTING: Ken Griffey Jr., .327, 1991
HRs: Gorman Thomas, 32, 1985
RBI: Alvin Davis, 116, 1984
STEALS: Harold Reynolds, 60, 1987
WINS: Mark Langston, 19, 1987
STRIKEOUTS: Mark Langston, 262, 1987

TEXAS RANGERS

TEAM DIRECTORY: General Partners: George W. Bush, Edward W. (Rusty) Rose; Pres.: J. Thomas Schieffer; VP/GM: Tom Grieve; VP-Business Oper.: John McMichael; VP-Adm.: Charles Wangner; Asst. GM-Player Pers./Scouting: Sandy Johnson; Dir. Player Dev.: Marty Scott; VP-Pub. Rel.: John Blake; Trav. Sec.: Dan Schimek; Mgr.: Bobby Valentine. Home: Arlington Stadium (43,508). Field distances: 330, l.f. line; 380, l.c.; 400, c.f.; 380, r.c.; 330, r.f. line. Spring training: Port Charlotte, Fla.

SCOUTING REPORT

HITTING: What's not to like in a lineup that includes Rafael Palmeiro (.322, 26, 88), Ruben Sierra (.307, 25, 116), Julio Franco (.341, 15, 78) and Juan Gonzalez (.264, 27, 102)? No wonder the 1991 Rangers led the majors in runs (829), finished third in team average (.270) and wound up third in homers (177).

But the production doesn't stop there. Brian Downing (.278, 17, 49) is a dangerous designated hitter at age 40. Kevin Reimer

Julio Franco became Rangers' first batting champ at .341.

had 20 homers and 69 RBI in 1991. Dean Palmer (15 homers in 268 at-bats) figures to hit 25 homers in a full season. Ivan Rodriguez, only 21, can only get better in his first full season. And ex-Phillie Dickie Thon, signed as a free agent, still has some pop in his bat. The only thing missing is speed. Franco is the only 30-steal threat now that Gary Pettis' playing time figures to be reduced.

PITCHING: Nolan Ryan (12-6, 2.91) kept rolling and Jose Guzman (13-7, 3.08) came back sound and effective in 1991. All the 45-year-old Ryan did last year was throw his seventh no-hitter and lead the majors in hits allowed per nine innings (5.31) and strikeouts per nine innings (10.6). But injury-riddled Bobby Witt (3-7, 6.09) and temperamental Kevin Brown (9-12, 4.40) need to step up to the 15-win category for this team to have a legitimate shot at its first division title. The fifth starter spot will be split among left-handers Brian Bohanon (4-3, 4.84) and John Barfield (4-4, 4.54) and 21-year-old right-hander Hector Fajardo (0-2, 5.68), who came from the Pirates in the Steve Buechele deal.

Closer Jeff Russell (6-4, 3.29) bounced back from elbow surgery to save 30 games, but it took him 40 opportunities to do so. Left-hander Kenny Rogers (10-10, 5.42) has settled back into a setup role and figures to have a much-improved season. Injuries gave Terry Mathews, Gerald Alexander and Barry Manuel experience in 1991 and they should be better for it.

FIELDING: A perennial problem got worse when Buechele was traded and the Rangers tied for 12th in fielding percentage at .979 in 1991. At least the strong-armed Rodriguez is behind the plate to cut down opponents' running games. Palmer is no Buechele at third, but should be average. Franco's reliability is diminishing at second and the Rangers are hoping Thon simply makes all the routine plays at shortstop. Right fielder Sierra got serious about his defense and improved markedly. Gonzalez will slide from center to left in the late innings, making room for the sterling glove of Pettis.

OUTLOOK: GM Tom Grieve and manager Bobby Valentine had their contracts extended once again and are locked up through 1993. But this time, the extension came with an implied mandate to win a title. Coming off a third-place finish and third consecutive winning season at 85-77, the Rangers could do exactly that in the AL West—but only if the pitching staff stays healthy and consistent.

TEXAS RANGERS 1992 ROSTER

MANAGER Bobby Valentine
Coaches—Ray Burris, Orlando Gomez, Toby Harrah, Tom House, Dave Oliver, Tom Robson

PITCHERS

No.	Name	1991 Club	W-L	IP	SO	ERA	B-T	Ht.	Wt.	Born
48	Alexander, Gerald	Oklahoma City	1-1	11	10	4.22	R-R	5-11	200	3/26/68 Baton Rouge, LA
		Texas	5-3	89	50	5.24				
27	Barfield, John	Texas	4-4	83	27	4.54	L-L	6-1	195	10/15/64 Pine Bluff, AR
45	Bohanon, Brian	Charlotte	1-0	12	7	3.86	L-L	6-2	220	8/1/68 Denton, TX
		Tulsa	0-1	12	6	2.31				
		Oklahoma City	0-4	46	37	2.91				
		Texas	4-3	61	34	4.84				
41	Brown, Kevin	Texas	9-12	211	96	4.40	R-R	6-4	195	3/14/65 McIntyre, GA
43	Chiamparino, Scott	Texas	1-0	22	8	4.03	L-R	6-2	205	8/22/66 San Mateo, CA
32	Fajardo, Hector	Augusta	4-3	60	79	2.69	R-R	6-4	200	11/6/70 Mexico
		Salem	0-1	8	7	2.35				
		Carolina	3-4	61	24	4.13				
		Pittsburgh	0-0	6	8	9.95				
		Buffalo	1-0	9	12	0.96				
		Texas	0-2	19	15	5.68				
23	Guzman, Jose	Oklahoma City	1-1	21	18	3.92	R-R	6-3	195	4/9/63 Puerto Rico
		Texas	13-7	170	125	3.08				
44	Manuel, Barry	Tulsa	2-7	68	53	3.29	R-R	5-11	185	8/12/65 Mamou, LA
		Texas	1-0	16	5	1.13				
38	Mathews, Terry	Oklahoma City	5-6	95	63	3.49	L-R	6-2	225	10/5/64 Alexandria, LA
		Texas	4-0	57	51	3.61				
—	Nen, Robb	Tulsa	0-2	28	23	5.79	R-R	6-4	200	11/28/69 San Pedro, CA
59	Pavlik, Roger	Oklahoma City	0-5	26	43	5.19	R-R	6-2	220	10/4/67 Houston, TX
37	Rogers, Kenny	Texas	10-10	110	73	5.42	L-L	6-1	205	11/10/64 Savannah, GA
40	Russell, Jeff	Texas	6-4	79	52	3.29	R-R	6-3	205	9/2/61 Cincinnati, OH
34	Ryan, Nolan	Texas	12-6	173	203	2.91	R-R	6-2	212	1/31/47 Refugio, TX
36	Witt, Bobby	Texas	3-7	89	82	6.09	R-R	6-2	205	5/11/64 Arlington, VA
		Oklahoma City	1-1	8	12	1.13				

CATCHERS

No.	Name	1991 Club	H	HR	RBI	Pct.	B-T	Ht.	Wt.	Born
—	Haselman, Bill	Oklahoma City	113	9	59	.256	R-R	6-3	205	5/25/66 Long Branch, NJ
12	Petralli, Geno	Texas	54	2	20	.271	L-R	6-1	190	9/25/59 Sacramento, CA
7	Rodriguez, Ivan	Texas	74	3	27	.264	R-R	5-9	205	11/30/71 Puerto Rico
		Tulsa	48	3	28	.274				

INFIELDERS

No.	Name	1991 Club	H	HR	RBI	Pct.	B-T	Ht.	Wt.	Born
—	Colon, Cris	Charlotte	78	3	27	.313	S-R	6-2	180	1/3/69 Venezuela
4	Fariss, Monty	Oklahoma City	134	13	73	.271	R-R	6-4	200	10/13/67 Cordell, OK
		Texas	8	1	6	.258				
14	Franco, Julio	Texas	201	15	78	.341	R-R	6-1	188	8/23/61 Dominican Republic
—	Frye, Jeff	Tulsa	152	4	41	.302	R-R	5-9	180	8/31/66 Oakland, CA
3	Hernandez, Jose	Tulsa	72	1	20	.239	R-R	6-1	180	7/14/69 Puerto Rico
		Oklahoma City	14	1	3	.304				
		Texas	18	0	4	.184				
9	Huson, Jeff	Texas	57	2	26	.213	L-R	6-3	180	8/15/64 Scottsdale, AZ
		Oklahoma City	3	0	2	.500				
20	Kunkel, Jeff	Texas		Injured			R-R	6-2	180	3/25/62 West Palm Beach, FL
39	Maurer, Rob	Oklahoma City	138	20	77	.301	L-L	6-3	210	1/7/67 Evansville, IN
		Texas	1	0	2	.063				
—	Oliva, Jose	Charlotte	92	1	44	.240	R-R	6-1	160	3/3/71 Dominican Republic
		Gulf Coast	1	0	1	.091				
25	Palmiero, Rafael	Texas	203	26	88	.322	L-L	6-0	188	9/24/64 Cuba
16	Palmer, Dean	Oklahoma City	70	22	59	.299	R-R	6-1	190	12/27/68 Tallahassee, FL
		Texas	50	15	37	.187				
—	Thon, Dickie	Philadelphia	136	9	44	.252	R-R	5-11	180	6/20/58 South Bend, IN

OUTFIELDERS

No.	Name	1991 Club	H	HR	RBI	Pct.	B-T	Ht.	Wt.	Born
8	Daugherty, Jack	Texas	28	1	16	.194	S-L	6-0	190	7/3/60 Hialeah, FL
		Oklahoma City	11	0	4	.143				
55	Downing, Brian	Texas	113	17	49	.278	R-R	5-10	195	10/9/50 Los Angeles, CA
19	Gonzalez, Juan	Texas	144	27	102	.264	R-R	6-3	210	10/16/69 Puerto Rico
33	Harris, Donald	Tulsa	102	11	53	.227	R-R	6-1	185	11/12/67 Waco, TX
		Texas	3	1	2	.375				
—	Peltier, Dan	Oklahoma City	79	3	31	.229	L-L	6-1	200	6/30/68 Clifton Park, NY
24	Pettis, Gary	Texas	61	0	19	.216	S-R	6-1	160	4/3/58 Oakland, CA
47	Reimer, Kevin	Texas	106	20	69	.269	L-R	6-2	220	6/28/64 Macon, GA
21	Sierra, Ruben	Texas	203	25	116	.307	S-R	6-1	200	10/6/65 Puerto Rico

RANGER PROFILES

JULIO FRANCO 30 6-1 188   Bats R Throws R

Won AL batting title with career-best .341 average . . . Became first Ranger to win crown, first AL second baseman since Rod Carew in 1975 and third AL right-handed hitter in the last 21 years . . . Has hit .300 or better in five of the last six seasons . . . All-Star for the third consecutive season since coming from Cleveland for Oddibe McDowell, Pete O'Brien and Jerry Browne . . . Scored a career-high 108 runs . . . Also established career high in homers (15) . . . Defensive range and reliability is diminishing, prompting thought of eventual move from second to first or DH . . . Earned $2.35 million in 1991, on first year of three-year extension . . . Born Aug. 23, 1961, in San Pedro de Macoris, D.R. . . . Phils signed him as undrafted free agent in 1978.

Year	Club	Pos.	G	AB	R	H	2B	3B	HR	RBI	SB	Avg.
1982	Philadelphia . . .	SS-3B	16	29	3	8	1	0	0	3	0	.276
1983	Cleveland	SS	149	560	68	153	24	8	8	80	32	.273
1984	Cleveland	SS	160	658	82	188	22	5	3	79	19	.286
1985	Cleveland	SS-2B	160	636	97	183	33	4	6	90	13	.288
1986	Cleveland	SS-2B	149	599	80	183	30	5	10	74	10	.306
1987	Cleveland	SS-2B	128	495	86	158	24	3	8	52	32	.319
1988	Cleveland	2B	152	613	88	186	23	6	10	54	25	.303
1989	Texas	2B	150	548	80	173	31	5	13	92	21	.316
1990	Texas	2B	157	582	96	172	27	1	11	69	31	.296
1991	Texas	2B	146	589	108	201	27	3	15	78	36	.341
	Totals		1367	5309	788	1605	242	40	84	671	219	.302

RAFAEL PALMEIRO 27 6-0 188   Bats L Throws L

Career-high 26 homers put to rest knock on his lack of power. Previous high was 14 . . . Ranked atop AL batting leaders for a month before dipping to a still-impressive .322 . . . Set club record by scoring 115 runs . . . Led majors with 49 doubles, another club record . . . Was second in majors with 336 total bases and third in hits with 203 . . . Continued to improve defensively at first base in his third full season at the position . . . Earned $1.475 million in 1991 . . . One of only three Cuban-born major leaguers . . . Born Sept. 24, 1964, in Havana, a few years before his family emigrated to Miami . . . Cubs drafted him in first round in 1985 . . . Rangers got him in nine-player deal that sent Mitch Williams to Chicago.

Year	Club	Pos.	G	AB	R	H	2B	3B	HR	RBI	SB	Avg.
1986	Chicago (NL) ..	OF	22	73	9	18	4	0	3	12	1	.247
1987	Chicago (NL) ..	OF-1B	84	221	32	61	15	1	14	30	2	.276
1988	Chicago (NL) ..	OF-1B	152	580	75	178	41	5	8	53	12	.307
1989	Texas	1B	156	559	76	154	23	4	8	64	4	.275
1990	Texas	1B	154	598	72	191	35	6	14	89	3	.319
1991	Texas	1B	159	631	115	203	49	3	26	88	4	.322
	Totals		727	2662	379	805	167	19	73	336	26	.302

RUBEN SIERRA 26 6-1 200   Bats S Throws R

Bounced back from subpar 1990 season with .307 average, 25 homers and 116 RBI . . . Became first Ranger to drive in 100-plus runs three times . . . In last six seasons, he is tied for fourth in majors in RBI . . . Finished among top five in AL in five offensive categories . . . Already is club's all-time leader in RBI and extra-base hits and is second in homers, runs, doubles and total bases . . . Scored 110 runs, one of three Rangers to top 100 mark . . . Made diligent effort to improve outfield defense and succeeded . . . Earned $2.65 million in 1991 . . . Born Oct. 6, 1965, in Rio Piedras, P.R. . . . One of several current Rangers signed by club bullpen coach Orlando Gomez, in November 1982.

Year	Club	Pos.	G	AB	R	H	2B	3B	HR	RBI	SB	Avg.
1986	Texas	OF	113	382	50	101	13	10	16	55	7	.264
1987	Texas	OF	158	643	97	169	35	4	30	109	16	.263
1988	Texas	OF	156	615	77	156	32	2	23	91	18	.254
1989	Texas	OF	162	634	101	194	35	14	29	119	8	.306
1990	Texas	OF	159	608	70	170	37	2	16	96	9	.280
1991	Texas	OF	161	661	110	203	44	5	25	116	16	.307
	Totals		909	3543	505	993	196	37	139	586	74	.280

JUAN GONZALEZ 22 6-3 210   Bats R Throws R

Missed qualifying as certain AL Rookie of the Year in 1991 by 20 at-bats, because he had 150 in two September callups prior to last season . . . Several scouts feel he eventually will be better than Ruben Sierra . . . Fit right into the middle of the Rangers' powerful lineup with 27 homers and 102 RBI, despite late fade . . . Hit only .150 in his last 128 at-bats . . . Only

18th player to drive in 100 runs in a season before his 22nd birthday ... Played most of time in center field, although his still-growing frame eventually will end up in left ... Another in the Rangers' line of standout Latins ... Born Oct. 16, 1969, in Vega Baja, P.R. ... Earned $120,000 in 1991 ... Signed as free agent in May 1986.

Year Club	Pos.	G	AB	R	H	2B	3B	HR	RBI	SB	Avg.
1989 Texas	OF	24	60	6	9	3	0	1	7	0	.150
1990 Texas	OF	25	90	11	26	7	1	4	12	0	.289
1991 Texas	OF	142	545	78	144	34	1	27	102	4	.264
Totals		191	695	95	179	44	2	32	121	4	.258

DEAN PALMER 23 6-1 190   Bats R Throws R

Forced promotion from Oklahoma City (AAA) on June 24 by slamming 22 homers and driving in 58 runs ... Finished with 15 homers in 268 big-league at-bats ... Twenty-six of his 50 hits were for extra bases ... Hit only .187 and struck out an alarming 96 times ... With trade of Steve Buechele, he figures to be a fixture at third base for several years ... Has a way to go to match Buechele's defense ... Committed nine errors, most of them on throws ... Born Dec. 27, 1968, in Tallahassee, Fla. ... Earned $100,000 in 1991 ... Third-round draft choice in 1986.

Year Club	Pos.	G	AB	R	H	2B	3B	HR	RBI	SB	Avg.
1989 Texas	3B-SS-OF	16	19	0	2	2	0	0	1	0	.105
1991 Texas	3B-OF	81	268	38	50	9	2	15	37	0	.187
Totals		97	287	38	52	11	2	15	38	0	.181

BRIAN DOWNING 41 5-10 195   Bats R Throws R

Signed as free agent late in spring training, he reached two significant milestones in 18th full season ... Hit 250th homer May 18 and recorded 2,000th hit Sept. 16 ... Became fifth AL player to hit at least 16 homers at 40 years old or older, joining Darrell Evans, Carlton Fisk, Reggie Jackson and Carl Yastrzemski ... Led off first inning with a home run four times in 1991, giving him 23 for his career ... Hit .429 as a pinch-hitter, highest mark in AL for 20 or more at-bats ... Used exclusively as DH for the fourth consecutive season ... He and Frank Tanana are only active 19-year vets who have never appeared in a World Series...Earned $425,000 in 1991...Born Oct. 9, 1950, in Los Angeles...Began career as undrafted free agent with White Sox in 1969...As free agent, re-signed $800,000 contract for '92.

Year Club	Pos.	G	AB	R	H	2B	3B	HR	RBI	SB	Avg.
1973 Chicago (AL) ..	OF-C-3B	34	73	5	13	1	0	2	4	0	.178
1974 Chicago (AL) ..	C-OF	108	293	41	66	12	1	10	39	0	.225
1975 Chicago (AL) ..	C	138	420	58	101	12	1	7	41	13	.240
1976 Chicago (AL) ..	C	104	317	38	81	14	0	3	30	7	.256
1977 Chicago (AL) ..	C-OF	69	169	28	48	4	2	4	25	1	.284
1978 California	C	133	412	42	105	15	0	7	46	3	.255
1979 California	C	148	509	87	166	27	3	12	75	3	.326
1980 California	C	30	93	5	27	6	0	2	25	0	.290
1981 California	OF-C	93	317	47	79	14	0	9	41	1	.249
1982 California	OF	158	623	109	175	37	2	28	84	2	.281
1983 California	OF	113	403	68	99	15	1	19	53	1	.246
1984 California	OF	156	539	65	148	28	2	23	91	0	.275
1985 California	OF	150	520	80	137	23	1	20	85	5	.263
1986 California	OF	152	513	90	137	25	4	20	95	4	.267
1987 California	OF	155	567	110	154	29	3	29	77	5	.272
1988 California	DH	135	484	80	117	18	2	25	64	3	.242
1989 California	DH	142	544	59	154	25	2	14	59	0	.283
1990 California	DH	96	330	47	90	18	2	14	51	0	.273
1991 Texas	DH	123	407	76	113	17	2	17	49	1	.278
Totals		2237	7533	1135	2010	342	28	265	1034	49	.267

IVAN RODRIGUEZ 20 5-9 205   Bats R Throws R

Was AL Rookie of the Year candidate despite not being recalled until June 19...Didn't turn 20 until after last season...Quickly established reputation as one of the game's best defensive catchers...Threw out 48.9 percent of would-be base-stealers, best mark among regular AL catchers...Also hit much better than expected, although five walks in combination with 280 at-bats shows he needs to develop patience...On morning of his recall, he was married in a ceremony at home plate of Drillers Stadium in Tulsa...Nicknamed "Pudge" in the minors because of stocky frame...Caught more games (88) than any teenager since Del Crandall in 1949...Born Nov. 30, 1971, in Vega Baja, P.R....Earned $100,000 last year...Signed as free agent in July 1988.

Year Club	Pos.	G	AB	R	H	2B	3B	HR	RBI	SB	Avg.
1991 Texas	C	88	280	24	74	16	0	3	27	0	.264

DICKIE THON 33 5-11 180   Bats R Throws R

Turned in another solid, injury-free season in 1991 as Phils' regular shortstop and signed one-year, free-agent contract with Rangers for $700,000 . . . His .252 batting average was second-highest among Phils' regulars . . . Had sixth career two-homer game Aug. 2 at Montreal . . . Began season with 5-for-29 slump but bounced back, showing he can still be consistent performer . . . Signed by Angels as non-drafted free agent in 1975 . . . Traded to Astros in 1981 . . . Became one of NL's brightest stars in 1983, leading league with 18 game-winning RBI . . . Career nearly ended when he was hit in head by Mike Torrez pitch in 1984 . . . Vision problems plagued him for years . . . Signed as free agent with Padres in 1988 . . . Contract was sold to to Phillies before 1989 season . . . Led NL shortstops in homers and RBI in 1989 . . . Born June 20, 1958, in South Bend, Ind . . . Earned $1,250,000 in 1991 . . . Tied with Barry Larkin for most DPs turned by NL shortstop in 1990.

Year	Club	Pos.	G	AB	R	H	2B	3B	HR	RBI	SB	Avg.
1979	California	2B-SS-3B	35	56	6	19	33	0	0	8	0	.339
1980	California	SS-2B-3B-1B	80	267	32	68	12	2	0	15	7	.255
1981	Houston	2B-SS-3B	49	95	13	26	6	0	0	3	6	.274
1982	Houston	SS-3B-2B	136	496	73	137	31	10	3	36	37	.276
1983	Houston	SS	154	619	81	177	28	9	20	79	34	.286
1984	Houston	SS	5	17	3	6	0	1	0	1	0	.353
1985	Houston	SS	84	251	26	63	6	1	6	29	8	.251
1986	Houston	SS	106	278	24	69	13	1	3	21	6	.248
1987	Houston	SS	32	66	6	14	1	0	1	3	3	.212
1988	San Diego	SS-3B-2B	95	258	36	68	12	2	1	18	19	.264
1989	Philadelphia	SS	136	435	45	118	18	4	15	60	6	.271
1990	Philadelphia	SS	149	552	54	141	20	4	8	48	12	.255
1991	Philadelphia	SS	146	539	44	136	18	4	9	44	11	.252
	Totals		1207	3929	443	1042	168	38	66	365	149	.265

KEVIN REIMER 27 6-2 220   Bats L Throws R

Manager Bobby Valentine thought enough of this guy's ability to cut Pete Incaviglia in spring training . . . Proved his manager right by slamming 20 homers and driving in 69 runs in 394 at-bats . . . Had only three homers in 130 at-bats prior to 1991 . . . Caught fire beginning July 28, hitting 15 homers and driving in 56 runs . . . One problem: he made Incaviglia look good in left field by comparison . . . Poor range and arm make him an ideal DH candidate . . . Born June 28, 1964, in Macon, Ga., but

was raised in British Columbia . . . Earned $115,000 in 1991 . . .
Eleventh-round pick in 1985 draft.

Year	Club	Pos.	G	AB	R	H	2B	3B	HR	RBI	SB	Avg.
1988	Texas	OF	12	25	2	3	0	0	1	2	0	.120
1989	Texas	DH	3	5	0	0	0	0	0	0	0	.000
1990	Texas	OF	64	100	5	26	9	1	2	15	0	.260
1991	Texas	OF	136	394	46	106	22	0	20	69	0	.269
	Totals		215	524	53	135	31	1	23	86	0	.258

JEFF RUSSELL 30 6-3 205   Bats R Throws R

Rebounded from surgery-marred 1990 season
to post 30 saves in 1991 . . . Failed to convert
10 opportunities, the most blown saves in AL
. . . On a staff that includes Nolan Ryan, he is
consistently clocked as the hardest thrower, in
the 95-96-mph range . . . Opponents hit .236
off him . . . Allowed 11 home runs after surrendering just five in 1989 and 1990 . . . Was
bothered by arm trouble for all but the first two months of the
season, when he was used heavily . . . Is club all-time save leader
with 83 and has top two single-season save totals . . . Saved 37 in
1989 . . . Came to Texas from Cincinnati for Buddy Bell in 1985
. . . Earned $2.45 million in 1991 . . . Born Sept. 2, 1961, in Cin-
cinnati . . . Reds drafted him in fifth round in 1979.

Year	Club	G	IP	W	L	Pct.	SO	BB	H	ERA
1983	Cincinnati	10	68⅓	4	5	.444	40	22	58	3.03
1984	Cincinnati	33	181⅔	6	18	.250	101	65	186	4.26
1985	Texas	13	62	3	6	.333	44	27	85	7.55
1986	Texas	37	82	5	2	.714	54	31	74	3.40
1987	Texas	52	97⅓	5	4	.556	56	52	109	4.44
1988	Texas	34	188⅔	10	9	.526	88	66	183	3.82
1989	Texas	71	72⅔	6	4	.600	77	24	45	1.98
1990	Texas	27	25⅓	1	5	.167	16	16	23	4.26
1991	Texas	68	79⅓	6	4	.600	52	26	71	3.29
	Totals	345	857⅓	46	57	.447	528	329	834	3.96

JOSE GUZMAN 28 6-3 195   Bats R Throws R

Great comeback story, winning 13 games after
not pitching in the majors since 1988 because
of career-threatening shoulder injuries . . . Also
posted a 3.08 ERA, 11th-best mark among AL
starters . . . Won nine games after All-Star
break, including six of last seven decisions . . .
Made first start May 23, when he walked nine
Twins in 3⅔ innings . . . Finished with 169⅔
innings, third-most on staff . . . Was cut in spring training, then

agreed to a minor-league contract with his only organization in an 11-year pro career that began as undrafted free agent in February 1981... Earned $365,000 in 1991... Born April 9, 1963, in Santa Isabel, P.R.

Year	Club	G	IP	W	L	Pct.	SO	BB	H	ERA
1985	Texas	5	32⅔	3	2	.600	24	14	27	2.76
1986	Texas	29	172⅓	9	15	.375	87	60	199	4.54
1987	Texas	37	208⅓	14	14	.500	143	82	196	4.67
1988	Texas	30	206⅔	11	13	.458	157	82	180	3.70
1991	Texas	25	169⅔	13	7	.650	125	84	152	3.08
	Totals	126	789⅔	50	51	.495	536	322	754	3.97

KEVIN BROWN 27 6-4 195   Bats R Throws R

Instead of developing into a top-line starter as expected, he took a step backwards in third season... Slipped to nine wins after posting 12 in each of his first two full seasons... ERA climbed above 4.00 for the first time in three seasons... Ran into an uncommon amount of bad luck, but made matters worse with emotional blowups... On the plus side, he did pitch a full season (210⅔ innings in 33 starts) for first time after succumbing to late-season arm weariness in each of his first two years... Earned only $320,000 in 1991 and staged a one-day spring holdout in protest... Rangers' first draft pick in 1986... Born March 14, 1965, in McIntyre, Ga.

Year	Club	G	IP	W	L	Pct.	SO	BB	H	ERA
1986	Texas	1	5	1	0	1.000	4	0	6	3.60
1988	Texas	4	23⅓	1	1	.500	12	8	33	4.24
1989	Texas	28	191	12	9	.571	104	70	167	3.35
1990	Texas	26	180	12	10	.545	88	60	175	3.60
1991	Texas	33	210⅔	9	12	.429	96	90	233	4.40
	Totals	92	610	35	32	.522	304	228	614	3.82

NOLAN RYAN 45 6-2 212   Bats R Throws R

''The Express' kept rolling... Added another no-hitter to his nature-defying feats. No-No No. 7 came May 1 against Toronto... Had majors' lowest oppenents' batting average (.174)... Struck out 203 in 173 innings, the 15th season he topped 200... Fanned AL-high 16 in his no-hitter... Enters 1992 with unmatched 5,511 strikeouts... Has made 548 consecutive starts without a relief appearance, another of his 40-plus major-league records... His 12 wins were most by any pitcher 44 or older since Tommy John's 13 in 1987 . . . Has won 10 or more games 20 times, putting him one season short of Don Sutton's record . . . Finished 5-1 after his second stint on the DL because of shoulder irritation . . . ERA of 2.91 was fifth-best in AL . . . Earned $3 million in 1991 . . . Signed two-year extension that also includes 10-year personal services contract with club upon retirement as player . . . Born Jan. 31, 1947, in Refugio, Tex. . . . Son Reid pitches at Texas Christian University . . . Mets drafted him in 10th round in 1965 . . . Rangers signed him as free agent prior to 1989 season.

Year	Club	G	IP	W	L	Pct.	SO	BB	H	ERA
1966	New York (NL)	2	3	0	1	.000	6	3	5	15.00
1968	New York (NL)	21	134	6	9	.400	133	75	93	3.09
1969	New York (NL)	25	89	6	3	.667	92	53	60	3.54
1970	New York (NL)	27	132	7	11	.389	125	97	86	3.41
1971	New York (NL)	30	152	10	14	.417	137	116	125	3.97
1972	California	39	284	19	16	.543	329	157	166	2.28
1973	California	41	326	21	16	.568	383	162	238	2.87
1974	California	42	333	22	16	.578	367	202	221	2.89
1975	California	28	198	14	12	.538	186	132	152	3.45
1976	California	39	284	17	18	.486	327	183	193	3.36
1977	California	37	299	19	16	.543	341	204	198	2.77
1978	California	31	235	10	13	.435	260	148	183	3.71
1979	California	34	223	16	14	.533	223	114	169	3.59
1980	Houston	35	234	11	10	.524	200	98	205	3.35
1981	Houston	21	149	11	5	.688	140	68	99	1.69
1982	Houston	35	250⅓	16	12	.571	245	109	196	3.16
1983	Houston	29	196⅓	14	9	.609	183	101	134	2.98
1984	Houston	30	183⅔	12	11	.522	197	69	143	3.04
1985	Houston	35	232	10	12	.455	209	95	205	3.80
1986	Houston	30	178	12	8	.600	194	82	119	3.34
1987	Houston	34	211⅔	8	16	.333	270	87	154	2.76
1988	Houston	33	220	12	11	.522	228	87	186	3.52
1989	Texas	32	239⅓	16	10	.615	301	98	162	3.20
1990	Texas	30	204	13	9	.591	232	74	137	3.44
1991	Texas	27	173	12	6	.667	203	72	102	2.91
	Totals	767	5163⅓	314	278	.530	5511	2686	3731	3.15

TOP PROSPECTS

MONTY FARISS 24 6-4 200   **Bats R Throws R**
Reached majors last September because of his bat . . . Hit .271 with 13 homers and 73 RBI for Oklahoma City (AAA) before promotion . . . Weak throwing arm and bouts of Steve Sax Disease have him scrambling for a position . . . Has moved from shortstop to second base to left field, but future may be at first base . . . Rangers' No. 1 pick in 1988 draft . . . Born Oct. 13, 1967, in Cordell, Okla.

ROB MAURER 25 6-3 210   Bats L Throws L

Has the numbers, if not a place to play as a first baseman behind Rafael Palmeiro . . . Hit .301 with 20 homers and 77 RBI for Oklahoma City (AAA) before September promotion . . . In 1990, he hit .300 with 21 homers and 78 RBI for Tulsa (AA) . . . Sixth-round draft choice in 1988 . . . Born Jan. 7, 1967, in Evansville, Ind.

MANAGER BOBBY VALENTINE: Set major-league mark for longest tenure at start of career without a division title . . . May 16 will mark start of eighth season since replacing Doug Rader . . . Has second-longest tenure with same team among AL managers as only Tigers' Sparky Anderson has stayed put longer . . . Career record is 536-564 after 85-77 finish in 1991 . . . That makes him by far the winningest and losingest manager in club history . . . A top-notch game manager, but has been dogged by personality conflicts, especially with veteran players . . . Cocky demeanor makes him unpopular figure around the league . . . Promising No. 1 pick whose career was reduced to utilityman status after he shattered his left leg crashing into the wall at Anaheim Stadium in 1973 . . . Successful restaurateur who has six establishments in native Connecticut and Arlington, Tex. . . . Wife Mary is the daughter of former Dodger pitcher Ralph Branca . . . Born May 13, 1950, in Stamford, Conn.

ALL-TIME RANGER SEASON RECORDS

BATTING: Julio Franco, .341, 1991
HRs: Larry Parrish, 32, 1987
RBI: Ruben Sierra, 119, 1989
STEALS: Bump Wills, 52, 1987
WINS: Ferguson Jenkins, 25, 1974
STRIKEOUTS: Nolan Ryan, 301, 1989

BALTIMORE ORIOLES

TEAM DIRECTORY: Pres.: Lawrence Lucchino; Exec. VP/GM: Roland Hemond; VP-Adm. Pers.: Calvin Hill; VPs: Robert Aylward, Martin Conway; Asst. GM-Player Dev. Dir.: Doug Melvin; Dir. Pub. Rel.: Rick Vaughn; Trav. Sec.: Phillip Itzoe; Mgr.: John Oates. Home: Oriole Park (48,003). Field distances: 333, l.f. line; 410, l.c.; 399, c.f.; 318, r.f. line. Spring training: Sarasota, Fla.

SCOUTING REPORT

HITTING: Cal Ripken Jr., coming off a year that saw him notch personal highs in average (.323), home runs (34) and RBI (114), must provide another monster season in 1992. Even with the 1991 AL MVP's huge contribution last summer, Baltimore finished 12th in the AL in hitting (.254) and 10th in runs (686).

AL MVP Cal Ripken Jr. has no days off, few off days.

The Orioles re-signed slugger Glenn Davis (.227, 10, 28) with the hope that he will be healthy this time. Davis missed 105 games last year after injuring the spinal accessory nerve in his neck, leaving Randy Milligan (.263, 16, 70) to provide the power. Joe Orsulak (.278, 5, 43) hopes to pick up where he left off after batting .335 from Aug. 2 until the end of the season. Mike Devereaux (.260, 19, 59) led the slow-footed Orioles with 16 of their 50 stolen bases.

PITCHING: To avoid another 67-95 finish, Baltimore must improve upon its 4.59 ERA of 1991 that was the worst mark in the majors and the second-highest in club history. To do that, the Orioles must find starters who can provide innings and keep their team in the game. The Orioles fell behind by at least three runs before the fourth inning 43 times last year and dropped 39 of those games.

Full seasons from Bob Milacki (10-9, 4.01) and Mike Mussina (4-5, 2.87) will help. More can be expected from big Ben McDonald (6-8, 4.84), if he avoids more of the injury problems that have plagued him. Storm Davis (3-9, 4.96 with the Royals) isn't the same pitcher he was as a first-time Oriole and free agent addition Rick Sutcliffe (6-5, 4.10 with the Cubs) is nothing more than a gamble.

The Orioles must ease the load on a bullpen that labored a major league-high 557⅔ innings. Relief ace Gregg Olson (4-6, 3.18, 31 Sv in 39 chances) may be a victim of the strain of too many curves, because he isn't what he used to be. Mike Flanagan excelled in short relief last year, but he is 40 years old.

FIELDING: Defensive excellence continues to be an Oriole trademark. Last season, they became the first team in major league history to commit fewer than 100 errors in three straight seasons. They committed a major league-low 91 errors and set a club record with 97 errorless games in 1991. The key to it all is the constant and steadying presence of Cal Ripken, who averaged one error per 73.4 chances at short in 1991. Brother Billy Ripken is almost that smooth at second base.

OUTLOOK: Baltimore has a grand new place to call home in Oriole Park at Camden Yards. It has an enthusiastic manager who is beginning his first full season in John Oates. It has a living legend at shortstop in Cal Ripken Jr. But it also has suspect starting pitching and a spotty offense. It will be a fun time at Camden Yards—until the reality of a mediocre home team sets in.

BALTIMORE ORIOLES 1992 ROSTER

MANAGER John Oates
Coaches—Greg Biagini, Dick Bosman, Elrod Hendricks, Davey Lopes,
Cal Ripken Sr.

PITCHERS

No.	Name	1991 Club	W-L	IP	SO	ERA	B-T	Ht.	Wt.	Born
43	Davis, Storm	Kansas City	3-9	114	53	4.96	R-R	6-4	225	12/26/61 Dallas, TX
—	De la Rosa, Francisco	Baltimore	0-0	4	1	4.50	S-R	5-11	195	3/3/66 Dominican Republic
		Rochester	4-1	84	61	2.67				
46	Flanagan, Mike	Baltimore	2-7	98	55	2.38	L-L	6-0	195	12/16/51 Manchester, NH
49	Frohwirth, Todd	Rochester	1-3	25	15	3.65	R-R	6-4	205	9/28/62 Milwaukee, WI
		Baltimore	7-3	96	77	1.87				
—	Hetzel, Eric	Pawtucket	9-5	116	83	3.57	R-R	6-3	180	9/25/63 Crowley, LA
—	Jones, Stacey	Hagerstown	0-1	30	26	1.78	R-R	6-6	225	5/26/67 Gadsden, AL
		Rochester	4-4	51	47	3.38				
		Baltimore	0-0	11	10	4.09				
—	Lewis, Richie	Harrisburg	6-5	75	82	3.74	R-R	5-10	175	1/25/66 Muncie, IN
		Indianapolis	1-0	28	22	3.58				
		Rochester	1-0	16	18	2.81				
19	McDonald, Ben	Baltimore	6-8	126	85	4.84	R-R	6-7	212	11/24/67 Baton Rouge, LA
		Rochester	0-1	7	7	7.71				
52	Mesa, Jose	Baltimore	6-11	124	64	5.97	R-R	6-3	222	5/22/66 Dominican Republic
		Rochester	3-3	51	48	3.86				
18	Milacki, Bob	Baltimore	10-9	184	108	4.01	R-R	6-4	234	7/28/64 Trenton, NJ
		Hagerstown	3-0	17	18	1.06				
42	Mussina, Mike	Rochester	10-4	122	107	2.87	R-R	6-2	185	12/8/68 Williamsport, PA
		Baltimore	4-5	88	52	2.87				
30	Olson, Gregg	Baltimore	4-6	74	72	3.18	R-R	6-4	209	10/11/66 Omaha, NE
—	Oquist, Mike	Hagerstown	10-9	166	136	4.06	R-R	6-2	170	5/30/68 La Junta, CO
—	Pennington, Brad	Kane County	0-2	23	43	5.87	L-L	6-5	210	4/14/69 Salem, IN
		Frederick	1-4	44	58	3.92				
45	Poole, Jim	Tex.-Balt.	3-2	42	38	2.36	L-L	6-2	203	4/28/66 Rochester, NY
		Rochester	3-2	29	25	2.79				
—	Rhodes, Arthur	Hagerstown	7-4	107	115	2.70	L-L	6-2	190	10/24/69 Waco, TX
		Baltimore	0-3	36	23	8.00				
40	Sutcliffe, Rick	Chicago (NL)	6-5	97	52	4.10	L-R	6-7	215	6/21/56 Independence, MO
—	Telford, Anthony	Rochester	12-9	157	115	3.95	R-R	6-0	189	3/6/66 San Jose, CA
		Baltimore	0-0	27	24	4.05				
32	Williamson, Mark	Baltimore	5-5	80	53	4.48	R-R	6-0	177	7/21/59 Corpus Christi, TX

CATCHERS

No.	Name	1991 Club	H	HR	RBI	Pct.	B-T	Ht.	Wt.	Born
—	Davares, Cesar	Frederick	59	3	29	.251	R-R	5-10	175	9/22/69 Dominican Republic
23	Hoiles, Chris	Baltimore	83	11	31	.243	R-R	6-0	208	3/20/65 Bowling Green, OH
—	Tackett, Jeff	Rochester	102	6	50	.236	R-R	6-2	206	12/1/65 Fresno, CA
		Baltimore	1	0	0	.125				

INFIELDERS

No.	Name	1991 Club	H	HR	RBI	Pct.	B-T	Ht.	Wt.	Born
—	Alexander, Manny	Frederick	143	3	42	.261	R-R	5-10	150	3/20/71 Dominican Republic
		Hagerstown	3	0	2	.333				
1	Bell, Juan	Baltimore	36	1	15	.172	S-R	5-11	176	3/29/68 Dominican Republic
37	Davis, Glenn	Baltimore	40	10	28	.227	R-R	6-3	200	3/28/61 Jacksonville, FL
		Hagerstown	6	1	3	.250				
10	Gomez, Leo	Rochester	26	6	19	.257	R-R	6-0	202	3/2/67 Puerto Rico
		Baltimore	91	16	45	.233				
—	Gutierrez, Ricky	Hagerstown	69	0	30	.236	R-R	6-1	175	5/23/70 Miami, FL
		Rochester	48	0	15	.306				
15	Horn, Sam	Baltimore	74	23	61	.233	L-L	6-5	247	11/2/63 Dallas, TX
36	Hulett, Tim	Baltimore	42	7	18	.204	R-R	6-0	190	1/12/60 Springfield, IL
39	Milligan, Randy	Baltimore	127	16	70	.263	R-R	6-1	235	11/27/61 San Diego, CA
3	Ripken, Bill	Baltimore	62	0	14	.216	R-R	6-1	182	12/16/64 Havre de Grace, MD
		Frederick	1	0	1	.250				
		Hagerstown	3	0	0	.600				
8	Ripken, Cal	Baltimore	210	34	114	.323	R-R	6-4	225	8/24/60 Havre de Grace, MD
21	Segui, David	Rochester	26	1	10	.271	S-L	6-1	200	7/19/66 Kansas City, KS
		Baltimore	59	2	22	.278				
25	Worthington, Craig	Baltimore	23	4	12	.225	R-R	6-0	200	4/17/65 Los Angeles, CA
		Rochester	17	2	9	.298				

OUTFIELDERS

No.	Name	1991 Club	H	HR	RBI	Pct.	B-T	Ht.	Wt.	Born
9	Anderson, Brady	Baltimore	59	2	27	.230	L-L	6-1	185	1/18/64 Silver Spring, MD
		Rochester	10	0	2	.385				
12	Devereaux, Mike	Baltimore	158	19	59	.260	R-R	6-0	193	4/10/63 Casper, WY
24	Evans, Dwight	Baltimore	73	6	38	.270	R-R	6-3	208	11/3/51 Santa Monica, CA
14	Martinez, Chito	Rochester	68	20	50	.322	L-L	5-10	180	12/19/65 Central America
		Baltimore	58	13	33	.269				
—	Mercedes, Luis	Rochester	125	2	36	.334	R-R	6-0	180	2/20/68 Dominican Republic
		Baltimore	11	0	2	.204				
6	Orsulak, Joe	Baltimore	135	5	43	.278	L-L	6-1	203	5/31/62 Glen Ridge, NJ

ORIOLE PROFILES

CAL RIPKEN Jr. 31 6-4 225　　　　　Bats R Throws R

Won his second AL MVP award with brilliant season . . . Joined Ernie Banks as only shortstops in major-league history to hit at least .300 with 30 home runs and 100 RBI . . . Set career highs with .323 average, 34 home runs, 114 RBI . . . One of four shortstops in major-league history to reach 30-homer plateau . . . One of eight big-league players to homer at least 20 times in each of first 10 seasons . . . Set club mark with 368 total bases . . . In past 50 years, only six AL players recorded as many total bases in a season . . . Topped majors in putouts (267), assists (529), total chances (807) and double plays (114) . . . Begins new season with 1,573 consecutive starts, having played in every game for nine consecutive seasons . . . Honored as AL Rookie of the Year in 1982 and AL MVP in 1983 . . . Born Aug. 24, 1960, in Havre de Grace, Md. . . . Orioles' second-round pick in 1978 draft . . . Best-paid shortstop in majors last year with $2,466,667 salary . . . Added Gold Glove in 1991.

Year	Club	Pos.	G	AB	R	H	2B	3B	HR	RBI	SB	Avg.
1981	Baltimore	SS-3B	23	39	1	5	0	0	0	0	0	.128
1982	Baltimore	SS-3B	160	598	90	158	32	5	28	93	3	.264
1983	Baltimore	SS	162	663	121	211	47	2	27	102	0	.318
1984	Baltimore	SS	162	641	103	195	37	7	27	86	2	.304
1985	Baltimore	SS	161	642	116	181	32	5	26	110	2	.282
1986	Baltimore	SS	162	627	98	177	35	1	25	81	4	.282
1987	Baltimore	SS	162	624	97	157	28	3	27	98	3	.252
1988	Baltimore	SS	161	575	87	152	25	1	23	81	2	.264
1989	Baltimore	SS	162	646	80	166	30	0	21	93	3	.257
1990	Baltimore	SS	161	600	78	150	28	4	21	84	3	.250
1991	Baltimore	SS	162	650	99	210	46	5	34	114	6	.323
	Totals		1638	6305	970	1762	340	33	259	942	28	.279

BILLY RIPKEN 27 6-1 182　　　　　Bats R Throws R

Looks to rebound after disappointing season . . . Finished with career lows in games (104), at-bats (287), hits (62) and RBI (14) . . . Disabled from July 17-Aug. 15 with strained rib cage . . . Fine second baseman matched career high of 53 consecutive errorless games (May 20-Sept. 9) . . . Tied for team lead with 11 sacrifice hits and owns 47 sacrifices in last three years . . . Much more outgoing than his famous older brother

Cal . . . Born Dec. 16, 1964, in Havre de Grace, Md. . . . Orioles' 11th-round choice in 1982 draft . . . His 1991 salary was $700,000.

Year	Club	Pos.	G	AB	R	H	2B	3B	HR	RBI	SB	Avg.
1987	Baltimore	2B	58	234	27	72	9	0	2	20	4	.308
1988	Baltimore	2B-3B	150	512	52	106	18	1	2	34	8	.207
1989	Baltimore	2B	115	318	31	76	11	2	2	26	1	.239
1990	Baltimore	2B	129	406	48	118	28	1	3	38	5	.291
1991	Baltimore	2B	104	287	24	62	11	1	0	14	0	.216
	Totals		556	1757	182	434	77	5	9	132	18	.247

RANDY MILLIGAN 30 6-1 235   Bats R Throws R

Quality offensive player salvaged career with Orioles . . . First baseman seemed to be headed nowhere in first eight pro seasons with Mets and Pirates organizations . . . Received only 83 major-league at-bats with those two organizations . . . Placed second to Cal Ripken Jr. last year in club RBI race with career-high 70 . . . Tailed off sharply late in season and did not drive in a run in final 14 games . . . A selective hitter, he drew club-high 84 walks . . . Enjoyed pair of two-homer games, May 5 vs. Oakland and Sept. 16 vs. Boston . . . Born Nov. 27, 1961, in San Diego . . . Turned out to be a steal as he was acquired from Pittsburgh for Peter Blohm following 1988 season . . . Began career with Mets as first-round choice in January 1981 draft . . . Earned modest $330,000 in 1991.

Year	Club	Pos.	G	AB	R	H	2B	3B	HR	RBI	SB	Avg.
1987	New York (NL)	PH-PR	3	1	0	0	0	0	0	0	0	.000
1988	Pittsburgh	1B-OF	40	82	10	18	5	0	3	8	1	.220
1989	Baltimore	1B	124	365	56	98	23	5	12	45	9	.268
1990	Baltimore	1B	109	362	64	96	20	1	20	60	6	.265
1991	Baltimore	1B-OF	141	483	57	127	17	2	16	70	0	.263
	Totals		417	1293	187	339	65	8	51	183	16	.262

JOE ORSULAK 29 6-1 203   Bats L Throws L

Looks to pick up where he left off in 1991 . . . Batted .335 from Aug. 2 to end of season . . . His torrid .384 August was highest average by an Oriole in any month since Eddie Murray's .385 in May 1984 . . . Ran off 21-game hitting streak, one shy of club record, from Aug. 2-25 . . . Set club record with 21 outfield assists . . . Can play all three outfield positions well . . . Born May 31, 1962, in Glen Ridge, N.J. . . . Acquired from Pittsburgh for Terry Crowley Jr. and Rico Rossy, following 1987 season . . . Pirates' sixth-round choice in 1980 draft . . . His 1991 salary was $1.1 million.

Year	Club	Pos.	G	AB	R	H	2B	3B	HR	RBI	SB	Avg.
1983	Pittsburgh	OF	7	11	0	2	0	0	0	1	0	.182
1984	Pittsburgh	OF	32	67	12	17	1	2	0	3	3	.254
1985	Pittsburgh	OF	121	397	54	119	14	6	0	21	24	.300
1986	Pittsburgh	OF	138	401	60	100	19	6	2	19	24	.249
1988	Baltimore	OF	125	379	48	109	21	3	8	27	9	.288
1989	Baltimore	OF	123	390	59	111	22	5	7	55	5	.285
1990	Baltimore	OF	124	413	49	111	14	3	11	57	6	.269
1991	Baltimore	OF	143	486	57	135	22	1	5	43	6	.278
	Totals		813	2544	339	704	113	26	33	226	77	.277

MIKE DEVEREAUX 28 6-0 193   Bats R Throws R

Center fielder provides spark at top of batting order . . . Blasted 16 of his career-high 19 home runs as a leadoff hitter, most by an Oriole lead-off man since Don Buford hit 19 in 1971 . . . Had 56 extra-base hits . . . Paced Orioles with 16 stolen bases, although he didn't attempt a steal in final 23 games . . . Born April 10, 1963, in Casper, Wy. . . . Acquired from Los Angeles for Mike Morgan prior to 1989 season . . . Dodgers' fifth-round pick in 1985 draft, out of Arizona State . . . High school track star . . . Will receive substantial raise after earning $210,000 in 1991.

Year	Club	Pos.	G	AB	R	H	2B	3B	HR	RBI	SB	Avg.
1987	Los Angeles . . .	OF	19	54	7	12	3	0	0	4	3	.222
1988	Los Angeles . . .	OF	30	43	4	5	1	0	0	2	0	.116
1989	Baltimore	OF	122	391	55	104	14	3	8	46	22	.266
1990	Baltimore	OF	108	367	48	88	18	1	12	49	13	.240
1991	Baltimore	OF	149	608	82	158	27	10	19	59	16	.260
	Totals		428	1463	196	367	63	14	39	160	54	.251

GLENN DAVIS 31 6-3 200   Bats R Throws R

Orioles didn't get expected return after paying heavy price to acquire him from Houston prior to last season . . . Birds sent Pete Harnisch, Curt Schilling and Steve Finley to Astros . . . Also paid deep price financially, because he received $3.275-million salary in 1991 . . . Power-hitting first baseman hurt spinal accessory nerve in his neck and was disabled April 26 . . . Missed 105 games before returning Aug. 19 . . . Homered and tied career high with five RBI in second game back, Aug. 20 at Texas . . . Began career with Astros, who selected him in secondary phase of January 1981 draft, out of University of Georgia . . . Born March 28, 1961, in Jacksonville, Fla. . . . Orioles re-signed him to two-year, $6.65-million deal after last season.

Year	Club	Pos.	G	AB	R	H	2B	3B	HR	RBI	SB	Avg.
1984	Houston	1B	18	61	6	13	5	0	2	8	0	.213
1985	Houston	1B-OF	100	350	51	95	11	0	20	64	0	.271
1986	Houston	1B	158	574	91	152	32	3	31	101	3	.265
1987	Houston	1B	151	578	70	145	35	2	27	93	4	.251
1988	Houston	1B	152	561	78	152	26	0	30	99	4	.271
1989	Houston	1B	158	581	87	156	26	1	34	89	4	.269
1990	Houston	1B	93	327	44	82	15	4	22	64	8	.251
1991	Baltimore	1B	49	176	29	40	9	1	10	28	4	.227
	Totals		879	3208	456	835	159	11	176	546	27	.260

BEN McDONALD 24 6-7 212   Bats R Throws R

Injuries have kept him from blossoming into dominant ace he was projected to be as first player taken in 1989 draft . . . Was disabled in April and for a second time in May with strained flexor muscle in elbow . . . Was activated June 30 after rehabilitation assignment at Rochester . . . Fired two-hitter over eight innings July 1 vs. Detroit in 10-2 win that marked his best effort of season . . . Did work at least six innings in 10 of final 14 starts . . . Season ended on sour note when he missed final four weeks with shoulder stiffness . . . Critics say he's not same power pitcher who fashioned 29-14 record in three years at LSU, including 14-4 as a senior, and fanned 373 in 308⅓ innings . . . Born Nov. 24, 1967, in Baton Rouge, La. . . . Despite inexperience, he commanded $441,667 salary in 1991.

Year	Club	G	IP	W	L	Pct.	SO	BB	H	ERA
1989	Baltimore	6	7⅓	1	0	1.000	3	4	8	8.59
1990	Baltimore	21	118⅔	8	5	.615	65	35	88	2.43
1991	Baltimore	21	126⅓	6	8	.429	85	43	126	4.84
	Totals	48	252⅓	15	13	.536	153	82	222	3.82

GREGG OLSON 25 6-4 209   Bats R Throws R

Not the dominant closer he was earlier in career . . . Earned 31 saves to rank seventh in AL, but also absorbed eight blown saves . . . Was helped by streak in which he converted 10 straight save tries from June 22-July 13 . . . Hot stretch was capped July 13 at Oakland, when he preserved combined no-hitter . . . Has career total of 95 saves . . . Appeared in team-high 72 games to tie for second in AL . . . Became first pitcher in club history with two 30-save seasons . . . Curve is not nearly the weapon it was when he entered league . . . Born Oct. 11, 1966, in Omaha, Neb. . . . First-round choice in 1988 draft and the fourth player picked overall . . . Received All-American honors in final two years at Auburn . . . Earned $505,000 in 1991 and signed a two-year, $3.75-million contract in December.

Year	Club	G	IP	W	L	Pct.	SO	BB	H	ERA
1988	Baltimore	10	11	1	1	.500	9	10	10	3.27
1989	Baltimore	64	85	5	2	.714	90	46	57	1.69
1990	Baltimore	64	74⅓	6	5	.545	74	31	57	2.42
1991	Baltimore	72	73⅔	4	6	.400	72	29	74	3.18
	Totals	210	244	16	14	.533	245	116	198	2.43

BOB MILACKI 27 6-4 234   Bats R Throws R

Returns as club leader in victories (10), starts (26), complete games (three), innings pitched (184) and strikeouts (108) . . . Accomplished that despite beginning season with Hagerstown (AA) . . . Was recalled April 25 . . . Improved control was a key to success . . . Walked only 18 batters in final 86 innings . . . Started and combined with Mike Flanagan, Mark Williamson and Gregg Olson on July 13 no-hitter at Oakland . . . In 1989, he became first rookie to top AL in starts in 71 years with 31 . . . Born July 28, 1964, in Trenton, N.J. . . . Selected by Orioles in second round of 1983 draft . . . Due for raise after earning $235,000 in 1991.

Year	Club	G	IP	W	L	Pct.	SO	BB	H	ERA
1988	Baltimore	3	25	2	0	1.000	18	9	9	0.72
1989	Baltimore	37	243	14	12	.538	113	88	233	3.74
1990	Baltimore	27	135⅓	5	8	.385	60	61	143	4.46
1991	Baltimore	31	184	10	9	.526	108	53	175	4.01
	Totals	98	587⅓	31	29	.517	299	211	560	3.86

MIKE FLANAGAN 40 6-0 195   Bats L Throws L

Former starter resurrected career as short reliever last season . . . Appeared in 64 games, most by an Orioles lefty since Tippy Martinez (65 in 1983) . . . Finished fourth in AL with 94⅓ relief innings . . . Held lefties to .181 batting average compared to .266 for righties . . . Was scored on in consecutive outings only twice . . . Beloved member of franchise provided appropriate end at Memorial Stadium when he pitched in final inning and struck out both batters he faced . . . Attended spring training on tryout basis without a contract . . . Later agreed to $250,000 salary... Born Dec. 16, 1951, in Manchester, N.H.... Began career with Orioles as seventh-round pick in 1973 draft... Traded to Toronto for pitchers Oswaldo Peraza and Jose Mesa, Aug. 31, 1987... Known for quick wit.

Year	Club	G	IP	W	L	Pct.	SO	BB	H	ERA
1975	Baltimore	2	10	0	1	.000	7	6	9	2.70
1976	Baltimore	20	85	3	5	.375	56	33	83	4.13
1977	Baltimore	36	235	15	10	.600	149	70	235	3.64
1978	Baltimore	40	281	19	15	.559	167	87	271	4.04
1979	Baltimore	39	266	23	9	.719	190	70	245	3.08
1980	Baltimore	37	251	16	13	.552	128	71	278	4.12
1981	Baltimore	20	116	9	6	.600	72	37	108	4.19
1982	Baltimore	36	236	15	11	.577	103	76	233	3.97
1983	Baltimore	20	125⅓	12	4	.750	50	31	135	3.30
1984	Baltimore	34	226⅔	13	13	.500	115	81	213	3.53
1985	Baltimore	15	86	4	5	.444	42	28	101	5.13
1986	Baltimore	29	172	7	11	.389	96	66	179	4.24
1987	Balt.-Tor.	23	144	6	8	.429	93	51	148	4.06
1988	Toronto	34	211	13	13	.500	99	80	220	4.18
1989	Toronto	30	171⅔	8	10	.444	47	47	186	3.93
1990	Toronto	5	20⅓	2	2	.500	5	8	28	5.31
1991	Baltimore	64	98⅓	2	7	.222	55	25	84	2.38
	Totals	484	2735⅓	167	143	.539	1474	867	2756	3.84

TOP PROSPECTS

CHITO MARTINEZ 26 5-10 180   Bats L Throws L

Right fielder proved to be a great find after being signed as a six-year minor-league free agent, Nov. 16, 1990... Made major-league debut July 5 vs. Yankees and became first Oriole in history to produce hits in each of his first six major-league games (8-for-21)... Finished third among AL rookies with 13 homers ... Hit .269 with 26 extra-base hits and 33 RBI in 216 at-bats with Orioles... Placed second in International League with 20 homers and hit .322 with 50 RBI in 211 at-bats with Rochester (AAA)... Born Dec. 19, 1965, in Belize, Central America... Grew up in New Orleans... Began career with Kansas City as sixth-round choice in 1984 draft.

LUIS MERCEDES 24 6-0 180   Bats R Throws R

Outstanding young hitter ranked second in International League with .334 average and had 23 steals for Rochester (AAA) in 1991 ... Captured batting titles in Carolina League (1989) and Eastern League (1990)... Left fielder made major-league debut Sept. 8 vs. Royals and drilled two hits... Wound up at .204 in 54 at-bats with Orioles... Born Feb. 20, 1968, in San Pedro de Macoris,

D.R. . . . Signed with Orioles as undrafted free agent, Feb. 16, 1987.

MIKE MUSSINA 23 6-2 185   **Bats R Throws R**
First-round selection in 1990 draft is ready to become a fixture in Orioles' rotation . . . Pitched into seventh inning in 10 of 12 starts with Orioles, including final eight . . . Made impressive debut Aug. 4 vs. White Sox, allowing one run in 7⅔ innings in tough 1-0 defeat . . . Went 10-4 with 2.87 ERA for Rochester (AAA) and 4-5 with 2.87 ERA for Orioles . . . Exceptional control is one of his great assets . . . Compiled 25-12 record in three years at Stanford, where he earned economics degree . . . Born Dec. 8, 1968, in Williamsport, Pa.

ARTHUR RHODES 22 6-2 190   **Bats L Throws L**
Frequently compared to Vida Blue . . . Went through some growing pains after jump from Hagerstown (AA) to majors Aug. 21 . . . Went 0-3 with 8.00 ERA, although Orioles were 4-4 in his eight appearances . . . Worked career-high seven innings, allowing three runs, in no-decision vs. Yankees Oct. 2, his final start . . . Was 7-4 with 2.70 ERA for Hagerstown . . . Taken by Baltimore in second round of 1988 draft . . . Born Oct. 24, 1969, in Waco, Tex., and still lives there . . . Brother Ricky pitches in Yankees' system.

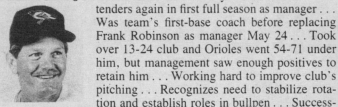

MANAGER JOHNNY OATES: Will try to make Orioles contenders again in first full season as manager . . . Was team's first-base coach before replacing Frank Robinson as manager May 24 . . . Took over 13-24 club and Orioles went 54-71 under him, but management saw enough positives to retain him . . . Working hard to improve club's pitching . . . Recognizes need to stabilize rotation and establish roles in bullpen . . . Successful minor-league manager . . . Captured Southern League championship with Nashville in first managerial stop in 1982 . . . Took regular-season title with Columbus in 1983, his second season in Yankees' system . . . Spent next four years as major-league coach with Cubs before returning to Orioles' organization after 16-year absence to manage Rochester . . . Took Red Wings to first league championship since 1974 and gained International League Manager of the Year honors in the process . . . Began catching career as Orioles' first-round choice in January 1967 draft . . . Also played for Braves, Phillies, Dodgers and Yankees in 10-year major-league career . . . Known primarily for intelligence he showed behind the plate . . . Born Jan. 21, 1946, in Sylva, Va.

ALL-TIME ORIOLE SEASON RECORDS

BATTING: Ken Singleton, .328, 1977
HRs: Frank Robinson, 49, 1966
RBI: Jim Gentile, 141, 1961
STEALS: Luis Aparicio, 57, 1964
WINS: Steve Stone, 25, 1980
STRIKEOUTS: Dave McNally, 202, 1968

Joe Orsulak was O's DiMag with 21-game hitting streak.

BOSTON RED SOX

TEAM DIRECTORY: Majority Owner and Chairwoman of the Board: Jean R. Yawkey; General Partner: Haywood C. Sullivan; Sr. VP/GM: Lou Gorman; VP-Baseball Dev.: Edward F. Kenney; Dir. Scouting: Eddie Kasko; Dir. Minor League Oper.: Edward P. Kenney; VP-Pub. Rel.: Dick Bresciani; Publicity Dir.: Josh Spofford; Trav. Sec.: Steve August; Mgr.: Butch Hobson. Home: Fenway Park (34,171). Field distances: 315, l.f. line; 379, l.c.; 390, c.f.; 420, deep c.f.; 380, deep r.f.; 302, r.f. line. Spring training: Winter Haven, Fla.

SCOUTING REPORT

HITTING: Boston traditionally fields a potent offensive club and this edition will be no exception.

Wade Boggs showed there is still plenty of life left in his bat by hitting .332, a dramatic 30-point rise from his career low the year before. Jody Reed (.283, 5, 60) set career highs last season with 175 hits and 54 multi-hit games and batted .306 over the final 132 games.

Tri-Cy winner Roger Clemens is Rocket Gibraltar.

Designated hitter Jack Clark is a force anywhere, but particularly in Fenway Park, where he hit 18 of his 28 home runs. The Red Sox expect Mo Vaughn (.260, 4, 32) to show more muscle than he did last year, when he supplied only one home run in the final 66 games. Mike Greenwell (.300, 9, 83) was shopped in the offseason, but nobody doubts that he can hit.

Ellis Burks (.251, 14, 56) will be a key figure if he can rebound from back problems that forced him to miss 21 of the final 23 games. That's because Burks is a source of speed on a team that doesn't have much. The Red Sox finished 13th in the AL with 59 stolen bases in 1991.

PITCHING: As always, Boston's hopes rest with Roger Clemens. No starting pitcher means more to his team. ''The Rocket'' won his third Cy Young award last season, topping the majors with 271⅓ innings, leading the AL with a 2.62 ERA and tying for the major league lead with 241 strikeouts en route to an 18-10 record.

Depth in the rotation was a concern, before former Cy Young winner Frank Viola (13-15, 3.97 with the Mets) was signed as a free agent and Joe Hesketh (12-4, 3.29) was re-signed. Left-hander Kevin Morton (6-5, 4.59) showed ability after being promoted from Pawtucket in early July. Injury-plagued Danny Darwin (3-6, 5.16), Matt Young (3-7, 5.18), Tom Bolton (8-9, 5.24) and Mike Gardiner (9-10, 4.85) are other possibilities.

All eyes in the bullpen will be focused on Jeff Reardon (1-4, 3.03, 40 Sv) as he takes aim at the all-time save record. Reardon opens the season needing 15 saves to erase Rollie Fingers' mark of 341.

FIELDING: Tony Pena is a Gold Glove catcher and a take-charge type behind the plate. He's durable—he caught a league-high 140 games—and he's good. He made only five errors in 929 total chances for a fine .995 fielding percentage. Boston must get better play from the shortstop position. Luis Rivera was guilty of 24 errors, most among AL shortstops.

OUTLOOK: Boston, 84-78 to tie for second in 1991, has an excellent shot at its third AL East title in five years, under new manager Butch Hobson. In Clemens, the Red Sox have a dominant starter no team in the division can match. Owner of a 77-26 record after Boston defeats, he simply does not permit ruinous losing streaks. The Red Sox have enough talent to take this weak division.

BOSTON RED SOX 1992 ROSTER

MANAGER Butch Hobson
Coaches—Gary Allenson, Al Bumbry, Rick Burleson, Rich Gale, Don Zimmer

PITCHERS

No.	Name	1991 Club	W-L	IP	SO	ERA	B-T	Ht.	Wt.	Born
50	Bolton, Tom	Boston	8-9	110	64	5.24	L-L	6-3	185	5/6/62 Nashville, TN
21	Clemens, Roger	Boston	18-10	217	241	2.62	R-R	6-4	220	8/4/62 Dayton, OH
44	Darwin, Danny	Boston	3-6	68	42	5.16	R-R	6-3	195	10/25/55 Bonham, TX
40	Dopson, John	Winter Haven	2-2	27	26	3.38	R-R	6-4	235	7/14/63 Baltimore, MD
		Boston	0-0	1	0	18.00				
52	Fischer, Tom	New Britain	8-11	134	85	4.09	L-L	5-11	195	3/23/67 West Bend, WI
		Pawtucket	0-2	10	8	9.58				
48	Fossas, Tony	Boston	3-2	57	29	3.47	L-L	6-0	187	9/23/57 Cuba
47	Gardiner, Mike	Pawtucket	7-1	58	42	2.34	S-R	6-0	200	10/19/65 Canada
		Boston	9-10	130	91	4.85				
38	Gray, Jeff	Boston	2-3	62	41	2.34	R-R	6-1	190	4/10/63 Alexandria, VA
27	Harris, Greg	Boston	11-12	173	127	3.85	S-R	6-0	175	11/2/55 Lynwood, CA
55	Hesketh, Joe	Boston	12-4	153	104	3.29	L-L	6-2	170	2/15/59 Lackawanna, NY
—	Hoy, Peter	New Britain	4-4	68	39	1.46	L-R	6-7	220	6/29/66 Canada
59	Irvine, Daryl	Pawtucket	1-1	33	19	3.00	R-R	6-3	195	11/15/64 Harrisonburg, VA
		Boston	0-0	18	8	6.00				
19	Kiecker, Dana	Pawtucket	2-3	38	23	3.79	R-R	6-3	195	2/25/61 Sleepy Eye, MN
		Boston	2-3	40	21	7.36				
60	Livernois, Derek	New Britain	3-2	28	31	3.25	L-R	6-1	185	4/17/67 Inglewood, CA
		Pawtucket	1-2	20	14	10.53				
51	Manzanillo, Josias	New Britain	2-2	50	35	2.90	R-R	6-0	190	10/16/87 Dominican Republic
		Pawtucket	5-5	103	65	5.61				
		Boston	0-0	1	1	18.00				
43	Morton, Kevin	Pawtucket	7-3	98	80	3.49	R-L	6-2	185	8/3/68 Norwalk, CT
		Boston	6-5	86	45	4.59				
54	Plympton, Jeff	Pawtucket	2-6	69	58	3.12	R-R	6-2	205	11/24/65 Framingham, MA
		Boston	0-0	5	2	0.00				
—	Quantrill, Paul	New Britain	2-1	35	18	2.06	L-R	6-1	175	11/3/68 Canada
		Pawtucket	10-7	156	75	4.45				
41	Reardon, Jeff	Boston	1-4	59	44	3.03	R-R	6-0	200	10/1/55 Dalton, MA
56	Taylor, Scott	New Britain	2-0	29	38	0.62	L-L	6-1	185	8/2/67 Defiance, OH
		Pawtucket	3-3	39	35	3.46				
—	Viola, Frank	New York (NL)	13-15	231	132	3.97	L-L	6-4	210	4/19/60 Hempstead, NY
30	Young, Matt	Pawtucket	1-0	8	7	4.50	L-L	6-3	210	8/9/58 Pasadena, CA
		Boston	3-7	89	69	5.18				

CATCHERS

No.	Name	1991 Club	H	HR	RBI	Pct.	B-T	Ht.	Wt.	Born
20	Marzano, John	Boston	30	0	9	.263	R-R	5-11	195	2/14/63 Philadelphia, PA
6	Pena, Tony	Boston	107	5	48	.231	R-R	6-0	185	6/4/57 Dominican Republic
22	Wedge, Eric	Winter Haven	5	1	1	.238	R-R	6-3	215	1/27/68 Fort Wayne, IN
		New Britain	2	0	2	.250				
		Pawtucket	38	5	18	.233				
		Boston	1	0	0	1.000				

INFIELDERS

No.	Name	1991 Club	H	HR	RBI	Pct.	B-T	Ht.	Wt.	Born
26	Boggs, Wade	Boston	181	8	51	.332	L-R	6-2	197	6/15/58 Omaha, NE
10	Brumley, Mike	Pawtucket	29	4	16	.269	S-R	5-10	175	4/9/63 Oklahoma City, OK
		Boston	25	0	5	.212				
25	Clark, Jack	Boston	120	28	87	.249	R-R	6-3	205	11/10/55 New Brighton, PA
45	Cooper, Scott	Pawtucket	134	15	72	.277	L-R	6-3	205	10/13/67 St. Louis, MO
		Boston	16	0	7	.457				
11	Naehring, Tim	Boston	6	0	3	.109	R-R	6-2	190	2/1/67 Cincinnati, OH
18	Quintana, Carlos	Boston	141	11	71	.295	R-R	6-2	220	8/26/65 Venezuela
3	Reed, Jody	Boston	175	5	60	.283	R-R	5-9	165	7/26/62 Tampa, FL
2	Rivera, Luis	Boston	107	8	40	.258	R-R	5-9	175	1/3/64 Puerto Rico
—	Valentin, John	New Britain	16	0	5	.198	R-R	6-0	170	2/18/67 Jersey City, NJ
		Pawtucket	87	9	49	.264				
42	Vaughn, Mo	Pawtucket	64	14	50	.274	L-R	6-1	225	12/15/67 Norwalk, CT
		Boston	57	4	32	.260				

OUTFIELDERS

No.	Name	1991 Club	H	HR	RBI	Pct.	B-T	Ht.	Wt.	Born
23	Brunansky, Tom	Boston	105	16	70	.229	R-R	6-4	220	8/20/60 Covina, CA
12	Burks, Ellis	Boston	119	14	56	.251	R-R	6-2	202	9/11/64 Vicksburg, MS
39	Greenwell, Mike	Boston	163	9	83	.300	L-R	6-0	200	7/18/63 Louisville, KY
17	Housie, Wayne	New Britain	123	6	26	.277	S-R	5-9	165	5/20/65 Hampton, VA
		Pawtucket	26	2	8	.329				
		Boston	2	0	0	.250				
—	McNeely, Jeff	Lynchburg	123	4	38	.322	R-R	6-2	190	10/18/70 Monroe, NC
29	Plantier, Phil	Pawtucket	91	16	61	.305	L-R	5-11	195	1/27/69 Manchester, NH
		Boston	49	11	35	.331				
16	Zupcic, Bob	Pawtucket	103	18	70	.240	R-R	6-4	225	8/18/68 Pittsburgh, PA
		Boston	4	1	3	.160				

RED SOX PROFILES

WADE BOGGS 33 6-2 197   Bats L Throws R

Great contact hitter will take aim at another batting title after placing second with .332 average in 1991, nine points behind Texas' Julio Franco . . . Third baseman rebounded after batting career-low .302 with career-high 68 strikeouts in 1990 . . . Has banged 40 or more doubles for seven straight seasons, joining Joe Medwick (1933-39) as only player to accomplish that . . . Fanned once every 20 plate appearances, making him toughest in AL to strike out . . . Hit .389 at Fenway, bringing career average there to .381. Ted Williams' career average at Fenway was .361 . . . On negative side, he finished with fewest hits (181) in full season since rookie year . . . Nagging injuries included sore back, strained groin muscle and sore right shoulder . . . Captured five of possible six batting titles from 1983-88, missing only in 1984 . . . Born June 15, 1958, in Omaha, Neb. . . . Red Sox' seventh-round pick in 1976 draft . . . Earned $2.7 million in 1991.

Year	Club	Pos.	G	AB	R	H	2B	3B	HR	RBI	SB	Avg.
1982	Boston	1B-3B-OF	104	338	51	118	14	1	5	44	1	.349
1983	Boston	3B	153	582	100	210	44	7	5	74	3	.361
1984	Boston	3B	158	625	109	203	31	4	6	55	3	.325
1985	Boston	3B	161	653	107	240	42	3	8	78	2	.368
1986	Boston	3B	149	580	107	207	47	2	8	71	0	.357
1987	Boston	3B-1B	147	551	108	200	40	6	24	89	1	.363
1988	Boston	3B	155	584	128	214	45	6	5	58	2	.366
1989	Boston	3B	156	621	113	205	51	7	3	54	2	.330
1990	Boston	3B	155	619	89	187	44	5	6	63	0	.302
1991	Boston	3B	144	546	93	181	42	2	8	51	1	.332
	Totals		1482	5699	1005	1965	400	43	78	637	15	.345

JACK CLARK 36 6-3 205   Bats R Throws R

Free-agent signee gave Red Sox power they had sought from DH slot . . . Joined Bobby Bonds as only major leaguers to hit 25 or more home runs for five different teams . . . Achieved highest homer total since 1987 . . . Fifteen of his 28 homers either tied game or put Red Sox ahead . . . Averaged one home run every 17.2 at-bats and Red Sox were 21-5 when he connected . . . His 18 home runs at Fenway represented highest total there since Tony Armas' 21 in 1984 . . . Very selective hitter worked 96 walks . . . Owned four consecutive 100-walk seasons before 1991 . . .

Typical slugger, he strikes out often . . . Fanned 133 times, sixth-highest total in AL . . . Outspoken team leader who has reputation for criticizing management . . . Born Nov. 10, 1955, in New Brighton, Pa. . . . Began career as Giants' 13th-round pick in 1973 draft . . . Earned whopping $2.9 million in 1991.

Year	Club	Pos.	G	AB	R	H	2B	3B	HR	RBI	SB	Avg.
1975	San Francisco	OF-3B	8	17	3	4	0	0	0	2	1	.235
1976	San Francisco	OF	26	102	14	23	6	2	2	10	6	.225
1977	San Francisco	OF	136	413	64	104	17	4	13	51	12	.252
1978	San Francisco	OF	156	592	90	181	46	8	25	98	15	.306
1979	San Francisco	OF-3B	143	527	84	144	25	2	26	86	11	.273
1980	San Francisco	OF	127	437	77	124	20	8	22	82	2	.284
1981	San Francisco	OF	99	385	60	103	19	2	17	53	1	.268
1982	San Francisco	OF	157	563	90	154	30	3	27	103	6	.274
1983	San Francisco	OF-1B	135	492	82	132	25	0	20	66	5	.268
1984	San Francisco	OF-1B	57	203	33	65	9	1	11	44	1	.320
1985	St. Louis	1B-OF	126	442	71	124	26	3	22	87	1	.281
1986	St. Louis	1B	65	232	34	55	12	2	9	23	1	.237
1987	St. Louis	1B-OF	131	419	93	120	23	1	35	106	1	.286
1988	New York (AL)	OF-1B	150	496	81	120	14	0	27	93	3	.242
1989	San Diego	1B-OF	142	455	76	110	19	1	26	94	6	.242
1990	San Diego	1B	115	334	59	89	12	1	25	62	4	.266
1991	Boston	DH	140	481	75	120	18	1	28	87	0	.249
	Totals		1913	6590	1086	1772	321	39	335	1147	76	.269

JODY REED 29 5-9 165   Bats R Throws R

Second baseman has developed into key figure on Red Sox . . . Set career highs with 175 hits, 54 multi-hit games, 60 RBI and 618 at-bats . . . Tied for fourth in AL with 42 doubles, his third straight season over 40 doubles . . . Known as warm-weather hitter . . . Batted .306 over final 132 games . . . Boston's top road hitter for second year in row at .304 . . . Hit .318 with men on base, .304 with runners in scoring position . . . Devastated arch-rival Yankees, batting .500 (27-for-54) against them last season, and he owns .384 lifetime mark against them . . . Born July 26, 1962, in Tampa . . . Red Sox' eighth-round pick in 1984 draft . . . Holds criminology degree from Florida State . . . Should receive significant increase from $800,000 salary in 1991.

Year	Club	Pos.	G	AB	R	H	2B	3B	HR	RBI	SB	Avg.
1987	Boston	SS-2B-3B	9	30	4	9	1	1	0	8	1	.300
1988	Boston	SS-2B-3B	109	338	60	99	23	1	1	28	1	.293
1989	Boston	SS-2B-3B-OF	146	524	76	151	42	2	3	40	4	.288
1990	Boston	2B-SS	155	598	70	173	45	0	5	51	4	.289
1991	Boston	2B-SS	153	618	87	175	42	2	5	60	6	.283
	Totals		572	2108	297	607	153	6	14	187	16	.288

MIKE GREENWELL 28 6-0 200   Bats L Throws R

Left fielder searches for improvement after somewhat disappointing season . . . Finished with career-low nine home runs . . . Bothered by various nagging injuries, including strained right groin and sore right knee . . . On positive side, his average reached .300 June 15 and did not dip below that level for rest of season . . . His average in June was lofty .364 . . . Able to fight off pitches when he has to . . . Averaged one strikeout every 17.1 plate appearances, making him third-toughest in AL to fan . . . Compiled .327 average vs. left-handers . . . Hit .307 with runners in scoring position . . . Topped Red Sox with 15 stolen bases . . . Fields auto racing team . . . Born July 18, 1963, in Louisville, Ky. . . . Boston's sixth-round pick in 1982 draft . . . Best-paid among Boston outfielders in 1991 at $2.55 million.

Year	Club	Pos.	G	AB	R	H	2B	3B	HR	RBI	SB	Avg.
1985	Boston	OF	17	31	7	10	1	0	4	8	1	.323
1986	Boston	OF	31	35	4	11	2	0	0	4	0	.314
1987	Boston	OF-C	125	412	71	135	31	6	19	89	5	.328
1988	Boston	OF	158	590	86	192	39	8	22	119	16	.325
1989	Boston	OF	145	578	87	178	36	0	14	95	13	.308
1990	Boston	OF	159	610	71	181	30	6	14	73	8	.297
1991	Boston	OF	147	544	76	163	26	6	9	83	15	.300
	Totals		782	2800	402	870	165	26	82	471	58	.311

TONY PENA 35 6-0 185   Bats R Throws R

Gold Glove catcher continues to give Red Sox the defense they sought when they signed him to three-year contract as a free agent on Nov. 27, 1989 . . . Caught AL-high 140 games . . . Made only five errors in 929 total chances for fine .995 fielding percentage . . . Pitchers like to work with him . . . Strong figure in clubhouse . . . Should rebound from sub-par offensive season in which he batted only .231 with 107 hits . . . Totals were lowest in both categories since 1987 . . . Born June 4, 1957, in Monte Cristi, Dominican Republic . . . Began career as free-agent signee with Pittsburgh in July 1975 . . . Pirates dealt him to St. Louis in April 1987 and he helped Cardinals reach World Series that year, batting .409 in the fall classic . . . Was paid $2.3 million in 1991.

Year	Club	Pos.	G	AB	R	H	2B	3B	HR	RBI	SB	Avg.
1980	Pittsburgh	C	8	21	1	9	1	1	0	1	0	.429
1981	Pittsburgh	C	66	210	16	63	9	1	2	17	1	.300
1982	Pittsburgh	C	138	497	53	147	28	4	11	63	2	.296
1983	Pittsburgh	C	151	542	51	163	22	3	15	70	6	.301
1984	Pittsburgh	C	147	546	77	156	27	2	15	78	12	.286
1985	Pittsburgh	C-1B	147	546	53	136	27	2	10	59	12	.249
1986	Pittsburgh	C-1B	144	510	56	147	26	2	10	52	9	.288
1987	St. Louis	C-1B-OF	116	384	40	82	13	4	5	44	6	.214
1988	St. Louis	C-1B	149	505	55	133	23	1	10	51	6	.263
1989	St. Louis	C-OF	141	424	36	110	17	2	4	37	5	.259
1990	Boston	C-1B	143	491	62	129	19	1	7	56	8	.263
	Totals		1350	4676	500	1275	212	23	89	528	67	.273

ROGER CLEMENS 29 6-4 220　　　　Bats R Throws R

Widely regarded as game's premier pitcher . . . Captured third AL Cy Young award after leading majors with 271⅓ innings, tying Mets' David Cone for major-league lead with 241 strikeouts and topping AL with 2.62 ERA and four shutouts . . . Will attempt to extend club record of consecutive 200-strikeout seasons to seven . . . Held opponents to .221 batting average . . . Vaulted Red Sox back into contention by winning all six of his decisions and posting 1.33 ERA from Aug. 26-Sept. 26 . . . Boasts 77-26 career mark in starts after Red Sox loss . . . Became only pitcher to gain league MVP, Cy Young and All-Star Game MVP honors in same season, accomplishing that in 1986 . . . Repeated as Cy Young winner in '87 to join Sandy Koufax (1965-66) and Jim Palmer (1975-76) as only consecutive winners . . . Holds club single-season strikeout record with 291 in 1988 . . . Born Aug. 4, 1962, in Dayton, Ohio . . . Boston's first pick in 1983 draft, out of University of Texas . . . One superstar who's worth the big money . . . Earned $2.6 million in 1991.

Year	Club	G	IP	W	L	Pct.	SO	BB	H	ERA
1984	Boston	21	133⅓	9	4	.692	126	29	146	4.32
1985	Boston	15	98⅓	7	5	.583	74	37	83	3.29
1986	Boston	33	254	24	4	.857	238	67	179	2.48
1987	Boston	36	281⅔	20	9	.690	256	83	248	2.97
1988	Boston	35	264	18	12	.600	291	62	217	2.93
1989	Boston	35	253⅓	17	11	.607	230	93	215	3.13
1990	Boston	31	228⅓	21	6	.778	209	54	193	1.93
1991	Boston	35	271⅓	18	10	.643	241	65	219	2.62
	Totals	241	1784⅓	134	61	.687	1665	490	1500	2.85

FRANK VIOLA 31 6-4 210   Bats L Throws L

Signed three-year, $13.9-million pact with Red Sox in December after season with Mets in which he suffered through career-worst seven-game losing streak from Aug. 8 until Sept. 29 . . . Mets averaged just 1.4 runs per game while he was losing 10 of last 11 decisions . . . Had All-Star first half, winning four straight starts and posting 2.12 ERA in June and July . . . Pitched scoreless inning after being invited to his third All-Star Game . . . Led NL with 0.86 ERA in April . . . Selected by Twins in second round of 1981 draft . . . Was AL Cy Young winner in 1988 and MVP of 1987 World Series . . . Traded to Mets for five pitchers, including Rick Aguilera and Kevin Tapani, July 31, 1989 . . . Born April 19, 1960, in Hempstead, N.Y. . . . Earned $3,166,667 in 1991 . . . Had been offered salary arbitration in December.

Year	Club	G	IP	W	L	Pct.	SO	BB	H	ERA
1982	Minnesota	22	126	4	10	.286	84	38	152	5.21
1983	Minnesota	35	210	7	15	.318	127	92	242	5.49
1984	Minnesota	35	257⅔	18	12	.600	149	73	225	3.21
1985	Minnesota	36	250⅔	18	14	.563	135	68	262	4.09
1986	Minnesota	37	245⅔	16	13	.552	191	83	257	4.51
1987	Minnesota	36	251⅔	17	10	.630	197	66	230	2.90
1988	Minnesota	35	255⅓	24	7	.774	193	54	236	2.64
1989	Minnesota	24	175⅔	8	12	.400	138	47	171	3.79
1989	New York (NL)	12	85⅓	5	5	.500	73	27	75	3.38
1990	New York (NL)	35	249⅔	20	12	.625	182	60	227	2.67
1991	New York (NL)	35	231⅓	13	15	.464	132	54	259	3.97
	Totals	342	2339	150	125	.545	1601	662	2336	3.72

JOE HESKETH 33 6-2 170   Bats L Throws L

Revived career after he was signed by Boston as free agent, July 31, 1990 . . . Was released by Montreal and Atlanta earlier that season . . . Success last year helped Red Sox contend . . . Joined rotation after All-Star break and fashioned 10-3 record with 3.00 ERA in 16 starts . . . Finished with career-high 12 victories and his 12-4 record represented best winning percentage in majors . . . Made 17 starts in all and worked into seventh inning in 11 of them . . . One key to success was superior control . . . Walked 2.05 batters per nine innings . . . Gets in trouble when location is poor . . . Allowed staff-high 19 home runs . . . Drafted by Montreal in second round in 1980 . . . Born Feb. 15, 1959, in Lackawanna, N.Y. . . . Accepted arbitration in December.

Year	Club	G	IP	W	L	Pct.	SO	BB	H	ERA
1984	Montreal	11	45	2	2	.500	32	15	38	1.80
1985	Montreal	25	155⅓	10	5	.667	113	45	125	2.49
1986	Montreal	15	82⅔	6	5	.545	67	31	92	5.01
1987	Montreal	18	28⅔	0	0	.000	31	15	23	3.14
1988	Montreal	60	72⅔	4	3	.571	64	35	63	2.85
1989	Montreal	43	48⅓	6	4	.600	44	26	54	5.77
1990	Mont.-Atl.	33	34	1	2	.333	24	14	32	5.29
1990	Boston	12	25⅔	0	4	.000	26	11	37	3.51
1991	Boston	39	153⅓	12	4	.750	104	53	142	3.29
	Totals	256	645⅔	41	29	.586	505	245	606	3.46

KEVIN MORTON 23 6-2 185   Bats R Throws L

Determined youngster shows promise . . . Gave Red Sox a lift last year after his contract was purchased from Pawtucket July 5 . . . Made major-league debut that day, beating Detroit, 10-1, with five-hit, nine-strikeout effort . . . Success down the stretch was encouraging . . . Posted 4-1 record with 3.60 ERA in six starts from Aug. 18-Sept. 17 . . . Labored into seventh inning in seven of 15 starts . . . Red Sox backed him with seven or more runs in four of his six wins . . . Born Aug. 3, 1968, in Norwalk, Conn. . . . Compiled 27-5 record at Seton Hall from 1987-89 . . . Boston's third pick in 1989 draft, he was supplemental choice for loss of free agent Bruce Hurst.

Year	Club	G	IP	W	L	Pct.	SO	BB	H	ERA
1991	Boston	16	86⅓	6	5	.545	45	40	93	4.59

JEFF REARDON 36 6-0 200   Bats R Throws R

Consistent closer is taking aim at all-time save record . . . Needs 15 saves to move ahead of Rollie Fingers (341) . . . Became fourth pitcher to reach 300-save plateau May 20 vs. Milwaukee . . . Has been able to stay healthy for most part and reward is unprecedented 10 straight 20-save seasons . . . Notched 40 saves in 49 chances last year to join Athletics' Dennis Eckersley as only relievers with three 40-save seasons . . . Prevented 14 of 18 inherited runners from scoring . . . Held opposition to .236 average, .157 by right-handed hitters . . . Possesses outstanding makeup for a closer . . . Recognizes blown saves as part of job and is able to quickly forget them . . . Born Oct. 1, 1955, in Dalton, Mass. . . . Began career with Mets as undrafted free agent in June

1977 . . . Earned $2,533,333 in 1991 . . . Signed with Red Sox as free agent prior to 1990 season, he earned $2,533,333 last season.

Year	Club	G	IP	W	L	Pct.	SO	BB	H	ERA
1979	New York (NL)	18	21	1	2	.333	10	9	12	1.71
1980	New York (NL)	61	110	8	7	.533	101	47	96	2.62
1981	N.Y. (NL)-Mont.	43	70	3	0	1.000	49	21	48	2.19
1982	Montreal	75	109	7	4	.636	86	36	87	2.06
1983	Montreal	66	92	7	9	.438	78	44	87	3.03
1984	Montreal	68	87	7	7	.500	79	37	70	2.90
1985	Montreal	63	87⅔	2	8	.200	67	26	68	3.18
1986	Montreal	62	89	7	9	.438	67	26	83	3.94
1987	Minnesota	63	80⅓	8	8	.500	83	28	70	4.48
1988	Minnesota	63	73	2	4	.333	56	15	68	2.47
1989	Minnesota	65	73	5	4	.556	46	12	68	4.07
1990	Boston	47	51⅓	5	3	.625	33	19	39	3.16
1991	Boston	57	59⅓	1	4	.200	44	16	54	3.03
	Totals	751	1002⅔	63	69	.477	799	336	850	3.03

TOP PROSPECTS

JEFF McNEELY 21 6-2 190   Bats R Throws R
Undoubtedly Boston's center fielder of future . . . Will eventually add much-needed speed to Red Sox lineup . . . Stole 38 bases for Lynchburg (A) last year and batted .322 with .436 on-base percentage . . . One of the best defensive outfielders in minors . . . Born Oct. 18, 1970, in Monroe, N.C. . . . Boston's fourth pick in 1989 draft . . . Was 1989 Junior College All-American at Spartanburg Methodist College in Spartanburg, S.C. . . . Was New York-Penn League All-Star for Elmira (A) in 1990, when he batted .313 and stole league-leading 39 bases.

FRANKIE RODRIGUEZ 19 6-0 175   Bats R Throws R
Debate rages about whether he should pitch or play shortstop . . . Remarkably strong arm gives him ability to do both . . . Possesses mid-90-mph fastball, but prefers to play every day at short . . . Hit .271 with six home runs and 31 RBI for Elmira (A) of New York-Penn League last season . . . Born Dec. 11, 1972, in Brooklyn, N.Y. . . . Taken in second round of 1990 draft, he signed June 2 and received $400,000 bonus.

JEFF PLYMPTON 26 6-2 205   Bats R Throws R
Could help Red Sox bullpen this year after solid Triple-A season in 1991 . . . Was 2-6 with 3.12 ERA and seven saves in 41 appearances for Pawtucket . . . Showed strikeout potential by fanning 58 in 69⅓ innings . . . Born Nov. 24, 1965, in Framingham, Mass. . . . Has progressed steadily since being Boston's 10th-

round choice in 1987 draft . . . Pitched for Maine in 1986 College World Series.

ERIC WEDGE 24 6-3 215   Bats R Throws R

Could figure as backup catcher with Red Sox . . . Batted .233 with five home runs and 18 RBI in 53 games at Pawtucket (AAA) . . . Lost time due to surgery on his left knee . . . Considered a skilled defensive catcher . . . Born Jan. 27, 1968, in Fort Wayne, Ind. . . . Obtained by Boston in third round of 1989 draft . . . Batted .380 in 83 games for Wichita State in 1989, helping school to 68-16 record and College World Series title.

MANAGER BUTCH HOBSON: Named manager last Oct. 8  in startling decision . . . Management fired successful Joe Morgan to make room for much younger man . . . Red Sox GM Lou Gorman feared losing him to another organization if he waited . . . Was thought to be in demand after guiding Pawtucket to 79-64 record in his only year managing at Triple-A level . . . Began minor-league managerial career in Mets' organization, handling Columbia (A) of South Atlantic League in 1987 and 1988 . . . Former Red Sox third baseman rejoined that organization when he was named to manage New Britain (AA) in 1989 . . . Club's 60-76 record in first season under him marked 13-game improvement . . . Piloted New Britain to final round of Eastern League playoffs in 1990 . . . Born Aug. 17, 1951, in Tuscaloosa, Ala. . . . Played baseball and football at University of Alabama, the latter under legendary coach Bear Bryant . . . Boston's eighth pick in 1973 draft . . . Became important run producer who wasn't afraid to get his uniform dirty . . . Full name: Clell Lavern Hobson.

ALL-TIME RED SOX SEASON RECORDS

BATTING: Ted Williams, .406, 1941
HRs: Jimmie Foxx, 50, 1938
RBI: Jimmie Foxx, 175, 1938
STEALS: Tommy Harper, 54, 1973
WINS: Joe Wood, 34, 1912
STRIKEOUTS: Roger Clemens, 291, 1988

CLEVELAND INDIANS

TEAM DIRECTORY: Owners: Richard Jacobs, David Jacobs; Pres./COO: Rick Bay; GM: John Hart; Dir. Player Dev.: Dan O'Dowd; Dir. Media Rel.: John Maroon; Trav. Sec.: Mike Seghi; Mgr.: Mike Hargrove. Home: Cleveland Stadium (74,483). Field distances: 320, l.f. line; 377, l.c.; 400, c.f.; 395, r.c.; 320, r.f. line. Spring training: Tucson, Ariz.

When he behaves, Albert is Belle of Indians' ball.

SCOUTING REPORT

HITTING: Cleveland has the personnel to make a better offensive showing than it did last year. Then again, it's hard to imagine that the 1992 Indians could show less punch than the '91 bunch.

Cleveland was last in the AL in runs with 576 (77 fewer than next-to-last California) and in home runs with 79 (36 fewer than the Angels). Only two teams hit for a poorer average than the Indians' .254 mark. Greater selectivity at the plate is one key to an offensive improvement. Cleveland's total of 449 walks was the second lowest in the AL.

Cleveland must have a full effort from Albert Belle (.282, 28, 95), who hasn't always provided that. Injury-plagued Sandy Alomar Jr., who batted a meager .217 with no home runs in 51 games, will provide a tremendous lift if he stays healthy. Carlos Baerga (.288, 11, 69) is developing into the talent the Indians thought he would be. Alex Cole (.295, 0, 21, 27 steals) provides speed. Mark Whiten and newly acquired speedster Kenny Lofton are two young outfielders with bright futures.

PITCHING: This looms as a tremendous trouble spot. The Indians finished ninth in the AL with a 4.23 ERA and subtracted their best starter, Greg Swindell, when it became obvious they could not sign him to a long-term contract.

The Indians dealt Swindell to Cincinnati and received two good young arms in return—Scott Scudder (6-9, 4.35) and Jack Armstrong (7-13, 5.48). Both are better than their performances with the Reds last year would indicate. Charles Nagy (10-15, 4.13) is coming into his own. Rod Nichols (2-11, 3.54) is significant because of his versatility. The Indians, giving up on Eric King (6-11, 4.60), didn't offer him a contract.

Right-hander Steve Olin bears a heavy burden in a bullpen that finished last in the AL with 33 saves. Olin accounted for 17 of those, including 11 in his last 12 tries.

FIELDING: Mike Hargrove will undoubtedly stress defense in his first full season as manager. The Indians were last in the AL with a .976 fielding percentage. Their 149 errors were 15 more than the next-to-last Yankees committed. Full seasons from Alomar, one of the game's finest catchers when he is sound, and the rifle-armed Whiten in right field will help.

CLEVELAND INDIANS 1992 ROSTER

MANAGER Mike Hargrove
Coaches—Rick Adair, Ken Bolek, Ron Clark, Jose Morales, Dave Nelson, Jeff Newman

PITCHERS

No.	Name	1991 Club	W-L	IP	SO	ERA	B-T	Ht.	Wt.	Born
—	Armstrong, Jack	Cincinnati	7-13	140	93	5.48	R-R	6-5	215	3/7/65 Englewood, NJ
		Nashville	2-0	37	23	2.65				
63	Bell, Eric	Canton-Akron	9-5	93	84	2.89	L-L	6-0	165	10/27/63 Modesto, CA
		Colorado Springs	2-1	25	16	2.13				
		Cleveland	4-0	18	7	0.50				
49	Boucher, Denis	Syracuse	2-1	57	28	3.18	R-L	6-1	195	3/7/88 Canada
		Tor.-Clev.	1-7	58	29	6.05				
		Colorado Springs	1-0	14	9	5.02				
—	Christopher, Mike	Albuquerque	7-2	77	67	2.44	R-R	6-5	205	11/3/63 Petersburg, VA
		Los Angeles	0-0	4	2	0.00				
—	Cook, Dennis	San Antonio	1-3	51	45	2.49	L-L	6-3	185	10/4/62 Lamarque, TX
		Albuquerque	7-3	92	84	3.63				
		Los Angeles	1-0	18	8	0.51				
45	DiPoto, Jerry	Canton-Akron	6-11	156	97	3.81	R-R	6-2	203	5/24/68 Jersey City, NJ
46	Egloff, Bruce	Cleveland	0-0	6	8	4.76	R-R	6-2	215	4/10/65 Denver CO
		Colorado Springs	1-2	29	17	3.38				
38	Hillegas, Shawn	Cleveland	3-4	83	66	4.34	R-R	6-2	223	8/21/64 Dos Palos, CA
64	Kramer, Tom	Canton-Akron	7-3	79	61	2.38	S-R	6-0	185	1/9/68 Cincinnati, OH
		Colorado Springs	1-0	11	18	0.79				
		Cleveland	0-0	5	4	17.36				
26	Lilliquist, Derek	San Diego	0-2	14	7	8.79	L-L	6-0	214	2/20/66 Winter Park, FL
		Las Vegas	4-6	105	89	5.38				
—	Mutis, Jeff	Canton-Akron	11-5	170	89	1.80	L-L	6-3	185	12/20/66 Allentown, PA
		Cleveland	0-3	12	6	11.68				
41	Nagy, Charles	Cleveland	10-15	211	109	4.13	L-R	6-3	200	5/5/67 Fairfield, CT
54	Nichols, Rod	Cleveland	2-11	137	76	3.54	R-R	6-2	190	12/29/64 Burlington, IA
31	Olin, Steve	Cleveland	3-6	44	36	4.47	R-R	6-2	190	10/10/65 Portland, OR
27	Otto, Dave	Colorado Springs	5-6	95	62	4.75	L-L	6-7	210	11/12/64 Chicago, IL
		Cleveland	2-8	100	47	4.23				
33	Scudder, Scott	Cincinnati	6-9	101	51	4.35	R-R	6-2	185	2/14/68 Paris, TX
57	Shaw, Jeff	Colorado Springs	6-3	76	55	4.64	R-R	6-2	185	7/7/66 Wash. Ct. House, OH
		Cleveland	0-5	72	31	3.36				
53	Wickander, Kevin	Colorado Springs	1-0	12	10	2.31	L-L	6-2	202	1/4/65 Fort Dodge, IA
		Canton-Akron	1-2	25	21	3.91				

CATCHERS

No.	Name	1991 Club	H	HR	RBI	Pct.	B-T	Ht.	Wt.	Born
15	Alomar, Sandy	Cleveland	40	0	7	.217	R-R	6-5	200	6/18/66 Puerto Rico
		Colorado Springs	14	1	10	.400				
4	Skinner, Joel	Cleveland	69	1	24	.243	R-R	6-4	204	2/21/61 LaJolla, CA

INFIELDERS

No.	Name	1991 Club	H	HR	RBI	Pct.	B-T	Ht.	Wt.	Born
9	Baerga, Carlos	Cleveland	171	11	69	.288	S-R	5-11	165	11/4/68 Puerto Rico
14	Browne, Jerry	Cleveland	66	1	29	.228	S-R	5-10	170	2/13/66 Virgin Islands
16	Fermin, Felix	Cleveland	111	0	31	.262	R-R	5-11	170	10/9/63 Dominican Republic
		Colorado Springs	2	0	1	.250				
44	Jefferson, Reggie	Nashville	31	3	20	.307	S-L	6-4	210	9/25/68 Tallahassee, FL
		Cincinnati	1	1	1	.143				
		Cleveland	20	2	12	.198				
		Canton-Akron	7	0	4	.280				
		Colorado Springs	42	3	21	.309				
10	Lewis, Mark	Colorado Springs	50	2	31	.279	R-R	6-1	190	11/30/69 Hamilton, OH
		Cleveland	83	0	30	.264				
42	Martinez, Carlos	Canton-Akron	97	11	73	.329	R-R	6-5	175	8/11/65 Venezuela
		Cleveland	73	5	30	.284				
20	Perezchica, Tony	Phoenix	51	8	34	.267	R-R	5-11	165	4/20/66 Mexico
		San Francisco	11	0	3	.229				
		Cleveland	8	0	0	.364				
—	Rhode, Dave	Tucson	94	1	40	.372	S-R	6-2	182	5/8/64 Los Altos, CA
		Houston	5	0	0	.122				
25	Thome, Jim	Canton-Akron	99	5	45	.337	L-R	6-3	205	8/27/70 Peoria, IL
		Colorado Springs	43	2	28	.285				
		Cleveland	25	1	9	.255				

OUTFIELDERS

No.	Name	1991 Club	H	HR	RBI	Pct.	B-T	Ht.	Wt.	Born
29	Aldrete, Mike	San Diego	0	0	1	.000	L-L	5-11	185	1/29/61 Carmel, CA
		Colorado Springs	22	0	8	.289				
		Cleveland	48	1	19	.262				
8	Belle, Albert	Cleveland	130	28	95	.282	R-R	6-2	200	8/25/66 Shreveport, LA
		Colorado Springs	20	2	16	.328				
2	Cole, Alex	Cleveland	114	0	21	.295	L-L	6-2	170	8/17/65 Fayetteville, NC
		Colorado Springs	6	0	3	.188				
1	Hill, Glenallen	Tor.-Clev.	57	8	25	.258	R-R	6-2	210	3/22/65 Santa Cruz, CA
—	Loften, Kenny	Tucson	168	2	50	.308	L-L	6-0	180	5/31/67 East Chicago, IN
		Houston	15	0	0	.203				
48	Pough, Clyde	Columbus	126	11	73	.304	R-R	6-0	173	12/25/69 Avon Park, FL
		Kinston	5	0	2	.167				
		Colorado Springs	0	0	0	.000				
12	Tinsley, Lee	Huntsville	68	2	24	.224	S-R	5-10	180	3/4/69 Shelbyville, KY
		Canton-Akron	41	3	8	.295				
23	Whiten, Mark	Tor.-Clev.	99	9	45	.243	S-R	6-3	215	11/25/66 Pensacola, FL

OUTLOOK: The Indians are stockpiling top prospects, then force-feeding them at the major league level. The approach will work if they are accurate in their assessment of the young talent, but that's always risky business. Cleveland, last at 57-105 in 1991, wound up with the youngest team in the majors by the end of last season (26.1 years old) after tying a club-record 53 different players. Pity Cleveland fans, who have gone since 1954 without a pennant, because this fresh-faced team will endure severe growing pains.

INDIAN PROFILES

ALBERT BELLE 25 6-2 200   Bats R Throws R

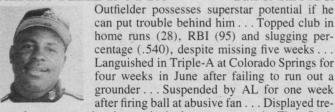

Outfielder possesses superstar potential if he can put trouble behind him . . . Topped club in home runs (28), RBI (95) and slugging percentage (.540), despite missing five weeks . . . Languished in Triple-A at Colorado Springs for four weeks in June after failing to run out a grounder . . . Suspended by AL for one week after firing ball at abusive fan . . . Displayed tremendous power when he crushed a home run onto the Tiger Stadium roof in left field in September . . . Was far better hitter on the road, where he batted .311 with 20 homers and 60 RBI, compared to .254 with eight homers, 35 RBI at Cleveland Stadium . . . Checked himself into Cleveland Clinic during 1990 season and was treated for alcoholism for 10 weeks . . . Born Aug. 25, 1966, in Shreveport, La. . . . Selected by Cleveland in second round of 1987 draft, after stellar career at Louisiana State . . . Earned $100,000 in 1991.

Year Club	Pos.	G	AB	R	H	2B	3B	HR	RBI	SB	Avg.
1989 Cleveland	OF	62	218	22	49	8	4	7	37	2	.225
1990 Cleveland	OF	9	23	1	4	0	0	1	3	0	.174
1991 Cleveland	OF	123	461	60	130	31	2	28	95	3	.282
Totals		194	702	83	183	39	6	36	135	5	.261

SANDY ALOMAR Jr. 25 6-5 200   Bats R Throws R

AL Rookie of the Year in 1990 will try to rebound from injury-filled sophomore season in 1991 . . . Disabled from May 15-June 18 with inflammation and irritation of right rotator cuff . . . Disabled from Aug. 6 until end of season with strained right hip flexor . . . Catcher missed 111 games overall . . . Gained election to All-Star Game despite lost time, becoming first Indian to start consecutive All-Star Games since Al Rosen in 1953-54 . . . He and Roberto of Toronto became only third set of brothers to start for same All-Star squad . . . Named *Baseball America*'s Minor League Player of the Year in 1988 and '89 . . . Born June 18, 1966, in Salinas, P.R. . . . Signed with San Diego as 17-year-old free agent in October 1983 . . . Father Sandy Sr. enjoyed 15-year major-league career . . . Earned $345,000 in 1991.

Year	Club	Pos.	G	AB	R	H	2B	3B	HR	RBI	SB	Avg.
1988	San Diego	PH	1	1	0	0	0	0	0	0	0	.000
1989	San Diego	C	7	19	1	4	1	0	1	6	0	.211
1990	Cleveland	C	132	445	60	129	26	2	9	66	4	.290
1991	Cleveland	C	51	184	10	40	9	0	0	7	0	.217
	Totals		191	649	71	173	36	2	10	79	4	.267

MARK WHITEN 25 6-3 215   Bats S Throws R

Regarded as one of keys to Indians' future since acquisition from Toronto with Glenallen Hill and Denis Boucher for Tom Candiotti and Turner Ward June 27 of last season . . . Owns one of the strongest outfield arms in either league . . . Tied for sixth in AL with 13 outfield assists . . . Paced all AL rookies in that category . . . Tied for second among AL rookies with 45 RBI . . . Missed 18 games in September with sprained left ankle . . . Seven of switch-hitter's nine homers came from left side . . . Put together 26 multi-hit games . . . Born Nov. 25, 1966, in Pensacola, Fla. . . . Began pro career with Toronto in 1989 as fifth-round draft choice . . . Earned $115,000 in 1991.

Year	Club	Pos.	G	AB	R	H	2B	3B	HR	RBI	SB	Avg.
1990	Toronto	OF	33	88	12	24	1	1	2	7	2	.273
1991	Tor.-Clev.	OF	116	407	46	99	18	7	9	45	4	.243
	Totals		149	495	58	123	19	8	11	52	6	.248

CARLOS BAERGA 23 5-11 165   Bats S Throws R

Youngster is ready to be an impact player... Moved permanently to second base on July 23 and immediately improved club's ability to turn double play... Finished as team leader in hits (171), runs (80) and games played (158)... Placed second on club with 11 homers and 69 RBI... Topped Indians with 48 multi-hit games... Significantly better hitter from the right side (.329) than from the left (.273)... Acquired with Chris James and Sandy Alomar Jr. from San Diego for Joe Carter prior to 1990 season... Born Nov. 4, 1968, in San Juan, P.R.... Originally signed as a free agent by Padres, Nov. 4, 1968... Due for increase after making only $165,000 in 1991.

Year	Club	Pos.	G	AB	R	H	2B	3B	HR	RBI	SB	Avg.
1990	Cleveland	3B-SS-2B	108	312	46	81	17	2	7	47	0	.260
1991	Cleveland	3B-2B-SS	158	593	80	171	28	2	11	69	3	.288
	Totals		266	905	126	252	45	4	18	116	3	.278

GLENALLEN HILL 27 6-2 210   Bats R Throws R

Will compete for outfield spot in first full season with Tribe... Was acquired last June from Toronto with Mark Whiten, Denis Boucher and cash for Tom Candiotti and Turner Ward... Went 2-for-4 in Indian debut vs. Baltimore, but bruised right foot in second game... Disc problem in lower back disabled him in September... Produced 18 multihit games, nine with Cleveland... Batted .273 with runners in scoring position, but only .203 from seventh inning on... Began career as Toronto's ninth-round pick in 1983... Spent eight years in the minors... Born March 22, 1965, in Santa Cruz, Cal.... Earned $170,000 in 1991.

Year	Club	Pos.	G	AB	R	H	2B	3B	HR	RBI	SB	Avg.
1989	Toronto	OF	19	52	4	15	0	0	1	7	2	.288
1990	Toronto	OF	84	260	47	60	11	3	12	32	8	.231
1991	Tor.-Clev.	OF	72	221	29	57	8	2	8	25	6	.258
	Totals		175	533	80	132	19	5	21	64	16	.248

ALEX COLE 26 6-2 170   Bats L Throws L

Indians need more than they got from him last year . . . Did lead club in walks (58), stolen bases (27) and on-base percentage (.386), but was not base-stealing threat he can be . . . Stole only nine bases in 21 attempts the entire first half . . . Did improve in second half, converting 18 of 23 stolen-base tries . . . Outfielder hit .292 before All-Star break, .296 after it . . . Obtained from St. Louis for Tom Lampkin, July 11, 1990 . . . Cards' second-round pick in 1985 draft . . . Born Aug. 17, 1965, in Fayetteville, N.C. . . . Earned $155,000 in 1991.

Year	Club	Pos.	G	AB	R	H	2B	3B	HR	RBI	SB	Avg.
1990	Cleveland	OF	63	227	43	68	5	4	0	13	40	.300
1991	Cleveland	OF	122	387	58	114	17	3	0	21	27	.295
	Totals		185	614	101	182	22	7	0	34	67	.296

CHARLES NAGY 24 6-3 200   Bats L Throws R

Should be mainstay in rotation for years to come . . . Led club in victories with 10 in first full major-league season . . . Tied Greg Swindell for team lead in starts (33) and placed second to him in innings pitched (211⅓) and complete games (six) . . . Was only 3-3 when he went the distance . . . Enjoyed much better results at home (6-5) than on road (4-10) . . . Taken by Cleveland in first round of 1988 draft as 17th player selected overall . . . Member of gold medal-winning team at 1988 Summer Olympics . . . Led Team USA with 1.05 ERA during 53-game summer schedule . . . Born May 5, 1967, in Fairfield, Conn. . . . Starred for two years at University of Connecticut . . . Salary was only $115,000 in 1991.

Year	Club	G	IP	W	L	Pct.	SO	BB	H	ERA
1990	Cleveland	9	45⅔	2	4	.333	26	21	58	5.91
1991	Cleveland	33	211⅓	10	15	.400	109	66	228	4.13
	Totals	42	257	12	19	.387	135	87	286	4.45

ROD NICHOLS 27 6-2 190   Bats R Throws R

Best assets are versatility and persistence... Ended 13-game losing streak dating back to Sept. 14, 1989 when he edged Oakland, 2-1, July 17... Fired four-hitter in that game... Showed another flash of brilliance when he blanked White Sox, 3-0, on three-hitter Aug. 25... Enjoyed best success in bullpen, where he was 0-1 with a 2.48 ERA covering 40 innings... Dropped 10 of 12 decisions with 3.98 ERA as starter ... Cleveland's fifth selection in 1985 draft, out of University of New Mexico... Born Dec. 29, 1964, in Burlington, Iowa... Earned $125,000 in 1991.

Year	Club	G	IP	W	L	Pct.	SO	BB	H	ERA
1988	Cleveland	11	69⅓	1	7	.125	31	23	73	5.06
1989	Cleveland	15	71⅔	4	6	.400	42	24	81	4.40
1990	Cleveland	4	16	0	3	.000	3	6	24	7.88
1991	Cleveland	31	137⅓	2	11	.154	76	30	145	3.54
	Totals	61	294⅓	7	27	.206	152	83	323	4.34

STEVE OLIN 26 6-2 190   Bats R Throws R

Will try to build on solid results that followed recall from Colorado Springs (AAA) last July 15... Posted team-leading 17 saves, converting all but five of 22 opportunities... Rattled off 11 saves in final 12 tries... Retired first batter only 23 of possible 47 times... Sixteenth-round choice in 1987 draft has far exceeded expectations... Sidearm style gives him immediate advantages because batters struggle to locate his release point... Played at Portland State... Born Oct. 10, 1965, in Portland, Ore.... Salary was $175,000 in 1991.

Year	Club	G	IP	W	L	Pct.	SO	BB	H	ERA
1989	Cleveland	25	36	1	4	.200	24	14	35	3.75
1990	Cleveland	50	92⅓	4	4	.500	64	26	96	3.41
1991	Cleveland	48	56⅓	3	6	.333	38	23	61	3.36
	Totals	123	184⅔	8	14	.364	126	63	192	3.46

TOP PROSPECTS

JIM THOME 21 6-3 205   Bats L Throws R
Ready to establish himself as big-league third baseman... Began

last year with Canton (AA) and batted .337 with five home runs, 45 RBI in 84 games ... Earned promotion to Colorado Springs (AAA), where he hit .285 with two homers, 28 RBI in 41 games ... Born Aug. 27, 1970, in Peoria, Ill. ... Cleveland's 13th selection in 1989 draft hit .255 with homer and nine RBI for Indians last year.

REGGIE JEFFERSON 23 6-4 210   **Bats S Throws L**
First baseman was acquired from Cincinnati for Tim Costo last June 14, after Reds had accidentally left him exposed to being claimed by other teams ... Reds' third choice in 1986 draft ... Born Sept. 25, 1968, in Tallahassee, Fla. ... Minor-league career marred by injuries ... Missed most of 1987 with right shin fracture ... Stress fracture in lower back finished his '90 season at end of May ... Hit .309 with three homers and 21 RBI in 136 at-bats for Colorado Springs (AAA).

DAVE ROHDE 27 6-2 180   **Bats S Throws R**
Second baseman traded in December by Astros with Kenny Lofton for Indian minor leaguers Eddie Taubensee and Willie Blair ... Best season was '91, when he hit .372 in 73 games with Tuscon (AAA) ... In 88 games with Houston in 1990 and '91, he batted .165 in 139 at-bats ... Slick fielder ... Born May 8, 1964, in Los Altos, Cal.

MANNY RAMIREZ 19 6-0 195   **Bats R Throws R**
First-round choice in 1991 draft as 13th pick overall is drawing rave reviews ... Center fielder batted .326 for Burlington to finish third in Appalachian League ... Topped that rookie league with 19 home runs and 63 RBI ... Born May 30, 1972, in Santiago, D.R., but raised in Bronx, N.Y.

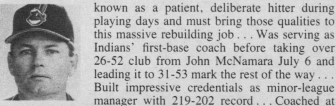

MANAGER MIKE HARGROVE: Former first baseman was known as a patient, deliberate hitter during playing days and must bring those qualities to this massive rebuilding job ... Was serving as Indians' first-base coach before taking over 26-52 club from John McNamara July 6 and leading it to 31-53 mark the rest of the way ... Built impressive credentials as minor-league manager with 219-202 record ... Coached at Batavia of New York-Penn League in 1986 ... Honored as Carolina League Manager of the Year the following season with runnerup Kinston . . . After year at AA Williamsport (AA), he was named Manager of the Year in 1989, when he guided Colorado Springs (AAA) to first-half championship of Pacific Coast League . . . Selected as *Baseball America's* top managerial prospect following that effort . . . Spent six-plus seasons with Cleveland during 12-year major-league career . . . Also played for Texas and San Diego . . . Named AL Rookie of the Year in 1974 . . . Led AL in walks in 1976 and '78 . . . Boasted .400 career on-base percentage . . . Born Oct. 26, 1949, in Perryton, Tex. . . . Wife Sharon co-authored "Safe at Home," a book about life of a baseball wife.

ALL-TIME INDIAN SEASON RECORDS

BATTING: Joe Jackson, .408, 1911
HRs: Al Rosen, 43, 1953
RBI: Hal Trosky, 162, 1936
STEALS: Miguel Dilone, 61, 1980
WINS: Jim Bagby, 31, 1920
STRIKEOUTS: Bob Feller, 348, 1946

DETROIT TIGERS

TEAM DIRECTORY: Owner: Tom Monaghan; Chairman/CEO: Jim Campbell; Pres./COO: Bo Schembechler; Sr. VP-Oper.: Bill Haase; Sr. VP-Player Procurement: Joe McDonald; Sr. VP-Major League Pers.: Jerry Walker; Sr. VP-Marketing, Radio, TV: Jeff Odenwald; VP-Pub. Rel.: Dan Ewald; Dir. Pub. Rel.: Greg Shea; Trav. Sec.: Bill Brown; Mgr.: Sparky Anderson. Home: Tiger Stadium (52,416). Field distances: 340, l.f. line; 365, l.c.; 440, c.f.; 370, r.c.; 325, r.f. line. Spring training: Lakeland, Fla.

SCOUTING REPORT

HITTING: Detroit's offense is largely an all-or-nothing approach. The Tigers topped the majors with 209 home runs in 1991,

Cecil Fielder squawked at being MVP runnerup again.

wearing the AL team home run crown for the fifth time in the last eight seasons. However, Detroit batters struck out 1,185 times, the second-highest single-season total in major league history behind the 1968 Mets, and the Tigers' .247 batting average was a league low in 1991.

Beefy Cecil Fielder (.261, 44, 133) is bidding to lead the majors in RBI for the third straight year. He is the first American Leaguer to pace the majors in RBI in consecutive seasons since Jimmie Foxx did it for the Philadelphia A's in 1932 and 1933. Perhaps this will be the season Fielder finally latches onto the league's MVP award, after consecutive runnerup finishes.

Mickey Tettleton (.263, 31, 89), Rob Deer (.179, 25, 64), Lou Whitaker (.279, 23, 78) and Tony Phillips (.284, 17, 72) are other sources of power for the Tigers, who placed second in the majors with 817 runs. Free agent import Dan Gladden (.247, 6, 52 with the Twins) should provide some speed.

PITCHING: Was Bill Gullickson a one-year wonder? The Tigers can only hope that his 20-9 record in 1991, which doubled his victory total of the year before with Houston, was no aberration. Gullickson, 33, had never before won more than 17 games in a season—and he did that in 1983, with Montreal.

Frank Tanana (13-12, 3.77) and Walt Terrell (12-14, 4.24) are two other key members of the rotation. They joined Gullickson in giving Detroit three starters with more than 200 innings. Mike Henneman (10-2, 2.88, 21 Sv) anchors a bullpen that leaves something to be desired in middle relief. The sturdy Henneman bears a greater burden than most closers. He's aiming for his fifth straight year with 60-plus appearances.

FIELDING: Shortstop Alan Trammell and second baseman Whitaker will team for a major league-record 15th consecutive season. Trammell's health will go a long way toward determining the fate of the Tigers as injuries limited him to a career-low 101 games last season. Whitaker, still one of the league's better second basemen, made only four errors last year.

OUTLOOK: Detroit will again be a factor in the AL East race. Sparky Anderson's Tigers almost always are. Their tie with Boston for second place last year at 84-78 marked the eighth time in the last nine seasons that they finished third or better. Detroit has assembled a lineup to terrorize opponents, particularly at Tiger Stadium, where they were 49-32 last summer. But pitching makes champions and the Tigers lack depth in their rotation and bullpen.

DETROIT TIGERS 1992 ROSTER

MANAGER Sparky Anderson
Coaches—Billy Consolo, Larry Herndon, Billy Muffett, Gene Roof, Dick Tracewski, Dan Whitmer

PITCHERS

No.	Name	1991 Club	W-L	IP	SO	ERA	B-T	Ht.	Wt.	Born
30	Aldred, Scott	Toledo	8-8	135	95	3.92	L-L	6-4	195	6/12/68 Flint, MI
		Detroit	2-4	57	35	5.18				
—	Cummings, Steve	Colorado Springs	0-4	27	15	6.08	S-R	6-2	205	7/15/64 Houston, TX
		Toledo	5-5	75	41	4.68				
—	DeSilva, John	London	5-4	74	80	2.81	R-R	6-0	193	9/30/67 Fort Bragg, NC
		Toledo	5-4	59	56	4.13				
—	Doherty, John	London	3-3	65	42	2.22	R-R	6-4	190	6/11/67 Bronx, NY
32	Gakeler, Dan	Toledo	2-3	44	32	3.50	R-R	6-6	210	5/1/64 Mt. Holly, NJ
		Detroit	1-4	74	43	5.74				
48	Gibson, Paul	Detroit	5-7	96	52	4.59	R-L	6-0	185	1/4/60 Center Moriches, NY
—	Gohr, Greg	London	0-0	11	10	0.00	R-R	6-3	210	10/29/67 Santa Clara, CA
		Toledo	10-8	148	96	4.61				
—	Groom, Buddy	London	7-1	52	39	3.48	L-L	6-2	200	7/10/65 Dallas, TX
		Toledo	2-5	75	49	4.32				
36	Gullickson, Bill	Detroit	20-9	226	91	3.90	R-R	6-3	220	2/20/59 Marshall, MN
16	Haas, David	Toledo	8-10	158	133	5.23	R-R	6-1	200	10/19/65 Independence, MO
		Detroit	1-0	11	6	6.75				
39	Henneman, Mike	Detroit	10-2	84	61	2.88	R-R	6-4	195	12/11/61 St. Charles, MO
46	Kiely, John	Toledo	4-2	72	60	2.13	R-R	6-3	210	10/4/64 Boston, MA
		Detroit	0-1	7	1	14.85				
—	Knudsen, Kurt	London	2-3	52	56	3.48	R-R	6-2	185	2/20/67 Arlington Heights, IL
		Toledo	1-2	18	28	1.47				
23	Leiter, Mark	Toledo	1-0	7	7	0.00	R-R	6-3	210	4/13/63 Joliet, IL
		Detroit	9-7	135	103	4.21				
43	Munoz, Mike	Toledo	2-3	54	38	3.83	L-L	6-3	195	7/12/65 Baldwin Park, CA
		Detroit	0-0	9	3	9.64				
31	Ritz, Kevin	Toledo	8-7	126	105	3.28	R-R	6-4	210	6/8/65 Eatontown, NJ
		Detroit	0-3	15	9	11.74				
26	Tanana, Frank	Detroit	13-12	217	107	3.77	L-L	6-3	195	7/3/53 Detroit, MI
35	Terrell, Walt	Detroit	12-14	219	80	4.24	R-R	6-1	215	5/11/58 Jeffersonville, IN

CATCHERS

No.	Name	1991 Club	H	HR	RBI	Pct.	B-T	Ht.	Wt.	Born
12	Rowland, Rich	Toledo	104	13	48	.272	R-R	6-1	210	2/25/67 Cloverdale, CA
		Detroit	1	0	1	.250				
20	Tettleton, Mickey	Detroit	132	31	89	.263	S-R	6-2	212	9/16/60 Oklahoma City, OK

INFIELDERS

No.	Name	1991 Club	H	HR	RBI	Pct.	B-T	Ht.	Wt.	Born
14	Bergman, Dave	Detroit	46	7	29	.237	L-L	6-2	190	6/6/53 Evanston, IL
—	Brogna, Rico	London	80	13	51	.273	L-L	6-2	190	4/18/70 Turner Falls, MA
		Toledo	29	2	13	.220				
45	Fielder, Cecil	Detroit	163	44	133	.261	R-R	6-3	240	9/21/63 Los Angeles, CA
24	Fryman, Travis	Detroit	144	21	91	.259	R-R	6-1	180	4/25/69 Lexington, KY
21	Livingstone, Scott	Toledo	100	3	52	.302	L-R	6-0	190	7/15/65 Dallas, TX
		Detroit	37	2	11	.291				
—	Phillips, Tony	Detroit	160	17	72	.284	S-R	5-10	175	4/25/59 Atlanta, GA
—	Rosario, Vince	Rich.-Tol.	127	1	48	.300	R-R	5-11	155	8/26/66 Dominican Republic
3	Trammell, Alan	Detroit	93	9	55	.248	R-R	6-0	175	2/21/58 Garden Grove, CA
1	Whitaker, Lou	Detroit	131	23	78	.279	L-R	5-11	180	5/12/57 New York, NY

OUTFIELDERS

No.	Name	1991 Club	H	HR	RBI	Pct.	B-T	Ht.	Wt.	Born
9	Barnes, Skeeter	Toledo	77	9	40	.330	R-R	5-10	180	3/7/57 Cincinnati, OH
		Detroit	46	5	17	.289				
22	Cuyler, Milt	Detroit	122	3	33	.257	S-R	5-10	175	10/7/68 Macon, GA
44	Deer, Rob	Detroit	80	25	64	.179	R-R	6-3	225	9/29/60 Orange, CA
—	Gladden, Dan	Minnesota	114	6	52	.247	R-R	5-11	181	7/7/57 San Jose, CA
25	Hare, Shawn	London	34	4	28	.272	L-R	6-2	190	3/26/67 St. Louis, MO
		Toledo	78	9	42	.310				
		Detroit	1	0	0	.053				
—	Hurst, Jody	London	52	8	24	.278	R-L	6-4	190	3/11/67 Meridian, MS
—	Ingram, Riccardo	London	114	18	64	.271	R-R	6-0	198	9/10/66 Douglas, GA
40	Pegues, Steve	London	65	6	26	.301	R-R	6-2	172	5/21/68 Pontotoc, MS
		Toledo	50	4	23	.225				
18	Pemberton, Rudy	Lakeland	86	3	36	.229	R-R	6-1	185	12/17/69 Dominican Republic

TIGER PROFILES

CECIL FIELDER 28 6-3 240   Bats R Throws R

Became first player to top majors in RBI in back-to-back seasons since Ernie Banks did it in 1958-59 . . . Fourth Tiger to lead AL in RBI in consecutive seasons and first since Bobby Veach (1917-18) . . . Remarkably consistent run producer drove in at least 18 runs every month last season . . . Home run derby with Oakland's Jose Canseco ended in tie for major-league lead at 44 . . . Became first player to clear bleachers at Milwaukee's County Stadium with mammoth 502-foot shot Sept. 14 . . . Beefy first baseman gained Detroit's attention by slamming 38 homers in 1989 for Hanshin Tigers, who had purchased him from Toronto after the 1988 season . . . Retains huge following in Japan, where he's known as "Wild Bear" . . . Born Sept. 21, 1963, in Los Angeles . . . Underpaid at $1.75 million in 1991 . . . Royals' fourth-round pick in 1982 was signed by Tigers as free agent prior to 1990 season.

Year	Club	Pos.	G	AB	R	H	2B	3B	HR	RBI	SB	Avg.
1985	Toronto	1B	30	74	6	23	4	0	4	16	0	.311
1986	Toronto	1B-3B-OF	34	83	7	13	2	0	4	13	0	.157
1987	Toronto	1B-3B	82	175	30	47	7	1	14	32	0	.269
1988	Toronto	1B-3B-2B	74	174	24	40	6	1	9	23	0	.230
1990	Detroit	1B	159	573	104	159	25	1	51	132	0	.277
1991	Detroit	1B	162	624	102	163	25	0	44	133	0	.261
	Totals		541	1703	273	445	69	3	126	349	0	.261

LOU WHITAKER 34 5-11 180   Bats L Throws R

Second baseman figures to team with shortstop Alan Trammell for record 15th consecutive season . . . Remains an extremely productive player . . . His 23 home runs and 78 RBI last year represented second-highest totals of his career . . . Paced Tigers with .391 on-base percentage that ranked 10th in AL . . . Second on club with 94 runs . . . A selective hitter who worked 90 walks, he is extremely difficult to strike out . . . Fanned only 45 times in 470 at-bats . . . Raised batting average 42 points from previous year . . . Made only four errors all year . . . Honored as AL Rookie of the Year in 1978 . . . Born May 12, 1957, in

Brooklyn, N.Y. . . . Fifth-round choice in 1975 draft . . . Earned $2 million in 1991.

Year	Club	Pos.	G	AB	R	H	2B	3B	HR	RBI	SB	Avg.
1977	Detroit	2B	11	32	5	8	1	0	0	2	2	.250
1978	Detroit	2B	139	484	71	138	12	7	3	58	7	.285
1979	Detroit	2B	127	423	75	121	14	8	3	42	20	.286
1980	Detroit	2B	145	477	68	111	19	1	1	45	8	.233
1981	Detroit	2B	109	335	48	88	14	4	5	36	5	.263
1982	Detroit	2B	152	560	76	160	22	8	15	65	11	.286
1983	Detroit	2B	161	643	94	206	40	6	12	72	17	.320
1984	Detroit	2B	143	558	90	161	25	1	13	56	6	.289
1985	Detroit	2B	152	609	102	170	29	8	21	73	6	.279
1986	Detroit	2B	144	584	95	157	26	6	20	73	13	.269
1987	Detroit	2B	149	604	110	160	38	6	16	59	13	.265
1988	Detroit	2B	115	403	54	111	18	2	12	55	2	.275
1989	Detroit	2B	148	509	77	128	21	1	28	85	6	.251
1990	Detroit	2B	132	472	75	112	22	2	18	60	8	.237
1991	Detroit	2B	138	470	94	131	26	2	23	78	4	.279
	Totals		1965	7163	1134	1962	327	62	190	859	128	.274

TONY PHILLIPS 32 5-10 175   Bats S Throws R

Joined Tigers in 1990 as free agent after nine years with Oakland organization and has been an excellent addition . . . Led Tigers with .284 batting average . . . Set career highs with 17 home runs and 72 RBI . . . Placed second to Cecil Fielder with 564 at-bats . . . Was third on club with 87 runs . . . Had 49 extra-base hits among his 160 hits . . . Frequently praised for his solid makeup . . . Significant member of A's World Series team in 1988 and '89 . . . Played every position except pitcher and catcher with A's . . . Born April 25, 1959, in Atlanta . . . Earned $1,566,667 in 1991.

Year	Club	Pos.	G	AB	R	H	2B	3B	HR	RBI	SB	Avg.
1982	Oakland	SS	40	81	11	17	2	2	0	8	2	.210
1983	Oakland	SS-2B-3B	148	412	54	102	12	3	4	35	16	.248
1984	Oakland	SS-2B-OF	154	451	62	120	24	3	4	37	10	.266
1985	Oakland	3B-2B	42	161	23	45	12	2	4	17	3	.280
1986	Oakland	SS-2B-3B	118	441	76	113	14	5	5	52	15	.256
1987	Oakland	2B-3B-SS-OF	111	379	48	91	20	0	10	46	7	.240
1988	Oakland	INF-OF	79	212	32	43	8	4	2	17	0	.203
1989	Oakland	INF-OF	143	451	48	118	15	6	4	47	3	.262
1990	Detroit	3B-2B-SS-OF	152	573	97	144	23	5	8	55	19	.251
1991	Detroit	OF-3B-2B-SS	146	564	87	160	28	4	17	72	10	.284
	Totals		1133	3725	538	953	158	34	58	386	85	.256

ALAN TRAMMELL 34 6-0 175   Bats R Throws R

Injury-plagued veteran shortstop will try to reassert himself after difficult season...Finished with career lows in games (101), at-bats (375) and hits (93)...Aggravated old knee injury before All-Star break...Troubled by severe ankle sprain after break...One of five Tigers in history with at least 200 stolen bases after his 11 steals last year gave him 210...
Has been the heart of the Tigers for many years now...Was MVP when Tigers won World Series in 1984, batting .450 with two homers and six RBI...Narrowly missed AL MVP award in 1987, placing second despite batting .416 in September to rally Detroit to AL East crown...Born Feb. 21, 1958, in Garden Grove, Cal....Second-round choice in 1976 draft...Best-paid Detroit player in 1991 at $2.2 million.

Year	Club	Pos.	G	AB	R	H	2B	3B	HR	RBI	SB	Avg.
1977	Detroit	SS	19	43	6	8	0	0	0	0	0	.186
1978	Detroit	SS	139	448	49	120	14	6	2	34	3	.268
1979	Detroit	SS	142	460	68	127	11	4	6	50	17	.276
1980	Detroit	SS	146	560	107	168	21	5	9	65	12	.300
1981	Detroit	SS	105	392	52	101	15	3	2	31	10	.258
1982	Detroit	SS	157	489	66	126	34	3	9	57	19	.258
1983	Detroit	SS	142	505	83	161	31	2	14	66	30	.319
1984	Detroit	SS	139	555	85	174	34	5	14	69	19	.314
1985	Detroit	SS	149	605	79	156	21	7	13	57	14	.258
1986	Detroit	SS	151	574	107	159	33	7	21	75	25	.277
1987	Detroit	SS	151	597	109	205	34	3	28	105	21	.343
1988	Detroit	SS	128	466	73	145	24	1	15	69	7	.311
1989	Detroit	SS	121	449	54	109	20	3	5	43	10	.243
1990	Detroit	SS	146	559	71	170	37	1	14	89	12	.304
1991	Detroit	SS-3B	101	375	57	93	20	0	9	55	11	.248
	Totals		1936	7077	1066	2023	349	50	161	865	210	.286

MICKEY TETTLETON 31 6-2 212   Bats S Throws R

Catcher was obtained from Baltimore for Jeff Robinson prior to last season and gave Tigers another big bat in their explosive lineup...Smashed previous career highs with 31 home runs and 89 RBI...His 31 homers more than doubled previous year's total and tied him for fifth in AL...Drew 101 walks to rank second to White Sox' Frank Thomas in that category
...Placed second on Tigers with .491 slugging percentage...Played in all but eight games...Born Sept. 16, 1960, in Oklahoma City, Okla....Oakland's fifth selection in 1981 draft...

Salvaged career after his release by A's just before start of 1988 season . . . Earned $1.6 million in 1991.

Year	Club	Pos.	G	AB	R	H	2B	3B	HR	RBI	SB	Avg.
1984	Oakland	C	33	76	10	20	2	1	1	5	0	.263
1985	Oakland	C	78	211	23	53	12	0	3	15	2	.251
1986	Oakland	C	90	211	26	43	9	0	10	35	7	.204
1987	Oakland	C-1B	82	211	19	41	3	0	8	26	1	.194
1988	Baltimore	C	86	283	31	74	11	1	11	37	0	.261
1989	Baltimore	C	117	411	72	106	21	2	26	65	3	.258
1990	Baltimore	C-1B-OF	135	444	68	99	21	2	15	51	2	.223
1991	Detroit	C-OF-1B	154	501	85	132	17	2	31	89	3	.263
	Totals			775	2348	334	568	96	8	105	323	18	.242

ROB DEER 31 6-3 225   Bats R Throws R

Continues to be long-ball threat, slamming at least 23 home runs in each of his six full major-league seasons . . . Power comes at a steep price, however . . . Led Tigers with 175 strikeouts . . . Batted career-low .179 . . . Average has declined for four straight years . . . Did draw 89 walks, third-highest total on club . . . Must work on selectivity . . . Quality outfielder with strong arm . . . Began career with San Francisco as fourth-round choice in 1978 draft . . . Dealt to Milwaukee for Dean Freeland and Eric Pilkington in 1986 . . . Born Sept. 29, 1960, in Orange, Cal. . . . Earned $1,966,667 in 1991.

Year	Club	Pos.	G	AB	R	H	2B	3B	HR	RBI	SB	Avg.
1984	San Francisco	OF	13	24	5	4	0	0	3	3	1	.167
1985	San Francisco	OF-1B	78	162	22	30	5	1	8	20	0	.185
1986	Milwaukee	OF-1B	134	466	75	108	17	3	33	86	5	.232
1987	Milwaukee	OF-1B	134	474	71	113	15	2	28	80	12	.238
1988	Milwaukee	OF	135	492	71	124	24	0	23	85	9	.252
1989	Milwaukee	OF	130	466	72	98	18	2	26	65	4	.210
1990	Milwaukee	OF 1B	134	440	57	92	15	1	27	69	2	.209
1991	Detroit	OF	134	448	64	80	14	2	25	64	1	.179
	Totals			892	2972	437	649	108	11	173	472	34	.218

BILL GULLICKSON 33 6-3 220   Bats R Throws R

Tigers' free-agent find of last season will try to continue success after being one of baseball's biggest surprises in 1991 . . . Registered career-high 20 victories, doubling his 1990 total with Houston . . . Previous career high was 17 victories, with Montreal in 1983 . . . His 20 victories tied him with Minnesota's Scott Erickson for AL lead . . . Went 11-4 before All-Star

break, 9-5 after it . . . One key to success was superb control . . .
Walked only 44, 13 of them intentional . . . Most thought he'd
never pitch in majors again after he spent 1988 and 1989 with
Japan's Yomiuri Giants . . . Born Feb. 20, 1959, in Marshall,
Minn. . . . Began career as Montreal's first-round choice in 1977
draft as second player taken overall behind Harold Baines . . .
Earned $1.825 million in 1991.

Year	Club	G	IP	W	L	Pct.	SO	BB	H	ERA
1979	Montreal	1	1	0	0	.000	0	0	2	0.00
1980	Montreal	24	141	10	5	.667	120	50	127	3.00
1981	Montreal	22	157	7	9	.438	115	34	142	2.81
1982	Montreal	34	236⅔	12	14	.462	155	61	231	3.57
1983	Montreal	34	242⅓	17	12	.586	120	59	230	3.75
1984	Montreal	32	226⅔	12	9	.571	100	37	230	3.61
1985	Montreal	29	181⅓	14	12	.538	68	47	187	3.52
1986	Cincinnati	37	244⅔	15	12	.556	121	60	245	3.38
1987	Cincinnati	27	165	10	11	.476	89	39	172	4.85
1987	New York (AL)	8	48	4	2	.667	28	11	46	4.88
1990	Houston	32	193⅓	10	14	.417	73	61	221	3.82
1991	Detroit	35	226⅓	20	9	.690	91	44	256	3.90
	Totals	315	2063⅓	131	109	.546	1080	503	2089	3.66

MIKE HENNEMAN 30 6-4 195   Bats R Throws R

Does quiet but very effective job as Tigers'
closer . . . Comes off third season with at least
20 saves and Willie Hernandez (1984-86) is the
only other Tiger to do that . . . Ranks fourth on
Tigers' all-time list with 80 career saves . . .
Aiming for fifth straight year with 60-plus appearances . . . Very difficult to beat at Tiger
Stadium, where he is 34-6 lifetime, including
7-0 last year . . . Born Dec. 11, 1961, in St. Charles, Mo. . . .
Third-round pick in 1984 draft . . . Helped Oklahoma State reach
College World Series in 1983 and 1984 . . . Earned $1.1 million
in 1991.

Year	Club	G	IP	W	L	Pct.	SO	BB	H	ERA
1987	Detroit	55	96⅔	11	3	.786	75	30	86	2.98
1988	Detroit	65	91⅓	9	6	.600	58	24	72	1.87
1989	Detroit	60	90	11	4	.733	69	51	84	3.70
1990	Detroit	69	94⅓	8	6	.571	50	33	90	3.05
1991	Detroit	60	84⅓	10	2	.833	61	34	81	2.88
	Totals	309	456⅔	49	21	.700	313	172	413	2.90

FRANK TANANA 38 6-3 195   Bats L Throws L

Continues as capable starter despite advancing age . . . Has won in double figures in seven of last eight years . . . Has pitched 200-plus innings six times in last eight years and 12 times overall . . . Ranks 62nd all-time with 220 career victories . . . Stands 16th on all-time strikeout list with 2,562 . . . Overpowering early in career, he has made outstanding adjustment to lost velocity . . . One of smartest pitchers in either league . . . Detroit native was born in Motor City, July 3, 1953 . . . Angels' first-round pick in 1971 draft . . . Best-paid Detroit pitcher in 1991 at $1.9 million . . . Obtained from Rangers for Duane James, June 20, 1985.

Year	Club	G	IP	W	L	Pct.	SO	BB	H	ERA
1973	California	4	26	2	2	.500	22	8	20	3.12
1974	California	39	269	14	19	.424	180	77	262	3.11
1975	California	34	257	16	9	.640	269	73	211	2.63
1976	California	34	288	19	10	.655	261	73	212	2.44
1977	California	31	241	15	9	.625	205	61	201	2.54
1978	California	33	239	18	12	.600	137	60	239	3.65
1979	California	18	90	7	5	.583	46	25	93	3.90
1980	California	32	204	11	12	.478	113	45	223	4.15
1981	Boston	24	141	4	10	.286	78	43	142	4.02
1982	Texas	30	194⅓	7	18	.280	87	55	199	4.21
1983	Texas	29	159⅓	7	9	.438	108	49	144	3.16
1984	Texas	35	246⅓	15	15	.500	141	81	234	3.25
1985	Texas-Detroit	33	215	12	14	.462	159	57	220	4.27
1986	Detroit	32	188⅓	12	9	.571	119	65	196	4.16
1987	Detroit	34	218⅔	15	10	.600	146	56	216	3.91
1988	Detroit	32	203	14	11	.560	127	64	213	4.21
1989	Detroit	33	223⅔	10	14	.417	147	74	227	3.58
1990	Detroit	34	176⅓	9	8	.529	114	66	190	5.31
1991	Detroit	33	217⅓	13	12	.520	107	78	217	3.77
	Totals	574	3797⅓	220	208	.514	2566	1110	3659	3.59

WALT TERRELL 33 6-1 215   Bats R Throws R

Tigers look for him to give them another solid season . . . His 12 victories last year marked his best total since he won 17 in 1987 . . . Will try to surpass 200-inning plateau for eighth time in nine years . . . Led Tigers with eight complete games . . . Hates to leave games early . . . Earned 100th career victory with 4-0 four-hitter at Yankee Stadium Aug. 10 . . . Sports 48-21 career record at Tiger Stadium . . . Sinkerballer benefits from tall grass in infield there . . . Must keep the ball down to have any chance for success . . . Signed to long-term deal and then released by Pittsburgh July 27, 1990, he was signed by Detroit almost immediately for major-league minimum of $100,000 . . . Born May 11, 1958, in Jeffersonville, Ind. . . . Rangers' 33rd-round pick in 1980.

Year	Club	G	IP	W	L	Pct.	SO	BB	H	ERA
1982	New York (NL)	3	21	0	3	.000	8	14	22	3.43
1983	New York (NL)	21	133⅔	8	8	.500	59	55	123	3.57
1984	New York (NL)	33	215	11	12	.478	114	80	232	3.52
1985	Detroit	34	229	15	10	.600	130	95	221	3.85
1986	Detroit	34	217⅓	15	12	.556	93	98	199	4.56
1987	Detroit	35	244⅔	17	10	.630	143	94	254	4.05
1988	Detroit	29	206⅓	7	16	.304	84	78	199	3.97
1989	San Diego	19	123⅓	5	13	.278	63	26	134	4.01
1989	New York (AL)	13	83	6	5	.545	30	24	102	5.20
1990	Pittsburgh	16	82⅔	2	7	.222	34	33	98	5.88
1990	Detroit	13	75⅓	6	4	.600	30	24	86	4.54
1991	Detroit	35	218⅔	12	14	.462	80	79	257	4.24
	Totals	285	1850	104	114	.477	868	700	1927	4.14

TOP PROSPECTS

SCOTT LIVINGSTONE 26 6-0 190   Bats L Throws R
Third baseman asserted himself by batting .291 in 44 games with Tigers . . . Batted .302 in 92 games with Toledo (AAA) . . . Doesn't have much power or speed, however . . . Finished with only three home runs and two steals for Toledo . . . Born July 15, 1965, in Dallas . . . Second selection in 1988 draft, out of Texas A&M.

RICHARD ROWLAND 25 6-1 210   Bats R Throws R
Catcher comes off solid season for Toledo (AAA) as he batted .272 with 13 home runs and 68 RBI . . . Topped Mud Hens in RBI . . . Had only four at-bats after promotion to Detroit, producing a single . . . Has made surprising rise since being 17th pick in 1988 draft . . . Born Feb. 25, 1967, in Cloverdale, Cal.

GREG GOHR 24 6-3 210   Bats R Throws R
Tigers like his potential . . . Compiled 10-8 record with 4.61 ERA in 26 starts for Toledo (AAA) . . . Placed second on Mud Hens' staff in innings pitched with 148⅓ . . . Has advanced rapidly through system . . . Detroit's first pick in 1989 draft, out of Santa Clara University . . . Born Oct. 29, 1967, in Santa Clara, Cal. . . . Topped Lakeland (A) in victories with 13-5 record in 1990.

SCOTT ALDRED 23 6-4 195　　　　**Bats L Throws L**
Appears set to join Tigers' rotation . . . Finished with 2-4 record
and 5.18 ERA in 11 starts for Tigers, but showed improvement
in final outings . . . Was 8-8 with a 3.92 ERA for Toledo
(AAA) . . . Can get strikeouts when he needs them . . . Born June
12, 1968, in Flint, Mich. . . . Tigers' 16th selection in 1988 draft.

RICO BROGNA 21 6-2 190　　　　**Bats L Throws L**
Hailed by manager Sparky Anderson as Tigers' first baseman of
future . . . Showed he wasn't quite ready for Triple-A in 1991 by
struggling to .220 average in 41 games for Toledo . . . Batted .273
with 13 homers and 51 RBI for London (AA) . . . Detroit's first-
round pick in 1988 . . . Born April 18, 1970, in Turner Falls,
Mass. . . . Heavily recruited as a tight end by Clemson.

MANAGER SPARKY ANDERSON: Deserves recognition as

one of game's great managers . . . Runnerup to
Minnesota's Tom Kelly as AL Manager of the
Year after doing another superlative job with
84-78 overachieving Tigers . . . First manager
to win World Series in both leagues . . . Named
Manager of the Year in both leagues . . . Led
world champion 1984 Tigers to club-record 104
victories . . . Has won 18 League Champion-
ship Series games . . . First major-league manager to win 700
games with two different teams . . . Boasts 20-year record of
1,921-1,524 . . . Record with Detroit stands at 1,058-938 . . . Became Tigers' manager June 12, 1979 . . . Big Red Machine won
five NL West titles, four pennants and two World Series under
him . . . Born Feb. 22, 1934, in Bridgewater, S.D. . . . Played in
minors for six seasons as infielder . . . Played for Philadelphia in
1959, his lone year as major leaguer . . . Only Dodgers' Tommy
Lasorda boasts longer continuous service among major-league
managers.

ALL-TIME TIGER SEASON RECORDS

BATTING: Ty Cobb, .420, 1911
HRs: Hank Greenberg, 58, 1938
RBI: Hank Greenberg, 183, 1937
STEALS: Ty Cobb, 96, 1915
WINS: Denny McLain, 31, 1968
STRIKEOUTS: Mickey Lolich, 308, 1971

MILWAUKEE BREWERS

TEAM DIRECTORY: Pres./CEO: Allan (Bud) Selig; Sr. VP-Baseball Oper.: Sal Bando; Sr. VP: Harry Dalton; Asst. VP-Baseball Oper.: Bruce Manno; Dir. Player Dev.: Fred Stanley; Dir. Communications: Laurel Prieb; Dir. Media Rel.: Tom Skibosh; Dir. Publications: Mario Ziino; Trav. Sec.: Jimmy Bank; Mgr.: Phil Garner. Home: Milwaukee County Stadium (53,192). Field distances: 315, l.f. line; 362, l.f.; 392, l.c.; 402, c.f.; 392, r.c.; 362, r.f.; 315, r.f. line. Spring training: Chandler, Ariz.

SCOUTING REPORT

HITTING: Offense isn't a problem for the Brewers, who hit .271 and generated 799 runs in 1991. Paul Molitor continues as Milwaukee's ignitor and he shows no sign of slowing down at age 35. He topped the majors with 216 hits and 133 runs and paced the AL with 13 triples in 1991. Robin Yount, 36, also remains productive, although he can undoubtedly improve on last year's sub-standard performance (.260, 10, 77). Yount is only 122 hits shy of the coveted 3,000 plateau.

Greg Vaughn has established himself as one of the game's young stars. He paced the Brewers with 27 home runs and 98 RBI and is an explosive player. He knocked in five or more runs five times. A full season from Gary Sheffield (.194, 2, 22) could make a difference in 1992. He played in only 50 games last season and must show he is fully recovered from surgery last August to repair an impingement in his left shoulder. Free agent defector Willie Randolph could be missed in the No. 2 hole, but that loss is eased by the re-signing of Jim Gantner.

PITCHING: Milwaukee re-signed Bill Wegman as a free agent, hoping he can do again for them what he did last year. In 1991, Wegman rebounded from two injury-filled seasons to set a career high in victories with a 15-7 record while posting a career-low 2.84 ERA. The Brewers also look to Jaime Navarro (15-12, 3.92) and Chris Bosio (14-10, 3.25) to be winning pitchers. Longtime closer Dan Plesac (2-7, 4.29, 8 Sv) no longer throws hard enough to retain that role, so he enters his first full season as a starter.

Doug Henry (2-1, 1.00) succeeded Plesac as the closer and excelled late last season. Henry ran off 15 saves in 16 opportunities and was overpowering much of the time, allowing only three of 17 inherited runners to score after his mid-July recall from the

Paul Molitor's 216 hits and 133 runs topped majors.

minors. However, Henry's supporting cast in the bullpen is extremely suspect.

FIELDING: This had been an area of great concern for Milwaukee, until last season. The Brewers committed only 118 errors, the second-fewest amount in franchise history. This marked a dramatic improvement, since the Brewers had been guilty of the most errors in the AL each of the previous two seasons.

OUTLOOK: No team in the majors was hotter than Milwaukee in the final two months of last season. The sizzling Brewers went 40-19 down the stretch to close with an 83-79 record, their first winning effort since 1988. Still, owner Bud Selig decided it was time to start over and will do that with new GM Sal Bando and Bando's choice as the new manager, inexperienced Phil Garner. The changes might help long term, but don't look for immediate results.

MILWAUKEE BREWERS 1992 ROSTER

MANAGER Phil Garner
Coaches—Bill Castro, Duffy Dyer, Mike Easler, Tim Foli, Don Rowe

PITCHERS

No.	Name	1991 Club	W-L	IP	SO	ERA	B-T	Ht.	Wt.	Born
—	Austin, James	Denver	6-3	44	37	2.45	R-R	6-2	200	12/7/63 Farmville, VA
		Milwaukee	0-0	9	3	8.31				
29	Bosio, Chris	Milwaukee	14-10	205	117	3.25	R-R	6-3	225	4/3/63 Carmichael, CA
16	Brown, Kevin	Denver	4-3	62	31	4.67	L-L	6-1	185	3/5/66 Oroville, CA
		Milwaukee	2-4	64	30	5.51				
21	Eldred, Cal	Denver	13-9	185	168	3.75	R-R	6-4	215	11/24/67 Cedar Rapids, IA
		Milwaukee	2-0	16	10	4.50				
58	Elvira, Narciso	Denver	0-4	80	52	5.96	L-L	5-10	160	10/29/67 Mexico
—	Fetters, Mike	Edmonton	2-7	61	43	4.87	R-R	6-4	212	12/19/64 Van Nuys, CA
		California	2-5	45	24	4.84				
59	George, Chris	Denver	4-5	85	65	2.33	R-R	6-2	200	9/24/66 Pittsburgh, PA
		Milwaukee	0-0	6	2	3.00				
56	Green, Otis	Stockton	9-1	75	106	1.92	L-L	6-2	192	3/11/64 Miami, FL
		El Paso	3-3	51	40	3.18				
28	Henry, Doug	Denver	3-2	58	47	2.18	R-R	6-4	185	12/10/63 Sacramento, CA
		Milwaukee	2-1	36	28	1.00				
49	Higuera, Ted	Denver	1-0	9	6	2.08	S-L	5-10	178	11/9/58 Mexico
		Milwaukee	3-2	36	33	4.46				
40	Holmes, Darren	Denver	9-5	138	103	4.25	S-R	5-11	175	3/12/66 Anchorville, MI
		Milwaukee	2-1	13	10	5.68				
62	Kiefer, Mark	El Paso	7-1	76	72	3.33	R-R	6-4	175	11/13/68 Orange, CA
		Denver	9-5	101	68	4.62				
34	Lee, Mark	Milwaukee	2-5	68	43	3.66	L-L	6-3	200	7/20/64 Williston, ND
48	Machado, Julio	Milwaukee	3-3	89	98	3.45	R-R	5-9	165	12/1/65 Venezuela
43	Miranda, Angel	El Paso	4-2	74	86	2.54	L-L	6-1	160	11/9/69 Puerto Rico
		Denver	0-1	12	14	6.17				
31	Navarro, Jaime	Milwaukee	15-12	234	114	3.92	R-R	6-4	210	3/27/67 Puerto Rico
41	Nunez, Edwin	Beloit	0-1	9	9	4.00	R-R	6-5	240	5/27/63 Puerto Rico
		Milwaukee	2-1	25	24	6.04				
47	Orosco, Jesse	Cleveland	2-0	46	36	3.74	R-L	6-2	185	4/21/57 Santa Barbara, CA
37	Plesac, Dan	Milwaukee	2-7	92	61	4.29	L-L	6-5	215	2/4/62 Gary, IN
33	Robinson, Ron	Milwaukee	0-1	4	0	6.23	R-R	6-4	235	3/24/62 Woodlake, CA
—	Ruffin, Bruce	Scranton	4-5	75	50	4.66	R-L	6-2	209	10/4/63 Lubbock, TX
		Philadelphia	4-7	119	85	3.78				
46	Wegman, Bill	Beloit	0-2	11	12	1.64	R-R	6-5	220	12/19/62 Cincinnati, OH
		Denver	0-0	7	1	2.57				
		Milwaukee	15-7	193	89	2.84				

CATCHERS

No.	Name	1991 Club	H	HR	RBI	Pct.	B-T	Ht.	Wt.	Born
27	Kmak, Joe	Denver	70	1	33	.238	R-R	6-0	185	5/3/63 Napa, CA
13	Nilsson, Dave	El Paso	104	5	57	.418	S-R	6-3	185	12/14/69 Australia
		Denver	22	1	14	.232				
5	Surhoff, B.J.	Milwaukee	146	5	68	.289	L-R	6-1	200	8/4/64 Bronx, NY

INFIELDERS

No.	Name	1991 Club	H	HR	RBI	Pct.	B-T	Ht.	Wt.	Born
17	Gantner, Jim	Milwaukee	149	2	47	.283	L-R	5-11	175	1/5/54 Eden, WI
57	Jaha, John	El Paso	167	30	134	.344	R-R	6-1	195	5/27/66 Portland, OR
67	Listach, Pat	El Paso	47	0	13	.253	R-R	5-9	170	9/12/67 Natchitoches, LA
		Denver	72	1	31	.252				
26	McIntosh, Tim	Denver	135	18	91	.292	R-R	5-11	195	3/21/65 Minneapolis, MN
		Milwaukee	4	1	1	.364				
4	Molitor, Paul	Milwaukee	216	17	75	.325	R-R	6-0	185	8/22/56 St. Paul, MN
11	Sheffield, Gary	Milwaukee	34	2	22	.194	R-R	5-11	190	11/18/68 Tampa, FL
9	Spiers, Bill	Milwaukee	117	8	54	.283	L-R	6-2	190	6/5/66 Orangeburg, SC
0	Stubbs, Franklin	Milwaukee	77	11	38	.213	L-L	6-2	209	10/21/60 Laurinburg, NC
2	Suero, William	Syracuse	78	1	28	.198	R-R	5-9	175	11/7/66 Dominican Republic
		Denver	27	0	15	.386				
51	Tatum, Jim	El Paso	158	18	128	.320	R-R	6-2	200	10/9/67 San Diego, CA

OUTFIELDERS

No.	Name	1991 Club	H	HR	RBI	Pct.	B-T	Ht.	Wt.	Born
8	Bichette, Dante	Milwaukee	106	15	59	.238	R-R	6-3	225	11/18/63 W. Palm Beach, FL
24	Hamilton, Darryl	Milwaukee	126	1	57	.311	L-R	6-1	180	12/3/64 Baton Rouge, LA
18	Olander, Jim	Denver	162	9	78	.325	R-R	6-1	185	2/21/63 Tucson, AZ
		Milwaukee	0	0	0	.000				
23	Vaughn, Greg	Milwaukee	132	27	98	.244	R-R	6-0	193	7/3/65 Sacramento, CA
19	Yount, Robin	Milwaukee	131	10	77	.260	R-R	6-0	180	9/16/55 Danville, IL

BREWER PROFILES

PAUL MOLITOR 35 6-0 185   **Bats R Throws R**

Injury-prone veteran stayed healthy in 1991 with dazzling results . . . Topped the majors with 216 hits and 133 runs . . . Paced AL with 13 triples . . . Recorded 2,000th career hit July 30 vs. Kansas City . . . Belted six leadoff home runs to tie Tommy Harper's club record, set in 1970, and boosted career total to 33, second all-time to Rickey Henderson . . . Hit for cycle May 15 against Minnesota's Kevin Tapani . . . Only three other Brewers have hit for the cycle . . . Undoubtedly the catalyst for Brewers' offense . . . His 39-game hitting streak in 1987 was AL's longest since Joe DiMaggio's record 56-gamer in 1941 . . . Born Aug. 22, 1956, in St. Paul, Minn. . . . Selected in first round of 1977 draft . . . Earned $3,233,333 in 1991.

Year	Club	Pos.	G	AB	R	H	2B	3B	HR	RBI	SB	Avg.
1978	Milwaukee	2B-SS-3B	125	521	73	142	26	4	6	45	30	.273
1979	Milwaukee	2B-SS	140	584	88	188	27	16	9	62	33	.322
1980	Milwaukee	2B-SS-3B	111	450	81	137	29	2	9	37	34	.304
1981	Milwaukee	OF	64	251	45	67	11	0	2	19	10	.267
1982	Milwaukee	3B-SS	160	666	136	201	26	8	19	71	41	.302
1983	Milwaukee	3B	152	608	95	164	28	6	15	47	41	.269
1984	Milwaukee	3B	13	46	3	10	1	0	0	6	1	.217
1985	Milwaukee	3B	140	576	93	171	28	3	10	48	21	.297
1986	Milwaukee	3B-OF	105	437	62	123	24	6	9	55	20	.281
1987	Milwaukee	3B-2B	118	465	114	164	41	5	16	75	45	.353
1988	Milwaukee	3B-2B	154	609	115	190	34	6	13	60	41	.312
1989	Milwaukee	3B-2B	155	615	84	194	35	4	11	56	27	.315
1990	Milwaukee	2B-1B-3B	103	418	64	119	27	6	12	45	18	.285
1991	Milwaukee	1B	158	665	133	216	32	13	17	75	19	.325
	Totals		1698	6911	1186	2086	369	79	148	701	381	.302

GREG VAUGHN 26 6-0 193   **Bats R Throws R**

Rising star topped Brewers last season with 27 home runs and 98 RBI . . . Knocked in five or more runs five times . . . No Brewer had ever done that more than twice in a season . . . Left fielder started quickly, crashing five home runs in April . . . Sizzled in June with seven homers and 28 RBI . . . Worst month was July, when he batted just .181 with three homers and nine RBI . . . Continues to bash Athletics, his favorite team as a youngster. He is batting .337 with 12 homers and 34 RBI in 25 career games against them...Born July 3, 1965, in Sacramento, Cal....First-round pick in 1986 draft, out of the University of Miami...Received business degree from Miami...A real bargain at a $190,000 salary in 1991.

Year	Club	Pos.	G	AB	R	H	2B	3B	HR	RBI	SB	Avg.
1989	Milwaukee	OF	38	113	18	30	3	0	5	23	4	.265
1990	Milwaukee	OF	120	382	51	84	26	2	17	61	7	.220
1991	Milwaukee	OF	145	542	81	132	24	5	27	98	2	.244
	Totals		303	1037	150	246	53	7	49	182	13	.237

ROBIN YOUNT 36 6-0 180   Bats R Throws R

Distinguished veteran should achieve cherished milestone this season with 3,000th hit as he begins year with 2,878...Stroked 2,000th career single Sept. 24 against Yankees' Eric Plunk, becoming only 37th player in history to reach that plateau...Recorded 800th multi-hit game Aug. 27 at Seattle...Slugged three game-winning home runs in extra innings... Brewers can't win without his offense...Still a quality center fielder...Was disabled in mid-July with kidneystones...Marked first stint on DL since 1978...AL MVP 1989...Born Sept. 16, 1955, in Danville, Ill....Selected in first round of 1973 draft... Switched from shortstop to center field in 1985 after shoulder surgery...Earned $3.2 million in 1991.

Year	Club	Pos.	G	AB	R	H	2B	3B	HR	RBI	SB	Avg.
1974	Milwaukee	SS	107	344	48	86	14	5	3	26	7	.250
1975	Milwaukee	SS	147	558	67	149	28	2	8	52	12	.267
1976	Milwaukee	SS-OF	161	638	59	161	19	3	2	54	16	.252
1977	Milwaukee	SS	154	605	66	174	34	4	4	49	16	.288
1978	Milwaukee	SS	127	502	66	147	23	9	9	71	16	.293
1979	Milwaukee	SS	149	577	72	154	26	5	8	51	11	.267
1980	Milwaukee	SS	143	611	121	179	49	10	23	87	20	.293
1981	Milwaukee	SS	96	377	50	103	15	5	10	49	4	.273
1982	Milwaukee	SS	156	635	129	210	46	12	29	114	14	.331
1983	Milwaukee	SS	149	578	102	178	42	10	17	80	12	.308
1984	Milwaukee	SS	160	624	105	186	27	7	16	80	14	.298
1985	Milwaukee	OF-1B	122	466	76	129	26	3	15	68	10	.277
1986	Milwaukee	OF-1B	140	522	82	163	31	7	9	46	14	.312
1987	Milwaukee	OF	158	635	99	198	25	9	21	103	19	.312
1988	Milwaukee	OF	162	621	92	190	38	11	13	91	22	.306
1989	Milwaukee	OF	160	614	101	195	38	9	21	103	19	.318
1990	Milwaukee	OF	158	587	98	145	17	5	17	77	15	.247
1991	Milwaukee	OF	130	503	66	131	20	4	10	77	6	.260
	Totals		2579	9997	1499	2878	518	120	235	1278	247	.288

A Brewer star was born in young Greg Vaughn.

GARY SHEFFIELD 23 5-11 190   Bats R Throws R

Youngster with vast potential may be entering pivotal year of career . . . Last season was virtually wiped out by injuries that held him to 50 games . . . Didn't perform well when he was in lineup . . . Didn't play after July 24 . . . Disabled from June 12-July 3 with a displaced extensor tendon in left wrist . . . Underwent surgery to repair impingement in left shoulder Aug. 23 . . . Even when he is healthy, there is question about whether he possesses desire to excel . . . Perceived as an angry young man . . . Clashed with Brewers' management more than once . . . Would probably benefit from a fresh start elsewhere . . . Born Nov. 18, 1968, in Tampa . . . Brewers' first-round choice in 1986 as sixth player picked overall . . . Salary was $400,000 in 1991.

Year	Club	Pos.	G	AB	R	H	2B	3B	HR	RBI	SB	Avg.
1988	Milwaukee	SS	24	80	12	19	1	0	4	12	3	.238
1989	Milwaukee	SS–3B	95	368	34	91	18	0	5	32	10	.247
1990	Milwaukee	3B	125	487	67	143	30	1	10	67	25	.294
1991	Milwaukee	3B	50	175	25	34	12	2	2	22	5	.194
	Totals		294	1110	138	287	61	3	21	133	43	.259

BILL WEGMAN 29 6-5 220   Bats R Throws R

Was rewarded with four-year, $9.5-million contract after rebounding from two injury-filled seasons to set career high in victories (15) while posting career-low ERA (2.84) in 1991 . . . Tied with Jaime Navarro for Milwaukee club lead in victories while ERA was best among Brewer starters . . . Worked more than 190 innings for fourth time . . . Missed much of 1990 season due to extensive elbow surgery . . . Was sidelined for extended period year before that after undergoing surgery to repair torn labrum . . . Made total of only 13 starts for Milwaukee in 1989 and 1990 . . . Born Dec. 19, 1962, in Cincinnati . . . Milwaukee's fifth-round selection in 1981 draft . . . Earned $440,000 in 1991.

Year	Club	G	IP	W	L	Pct.	SO	BB	H	ERA
1985	Milwaukee	3	17⅔	2	0	1.000	6	3	17	3.57
1986	Milwaukee	35	198⅓	5	12	.294	82	43	217	5.13
1987	Milwaukee	34	225	12	11	.522	102	53	229	4.24
1988	Milwaukee	32	199	13	13	.500	84	50	207	4.12
1989	Milwaukee	11	51	2	6	.250	27	21	69	6.71
1990	Milwaukee	8	29⅔	2	2	.500	20	6	37	4.85
1991	Milwaukee	28	193⅓	15	7	.682	89	40	176	2.84
	Totals	151	914	51	51	.500	410	216	952	4.25

TEDDY HIGUERA 33 5-10 178   Bats S Throws L

Longtime ace appears to be at or near the end . . . Will try to resume pitching after surgery Aug. 23 to repair labrum and rotator cuff . . . Labrum was worked on arthroscopically but rotator had to be done surgically . . . Made only six starts last year, none after June 29 . . . Only highlight of season was brilliant performance in matchup that delighted Mexico. He opposed

Angels' Fernando Valenzuela and struck out 10 in six innings to defeat him . . . Brewers' all-time strikeout leader . . . Also set club single-season mark with 240 strikeouts in 1987 . . . Placed second in 1985 AL Rookie of the Year voting . . . Contract was purchased from Juarez of Mexican League, Sept. 13, 1983 . . . Born Nov. 9, 1958, in Los Mochis, Mexico . . . Earned $2,833,333 in 1991, the start of four-year, $13-million contract.

Year	Club	G	IP	W	L	Pct.	SO	BB	H	ERA
1985	Milwaukee	32	212⅓	15	8	.652	127	63	186	3.90
1986	Milwaukee	34	248⅓	20	11	.645	207	74	226	2.79
1987	Milwaukee	35	261⅔	18	10	.643	240	87	236	3.85
1988	Milwaukee	31	227⅓	16	9	.640	192	59	168	2.45
1989	Milwaukee	22	135⅓	9	6	.600	91	48	125	3.46
1990	Milwaukee	27	170	11	10	.524	129	50	167	3.76
1991	Milwaukee	7	36⅓	3	2	.600	33	10	37	4.46
	Totals	188	1291⅓	92	56	.622	1019	391	1145	3.37

JAIME NAVARRO 25 6-4 210   Bats R Throws R

Brewers look to him for another yeoman's effort . . . Tied with Minnesota's Jack Morris for third in AL with 10 complete games . . . First Brewer pitcher to go the distance that many times since Teddy Higuera had 14 complete games in 1987 . . . Ranked ninth in league with 234 innings . . . Established career highs in every category . . . Best month was May, when he won four of six decisions and posted 2.59 ERA . . . Enjoyed four-game winning streak from Aug. 7-23 . . . Born March 27, 1967, in Bayamon, P.R. . . . Third-round pick in 1987 draft, out of Miami-Dade Center College . . . Father Julio pitched in majors from 1962-70 . . . Earned $190,000 in 1991.

Year	Club	G	IP	W	L	Pct.	SO	BB	H	ERA
1989	Milwaukee	19	109⅔	7	8	.467	56	32	119	3.12
1990	Milwaukee	32	149⅓	8	7	.533	75	41	176	4.46
1991	Milwaukee	34	234	15	12	.556	114	73	237	3.92
	Totals	85	493	30	27	.526	245	146	532	3.91

CHRIS BOSIO 28 6-3 225   Bats R Throws R

Will try to build on big second half . . . Won eight of final 11 decisions after struggling to 6-7 record at the All-Star break . . . Strong finish was highlighted by his only shutout of season, 2-0 at New York Sept. 17 . . . Fired career-best two-hitter in that game despite striking out only one batter . . . Surpassed 200 innings for second time in career . . . Went 3-2 in April with 2.00 ERA to boost career record for first month to 16-4 with 1.94 ERA . . . Rebounded from injury-filled 1990 that included two knee operations . . . Born April 3, 1963, in Carmichael, Cal. . . . Selected in second round of January 1982 draft . . . Earned $875,000 in 1991.

Year	Club	G	IP	W	L	Pct.	SO	BB	H	ERA
1986	Milwaukee	10	34⅔	0	4	.000	29	13	41	7.01
1987	Milwaukee	46	170	11	8	.579	150	50	187	5.24
1988	Milwaukee	38	182	7	15	.318	84	38	190	3.36
1989	Milwaukee	33	234⅔	15	10	.600	173	48	225	2.95
1990	Milwaukee	20	132⅔	4	9	.308	76	38	131	4.00
1991	Milwaukee	32	204⅔	14	10	.583	117	58	187	3.25
	Totals	179	958⅔	51	56	.477	629	245	961	3.79

DAN PLESAC 30 6-5 215   Bats L Throws L

Longtime relief ace faces first full season as starter . . . No longer has hard stuff to fill closer's role . . . Will have to refine other pitches to make up for mediocre fastball . . . Although he began last year in pen, he wasn't used in save situation until May 15 . . . Didn't record second save until June 15 . . . After 311 big-league relief appearances, he made debut as starter Aug. 10 in Texas and won, 5-2 . . . Brewers' all-time saves leader with 132 . . . Surpassed Rollie Fingers for that honor when he registered 98th save, Sept. 16, 1989 . . . Born Feb. 4, 1962, in Gary, Ind. . . . First-round choice in 1983 draft . . . Earned $2,266,667 in 1991.

Year	Club	G	IP	W	L	Pct.	SO	BB	H	ERA
1986	Milwaukee	51	91	10	7	.588	75	29	81	2.97
1987	Milwaukee	57	79⅓	5	6	.455	89	23	63	2.61
1988	Milwaukee	50	52⅓	1	2	.333	52	12	46	2.41
1989	Milwaukee	52	61⅓	3	4	.429	52	17	47	2.35
1990	Milwaukee	66	69	3	7	.300	65	31	67	4.43
1991	Milwaukee	45	92⅓	2	7	.222	61	39	92	4.29
	Totals	321	445⅓	24	33	.421	394	151	396	3.25

DOUG HENRY 28 6-4 185   Bats R Throws R

Has chance to be superior closer if his work late last season is any indication . . . Rattled off 15 saves in 16 opportunities . . . Recorded first big-league save Aug. 10 at Texas . . . Allowed only three of 17 inherited runners to score following July 14 recall from Denver . . . Fanned 28 batters in 36 innings and was overpowering much of the time . . . Did walk 14 and must concentrate on reducing that total . . . Extremely assertive pitcher, he is not afraid to challenge hitters... Went 3-2 with 2.18 ERA and 14 saves for Denver (AAA) prior to promotion... Lost virtually all of 1989 season to elbow injury that required surgery... Born Dec. 10, 1963, in Sacramento, Cal.... Taken in eighth round of 1985 draft, out of Arizona State... Earned $100,000 in 1991.

Year	Club	G	IP	W	L	Pct.	SO	BB	H	ERA
1991	Milwaukee	32	36	2	1	.667	28	14	16	1.00

TOP PROSPECTS

CAL ELDRED 24 6-4 215   Bats R Throws R
First-round selection in 1989 draft appears ready for Brewers' rotation... Topped American Association with 168 strikeouts for Denver (AAA), although he lost velocity late in season... After 3-8 start, he rolled to 10-1 record with 2.35 ERA in last 13 starts... Defeated Yankees, 5-4, in his first major-league start Sept. 24, becoming first Brewer starter to win debut since Rickey Keeton in 1980... Born Nov. 24, 1967, in Cedar Rapids, Iowa.

DAVID NILSSON 22 6-3 185   Bats S Throws R
Catcher is on course to become third Australian to reach majors, joining Joe Quinn (1884-1901) and Craig Shipley (1986-87)... Born Dec. 14, 1969, in Brisbane, Queensland, Australia... Spent most of last season with El Paso (AA), where he hit .418, before promotion to Denver (AAA)... His .366 batting average overall was the highest by a minor-league player last year... Expected to be ready for spring training after surgery in late August for a loose left shoulder socket.

CHRIS GEORGE 25 6-2 200   Bats R Throws R
Could be a factor in bullpen this year... Owns 45 career saves in minors... Appears best-suited as set-up man... Served in that capacity for Doug Henry with Denver (AAA) before Henry's promotion in mid-July, then he capably handled closer role for Zephyrs... Went 4-5 with 2.33 ERA and four saves... Born Sept. 24, 1966, in Pittsburgh... Seventh-round choice in 1988 draft.

MARK KIEFER 23 6-4 175   Bats R Throws R
Drew attention to abilities by being the MVP in Triple-A Alliance Championship Series against Columbus, Yankees' affiliate... Split season between El Paso (AA) and Denver... Compiled

16-6 record with 4.07 ERA overall . . . Born Nov. 13, 1968, in Orange, Cal. . . . Brewers' 21st-round pick in 1987 draft . . . Brother Steve was a former Brewer infielder.

MANAGER PHIL GARNER: Faces season of scrutiny after being given a three-year contract to replace Tom Trebelhorn in Brewers' dugout, despite lack of any managerial experience . . . Served for three seasons as Astros' coach after retirement as player in 1988 . . . New Brewer GM Sal Bando said he based decision on this ex-Oakland teammate's potential . . . Should succeed if he brings qualities to managing that he once took to field . . . Vows to be aggressive, take-charge manager . . . Earned nickname "Scrap Iron" for toughness he displayed as member of Pirates in late 1970's . . . Enjoyed 14-year major-league career with Oakland, Pittsburgh, Houston, Los Angeles and San Francisco . . . Recognized as All-Star in 1976, 1980 and 1981 . . . Excelled in 1979 postseason for Pittsburgh, batting .417 in playoffs and tying seven-game World Series record with .500 average . . . Born April 30, 1949, in Jefferson City, Tenn. . . . Was an All-American at University of Tennessee.

ALL-TIME BREWER SEASON RECORDS

BATTING: Paul Molitor, .353, 1987
HRs: Gorman Thomas, 45, 1979
RBI: Cecil Cooper, 126, 1983
STEALS: Paul Molitor, 45, 1987
WINS: Mike Caldwell, 22, 1978
STRIKEOUTS: Ted Higuera, 240, 1987

NEW YORK YANKEES

TEAM DIRECTORY: Managing General Partner: Robert Neder-lander; Principal Owner: George Steinbrenner III; VP/GM: Gene Michael; VP-Player Dev. and Scouting: Brian Sabean; Dir. Scouting: Bill Livesey; Sr. VP: Arthur Richman; Dir. Media Rel.: Jeff Idelson; Trav. Sec.: David Szen; Mgr.: Bucky Showalter. Home: Yankee Stadium (57,545). Field distances: 312, l.f. line; 379, l.f.; 411, l.c.; 410, c.f.; 385, r.c.; 310, r.f. line. Spring training: Fort Lauderdale, Fla.

SCOUTING REPORT

HITTING: Signing of KC free agent Danny Tartabull (.316, 31, 100) brings mighty bat to Yankee Stadium. His .593 slugging percentage topped the majors. Much still depends on whether Don Mattingly (.288, 9, 68) can overcome chronic back problems and relocate the form that enabled him to bat above .300 for six con-secutive seasons, from 1984-90, and knock in more than 100 runs five times in that span.

Roberto Kelly (.267, 20, 69) may be ready to become an impact player. He was one of only three American Leaguers last season

Can Yankee slipper Don Mattingly come back strong?

to produce at least 20 home runs and steal at least 20 bases—Kelly swiped a team-leading 32—and accomplished that despite missing six weeks with a sprained wrist. Matt Nokes (.268, 24, 77), Mel Hall (.285, 19, 80) and Kevin Maas (.220, 23, 63) provide power from the left side, critical at Yankee Stadium.

The Yankees spent much of the offseason shopping Steve Sax to make room for young Pat Kelly (.242, 3, 23) at second base. And they signed A's free agent second baseman-shortstop Mike Gallego (.247, 12, 49). In trading Sax to the White Sox in the Melido Perez deal, the Yankees gave up the man who led the club last year in batting average (.304), hits (198), multi-hit games (58), doubles (38) and runs (85).

PITCHING: Poor starting pitching has marked the decline of the Yankees and the rotation will again be a cause of great concern. Last year, Yankee starters were 45-68 with a 5.07 ERA. They were last in the AL with only three complete games.

Can 1991 surprise Scott Sanderson (16-10, 3.81) do for the Yankees what he did for them last year, when he accounted for 22.5 percent of the team's victory total? Melido Perez (8-7, 3.12, 1 Sv with the White Sox) will be a key figure, as will brother Pascual (12-4, 3.18), who the Yankees hope has fully recovered from rotator cuff surgery performed in August 1990. The Yankees are also counting on veteran Tim Leary (4-10, 6.49) to regain the movement in his split-finger fastball, another iffy proposition.

Steve Farr (5-5, 2.19, 23 Sv in 29 chances) is back for his second full season as the team's closer, but Steve Howe (3-1, 1.68, 3 Sv) went bust again last winter. Durable, versatile Greg Cadaret (8-6, 3.62) is a valuable member of the staff.

FIELDING: Mattingly's back problems have not lessened his defensive brilliance. He was honored with his sixth Gold Glove in seven years. In an attempt to solve their third third-base problem, the Yankees, who finished in a tie for next to last in the AL with a .979 fielding mark, acquired Charlie Hayes from Philadelphia. Catcher Nokes threw out only 24 percent (31 of 129) of would-be base-stealers last season.

OUTLOOK: The Yankees have not finished higher than fourth in the AL East since 1986 and wound up fifth last year with a 71-91 record that was the fourth-worst in the majors. Out of the front-office chaos in the offseason, there were finally the free-agent signings of Tartabull and Gallego. But new manager Buck Showalter, given a one-year contract, better not make plans for '93.

NEW YORK YANKEES 1992 ROSTER

MANAGER Buck Showalter
Coaches—Clete Boyer, Tony Cloninger, Mark Connor, Frank Howard,
Russ Meyer, Ed Napoleon

PITCHERS

No.	Name	1991 Club	W-L	IP	SO	ERA	B-T	Ht.	Wt.	Born
25	Cadaret, Greg	New York (AL)	8-6	122	105	3.62	L-L	6-3	214	2/27/62 Detroit, MI
26	Farr, Steve	New York (AL)	5-5	70	60	2.19	R-R	5-11	200	12/12/56 Cheverly, MD
63	Gardella, Mike	Albany	4-5	78	64	3.82	L-L	5-10	195	1/18/67 Bronx, NY
35	Guetterman, Lee	New York (AL)	3-4	88	35	3.68	L-L	6-8	230	11/22/58 Chattanooga, TN
42	Habyan, John	New York (AL)	4-2	90	70	2.30	R-R	6-2	191	1/29/64 Bayshore, NY
57	Howe, Steve	Columbus	2-1	18	13	0.00	L-L	5-11	198	3/10/58 Pontiac, MI
		New York (AL)	3-1	48	34	1.68				
43	Johnson, Jeff	Columbus	4-0	62	40	2.61	R-L	6-3	206	8/4/66 Durham, NC
		New York (AL)	6-11	127	62	5.95				
33	Kamieniecki, Scott	Columbus	6-3	76	58	2.36	R-R	6-0	197	4/19/64 Mt. Clemens, MI
		New York (AL)	4-4	55	34	3.90				
54	Leary, Tim	New York (AL)	4-10	121	83	6.49	R-R	6-3	218	12/23/58 Santa Monica, CA
—	Martel, Ed	Albany	13-6	163	141	2.81	R-R	6-1	190	3/2/69 Mt. Clemens, MI
45	Mills, Alan	Columbus	7-5	114	77	4.43	R-R	6-1	190	10/18/66 Lakeland, FL
		New York (AL)	1-1	16	11	4.41				
—	Monteleone, Rich	Columbus	1-3	47	51	2.12	R-R	6-2	236	3/22/63 Tampa, FL
		New York (AL)	3-1	47	34	3.64				
—	Munoz, Roberto	Ft. Lauderdale	5-8	108	53	2.33	R-R	6-7	210	3/3/68 Puerto Rico
		Columbus	0-1	3	2	24.00				
—	Perez, Melido	Chicago (AL)	8-7	136	128	3.12	R-R	6-4	185	2/15/66 Dominican Republic
34	Perez, Pascual	New York (AL)	2-4	74	41	3.18	R-R	6-3	183	5/17/57 Dominican Republic
21	Sanderson, Scott	New York (AL)	16-10	208	130	3.81	R-R	6-5	200	7/22/56 Dearborn, MI
59	Smith, Willie	Albany	7-7	108	104	4.15	R-R	6-6	240	8/27/67 Savannah, GA
—	Springer, Russ	Ft. Lauderdale	5-9	152	138	3.49	R-R	6-4	195	11/7/68 Alexandria, LA
		Albany	1-0	15	16	1.80				
—	Stanford, Larry	Albany	2-3	62	61	1.89	R-R	6-3	205	9/24/67 Manchester, CT
41	Taylor, Wade	Columbus	4-1	61	36	3.54	R-R	6-1	193	10/19/65 Mobile, AL
		New York (AL)	7-12	116	72	6.27				

CATCHERS

No.	Name	1991 Club	H	HR	RBI	Pct.	B-T	Ht.	Wt.	Born
53	Ausmus, Brad	Prince William	70	2	30	.304	R-R	5-11	185	4/14/69 New Haven, CT
		Albany	61	1	29	.266				
12	Leyritz, Jim	Columbus	72	11	48	.267	R-R	6-0	190	12/27/63 Lakewood, OH
		New York (AL)	14	0	4	.182				
38	Nokes, Matt	New York (AL)	122	24	77	.268	L-R	6-1	191	10/31/63 San Diego, CA
—	Ramos, John	Columbus	116	10	63	.308	R-R	6-0	190	8/6/65 Tampa, FL
		New York (AL)	8	0	3	.308				

INFIELDERS

No.	Name	1991 Club	H	HR	RBI	Pct.	B-T	Ht.	Wt.	Born
20	Espinoza, Alvaro	New York (AL)	123	5	33	.256	R-R	6-0	190	2/19/62 Venezuela
—	Gallego, Mike	Oakland	119	12	49	.247	R-R	5-8	160	10/31/60 Whittier, CA
—	Hayes, Charlie	Philadelphia	106	12	53	.230	R-R	6-0	205	5/29/65 Hattiesburg, MS
14	Kelly, Pat	Columbus	39	5	19	.336	R-R	6-0	180	10/14/67 Philadelphia, PA
		New York (AL)	72	3	23	.242				
24	Maas, Kevin	New York (AL)	110	23	63	.220	L-L	6-3	206	1/20/65 Castro Valley, CA
23	Mattingly, Don	New York (AL)	169	9	68	.288	L-L	6-0	193	4/20/61 Evansville, IN
—	Silvestri, Dave	Albany	134	19	83	.262	R-R	6-0	180	9/29/67 St. Louis, MO
—	Snow, J.T.	Albany	133	13	76	.279	S-L	6-2	202	2/26/68 Long Beach, CA
18	Velarde, Randy	New York (AL)	45	1	15	.245	R-R	6-0	190	11/24/62 Midland, TX

OUTFIELDERS

No.	Name	1991 Club	H	HR	RBI	Pct.	B-T	Ht.	Wt.	Born
29	Barfield, Jesse	New York (AL)	64	17	48	.225	R-R	6-1	201	10/29/59 Joliet, IL
27	Hall, Mel	New York (AL)	140	19	80	.285	L-L	6-1	218	9/16/60 Lyons, NY
36	Humphreys, Mike	Columbus	117	9	53	.283	R-R	6-0	185	4/10/67 Dallas, TX
		New York (AL)	8	0	3	.200				
39	Kelly, Roberto	New York (AL)	130	20	69	.267	R-R	6-2	192	10/1/64 Panama
31	Meulens, Hensley	New York (AL)	64	6	29	.222	R-R	6-3	212	6/23/67 Curacao
4	Tartabull, Danny	Kansas City	153	31	100	.316	R-R	6-1	210	10/30/62 Miami, FL
51	Williams, Bernie	Columbus	90	8	37	.294	S-R	6-2	196	9/13/68 Puerto Rico
		New York (AL)	76	3	34	.238				
62	Williams, Gerald	Albany	50	5	32	.286	R-R	6-2	190	8/10/66 New Orleans, LA
		Columbus	51	2	27	.258				

YANKEE PROFILES

DON MATTINGLY 30 6-0 193   Bats L Throws L

Failed to reach double figures in home runs for second straight year . . . Inoperable disc problems have forced more upright stance at expense of power . . . Has fallen far short of 100 RBI three of last four years after running off four straight seasons of 110 or more . . . Remains a Gold Glove first baseman . . . Named 10th captain in Yankees' history before last season . . . Had run-in with front office when he was benched Aug. 15 for refusing to cut his collar-length hair . . . Secured batting title in first full major-league season with .343 mark in 1984 . . . Outdid that in 1985 by gaining AL MVP honors with 145 RBI, most by a Yankee since Joe DiMaggio's 155 in 1948 . . . Established club records with 238 hits and 53 doubles in 1986 . . . Set major-league mark with six grand slams in 1987 and tied another standard by homering in eight consecutive games . . . Born April 20, 1961, in Evansville, Ind. . . . Selected in 19th round of 1979 draft . . . Earned $3.42 million in 1991.

Year	Club	Pos.	G	AB	R	H	2B	3B	HR	RBI	SB	Avg.
1982	New York (AL)	OF-1B	7	12	0	2	0	0	0	1	0	.167
1983	New York (AL)	OF-1B-2B	91	279	34	79	15	4	4	32	0	.283
1984	New York (AL)	1B-OF	153	603	91	207	44	2	23	110	1	.343
1985	New York (AL)	1B	159	652	107	211	48	3	35	145	2	.324
1986	New York (AL)	1B-3B	162	677	117	238	53	2	31	113	0	.352
1987	New York (AL)	1B	141	569	93	186	38	2	30	115	1	.327
1988	New York (AL)	1B-OF	144	599	94	186	37	0	18	88	1	.311
1989	New York (AL)	1B-OF	158	631	79	191	37	2	23	113	3	.303
1990	New York (AL)	1B-OF	102	394	40	101	16	0	5	42	1	.256
1991	New York (AL)	1B	152	587	64	169	35	0	9	68	2	.288
	Totals		1269	5003	719	1570	323	15	178	827	11	.314

DANNY TARTABULL 29 6-1 210   Bats R Throws R

Free agent KC outfielder became a Yankee in January with five-year, $25.5-million contract after remarkable offensive season . . . His .593 slugging percentage led the majors . . . His 31 homers almost doubled total of runnerup on Royals, Kirk Gibson (16) . . . His 100 RBI were 36 more than runnerup Brian McRae's total . . . Also led club in hitting (.316) and on-base percentage (.397) . . . Made first appearance in All-Star Game . . . Earned $2.25 million in 1991 . . . Reds' third-round pick in 1980 . . . Acquired from Mariners for Scott Bankhead and Steve Shields plus outfielder Mike Kingery prior to 1987 season . . . Son of former major-league outfielder Jose . . . Born Oct. 30, 1962, in Miami . . . A third-round pick of Reds in 1980 free agent draft.

Year	Club	Pos.	G	AB	R	H	2B	3B	HR	RBI	SB	Avg.
1984	Seattle.......	SS-2B	10	20	3	6	1	0	2	7	0	.300
1985	Seattle.......	SS-3B	19	61	8	20	7	1	1	7	1	.328
1986	Seattle.......	OF-2B-3B	137	511	76	138	25	6	25	96	4	.270
1987	Kansas City ...	OF	158	582	95	180	27	3	34	101	9	.309
1988	Kansas City ...	OF	146	507	80	139	38	4	26	102	8	.274
1989	Kansas City ...	OF	133	441	54	118	22	0	18	62	4	.268
1990	Kansas City ...	OF	88	313	41	84	19	0	15	60	1	.268
1991	Kansas City ...	OF	132	484	78	153	35	3	31	100	6	.316
	Totals		823	2919	435	838	174	16	152	535	33	.287

MATT NOKES 28 6-1 191   Bats L Throws L

Gives Yankees power at catcher's position . . . Tied Detroit's Mickey Tettleton for homer lead among major-league catchers with 24 . . . Total was highest by a Yankee catcher since Elston Howard's 28 in 1963 and most by a left-handed-hitting Yankee catcher since Yogi Berra's 30 in 1956 . . . Giants' 20th-round pick in 1981 . . . Threw out only 31 of 129 would-be base-stealers, a meager 24 percent . . . Needs work on calling a game . . . Gained AL's attention in 1987 by becoming first Tiger rookie to hit 30 homers since Rudy York in 1937 . . . Born Oct. 31, 1963, in San Diego . . . Acquired from Detroit for Clay Parker and Lance McCullers, June 4, 1990 . . . Earned $887,500 in 1991.

Year	Club	Pos.	G	AB	R	H	2B	3B	HR	RBI	SB	Avg.
1985	San Francisco	C	19	53	3	11	2	0	2	5	0	.208
1986	Detroit.......	C	7	24	2	8	1	0	1	2	0	.333
1987	Detroit.......	C-OF-3B	135	461	69	133	14	2	32	87	2	.289
1988	Detroit.......	C	122	382	53	96	18	0	16	53	0	.251
1989	Detroit.......	C	87	268	15	67	10	0	9	39	1	.250
1990	Det.-NY (AL)	C-OF	136	351	33	87	9	1	11	40	2	.248
1991	New York (AL)	C	135	456	52	122	20	0	24	77	3	.268
	Totals		641	1995	227	524	74	3	95	303	8	.263

MIKE GALLEGO 31 5-8 160   Bats R Throws R

A's free agent signed three-year, $5.1-million contract with Yanks in January . . . Slammed 12 homers, one more than his career total prior to 1991 . . . Also drove in a career-high 48 runs . . . Became a regular player for first time when shortstop Walt Weiss tore ligaments in his ankle . . . Also set career highs in games (159), at-bats (482), runs (67), hits (119), doubles (15)

and walks (67)... Played his usual sparkling defense at second base, where he committed only seven errors in 129 games... Made five more errors in 52 games at shortstop... Earned $565,000 in 1991... Born Oct. 31, 1960, in Whittier, Cal.... A's drafted him in second round in 1981.

Year	Club	Pos.	G	AB	R	H	2B	3B	HR	RBI	SB	Avg.
1985	Oakland	2B-SS-3B	76	77	13	16	5	1	1	9	1	.208
1986	Oakland	2B-3B-SS	20	37	2	10	2	0	0	4	0	.270
1987	Oakland	2B-3B-SS	72	124	18	31	6	0	2	14	0	.250
1988	Oakland	2B-SS-3B	129	277	38	58	8	0	2	20	2	.209
1989	Oakland	SS-2B-3B	133	357	45	90	14	2	3	30	7	.252
1990	Oakland	2B-SS-3B-OF	140	389	36	80	13	2	3	34	5	.206
1991	Oakland	2B-SS	159	482	67	119	15	4	12	49	6	.247
	Totals		729	1743	219	404	63	9	23	160	21	.232

MEL HALL 31 6-1 218   Bats L Throws L

Veteran comes off career year... Responded when playing time was threatened to set career highs with 19 home runs and team-leading 80 RBI... Showed ability to handle left-handers for first time... Batted above .300 against them after beginning year with .164 career average vs. southpaws... Started 123 games, 57 in right field, 56 in left, 10 as DH... Capable outfielder, although teams can run on his arm... Made big effort to change bad-boy image that hurt him in past, leading headline writers to describe him as "Mellow Mel"... Born Sept. 16, 1960, in Lyons, N.Y.... Acquired from Cleveland for Joel Skinner and Turner Ward prior to 1989 season... Salary was $1.1 million in 1991... Cubs' second-round pick in 1978.

Year	Club	Pos.	G	AB	R	H	2B	3B	HR	RBI	SB	Avg.
1981	Chicago (NL)	OF	10	11	1	1	0	0	1	2	0	.091
1982	Chicago (NL)	OF	24	80	6	21	3	2	0	4	0	.263
1983	Chicago (NL)	OF	112	410	60	116	23	5	17	56	6	.283
1984	Chicago (NL)	OF	48	150	25	42	11	3	4	22	2	.280
1984	Cleveland	OF	83	257	43	66	13	1	7	30	1	.257
1985	Cleveland	OF	23	66	7	21	6	0	0	12	0	.318
1986	Cleveland	OF	140	442	68	131	29	2	18	77	6	.296
1987	Cleveland	OF	142	485	57	136	21	1	18	76	5	.280
1988	Cleveland	OF	150	515	69	144	32	4	6	71	7	.280
1989	New York (AL)	OF	113	361	54	94	9	0	17	58	0	.260
1990	New York (AL)	OF	113	360	41	93	23	2	12	46	0	.258
1991	New York (AL)	OF	141	492	67	140	23	2	19	80	0	.285
	Totals		1099	3629	498	1005	193	22	119	534	27	.277

ROBERTO KELLY 27 6-2 192   Bats R Throws R

Has chance for stardom if he can stay healthy . . . Joined Jose Canseco and Joe Carter as only American Leaguers to record at least 20 home runs and 20 stolen bases . . . Set career highs in home runs (20) and RBI (69), despite being disabled from July 6-Aug. 13 with a sprained right wrist . . . Piled up 10 home runs and 33 RBI in 51 games after returning from injury . . . Accounted for seven of Yankees' last 18 home runs . . . Has power to opposite field, although he remains essentially a line-drive hitter . . . Led club with 32 stolen bases . . . Shifted to left field because rookie Bernie Williams replaced him in center during his injury . . . Has blossomed offensively in big leagues . . . Compiled only a .260 average in minors . . . Born Oct. 1, 1964, in Panama City, Panama . . . Signed as free agent by Yanks in February 1982 . . . Will break million-dollar barrier after $900,000 salary in 1991.

Year	Club	Pos.	G	AB	R	H	2B	3B	HR	RBI	SB	Avg.
1987	New York (AL)	OF	23	52	12	14	3	0	1	7	9	.269
1988	New York (AL)	OF	38	77	9	19	4	1	1	7	5	.247
1989	New York (AL)	OF	137	441	65	133	18	3	9	48	35	.302
1990	New York (AL)	OF	162	641	85	183	32	4	15	61	42	.285
1991	New York (AL)	OF	126	486	68	130	22	2	20	69	32	.267
	Totals		486	1697	239	479	79	10	46	192	123	.282

MELIDO PEREZ 26 6-4 185   Bats R Throws R

Joins older brother Pascual following deal that sent Steve Sax to White Sox . . . Horrible as starter, he went to middle relief and became a dominating force . . . Finished 8-7 with 3.12 ERA and one save after posting 1-4 record and 4.65 ERA in eight starts . . . Has devastating split-finger pitch and is especially tough when he's throwing his fastball for strikes . . . Had rain-shortened no-hitter vs. Yanks in 1990 stricken from record books . . . Born Feb. 15, 1966, in San Cristobal, D.R. . . . Royals signed him as free agent in July 1983 . . . Earned $343,000 in 1991.

Year	Club	G	IP	W	L	Pct.	SO	BB	H	ERA
1987	Kansas City	3	10⅓	1	1	.500	5	5	18	7.84
1988	Chicago (AL)	32	197	12	10	.545	138	72	186	3.79
1989	Chicago (AL)	31	183⅓	11	14	.440	141	90	187	5.01
1990	Chicago (AL)	35	197	13	14	.481	161	86	177	4.61
1991	Chicago (AL)	49	135⅔	8	7	.533	128	52	111	3.12
	Totals	150	723⅓	45	46	.495	573	305	679	4.26

SCOTT SANDERSON 35 6-5 200   Bats R Throws R

Obtained from Oakland for a mere $100 prior to last season, he proved to be a great find for Yankees . . . His 16 victories more than doubled the total of club's next highest winner . . . Only Yankee starter to provide at least 200 innings . . . Made sensational debut, carrying no-hitter into ninth inning April 10 in Detroit before Tony Phillips led off with a double. Combined with Greg Cadaret for 4-0 victory and one-hitter . . . Added complete-game one-hitter July 11 in California, zipping Angels, 2-0. Luis Polonia doubled to open fourth inning in that one . . . Named to All-Star staff for first time with 9-3 record at the break . . . Location and guile compensate for lack of velocity . . . Began career as Expos' third-round choice in 1977 draft . . . Born July 22, 1956, in Dearborn, Mich. . . . Earned $2,125,000 in 1991.

Year	Club	G	IP	W	L	Pct.	SO	BB	H	ERA
1978	Montreal	10	61	4	2	.667	50	21	52	2.51
1979	Montreal	34	168	9	8	.529	138	54	148	3.43
1980	Montreal	33	211	16	11	.593	125	56	206	3.11
1981	Montreal	22	137	9	7	.563	77	31	122	2.96
1982	Montreal	32	224	12	12	.500	158	58	212	3.46
1983	Montreal	18	81⅓	6	7	.462	55	20	98	4.65
1984	Chicago (NL)	24	140⅔	8	5	.615	76	24	140	3.14
1985	Chicago (NL)	19	121	5	6	.455	80	27	100	3.12
1986	Chicago (NL)	37	169⅔	9	11	.450	124	37	165	4.19
1987	Chicago (NL)	32	144⅔	8	9	.471	106	50	156	4.29
1988	Chicago (NL)	11	15⅓	1	2	.133	6	3	13	5.28
1989	Chicago (NL)	37	146⅓	11	9	.550	86	31	155	3.94
1990	Oakland	34	206	17	11	.607	128	66	205	3.88
1991	New York (AL)	34	208	16	10	.615	130	29	200	3.81
	Totals	377	2034⅓	131	110	.544	1339	507	1972	3.61

STEVE FARR 35 5-11 200   Bats R Throws R

Free-agent signee enters second season with Yankees after adequately replacing all-time save leader Dave Righetti in first year . . . Recorded career-high 23 saves in 29 chances and now has career total of 73 saves . . . Makes up in finesse what he lacks in velocity . . . Works the corners extremely well and helps himself greatly by pitching inside . . . Allowed only seven of 30 inherited runners to score . . . Retired first batter he faced on 39 of 60 occasions . . . Limited right-handed hitters to .204 average . . . Rugged competitor insisted on pitching final month despite sore shoulder . . . Began career as undrafted free agent with Pirates and pitched seven-plus seasons in minors before breaking in with Cleveland in 1984... Born Dec. 12, 1956, in Cheverly, Md.... Yankees' best-paid pitcher with $2.4-million salary in 1991.

Year	Club	G	IP	W	L	Pct.	SO	BB	H	ERA
1984	Cleveland	31	116	3	11	.214	83	46	106	4.58
1985	Kansas City	16	37⅔	2	1	.667	36	20	34	3.11
1986	Kansas City	56	109⅓	8	4	.667	83	39	90	3.13
1987	Kansas City	47	91	4	3	.571	88	44	97	4.15
1988	Kansas City	62	82⅔	5	4	.556	72	30	74	2.50
1989	Kansas City	51	63⅓	2	5	.286	56	22	75	4.12
1990	Kansas City	57	127	13	7	.650	94	48	99	1.98
1991	New York (AL)	60	70	5	5	.500	60	20	57	2.19
	Totals	380	697	42	40	.512	572	269	632	3.22

GREG CADARET 30 6-3 214   Bats L Throws L

Versatility and durability make him an asset... Has helped Yankees as starter and reliever... Made team-high 68 appearances last season, fifth-highest total in club history... Allowed only 14 of 44 inherited runners to score... Did not permit a homer to a left-handed hitter... Made five starts when rotation needed a lift and went 3-1 during that stretch, despite 6.00 ERA ... More effective as starter than ERA would indicate... Yearns to be a closer, but must improve control first... Born Feb. 27, 1962, in Detroit... Athletics' 11th-round pick in 1983 was acquired from Oakland with Eric Plunk and Luis Polonia for Rickey Henderson, June 21, 1989... Earned $620,000 in 1991.

Year	Club	G	IP	W	L	Pct.	SO	BB	H	ERA
1987	Oakland	29	39⅔	6	2	.750	30	24	37	4.54
1988	Oakland	58	71⅓	5	2	.714	64	36	60	2.89
1989	Oak.-N.Y. (AL)	46	120	5	5	.500	80	57	130	4.05
1990	New York (AL)	54	121½	5	4	.556	80	64	120	4.15
1991	New York (AL)	68	121⅔	8	6	.571	105	59	110	3.62
	Totals	255	474⅓	29	19	.604	359	240	457	3.83

PASCUAL PEREZ 34 6-3 183   Bats R Throws R

Looking to give Yankees first full season in final year of three-year, $5.7-million contract he signed with them as free agent prior to 1990 ... Did not pitch after April in 1990 and underwent rotator cuff surgery Aug. 9 of that year ... Rejoined the Yankees May 14 after extended spring training last season, but made only four starts before being disabled with shoulder stiffness... Was activated again Aug. 16 and remained in rotation until end of season . . . Pitched consistently well during second stint despite poor support . . . Ended string of 11 consecutive winless starts with 3-0 combined shutout in Cleveland Sept. 27 . . . Still has good velocity, but must concentrate on changing speeds more . . . Revels in eccentricities . . . Began career as undrafted free agent in Pirates' organization in 1976 . . . Born May 17, 1957, in San Cristobal, D.R. . . . Earned $2,133,333 in 1991.

Year	Club	G	IP	W	L	Pct.	SO	BB	H	ERA
1980	Pittsburgh	2	12	0	1	.000	7	2	15	3.75
1981	Pittsburgh	17	86	2	7	.222	46	34	92	3.98
1982	Atlanta	16	79⅓	4	4	.500	29	17	85	3.06
1983	Atlanta	33	215⅓	15	8	.652	144	51	213	3.43
1984	Atlanta	30	211⅔	14	8	.636	145	51	208	3.74
1985	Atlanta	22	95⅓	1	13	.071	57	57	115	6.14
1987	Montreal	10	70⅓	7	0	1.000	58	16	52	2.30
1988	Montreal	27	188	12	8	.600	131	44	133	2.44
1989	Montreal	33	198⅓	9	13	.409	152	45	178	3.31
1990	New York (AL)	3	14	1	2	.333	12	3	8	1.29
1991	New York (AL)	14	73⅔	2	4	.333	41	24	68	3.18
	Totals	207	1244	67	68	.496	822	344	1167	3.44

TOP PROSPECTS

BRIEN TAYLOR 20 6-3 205　　　　　**Bats L Throws L**
Received record $1.55-million minor-league contract day before he was to attend junior college in North Carolina . . . Sat out summer after Yankees made him first high-school pitcher taken with top choice in draft since David Clyde in 1973 . . . *USA TODAY*'s Player of the Year in 1991, when he went 9-2 with a 0.47 ERA at East Carteret High in Beaufort, N.C. . . . Registered back-to-back no-hitters . . . Once struck out 20 of 21 batters . . . His overpowering fastball has been clocked as high as 98 mph . . . Will use time in minors to develop breaking pitches . . . Born Dec. 26, 1971, in Beaufort, N.C.

GERALD WILLIAMS 25 6-2 190　　　　　**Bats R Throws R**
Figures prominently in outfield plans for future . . . Batted .258 with two home runs and 27 RBI in 61 games for Columbus (AAA) after beginning season with Albany (AA) and hitting .286 with five homers and 32 RBI in 45 games there . . . Remains a raw talent offensively . . . Possesses very strong arm . . . Right fielder has range of a center fielder . . . Born Aug. 10, 1966, in New Orleans . . . Outstanding choice as 14th-round selection in 1987 draft . . . Product of Grambling State . . . Led organization with 101 RBI in 1990, when he split season between Fort Lauderdale (A) and Albany.

CARL EVERETT 20 6-0 190   Bats S Throws R

Yankees' first-round selection in 1990 has not disappointed . . . Center fielder batted .271 for Greensboro (A), despite striking out 122 times in 468 at-bats . . . Topped club with 97 runs scored . . . Although he hit only four home runs with 40 RBI, Yankees are confident power will come with maturity . . . Born June 3, 1971, in Tampa . . . Graduated from Hillsborough High School, which produced Dwight Gooden . . . Will be brought along slowly.

MANAGER BUCK SHOWALTER: Became youngest manager in majors when he was given one-year contract Oct. 29 . . . Selected under bizarre set of circumstances . . . Was named 22 days after GM Gene Michael had ruled him out . . . At first, Michael said he sought candidate with major-league managerial experience, but he was later persuaded by upper management to reconsider . . . Budget considerations were a factor since he came more cheaply than veteran man would have . . . Had been Yankees' third-base coach since June 6, 1990 and is extremely popular among players . . . Built reputation as bright baseball mind during extremely successful minor-league managerial career . . . Compiled 360-207 record in five seasons and never suffered a losing campaign . . . Won championships in New York-Penn League (1985), Florida State League (1987) and Eastern League (1989) . . . Named Eastern League Manager of the Year in championship season, when Albany rolled up 92-48 record . . . Played in Yankees' minor-league system from 1977-83 without ever playing a major-league game . . . Born May 23, 1956, in DeFuniak Springs, Fla.

ALL-TIME YANKEE SEASON RECORDS

BATTING: Babe Ruth, .393, 1923
HRs: Roger Maris, 61, 1961
RBI: Lou Gehrig, 184, 1931
STEALS: Rickey Henderson, 93, 1988
WINS: Jack Chesbro, 41, 1904
STRIKEOUTS: Ron Guidry, 248, 1978

TORONTO BLUE JAYS

TEAM DIRECTORY: Chairman: W.R.R. Ferguson; Vice Chairman/CEO: P.N.T. Widdrington; Pres./COO: Paul Beeston; Exec. VP-Baseball: Pat Gillick; VP-Baseball: Al LaMacchia, Bob Mattick; Dir. Pub. Rel.: Howard Starkman; Trav. Sec.: John Brioux; Mgr.: Cito Gaston. Home: Skydome (50,300). Field distances: 330, l.f. line; 375, l.c.; 400, c.f.; 375, r.c.; 330, r.f. line. Spring training: Dunedin, Fla.

SCOUTING REPORT

HITTING: Toronto featured three candidates for the league's MVP award last season and that says much about the nature of this team's offense. This is no one-man wrecking crew.

Joe Carter (.273, 33, 108) wields the biggest bat. He ranked fourth in the AL in home runs and sixth in RBI with 38 more than the next Blue Jay. But where would Carter be without Devon White (.282, 17, 60) and Roberto Alomar (.295, 9, 69, 53 steals) as table-setters? The Blue Jays placed second in the AL with 148 steals as Alomar and White combined for 86 of them.

The Blue Jays think John Olerud (.256, 17, 68) will continue to improve. Kelly Gruber (.252, 20, 65) can be counted on for more production if he avoids the injuries that limited him to 113 games last year. And free agent addition Dave Winfield (.262, 28, 86 with the Angels) still has plenty of life in his bat at age 40.

PITCHING: Pitching is the main ingredient here. Toronto's pitching was clearly superior to that in the rest of the AL last season. The Blue Jays topped the league with a 3.50 ERA while holding opponents to a league-best .238 batting average. This staff is again well-stocked—especially after the signing of free agent Jack Morris (18-12, 3.43 with the Twins), fresh from his postseason heroics.

Jimmy Key (16-12, 3.05), Todd Stottlemyre (15-8, 3.78) and David Wells (15-10, 3.72) are all dependable winners, assuming the leg Key broke in the offseason heals. Jose Guzman (10-3, 2.99) is a young right-hander with big potential.

Toronto's bullpen is even more impressive than its rotation. The Blue Jays paced the AL with 60 saves and it's not hard to see why. While some teams scrap for one closer, Toronto has two in Tom Henke (0-2, 2.32, 32 Sv) and Duane Ward (7-6, 2.77,

Joe Carter has driven in 100 for three teams since '89.

23 Sv). Henke will bear some watching, though, because he suffered from tendinitis last September.

FIELDING: When it comes to strength up the middle, Toronto has lots of it. Alomar, at second base, and White, in center field, give the Blue Jays a pair of returning Gold Glove winners. Barring injury, the far-ranging Alomar will be an All-Star second baseman for years to come and the speedy White was guilty of only one error last season.

OUTLOOK: Toronto's talent has been enough to produce nine consecutive winning seasons, a streak no other major league club can match. It's been enough to give the Blue Jays two AL East titles in the last three years. But it hasn't been enough to bring the franchise its first pennant and the Blue Jays were a dispirited group after Minnesota blitzed them in five games in the ALCS last October. The Blue Jays face another pressure-filled season and probably another heart-rending finish.

TORONTO BLUE JAYS 1992 ROSTER

MANAGER Cito Gaston
Coaches—Bob Bailor, Galen Cisco, Rich Hacker, Larry Hisle, John Sullivan, Gene Tenace

PITCHERS

No.	Name	1991 Club	W-L	IP	SO	ERA	B-T	Ht.	Wt.	Born
46	Dayley, Ken	Dunedin	0-0	6	2	0.00	L-L	6-0	180	2/25/59 Jerome, ID
		Syracuse	0-1	14	13	9.64				
		Toronto	0-0	4	3	6.23				
66	Guzman, Juan	Syracuse	4-5	67	67	4.03	R-R	5-11	195	8/10/66 Dominican Republic
		Toronto	10-3	139	123	2.99				
50	Henke, Tom	Toronto	0-2	50	53	2.32	R-R	6-5	225	12/21/57 Kansas City, MO
41	Hentgen, Pat	Syracuse	8-9	171	155	4.47	R-R	6-2	200	11/13/68 Detroit, MI
		Toronto	0-0	7	3	2.45				
26	Horsman, Vince	Knoxville	4-1	81	80	2.34	R-L	6-2	180	3/9/67 Canada
		Toronto	0-0	4	2	0.00				
22	Key, Jimmy	Toronto	16-12	209	125	3.05	R-L	6-1	185	4/22/61 Huntsville, AL
28	Leiter, Al	Dunedin	0-0	10	5	1.86	L-L	6-3	215	10/23/65 Toms River, NJ
		Toronto	0-0	2	1	27.00				
45	MacDonald, Bob	Syracuse	1-0	6	8	4.50	L-L	6-3	208	4/27/65 East Orange, NJ
		Toronto	3-3	54	24	2.85				
47	Morris, Jack	Minnesota	18-12	247	163	3.43	R-R	6-3	200	5/16/55 St. Paul, MN
37	Stieb, Dave	Toronto	4-3	60	29	3.17	R-R	6-1	195	7/22/57 Santa Ana, CA
30	Stottlemyre, Todd	Toronto	15-8	219	116	3.78	L-R	6-3	195	5/20/65 Yakima, WA
40	Timlin, Mike	Toronto	11-6	108	85	3.16	R-R	6-4	205	3/10/66 Midland, TX
52	Trlicek, Rick	Knoxville	2-5	51	55	2.45	R-R	6-3	200	4/26/69 Houston, TX
31	Ward, Duane	Toronto	7-6	107	132	2.77	R-R	6-4	215	5/28/64 Parkview, NM
53	Weathers, Dave	Knoxville	10-7	139	114	2.45	R-R	6-3	205	9/25/69 Lawrenceburg, TN
		Toronto	1-0	15	13	4.91				
36	Wells, David	Toronto	15-10	196	106	3.72	L-L	6-4	225	5/20/63 Torrance, CA

CATCHERS

No.	Name	1991 Club	H	HR	RBI	Pct.	B-T	Ht.	Wt.	Born
10	Borders, Pat	Toronto	71	5	36	.244	R-R	6-2	200	5/14/63 Columbus, OH
54	Knorr, Randy	Knoxville	13	0	4	.176	R-R	6-2	205	11/12/68 San Gabriel, CA
		Syracuse	89	5	44	.260				
		Toronto	0	0	0	.000				
21	Myers, Greg	Toronto	81	8	36	.262	L-R	6-2	205	4/14/66 Riverside, CA

INFIELDERS

No.	Name	1991 Club	H	HR	RBI	Pct.	B-T	Ht.	Wt.	Born
12	Alomar, Roberto	Toronto	188	9	69	.295	S-R	6-0	185	2/5/68 Puerto Rico
17	Gruber, Kelly	Toronto	108	20	65	.252	R-R	6-0	180	2/26/62 Bellaire, TX
--	Kent, Jeff	Knoxville	114	12	61	.256	R-R	6-1	185	3/7/66 Bellflower, CA
4	Lee, Manuel	Toronto	104	0	29	.234	S-R	5-9	166	6/17/65 Dominican Republic
—	Martinez, Domingo	Syracuse	146	17	83	.313	R-R	6-2	215	8/4/67 Dominican Republic
	Mulliniks, Rance	Toronto	60	2	24	.250	L-R	6-0	175	1/5/56 Tulare, CA
9	Olerud, John	Toronto	116	17	68	.256	L-L	6-5	210	8/5/68 Seattle, WA
16	Quinlan, Tom	Syracuse	112	10	49	.240	R-R	6-3	210	3/27/68 St. Paul, MN
33	Sprague, Ed	Syracuse	32	5	25	.364	R-R	6-2	215	7/25/67 Castro Valley, CA
		Toronto	44	4	20	.275				
15	Tabler, Pat	Toronto	40	1	21	.216	R-R	6-2	200	2/2/58 Hamilton, OH
1	Zosky, Eddie	Syracuse	135	6	39	.264	R-R	6-0	175	2/10/68 Whittier, CA
		Toronto	4	0	2	.148				

OUTFIELDERS

No.	Name	1991 Club	H	HR	RBI	Pct.	B-T	Ht.	Wt.	Born
14	Bell, Derek	Syracuse	158	13	93	.346	R-R	6-2	200	12/11/68 Tampa, FL
		Toronto	4	0	1	.143				
29	Carter, Joe	Toronto	174	33	108	.273	R-R	6-3	220	3/7/60 Oklahoma City, OK
20	Ducey, Rob	Syracuse	78	8	40	.293	L-R	6-2	180	5/24/65 Canada
		Toronto	16	1	4	.235				
23	Maldonado, Candy	Mil.-Tor.	72	12	48	.250	R-R	6-0	195	10/5/60 Puerto Rico
—	Perez, Robert	Dunedin	145	4	50	.302	R-R	6-3	195	6/4/69 Venezuela
		Syracuse	4	0	1	.200				
—	Thompson, Ryan	Knoxville	97	8	40	.241	R-R	6-3	200	11/4/67 Chestertown, MD
24	Ward, Turner	Syracuse	72	7	32	.330	S-R	6-2	200	4/11/65 Orlando, FL
		Toronto	27	0	7	.239				
19	White, Devon	Toronto	181	17	60	.282	S-R	6-2	185	12/29/62 Jamaica
—	Wilson, Nigel	Dunedin	137	12	55	.301	L-L	6-1	185	1/12/70 Canada
32	Winfield, Dave	California	149	28	86	.262	R-R	6-6	246	10/3/51 St. Paul, MN

BLUE JAY PROFILES

JOE CARTER 32 6-3 220   Bats R Throws R

His run production will again be key to Blue Jays' hopes... Gave Blue Jays big bat they hoped for when they acquired him with Roberto Alomar from San Diego for Fred McGriff and Tony Fernandez prior to 1991 season... Ranked fourth in AL in home runs (33), sixth in RBI (108), fifth in total bases (321) and tied for second in extra-base hits (78)... First player in history to rack up three consecutive 100-RBI seasons for three different teams... Honored as an All-Star for first time ... AL Player of the Month in June, when his 11 home runs tied a club record for homers in one month... Topped Blue Jays with 13 outfield assists... Clouted 200th career homer Aug. 9 vs. Boston... Batted .263 with one home run, four RBI in ALCS ... Postseason performance was diminished by a sprained ankle suffered in Game 3... Has played 505 consecutive games, second-longest streak to Cal Ripken among actives... Born March 7, 1960, in Oklahoma City, Okla.... Earned $1,883,334 in 1991 ... Cubs chose him second overall in 1981 draft.

Year	Club	Pos.	G	AB	R	H	2B	3B	HR	RBI	SB	Avg.
1983	Chicago (NL) ..	OF	23	51	6	9	1	1	0	1	1	.176
1984	Cleveland	OF-1B	66	244	32	67	6	1	13	41	2	.275
1985	Cleveland	OF-1B-2B-3B	143	489	64	128	27	0	15	59	24	.262
1986	Cleveland	OF-1B	162	663	108	200	36	9	29	121	29	.302
1987	Cleveland	OF-1B	149	588	83	155	27	2	32	106	31	.264
1988	Cleveland	OF	157	621	85	168	36	6	27	98	27	.271
1989	Cleveland	OF-1B	162	651	84	158	32	4	35	105	13	.243
1990	San Diego	OF-1B	162	634	79	147	27	1	24	115	22	.232
1991	Toronto	OF	162	638	89	174	42	3	33	108	20	.273
	Totals		1186	4579	630	1206	234	27	208	754	169	.263

DEVON WHITE 29 6-2 180   Bats S Throws R

Blossomed with Toronto after disappointing stay with Angels... Set career highs in batting average (.282), runs (110), hits (181) and walks (55)... Brilliant center fielder topped all AL outfielders with .998 fielding percentage (one error) and won Gold Glove... Clubbed 17 home runs, 12 leading off an inning... Enjoyed fine ALCS, batting .364... Acquired from Angels with Willie Fraser and Marcus Moore for Junior Felix, Luis Sojo and Ken Rivers prior to 1991 season... Born

Dec. 29, 1962, in Kingston, Jamaica . . . Earned $750,000 in 1991 . . . Angels' sixth-round pick in 1981.

Year	Club	Pos.	G	AB	R	H	2B	3B	HR	RBI	SB	Avg.
1985	California	OF	21	7	7	1	0	0	0	0	3	.143
1986	California	OF	29	51	8	12	1	1	1	3	6	.235
1987	California	OF	159	639	103	168	33	5	24	87	32	.263
1988	California	OF	122	455	76	118	22	2	11	51	17	.259
1989	California	OF	156	636	86	156	18	13	12	56	44	.245
1990	California	OF	125	443	57	96	17	3	11	44	21	.217
1991	Toronto	OF	156	642	110	181	40	10	17	60	33	.282
	Totals		768	2873	447	732	131	34	76	301	156	.255

ROBERTO ALOMAR 24 6-0 185   Bats S Throws R

Joined George Bell as only Blue Jays in history to be voted to All-Star Game . . . Became 55th player in major-league history to homer from both sides of the plate in the same game, accomplishing that against the White Sox May 10 . . . Tied club record with four stolen bases June 8 at Baltimore . . . Ranked second in AL with career-high 53 steals . . . Swiped third base 17 times . . . Led both teams with .474 average in ALCS . . . Brother Sandy is standout catcher with Indians . . . Born Feb. 5, 1968, in Salinas, P.R. . . . Earned $1.25 million and Gold Glove in 1991 . . . Padres signed him as free agent in February 1985, then dealt him to Toronto prior to last season.

Year	Club	Pos.	G	AB	R	H	2B	3B	HR	RBI	SB	Avg.
1988	San Diego	2B	143	545	84	145	24	6	9	41	24	.266
1989	San Diego	2B	158	623	82	184	27	1	7	56	42	.295
1990	San Diego	2B-SS	147	586	80	168	27	5	6	60	24	.287
1991	Toronto	2B	161	637	88	188	41	11	9	69	53	.295
	Totals		609	2391	334	685	119	23	31	226	143	.286

DAVE WINFIELD 40 6-6 246   Bats R Throws R

Free agent signed one-year, $2.3-million contract with Blue Jays in December after solid season with Angels marked by contrast . . . Had .280 average, 18 homers and 57 RBI at All-Star break . . . Finished at .262, hitting only 10 more homers and driving in just 29 second-half runs . . . Highlight was passing 400-homer plateau . . . Brilliant career has included seven 100-plus RBI seasons, 12 All-Star Game appearances, five Gold

Gloves and Comeback Player of the Year Award in 1990 . . . Came to Angels from Yankees for sore-armed Mike Witt on May 11, 1990 . . . Earned $3.3 million in 1991 . . . Born Oct. 3, 1951, in St. Paul, Minn.

Year	Club	Pos.	G	AB	R	H	2B	3B	HR	RBI	SB	Avg.
1973	San Diego	OF-1B	56	141	9	39	4	1	3	12	0	.277
1974	San Diego	OF	145	498	57	132	18	4	20	75	9	.265
1975	San Diego	OF	143	509	74	136	20	2	15	76	23	.267
1976	San Diego	OF	137	492	81	139	26	4	13	69	26	.283
1977	San Diego	OF	157	615	104	169	29	7	25	92	16	.275
1978	San Diego	OF-1B	158	587	88	181	30	5	24	97	21	.308
1979	San Diego	OF	159	597	97	184	27	10	34	118	15	.308
1980	San Diego	OF	162	558	89	154	25	6	20	87	23	.276
1981	New York (AL)	OF	105	388	52	114	25	1	13	68	11	.294
1982	New York (AL)	OF	140	539	84	151	24	8	37	106	5	.280
1983	New York (AL)	OF	152	598	99	169	26	8	32	116	15	.283
1984	New York (AL)	OF	141	567	106	193	34	4	19	100	6	.340
1985	New York (AL)	OF	155	633	105	174	34	6	26	114	19	.275
1986	New York (AL)	OF-3B	154	565	90	148	31	5	24	104	6	.262
1987	New York (AL)	OF	156	575	83	158	22	1	27	97	5	.275
1988	New York (AL)	OF	149	559	96	180	37	2	25	107	9	.322
1989	New York (AL)				Injured							
1990	NY (AL)-Cal. . . .	OF	132	475	70	127	21	2	21	78	0	.267
1991	California	OF	150	568	75	149	27	4	28	86	7	.262
	Totals		2551	9464	1459	2697	460	80	406	1602	216	.285

JACK MORRIS 36 6-3 200   Bats R Throws R

Twins' free agent did it again, this time moving north of the border for a two-year, $10.85-million contract with a third-year option for $5.15 million . . . Was World Series MVP and pitched 10-inning, 1-0 Game 7 shutout vs. Braves . . . Posted 18 regular-season victories, made his fifth All-Star Game appearance and first start and notched two wins in the ALCS— against Toronto—and two more in World Series . . . Notched 1.17 ERA in World Series . . . Signed as free agent before last season to be staff workhorse and did exactly that . . . Totaled 246⅔ innings . . . Pitcher of the 1980s isn't too bad in 1990s . . . Has 33 victories in last two years . . . Has 216 wins in potential Hall of Fame career, rank fourth among active pitchers . . . Also is fourth among actives in strikeouts and innings pitched . . . Earned $3 million in 1991 . . . Born May 16, 1955, in St. Paul, Minn. . . . Tigers' fifth-round pick in 1976.

Year	Club	G	IP	W	L	Pct.	SO	BB	H	ERA
1977	Detroit	7	46	1	1	.500	28	23	38	3.72
1978	Detroit	28	106	3	5	.375	48	49	107	4.33
1979	Detroit	27	198	17	7	.708	113	59	179	3.27
1980	Detroit	36	250	16	15	.516	112	87	252	4.18
1981	Detroit	25	198	14	7	.667	97	78	153	3.05
1982	Detroit	37	266⅓	17	16	.515	135	96	247	4.06
1983	Detroit	37	293⅔	20	13	.606	232	83	257	3.34
1984	Detroit	35	240⅓	19	11	.633	148	87	221	3.60
1985	Detroit	35	257	16	11	.593	191	110	212	3.33
1986	Detroit	35	267	21	8	.724	223	82	229	3.27
1987	Detroit	34	266	18	11	.621	208	93	227	3.38
1988	Detroit	34	235	15	13	.536	168	83	225	3.94
1989	Detroit	24	170⅓	6	14	.300	115	59	189	4.86
1990	Detroit	36	249⅔	15	18	.455	162	97	231	4.51
1991	Minnesota	35	246⅔	18	12	.600	163	92	226	3.43
	Totals	465	3290	216	162	.571	2143	1178	2993	3.71

TOM HENKE 34 6-5 225　　　　　Bats R Throws R

Fine closer shows no sign of slowing down . . . Ranked sixth in AL with 32 saves . . . Established major-league record by converting 25 consecutive saves from April 9 to Aug. 7 . . . Didn't blow a save until Milwaukee's Paul Molitor slammed a three-run homer against him in the ninth inning Aug. 13 . . . Has averaged at least one strikeout per inning in each of last seven seasons . . . Owns career rate of 10.41 strikeouts per nine innings, highest in major-league history among pitchers with at least 500 innings . . . Received two cortisone injections in September to treat tendinitis . . . Not used in a save situation in postseason . . . Born Dec. 21, 1957, in Kansas City, Mo. . . . Has 186 career saves . . . Rangers' secondary phase pick in 1980 was plucked by Toronto in January 1985 compensation pool for loss of free agent Cliff Johnson . . . Bricklayer by trade, he earned $2,968,667 playing ball in 1991.

Year	Club	G	IP	W	L	Pct.	SO	BB	H	ERA
1982	Texas	8	15⅔	1	0	1.000	9	8	14	1.15
1983	Texas	8	16	1	0	1.000	17	4	16	3.38
1984	Texas	25	28⅓	1	1	.500	25	20	36	6.35
1985	Toronto	28	40	3	3	.500	42	8	29	2.03
1986	Toronto	63	91⅓	9	5	.643	118	32	63	3.35
1987	Toronto	72	94	0	6	.000	128	25	62	2.49
1988	Toronto	52	68	4	4	.500	66	24	60	2.91
1989	Toronto	64	89	8	3	.727	116	25	66	1.92
1990	Toronto	61	74⅔	2	4	.333	75	19	58	2.17
1991	Toronto	49	50⅓	0	2	.000	53	11	33	2.32
	Totals	430	567⅓	29	28	.509	649	176	437	2.68

JIMMY KEY 30 6-1 185   Bats R Throws L

One of the most dependable starters in either league . . . He and Frank Viola are only two major-league pitchers to post 12 or more victories in each of last seven seasons . . . Fashioned 10-4 record at the break, not allowing more than three earned runs in any start, and received second All-Star selection . . . Was winning pitcher in All-Star Game . . . Gained 100th career triumph Aug. 26 at Baltimore . . . Made one post-season start, receiving a no-decision in Game 3. Permitted two runs in six innings in that start . . . Won ERA title with 2.76 mark in 1987 and placed second to Roger Clemens in AL Cy Young voting . . . Born April 22, 1961, in Huntsville, Ala. . . . Toronto's third-round choice in 1982 draft . . . Earned $2,166,667 in 1991.

Year	Club	G	IP	W	L	Pct.	SO	BB	H	ERA
1984	Toronto	63	62	4	5	.444	44	32	70	4.65
1985	Toronto	35	212⅔	14	6	.700	85	50	188	3.00
1986	Toronto	36	232	14	11	.560	141	74	222	3.57
1987	Toronto	36	261	17	8	.680	161	66	210	2.76
1988	Toronto	21	131⅓	12	5	.706	65	30	127	3.29
1989	Toronto	33	216	13	14	.481	118	27	226	3.88
1990	Toronto	27	154⅔	13	7	.650	88	22	169	4.25
1991	Toronto	33	209⅓	16	12	.571	125	44	207	3.05
	Totals	284	1479	103	68	.602	827	345	1419	3.41

DAVID WELLS 28 6-4 225   Bats L Throws L

Quality left-hander possesses versatility to start or relieve . . . Began last season as starter, winning seven straight decisions from May 31 to July 24 . . . Dropped next five decisions, however, from July 29 to Aug. 24 . . . Missed start on Aug. 19 with tired arm and was sent to bullpen Sept. 13 . . . Went 1-0 with one save and 3.44 ERA in 18⅓ relief innings . . . Vulnerable to long ball . . . Yielded team-high 24 home runs, 21 of them to right-handed batters . . . Born May 20, 1963, in Torrance, Cal. . . . Toronto's second-round choice in 1982 draft . . . Salary was $800,000 in 1991.

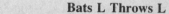

Year	Club	G	IP	W	L	Pct.	SO	BB	H	ERA
1987	Toronto	18	29⅓	4	3	.571	32	12	37	3.99
1988	Toronto	41	64⅓	3	5	.375	56	31	65	4.62
1989	Toronto	54	86⅓	7	4	.636	78	28	66	2.40
1990	Toronto	43	189	11	6	.647	115	45	165	3.14
1991	Toronto	40	198⅓	15	10	.600	106	49	188	3.72
	Totals	196	567⅓	40	28	.588	387	165	521	3.44

TODD STOTTLEMYRE 26 6-3 195   Bats L Throws R

Can look forward to many successful seasons ... Used fast start last year to register first winning record ... Jumped out to 5-0 mark after seven starts ... Was 8-2 after 14 starts ... Lasted six or more innings in all but 10 starts ... Boasts back-to-back seasons of 200-plus innings ... Very effective at SkyDome, where he was 9-3 with a 3.96 ERA in 17 starts ... Pitched poorly in only playoff start, surrendering four runs and seven hits in 3⅔ innings in 9-3 Game 4 loss ... Born May 20, 1965, in Yakima, Wash. ... Selected in first round of 1985 draft and was third player picked overall ... Son of former Yankee pitcher and current Met pitching coach Mel ... A bargain at $315,000 salary in 1991.

Year	Club	G	IP	W	L	Pct.	SO	BB	H	ERA
1988	Toronto	28	98	4	8	.333	67	46	109	5.69
1989	Toronto	27	127⅔	7	7	.500	63	44	137	3.88
1990	Toronto	33	203	13	17	.433	115	69	214	4.34
1991	Toronto	34	219	15	8	.652	116	75	194	3.78
	Totals	122	647⅔	39	40	.494	361	234	654	4.27

TOP PROSPECTS

DEREK BELL 23 6-2 200   Bats R Throws R

Baseball America's Minor League Player of the Year and the first member of Blue Jays' organization to receive the honor ... Named International League MVP after leading circuit in batting average (.346), hits (158), RBI (93), total bases (243) and runs (89) for Syracuse (AAA) ... Credits success to improved patience at plate ... Blue Jays think he can be above-average outfielder if he's willing to work at it ... Moody player on occasion ... Born Dec. 11, 1968, in Tampa ... Toronto's second-round pick in 1987.

EDDIE ZOSKY 24 6-0 175   Bats R Throws R

Should be ready to establish himself as Blue Jays' shortstop ... Has already built reputation for rifle arm and great range ... Few infielders compare to this International League All-Star in arm strength ... Batted .264 in 119 games for Syracuse (AAA) ... Should be able to hold his own offensively ... Born Feb. 10, 1968, in Whittier, Cal. ... Toronto's first-round pick in 1989 draft.

DAVE WEATHERS 22 6-3 205   Bats R Throws R

Toronto showed its regard for him with promotion from Knoxville (AA) to big leagues Aug. 2, when an injury created a bullpen opening . . . Contributed by allowing only one run in eight innings before being returned to Knoxville . . . Used almost exclusively as starter in minors . . . Tied for team lead in victories at Knoxville with 10-7 record to go with 2.45 ERA . . . Born Sept. 25, 1969, in Lawrenceburg, Tenn. . . . Toronto's third-round selection in 1988 draft.

MANAGER CITO GASTON: Under pressure to produce Toronto's first pennant, despite being part of two AL East championships in three years . . . Took over club May 31, 1989 and Blue Jays went on to division crown . . . Was under fire last year after eventual World Series champion Minnesota ousted Blue Jays from ALCS in five games . . . Severest criticism involved his handling of pitching staff in postseason . . . Some are uncomfortable with his soft-spoken, unemotional approach . . . Was plagued by severe back pain for much of last season . . . Hospitalized from Aug. 21-31 with sciatica . . . Turned over team to Gene Tenace with 2½-game lead in AL East and returned to find lead exactly as he had left it . . . Originally signed as player by Milwaukee Braves . . . Selected by San Diego in 1969 NL expansion draft, beginning 10-year major-league career . . . Represented San Diego in 1970 All-Star Game . . . Traded by Padres to Atlanta following 1974 season . . . Made coaching debut as Braves' minor-league batting instructor in 1981 . . . Made significant strides working with Blue Jays hitters in 1982 as team average improved 36 points . . . Born March 17, 1944, in San Antonio . . . Owns 235-182 major-league managerial record, a .564 winning percentage, after last year's 91-71 finish.

ALL-TIME BLUE JAY SEASON RECORDS

BATTING: Tony Fernandez, .322, 1987
HRs: George Bell, 47, 1987
RBI: George Bell, 134, 1987
STEALS: Damaso Garcia, 54, 1982
WINS: Dave Stieb, 18, 1990
STRIKEOUTS: Dave Stieb, 198, 1984

INSIDE THE
NATIONAL LEAGUE

By JOHN BELIS and KEVIN KERNAN
Bridgewater (N.J.)   *San Diego Union*
Courier-Post

	East	*West*
PREDICTED	New York Mets	Cincinnati Reds
ORDER	Chicago Cubs	Atlanta Braves
OF	St. Louis Cardinals	San Francisco Giants
FINISH	Pittsburgh Pirates	Los Angeles Dodgers
	Philadelphia Phillies	San Diego Padres
	Montreal Expos	Houston Astros

Playoff Winner: Cincinnati

EAST DIVISION

		Owner		Morning Line Manager
1	**METS** Orange, white & blue Have the horses now	N. Doublday/F. Wilpon	1991 W 77 L 84	3-1 Jeff Torborg
2	**CUBS** Royal blue & white Due for a good race	Tribune Co.	1991 W 77 L 83	7-2 Jim Lefebvre
3	**CARDINALS** Red & white Rapidly making strides	August A. Busch III	1991 W 84 L 78	5-1 Joe Torre
4	**PIRATES** Old gold, white & black Starting to fade	Douglas Danforth	1991 W 98 L 64	8-1 Jim Leyland
5	**PHILLIES** Crimson & white Can't go the distance	William Y. Giles	1991 W 78 L 84	10-1 Jim Fregosi
6	**EXPOS** Scarlet, white & royal blue Too much competition	Claude Brochu	1991 W 71 L 90	20-1 Tom Runnells

Riverfront Stakes

116th Running. National League Race. Distance: 162 games plus playoff. Payoff (based on '91): $119,579.66 per winning player, World Series; $73,323.41 per losing player, World Series. A field of 12 entered in two divisions.

Track Record: 116 wins—Chicago, 1906

WEST DIVISION		Owner		Morning Line Manager
1	**REDS** Red & white Return to '90 form	Marge Schott	1991 W 74 L 88	3-1 Lou Piniella
2	**BRAVES** Royal blue & white Armed and dangerous	W. Bartholomay/S. Kasten	1991 W 94 L 68	4-1 Bobby Cox
3	**GIANTS** White, orange & black Must prove can go the distance	Bob Lurie	1991 W 75 L 87	10-1 Roger Craig
4	**DODGERS** Royal blue & white Could be in race if new parts click	Peter O'Malley	1991 W 93 L 69	15-1 Tommy Lasorda
5	**PADRES** Brown, gold & white Still not enough horses	Tom Werner	1991 W 84 L 78	40-1 Greg Riddoch
6	**ASTROS** Orange & white Move down in class	John J. McMullen	1991 W 65 L 97	100-1 Art Howe

New-look **REDS** nip **BRAVES** in photo finish as **GIANTS** falter down the stretch. **DODGERS** make a bid. **PADRES** throw their jockey at the turn. **ASTROS** leave it in the barn.

METS move fast out of the gate and set the pace in the face of a final charge by **CUBS** and the **CARDINALS**. Defending champion **PIRATES** barely hold off **PHILLIES**. **EXPOS** are out of the running even before the bugle calls.

CHICAGO CUBS

TEAM DIRECTORY: Chairman: Stanton Cook; Exec. VP-Baseball Operations: Larry Himes; VP-Scouting and Player Development: Dick Balderson; Dir. Media Rel.: Sharon Pannozzo; Trav. Sec.: Peter Durso; Mgr.: Jim Lefebvre. Home: Wrigley Field (38,712). Field distances: 355, l.f. line; 400, c.f.; 353, r.f. line. Spring training: Mesa, Ariz.

SCOUTING REPORT

HITTING: Offense was not the Cubs' problem last season. Their .253 team batting average was the fifth-best mark in the NL, they led the league in runs (734) and they were second in home runs (159). Playing in the "friendly confines," this team still has plenty of firepower to keep things interesting in 1992.

Ryne Sandberg (.291, 26, 100) is among the most consistent, most productive players in baseball and he has the added incentive of playing for a new contract. George Bell (.285, 25, 86) proved to be a valuable addition after switching leagues as a free agent.

Andre Dawson (.272, 31, 104) turns 38 this summer, but has put together back-to-back 100 RBI seasons and shows no signs of letting up. Mark Grace (.273, 8, 58) saw all of his numbers dip in 1991, but he still had 28 doubles and reached base over 200 times for a fourth straight year. Shawon Dunston (.260, 12, 50) gives the Cubs plenty of production for a shortstop and he figures to thrive after getting the security of a new four-year contract.

PITCHING: Devastated by injuries, this staff ranked at or near the bottom in most categories in 1991. The Cubs' 4.03 ERA tied for 11th in the NL, they had a league-low four shutouts and allowed opponents a league-high .257 batting average. Obviously, this is one area which must improve in 1992.

Greg Maddux (15-11, 3.35) has been the one bright spot in the rotation, surpassing 200 innings for four straight years. Last season, he led the NL in games started (37) and finished second in strikeouts (198). Free agent signee Mike Morgan (14-10, 2.78 with the Dodgers in 1991) should give the Cubs a reliable No. 2 starter.

Fragile Danny Jackson (1-5, 6.75) must bounce back from a groin injury to regain his 20-win form and prove he wasn't a bad investment. Mike Harkey (0-2, 5.30) has enormous potential, but

Thoroughbred Greg Maddux logged NL-leading 263 innings.

his status remains uncertain following shoulder surgery. Closer Dave Smith (0-6, 6.00, 17 Sv) is coming off knee surgery at 37, so Paul Assenmacher (7-8, 3.24, 15 Sv) figures to be the main cog in a bullpen by committee.

FIELDING: The Cubs tied for the NL lead with a .982 fielding percentage last year. Nine-time Gold Glove second baseman Sandberg hasn't committed a throwing error since 1990 and he anchors an infield which includes Grace, who led all NL first basemen in total chances, and Dunston, whose range and arm are second to none. Dawson might be slowing down in right field and Bell is a liability in left field, leading the league's outfielders with 10 errors in 1991. Maddux has won two straight Gold Gloves and improves the defense when he's on the mound.

OUTLOOK: If the pitching improves, the Cubs can be contenders, rising from the ashes of last year's 77-83, fourth-place finish. GM Larry Himes and manager Jim Lefebvre are both looking for an instant revival in 1992, because this team is starting to show some age.

CHICAGO CUBS 1992 ROSTER

MANAGER Jim Lefebvre
Coaches—Billy Connors, Chuck Cottier, Sammy Ellis, Jose Martinez,
Tom Trebelhorn

PITCHERS

No.	Name	1991 Club	W-L	IP	SO	ERA	B-T	Ht.	Wt.	Born
45	Assenmacher, Paul	Chicago (NL)	7-8	.103	117	3.24	L-L	6-3	200	12/10/60 Detroit, MI
47	Boskie, Shawn	Iowa	2-2	45	29	3.57	R-R	6-3	205	3/28/67 Hawthorne, NV
		Chicago (NL)	4-9	129	62	5.23				
52	Bullinger, Jim	Charlotte	9-9	143	128	3.53	R-R	6-2	185	8/21/65 New Orleans, LA
		Iowa	3-4	47	30	5.40				
49	Castillo, Frank	Iowa	3-1	25	20	2.52	R-R	6-1	180	4/1/69 El Paso, TX
		Chicago (NL)	6-7	112	73	4.35				
33	Dickson, Lance	Iowa	4-4	101	101	3.11	R-L	6-1	185	10/19/69 Fullerton, CA
22	Harkey, Mike	Chicago (NL)	0-2	19	15	5.30	R-R	6-5	220	10/25/66 San Diego, CA
44	Hartsock, Jeff	Albuquerque	12-6	154	123	3.80	R-R	6-0	190	11/19/66 Fairfield, OH
32	Jackson, Danny	Iowa	0-0	5	4	1.80	R-L	6-0	205	1/5/62 San Antonio, TX
		Chicago (NL)	1-5	71	31	6.75				
50	Lancaster, Les	Chicago (NL)	9-7	156	102	3.52	R-R	6-2	200	4/21/62 Dallas, TX
31	Maddux, Greg	Chicago (NL)	15-11	263	198	3.35	R-R	6-0	170	4/14/66 San Angelo, TX
35	McElroy, Chuck	Chicago (NL)	6-2	101	92	1.95	L-L	6-0	180	10/1/67 Galveston, TX
36	Morgan, Mike	Los Angeles	14-10	236	140	2.78	R-R	6-2	222	10/8/59 Tulare, CA
30	Scanlan, Bob	Iowa	2-0	18	15	2.95	R-R	6-7	215	8/9/66 Los Angeles, CA
		Chicago (NL)	7-8	111	44	3.89				
51	Slocumb, Heathcliff	Chicago (NL)	2-1	63	34	3.45	R-R	6-3	210	6/7/66 Jamaica, NY
		Iowa	1-0	13	9	4.05				
42	Smith, Dave	Chicago (NL)	0-6	33	16	6.00	R-R	6-1	195	1/21/55 San Francisco, CA
43	Wendell, Turk	Greenville	11-3	148	122	2.56	S-R	6-2	175	5/19/67 Pittsfield, MA
		Richmond	0-2	21	18	3.43				

CATCHERS

No.	Name	1991 Club	H	HR	RBI	Pct.	B-T	Ht.	Wt.	Born
7	Girardi, Joe	Chicago (NL)	8	0	4	.222	R-R	5-11	195	10/1/64 Peoria, IL
		Iowa	9	0	6	.191				
—	Pedre, George	Memphis	92	9	59	.259	R-R	5-11	210	10/12/66 Culver City, CA
		Omaha	25	1	4	.216				
		Kansas City	5	0	3	.263				
19	Villanueva, Hector	Chicago (NL)	53	13	32	.276	R-R	6-1	220	10/2/64 Puerto Rico
		Iowa	9	2	9	.360				
2	Wilkins, Rick	Iowa	29	5	14	.271	L-R	6-2	210	6/4/67 Jacksonville, FL
		Chicago (NL)	45	6	22	.222				

INFIELDERS

No.	Name	1991 Club	H	HR	RBI	Pct.	B-T	Ht.	Wt.	Born
21	Arias, Alex	Charlotte	134	4	47	.275	R-R	6-3	185	11/20/67 New York, NY
37	Castellano, Pedro	Winston-Salem	139	10	87	.303	R-R	6-1	175	3/11/70 Venezuela
		Charlotte	8	0	2	.421				
12	Dunston, Shawon	Chicago (NL)	128	12	50	.260	R-R	6-1	175	3/21/63 Brooklyn, NY
17	Grace, Mark	Chicago (NL)	169	8	58	.273	L-L	6-2	190	6/28/64 Winston-Salem, NC
9	Paulino, Elvin	Charlotte	118	24	81	.257	L-R	6-1	190	11/6/67 Dominican Republic
10	Salazar, Luis	Chicago (NL)	86	14	38	.258	R-R	5-10	190	5/19/56 Venezuela
15	Sanchez, Rey	Iowa	121	2	48	.290	R-R	5-9	165	10/5/67 Puerto Rico
		Chicago (NL)	6	0	2	.261				
23	Sandberg, Ryne	Chicago (NL)	170	26	100	.291	R-R	6-2	180	9/18/59 Spokane, WA
25	Scott, Gary	Chicago (NL)	13	1	5	.165	R-R	6-0	175	8/22/68 New Rochelle, NY
		Iowa	48	3	34	.208				
1	Strange, Doug	Iowa	149	8	56	.293	S-R	6-2	170	4/13/64 Greenville, SC
		Chicago (NL)	4	0	1	.444				
16	Vizcaino, Jose	Chicago (NL)	38	0	10	.262	S-R	6-1	180	3/26/68 Dominican Republic

OUTFIELDERS

No.	Name	1991 Club	H	HR	RBI	Pct.	B-T	Ht.	Wt.	Born
11	Bell, George	Chicago (NL)	159	25	86	.285	R-R	6-1	202	10/21/59 Dominican Republic
29	Dascenzo, Doug	Chicago (NL)	61	1	18	.255	S-L	5-8	160	6/30/64 Cleveland, OH
8	Dawson, Andre	Chicago (NL)	153	31	104	.272	R-R	6-3	195	7/10/54 Miami, FL
28	Landrum, Ced	Iowa	44	1	11	.336	L-R	5-8	170	9/3/63 Butler, AL
		Chicago (NL)	20	0	6	.233				
27	May, Derrick	Iowa	92	3	49	.297	L-R	6-4	206	7/14/68 Rochester, NY
		Chicago (NL)	5	1	3	.227				
34	Roberson, Kevin	Charlotte	130	19	67	.256	S-R	6-4	210	1/29/68 Decatur, IL
18	Smith, Dwight	Chicago (NL)	38	3	21	.228	L-R	5-11	175	11/8/63 Tallahassee, FL
24	Walker, Chico	Chicago (NL)	96	6	34	.257	S-R	5-9	185	11/26/58 Jackson, MS
20	Walton, Jerome	Chicago (NL)	59	5	17	.219	R-R	6-1	175	7/8/65 Newman, GA

CUB PROFILES

RYNE SANDBERG 32 6-2 180   Bats R Throws R

His home run total was down (26), following spectacular 1990 season, but "Ryno" remains Ernie Banks' heir to title of "Mr. Cub" . . . Has appeared in more games at second base than any other Cub, surpassing Johnny Evers (1,368) . . . Finished third in NL in runs (104), sixth in hits (170), walks (87) and total bases (284), seventh in RBI (100) and on-base percentage (.379) . . . Made eighth consecutive All-Star appearance and seventh start . . . Got ninth Gold Glove . . . Has not committed throwing error since July 4, 1990 . . . Ranks third in club history in stolen bases . . . Stands fifth among all-time second basemen in career homers . . . Hit 200th career homer Aug. 18 off Phils' Danny Cox . . . Had 18th two-homer game July 27 against Braves, including second inside-the-park job of career . . . Had four four-hit games for career total of 26 . . . Selected by Phillies in 20th round of 1978 draft . . . Traded to Cubs with Larry Bowa for Ivan DeJesus in 1982 . . . Born Sept. 18, 1959, in Spokane, Wash. . . . Earned $2,650,000 in 1991.

Year	Club	Pos.	G	AB	R	H	2B	3B	HR	RBI	SB	Avg.
1981	Philadelphia . . .	SS-2B	13	6	2	1	0	0	0	0	0	.167
1982	Chicago (NL) . .	3B-2B	156	635	103	172	33	5	7	54	32	.271
1983	Chicago (NL) . .	2B-SS	158	633	94	165	25	4	8	48	37	.261
1984	Chicago (NL) . .	2B	156	636	114	200	36	19	19	84	32	.314
1985	Chicago (NL) . .	2B-SS	153	609	113	186	31	6	26	83	54	.305
1986	Chicago (NL) . .	2B	154	627	68	178	28	5	14	76	34	.284
1987	Chicago (NL) . .	2B	132	523	81	154	25	2	16	59	21	.294
1988	Chicago (NL) . .	2B	155	618	77	163	23	8	19	69	25	.264
1989	Chicago (NL) . .	2B	157	606	104	176	25	5	30	76	15	.290
1990	Chicago (NL) . .	2B	155	615	116	188	30	3	40	100	25	.306
1991	Chicago (NL) . .	2B	158	585	104	170	32	2	26	100	22	.291
	Totals		1547	6093	976	1753	288	59	205	749	207	.288

ANDRE DAWSON 37 6-3 195   Bats R Throws R

Age hasn't slowed down the "Hawk" . . . Right fielder still loves hitting at Wrigley . . . He and Ryne Sandberg became first Cubs to post consecutive 100-RBI seasons since Ron Santo in 1969-70 . . . Despite playing most of career in Montreal, he ranks ninth on Cubs' all-time home run list . . . Had 35th multiple home run game Oct. 6 against Cardinals . . . Hit sixth career grand slam April 21 at Pittsburgh off Bob Patterson, two days after hitting pinch slam off Pirates' Stan Belinda . . . Selected to NL All-Star team for eighth time and homered off Roger Clemens . . . Finished fourth in NL in homers (31), sixth in RBI (104), ninth in total bases (275) . . . Has finished among top 10 in batting race five times . . . He and Willie Mays are only players in history to surpass 2,000 hits, 300 homers and 300 steals . . . Born July 10, 1954, in Miami . . . Selected by Expos in 11th round of 1975 draft . . . Signed with Cubs as free agent in 1987 and won NL MVP . . . Highest-paid Cub at $3.3 million in 1991.

Year	Club	Pos.	G	AB	R	H	2B	3B	HR	RBI	SB	Avg.
1976	Montreal	OF	24	85	9	20	4	1	0	7	1	.235
1977	Montreal	OF	139	525	64	148	26	9	19	65	21	.282
1978	Montreal	OF	157	609	84	154	24	8	25	72	28	.253
1979	Montreal	OF	155	639	90	176	24	12	25	92	35	.275
1980	Montreal	OF	151	577	96	178	41	7	17	87	34	.308
1981	Montreal	OF	103	394	71	119	21	3	24	64	26	.302
1982	Montreal	OF	148	608	107	183	37	7	23	83	39	.301
1983	Montreal	OF	159	633	104	189	36	10	32	113	25	.299
1984	Montreal	OF	138	533	73	132	23	6	17	86	13	.248
1985	Montreal	OF	139	529	65	135	27	2	23	91	13	.255
1986	Montreal	OF	130	496	65	141	32	2	20	78	18	.284
1987	Chicago (NL)	OF	153	621	90	178	24	2	49	137	11	.287
1988	Chicago (NL)	OF	157	591	78	179	31	8	24	79	12	.303
1989	Chicago (NL)	OF	118	416	62	105	18	6	21	77	8	.252
1990	Chicago (NL)	OF	147	529	72	164	28	5	27	100	16	.310
1991	Chicago (NL)	OF	149	563	69	153	21	4	31	104	4	.272
	Totals		2167	8348	1199	2354	417	92	377	1335	304	.282

GEORGE BELL 32 6-1 202   Bats R Throws R

Had no trouble adjusting to NL pitching, putting up his best homer numbers since 1987 after signing with Cubs as free agent before 1991 season . . . Finished eighth in league in multi-hit games (47) . . . Combined with Andre Dawson to become first Cub outfield duo to reach 25-homer mark since George Altman and Billy Williams in 1961 . . . Had 16th multi-homer game of career July 30 at Cincinnati . . . After hitting just .236 in first 39 games, he exploded over next 43 games with .351 average, eight homers and 31 RBI . . . Signed with Phillies as free agent in 1978 . . . Claimed by Blue Jays in Rule 5 draft following 1980 season . . . Named American League MVP in 1987 . . . Born Oct. 21, 1959, in San Pedro de Macoris, D.R . . . Earned $2.1 million in 1991 . . . An adventure defensively in left field.

Year	Club	Pos.	G	AB	R	H	2B	3B	HR	RBI	SB	Avg.
1981	Toronto	OF	60	163	19	38	2	1	5	12	3	.233
1983	Toronto	OF	39	112	5	30	5	4	2	17	1	.268
1984	Toronto	OF-3B	159	606	85	177	39	4	26	87	11	.292
1985	Toronto	OF-1B	157	607	87	167	28	6	28	95	21	.275
1986	Toronto	OF-3B	159	641	101	198	38	6	31	108	7	.309
1987	Toronto	OF-2B-3B	156	610	111	188	32	4	47	134	5	.308
1988	Toronto	OF	156	614	78	165	27	5	24	97	4	.269
1989	Toronto	OF	153	613	88	182	41	2	18	104	4	.297
1990	Toronto	OF	142	562	67	149	25	0	21	86	3	.265
1991	Chicago (NL) . .	OF	149	558	63	159	27	0	25	86	2	.285
	Totals		1330	5086	704	1453	264	32	227	826	61	.286

MARK GRACE 27 6-2 190   Bats L Throws L

After finishing among top 10 hitters during first three years in NL, he saw his average slip to .273 in 1991 following late-season slump . . . Went without homer from July 17-Sept. 25 . . . Still among most consistent hitters in baseball, he had career-high, 19-game hitting streak spanning July and August . . . Reached base by hit or walk more than 200 times for fourth straight year . . . Had second career two-homer game July 4 against Pirates, including game-winning, 11th-inning shot off Bill Landrum . . . Finished ninth in NL in hits . . . Mild-mannered first baseman suffered first career ejection after disputing called third strike in San Diego June 16 . . . Selected by Cubs in 24th round of 1985 draft . . . Born June 28, 1964, in Winston-Salem, N.C. . . . Earned $1.2 million in 1991.

Year	Club	Pos.	G	AB	R	H	2B	3B	HR	RBI	SB	Avg.
1988	Chicago (NL) . .	1B	134	486	65	144	23	4	7	57	3	.296
1989	Chicago (NL) . .	1B	142	510	74	160	28	3	13	79	14	.314
1990	Chicago (NL) . .	1B	157	589	72	182	32	1	9	82	15	.309
1991	Chicago (NL) . .	1B	160	619	87	169	28	5	8	58	3	.273
	Totals		593	2204	298	655	111	13	37	276	35	.297

SHAWON DUNSTON 29 6-1 175   Bats R Throws R

Probably has best tools of any shortstop in baseball, including rifle arm, but is plagued by inconsistency . . . A favorite of ex-manager Don Zimmer, he was shaken by Zim's dismissal and struggled badly during first half of 1991 . . . Came on strong in second half, including 14-game hitting streak in August . . . Batted .374 during 31-game stretch spanning August and

September . . . Hot streak began when he started swinging one of Andre Dawson's heavier bats . . . Had four-hit game Aug. 15 against Expos . . . During slump, he shared shortstop job with Jose Vizcaino . . . Early 2-for-29 tailspin dropped average to .200 . . . Made six errors in first 31 games . . . Passed up free agency, signing $12-million, four-year deal with Cubs the final weekend of season . . . First player chosen in 1982 draft . . . Led NL shortstops with 17 homers in 1986 . . . Born March 21, 1963, in Brooklyn, N.Y. . . . Earned $2.1 million in 1991.

Year	Club	Pos.	G	AB	R	H	2B	3B	HR	RBI	SB	Avg.
1985	Chicago (NL) . .	SS	74	250	40	65	12	4	4	18	11	.260
1986	Chicago (NL) . .	SS	150	581	66	145	36	3	17	68	13	.250
1987	Chicago (NL) . .	SS	95	346	40	85	18	3	5	22	12	.246
1988	Chicago (NL) . .	SS	155	575	69	143	23	6	9	56	30	.249
1989	Chicago (NL) . .	SS	138	471	52	131	20	6	9	60	19	.278
1990	Chicago (NL) . .	SS	146	545	73	143	22	8	17	66	25	.262
1991	Chicago (NL) . .	SS	142	492	59	128	22	7	12	50	21	.260
	Totals		900	3260	399	840	153	37	73	340	131	.258

GREG MADDUX 25 6-0 170   Bats R Throws R

Ace of Cubs' staff since 1988 has established himself among most consistent pitchers in majors . . . Surpassed 200 innings for fourth straight year, longest such string by a Cub pitcher since Rick Reuschel (1973-80) . . . Led NL in games started (37) and innings pitched (263) . . . Ranked second in strikeouts (198) and fourth in complete games (seven) . . . Equaled career high with 10 strikeouts at San Francisco June 21 . . . Committed throwing error Sept. 13, snapping string of 68 straight errorless starts dating back to 1989 . . . Hit first major-league homer June 16 at San Diego . . . His shutout in Houston July 20 was Cubs' first in 11 months . . . Selected by Cubs in second round of 1984 draft . . . Made major-league debut Sept. 7, 1986 at Cincinnati, beating Reds to become youngest pitcher to win complete game in NL that season . . . Finished third in 1989 Cy Young voting . . . Born April 14, 1966, in San Angelo, Tex. . . . Earned $2.4 million in 1991 and a Gold Glove.

Year	Club	G	IP	W	L	Pct.	SO	BB	H	ERA
1986	Chicago (NL)	6	31	2	4	.333	20	11	44	5.52
1987	Chicago (NL)	30	155⅔	6	14	.300	101	74	181	5.61
1988	Chicago (NL)	34	249	18	8	.692	140	81	230	3.18
1989	Chicago (NL)	35	238⅓	19	12	.613	135	82	222	2.95
1990	Chicago (NL)	35	237	15	15	.500	144	71	242	3.46
1991	Chicago (NL)	37	263	15	11	.577	198	66	232	3.35
	Totals.	177	1174	75	64	.540	738	385	1151	3.61

MIKE MORGAN 32 6-2 222   Bats R Throws R

As free agent, he signed four-year, $12.5-million contract with Cubs after becoming Dodgers' most consistent starter and second-biggest winner with career-high 14 victories in '91 . . . Ranked eighth in NL in ERA with 2.78 mark . . . Threw two-hitter April 30 vs. Montreal but lost, 1-0 . . . Started the year by hurling 19 consecutive scoreless innings . . . Went to first All-Star Game, as Ramon Martinez' replacement . . . Surrendered just two earned runs or less in 22 of 33 starts . . . Traded to Dodgers from Orioles for Mike Devereaux prior to 1989 season . . . Huge fan of UNLV basketball team . . . Earned $650,000 last season . . . Selected by the A's in the first round of 1978 draft . . . Found himself starting in the majors at 18, as part of Charlie Finley's sideshow, going 0-3 before being sent to Vancouver (AAA) . . . Since inception of amateur draft in '65, only eight other pitchers have made their pro debut in majors . . . Born Oct. 8, 1959, in Tulsa, Okla.

Year	Club	G	IP	W	L	Pct.	SO	BB	H	ERA
1978	Oakland	3	12	0	3	.000	0	8	19	7.50
1979	Oakland	13	77	2	10	.167	17	50	102	5.96
1982	New York (AL)	30	150⅓	7	11	.389	71	67	167	4.37
1983	Toronto	16	45⅓	0	3	.000	22	21	48	5.16
1985	Seattle	2	6	1	1	.500	2	5	11	12.00
1986	Seattle	37	216⅓	11	17	.393	116	86	243	4.53
1987	Seattle	34	207	12	17	.414	85	53	245	4.65
1988	Baltimore	22	71⅓	1	6	.143	29	23	70	5.43
1989	Los Angeles	40	152⅔	8	11	.421	72	33	130	2.53
1990	Los Angeles	33	211	11	15	.423	106	60	216	3.75
1991	Los Angeles	34	236⅓	14	10	.583	140	61	197	2.78
	Totals	264	1385⅓	67	104	.392	660	467	1448	4.10

PAUL ASSENMACHER 31 6-3 200   Bats L Throws L

Workhorse of Cub bullpen for two straight years . . . Was especially effective during second half when Dave Smith was unavailable . . . Finished with career-high 15 saves . . . Became first Cub reliever to strike out 100-plus since Lee Smith in 1985 . . . Second in NL with 75 appearances . . . After going 3-4 with 3.84 ERA before All-Star break, he put together solid four-week stretch of 4-0 and 1.96 ERA . . . Blew six of first 15 save opportunities . . . Made first error in 323 major-league games, falling nine short of Rob Murphy's record for errorless games at start of career . . . Signed by Braves as non-drafted free agent in

1983 . . . Traded to Cubs for Pat Gomez and Kelly Mann, Aug. 24, 1989 . . . As rookie in 1986, he had third-lowest ERA among NL relievers . . . Involved in 17 Cub victories in 1990 while saving 10 games and finishing second in NL in appearances . . . Born Dec. 10, 1960, in Detroit . . . Earned $1 million in 1991.

Year	Club	G	IP	W	L	Pct.	SO	BB	H	ERA
1986	Atlanta	61	68⅓	7	3	.700	56	26	61	2.50
1987	Atlanta	52	54⅔	1	1	.500	39	24	58	5.10
1988	Atlanta	64	79⅓	8	7	.533	71	32	72	3.06
1989	Atl.-Chi. (NL)	63	76⅔	3	4	.429	79	28	74	3.99
1990	Chicago (NL)	74	103	7	2	.778	95	36	90	2.80
1991	Chicago (NL)	75	102⅔	7	8	.467	117	31	85	3.24
	Totals	389	484⅔	33	25	.569	457	177	440	3.34

DAVE SMITH 37 6-1 195   Bats R Throws R

Veteran reliever was signed as new-look free agent before 1991 season, but his first year in Chicago was ruined by injuries . . . Disabled from July 23-Sept. 1 with torn medial collateral ligament in right knee, requiring arthroscopic surgery . . . Sidelined again after undergoing surgery Sept. 16 to remove cyst from right knee . . . His 17 saves were his lowest total since 1984, but he still tied for seventh in NL . . . Opponents batted .302 against him . . . Has 216 career saves, two shy of tying Gene Garber for ninth place on all-time list . . . Blew five of first 21 save opportunities with Cubs . . . Squandered three straight chances after converting first four save opportunities . . . Used frequently during early months, he was on pace for most appearances of career . . . Selected by Astros in eighth round of 1976 draft . . . Recorded career-high 33 saves in 1986 . . . Born Jan. 21, 1955, in San Francisco . . . Earned $1.9 million in 1991.

Year	Club	G	IP	W	L	Pct.	SO	BB	H	ERA
1980	Houston	57	103	7	5	.583	85	32	90	1.92
1981	Houston	42	75	5	3	.625	52	23	54	2.76
1982	Houston	49	63⅓	5	4	.556	28	31	69	3.84
1983	Houston	42	72⅔	3	1	.750	41	36	72	3.10
1984	Houston	53	77⅓	5	4	.556	45	20	60	2.21
1985	Houston	64	79⅓	9	5	.643	40	17	69	2.27
1986	Houston	54	56	4	7	.364	46	22	39	2.73
1987	Houston	50	60	2	3	.400	73	21	39	1.65
1988	Houston	51	57⅓	4	5	.444	38	19	60	2.67
1989	Houston	52	58	3	4	.429	31	19	49	2.64
1990	Houston	49	60⅓	6	6	.500	50	20	45	2.39
1991	Chicago (NL)	35	33	0	6	.000	16	19	39	6.00
	Totals	598	795⅓	53	53	.500	545	279	685	2.67

DANNY JACKSON 30 6-0 205　　　　　**Bats R Throws L**

Free-agent bust during first season with Cubs . . . Disabled from April 20-June 9 with strained left groin and again from June 20-Aug. 3 with lower abdominal strain . . . Was Opening Day starter and loser against Cardinals at Wrigley . . . First Cub pitcher to debut as Opening Day starter since Fred Norman in 1964 and club's first lefty Opening Day pitcher since Dick Ellsworth in 1965 . . . Problems began April 19 in Pittsburgh when he strained groin after pitching just two innings . . . Earned his only victory June 14 at San Diego . . . Demoted to bullpen in September . . . Made first relief appearance since 1987 . . . Royals made him first player chosen in secondary phase of January 1982 draft . . . Traded to Reds before 1988 season . . . Finished second in 1988 Cy Young voting . . . Born Jan. 5, 1962, in San Antonio . . . Most overpaid Cub at $2,625,000 in 1991.

Year	Club	G	IP	W	L	Pct.	SO	BB	H	ERA
1983	Kansas City	4	19	1	1	.500	9	6	26	5.21
1984	Kansas City	15	76	2	6	.250	40	35	84	4.26
1985	Kansas City	32	208	14	12	.538	114	76	209	3.42
1986	Kansas City	32	185⅔	11	12	.478	115	79	177	3.20
1987	Kansas City	36	224	9	18	.333	152	109	219	4.02
1988	Cincinnati	35	260⅔	23	8	.742	161	71	206	2.73
1989	Cincinnati	20	115⅔	6	11	.353	70	57	122	5.60
1990	Cincinnati	22	117⅓	6	6	.500	76	40	119	3.61
1991	Chicago (NL)	17	70⅔	1	5	.167	31	48	89	6.75
	Totals	213	1277	73	79	.480	765	521	1251	3.83

TOP PROSPECTS

LANCE DICKSON 22 6-1 185　　　　　**Bats R Throws L**

Despite stress fracture of right foot which cut short his second pro season, he remains one of brightest pitching prospects in baseball . . . Struck out 101 batters in 101 innings for Iowa (AAA) while going 4-4 with 3.11 ERA in 1991 . . . Has outstanding curve and good poise . . . Selected by Cubs in first round of 1990 draft . . . In 11 starts during first minor-league season, he went 7-3 with 0.94 ERA at three levels of Cubs' system . . . Also made three major-league starts in 1990, going 0-3 with 7.24 ERA after reaching big leagues faster than any Cub draft selection since Burt Hooten in 1971 . . . Born Oct. 19, 1969, in Fullerton, Cal.

REY SANCHEZ 24 5-9 165   Bats R Throws R

Highly regarded shortstop batted .290 with 16 doubles, five triples, two homers and 46 RBI for Iowa (AAA) while striking out only 27 times in 417 at-bats . . . Had 11-game hitting streak . . . Led American Association shortstops with .971 fielding percentage . . . Started for NL squad in Triple-A All-Star Game and was selected to American Association postseason all-star team . . . Was American Association Player of the Month for June, batting .344 with 27 RBI . . . Promoted to big leagues Sept. 6 . . . Recorded first hit and RBI off Pirates' Doug Drabek Sept. 17 . . . Missed 1990 season with medial collateral ligament tear in right elbow . . . Selected by Rangers in 13th round of 1986 draft . . . Traded to Cubs in 1990 . . . Born Oct. 5, 1967, in Rio Piedras, P.R.

DERRICK MAY 23 6-4 205   Bats L Throws R

Good-hitting outfielder was slowed by injuries during second full season with Iowa (AAA) . . . Missed more than six weeks with broken right wrist and lost another 18 days after reinjuring it . . . Batted .297 with 18 doubles, three homers and 49 RBI in just 82 games . . . Recalled to big leagues Sept. 6 and hit .227 in 22 at-bats . . . Had hitting streaks of 20 and 23 games for Iowa in 1990 while finishing fifth in American Association batting race . . . Ranked among top five in batting average in four of first five pro seasons . . . Son of former major-league outfielder Dave May . . . Selected by Cubs in first round of 1986 draft . . . Born July 14, 1968, in Rochester, N.Y.

GARY SCOTT 23 6-0 175   Bats R Throws R

After sensational spring training, he became Cubs' regular third baseman but hit just .165 with five RBI during six-week trial . . . Demoted to Iowa (AAA) where he continued to struggle, hitting .208 . . . Broken hand ended disappointing season, but he's still regarded as outstanding prospect . . . Named Cub organization's Minor League Player of the Year in 1990 after batting .298 with 16 homers and 87 RBI in 137 games for Winston-Salem (A) and Charlotte (AA) . . . Named 1990 Carolina League MVP . . . Selected by Cubs in second round of 1989 draft . . . Born Aug. 22, 1968, in New Rochelle, N.Y.

MANAGER JIM LEFEBVRE: Begins first season as Cubs' skipper with impressive credentials . . . Most successful Seattle Mariners' manager ever, he was fired following 1991 season despite leading team to first winning record in franchise history (85-77) . . . Mariners' record improved during each of his three seasons . . . Overall record of 235-251 represented better winning percentage (.484) than any of previous eight Seattle managers . . . Born Jan. 7, 1943, in Hawthorne, Cal. . . . Compiled .251 lifetime average during eight-year big-league career as switch-hitting infielder with Dodgers . . . Named NL Rookie of the Year in 1965 . . . Made All-Star team in 1966 while hitting career-high 24 homers . . . Played four seasons with Lotte Orions of Japanese League, becoming only second man (Johnny Logan was the other) to play on World Series winner and a Japanese champion . . . Began managing career with Lethbridge of Pioneer (A) League in 1978 . . . Coached with Giants and Dodgers before becoming Giants' director of player development in 1983 . . . Returned to managing in 1985, leading Phoenix (AAA) to division title and was named *Baseball America's* Minor League Manager of the Year . . . Collaborated with father Ben to coauthor *The Making of a Hitter*.

ALL-TIME CUB SEASON RECORDS

BATTING: Rogers Hornsby, .380, 1929
HRs: Hack Wilson, 56, 1930
RBI: Hack Wilson, 190, 1930
STEALS: Frank Chance, 67, 1903
WINS: Mordecai Brown, 29, 1908
STRIKEOUTS: Ferguson Jenkins, 274, 1970

MONTREAL EXPOS

TEAM DIRECTORY: Pres.-General Partner: Claude Brochu; VP/GM: Dan Duquette; VP-Baseball Oper.: Bill Stoneham; Dir. Media Rel.: Richard Griffin; Dir. Media Services: Monique Giroux; Trav. Sec.: Erik Ostling; Mgr.: Tom Runnells. Home: Olympic Stadium (43,739). Field distances: 325, l.f. line; 375, l.c.; 404, c.f.; 375, r.c.; 325, r.f. line. Spring training: West Palm Beach, Fla.

SCOUTING REPORT

HITTING: The Expos scored the fewest runs (579) in the NL and they were 10th in home runs (95) in 1991. And they enter this season without Andres Galarraga, who used to be the big gun in the middle of their lineup. Still, the Expos have a wealth of young talent, so there's reason to be optimistic.

Ivan Calderon (.300, 19, 75) made a quick adjustment to the NL, leading the team in homers and RBI during his first season in Montreal, despite playing with an injured shoulder. Larry Walker (.290, 16, 64) is coming off a solid sophomore season and Marquis Grissom (.267, 6, 39) led the league with 76 stolen

Ivan Calderon conquered Mount .300 in Canadian debut.

bases. Delino DeShields (.238, 10, 51, 56 steals) is a future star while youngsters Bret Barberie (.353, 2, 18) and John Vander Wal (.293, 15, 71 for AAA Indianapolis) look promising.

Twenty-year-old rookie shortstop Wil Cordero (.261, 11, 52 at Indianapolis) is so advanced that he'll be given a chance to win the starting job from incumbent Spike Owen this spring. The Expos are counting on steady veteran Tim Wallach (.225, 13, 73) to rebound from a disappointing season. By claiming aging former star Gary Carter on waivers from the Dodgers, they showed how badly they need help behind the plate, even with the acquisition of Darrin Fletcher from the Phillies.

PITCHING: Expo pitchers tied for the NL lead with 14 shutouts in 1991 and most of these guys are just beginning their careers. Staff anchor Dennis Martinez (14-11, 2.39, 5 shutouts) is the exception. At 36, Martinez is still one of the premier pitchers in baseball and he proved it last summer with a perfect game.

Mark Gardner (9-11, 3.85) also has shown no-hit stuff. He worked nine innings of no-hit ball in Los Angeles, but lost the game in the 10th. Chris Nabholz (8-7, 3.63), Brian Barnes (5-8, 4.22) and Chris Haney (3-7, 4.04) all are improving young pitchers who could make up a solid rotation. And the Expos strengthened their staff when they acquired Ken Hill (11-10, 3.57 with the Cardinals) in the trade for Galarraga.

Barry Jones, last year's bullpen closer, was traded to the Phillies and the Expos are hoping John Wetteland can step into that role. Wetteland (4-3, 2.79, 20 Sv for AAA Albuquerque) made a quick trip across the continent during the offseason, moving from the Dodgers to the Reds before coming to Montreal in a December trade for Dave Martinez.

FIELDING: Wallach, a former Gold Glove winner, led all NL third basemen with a .968 fielding percentage in 1991 and Grissom led all outfielders with 15 assists. On the negative side, DeShields committed a league-high 27 errors at second base and Expos catchers were charged with 22 passed balls, the most in the NL. Losing Galarraga, the slick first baseman, also hurts the defense.

OUTLOOK: Rookie manager Tom Runnells suffered growing pains along with his team in 1991 as the Expos finished in the basement with a 71-90 record. If the young players continue to develop, the Expos could dramatically improve that record in 1992, but they're probably at least a year away from being serious contenders.

MONTREAL EXPOS 1992 ROSTER

MANAGER Tom Runnells
Coaches—Felipe Alou, Tommy Harper, Joe Kerrigan, Jerry Manuel, Jay Ward

PITCHERS

No.	Name	1991 Club	W-L	IP	SO	ERA	B-T	Ht.	Wt.	Born
47	Barnes, Brian	Montreal	5-8	160	117	4.22	L-L	5-9	170	3/25/67 Roanoke Rapids, NC
		W. Palm Beach	0-0	7	6	0.00				
		Indianapolis	2-1	11	10	1.64				
46	Bottenfield, Kent	Indianapolis	8-15	166	108	4.06	S-R	6-3	225	11/14/68 Portland, OR
49	Farmer, Howard	Indianapolis	6-4	105	67	3.86	R-R	6-3	192	1/18/66 Gary, IN
39	Fassero, Jeff	Indianapolis	3-0	18	12	1.47	L-L	6-1	195	1/5/63 Springfield, IL
		Montreal	2-5	55	42	2.44				
41	Frey, Steve	Montreal	0-1	40	21	4.99	R-L	5-9	170	7/26/63 Southampton, PA
		Indianapolis	3-1	36	45	1.51				
28	Gardner, Mark	Indianapolis	2-0	31	38	3.48	R-R	6-1	200	3/1/62 Los Angeles, CA
		Montreal	9-11	168	107	3.85				
42	Haney, Chris	Harrisburg	5-3	83	68	2.16	L-L	6-3	185	11/16/68 Baltimore, MD
		Indianapolis	1-1	10	8	4.35				
		Montreal	3-7	85	51	4.04				
44	Hill, Ken	St. Louis	11-10	181	121	3.57	R-R	6-2	175	12/14/65 Lynn, MA
		Louisville	0-0	1	2	0.00				
56	Hurst, Jonathan	Harrisburg	5-0	42	34	0.86	R-R	6-3	175	10/20/66 New York, NY
		Tulsa	2-1	25	17	2.16				
		Miami	8-2	99	91	2.90				
32	Martinez, Dennis	Montreal	14-11	222	123	2.39	R-R	6-1	180	5/14/55 Nicaragua
43	Nabholz, Chris	Montreal	8-7	154	99	3.63	L-L	6-5	212	1/5/67 Harrisburg, PA
		Indianapolis	2-2	19	16	1.86				
48	Piatt, Doug	Indianapolis	8-4	47	61	3.45	L-R	6-1	190	9/26/65 Beaver, PA
		Montreal	0-0	35	29	2.60				
—	Risley, Bill	Chattanooga	5-7	108	77	3.16	R-R	6-2	215	5/29/67 Chicago, IL
		Nashville	3-5	44	32	4.91				
51	Rojas, Mel	Montreal	3-3	48	37	3.75	R-R	5-11	185	12/10/66 Dominican Republic
		Indianapolis	4-2	53	55	4.10				
55	Sampen, Bill	Montreal	9-5	92	52	4.00	R-R	6-2	195	1/18/63 Lincoln, IL
		Indianapolis	4-0	40	41	2.04				
40	Wainhouse, David	Harrisburg	2-2	52	46	2.60	L-R	6-2	185	11/7/67 Canada
		Indianapolis	2-0	29	13	4.08				
		Montreal	0-1	3	1	6.75				
—	Wetteland, John	Albuquerque	4-3	61	55	2.79	R-R	6-2	195	8/21/66 San Mateo, CA
		Los Angeles	1-0	9	9	0.00				
57	Young, Pete	Harrisburg	7-5	90	74	2.60	R-R	6-0	225	3/19/68 Meadville, MS

CATCHERS

No.	Name	1991 Club	H	HR	RBI	Pct.	B-T	Ht.	Wt.	Born
8	Carter, Gary	Los Angeles	61	6	26	.246	R-R	6-2	214	4/8/54 Culver City, CA
15	Colbrunn, Greg	Montreal	Did not play				R-R	6-0	190	7/26/69 Fontana, CA
—	Fletcher, Darrin	Scranton	87	8	50	.284	L-R	6-1	199	10/3/66 Elmhurst, IL
		Philadelphia	31	1	12	.228				
54	Kremers, Jimmy	Indianapolis	70	11	42	.241	L-R	6-3	210	10/6/65 Little Rock, AR
53	Laker, Tim	W. Palm Beach	77	5	33	.231	R-R	6-2	185	11/27/69 Encino, CA
		Harrisburg	10	1	5	.286				
58	Natal, Robert	Harrisburg	86	13	53	.256	R-R	5-11	190	11/13/65 Long Beach, CA
		Indianapolis	13	0	9	.317				
2	Reyes, Gilberto	Montreal	45	0	13	.217	R-R	6-2	212	12/10/63 Dominican Republic

INFIELDERS

No.	Name	1991 Club	H	HR	RBI	Pct.	B-T	Ht.	Wt.	Born
25	Barberie, Bret	Indianapolis	68	10	48	.312	S-R	5-11	185	8/16/67 Long Beach, CA
		Montreal	48	2	18	.353				
52	Canale, George	Denver	64	10	47	.234	L-R	6-1	190	8/11/65 Memphis, TN
		Milwaukee	6	3	10	.176				
12	Cordero, Wilfredo	Indianapolis	94	11	52	.261	R-R	6-2	185	10/3/71 Puerto Rico
4	DeShields, Delino	Montreal	134	10	51	.238	L-R	6-1	170	1/15/69 Seaford, DE
16	Foley, Tom	Montreal	35	0	15	.208	L-R	6-1	175	9/9/59 Columbus, GA
11	Owen, Spike	Montreal	108	3	26	.255	S-R	5-10	170	4/19/61 Cleburne, TX
29	Wallach, Tim	Montreal	130	13	73	.225	R-R	6-3	200	9/14/57 Huntington Park, CA

OUTFIELDERS

No.	Name	1991 Club	H	HR	RBI	Pct.	B-T	Ht.	Wt.	Born
18	Alou, Moises	Montreal	Injured				R-R	6-3	190	7/3/66 Atlanta, GA
22	Calderon, Ivan	Montreal	141	19	75	.300	R-R	6-1	220	3/19/62 Puerto Rico
9	Grissom, Marquis	Montreal	149	6	39	.267	R-R	5-11	190	4/17/67 Atlanta, GA
5	Reed, Darren	Montreal	Injured				R-R	6-1	205	10/16/65 Ventura, CA
59	Stairs, Matt	Harrisburg	168	13	78	.333	R-R	5-9	175	2/27/69 Canada
23	Vander Wal, John	Indianapolis	140	15	71	.293	L-L	6-2	190	4/29/66 Grand Rapids, MI
		Montreal	13	1	8	.213				
33	Walker, Larry	Montreal	141	16	64	.290	L-L	6-3	210	12/1/66 Canada

EXPO PROFILES

IVAN CALDERON 30 6-1 220   Bats R Throws R

During first year in Montreal, this left fielder led Expos in RBI (75) and homers (19) despite injuries that shortened his season . . . Finished 10th in NL batting race at .300 . . . Homered in three consecutive games in August . . . Drove in 29 of 39 runners from third base with less than two out . . . Sidelined briefly in May with jammed left shoulder, in July with fluid drained from left knee and in September with sore elbow . . . Named Expos' Player of the Month in April (.284, three homers, 15 RBI) and May (.330, 4, 20) . . . Obtained from White Sox with Barry Jones for Tim Raines prior to last season . . . Led White Sox in 1990 in RBI, hits, runs, multi-hit games (42), total bases (256), extra-base hits (60), sac flies (eight), at-bats and doubles . . . Earned $2.2 million in 1991 . . . Born March 19, 1962, in Fajardo, P.R.

Year	Club	Pos.	G	AB	R	H	2B	3B	HR	RBI	SB	Avg.
1984	Seattle	OF	11	24	2	5	1	0	1	1	1	.208
1985	Seattle	OF-1B	67	210	37	60	16	4	8	28	4	.286
1986	Sea.-Chi. (AL)	OF	50	164	16	41	7	1	2	15	3	.250
1987	Chicago (AL) . .	OF	144	542	93	159	38	2	28	83	10	.293
1988	Chicago (AL) . .	OF	73	264	40	56	14	0	14	35	4	.212
1989	Chicago (AL) . .	OF-1B	157	622	83	178	34	9	14	87	7	.286
1990	Chicago (AL) . .	OF-1B	158	607	85	166	44	2	14	74	32	.273
1991	Montreal	OF-1B	134	470	69	141	22	3	19	75	31	.300
	Totals		794	2903	425	806	176	21	100	398	92	.278

LARRY WALKER 25 6-3 210   Bats L Throws R

Brought speed, power and defense to right field, a combination Expos had lacked since Andre Dawson's departure in 1987 . . . Improved on almost all of his rookie statistics in 1991 . . . Led Expos in doubles (30) and was second in homers (16) . . . During 45-game stretch spanning August and September, he batted .353 with 18 doubles, seven homers and 27 RBI . . . Tied club record with three doubles Aug. 7 at St. Louis . . . Had nine-game hitting streak in June and career-high 10-game streak in August . . . Hit first career pinch homer July 21 against Giants' Jeff Brantley . . . Broke out of 0-for-10 slump June 22 with longest career homer, a 450-foot shot off Jack Armstrong in Cincinnati . . . Tied club record with two outfield assists in one inning April

26 against Cardinals . . . Expos' Player of the Month in August, batting .376 with four homers and 12 RBI . . . Signed by Expos as free agent in 1984 . . . Earned $185,000 in 1991 . . . Born Dec. 1, 1966, in Maple Ridge, B.C.

Year	Club	Pos.	G	AB	R	H	2B	3B	HR	RBI	SB	Avg.
1989	Montreal	OF	20	47	4	8	0	0	0	4	1	.170
1990	Montreal	OF	133	419	59	101	18	3	19	51	21	.241
1991	Montreal	OF-1B	137	487	59	141	30	2	16	64	14	.290
	Totals		290	953	122	250	48	5	35	119	36	.262

MARQUIS GRISSOM 24 5-11 190   Bats R Throws R

Led NL in steals with 76 during second full season . . . Finished fourth in triples with nine . . . Stole three bases in a game four times . . . Center fielder had assists in four consecutive games from June 10-13 . . . Had streak of seven straight games with at least one steal snapped June 4 . . . His speed intimidates infielders . . . Reached base eight times on infield errors and also had 31 infield hits among first 93 singles . . . None of the first 50 infield singles of his career were bunts . . . Had five-hit games June 7 at Atlanta and June 26 at New York . . . Joined Andre Dawson as only Expos with two five-hit games in one season . . . Homered in three consecutive games from May 5-7 . . . Had career-high five RBI April 28 at St. Louis, including grand slam . . . Selected by Expos in third round of 1988 draft . . . Earned $140,000 in 1991 . . . Born April 17, 1967, in Atlanta.

Year	Club	Pos.	G	AB	R	H	2B	3B	HR	RBI	SB	Avg.
1989	Montreal	OF	26	74	16	19	2	0	1	2	1	.257
1990	Montreal	OF	98	288	42	74	14	2	3	29	22	.257
1991	Montreal	OF	148	558	73	149	23	9	6	39	76	.267
	Totals		272	920	131	242	39	11	10	70	99	.263

SPIKE OWEN 30 5-10 170   Bats S Throws R

Among most sure-handed shortstops in baseball, he made just eight errors in 1991 . . . Led NL shortstops in fielding percentage in 1989 and 1990 . . . Started 1990 season with record 63 straight errorless games . . . Made two errors in a game for first time in NL career Aug. 13 . . . Finished sixth in NL in triples with eight . . . Tied career high with four hits Sept. 4 against Braves . . . During 46-game stretch in August and September, he batted .300 with seven doubles and two triples . . . His homer May 10 against Padres' Ed Whitson was his first since June 7, 1990 . . . Didn't homer again until July 1 against Mets' Frank Viola . . . Selected by Mariners in first round of 1982 draft . . . Traded to Red Sox Aug. 19, 1986, in time to help Boston reach World Series . . . Traded to Expos with Dan Gakeler for John Dopson and Luis Rivera before 1989 season . . . Born April 19, 1961, in Austin, Tex. . . . Named Southwest Conference Player of the Year for Texas in 1981 . . . Earned $1,033,333 in 1991.

Year	Club	Pos.	G	AB	R	H	2B	3B	HR	RBI	SB	Avg.
1983	Seattle	SS	80	306	36	60	11	3	2	21	10	.196
1984	Seattle	SS	152	530	67	130	18	8	3	43	16	.245
1985	Seattle	SS	118	352	41	91	10	6	6	37	11	.259
1986	Sea.-Bos.	SS	154	528	67	122	24	7	1	45	4	.231
1987	Boston	SS	132	437	50	113	17	7	2	48	11	.259
1988	Boston	SS	89	257	40	64	14	1	5	18	0	.249
1989	Montreal	SS	142	437	52	102	17	4	6	41	3	.233
1990	Montreal	SS	149	453	55	106	24	5	5	35	8	.234
1991	Montreal	SS	139	424	39	108	22	8	3	26	2	.255
	Totals		1155	3724	447	896	157	49	33	314	65	.241

TIM WALLACH 34 6-3 200   Bats R Throws R

Expos' all-time leader in games played at third base has been fixture since 1982 . . . Never spent day on disabled list despite numerous injuries . . . One of just 10 regular players in majors to play each year in 1980s without doing any time on DL . . . Third on Expos' all-time hit list behind Tim Raines and Andre Dawson . . . Had disappointing offensive season, but was second on team in RBI (73) . . . Suffered through homerless streak from July 20-Aug. 26 before finally going deep against Atlanta's Armando Reynosa . . . Missed three games in July with severely sprained right ankle, snapping string of 183 consecutive starts . . . First batter in 1991 to homer against Reds' Rob Dibble . . . Homered in back-to-back games three times . . . Had consecutive three-hit games June 5-6 . . . Had nine-game hitting streak in April . . . Collected 1,500th hit with bases-empty homer June 12 . . . Picked 10th overall by Expos in 1979 draft . . . Earned

$1,906,500 in 1991 . . . Born Sept. 14, 1957, in Huntington Park, Cal.

Year	Club	Pos.	G	AB	R	H	2B	3B	HR	RBI	SB	Avg.
1980	Montreal	OF-1B	5	11	1	2	0	0	1	2	0	.182
1981	Montreal	OF-1B-3B	71	212	19	50	9	1	4	13	0	.236
1982	Montreal	3B-OF-1B	158	596	89	160	31	3	28	97	6	.268
1983	Montreal	3B	156	581	54	156	33	3	19	70	0	.269
1984	Montreal	3B-SS	160	582	55	143	25	4	18	72	3	.246
1985	Montreal	3B	155	569	70	148	36	3	22	81	9	.260
1986	Montreal	3B	134	480	50	112	22	1	18	71	8	.233
1987	Montreal	3B-P	153	593	89	177	42	4	26	123	9	.298
1988	Montreal	3B-2B	159	592	52	152	32	5	12	69	2	.257
1989	Montreal	3B-P	154	573	76	159	42	0	13	77	3	.277
1990	Montreal	3B	161	626	69	185	37	5	21	96	6	.296
1991	Montreal	3B	151	577	60	130	22	1	13	73	2	.225
	Totals		1617	5992	684	1574	331	30	195	846	48	.263

DELINO DeSHIELDS 23 6-1 170   Bats L Throws R

Touched by sophomore jinx in 1991 . . . Struck out 151 times, most in NL . . . Sometimes shaky at second base, he led Expos with 27 errors . . . Finished third in NL in stolen bases (56) and fourth in walks (95) . . . Had .440 on-base percentage as first batter of a game, .347 mark overall . . . Set club record by being caught stealing 23 times, breaking his own mark of 22 . . . Had seven multiple-steal games, including three steals June 22 against Reds . . . Hit six homers leading off an inning and two leading off a game . . . His homers June 4-5 against Astros' Pete Harnisch and Jim Clancy were the first he had ever hit with a runner on base . . . Tied career highs June 5 with four hits and four RBI . . . Also had four-hit game in major-league debut in 1990 . . . Had six straight hits and reached base seven straight times June 4-5 . . . Had 10-game hitting streak in July . . . Selected by Expos in first round of 1987 draft . . . Earned $215,000 in 1991 . . . Born Jan. 15, 1969, in Seaford, Del.

Year	Club	Pos.	G	AB	R	H	2B	3B	HR	RBI	SB	Avg.
1990	Montreal	2B	129	499	69	144	28	6	4	45	42	.289
1991	Montreal	2B	151	563	83	134	15	4	10	51	56	.238
	Totals		280	1062	152	278	43	10	14	96	98	.262

DENNIS MARTINEZ 36 6-1 180   Bats R Throws R

One of the game's most consistent starting pitchers earned place in history with perfect game at Los Angeles July 28 ... It was only the 15th perfect game ever pitched in big leagues and the first since Tom Browning's in 1988, also against Dodgers ... Led NL in ERA (2.39), shutouts (five) and complete games (nine) ... Ranked sixth in opponents' batting average (.226) ... Led Expos in victories, ERA, games started, strikeouts and nearly every other pitching category ... A recovering alcoholic, he re-established himself as a star in Montreal after Orioles gave up on him in 1986 ... Had 11-game winning streak in 1989 ... Traded to Expos for Rene Gonzales, June 16, 1986 ... Bypassed second-look free agency before 1991 season, signing three-year, $9.5-million contract with Expos ... Highest-paid Expo earned $3,333,333 in 1991 ... Born May 14, 1955, in Granada, Nicaragua.

Year	Club	G	IP	W	L	Pct.	SO	BB	H	ERA
1976	Baltimore	4	28	1	2	.333	18	8	23	2.57
1977	Baltimore	42	167	14	7	.667	107	64	157	4.10
1978	Baltimore	40	276	16	11	.593	142	93	257	3.25
1979	Baltimore	40	292	15	16	.484	132	78	279	3.67
1980	Baltimore	25	100	6	4	.600	42	44	103	3.96
1981	Baltimore	25	179	14	5	.737	88	62	173	3.32
1982	Baltimore	40	252	16	12	.571	111	87	262	4.21
1983	Baltimore	32	153	7	16	.304	71	45	209	5.53
1984	Baltimore	34	141⅔	6	9	.400	77	37	145	5.02
1985	Baltimore	33	180	13	11	.542	68	63	203	5.15
1986	Baltimore	4	6⅔	0	0	.000	2	2	11	6.75
1986	Montreal	19	98	3	6	.333	63	28	103	4.59
1987	Montreal	22	144⅔	11	4	.733	84	40	133	3.30
1988	Montreal	34	235⅓	15	13	.536	120	55	215	2.72
1989	Montreal	34	232	16	7	.696	142	49	227	3.18
1990	Montreal	32	226	10	11	.476	156	49	191	2.95
1991	Montreal	31	222	14	11	.560	123	62	187	2.39
	Totals	491	2933⅓	177	145	.550	1546	866	2878	3.71

KEN HILL 26 6-2 175   Bats R Throws R

Came from Cardinals in November trade for Andres Galarraga ... Lanky right-hander showed signs of reaching potential with strong finish in September ... Spent three weeks on DL with injured elbow ... During next five starts after being activated Sept. 1, he allowed just six earned runs on 18 hits while compiling 1.29 ERA ... Was winless in nine straight decisions before hot streak yet still managed to reach career highs in victories (11) and strikeouts (121)... Won three straight decisions in May while allowing just three earned runs for 1.19 ERA ... Limited opponents to .224 batting average, fourth-best mark in NL... Born Dec. 14, 1965, in Lynn, Mass.... Signed with Tigers as non-drafted free agent in 1985... Traded to Cards with Mike Laga for Mike Heath, Aug. 10, 1986... His 33 starts in 1989 were most by a Cardinal rookie since Reggie Cleveland had 34 in 1971... Earned $155,000 in 1991.

Year	Club	G	IP	W	L	Pct.	SO	BB	H	ERA
1988	St. Louis	4	14	0	1	.000	6	6	16	5.14
1989	St. Louis	33	196⅔	7	15	.318	112	99	186	3.80
1990	St. Louis	17	78⅔	5	6	.455	58	33	79	5.49
1991	St. Louis	30	181⅓	11	10	.524	121	67	147	3.57
	Totals	84	470⅔	23	32	.418	297	205	428	4.03

MARK GARDNER 30 6-1 200   Bats R Throws R

Pitched in hard luck throughout second big-league season... Threw nine no-hit innings in Los Angeles July 26, but lost no-hitter and game in 10th, 1-0... Became seventh player in major-league history to lose no-hitter in 10th as Lenny Harris led off inning with infield single and Eddie Murray also singled before he was removed... During four-week stretch at midseason, he went 2-3 despite 1.66 ERA... Finished second among Expos starters to Dennis Martinez in most categories, including victories, games started and innings pitched... Finished 10th in NL in opponents' batting average (.230)... Selected by Expos in eighth round of 1985 draft... Underwent surgery following 1990 season to repair small posterior labrum tear in shoulder... Born March 1, 1962, in Los Angeles... Earned $185,000 in 1991... Expos' eighth-round draft pick in 1985.

Year	Club	G	IP	W	L	Pct.	SO	BB	H	ERA
1989	Montreal	7	26⅓	0	3	.000	21	11	26	5.13
1990	Montreal	27	152⅔	7	9	.438	135	61	129	3.42
1991	Montreal	27	168⅓	9	11	.450	107	75	139	3.85
	Totals	61	347⅓	16	23	.410	263	147	294	3.76

TOP PROSPECTS

WIL CORDERO 20 6-2 185   Bats R Throws R

Youngest player ever invited to Expos' major-league camp in 1989 ... Florida State League All-Star shortstop in 1989... Following

1990 season spent with Jacksonville (AA), he played winter ball for Mayaguez and was selected Rookie of the Year in Puerto Rican League and All-Star shortstop . . . Born Oct. 3, 1971, in Maya-guez, P.R. . . . Signed with Expos as free agent in 1988 . . . Has good range defensively and was batting .261 with 11 homers and 52 RBI for Indianapolis (AAA) before being sidelined the rest of the season with broken hand sustained when he was hit by pitch.

CHRIS HANEY 23 6-3 185   **Bats L Throws L**
Split time in 1991 between Harrisburg (AA), Indianapolis (AAA) and Montreal . . . Was 5-3 with 2.16 ERA for Harrisburg, com-pleting three of 12 starts while striking out 68 batters in 83 innings . . . Went 1-1 in only two appearances for Indianapolis . . . Started 16 games for Expos, going 3-7 with 4.04 ERA . . . Member of 1989 Team USA . . . Born Nov. 16, 1968, in Baltimore . . . Selected by Expos in third round of 1990 draft . . . Son of former major leaguer Larry Haney . . . Attended North Carolina-Charlotte.

JOHN VANDER WAL 25 6-2 190   **Bats L Throws L**
Hard-hitting outfielder came out of nowhere to become hot pros-pect in 1991 . . . Began season as extra outfielder for Indianapolis (AAA) and finished it as American Association's ninth-best hitter . . . Batted .293 with 36 doubles, eight triples, 15 homers and 71 RBI . . . Left-handed hitter who doesn't mind facing left-handed pitching . . . Selected by Expos in third round of 1987 draft . . . Attended Western Michigan . . . Hit .213 with eight RBI in 61 at-bats with Expos last season . . . Born April 29, 1966, in Grand Rapids, Mich.

DOUG PIATT 26 6-1 190   **Bats L Throws R**
Right-handed reliever appeared in 44 games for Indianapolis (AAA), compiling 13 saves and 3.45 ERA while striking out 61 batters in 47 innings . . . Made 21 appearances for Expos, putting together 13-inning scoreless stretch . . . Finished with 2.60 ERA and 29 strikeouts in 34 innings for Montreal . . . Could be Expos' closer in 1992 . . . Held Southern League opponents to .175 batting average while pitching for Jacksonville (AA) in 1990 and had 14 saves in Mexican Winter League . . . Born Sept. 26, 1965, in Bea-ver, Pa. . . . Signed by Indians as non-drafted free agent in 1988 . . . Traded to Expos July 27, 1989 for Ricky Carriger . . . Saved 45 games during minor-league career . . . Attended Western Ken-tucky.

Dennis Martinez was picture of perfection vs. Dodgers.

BRET BARBERIE 24 5-11 185   **Bats S Throws R**
An excellent outfielder, he batted .312 for Indianapolis (AAA) with 10 doubles, four triples, 10 homers and 48 RBI in just 218 at-bats . . . Promoted to Expos Aug. 1 . . . Can play second, shortstop or third and switch-hits with power . . . Batted .353 with 12 doubles . . . Selected by Expos in eighth round of 1988 draft . . . Member of 1988 U.S. Olympic team . . . Graduate of USC . . . Hit .260 with 18 doubles, seven homers, 56 RBI and 20 steals for Jacksonville (AA) in 1990 . . . Born Aug. 16, 1967, in Long Beach, Cal.

MANAGER TOM RUNNELLS: Became youngest manager in majors when he replaced Buck Rodgers June 3 . . . Expos were last-place team with 20-29 record under Rodgers and remained last going 51-61 the rest of the way . . . Was given generous $450,000 salary and signed through 1992 . . . Groomed for job by former GM Dave Dombrowski, who never got along with Rodgers . . . Made rookie mistakes but showed strong desire to learn, even questioning veteran catcher Ron Hassey about Tony La Russa's methods . . . Was in second year as Expos' third-base coach and infield instructor before being elevated to manager . . . Named 1989 American Association Manager of the Year after leading Indianapolis to league championship . . . Was good-fielding second baseman in Giants' system, batting .240 during brief big-league trials in 1985 and 1986 . . . Born April 17, 1955, in Greeley, Col.

ALL-TIME EXPO SEASON RECORDS

BATTING: Tim Raines, .334, 1986
HRs: Andre Dawson, 32, 1983
RBI: Tim Wallach, 123, 1987
STEALS: Ron LeFlore, 97, 1980
WINS: Ross Grimsley, 20, 1978
STRIKEOUTS: Bill Stoneman, 251, 1971

NEW YORK METS

TEAM DIRECTORY: Chairman: Nelson Doubleday; Pres.: Fred Wilpon; COO/Sr. Exec. VP: Frank Cashen; Exec. VP/GM: Al Harazin; Asst. VP-Baseball Oper.: Gerry Hunsicker; Dir. Scouting: Roland Johnson; Minor League Coordinator: Bobby Floyd; Dir. Pub. Rel.: Jay Horwitz; Trav. Sec.: Bob O'Hara; Mgr.: Jeff Torborg. Home: Shea Stadium (55,601). Field distances: 338, l.f. line; 371, l.c.; 410, c.f.; 371, r.c.; 388, r.f. line. Spring training: Port St. Lucie, Fla.

SCOUTING REPORT

HITTING: This lineup still has holes, but it's a completely different group from the one that batted just .244 last season while finishing eighth in the NL with 640 runs. Kevin McReynolds, Gregg Jefferies and Hubie Brooks are all gone.

Free agent imports Bobby Bonilla (.302, 18, 100 with the Pirates) and Eddie Murray (.260, 19, 96 with the Dodgers) are both legitimate run producers who will strengthen the middle of the Mets' lineup. They'll combine with Howard Johnson (.259, 38, 117, 30 steals), who is coming off his best season.

Leadoff man Vince Coleman (.255, 1, 17) must bounce back from a hamstring injury which limited him to a career-low 37 stolen bases. Dave Magadan (.258, 4, 51) is trying to rebound from surgery on both shoulders. Free agent signee Willie Randolph (.327, 0, 54 with the Brewers) proved he could still set the table at 37 and versatile Bill Pecota (.286, 6, 45 with the Royals) will get his at-bats, too. The bottom of the lineup still looks pretty soft with shortstop Kevin Elster (.241, 6, 36) and rookie catcher Todd Hundley (.273, 14, 66 at AAA Tidewater), who has yet to prove he can hit in the big leagues.

PITCHING: If everybody is healthy, the Mets once again have the best starting rotation in baseball. Unfortunately, three of their big guys had physical problems last year and two of them are coming off surgery. Dwight Gooden (13-7, 3.60) didn't pitch a game after Aug. 22 and he had rotator cuff surgery in September. It's questionable whether he can still be a premier pitcher.

Bret Saberhagen (13-8, 3.07 with the Royals), a two-time AL Cy Young winner, replaces free agent defector Frank Viola in the rotation. But the tendinitis-plagued Saberhagen has had a roller-coaster career, with bad years following good ones, and he has

Nouveau Straw Bobby Bonilla figures to stir Mets.

also spent time on the disabled list in each of the past two seasons.

Sid Fernandez (1-3, 2.86) had arthroscopic knee surgery in September. He dropped 35 pounds over the winter, which should mean less pressure on his knee, and that might allow him to finally reach his potential. David Cone (14-14, 3.29, 241 Ks) led the NL in strikeouts the last two seasons and could be a 20-game winner. Closer John Franco (5-9, 2.93, 30 Sv) remains one of the best in the business, but he could use some help.

FIELDING: The Mets were 11th in the NL with a .977 fielding percentage and there still aren't many Gold Glove candidates in the revamped version. The outfield looks especially weak with two ex-third basemen, Bonilla and Johnson, along with the erratic Coleman. Murray and Randolph improve the right side of the infield, Elster is solid at shortstop and Hundley is a good catcher. Magadan's range at third base is limited, but Pecota should ease the pain there. Dave Gallagher and Daryl Boston will improve the outfield defense, if they get a chance to play.

OUTLOOK: If the pitchers stay healthy, the Mets could win the division. New manager Jeff Torborg will be a positive influence and the clubhouse atmosphere should improve. The Mets are ready to erase the nightmare of last year's 77-84, fifth-place finish.

NEW YORK METS 1992 ROSTER

MANAGER Jeff Torborg
Coaches—Mike Cubbage, Barry Foote, Dave LaRoche, Tom McCraw, Mel Stottlemyre

PITCHERS

No.	Name	1991 Club	W-L	IP	SO	ERA	B-T	Ht.	Wt.	Born
46	Bross, Terry	Tidewater	2-0	33	23	4.36	R-R	6-9	230	3/30/66 El Paso, TX
		Williamsport	2-0	25	28	2.49				
44	Burke, Tim	New York (NL)	0-0	10	5	1.80				
		Mont.-NY (NL)	6-7	102	59	3.36	R-R	6-3	205	2/19/59 Omaha, NE
36	Castillo, Tony	Richmond	5-6	118	78	2.90	L-L	5-10	188	3/1/63 Venezuela
		Atl.-NY (NL)	2-1	32	18	3.34				
17	Cone, David	New York (NL)	14-14	233	241	3.29	L-R	6-1	190	1/2/63 Kansas City, MO
50	Fernandez, Sid	St. Lucie	0-0	3	4	0.00	L-L	6-1	230	10/12/62 Honolulu, HI
		Williamsport	0-0	6	5	0.00				
		Tidewater	1-0	16	22	1.15				
		New York (NL)	1-3	44	31	2.86				
31	Franco, John	New York (NL)	5-9	55	45	2.93	L-L	5-10	185	9/17/60 Brooklyn, NY
16	Gooden, Dwight	New York (NL)	13-7	190	150	3.60	R-R	6-3	210	11/16/64 Tampa, FL
32	Hillman, Eric	Tidewater	5-12	162	91	4.01	L-L	6-10	225	4/27/66 Gary, IN
40	Innis, Jeff	New York (NL)	0-2	85	47	2.66	R-R	6-1	180	7/5/62 Decatur, IL
35	Johnstone, John	Williamsport	7-9	165	99	3.97	R-R	6-3	195	11/25/68 Liverpool, NY
—	Rosenberg, Steve	Las Vegas	2-4	68	61	7.54	L-L	6-0	185	10/31/64 Brooklyn, NY
		San Diego	1-1	12	6	6.94				
—	Saberhagen, Bret	Kansas City	13-8	196	136	3.07	R-R	6-1	200	4/11/64 Chicago Heights, IL
48	Schourek, Pete	New York (NL)	5-4	86	67	4.27	L-L	6-5	195	5/10/69 Austin, TX
		Tidewater	1-1	25	17	2.52				
43	Simons, Doug	New York (NL)	2-3	61	38	5.19	L-L	6-0	160	9/15/66 Bakersfield, CA
34	Valera, Julio	Tidewater	10-10	176	117	3.83	R-R	6-2	215	10/13/68 Puerto Rico
		New York (NL)	0-0	2	3	0.00				
66	Vasquez, Julian	St. Lucie	3-2	64	56	0.28	R-R	6-3	165	5/24/68 Dominican Republic
63	Vitko, Joe	S. Lucie	11-8	140	105	2.24	R-R	6-8	210	2/1/70 Somerville, NJ
47	Whitehurst, Wally	New York (NL)	7-12	133	87	4.19	R-R	6-3	195	4/11/64 Shreveport, LA
—	Young, Anthony	Tidewater	7-9	164	93	3.73	R-R	6-2	200	1/19/66 Houston, TX
		New York (NL)	2-5	49	20	3.10				

CATCHERS

No.	Name	1991 Club	H	HR	RBI	Pct.	B-T	Ht.	Wt.	Born
64	Fordyce, Brook	St. Lucie	97	7	55	.239	R-R	6-1	185	5/7/70 New London, CT
8	Hundley, Todd	Tidewater	124	14	66	.273	S-R	5-11	185	5/27/69 Martinsville, VA
		New York (NL)	8	1	7	.133				
5	O'Brien, Charlie	New York (NL)	31	2	14	.185	R-R	6-2	190	5/1/61 Tulsa, OK
2	Sasser, Mackey	New York (NL)	62	5	35	.272	L-R	6-1	210	8/3/62 Fort Gaines, GA

INFIELDERS

No.	Name	1991 Club	H	HR	RBI	Pct.	B-T	Ht.	Wt.	Born
13	Baez, Kevin	Tidewater	36	0	13	.171	R-R	6-0	170	1/10/67 Brooklyn, NY
23	Donnels, Chris	Tidewater	87	8	56	.303	L-R	6-0	185	4/21/66 Los Angeles, CA
		New York (NL)	20	0	5	.225				
15	Elster, Kevin	New York (NL)	84	6	36	.241	R-R	6-2	200	8/3/64 San Pedro, CA
26	Hansen, Terrel	Tidewater	100	12	62	.272	R-R	6-3	210	9/25/61 Bremerton, WA
18	Magadan, Dave	New York (NL)	108	4	51	.258	L-R	6-3	200	9/30/62 Tampa, FL
33	Murray, Eddie	Los Angeles	150	19	96	.260	S-R	6-2	224	2/24/56 Los Angeles, CA
65	Navarro, Tito	Williamsport	139	2	42	.288	S-R	5-10	155	9/12/70 Puerto Rico
3	Noboa, Junior	Montreal	23	1	2	.242	R-R	5-10	165	11/10/64 Dominican Republic
—	Pecota, Bill	Kansas City	114	6	45	.286	R-R	6-2	190	2/16/60 Redwood City, CA

OUTFIELDERS

No.	Name	1991 Club	H	HR	RBI	Pct.	B-T	Ht.	Wt.	Born
25	Bonilla, Bobby	Pittsburgh	174	18	100	.302	S-R	6-3	240	2/23/63 New York, NY
6	Boston, Daryl	New York (NL)	70	4	21	.275	L-L	6-3	195	1/4/63 Cincinnati, OH
45	Carreon, Mark	New York (NL)	66	4	21	.260	R-L	6-0	195	7/9/63 Chicago, IL
5	Coleman, Vince	New York (NL)	71	1	17	.255	S-R	6-1	185	9/22/61 Jacksonville, FL
—	Gallagher, Dave	California	79	1	30	.293	R-R	6-0	184	9/20/60 Trenton, NJ
62	Howell, Pat	Williamsport	77	1	26	.281	S-R	5-11	155	8/31/68 Mobile, AL
		St. Lucie	54	0	10	.220				
20	Johnson, Howard	New York (NL)	146	38	117	.259	S-R	5-10	195	11/29/60 Clearwater, FL

MET PROFILES

BOBBY BONILLA 29 6-3 240   Bats S Throws R

Proved himself to be true "money player" by putting together another excellent season during contract option year with Pirates and then signing a five-year, guaranteed contract with Mets worth $29 million . . . Mets plan to use him in outfield . . . Led NL in doubles . . . Finished fourth in hits (174), runs (102) and on-base percentage (.391), fifth in walks (90), sixth in batting (.302) and total bases (284) . . . Went 7-for-23 with two doubles in NLCS, but drove in just one run . . . Had career-best 18-game hitting streak in August and 10-game streak in July . . . Pirates' regular right fielder also made 60 starts at third base . . . Missed just nine games in last four seasons . . . Signed by Pirates as non-drafted free agent in 1981 . . . Claimed by White Sox in December 1985 major-league draft . . . Traded back to Pirates for Jose DeLeon, July 23, 1986 . . . Born Feb. 23, 1963, in New York . . . Runnerup to Barry Bonds in 1990 NL MVP voting . . . Earned $2.4 million in 1991.

Year	Club	Pos.	G	AB	R	H	2B	3B	HR	RBI	SB	Avg.
1986	Chicago (AL) . .	OF-1B	75	234	27	63	10	2	2	26	4	.269
1986	Pittsburgh	OF-1B-3B	63	192	28	46	6	2	1	17	4	.240
1987	Pittsburgh	3B-OF-1B	141	466	58	140	33	3	15	77	3	.300
1988	Pittsburgh	3B	159	584	87	160	32	7	24	100	3	.274
1989	Pittsburgh	3B-1B-OF	163	616	96	173	37	10	24	86	8	.281
1990	Pittsburgh	OF-3B-1B	160	625	112	175	39	7	32	120	4	.280
1991	Pittsburgh	OF-3B-1B	157	577	102	174	44	6	18	100	2	.302
	Totals		918	3294	510	931	201	37	116	526	28	.283

HOWARD JOHNSON 31 5-10 195   Bats S Throws R

"HoJo" might have won NL MVP if Mets had been serious contenders in 1991 . . . Led NL in homers (38), RBI (117) and extra-base hits (76) . . . Was second in runs (108) and slugging percentage (.535), third in total bases (302), ninth in walks (78) . . . Smashed Mets' single-season RBI record of 108, set by Darryl Strawberry in 1990 . . . Broke own NL record for homers by switch-hitter, 36 set in 1989 . . . Had third "30-30"

season . . . Homered from both sides of plate Aug. 31 in Cincinnati
. . . Played shortstop and third base before making switch to right
field after Labor Day . . . Only negative was major-league-high 31
errors . . . Voted NL Player of the Month in September, batting
.296 with 10 homers and 28 RBI . . . Selected by Tigers in first
round of January 1979 draft's secondary phase . . . Traded to Mets
for Walt Terrell following 1984 season . . . Had breakthrough season in 1987 after finally winning regular job at third base . . . Born
Nov. 29, 1960, in Clearwater, Fla. . . . Earned $2,166,667 in
1991.

Year	Club	Pos.	G	AB	R	H	2B	3B	HR	RBI	SB	Avg.
1982	Detroit	3B-OF	54	155	23	49	5	0	4	14	7	.316
1983	Detroit	3B	27	66	11	14	0	0	3	5	0	.212
1984	Detroit	3B-SS-1B-OF	116	355	43	88	14	1	12	50	10	.248
1985	New York (NL)	3B-SS	126	389	38	94	18	4	11	46	6	.242
1986	New York (NL)	3B-SS-OF	88	220	30	54	14	0	10	39	8	.245
1987	New York (NL)	3B-SS-OF	157	554	93	147	22	1	36	99	32	.265
1988	New York (NL)	3B-SS	148	495	85	114	21	1	24	68	23	.230
1989	New York (NL)	3B-SS	153	571	104	164	41	3	36	101	41	.287
1990	New York (NL)	3B-SS	154	590	89	144	37	3	23	90	34	.244
1991	New York (NL)	3B-OF-SS	156	564	108	146	34	4	38	117	30	.259
	Totals		1179	3959	624	1014	206	17	197	629	191	.256

VINCE COLEMAN 30 6-1 185   Bats S Throws R

One of greatest base-stealers in history, he must
prove he can bounce back from hamstring injury which ruined his first year in New York
. . . Was leading NL with 33 steals when
strained left hamstring put him on DL June 15
. . . Activated July 24, but was sidelined again
with same injury from Aug. 13-Oct. 1 . . . Finished with lowest stolen-base total of career
(37), but still ranked seventh in NL . . . Last season snapped string
of six consecutive seasons leading NL in steals . . . Selected by
Cardinals in 10th round of 1982 draft . . . Established all-time pro
mark with 145 steals for Macon (A) in 1983, when he also batted
.350 . . . Set major-league record with 50 straight steals spanning
1988 and 1989 . . . Signed with Mets as free agent following 1990
season and made switch from left to center . . . Born Sept. 22,

1961, in Jacksonville, Fla. . . . Played football at Florida A&M
. . . Earned $3,112,500 in 1991.

Year	Club	Pos.	G	AB	R	H	2B	3B	HR	RBI	SB	Avg.
1985	St. Louis	OF	151	636	107	170	20	10	1	40	110	.267
1986	St. Louis	OF	154	600	94	139	13	8	0	29	107	.232
1987	St. Louis	OF	151	623	121	180	14	10	3	43	109	.289
1988	St. Louis	OF	153	616	77	160	20	10	3	38	81	.260
1989	St. Louis	OF	145	563	94	143	21	9	2	28	65	.254
1990	St. Louis	OF	124	497	73	145	18	9	6	39	77	.292
1991	New York (NL)	OF	72	278	45	71	7	5	1	17	37	.255
	Totals		950	3813	611	1008	113	61	16	234	586	.264

EDDIE MURRAY 36 6-2 224   Bats S Throws R

Free agent first baseman signed two-year, $7.5-
million contract with Mets after average plum-
meted 70 points from .330, second-best mark
in NL in 1990, to .260 with Dodgers last season
. . . Still has knack of hitting home runs at the
right time as 11 of his 19 homers put the Dodgers ahead or tied the game . . . Hit only .217
with six home runs from the right side . . . Hit
.295 with 13 homers left-handed . . . Nearing the end of a great
career . . . In three pinch-hit appearances, he had two hits, including a homer and four RBI . . . Named to the All-Star team for
eighth time, first in NL . . . Born Feb. 24, 1956, in Los Angeles
. . . Spent 12 years with the Orioles before being traded to the
Dodgers for Brian Holton, Ken Howell and Juan Bell prior to
1989 season . . . Has 398 career homers, 25th on the all-time list
and tops among active players . . . Earned $2,628,164 last season
. . . Drafted by Orioles in third round of 1983 draft.

Year	Club	Pos.	G	AB	R	H	2B	3B	HR	RBI	SB	Avg.
1977	Baltimore	OF-1B	160	611	81	173	29	2	27	88	0	.283
1978	Baltimore	1B-3B	161	610	85	174	32	3	27	95	6	.285
1979	Baltimore	1B	159	606	90	179	30	2	25	99	10	.295
1980	Baltimore	1B	158	621	100	186	36	2	32	116	7	.300
1981	Baltimore	1B	99	378	57	111	21	2	22	78	2	.294
1982	Baltimore	1B	151	550	87	174	30	1	32	110	7	.316
1983	Baltimore	1B	156	582	115	178	30	3	33	111	5	.306
1984	Baltimore	1B	162	588	97	180	26	3	29	110	10	.306
1985	Baltimore	1B	156	583	111	173	37	1	31	124	5	.297
1986	Baltimore	1B	137	495	61	151	25	1	17	84	3	.305
1987	Baltimore	1B	160	618	89	171	28	3	30	91	1	.277
1988	Baltimore	1B	161	603	75	171	27	2	28	84	5	.284
1989	Los Angeles	1B-3B	160	594	66	147	29	1	20	88	7	.247
1990	Los Angeles	1B	155	558	96	184	22	3	26	95	8	.330
1991	Los Angeles	1B-3B	153	576	69	150	23	1	19	96	10	.260
	Totals		2288	8573	1279	2502	425	30	398	1469	86	.292

WILLIE RANDOLPH 37 5-11 171   Bats R Throws R

Brewer free agent slated to be new Met second baseman after signing one-year, $850,000 contract . . . Tied with Seattle's Ken Griffey Jr. for third in AL batting race at .327 . . . Became regular second baseman in early August and batted .371 that month . . . Recorded pair of four-hit games, June 1 vs. Yankees and Sept. 30 vs. Red Sox . . . Range at second base is reduced but still turns double play with remarkable ease . . . Earned only $500,000 in 1991 . . . Born July 6, 1954, in Holly Hill, S.C. . . . Will be remembered as integral part of Yankees' world championship teams in 1977 and 1978.

Year	Club	Pos.	G	AB	R	H	2B	3B	HR	RBI	SB	Avg.
1975	Pittsburgh	2B-3B	30	61	9	10	1	0	0	3	1	.164
1976	New York (AL)	2B	125	430	59	115	15	4	1	40	37	.267
1977	New York (AL)	2B	147	551	91	151	28	11	4	40	13	.274
1978	New York (AL)	2B	134	499	87	139	18	6	3	42	36	.279
1979	New York (AL)	2B	153	574	98	155	15	13	5	61	33	.270
1980	New York (AL)	2B	138	513	99	151	23	7	7	46	30	.294
1981	New York (AL)	2B	93	357	59	83	14	3	2	24	14	.232
1982	New York (AL)	2B	144	553	85	155	21	4	3	36	16	.280
1983	New York (AL)	2B	104	420	73	117	21	1	2	38	12	.279
1984	New York (AL)	2B	142	564	86	162	24	2	2	31	10	.287
1985	New York (AL)	2B	143	497	75	137	21	2	5	40	16	.276
1986	New York (AL)	2B	141	492	76	136	15	2	5	50	15	.276
1987	New York (AL)	2B	120	449	96	137	24	2	7	67	11	.305
1988	New York (AL)	2B	110	404	43	93	20	1	2	34	8	.230
1989	Los Angeles ...	2B	145	549	62	155	18	0	2	36	7	.282
1990	Los Angeles ...	2B	26	96	15	26	4	0	1	9	1	.271
1990	Oakland	2B	93	292	37	75	9	3	1	21	6	.257
1991	Milwaukee	2B	124	431	60	141	14	3	0	54	4	.327
	Totals		2012	7732	1210	2138	305	64	52	672	270	.277

BILL PECOTA 32 6-2 190   Bats R Throws R

New Met came in December trade with Bret Saberhagen that sent Kevin McReynolds, Gregg Jefferies and Keith Miller to Royals . . . Career utilityman capitalized on first opportunity to play regularly . . . His numbers—.286 average, 45 RBI and 16 steals—make you wonder why he never got a chance at KC before Hal McRae arrived . . . Played mostly third base, but also saw a lot of time at second base and Mets plan to use him at both spots, too . . . Committed only four errors in 125 games . . . His 398 at-bats were 158 more than previous single-season high . . . Had only 686 career at-bats in parts of five seasons

before 1991 . . . Earned $307,500 last year . . . Had been in Royals'
organization since being picked in 10th round of 1981 draft . . .
Born Feb. 16, 1960, in Redwood City, Cal.

Year	Club	Pos.	G	AB	R	H	2B	3B	HR	RBI	SB	Avg.
1986	Kansas City . . .	3B-SS	12	29	3	6	2	0	0	2	0	.207
1987	Kansas City . . .	SS-3B-2B	66	156	22	43	5	1	3	14	5	.276
1988	Kansas City . . .	INF-OF-C	90	178	25	37	3	3	1	15	7	.208
1989	Kansas City . . .	INF-OF	65	83	21	17	4	2	3	5	5	.205
1990	Kansas City . . .	INF-OF	87	240	43	58	15	2	5	20	8	.242
1991	Kansas City . . .	INF-OF-C	125	398	53	114	23	2	6	45	16	.286
	Totals		445	1084	167	275	52	10	18	101	41	.254

BRET SABERHAGEN 27 6-1 200   Bats R Throws R

After eight years as a Royal, this two-time Cy
Young winner (1985, 1989) joined Mets with
Bill Pecota in December deal for Kevin
McReynolds, Gregg Jefferies and Keith Miller
. . . Bouncing back from elbow surgery, he fin-
ished 13-8 with 3.07 ERA last year . . . High-
light was no-hitter against Chicago Aug. 26 . . .
Allowed only 210 base-runners in 196⅓ in-
nings . . . Missed month with shoulder tendinitis . . . World Series
MVP in 1989 . . . Comeback Player of Year in 1987 . . . Picked by
Royals in 19th round of 1982 draft . . . Earned $2,950,000 in 1991
. . . Born April 11, 1964, in Chicago Heights, Ill.

Year	Club	G	IP	W	L	Pct.	SO	BB	H	ERA
1984	Kansas City	38	157⅔	10	11	.476	73	36	138	3.48
1985	Kansas City	32	235⅓	20	6	.769	158	38	211	2.87
1986	Kansas City	30	156	7	12	.368	112	29	165	4.15
1987	Kansas City	33	257	18	10	.643	163	53	246	3.36
1988	Kansas City	35	260⅔	14	16	.467	171	59	271	3.80
1989	Kansas City	36	262⅓	23	6	.793	193	43	209	2.16
1990	Kansas City	20	135	5	9	.357	87	28	146	3.27
1991	Kansas City	28	196⅓	13	8	.619	136	45	165	3.07
	Totals	252	1660⅓	110	78	.585	1093	331	1551	3.2'

DWIGHT GOODEN 27 6-3 210   Bats R Throws R

''Doc'' still ranks as one of the game's top
pitchers, but his career could be in jeopardy
following shoulder surgery . . . His 1991 season
ended Aug. 22 when he left game with shoulder
stiffness after pitching five innings against Cardinals . . . Had arthroscopic surgery Sept. 7 to
repair cartilage tear, remove loose fragments
and fix small tear in rotator cuff . . . His .714
career winning percentage is best in history for pitchers with 1,500

or more innings . . . Recorded 1,500th career strikeout July 11 . . .
Ranked third in NL in strikeouts at time of injury and still finished
ninth with 150 . . . Pitched 21st career shutout June 15 against
Astros . . . Fanned 14 Expos April 13, throwing 149 pitches in
only second start of season . . . Selected by Mets in first round of
1982 draft . . . Was NL Rookie of the Year in 1984 and Cy Young
winner in 1985 . . . Born Nov. 16, 1964, in Tampa . . . Earned
$2,466,667 in 1991.

Year	Club	G	IP	W	L	Pct.	SO	BB	H	ERA
1984	New York (NL)	31	218	17	9	.654	276	73	161	2.60
1985	New York (NL)	35	276⅔	24	4	.857	268	69	198	1.53
1986	New York (NL)	33	250	17	6	.739	200	80	197	2.84
1987	New York (NL)	25	179⅔	15	7	.682	148	53	162	3.21
1988	New York (NL)	34	248⅓	18	9	.667	175	57	242	3.19
1989	New York (NL)	19	118⅓	9	4	.692	101	47	93	2.89
1990	New York (NL)	34	232⅔	19	7	.731	223	70	229	3.83
1991	New York (NL)	27	190	13	7	.650	150	56	185	3.60
	Totals	238	1713⅔	-132	53	.714	1541	505	1467	2.91

JOHN FRANCO 31 5-10 185   Bats L Throws L

Still a top bullpen closer, he pitched fewest
innings of career in 1991, because Mets had so
few leads to protect . . . Tied for third in NL
with 30 saves . . . Gained 200th career save July
6 in Philadelphia . . . Ranks 11th on all-time
save list with 211 . . . Recorded at least 30 saves
for fifth straight season . . . Has converted 86
percent of save opportunities since 1988 . . .
Went three weeks between save chances from July 16-Aug. 8 . . .
Chalked up six saves and a victory in final seven appearances after
returning from back injury which sidelined him for 11 days in
June . . . Mets made 14 errors behind him . . . Selected by Dodgers
in fifth round of 1981 draft . . . Traded to Reds in 1983 . . . Dealt
to Mets for Randy Myers following 1989 season . . . Led NL in
saves in 1988 and 1990 . . . Four-time All-Star . . . Saved 39 games
in 42 opportunities in 1988 . . . Born Sept. 17, 1960, in Brooklyn,
N.Y. . . . Earned $2,633,333 in 1991.

Year	Club	G	IP	W	L	Pct.	SO	BB	H	ERA
1984	Cincinnati	54	79⅓	6	2	.750	55	36	74	2.61
1985	Cincinnati	67	99	12	3	.800	61	40	83	2.18
1986	Cincinnati	74	101	6	6	.500	84	44	90	2.94
1987	Cincinnati	68	82	8	5	.615	61	27	76	2.52
1988	Cincinnati	70	86	6	6	.500	46	27	60	1.57
1989	Cincinnati	60	80⅔	4	8	.333	60	36	77	3.12
1990	New York (NL)	55	67⅔	5	3	.625	56	21	66	2.53
1991	New York (NL)	52	55⅓	5	9	.357	45	18	61	2.93
	Totals	500	651	52	42	.553	468	249	587	2.53

DAVID CONE 29 6-1 190   Bats L Throws R

Could be ace of Mets staff if he harnesses talent and controls emotions . . . Led NL in strikeouts for second straight season with 241, but settled for .500 record again . . . Took no-hitter into eighth inning against Cardinals Sept. 20, but Felix Jose broke it up with double . . . Retired first 16 batters against Giants May 3 before Mike Felder singled with two outs in sixth . . . Fanned NL-record 19 Phillies while pitching three-hit shutout Oct. 6 . . . Became 13th pitcher in NL history to strike out side on nine pitches Aug. 30 at Cincinnati . . . Had 1.10 ERA over five starts from May 24-June 14 . . . Also had inconsistent stretches, going winless between July 29-Aug. 25 and Aug. 30-Sept. 20 . . . Selected by Royals in third round of 1981 draft . . . Traded to Mets with Chris Jelic for Ed Hearn, Rick Anderson and Mauro Gozzo before 1987 season . . . Became fourth 20-game winner in Met history in 1988, when his .870 winning percentage was sixth-best in history . . . Born Jan. 2, 1963, in Kansas City . . . Earned $2,350,000 in 1991.

Year	Club	G	IP	W	L	Pct.	SO	BB	H	ERA
1986	Kansas City	11	22⅔	0	0	.000	21	13	29	5.56
1987	New York (NL)	21	99⅓	5	6	.455	68	44	87	3.71
1988	New York (NL)	35	231⅓	20	3	.870	213	80	178	2.22
1989	New York (NL)	34	219⅔	14	8	.636	190	74	183	3.52
1990	New York (NL)	31	211⅔	14	10	.583	233	65	177	3.23
1991	New York (NL)	34	232⅔	14	14	.500	241	73	204	3.29
	Totals	166	1017⅓	67	41	.620	966	349	858	3.18

SID FERNANDEZ 29 6-1 230   Bats L Throws L

"El Sid" continues to frustrate Mets with unfulfilled potential . . . His 1991 season was washout because of injuries . . . Suffered non-displaced fracture of ulna bone when hit by batted ball in first exhibition outing . . . Sidelined until July 19 when he pitched six innings in first start against Dodgers, giving up one run on three hits . . . Made just eight starts before being sidelined again by left knee injury . . . Underwent arthroscopic surgery Sept. 7 to repair breakdown of cartilage under kneecap and tear in front part of medial cartilage . . . Condition was exacerbated by his never-ending weight problem . . . His 2.86 ERA was best among Met starters . . . Selected by Dodgers in third round of 1981 draft . . . Traded to Mets for Bob Bailor and Carlos Diaz before 1984 season . . . Held opponents to .200 batting average in 1990, .198 in 1989 and .191 in 1988 . . . Two-time All-Star . . . Born Oct. 12, 1962, in Honolulu . . . Earned $2,166,667 in 1991.

Year	Club	G	IP	W	L	Pct.	SO	BB	H	ERA
1983	Los Angeles.	2	6	0	1	.000	9	7	7	6.00
1984	New York (NL)	15	90	6	6	.500	62	34	74	3.50
1985	New York (NL)	26	170⅓	9	9	.500	180	80	108	2.80
1986	New York (NL)	32	204⅓	16	6	.727	200	91	161	3.52
1987	New York (NL)	28	156	12	8	.600	134	67	130	3.81
1988	New York (NL)	31	187	12	10	.545	189	70	127	3.03
1989	New York (NL)	35	219⅓	14	5	.737	198	75	157	2.83
1990	New York (NL)	30	179⅓	9	14	.391	181	67	130	3.46
1991	New York (NL)	8	44	1	3	.250	31	9	36	2.86
	Totals.	207	1256⅓	79	62	.560	1184	500	930	3.25

TOP PROSPECTS

TODD HUNDLEY 22 5-11 185　　　　　　**Bats S Throws R**
Figures to be Mets' No. 1 catcher in 1992 . . . No question about his receiving skills and fewer questions about his bat . . . Spent full season with Tidewater (AAA) in 1991 and put together best offensive year, batting .273 with 24 doubles, 14 homers and 66 RBI . . . Made major-league debut in 1990, hitting .209 in 67 at-bats, and hit .133 in 60 at-bats for Mets last year . . . Selected by Mets in second round of 1987 draft . . . Threw out 48 percent of runners attempting to steal for Jackson (AA) in 1990 . . . Named to South Atlantic League All-Star team in 1989 . . . Son of former major-league catcher Randy Hundley . . . Born May 27, 1969, in Martinsville, Va.

ANTHONY YOUNG 26 6-2 200　　　　　　**Bats R Throws R**
Late-season promotee stepped into starting rotation when Mets' staff was devastated by injuries and made big impression . . . Earned first big-league victory Sept. 3, striking out six while limiting Astros to one run over seven innings . . . Made eight starts for Mets, going 2-5 with 3.10 ERA . . . Started 25 games for Tidewater (AAA), compiling 7-9 record and 3.73 ERA . . . Selected by Mets in 38th round of 1987 draft after playing football and baseball at University of Houston . . . Named 1990 Texas League Pitcher of the Year after going 15-3 with 1.65 ERA for Jackson (AA) . . . Born Jan. 19, 1966, in Houston.

CHRIS DONNELS 25 6-0 185   **Bats L Throws R**
Batted .303 for Tidewater (AAA) with 18 doubles, eight homers
and 56 RBI . . . Can play first or third base . . . Called up to Mets
three times in 1991, he had first two-hit game Sept. 12 in Chicago
. . . Hit .225 in 89 at-bats . . . Selected by Mets in first round of
1987 draft . . . Named 1989 Florida State League MVP after hitting
.313 with 23 doubles, 17 homers and 78 RBI for St. Lucie
(A) . . . Named to Texas League All-Star Game in 1990, when he
hit .272 for Jackson (AA) with 24 doubles, 12 homers and 63
RBI . . . Born April 21, 1966, in Los Angeles.

MANAGER JEFF TORBORG: Mets hope can bring discipline
and intensity back to their clubhouse . . . Signed
four-year contract five days after season ended,
replacing fired Buddy Harrelson . . . Lifelong
New Jersey resident was anxious to return home
. . . Left White Sox with two years remaining
on contract after building them into contenders
. . . Named AL Manager of the Year in 1990,
his second season in Chicago, when he led
youngest team in majors to surprising 94-68 record, a 25-game
improvement from 1989 . . . Known for intense preparation, he
probably leads majors in pre-game meetings . . . Became White
Sox manager in 1989 after 10 years as Yankee coach . . . Replaced
Frank Robinson as Indians' manager June 19, 1977 and compiled
157-201 record before being replaced midway through 1979 . . .
Played 10 years in majors with Dodgers and Angels, catching no-
hitters by Sandy Koufax (1965), Bill Singer (1970) and Nolan
Ryan (1973) . . . Also was behind plate when Don Drysdale threw
fifth consecutive shutout in 1968 . . . Compiled .214 lifetime batting average . . . Led NCAA with .537 average during senior year
at Rutgers . . . Cumulative managerial record is 407-436 . . . Born
Nov. 26, 1941, in Westfield, N.J.

ALL-TIME MET SEASON RECORDS

BATTING: Cleon Jones, .340, 1969
HRs: Darryl Strawberry, 39, 1987, 1988
RBI: Howard Johnson, 117, 1991
STEALS: Mookie Wilson, 58, 1982
WINS: Tom Seaver, 25, 1969
STRIKEOUTS: Tom Seaver, 289, 1971

PHILADELPHIA PHILLIES

TEAM DIRECTORY: Pres.: William Y. Giles; Exec. VP: David Montgomery; VP/GM: Lee Thomas; Player Pers. Adm.: Ed Wade; VP-Pub. Rel.: Larry Shenk; Trav. Sec.: Eddie Ferenz; Mgr.: Jim Fregosi. Home: Veterans Stadium (64,538). Field distances: 330, l.f. line; 408, c.f.; 330, r.f. line. Spring training: Clearwater, Fla.

SCOUTING REPORT

HITTING: The Phillies ranked last in the NL in batting average (.241) and on-base percentage (.303) while finishing 11th in runs (629) in 1991. That's why they were so disappointed when they failed to land free agent Bobby Bonilla. And, for the first time in a decade, the Phils are going into a season without offensive stalwart Von Hayes, who was dealt to the Angels.

Basically, the Phillies need to stay away from the crippling injuries that ravaged their lineup last year. Lenny Dykstra (.297, 3, 12, 24 steals) must rebound from the automobile accident which ruined his 1991 season and prove that his 1990 achievements were no fluke. Darren Daulton (.196, 12, 42), a passenger in Dykstra's car, also needs to regain the form he displayed in 1990, when he led all NL catchers in most offensive categories.

John Kruk (.294, 21, 92) is primed for another big season and Dave Hollins (.298, 6, 21), who had an outstanding second half after winning the job at third base, will get a chance to show whether he can do it for a full season. Free agent signee Mariano Duncan (.258, 12, 40 with the Reds) was a .300 hitter two years ago and he could add a lot of offense at either of the middle infield positions. Dale Murphy (.252, 18, 81) and Ricky Jordan (.272, 9, 49) can both be run producers.

PITCHING: Very quietly, the Phillies have built a pretty solid pitching staff. Their 3.86 ERA was not spectacular, but they finished with 16 complete games and 11 shutouts while limiting opponents to a .246 batting average, the fourth-lowest mark in the NL. Their rotation will be even better in 1992 if former ace Ken Howell can return from the shoulder surgery that sidelined him for all of last season.

Terry Mulholland (16-13, 3.61) has developed into one of the NL's better pitchers. Tommy Greene (13-7, 3.38) is a strikeout pitcher who put together a string of 29 consecutive scoreless innings last year. Both Mulholland and Greene have pitched no-

Phils aren't whole without their Lenny Wallbanger.

hitters within the past two seasons.

Jose DeJesus (10-9, 3.42) will be spectacular if he ever improves his control. Kyle Abbott (14-10, 3.99 for AAA Edmonton), obtained for Hayes, will also be given a chance to make the rotation. Barry Jones (4-9, 3.35, 13 Sv with the Expos) bolsters the bullpen, aiding irrepressible and unhittable closer Mitch Williams (12-5, 2.34, 30 Sv).

FIELDING: The Phillies turned the fewest double plays (111) in the NL last season, but their other defensive numbers were in the middle of the pack. Ex-Brewer Dale Sveum and the versatile Duncan will bolster the middle infield and rookie shortstop Kim Batiste might be ready for prime time. Kruk made just two errors at first base last season, but Hollins committed seven in only 36 games at third. A healthy Dykstra in center will improve the outfield defense.

OUTLOOK: Jim Fregosi turned the Phillies into a respectable team after being named manager last April. Their 78-84, third-place finish was an achievement considering all the injuries. Pitching might keep the Phillies in the race in 1992, but this team probably doesn't have enough firepower to win yet.

PHILADELPHIA PHILLIES 1992 ROSTER

MANAGER Jim Fregosi
Coaches—Larry Bowa, Denis Menke, Johnny Podres, Mel Roberts, Mike Ryan, John Vukovich

PITCHERS

No.	Name	1991 Club	W-L	IP	SO	ERA	B-T	Ht.	Wt.	Born
—	Abbott, Kyle	Edmonton	14-10	180	120	3.99	L-L	6-2	200	2/18/68 Newburyport, MA
		California	1-2	20	12	4.58				
40	Ashby, Andy	Scranton	11-11	161	113	3.46	R-R	6-5	180	7/11/67 Kansas City, MO
		Philadelphia	1-5	42	26	6.00				
25	Ayrault, Bob	Scranton	8-5	99	103	4.83	R-R	6-4	230	4/27/66 S. Lake Tahoe, CA
22	Borland, Toby	Reading	8-3	77	72	2.70	R-R	6-6	180	5/29/69 Quilman, LA
51	Brantley, Cliff	Reading	4-3	70	51	1.94	R-R	6-1	190	4/12/68 Staten Island, NY
		Scranton	2-4	47	28	3.80				
		Philadelphia	2-2	32	25	3.41				
—	Chapin, Darrin	Columbus	10-3	78	69	1.95	R-R	6-0	170	2/1/66 Warren, OH
		New York (AL)	0-1	5	5	5.06				
38	Combs, Pat	Philadelphia	2-6	64	41	4.90	L-L	6-4	207	10/29/66 Newport, RI
		Scranton	2-2	27	14	6.67				
54	DeJesus, Jose	Philadelphia	10-9	182	118	3.42	R-R	6-5	195	1/6/65 Brooklyn, NY
49	Greene, Tommy	Philadelphia	13-7	208	154	3.38	R-R	6-5	225	4/6/67 Lumberton, NC
48	Grimsley, Jason	Scranton	2-3	52	43	4.35	R-R	6-3	182	8/7/67 Cleveland, TX
		Philadelphia	1-7	61	42	4.87				
42	Hartley, Mike	LA-Phil.	4-1	83	63	4.21	R-R	6-1	197	8/31/61 Hawthorne, CA
43	Howell, Ken	Scranton	2-0	25	20	5.11	R-R	6-3	237	11/28/60 Detroit, MI
—	Jones, Barry	Montreal	4-9	89	46	3.35	R-R	6-4	225	2/15/63 Centerville, IN
45	Mulholland, Terry	Philadelphia	16-13	232	142	3.61	K-L	6-3	207	3/9/63 Uniontown, PA
39	Ritchie, Wally	Scranton	1-0	26	25	2.42	L-L	6-2	180	7/12/65 Glendale, CA
		Philadelphia	1-2	50	26	2.50				
50	Searcy, Steve	Detroit	1-2	41	32	8.41	L-L	6-1	195	6/5/64 Knoxville, TN
		Philadelphia	2-1	30	21	4.15				
29	Williams, Mitch	Philadelphia	12-5	88	84	2.34	L-L	6-4	205	11/17/64 Santa Ana, CA

CATCHERS

No.	Name	1991 Club	H	HR	RBI	Pct.	B-T	Ht.	Wt.	Born
10	Daulton, Darren	Philadelphia	56	12	42	.196	L-R	6-2	200	1/3/62 Arkansas City, KS
		Reading	1	0	0	.250				
		Scranton	2	1	1	.222				
57	Lindsey, Doug	Reading	81	1	34	.259	R-R	6-2	200	9/22/67 Austin, TX

INFIELDERS

No.	Name	1991 Club	H	HR	RBI	Pct.	B-T	Ht.	Wt.	Born
6	Backman, Wally	Philadelphia	45	0	15	.243	S-R	5-9	168	9/22/59 Hillsboro, OR
—	Batiste, Kim	Scranton	135	1	41	.292	R-R	6-0	175	3/15/68 New Orleans, LA
		Philadelphia	6	0	1	.222				
7	Duncan, Mariano	Cincinnati	86	12	40	.258	R-R	6-0	185	3/13/63 Dominican Republic
15	Hollins, David	Scranton	61	8	35	.266	S-R	6-1	207	5/25/66 Buffalo, NY
		Philadelphia	45	6	21	.298				
17	Jordan, Ricky	Philadelphia	82	9	49	.272	R-R	6-3	209	5/26/65 Richmond, CA
28	Kruk, John	Philadelphia	158	21	92	.294	L-L	5-10	200	2/9/61 Charleston, WV
12	Morandini, Mickey	Scranton	12	1	9	.261	L-R	5-11	167	4/22/66 Kittanning, PA
		Philadelphia	81	1	20	.249				
—	Sveum, Dale	Milwaukee	64	4	43	.241	S-R	6-3	185	11/23/63 Richmond, CA

OUTFIELDERS

No.	Name	1991 Club	H	HR	RBI	Pct.	B-T	Ht.	Wt.	Born
—	Amaro, Ruben	Edmonton	154	3	42	.326	S-R	5-10	170	2/12/65 Philadelphia, PA
		California	5	0	2	.217				
26	Dostal, Bruce	Reading	114	5	34	.313	L-L	6-0	195	3/10/65 Montville, NJ
16	Castillo, Braulio	San Antonio	89	8	48	.300	R-R	6-0	160	5/13/68 Dominican Republic
		Scranton	21	0	15	.350				
		Philadelphia	9	0	2	.173				
44	Chamberlain, Wes	Scranton	37	2	20	.257	R-R	6-2	210	4/13/66 Chicago, IL
		Philadelphia	92	13	50	.240				
4	Dykstra, Lenny	Philadelphia	73	3	12	.297	L-L	5-10	180	2/10/63 Santa Ana, CA
19	Lindeman, Jim	Scranton	11	2	7	.275	R-R	6-1	200	1/10/62 Evanston, IL
		Philadelphia	32	0	12	.337				
27	Longmire, Anthony	Reading	93	9	56	.288	L-R	6-1	195	8/12/68 Vallejo, CA
		Scranton	29	0	9	.261				
3	Murphy, Dale	Philadelphia	137	18	81	.252	R-R	6-4	220	3/12/56 Portland, OR
34	Peguero, Julio	Scranton	138	2	39	.273	S-R	6-0	160	9/7/68 Dominican Republic
24	Williams, Cary	Reading	117	6	62	.278	R-R	6-3	190	7/29/69 San Antonio, TX

PHILLIE PROFILES

JOHN KRUK 31 5-10 200　　　　　　Bats L Throws L

When injuries devastated Phils' lineup in 1991, he stepped forward, putting together most productive season of career . . . First baseman set career highs in hits (158), doubles (27), homers (21), runs (84) and RBI (92) . . . Was rewarded with three-year, $7.2-million contract extension in September . . . Hit pair of homers, including third career grand slam, and drove in five runs in 5-4 win over Cubs Sept. 25 . . . Had 15-game hitting streak in September during which he batted .405 with five homers, five doubles and 13 RBI . . . Went 2,681 plate appearances without being hit by pitch before Pirates' Randy Tomlin plunked him Aug. 21 . . . Made first trip to All-Star Game . . . Tied Mike Schmidt's club record with 20 RBI in April . . . Selected by Padres in third round of 1981 draft's secondary phase . . . Traded to Phillies June 3, 1989 with Randy Ready for Chris James . . . Born Feb. 9, 1961, in Charleston, W. Va. . . . Earned $1,175,000 in 1991.

Year	Club	Pos.	G	AB	R	H	2B	3B	HR	RBI	SB	Avg.
1986	San Diego	OF-1B	122	278	33	86	16	2	4	38	2	.309
1987	San Diego	OF-1B	138	447	72	140	14	2	20	91	18	.313
1988	San Diego	1B-OF	120	378	54	91	17	1	9	44	5	.241
1989	S.D.-Phil.	OF-1B	112	357	53	107	13	6	8	44	3	.300
1990	Philadelphia . . .	OF-1B	142	443	52	129	25	8	7	67	10	.291
1991	Philadelphia . . .	1B-OF	152	538	84	158	27	6	21	92	7	.294
	Totals		786	2441	348	711	112	25	69	376	45	.291

LENNY DYKSTRA 29 5-10 180　　　　　Bats L Throws L

A burgeoning superstar who is almost a cartoon character . . . His Dead-End Kid approach to life took dark turn in 1991 when May 6 auto accident ruined his season as well as catcher Darren Daulton's . . . Center fielder suffered broken clavicle and three fractured ribs . . . Returned to lineup July 15 and immediately hit safely in 10 of 11 games, going 18-for-45 with six multi-hit games and four steals . . . His season ended Aug. 26 when he fractured collarbone again after colliding with outfield wall in Cincinnati . . . Attained stardom in 1990, leading NL in on-base percentage (.418) and hits while finishing fourth in batting (.325) and walks (89), fifth in runs and seventh in doubles . . . Selected by Mets in 12th round of 1981 draft . . . Traded to Phillies with Roger McDowell for Juan Samuel, June 18, 1989 . . . Born

Feb. 10, 1963, in Santa Ana, Cal. . . . Earned $2,216,000 in 1991 . . . Batted .304 in 1986 NLCS against Astros and .429 in 1988 NLCS against Dodgers.

Year	Club	Pos.	G	AB	R	H	2B	3B	HR	RBI	SB	Avg.
1985	New York (NL)	OF	83	236	40	60	9	3	1	19	15	.254
1986	New York (NL)	OF	147	431	77	127	27	7	8	45	31	.295
1987	New York (NL)	OF	132	431	86	123	37	3	10	43	27	.285
1988	New York (NL)	OF	126	429	57	116	19	3	8	33	30	.270
1989	N.Y.(NL)-Phil.	OF	146	511	66	121	32	4	7	32	30	.237
1990	Philadelphia . . .	OF	149	590	106	192	35	3	9	60	33	.325
1991	Philadelphia . . .	OF	63	246	48	73	13	5	3	12	24	.297
	Totals		846	2874	480	812	172	28	46	244	190	.283

DALE SVEUM 28 6-3 185   Bats B Throws R

Acquired by Phillies from Brewers in December trade for pitcher Bruce Ruffin . . . Played shortstop, third and second in 1991, finally showing signs of bouncing back from broken leg which has hampered career since 1988 . . . Missed entire 1989 regular season while recovering from tendinitis resulting from the leg injury . . . Also underwent arthroscopic shoulder surgery in 1989 . . . Split 1990 between Denver (AAA) and Milwaukee, starting games at all four infield positions . . . Reached big leagues in 1986 when injury sidelined Paul Molitor and had career-high 14-game hitting streak . . . Named to Topps All-Rookie team at third base . . . Had three-homer game against Angels as ninth-place hitter in 1987 . . . Born Nov. 23, 1963, in Richmond, Cal. . . . Earned $275,000 in 1991.

Year	Club	Pos.	G	AB	R	H	2B	3B	HR	RBI	SB	Avg.
1986	Milwaukee	3B-SS-2B	91	317	35	78	13	2	7	35	4	.246
1987	Milwaukee	SS-2B	153	535	86	135	27	3	25	95	2	.252
1988	Milwaukee	SS-2B	129	467	41	113	14	4	9	51	1	.242
1990	Milwaukee	3B-2B-1B-SS	48	117	75	23	7	0	1	12	0	.197
1991	Milwaukee	SS-2B-3B	90	266	33	64	19	1	4	43	2	.241
	Totals		511	1702	210	413	80	10	46	236	9	.243

DALE MURPHY 36 6-4 220   Bats R Throws R

Baseball's all-time class act is no longer a superstar but still can be a dangerous hitter . . . Led Phillies in doubles (33) . . . Was second in homers (18) and RBI (81) . . . His 440-foot homer to center against Cubs Aug. 6 was longest by a Phillie at Veterans Stadium in 1991 . . . Collected 2,000th career hit May 29 against Expos . . . Right fielder went homerless from

July 4 until Aug. 3 . . . Dropped from fifth to sixth in lineup in late July while in 4-for-34 skid . . . Went 4-for-4 against Mets July 6, snapping 3-for-21 slump . . . Finished ninth in NL in doubles . . . Selected by Braves in first round of 1974 draft . . . Seven-time All-Star . . . Named NL MVP in both 1982 and 1983 . . . Won five straight Gold Gloves . . . Traded to Phillies with Tommy Greene for Jeff Parrett, Aug. 3, 1990 . . . Left as Atlanta's all-time leader in 10 categories, including doubles, homers and RBI . . . Born March 12, 1956, in Portland, Ore. . . . Earned $2.5 million in 1991.

Year Club	Pos.	G	AB	R	H	2B	3B	HR	RBI	SB	Avg.
1976 Atlanta.......	C	19	65	3	17	6	0	0	9	0	.262
1977 Atlanta.......	C	18	76	5	24	8	1	2	14	0	.316
1978 Atlanta.......	C-1B	151	530	66	120	14	3	23	79	11	.226
1979 Atlanta.......	1B-C	104	384	53	106	7	2	21	57	6	.276
1980 Atlanta.......	OF-1B	156	569	98	160	27	2	33	89	9	.281
1981 Atlanta.......	OF-1B	104	369	43	91	12	1	13	50	14	.247
1982 Atlanta.......	OF	162	598	113	168	23	2	36	109	23	.281
1983 Atlanta.......	OF	162	589	131	178	24	4	36	121	30	.302
1984 Atlanta.......	OF	162	607	94	176	32	8	36	100	19	.290
1985 Atlanta..:....	OF	162	616	118	185	32	2	37	111	10	.300
1986 Atlanta.......	OF	160	614	89	163	29	7	29	83	7	.265
1987 Atlanta.......	OF	159	566	115	167	27	1	44	105	16	.295
1988 Atlanta.......	OF	156	592	77	134	35	4	24	77	3	.226
1989 Atlanta.......	OF	154	574	60	131	16	0	20	84	3	.228
1990 Atl.-Phil......	OF	154	563	60	138	23	1	24	83	9	.245
1991 Philadelphia ...	OF	153	544	66	137	33	1	18	81	1	.252
Totals........		2136	7856	1191	2095	348	39	396	1252	161	.267

TERRY MULHOLLAND 29 6-3 207   Bats R Throws R

Established himself as ace of Phils' staff in 1991 . . . Finished third in NL in complete games (eight) and shutouts (three), fourth in victories (16) and sixth in innings pitched (232) . . . Led staff in wins, innings pitched, starts and walk-strikeout ratio . . . Pitched all three of his shutouts in September and October, including three-hitter at Houston and two-hitter against Expos . . . Had career-high 12-strikeout game against Cardinals July 4 . . . His 16 wins were most by a Phillie since Shane Rawley had 17 in 1987 . . . Had four-game winning streak and three three-game winning streaks . . . Survived seven-game June slump during which he went 1-6 with 7.34 ERA . . . Selected by Giants in first round of 1984 draft . . . Traded to Phillies with Dennis Cook and Charlie Hayes, June 18, 1989 . . . Pitched first

Terry Mulholland emerged as ace of Phils' young staff.

nine-inning no-hitter in Veterans Stadium history Aug. 15, 1990 against Giants... Born March 9, 1963, in Uniontown, Pa.... Earned $475,000 in 1991.

Year	Club	G	IP	W	L	Pct.	SO	BB	H	ERA
1986	San Francisco	15	54⅔	1	7	.125	27	35	51	4.94
1988	San Francisco	9	46	2	1	.667	18	7	50	3.72
1989	S.F.-Phil.	25	115⅓	4	7	.364	66	36	137	4.92
1990	Philadelphia	33	180⅔	9	10	.474	75	42	172	3.34
1991	Philadelphia	34	232	16	13	.552	142	49	231	3.61
	Totals	116	628⅔	32	38	.457	328	169	641	3.89

TOMMY GREENE 24 6-5 225   Bats R Throws R

Stepped into spotlight May 23 by pitching no-hitter in Montreal while striking out career-high 10 batters... Before then, he had made nine relief appearances and just two starts... Became first Phillie since Steve Carlton in 1972 to hurl consecutive shutouts against a team when he blanked Expos twice in a row... String of 29 consecutive scoreless innings was snapped June 2 on two-run homer by Barry Bonds... Went 4-1 in September... Finished sixth in NL in winning percentages (.650) and eighth in strikeouts (154)... Hit two homers... Selected by Braves in first round of 1985 draft... Traded to Phillies with Dale Murphy for Jeff Parrett, Aug. 3, 1990... Named Braves' 1986 Minor League Pitcher of the Year... Pitched three-hit shutout against Astros for first big-league win in 1989... Born April 6, 1967, in Lumberton, N.C.... Earned $115,000 in 1991.

Year	Club	G	IP	W	L	Pct.	SO	BB	H	ERA
1989	Atlanta	4	26⅓	1	2	.333	17	6	22	4.10
1990	Atl.-Phil.	15	51⅓	3	3	.500	21	26	50	5.08
1991	Philadelphia	36	207⅔	13	7	.650	154	66	177	3.38
	Totals	55	285⅓	17	12	.586	192	98	249	3.75

MITCH WILLIAMS 27 6-4 205   Bats L Throws L

"Wild Thing" seemed rejuvenated after being traded by Cubs to Phillies on eve of 1991 opener... Bounced back from injury-plagued 1990 season... His 30 saves in 1991 were second-highest single-season total in Phils' history, trailing only Steve Bedrosian's 40 in 1987... Broke Al Holland's club record for saves by a lefty (29 in 1983)... Opponents hit just .121 against him with runners in scoring position... NL Pitcher of the

Month in August, going 8-1 with five saves and 1.21 ERA . . .
Eight wins in a month was major-league record for a reliever . . .
Tied for third in NL in saves and boosted career total to 114 . . .
Selected by Padres in eighth round of 1982 draft . . . Traded to
Rangers in 1985 and to Cubs before 1989 season . . . Had career-
best 36 saves in 1989 while leading NL with 76 appearances . . .
Traded to Phillies for Chuck McElroy and Bob Scanlon . . . Born
Nov. 17, 1964, in Santa Ana, Cal. . . . Earned $1.5 million in
1991 . . . Free agent re-signed three-year $9.2-million pact in De-
cember.

Year	Club	G	IP	W	L	Pct.	SO	BB	H	ERA
1986	Texas	80	98	8	6	.571	90	79	69	3.58
1987	Texas	85	108⅔	8	6	.571	129	94	63	3.23
1988	Texas	67	68	2	7	.222	61	47	48	4.63
1989	Chicago (NL)	76	81⅔	4	4	.500	67	52	71	2.64
1990	Chicago (NL)	59	66⅓	1	8	.111	55	50	60	3.93
1991	Philadelphia	69	88⅓	12	5	.706	84	62	56	2.34
	Totals	436	511	35	36	.493	486	384	367	3.33

JOSE DeJESUS 26 6-5 195   Bats R Throws R

Showed enormous talent during first full big-
league season but lack of control prevented him
from being a big winner . . . Led NL with 128
walks . . . Yielded six or more walks in eight
starts, including eight-walk game in 7-3 win at
Los Angeles May 12 . . . Had career-high five-
game winning streak spanning July and August
. . . His 13 strikeouts against Braves Aug. 31
was career high and most by a Phillie since John Denny fanned
13 in 1985 . . . Recorded first career save June 5 at Atlanta . . .
Named Phillies' Player of the Month in June after going 4-1 with
3.23 ERA . . . Opponents batted .224, fourth-lowest mark in NL
. . . Half of his six career complete games have come against Mets
. . . Signed by Royals as free agent in 1983 . . . Traded to Phillies
for Steve Jeltz before 1990 season . . . Promoted to majors June 2
and allowed five hits or less in all but four of 22 starts . . . Born
Jan. 6, 1965, in Brooklyn, N.Y. . . . Earned $145,000 in 1991.

Year	Club	G	IP	W	L	Pct.	SO	BB	H	ERA
1988	Kansas City	2	2⅔	0	1	.000	2	5	6	27.00
1989	Kansas City	3	8	0	0	.000	2	8	7	4.50
1990	Philadelphia	22	130	7	8	.467	87	73	97	3.74
1991	Philadelphia	31	181⅔	10	9	.526	118	128	147	3.42
	Totals	58	322⅓	17	18	.486	209	214	257	3.77

BARRY JONES 29 6-4 225   **Bats R Throws R**

Changed teams for second straight winter, coming to Phillies from Montreal in December trade for Darrin Fletcher... Was Expos' bullpen closer, leading team with 13 saves... In 1990, with White Sox, established himself as top setup man in baseball as he had a hand in 30 of Bob Thigpen's major-league record 57 saves ... Recorded just one save himself in 1990... Selected by Pirates in third round of 1984 draft... Traded to White Sox in August 1988 for Dave LaPoint... Traded to Expos before 1991 season with Ivan Calderon for Tim Raines... Entering second season of two-year contract, plus an option, signed prior to trade to Expos... Earned $875,000 in 1991... Born Feb. 15, 1963, in Centerville, Ind.

Year	Club	G	IP	W	L	Pct.	SO	BB	H	ERA
1986	Pittsburgh	26	37⅓	3	4	.429	29	21	29	2.89
1987	Pittsburgh	32	43⅓	2	4	.333	28	23	55	5.61
1988	Pittsburgh	42	56⅓	1	1	.500	31	21	57	3.04
1988	Chicago (AL)	17	26	2	2	.500	17	17	15	2.42
1989	Chicago (AL)	22	30⅓	3	2	.600	17	8	22	2.37
1990	Chicago (AL)	65	74	11	4	.733	45	33	62	2.31
1991	Montreal	77	88⅔	4	9	.308	46	33	76	3.35
	Totals	281	356	26	26	.500	213	156	316	3.16

TOP PROSPECTS

RUBEN AMARO Jr. 27 5-10 170   **Bats S Throws R**
Returns to native Philadelphia with Kyle Abbott for Von Hayes ... Switch-hitting outfielder stole 26 bases and hit .326 for Edmonton (AAA) in 1991... Versatile utility player is son of former major leaguer with same name... Eleventh-round pick in 1987 draft... Born Feb. 12, 1965, in Philadelphia.

ANDY ASHBY 24 6-5 180   **Bats R Throws R**
Control problems might be only factor holding back this big right-hander... Walked 60 batters in 161 innings for Scranton (AAA), but also struck out 113 and his 3.46 ERA was sixth-best in league ... Pitched 20 straight hitless innings... Went 1-5 with 6.00 ERA in eight starts with Phillies... Picked up first big-league victory Sept. 24 in Chicago... Signed as non-drafted free agent in 1986 ... Pitched 30 consecutive scoreless innings for Reading (AA) in 1990 and was named Phillies' Minor League Pitcher of the Year ... Born July 11, 1967, in Kansas City.

KIM BATISTE 24 6-0 175   Bats R Throws R

Could become Phillies' regular shortstop in 1992 . . . Phillies like his arm, range, speed and overall athleticism . . . Held his own following promotion to majors in September, collecting six hits in 27 at-bats . . . Batted .292 for Scranton (AAA) with 25 doubles and 18 stolen bases . . . Selected by Phillies in third round of 1987 draft . . . Ranked fifth in Eastern League in both hits and stolen bases for Reading (AA) in 1990 . . . Born March 15, 1968, in New Orleans.

DOUG LINDSEY 24 6-2 200   Bats R Throws R

Solid defensive catcher who committed just three errors in 94 games for Reading (AA) while batting .259 with 13 doubles and 34 RBI . . . Voted best defensive catcher in Eastern League . . . Threw out 46 of 100 would-be base-stealers . . . Called up to Phillies in September when both Darren Daulton and Steve Lake were injured but got just three at-bats . . . Selected by Phillies in sixth round of 1987 draft . . . Born Sept. 22, 1967, in Austin, Tex.

TONY LONGMIRE 23 6-1 195   Bats L Throws R

Good-hitting outfielder can do it all . . . Hits for average and power, also can run and throw . . . Hit .288 for Reading (AA) with 23 doubles, nine homers, 56 RBI and 10 stolen bases in just 323 at-bats . . . Split time in 1991 between Reading and Scranton (AAA), where he hit .261 . . . Selected by Pirates in eighth round of 1986 draft . . . Acquired by Phillies as player to be named in trade for Carmelo Martinez, Aug. 30, 1990 . . . Missed most of 1990 season with broken wrist sustained in winter ball . . . Born Aug. 12, 1968, in Vallejo, Cal.

BRAULIO CASTILLO 23 6-0 160   Bats R Throws R

Changing organizations at midseason didn't hurt this good-hitting outfielder's performance . . . Batted .300 for San Antonio (AA) with 19 doubles, three triples, eight homers, 48 RBI and 22 steals . . . Hit .350 with nine doubles and 15 RBI in just 16 games for Scranton (AAA) before being called up to majors in August . . . Singled off Cubs' Les Lancaster in major-league debut Aug. 18 . . . Three of his nine big-league hits were doubles . . . Signed by Dodgers as free agent in 1985 . . . Traded to Phillies with Mike Hartley for Roger McDowell, July 31, 1991 . . . Born May 13, 1968, in Elias Pina, D.R.

KYLE ABBOTT 24 6-2 200   Bats L Throws L

Highly regarded, hard-throwing southpaw made for two Angel Abbotts, but now he's a Phillie, traded with Ruben Amaro Jr. for Von Hayes . . . Went 1-2 with 4.58 ERA in five appearances, including three starts, after September promotion to Angels . . . Was 14-10 with 3.99 ERA for Edmonton (AAA) . . . First-round pick in 1989 draft . . . Born Feb. 18, 1968, in Newbury Port, Maine.

MANAGER JIM FREGOSI: Took over Phillies just 13 games into 1991 season when Nick Leyva was fired after getting off to 4-9 start . . . Brought upbeat approach to job despite having to contend with inconsistent pitching and numerous injuries to regular players . . . Put together 13-game winning streak in August . . . Phillies went 74-75 under his guidance, finishing third . . . Overall managing record is 504-550 . . . Managed Angels from 1978-81, winning AL West title in 1979 before losing ALCS to Orioles . . . Replaced by Gene Mauch after 22-25 start in 1981 . . . Between big-league jobs, he managed Louisville (AAA) from 1983-86, winning two division championships and two Manager of the Year awards . . . Replaced Tony La Russa as White Sox skipper in 1986 and had three straight fifth-place finishes before being released after 1988 season . . . Six-time All-Star shortstop played with Angels, Mets, Rangers and Pirates from 1961-78 . . . Best season was 1970 when he batted .278 with 22 homers and 82 RBI . . . Batted .265 during 18-year career . . . Gold Glove winner in 1967 . . . Held Angels' all-time records for games, at-bats, runs, hits, doubles, triples, extra-base hits and total bases . . . Lives in infamy among Mets fans as key player acquired from Angels in 1971 trade for Nolan Ryan . . . Born April 4, 1942, in San Francisco.

ALL-TIME PHILLIE SEASON RECORDS

BATTING: Frank O'Doul, .398, 1929
HRs: Mike Schmidt, 48, 1980
RBI: Chuck Klein, 170, 1930
STEALS: Juan Samuel, 72, 1984
WINS: Grover Alexander, 33, 1916
STRIKEOUTS: Steve Carlton, 310, 1972

PITTSBURGH PIRATES

TEAM DIRECTORY: Chairman: Douglas Danforth; Pres.: Mark Sauer; GM: Cameron Bonifay; VP-Pub. Rel.: Rick Cerrone; Dir. Media Rel.: Jim Trdinich; Trav. Sec.: Greg Johnson; Mgr.: Jim Leyland. Home: Three Rivers Stadium (58,729). Field distances: 335, l.f. line; 375, l.c.; 400, c.f.; 375, r.c.; 335, r.f. line. Spring training: Bradenton, Fla.

SCOUTING REPORT

HITTING: The Pirates were the best offensive team in the NL last season, leading the NL in batting average (.263), runs (768), doubles (259) and on-base percentage (.338). But it's unlikely that the Bucs can duplicate those numbers without cleanup hitter Bobby Bonilla, who defected to the Mets as a free agent.

Barry Bonds (.292, 25, 116) has put together two straight outstanding years and he has the added incentive of playing for an enormous contract when he's eligible for free agency at the end of this season. But he might be less effective without Bonilla hitting in front of him.

Andy Van Slyke (.265, 17, 83) is a solid performer, yet he still struggles against left-handed pitching. Steve Buechele (.262, 22, 85 with the Rangers and Pirates) is coming off a career year and must prove that he can do it again. Orlando Merced (.275, 10, 50) had a fine rookie year as a platoon first baseman and may get a chance to play every day. Jay Bell (.270, 16, 67) provides excellent offense for a shortstop and Jose Lind (.265, 3, 54) isn't bad for a second baseman. John Wehner, who batted .340 in just 106 at-bats before injuring his back, might be a big plus if he's healthy and the Pirates find a place for him.

PITCHING: Most of the key performers return from a pitching staff that tied for the NL lead in complete games (18) and saves (51) while finishing second in the league with a 3.44 ERA.

Ace Doug Drabek (15-14, 3.07) is still the rock in this rotation and he needs another big year with free agency on the horizon. John Smiley (20-8, 3.08) had a career year, but must bounce back from a nightmarish NLCS in which he was bombed twice by the Braves. Zane Smith (16-10, 3.20) also had his best season and Randy Tomlin (8-7, 2.98) led the team in ERA. Counting on a return to full health of Bob Walk (9-2, 3.60), the Pirates re-signed him to a two-year contract.

Barry Bonds has 58 HRs and 230 RBI the last two seasons.

The Pirates still lack a dominant closer in their bullpen, but they've gotten a lot of mileage out of a committee featuring Bill Landrum (4-4, 3.18, 17 Sv), Stan Belinda (7-5, 3.45, 16 Sv), Rosario Rodriguez (1-1, 4.11, 6 Sv), Roger Mason (3-2, 3.03, 3 Sv) and Vicente Palacios (6-3, 3.75, 3 Sv).

FIELDING: Losing Bonilla didn't hurt the Pirates' defense, because he was one of their few weak links. Van Slyke has won four straight Gold Gloves in center field and Bonds has won two straight in left field. Lind has excellent range at second base, Buechele is a fine third baseman and Bell led all NL shortstops in total chances. Mike LaVallicre had the top fielding percentage (.998) of any NL catcher.

OUTLOOK: No NL team has won three consecutive divisional titles since the 1976-78 Phillies. Manager Jim Leyland did an excellent job keeping the Pirates focused last season and they went 98-64 to repeat as NL East champs. It won't happen again. There's still enough talent here for the Pirates to be contenders, but they'll find it difficult to rebound from a second straight playoff flop and from the loss of Bonilla.

PITTSBURGH PIRATES 1992 ROSTER

MANAGER Jim Leyland
Coaches—Terry Collins, Rich Donnelly, Milt May, Ray Miller, Tommy Sandt

PITCHERS

No.	Name	1991 Club	W-L	IP	SO	ERA	B-T	Ht.	Wt.	Born
60	Ausanio, Joe	Carolina	0-0	3	2	0.00	R-R	6-1	205	12/9/65 Kingston, NY
		Buffalo	2-2	30	26	3.86				
50	Belinda, Stan	Pittsburgh	7-5	78	71	3.45	R-R	6-3	200	8/6/66 Huntingdon, PA
—	Cole, Victor	Omaha	1-1	13	12	4.15	R-R	5-10	160	1/23/68 Soviet Union
		Buffalo	1-2	24	23	3.75				
		Carolina	0-2	28	32	1.91				
15	Drabek, Doug	Pittsburgh	15-14	235	142	3.07	R-R	6-1	185	7/25/62 Victoria, TX
26	Heaton, Neal	Pittsburgh	3-3	69	34	4.33	L-L	6-1	205	3/3/60 Jamaica, NY
43	Landrum, Bill	Pittsburgh	4-4	76	45	3.18	R-R	6-2	205	8/17/58 Columbia, SC
48	Mason, Roger	Buffalo	9-5	123	80	3.08	R-R	6-6	220	9/18/58 Bellaire, MI
		Pittsburgh	3-2	30	21	3.03				
64	Miller, Paul	Carolina	7-2	89	69	2.42	R-R	6-5	215	4/27/65 Burlington, WI
		Buffalo	5-2	67	30	1.48				
		Pittsburgh	0-0	5	2	5.40				
56	Minor, Blas	Buffalo	2-2	36	25	5.75	R-R	6-3	195	3/20/66 Merced, CA
		Carolina	0-0	13	18	2.84				
58	Palacios, Vicente	Pittsburgh	6-3	82	64	3.75	R-R	6-3	195	7/19/63 Mexico
		Buffalo	0-0	6	7	1.42				
38	Patterson, Bob	Pittsburgh	4-3	66	57	4.11	R-L	6-2	192	5/16/59 Jacksonville, FL
34	Reed, Rick	Buffalo	14-4	168	102	2.15	R-R	6-0	205	8/16/64 Huntington, WV
		Pittsburgh	0-0	4	2	10.38				
30	Rodriguez, Rosario	Buffalo	4-3	51	43	3.00	R-L	6-0	190	7/8/69 Mexico
		Pittsburgh	1-1	15	10	4.11				
35	Roesler, Mike	Carolina	2-4	26	31	4.91	R-R	6-5	200	9/12/63 Ft. Wayne, IN
		Buffalo	5-4	48	33	3.56				
57	Smiley, John	Pittsburgh	20-8	208	129	3.08	L-L	6-4	200	3/17/65 Phoenixville, PA
41	Smith, Zane	Pittsburgh	16-10	228	120	3.20	L-L	6-2	200	12/28/60 Madison, WI
29	Tomlin, Randy	Pittsburgh	8-7	175	104	2.98	L-L	5-11	179	6/14/66 Bainbridge, MD
17	Walk, Bob	Pittsburgh	9-2	115	87	3.60	R-R	6-4	217	11/26/56 Van Nuys, CA

CATCHERS

No.	Name	1991 Club	H	HR	RBI	Pct.	B-T	Ht.	Wt.	Born
12	LaValliere, Mike	Pittsburgh	97	3	41	.289	L-R	5-10	205	8/18/60 Charlotte, NC
14	Prince, Tom	Pittsburgh	9	1	2	.265	R-R	5-11	185	8/13/64 Kankakee, IL
		Buffalo	46	6	32	.208				
77	Romero, Mandy	Carolina	70	3	31	.217	S-R	5-11	196	10/19/67 Miami, FL
11	Slaught, Don	Pittsburgh	65	1	29	.295	R-R	6-1	190	9/11/58 Long Beach, CA

INFIELDERS

No.	Name	1991 Club	H	HR	RBI	Pct.	B-T	Ht.	Wt.	Born
3	Bell, Jay	Pittsburgh	164	16	67	.270	R-R	6-1	185	12/11/65 Pensacola, FL
22	Buechele, Steve	Texas	111	18	66	.267	R-R	6-2	200	9/26/61 Lancaster, CA
		Pittsburgh	28	4	19	.246				
51	Garcia, Carlos	Buffalo	123	7	60	.266	R-R	6-1	185	10/15/67 Venezuela
		Pittsburgh	6	0	1	.250				
7	King, Jeff	Pittsburgh	26	4	18	.239	R-R	6-1	185	12/26/64 Marion, IN
		Buffalo	4	0	2	.222				
13	Lind, Jose	Pittsburgh	133	3	54	.265	R-R	5-11	175	5/1/64 Puerto Rico
6	Merced, Orlando	Buffalo	2	0	2	.167	S-R	5-11	175	11/2/66 Puerto Rico
		Pittsburgh	113	10	50	.275				
2	Redus, Gary	Pittsburgh	62	7	24	.246	R-R	6-1	195	11/1/56 Tanner, AL
27	Richardson, Jeff	Buffalo	48	1	24	.258	R-R	6-2	180	8/26/65 Grand Island, NE
		Pittsburgh	1	0	0	.250				
—	Shelton, Ben	Salem	53	14	56	.261	R-L	6-3	210	9/21/69 Chicago, IL
		Carolina	39	1	19	.231				
52	Wehner, John	Carolina	62	3	21	.265	R-R	6-3	204	6/29/67 Pittsburgh, PA
		Buffalo	34	1	15	.304				
		Pittsburgh	36	0	7	.340				

OUTFIELDERS

No.	Name	1991 Club	H	HR	RBI	Pct.	B-T	Ht.	Wt.	Born
24	Bonds, Barry	Pittsburgh	149	25	116	.292	L-L	6-1	190	7/24/64 Riverside, CA
47	Bullett, Scott	Augusta	109	1	36	.284	L-L	6-2	200	12/25/68 Martinsburg, WV
		Salem	52	2	15	.333				
		Pittsburgh	0	0	0	.000				
—	Martin, Albert	Greenville	73	7	38	.243	L-L	6-2	220	11/24/67 West Covina, CA
		Richmond	42	5	18	.278				
23	McClendon, Lloyd	Pittsburgh	47	7	24	.288	R-R	5-11	210	1/11/59 Gary, IN
—	McDaniel, Terry	Tidewater	99	9	42	.248	S-R	5-9	205	12/6/66 Kansas City, MO
		New York (NL)	6	0	2	.207				
—	Ratliff, Daryl	Salem	103	2	23	.293	R-R	6-1	180	10/15/69 Santa Cruz, CA
		Carolina	20	0	9	.215				
18	Van Slyke, Andy	Pittsburgh	130	17	83	.265	L-R	6-2	195	12/21/60 Utica, NY
42	Varsho, Gary	Pittsburgh	51	4	23	.273	L-R	5-11	190	6/20/61 Marshfield, WI

PIRATE PROFILES

BARRY BONDS 27 6-1 190   Bats L Throws L

Arguably the best all-around player in baseball but his outstanding 1991 season was overshadowed by disappointing postseason for second straight year . . . Went 4-for-27 with no RBI and just one extra-base hit in NLCS, was 0-for-16 with runners on base and, in 13 postseason games, has just one RBI . . . Led NL in on-base percentage (.410), second in RBI (116) and walks (107), fourth in slugging percentage (.514), fifth in stolen bases (43), 10th in total bases (262) . . . Named NL Player of the Month for July, after batting .362 with six homers, 29 RBI, 20 runs and 15 steals . . . Recognized as best left fielder in NL, winning first Gold Glove in 1990 along with NL MVP honors . . . Average dipped to .162 in May of last season as he went 60 at-bats between extra-base hits . . . Selected by Pirates in first round of 1985 draft . . . Born July 24, 1964, in Riverside, Cal. . . . Son of former major-league star Bobby . . . Earned $2.3 million in 1991 and added Gold Glove.

Year	Club	Pos.	G	AB	R	H	2B	3B	HR	RBI	SB	Avg.
1986	Pittsburgh	OF	113	413	72	92	26	3	16	48	36	.223
1987	Pittsburgh	OF	150	551	99	144	34	9	25	59	32	.261
1988	Pittsburgh	OF	144	538	97	152	30	5	24	58	17	.283
1989	Pittsburgh	OF	159	580	96	144	34	6	19	58	32	.248
1990	Pittsburgh	OF	151	519	104	156	32	3	33	114	52	.301
1991	Pittsburgh	OF	153	510	95	149	28	5	25	116	43	.292
	Totals		870	3111	563	837	184	31	142	453	212	.269

ANDY VAN SLYKE 31 6-2 195   Bats L Throws R

Perennial Gold Glove center fielder committed just one error in 1991 . . . Put together strong final three months offensively after batting average had dipped to .212 . . . Tied for eighth in NL in triples (seven) . . . Homered off Tom Glavine in first at-bat of NLCS and had RBI double in second at-bat, but drove in no other runs in series, going 4-for-25 overall . . . Missed 10 games spanning July and August with pulled muscle in lower left back . . . Still struggles against most left-handed pitchers . . . Had streak of 103 errorless games . . . Hit in 10 straight games and had RBI in seven consecutive games spanning June and July . . . Homered in three straight games after going homerless for 27 games . . . Selected by Cardinals in first round of 1979 draft . . . Traded to Pirates with Mike LaValliere and Mike Dunne for Tony Pena before 1987 season . . . Born Dec. 21, 1960, in Utica, N.Y. . . . Earned $2,150,000 in 1991 . . . Did guest appearance as weatherman on Pittsburgh TV station.

Year	Club	Pos.	G	AB	R	H	2B	3B	HR	RBI	SB	Avg.
1983	St. Louis	OF-1B-3B	101	309	51	81	15	5	8	38	21	.262
1984	St. Louis	OF-1B-3B	137	361	45	88	16	4	7	50	28	.244
1985	St. Louis	OF-1B	146	424	61	110	25	6	13	55	34	.259
1986	St. Louis	OF-1B	137	418	48	113	23	7	13	61	21	.270
1987	Pittsburgh	OF-1B	157	564	93	165	36	11	21	82	34	.293
1988	Pittsburgh	OF	154	587	101	169	23	15	25	100	30	.288
1989	Pittsburgh	OF-1B	130	476	64	113	18	9	9	53	16	.237
1990	Pittsburgh	OF	136	493	67	140	26	6	17	77	14	.284
1991	Pittsburgh	OF	138	491	87	130	24	7	17	83	10	.265
	Totals		1236	4123	617	1109	206	70	130	599	208	.269

JAY BELL 26 6-1 185   Bats R Throws R

Emerged as star during NLCS, leading all players with 12 hits while batting .414 with two doubles and a homer . . . Also made alert appeal play at third base in Game 5 after noticing Dave Justice missed bag, ultimately giving Pirates 1-0 victory . . . Led majors with 30 sacrifice bunts . . . Tied for sixth in NL in triples (8) and runs (96) . . . Second in homers (16) and RBI (67) among NL shortstops . . . Had career-best 10-game hitting streak in August . . . Became only third Pirate shortstop in history to hit over 15 homers . . . Went 20 games without RBI in August . . . Hit four homers at Astrodome . . . Hit second career grand slam . . . Selected by Twins in first round of 1984 draft . . . Traded to Indians in 1985 for Bert Blyleven . . . Traded to Pirates before 1987 season for Felix Fermin . . . Born Dec. 11, 1965, in Pensacola, Fla. . . . Earned $360,000 in 1991 . . . Led NL shortstops in 1990 in games played, putouts and total chances.

Year	Club	Pos.	G	AB	R	H	2B	3B	HR	RBI	SB	Avg.
1986	Cleveland	2B	5	14	3	5	2	0	1	4	0	.357
1987	Cleveland	SS	38	125	14	27	9	1	2	13	2	.216
1988	Cleveland	SS	73	211	23	46	5	1	2	21	4	.218
1989	Pittsburgh	SS	78	271	33	70	13	3	2	27	5	.258
1990	Pittsburgh	SS	159	583	93	148	28	7	7	52	10	.254
1991	Pittsburgh	SS	157	608	96	164	32	8	16	67	10	.270
	Totals		510	1812	262	460	89	20	30	184	31	.254

STEVE BUECHELE 30 6-2 200   Bats R Throws R

Free agent remained a Buc, re-signing three-year, $11-million pact... "Boo" came to Pirates from Rangers in late-season trade, filling hole at third base after both Jeff King and John Wehner were injured... Hit first NL homer Sept. 4 against Giants' Bud Black... Set AL record for best-fielding percentage by a third baseman (.991), breaking Don Money's .989 mark set in 1974... Tied NLCS record with five straight hits spanning Games 3 and 4... Went 3-for-3 in Game 4... Was 7-for-23 in NLCS with two doubles but no RBI... Committed two errors in first 14 games for Pirates after making only three miscues in 121 games for Rangers... Became eighth Pirate third baseman in 1991... Selected by Rangers in fifth round of 1982 draft... Traded to Pirates for minor-league pitchers Kurt Miller and Hector Fajardo Aug. 30... Born Sept. 26, 1961, in Lancaster, Cal.... Earned $775,000 in 1991... Showed good timing, having best season during final year of contract.

Year	Club	Pos.	G	AB	R	H	2B	3B	HR	RBI	SB	Avg.
1985	Texas	3B-2B	69	219	22	48	6	3	6	21	3	.219
1986	Texas	3B-2B-0F	153	461	54	112	19	2	18	54	5	.243
1987	Texas	3B-2B-0F	136	363	45	86	20	0	13	50	2	.237
1988	Texas	3B-2B	155	503	68	126	21	4	16	58	2	.250
1989	Texas	3B-2B	155	486	60	114	22	2	16	59	1	.235
1990	Texas	3B-2B	91	251	30	54	10	0	7	30	1	.215
1991	Texas	3B-2B-SS	121	416	58	111	17	2	18	66	0	.267
1991	Pittsburgh	3B	31	114	16	28	5	1	4	19	0	.246
	Totals		911	2813	353	679	120	14	98	357	14	.241

JOSE LIND 27 5-11 175   Bats R Throws R

Solid second baseman with outstanding range... Unsung hero while helping Pirates win back-to-back division titles... Put together good offensive season in 1991, reaching career highs in RBI, triples and home runs... His fifth inning RBI single off Tom Glavine gave Pirates 1-0 win in Game 5 of NLCS... Committed just two errors after July 22, finishing season with nine... Had 56-game errorless streak in 1990 while compiling .991 fielding percentage and leading NL second basemen in putouts (330)... Hit for cycle in 1990 NLCS vs. Reds, going 5-for-21... Cousin of former major-league shortstop Onix Concepcion... Brother Orlando pitched in Pirate organization for seven years . . . Born May 1, 1964, in Toabaja, P.R . . . Signed by Pirates as non-drafted free agent in 1982 . . . Earned $575,000 in 1991.

Year Club	Pos.	G	AB	R	H	2B	3B	HR	RBI	SB	Avg.
1987 Pittsburgh	2B	35	143	21	46	8	4	0	11	2	.322
1988 Pittsburgh	2B	154	611	82	160	24	4	2	49	15	.262
1989 Pittsburgh	2B	153	578	52	134	21	3	2	48	15	.232
1990 Pittsburgh	2B	152	514	46	134	28	5	1	48	8	.261
1991 Pittsburgh	2B	150	502	53	133	16	6	3	54	7	.265
Totals		644	2348	254	607	97	22	8	210	47	.259

ORLANDO MERCED 25 5-11 175   Bats S Throws R

Rookie first baseman did fine job replacing Sid Bream, and was runnerup to Astros' Jeff Bagwell in Rookie of the Year race . . . Recalled from Buffalo (AAA) April 15 and made immediate impact, hitting .318 in April and .362 in May before slumping to .152 in June . . . Rebounded with .317 average in July . . . Hit first big-league homer against Astros' Pete Harnisch May 3 . . . Homered off John Smoltz on first pitch of NLCS Game 3. Also led off Game 7 with single off Smoltz . . . Had just nine at-bats in playoffs, because he platooned with Gary Redus . . . Became Pirates' leadoff man against right-handed pitchers . . . Attended 1991 Instructional League to learn to play outfield . . . Named to American Association All-Star team in 1990 while leading Buffalo in RBI (55) in just 101 games . . . Signed with Pirates as undrafted free agent in 1985 . . . Born Nov. 2, 1966, in San Juan, P.R. . . . Earned major-league minimum of $100,000 in 1991.

Year Club	Pos.	G	AB	R	H	2B	3B	HR	RBI	SB	Avg.
1990 Pittsburgh	OF-C	25	24	3	5	1	0	0	0	0	.208
1991 Pittsburgh	1B-OF	120	411	83	113	17	2	10	50	8	.275
Totals		145	435	86	118	18	2	10	50	8	.271

DOUG DRABEK 29 6-1 185   Bats R Throws R

Followed up Cy Young season with another solid year despite getting off to sluggish 1-6 start . . . Finished fourth in NL in innings pitched (234⅔), seventh in complete games (five), 10th in ERA (3.07) . . . Opponents stole 29 bases on him, most in NL . . . Pitched six shutout innings in Game 1 of NLCS before leaving with strained right hamstring sustained while trying to stretch double . . . Pitched complete game in Game 6, but took 1-0 loss on ninth-inning run . . . NLCS ERA was 0.60 . . . Pitched Pirates' division-clinching victory two years in a row . . . Hurled one-hitter at St. Louis on Memorial Day . . . Selected by White Sox in 11th round of 1983 draft . . . Traded to Yankees in 1984 as player to be named in Roy Smalley deal . . . Sent to Pirates before 1987 season in six-player trade . . . Born July 25, 1962, in Victoria, Tex. . . . Earned $3,350,000 in 1991 . . . Led NL in victories (22) and winning percentage (.786) in 1990.

Year	Club	G	IP	W	L	Pct.	SO	BB	H	ERA
1986	New York (AL)	27	131⅔	7	8	.467	76	50	126	4.10
1987	Pittsburgh	29	176⅓	11	12	.478	120	46	165	3.88
1988	Pittsburgh	33	219⅓	15	7	.682	127	50	194	3.08
1989	Pittsburgh	35	244⅓	14	12	.538	123	69	215	2.80
1990	Pittsburgh	33	231⅓	22	6	.786	131	56	190	2.76
1991	Pittsburgh	35	234⅔	15	14	.517	142	62	245	3.07
	Totals	192	1237⅔	84	59	.587	719	333	1135	3.19

ZANE SMITH 31 6-2 200   Bats L Throws L

First full season in Pittsburgh was best of his career as he established himself among top lefties in league . . . Tied for third in NL in shutouts (three) . . . Ranked fourth in victories (16), fifth in complete games (six) . . . Averaged just 1.1 walks per nine innings . . . Went 5-1 with 1.87 ERA in May . . . Pitched one-hitter against Cardinals May 29 . . . Was outstanding in NLCS, allowing one run in 14⅔ innings while striking out 10 . . . Took 1-0 loss in Game 2 . . . Started on three days' rest in Game 5 and shut out Braves for 7⅔ innings, getting victory in tense 1-0 contest . . . Finished second in NL in ERA in 1990, going 4-0 with 1.42 ERA in first five starts after joining Pirates in August . . . Selected by Braves in third round of 1982 draft . . . Traded to Expos in July 1989 . . . Dealt to Pirates for Scott Ruskin, Willie Greene and Moises Alou, Aug. 8, 1990 . . . Born Dec. 28, 1960, in Madison, Wisc . . . Earned $2,225,000 in 1991.

Year	Club	G	IP	W	L	Pct.	SO	BB	H	ERA
1984	Atlanta	3	20	1	0	1.000	16	13	16	2.25
1985	Atlanta	42	147	9	10	.474	85	80	135	3.80
1986	Atlanta	38	204⅔	8	16	.333	139	105	209	4.05
1987	Atlanta	36	242	15	10	.600	130	91	245	4.09
1988	Atlanta	23	140⅓	5	10	.333	59	44	159	4.30
1989	Atl.-Mont.	48	147	1	13	.071	93	52	141	3.49
1990	Mont.-Pitt.	33	215⅓	12	9	.571	130	50	196	2.55
1991	Pittsburgh	35	228	16	10	.615	120	29	234	3.20
	Totals	258	1344⅓	67	78	.462	772	464	1335	3.58

JOHN SMILEY 27 6-4 200   Bats L Throws L

Enjoyed best season of career but was a playoff goat, getting bombed in both NLCS starts . . . Won final seven regular-season decisions to become 20-game winner for first time . . . Tied with Tom Glavine for NL lead in victories with 20 . . . Gave up just seven first-inning runs in 32 starts, but surrendered seven runs in two playoff starts . . . Lasted just two innings in Game 3, yielding five runs on five hits while taking loss in 10-3 rout . . . Blasted again in Game 7 as he failed to last an inning because Braves scored three times . . . Became first Pirate lefty to win 20 games since John Candelaria (1977) . . . Fractured left hand ruined 1990 season . . . Tied Doug Drabek in 1989 for club lead in complete games (eight) and strikeouts (123) . . . Selected by Pirates in 12th round of 1983 draft . . . Born March 17, 1965, in Phoenixville, Pa. . . . Earned $1,050,000 in 1991.

Year	Club	G	IP	W	L	Pct.	SO	BB	H	ERA
1986	Pittsburgh	12	11⅔	1	0	1.000	9	4	4	3.86
1987	Pittsburgh	63	75	5	5	.500	58	50	69	5.76
1988	Pittsburgh	34	205	13	11	.542	129	46	185	3.25
1989	Pittsburgh	28	205⅓	12	8	.600	123	49	174	2.81
1990	Pittsburgh	26	149⅓	9	10	.474	86	36	161	4.64
1991	Pittsburgh	33	207⅔	20	8	.714	129	44	194	3.08
	Totals	196	854	60	42	.588	534	229	787	3.57

RANDY TOMLIN 25 5-11 179   Bats L Throws L

Led Pirates in ERA (2.98) during first full season in big leagues . . . Pitched consecutive shutouts against Braves and Reds July 15-21, first back-to-back blankings by a Pirate since Rick Reuschel (1987) . . . Finished eighth in NL in ERA . . . Didn't lose on the road until Aug. 1 in St. Louis . . . Began season with three straight victories, but lost three decisions in a row from May 23-June 13 . . . Started NLCS Game 4 and pitched six innings, giving up two runs on six hits while getting no-decision . . . Allowed two earned runs or less in 19 of first 25 major-league starts . . . Named Pirates' Minor League Pitcher of the Year in 1990 and named to Eastern League All-Star team . . . Set Harrisburg (AA) club record with 2.28 ERA . . . Called up to big leagues Aug. 6, beating Phillies in debut . . . Selected by Pirates in 18th round of 1988 draft . . . Born June 14, 1966, in Bainbridge,

Md. . . . A bargain in 1991 with a $120,000 salary.

Year	Club	G	IP	W	L	Pct.	SO	BB	H	ERA
1990	Pittsburgh	12	77⅔	4	4	.500	42	12	62	2.55
1991	Pittsburgh	31	175	8	7	.533	104	54	170	2.98
	Totals	43	252⅔	12	11	.522	146	66	232	2.85

BILL LANDRUM 33 6-2 205   Bats R Throws R

Biggest name in Pirates' ''no-game'' bullpen . . . Led team in saves (17) for third straight season . . . Also led in games finished (43) and appearances (61) . . . Didn't blow a save until July 1 while going 15-for-15 in save opportunities . . . Had few save chances in second half and was sidelined in September with tender arm . . . Picked up final save Aug. 28 in Los Angeles . . . Far more successful in Three Rivers Stadium than on road, he allowed just one earned run in first 24 home appearances . . . Allowed only two of 26 batters to reach base during three-week stretch at midseason . . . Gave up three homers in Chicago . . . Signed by Cubs as non-drafted free agent in 1980 . . . Signed free-agent deal with Pirates before 1989 season . . . Saved 26 games in first season with Pirates . . . Born Aug. 17, 1958, in Columbia, S.C. . . . Earned $820,000 in 1991.

Year	Club	G	IP	W	L	Pct.	SO	BB	H	ERA
1986	Cincinnati	10	13⅓	0	0	.000	14	4	23	6.75
1987	Cincinnati	44	65	3	2	.600	42	34	68	4.71
1988	Chicago (NL)	7	12⅓	1	0	1.000	6	3	19	5.84
1989	Pittsburgh	56	81	2	3	.400	51	28	60	1.67
1990	Pittsburgh	54	71⅔	7	3	.700	39	21	69	2.13
1991	Pittsburgh	61	76⅓	4	4	.500	45	19	76	3.18
	Totals	232	319⅓	17	12	.586	197	109	315	3.13

TOP PROSPECTS

JOHN WEHNER 24 6-3 204   Bats R Throws R

Big third baseman was called up to majors July 15 and made sensational debut, hitting .340 with seven doubles in just 106 at-bats before being sidelined for remainder of 1991 with back injury . . . Became first Pirate rookie to have five-hit game (July 23 vs. Braves) since Richie Zisk (1973) . . . Split first half of season between Carolina (AA), where he hit .265, and Buffalo (AAA), where he batted .304 . . . Selected by Pirates in seventh round of 1988 draft . . . In 1990 for Harrisburg (AA), he led Eastern League third basemen in games, putouts, assists, total chances and double plays . . . Batted .301 with 32 doubles and 14 homers for Salem (A) in 1989 . . . Born June 29, 1967, in Pittsburgh.

CARLOS GARCIA 24 6-1 185　　　　**Bats R Throws R**
Solid defensive shortstop with speed and some power . . . Hit .266 for Buffalo (AAA) with 21 doubles, six triples, seven homers and 60 RBI . . . Stole 30 bases and was caught just seven times . . . Called up to Pirates for four days at midseason and again in September, hitting .250 in 24 at-bats . . . Signed by Pirates as non-drafted free agent in 1987 . . . Eastern League All-Star with Harrisburg (AA) in 1990 before being promoted to Buffalo, where he hit safely in first 10 games . . . Singled off Cubs' Bill Long in first major-league at-bat, Sept. 20, 1990 . . . Born Oct. 15, 1967, in Tachira, Venezuela.

SCOTT BULLETT 23 6-2 200　　　　**Bats S Throws L**
Speedy outfielder made so much progress in 1991 that Pirates promoted him from Salem (A) to majors Sept. 1 . . . Used mostly as pinch-runner during Pirates' stretch drive to clinch pennant . . . Enjoyed outstanding season split between Augusta (A) and Salem, hitting combined .298 with 28 doubles, 11 triples, 51 RBI and 63 stolen bases . . . Signed with Pirates as free agent in 1988 . . . Batted .301 and stole 30 bases in just 74 games for Welland (A) in 1990 . . . Born Dec. 25, 1968, in Martinsburg, W. Va.

ROSARIO RODRIGUEZ 22 6-0 195　　　**Bats R Throws L**
Played important role in Pirates' bullpen after being called up from Buffalo (AAA) Aug. 16 . . . Notched first major-league save at San Diego Aug. 30 . . . Finished with six saves, 1-1 record and 4.11 ERA . . . Allowed just eight hits, all singles, in first 14 appearances . . . For Buffalo, he went 4-3 with eight saves and 3.00 ERA, striking out 43 batters in 51 innings . . . Acquired by Reds from Nuevo Laredo of Mexican League in 1987 . . . Picked up on waivers by Pirates following 1990 season . . . Born July 8, 1969, in Los Mochis, Mexico.

MANAGER JIM LEYLAND: One of the most highly regarded  skippers in baseball, he won even more praise in 1991 by guiding Pirates to second straight NL East title . . . Became first NL manager to win back-to-back division races since 1978 . . . Had celebrated blowup with Barry Bonds during spring training which set tone for season . . . Runs loose clubhouse and usually maintains low profile, but he has also thrown furniture to make a point . . . Built Pirates from scratch, taking over last-place team in 1986 and getting Bucs into contention by 1988 . . . Named 1990 NL Manager of the Year by both Baseball Writers Association and *The Sporting News* managers' poll after winning first division title . . . Career minor-leaguer spent 22 years in baseball before becoming Pirates manager . . . Signed first professional contract with Tigers in 1963 and served that organization as player, minor-league coach and minor-league manager until 1981 . . . Just 26 years old when he became manager in 1971 . . . His teams reached playoffs in five of last six seasons in minors, winning three league championships . . . Named Manager of the Year three straight seasons . . . Coached third base for White Sox from 1982-85 under Tony La Russa, who remains a close friend . . . Born Dec. 15, 1944, in Toledo, Ohio . . . Managerial record in majors is 497-475.

ALL-TIME PIRATE SEASON RECORDS

BATTING: Arky Vaughan, .385, 1935
HRs: Ralph Kiner, 54, 1949
RBI: Paul Waner, 131, 1927
STEALS: Omar Moreno, 96, 1980
WINS: Jack Chesbro, 28, 1902
STRIKEOUTS: Bob Veale, 276, 1965

ST. LOUIS CARDINALS

TEAM DIRECTORY: Chairman: August A. Busch III: Pres./CEO: Fred L. Kuhlmann; Exec. VP/COO: Stuart Meyer; VP/GM: Dal Maxvill; Dir. Player Pers.: Ted Simmons; Dir. Pub. Rel.: Jeff Wehling; Mgr. Pub. Rel.: Brian Bartow; Trav. Sec.: C.J. Cherre; Mgr.: Joe Torre. Home: Busch Stadium (54,224). Field distances: 330, l.f. line; 414, c.f.; 330, r.f. line. Spring training: St. Petersburg, Fla.

SCOUTING REPORT

HITTING: The fences have been moved in at Busch Stadium and that should result in better power numbers for the Cardinals, who were last in the NL with only 68 homers in 1991. The Cards' overall production wasn't bad, however. Their .255 average was the fourth-best mark in the league and they ranked sixth with 651 runs.

Andres Galarraga (.219, 9, 33 with the Expos) will appreciate the shortened fences. Hampered by knee surgery, he suffered through his worst season in 1991 before the Expos traded him to St. Louis for pitcher Ken Hill. If Galarraga regains his form, he'll give the Cardinals the big bopper they'll need to support Pedro Guerrero (.272, 8, 70) in the middle of their lineup.

Todd Zeile (.280, 11, 81), who led Cards in RBI and homers, should also benefit from Busch's shorter dimensions. Felix Jose (.305, 8, 77) looks like a legitimate star. Ray Lankford (.251, 9, 69) stole 44 bases and will be a force, Ozzie Smith (.285, 3, 50, 35 steals) is still a pro, Tom Pagnozzi (.264, 2, 57) was surprisingly productive and Milt Thompson (.307, 6, 34) excelled as a role player. Bernard Gilkey (.216, 5, 20) is still in the picture despite a disappointing rookie season.

PITCHING: If Joe Magrane and Todd Worrell can bounce back from injuries, St. Louis will have a solid staff. Magrane, an 18-game winner in 1989, missed the entire 1991 season following elbow surgery. Worrell, who saved 121 games from 1986-89, hasn't pitched in two years because of elbow and shoulder problems, but he was throwing 90-plus-mph in the Instructional League.

The bullpen is already in good shape with Lee Smith (6-3, 2.34). At 34, he's better than ever, setting an NL record with 47 saves last year. Cris Carpenter (10-4, 4.23) and Scott Terry (4-4, 2.80, 1 Sv) did well as setup men.

Acquiring Felix Jose proved to be sharp deal of Cards.

The Cards are so deep in starters that they were able to trade Hill, an 11-game winner coming off his best season. Bryn Smith (12-9, 3.85), Bob Tewksbury (11-12, 3.25), Omar Olivares (11-7, 3.71), Jose DeLeon (5-9, 2.71) and Rheal Cormier (4-5, 4.12) give St. Louis a surplus of arms.

FIELDING: Adding Galarraga at first base gives the Cardinals three Gold Glove winners as he won the award in 1989 and 1990. Ozzie Smith has won 12 straight Gold Gloves and remains the standard by which other shortstops are measured. Pagnozzi, in his first season as the regular catcher, also won a Gold Glove. Lankford tied Brett Butler for the NL lead in total chances by an outfielder (380) and Jose Oquendo is among the best at second base. Converted catcher Zeile (25 errors) should improve at third base, but Guerrero looms as a liability in left.

OUTLOOK: Manager Joe Torre surprised everybody last season by taking the Cardinals to an 84-78, second-place finish, despite having a lineup filled with unknowns. If Magrane and Galarraga have big years and if the young players continue to improve, it might be enough to push this team over the top. In a division with no overwhelming favorite, the Cardinals have as good a chance as anybody.

ST. LOUIS CARDINALS 1992 ROSTER

MANAGER Joe Torre
Coaches—Don Baylor, Joe Coleman, Dave Collins, Bucky Dent, Gaylen Pitts, Red Schoendienst

PITCHERS

No.	Name	1991 Club	W-L	IP	SO	ERA	B-T	Ht.	Wt.	Born
49	Agosto, Juan	St. Louis	5-3	86	34	4.81	L-L	6-2	190	2/23/58 Puerto Rico
44	Carpenter, Cris	St. Louis	10-4	66	47	4.23	R-R	6-1	185	4/5/65 St. Augustine, FL
55	Clark, Mark	Arkansas	5-5	92	76	4.00	R-R	6-5	225	5/12/68 Bath, IL
		Louisville	3-2	45	29	2.98				
		St. Louis	1-1	22	13	4.03				
—	Compres, Fidel	Arkansas	4-2	32	18	3.94	R-R	6-0	165	5/10/65 Dominican Republic
		Louisville	0-2	15	7	3.07				
52	Cormier, Rheal	Louisville	7-9	128	74	4.23	L-L	5-10	185	4/23/67 Canada
		St. Louis	4-5	68	38	4.12				
48	DeLeon, Jose	St. Louis	5-9	163	118	2.71	R-R	6-3	226	12/20/60 Dominican Republic
35	DiPino, Frank	Louisville	0-0	1	0	36.00	L-L	6-0	194	10/22/56 Syracuse, NY
—	Ericks, John	Arkansas	5-14	140	103	4.77	R-R	6-7	220	9/16/67 Oaklawn, IL
32	Magrane, Joe	Injured					R-L	6-6	230	7/2/64 Des Moines, IA
22	McClure, Bob	California	0-0	10	5	9.31	R-L	5-11	188	4/29/53 Oakland, CA
		St. Louis	1-1	23	15	3.13				
—	Milchin, Mike	Arkansas	3-2	35	38	3.06	L-L	6-3	190	2/28/68 Knoxville, TN
		Louisville	5-9	94	47	5.07				
26	Olivares, Omar	St. Louis	11-7	167	91	3.71	R-R	6-1	193	7/6/67 Puerto Rico
		Louisville	1-2	36	27	3.47				
36	Smith, Bryn	St. Louis	12-9	199	94	3.85	R-R	6-2	205	8/11/55 Marietta, CA
47	Smith, Lee	St. Louis	6-3	73	67	2.34	R-R	6-6	269	12/4/57 Jamestown, LA
37	Terry, Scott	St. Louis	4-4	80	52	2.80	R-R	5-11	195	11/21/59 Hobbs, NM
39	Tewksbury, Bob	St. Louis	11-12	191	75	3.25	R-R	6-4	208	11/30/60 Concord, NH
38	Worrell, Todd	Louisville	0-0	3	4	18.00	R-R	6-5	222	9/28/59 Arcadia, CA

CATCHERS

No.	Name	1991 Club	H	HR	RBI	Pct.	B-T	Ht.	Wt.	Born
—	Fernandez, Jose	Arkansas	65	12	28	.228	L-R	6-3	210	8/24/67 New York, NY
29	Gedman, Rich	St. Louis	10	3	8	.106	L-R	6-0	211	9/26/59 Worcester, MA
19	Pagnozzi, Tom	St. Louis	121	2	57	.264	R-R	6-1	190	7/30/62 Tucson, AZ

INFIELDERS

No.	Name	1991 Club	H	HR	RBI	Pct.	B-T	Ht.	Wt.	Born
18	Alicea, Luis	Louisville	44	4	19	.393	S-R	5-9	177	7/29/65 Puerto Rico
		St. Louis	13	0	0	.191				
33	Brewer, Rod	Louisville	86	8	52	.225	L-L	6-3	218	2/24/66 Eustis, FL
		St. Louis	1	0	1	.077				
—	Carmona, Greg	Arkansas	6	0	1	.182	S-R	6-0	150	5/9/68 Dominican Republic
		Louisville	25	2	10	.175				
—	Galarraga, Andres	Montreal	82	9	33	.219	R-R	6-3	235	6/18/61 Venezuela
28	Guerrero, Pedro	St. Louis	116	8	70	.272	R-R	6-0	197	6/29/56 Dominican Republic
10	Hudler, Rex	St. Louis	47	1	15	.227	R-R	6-0	195	9/2/60 Tempa, AZ
8	Jones, Tim	Louisville	78	5	29	.255	L-R	5-10	175	12/1/62 Sumter, SC
		St. Louis	4	0	2	.167				
11	Oquendo, Jose	St. Louis	88	1	26	.240	S-R	5-10	171	7/4/63 Puerto Rico
7	Pena, Geronimo	St. Louis	45	5	17	.243	S-R	6-1	195	3/29/67 Dominican Republic
21	Perry, Gerald	St. Louis	58	6	36	.240	L-R	6-0	201	10/30/60 Savannah, GA
5	Royer, Stan	Louisville	133	14	74	.254	R-R	6-3	221	8/31/67 Olney, IL
		St. Louis	6	0	1	.286				
1	Smith, Ozzie	St. Louis	157	3	50	.285	S-R	5-10	168	12/26/54 Mobile, AL
2	Wilson, Craig	St. Louis	14	0	13	.171	R-R	5-11	208	11/28/64 Anne Arundel, MD
27	Zeile, Todd	St. Louis	158	11	81	.280	R-R	6-1	190	9/9/65 Van Nuys, CA

OUTFIELDERS

No.	Name	1991 Club	H	HR	RBI	Pct.	B-T	Ht.	Wt.	Born
23	Gilkey, Bernard	St. Louis	58	5	20	.216	R-R	6-0	190	9/24/66 St. Louis, MO
		Louisville	6	0	2	.146				
—	Jordan, Brian	Louisville	56	4	24	.264	R-R	6-1	205	3/29/67 Baltimore, MD
34	Jose, Felix	St. Louis	173	8	77	.305	S-R	6-1	221	5/8/65 Dominican Republic
16	Lankford, Ray	St. Louis	142	9	69	.251	L-L	5-11	198	6/5/67 Modesto, CA
—	Maclin, Lonnie	Louisville	94	4	37	.287	L-L	5-11	185	2/17/67 Clayton, MO
25	Thompson, Milt	St. Louis	100	6	34	.307	L-R	5-11	200	1/5/59 Washington, DC

CARDINAL PROFILES

FELIX JOSE 26 6-1 221   Bats S Throws R

Right fielder established himself as star during first full season with Cards . . . Made run at NL batting title before finishing fifth at .305 . . . Ranked second in NL in doubles (40) and multi-hit games (51) and fifth in hits (173) . . . Had first two-homer game of career and five RBI in Sept. 1 win at San Francisco . . . Had five four-hit games . . . Led Cards in batting, hits and extra-base hits (54) and was second in RBI . . . Batted over .350 with runners in scoring position and over .400 with runner on third . . . Born May 8, 1965, in Santo Domingo, D.R. . . . Signed by Athletics as non-drafted free agent in 1984 . . . Acquired by Cards with Stan Royer and Daryl Green in trade for Willie McGee, Aug. 30, 1990 . . . Batted .317 with 28 doubles and 83 RBI for Tacoma (AAA) in 1988 before making major-league debut with A's . . . Spent first full season in majors in 1990, compiling seven-game hitting streak with A's before trade to St. Louis . . . One of the biggest bargains in baseball with $160,000 salary in 1991.

Year Club	Pos.	G	AB	R	H	2B	3B	HR	RBI	SB	Avg.
1988 Oakland	OF	8	6	2	2	1	0	0	1	1	.333
1989 Oakland	OF	20	57	3	11	2	0	0	5	0	.193
1990 Oakland	OF	101	341	42	90	12	0	8	39	8	.264
1990 St. Louis	OF	25	85	12	23	4	1	3	13	4	.271
1991 St. Louis	OF	154	568	69	173	40	6	8	77	20	.305
Totals		308	1057	128	299	59	7	19	135	33	.283

TODD ZEILE 26 6-1 190   Bats R Throws R

Played huge role in Cards' 1991 success story by making transition from catcher to third baseman . . . Led team in errors with 25, yet also made outstanding plays and showed steady improvement . . . Led Cards in RBI (81) and homers (11) and was second in doubles (36) and extra-base hits (50) . . . Finished third in NL in doubles . . . Batted second, third, fourth, fifth and sixth in lineup . . . Bounced back from disappointing 1990 rookie season when he failed to live up to hype . . . Born Sept. 9, 1965, in Van Nuys, Cal. . . . Selected by Cards in third round of 1986 draft . . . Team MVP and All-Pac 10 at UCLA . . . Named

Midwest League's co-MVP in 1987 while driving in 106 runs for Springfield (A) . . . Named Texas League's best defensive catcher in 1988 while collecting 32 doubles, 19 homers and 75 RBI for Arkansas (AA) . . . Had 26 doubles, 19 homers and 85 RBI for Louisville (AAA) in 1989 . . . A bargain at $160,000 salary in 1991.

Year	Club	Pos.	G	AB	R	H	2B	3B	HR	RBI	SB	Avg.
1989	St. Louis	C	28	82	7	21	3	1	1	8	0	.256
1990	St. Louis	C–3B–1B–OF	144	495	62	121	25	3	15	57	2	.244
1991	St. Louis	3B	155	565	76	158	36	3	11	81	17	.280
	Totals		327	1142	145	300	64	7	27	146	19	.263

PEDRO GUERRERO 35 6-0 197   Bats R Throws R

Injuries ruined 1991 season for first baseman, who was making salary drive in final year of contract . . . Suffered hairline fracture of bone in lower left leg after colliding with Tom Pagnozzi July 7 and was on DL until Aug. 20 . . . Batted just .179 with seven RBI during next four weeks after being reactivated . . . Still a clutch hitter, he batted over .300 with runners in scoring position . . . Bothered by bad shoulder, he struggled through 5-for–52 slump in August and September . . . Had 10-game hitting streak before leg injury . . . Homered three times during five-game stretch in early July . . . Went homerless between May 18 and June 25 . . . Had just one extra-base hit between April 17 and May 17 . . . Born June 29, 1956, in San Pedro de Macoris, D.R. . . . Signed as free agent by Indians in 1973 . . . Traded to Dodgers in 1974 and acquired by Cards for John Tudor, Aug. 16, 1988 . . . Earned $2,283,000 in 1991 . . . Accepted arbitration in December.

Year	Club	Pos.	G	AB	R	H	2B	3B	HR	RBI	SB	Avg.
1978	Los Angeles . . .	1B	5	8	3	5	0	1	0	1	0	.625
1979	Los Angeles . . .	OF-1B-3B	25	62	7	15	2	0	2	9	2	.242
1980	Los Angeles . . .	OF-INF	75	183	27	59	9	1	7	31	2	.322
1981	Los Angeles . . .	OF-3B-1B	98	347	46	104	17	2	12	48	5	.300
1982	Los Angeles . . .	OF-3B	150	575	87	175	27	5	32	100	22	.304
1983	Los Angeles . . .	3B-1B	160	584	87	174	28	6	32	103	23	.296
1984	Los Angeles . . .	OF-3B-1B	144	535	85	162	29	4	16	72	9	.303
1985	Los Angeles . . .	OF-3B-1B	137	487	99	156	22	2	33	87	12	.320
1986	Los Angeles . . .	OF-1B	31	61	7	15	3	0	5	10	0	.246
1987	Los Angeles . . .	OF-1B	152	545	89	184	25	2	27	89	9	.338
1988	L.A.-St.L	1B-3B-OF	103	364	40	104	14	2	10	65	4	.286
1989	St. Louis	1B	162	570	60	177	42	1	17	117	2	.311
1990	St. Louis	1B	136	498	42	140	31	1	13	80	1	.281
1991	St. Louis	1B	115	427	41	116	12	1	8	70	4	.272
	Totals		1493	5246	720	1586	261	28	214	882	95	.302

OZZIE SMITH 37 5-10 168   Bats S Throws R

The ''Wiz'' just becomes more amazing with each passing year, strengthening credentials as greatest shortstop ever ... Made only eight errors in 1991 ... Had 68-game errorless streak before committing first miscue June 23 ... Reached 20-steal mark for 14th straight season and hit 30-steal plateau for 10th time ... Finished seventh in NL in walks (83), sixth in on-base percentage (.380), and runs (96) and eighth in steals (35) ... Averaged just one strikeout per 17 at-bats ... One of six active players to collect 100 hits in 14 straight seasons ... Named NL's smartest player in 1990 managers' poll ... Won 12th straight Gold Glove in 1991 ... Born Dec. 26, 1954, in Mobile, Ala. ... Selected by Padres in fourth round of 1977 draft ... Became San Diego's regular shortstop in 1978 after just 68 games in minors ... Traded to Cards for Garry Templeton before 1982 season ... Finished second in 1987 MVP voting ... Earned $2,225,000 in 1991.

Year Club	Pos.	G	AB	R	H	2B	3B	HR	RBI	SB	Avg.
1978 San Diego	SS	159	590	69	152	17	6	1	46	40	.258
1979 San Diego	SS	156	587	77	124	18	6	0	27	28	.211
1980 San Diego	SS	158	609	67	140	18	5	0	35	57	.230
1981 San Diego	SS	110	450	53	100	11	2	0	21	22	.222
1982 St. Louis	SS	140	488	58	121	24	1	2	43	25	.248
1983 St. Louis	SS	159	552	69	134	30	6	3	50	34	.243
1984 St. Louis	SS	124	412	53	106	20	5	1	44	35	.257
1985 St. Louis	SS	158	537	70	148	22	3	6	54	31	.276
1986 St. Louis	SS	153	514	67	144	19	4	0	54	31	.280
1987 St. Louis	SS	158	600	104	182	40	4	0	75	43	.303
1988 St. Louis	SS	153	575	80	155	27	1	3	51	57	.270
1989 St. Louis	SS	155	593	82	162	30	8	2	50	29	.273
1990 St. Louis	SS	143	512	61	130	21	1	1	50	32	.254
1991 St. Louis	SS	150	550	96	157	30	3	3	50	35	.285
Totals		2076	7569	1006	1955	327	55	22	650	499	.258

RAY LANKFORD 24 5-11 198   Bats L Throws L

Rookie center fielder was spectacular at times ... Led NL in triples with 15 and was fourth in stolen bases (44) ... Hit for cycle against Mets Sept. 15, becoming first Card to accomplish that feat since Willie McGee in 1984 ... His 15 triples were most by a Cardinal since McGee had 18 in 1985 ... First St. Louis rookie since Bake McBride (1974) to reach 50 RBI and 30 steals ... Batted second, third, sixth and seventh in lineup before settling in as leadoff man ... Far more productive in late-inning situations . . . Had two-homer game Sept. 1 at San Francisco . . . Had 12-game hitting streak in August . . . Born June 5, 1967, in Modesto, Cal. . . . Selected by Cards in third round of 1987 draft . . . Named Texas League MVP in 1989 . . . Worth much more than his $125,000 salary in 1991.

Year	Club	Pos.	G	AB	R	H	2B	3B	HR	RBI	SB	Avg.
1990	St. Louis	OF	39	126	12	36	10	1	3	12	8	.286
1991	St. Louis	OF	151	566	83	142	23	15	9	69	44	.251
	Totals		190	692	95	178	33	16	12	81	52	.257

TOM PAGNOZZI 29 6-1 190　　　　Bats R Throws R

Always an outstanding defensive catcher, he was finally given chance to be regular in 1991 and he responded with solid offensive season . . . Batted .272 during first half before slowing down after All-Star break . . . His nine steals were most by a Card catcher since Tim McCarver had nine in 1966 . . . Hit first five triples of career . . . Batted .364 during 18-game stretch in September . . . Established career highs in hits (121), doubles (24) and RBI (57) . . . Threw out 47 percent of would-be base-stealers . . . Had 88-game errorless streak snapped Aug. 12 by his first error since April 17 . . . Born July 30, 1962, in Tucson, Ariz. . . . Selected by Cards in eighth round of 1983 draft . . . All-Southwestern Conference at Arkansas . . . Made major-league debut in 1987 after Tony Pena suffered thumb injury . . . Earned $310,000 in 1991 and a Gold Glove.

Year	Club	Pos.	G	AB	R	H	2B	3B	HR	RBI	SB	Avg.
1987	St. Louis	C-1B	27	48	8	9	1	0	2	9	1	.188
1988	St. Louis	1B-C-3B	81	195	17	55	9	0	0	15	0	.282
1989	St. Louis	C-1B-3B	52	80	3	12	2	0	0	3	0	.150
1990	St. Louis	C-1B	69	220	20	61	15	0	2	23	1	.277
1991	St. Louis	C-1B	140	459	38	121	24	5	2	57	9	.264
	Totals		369	1002	86	258	51	5	6	107	11	.257

ANDRES GALARRAGA 30 6-3 235　　　Bats R Throws R

Slowed by injuries, the "Cat" struggled through worst offensive season of career and wound up being traded by Expos to Cardinals for pitcher Ken Hill . . . Disabled with strained left hamstring from May 26-July 4 . . . Had arthroscopic surgery June 8 to repair damage to undersurface of left kneecap . . . Batted just .183 with three doubles and three homers in first 48 games after being reactivated ... Drove ball onto Waveland Avenue in Chicago Aug. 15 for first homer since May 19 ... Stole home July 24 in San Diego for second time in career ... Hit 100th career homer May 19 at San Francisco ... Had four hits May 6 against Giants ... Still among best-fielding first basemen in game ... Expos missed his glove as much as his bat, committing 43 infield errors in first 53 games without him ... Signed by Expos as amateur free agent in 1979 ... Earned an inflated $2,366,667 in 1991 ... Born June 18, 1961, in Caracas, Venezuela.

Year	Club	Pos.	G	AB	R	H	2B	3B	HR	RBI	SB	Avg.
1985	Montreal	1B	24	75	9	14	1	0	2	4	1	.187
1986	Montreal	1B	105	321	39	87	13	0	10	42	6	.271
1987	Montreal	1B	147	551	72	168	40	3	13	90	7	.305
1988	Montreal	1B	157	609	99	184	42	8	29	92	13	.302
1989	Montreal	1B	152	572	76	147	30	1	23	85	12	.257
1990	Montreal	1B	155	579	65	148	29	0	20	87	10	.256
1991	Montreal	1B	107	375	34	82	13	2	9	33	5	.219
	Totals		847	3082	394	830	168	14	106	433	54	.269

BOB TEWKSBURY 31 6-4 208   Bats R Throws R

Journeyman starter spent first full season in majors and proved he belonged with career bests in victories (11), strikeouts (75), games started (30) and innings pitched (191) ... Was especially effective in day games, posting 1.62 ERA during one five-game stretch ... Allowed just one earned run during three-game surge in July ... Snapped five-start winless streak with complete-game victory against Reds July 26 ... Fanned career-high eight batters in home opener against Phillies ... Averaged less than two walks per nine innings ... Born Nov. 30, 1960, in Concord, N.H. ... Selected by Yankees in 19th round of 1981 draft ... Traded to Cubs in 1987 ... Signed as minor-league free agent by Cards before 1989 season ... Moved into Cards' rotation in 1990 and became most consistent starter, throwing back-to-back shutouts, including one-hitter against Astros ... Deserved more than his $160,000 salary in 1991.

Year	Club	G	IP	W	L	Pct.	SO	BB	H	ERA
1986	New York (AL)	23	130⅓	9	5	.643	49	31	144	3.31
1987	New York (AL)	8	33⅓	1	4	.200	12	7	47	6.75
1987	Chicago (NL)	7	18	0	4	.000	10	13	32	6.50
1988	Chicago (NL)	1	3⅓	0	0	.000	1	2	6	8.10
1989	St. Louis	7	30	1	0	1.000	17	10	25	3.30
1990	St. Louis	28	145⅓	10	9	.526	50	15	151	3.47
1991	St. Louis	30	191	11	12	.478	75	38	206	3.25
	Totals	104	551⅓	32	34	.485	214	116	611	3.67

BRYN SMITH 36 6-2 205   Bats R Throws R

Veteran right-hander became workhorse of staff in 1991, after Joe Magrane was lost to season-ending injury . . . Posted 100th career victory Aug. 9 at Pittsburgh . . . Two of his three complete games came against Astros . . . Has reached double figures in victories seven times . . . Inherited Magrane's role as Opening Day starter and responded with solid seven-inning effort to beat Cubs . . . Pitched three-hitter May 18 against Astros, his first complete game since 1989 . . . Hurled another three-hitter against Expos Sept. 23 . . . Has always been more successful on artificial surfaces . . . Averaged just two walks per nine innings . . . Among the best-hitting pitchers in baseball, he had eight-game hitting streak . . . Recorded 1,000th strikeout Sept. 5 . . . Born Aug. 11, 1955, in Marietta, Ga. . . . Signed by Orioles as non-drafted free agent in 1974 . . . Traded to Expos in 1977 . . . Signed as free agent by Cards before 1990 season . . . Earned $2,133,333 in 1991.

Year	Club	G	IP	W	L	Pct.	SO	BB	H	ERA
1981	Montreal	7	13	1	0	1.000	9	3	14	2.77
1982	Montreal	47	79⅓	2	4	.333	50	23	81	4.20
1983	Montreal	49	155⅓	6	11	.353	101	43	142	2.49
1984	Montreal	28	179	12	13	.480	101	51	178	3.32
1985	Montreal	32	222⅓	18	5	.783	127	41	193	2.91
1986	Montreal	30	187⅓	10	8	.555	105	63	182	3.94
1987	Montreal	26	150⅓	10	9	.526	94	31	164	4.37
1988	Montreal	32	198	12	10	.545	122	32	179	3.00
1989	Montreal	33	215⅔	10	11	.476	129	54	177	2.84
1990	St. Louis	26	141⅓	9	8	.529	78	30	160	4.27
1991	St. Louis	31	198⅔	12	9	.571	94	45	188	3.85
	Totals	341	1740⅓	102	88	.537	1010	416	1658	3.43

LEE SMITH 34 6-6 269   Bats R Throws R

Still one of most intimidating bullpen closers in the game . . . Seems to be getting better with age . . . Set NL record with 47 saves while leading league by 16 . . . Broke Bruce Sutter's league record of 45 saves . . . Has 312 career saves and is fifth pitcher to record 300 saves, joining Rollie Fingers, Goose Gossage, Jeff Reardon and Sutter . . . Has nine straight 20-save seasons and six 30-save years . . . Converted 15 straight save opportunities between Aug. 18, 1990 and May 3, 1991 . . . Se-

lected by Cubs in second round of 1975 draft . . . Traded to Red
Sox before 1988 season and dealt to Cards for Tom Brunansky,
May 4, 1990 . . . Recorded first major-league save Aug. 29, 1981
in Los Angeles . . . Made permanent switch to bullpen in 1982 and
led Cubs with 17 saves . . . His 36 saves in 1987 were career best
until 1991 . . . Born Dec. 4, 1957, in Jamestown, La. . . . Highest-
paid Cardinal at $2,666,666 in 1991.

Year	Club	G	IP	W	L	Pct.	SO	BB	H	ERA
1980	Chicago (NL)	18	22	2	0	1.000	17	14	21	2.86
1981	Chicago (NL)	40	67	3	6	.333	50	31	57	3.49
1982	Chicago (NL)	72	117	2	5	.286	99	37	105	2.69
1983	Chicago (NL)	66	103⅓	4	10	.286	91	41	70	1.65
1984	Chicago (NL)	69	101	9	7	.563	86	35	98	3.65
1985	Chicago (NL)	65	97⅔	7	4	.636	112	32	87	3.04
1986	Chicago (NL)	66	90⅓	9	9	.500	93	42	69	3.09
1987	Chicago (NL)	62	83⅔	4	10	.286	96	32	84	3.12
1988	Boston	64	83⅔	4	5	.444	96	37	72	2.80
1989	Boston	64	70⅔	6	1	.857	96	33	53	3.57
1990	Boston	11	14⅓	2	1	.667	17	9	13	1.88
1990	St. Louis	53	68⅔	3	4	.429	70	20	58	2.10
1991	St. Louis	67	73	6	3	.667	67	13	70	2.34
	Totals	717	992⅓	61	65	.484	990	376	857	2.84

TOP PROSPECTS

RHEAL CORMIER 24 5-10 185　　　　　**Bats L Throws L**
Rookie left-hander gave Cards big boost after being promoted to
big leagues in August . . . Won major-league debut Aug. 15, beating Mets . . . It was first victory by a Card lefty in 121 games . . .
Worked into sixth inning in each of first eight starts . . . In four
starts against Mets, he compiled 2.15 ERA . . . Struck out eight
batters at Los Angeles Sept. 4 . . . Pitched complete-game victory
over Mets Sept. 15, first complete game by a St. Louis rookie
since Ken Hill in 1989 . . . Overall, he made 10 starts, going 4-5
with 4.12 ERA . . . Was 7-9 with three shutouts for Louisville
(AAA) . . . Selected by Cards in sixth round of 1988 draft . . .
Pitched for 1988 Canadian Olympic team . . . In 1989, his first pro
season, he compiled 2.23 ERA for St. Petersburg (A) . . . Born
April 23, 1967, in Moncton, Canada.

MARK CLARK 23 6-5 225　　　　　**Bats R Throws R**
Big right-hander made rapid rise through Cardinals system during
fourth pro season, beginning at Arkansas (AA), jumping to Louisville (AAA) and finishing in big leagues . . . Went 5-5 with 4.00

ERA and 76 strikeouts in 92 innings for Arkansas . . . Was 3-2 with 2.98 ERA for Louisville before being called up to St. Louis in September . . . Pitched into seventh inning, giving up just two runs against Mets in first major-league start . . . Appeared in seven games, going 1-1 with 4.03 ERA . . . Selected by Cards in ninth round of 1988 draft . . . Led Texas League with five complete games in 1990 . . . Led South Atlantic League in victories (14) in 1989 . . . Born May 12, 1968, in Bath, Ill.

STAN ROYER 24 6-3 221   **Bats R Throws R**
Another bonus from Athletics in the Willie McGee trade, this big third baseman batted .254 with 14 homers and 74 RBI for Louisville in first full Triple-A season . . . Called up to St. Louis in September, he made major-league debut with pinch single against Pirates . . . Overall, he hit .286 in 21 big-league at-bats . . . Selected by Athletics in first round of 1988 draft . . . Hit 28 doubles for Modesto (A) in 1989 . . . Had 29 doubles and 89 RBI for Huntsville (AA) in 1990 . . . Born Aug. 31, 1967, in Olney, Ill.

ROD BREWER 26 6-3 218   **Bats L Throws L**
Slick-fielding first baseman had eight homers and 52 RBI during second full season at Louisville (AAA) . . . Batted .240 in 14 big-league games in September 1990 . . . Called up to St. Louis again last September and had just one hit in 13 at-bats . . . Batted .251 with 12 homers for Louisville in 1990, when his 83 RBI ranked second in American Association and led organization . . . Compiled .990 fielding percentage while leading league's first baseman in games, putouts, assists, total chances and double plays . . . Selected by Cardinals in fifth round of 1987 draft . . . Lettered in football and baseball at University of Florida . . . Born Feb. 24, 1966, in Eustis, Fla.

MANAGER JOE TORRE: A very popular player in St. Louis from 1969-74, he created new legend for himself in 1991 . . . Took team filled with unproven players and led it to surprising second-place finish in first full season as Cards' manager . . . Left job as Angels broadcaster to manage again Aug. 1, 1990, after Whitey Herzog voluntarily stepped down . . . Went 24-34 with last-place club over final two months but used that time to lay foundations for 1991 . . . Boldest move was switching Todd

Zeile from catcher to third base and it paid big dividends . . . Made managerial debut with Mets May 31, 1977, replacing Joe Frazier to become first player-manager in NL since Solly Hemus with the Cards in 1959 . . . Went 286-420 in five seasons with Mets, never finishing higher than fifth . . . Named AP Manager of the Year in 1982 after winning division title in first season with Braves . . . Never finished lower than second during three years in Atlanta . . . Spent six seasons broadcasting before returning to dugout in 1990 . . . Batted .297 with 252 doubles and 1,185 RBI during 18-year major-league career . . . Played in eight All-Star Games and was named NL MVP in 1971 after hitting .363 with 24 homers and 137 RBI . . . Born July 18, 1940, in Brooklyn, N.Y. . . . Overall managerial record is 651-751.

ALL-TIME CARDINAL SEASON RECORDS

BATTING: Rogers Hornsby, .424, 1924
HRs: Johnny Mize, 43, 1940
RBI: Joe Medwick, 154, 1937
STEALS: Lou Brock, 118, 1974
WINS: Dizzy Dean, 30, 1934
STRIKEOUTS: Bob Gibson, 274, 1970

ATLANTA BRAVES

TEAM DIRECTORY: Chairman: Bill Bartholomay; Pres.: Stan Kasten; Sr. VP/Asst. to Pres.: Hank Aaron; Exec. VP/GM: John Schuerholz; Dir. Scouting and Player Development: Chuck LaMar; Dir. Pub. Rel.: Jim Schultz; Trav. Sec.: Bill Acree; Mgr.: Bobby Cox. Home: Atlanta-Fulton County Stadium (52,007). Field distances: 330, l.f. line; 402, c.f.; 330, r.f. line. Spring training: West Palm Beach, Fla.

SCOUTING REPORT

HITTING: One more hit or one less base-running mistake and the Braves would have won their first world championship since

NL MVP Terry Pendleton simply showed Braves how to win.

Milwaukee beat the Yankees in 1957. Still, 1991 was a year of achievement and a big part of the Braves' success was due to improved hitting.

The addition of NL MVP and batting champ Terry Pendleton (.319, 22, 86), Otis Nixon (.297, 81 runs, 72 steals) and Sid Bream (.253, 11, 45) helped raise the Braves' on-base percentage from .311 in 1990 to .328 in 1991, second only to the Pirates' .338. Ron Gant put up some spectacular numbers with 32 homers, 105 RBI and 34 stolen bases. Sweet-swinging Dave Justice (.275, 21, 87) showed he was no rookie fluke, despite missing nearly two months of the season with back problems.

Rookie Brian Hunter showed his clutch capabilities, hitting .356 with runners on third and .357 with the bases loaded. Despite his fielding flubs and base-running boners, Lonnie Smith (.275, 7, 44) proved valuable off the bench.

PITCHING: When he was GM, Bobby Cox created this staff and now, as manager, he will reap the rewards for years to come. Steve Avery (18-8, 3.38) established himself as one of the top power pitchers in the game. John Smoltz went on a 12-2 second-half surge to finish 14-13 with a 3.80 ERA and Tom Glavine captured NL Cy Young honors with his 20-11, 2.55 season. Charlie Leibrandt (15-13, 3.49) also helped enable the Braves to finish third in the NL with a 3.49 ERA after they had finished last in 1990 at 4.58.

GM John Schuerholz made one valuable addition after another, but his acquisition of reliever Alejandro Pena (2-0, 1.40, 11 Sv as a Brave) from the Mets put the team over the top after Juan Berenguer (0-3, 2.24, 17 Sv) came up with an arm injury that sidelined him Aug. 12.

FIELDING: There's no statistic to measure how much catcher Greg Olson masterfully aided the Braves' young pitching staff. As for numbers, the Braves finished with a .978 fielding percentage, the third-worst mark in the league. Pendleton and Bream secured the corners. Mark Lemke was thought of as just another solid defensive second baseman before his .417 World Series turned him into the Braves' version of Mighty Mouse.

OUTLOOK: In the end, the game always comes down to pitching. That's why the Braves were able to finish 94-68 to win the West and went on to capture the pennant in 1991. Expect them to contend for another in 1992 under Cox, one of the best managers in baseball.

ATLANTA BRAVES 1992 ROSTER

MANAGER Bobby Cox
Coaches—Jim Beauchamp, Pat Corrales, Clarence Jones, Leo Mazzone,
Jimy Williams, Ned Yost

PITCHERS

No.	Name	1991 Club	W-L	IP	SO	ERA	B-T	Ht.	Wt.	Born
33	Avery, Steve	Atlanta	18-8	210	137	3.38	L-L	6-4	190	4/14/70 Trenton, MI
48	Berenguer, Juan	Atlanta	0-3	64	53	2.24	R-R	5-11	220	11/30/54 Panama
36	Bielecki, Mike	Chi. (NL)-Atl.	13-11	174	75	4.46	R-R	6-3	195	7/31/59 Baltimore, MD
67	Burlingame, Dennis	Durham	11-7	161	95	3.01	R-R	6-4	200	6/17/69 Woodbury, NJ
40	Freeman, Marvin	Atlanta	1-0	48	34	3.00	R-R	6-7	222	4/10/63 Chicago, IL
47	Glavine, Tom	Atlanta	20-11	247	192	2.55	L-L	6-0	175	3/25/66 Concord, MA
56	Gomez, Pat	Richmond	2-9	82	41	4.39	L-L	5-11	185	3/17/68 Roseville, CA
		Greenville	5-2	80	71	1.81				
32	Leibrandt, Charlie	Atlanta	15-13	230	128	3.49	R-L	6-3	200	10/4/56 Chicago, IL
50	Mercker, Kent	Atlanta	5-3	73	62	2.58	L-L	6-2	195	2/1/68 Dublin, OH
63	Murray, Matt	Durham	1-0	7	7	1.29	L-R	6-6	200	9/26/70 Boston, MA
62	Nied, David	Greenville	7-3	90	101	2.41	R-R	6-2	175	12/22/68 Dallas, TX
		Durham	8-3	81	77	1.56				
26	Pena, Alejandro	NY (NL)-Atl.	8-1	82	62	2.40	R-R	6-1	203	6/25/59 Dominican Republic
42	Reynoso, Armando	Atlanta	2-1	21	10	6.17	R-R	6-0	186	5/1/66 Mexico
		Richmond	10-6	131	97	2.61				
51	Rivera, Ben	Greenville	11-8	159	116	3.57	R-R	6-6	210	1/11/69 Dominican Republic
25	Smith, Pete	Macon	0-0	14	14	6.38	R-R	6-2	200	2/27/66 Weymouth, MA
		Atlanta	1-3	48	29	5.06				
29	Smoltz, John	Atlanta	14-13	230	148	3.80	R-R	6-3	185	5/15/67 Detroit, MI
30	Stanton, Mike	Atlanta	5-5	78	54	2.88	L-L	6-1	190	6/2/67 Houston, TX
43	Wohlers, Mark	Richmond	1-0	26	22	1.03	R-R	6-4	207	1/23/70 Holyoke, MA
		Greenville	0-0	31	44	0.57				
		Atlanta	3-1	20	13	3.20				

CATCHERS

No.	Name	1991 Club	H	HR	RBI	Pct.	B-T	Ht.	Wt.	Born
11	Berryhill, Damon	Chi. (NL)-Atl.	30	5	14	.188	S-R	6-0	205	12/3/63 South Laguna, CA
19	Cabrera, Francisco	Richmond	31	7	24	.261	R-R	6-3	193	10/10/66 Dominican Republic
		Atlanta	23	4	23	.242				
8	Heath, Mike	Atlanta	29	1	12	.209	R-R	5-11	180	2/5/55 Tampa, FL
64	Lopez, Javier	Durham	94	11	51	.245	R-R	6-3	185	11/5/70 Puerto Rico
10	Olson, Greg	Atlanta	99	6	44	.241	R-R	6-0	200	9/6/60 Marshall, MN
—	Willard, Jerry	Atlanta	3	1	4	.214	L-R	6-2	195	3/14/60 Oxnard, CA

INFIELDERS

No.	Name	1991 Club	H	HR	RBI	Pct.	B-T	Ht.	Wt.	Born
2	Belliard, Rafael	Atlanta	88	0	27	.249	R-R	5-6	160	10/24/61 Dominican Republic
4	Blauser, Jeff	Atlanta	91	11	54	.259	R-R	6-0	170	11/8/65 Los Gatos, CA
12	Bream, Sid	Atlanta	67	11	45	.253	L-L	6-4	220	8/3/60 Carlisle, PA
65	Caraballo, Ramon	Durham	111	6	52	.250	S-R	5-7	150	5/23/69 Dominican Republic
45	Castilla, Vinny	Richmond	54	7	36	.225	R-R	6-1	175	7/4/67 Mexico
		Atlanta	1	0	0	.200				
		Greenville	70	7	44	.270				
14	Hunter, Brian	Richmond	47	10	30	.260	R-L	6-0	195	3/4/68 Torrance, CA
		Atlanta	68	12	50	.251				
20	Lemke, Mark	Atlanta	63	2	23	.234	S-R	5-9	167	8/13/65 Utica, NY
—	Lyons, Steve	Boston	51	4	17	.241	L-R	6-3	195	6/3/60 Tacoma, WA
9	Pendleton, Terry	Atlanta	187	22	86	.319	S-R	5-9	195	7/16/60 Los Angeles, CA
15	Treadway, Jeff	Atlanta	98	3	32	.320	L-R	5-11	170	1/22/63 Columbus, GA

OUTFIELDERS

No.	Name	1991 Club	H	HR	RBI	Pct.	B-T	Ht.	Wt.	Born
5	Gant, Ron	Atlanta	141	32	105	.251	R-R	6-0	172	3/2/65 Victoria, TX
16	Gregg, Tommy	Atlanta	20	1	4	.187	L-L	6-1	190	7/29/63 Boone, NC
23	Justice, David	Atlanta	109	21	87	.275	L-L	6-3	195	4/14/66 Cincinnati, OH
17	Mitchell, Keith	Greenville	70	10	47	.327	R-R	5-10	180	8/6/69 San Diego, CA
		Atlanta	21	2	5	.318				
		Richmond	31	2	17	.326				
66	Nieves, Melvin	Durham	53	9	25	.264	S-R	6-2	186	12/28/71 Puerto Rico
1	Nixon, Otis	Atlanta	119	0	26	.297	S-R	6-2	180	1/9/59 Evergreen, NC
24	Sanders, Deion	Atlanta	21	4	13	.191	L-L	6-1	195	8/9/67 Ft. Myers, FL
		Richmond	34	5	16	.252				
27	Smith, Lonnie	Atlanta	97	7	44	.275	R-R	5-9	170	12/22/55 Chicago, IL

BRAVE PROFILES

TERRY PENDLETON 31 5-9 195   Bats S Throws R

Third baseman signed four-year, $10.2-million contract before last season after seven years with the Cardinals . . . Returned the highest dividend of any free-agent signing in Braves' history . . . A career .259 hitter entering the season, he won the NL batting title at .319 and was named MVP . . . Became the first Brave to lead NL in batting and hits (187) since Ralph Garr did it in 1974 . . . Also finished tied for first in NL in total bases (303) and first in multiple-hit games (52) . . . Was third in slugging percentage (.517) . . . Set a career high with 22 homers . . . Started every game from June 15 through Oct. 5 . . . Batted .320 with runners in scoring position . . . Batted .353 in his last 28 games, but just .167 in NLCS . . . Rebounded in World Series with .367 mark and two homers . . . Born July 16, 1960, in Los Angeles . . . Selected by St. Louis in first round of 1982 draft . . . Earned $1.75 million last season.

Year	Club	Pos.	G	AB	R	H	2B	3B	HR	RBI	SB	Avg.
1984	St. Louis	3B	67	262	37	85	16	3	1	33	20	.324
1985	St. Louis	3B	149	559	56	134	16	3	5	69	17	.240
1986	St. Louis	3B-OF	159	578	56	138	26	5	1	59	24	.239
1987	St. Louis	3B	159	583	82	167	29	4	12	96	19	.286
1988	St. Louis	3B	110	391	44	99	20	2	6	53	3	.253
1989	St. Louis	3B	162	613	83	162	28	5	13	74	9	.264
1990	St. Louis	3B	121	447	46	103	20	2	6	58	7	.230
1991	Atlanta	3B	153	586	94	187	34	8	22	86	10	.319
	Totals		1080	4019	498	1075	189	32	66	528	109	.267

DAVID JUSTICE 25 6-3 195   Bats L Throws L

One of the impact players of the '90s . . . Despite missing nearly two months with a strained back, right fielder collected 21 homers and 87 RBI in only 109 games . . . Helped win NL West by hitting two-run homer in ninth inning to beat Reds' Rob Dibble, 7-6, Oct. 1 . . . Was leading NL with 51 RBI when he was disabled June 27 . . . Braves went 31-14 after he returned to lineup Aug. 20 . . . Hit .347 with runners in scoring position . . . Takes himself too seriously and takes too many good pitches looking for perfect pitch to drive . . . Has great arm, but shows it off too much making the risky throw . . . Missed third base in Game 5 of NLCS . . . Knocked in five runs in World Series Game 5 win over Twins, but had only one other RBI for the rest of Series . . . Earned $296,000 last season . . . Born April 14, 1966, in Cincinnati . . . Selected by Braves in fourth round of 1985 draft.

Year Club	Pos.	G	AB	R	H	2B	3B	HR	RBI	SB	Avg.
1989 Atlanta	OF	16	51	7	12	3	0	1	3	2	.235
1990 Atlanta	1B-OF	127	439	76	124	23	2	28	78	11	.282
1991 Atlanta	OF	109	396	67	109	25	1	21	87	8	.275
Totals		252	886	150	245	51	3	50	168	21	.277

RON GANT 27 6-0 172   Bats R Throws R

Became only the third player in major-league history to produce back-to-back 30-homer, 30-steal seasons. Other two are Willie Mays and Bobby Bonds . . . First Brave to drive in more than 100 runs since Dale Murphy did it in 1987 . . . Finished third in NL with 32 homers, second with 70 extra-base hits, fifth in runs (101), fifth in RBI (105), eighth in total bases (278), fifth in doubles (35) and ninth in stolen bases (34) . . . Set NLCS record with seven steals . . . Produced just one extra-base hit in World Series . . . Was sent to Class A in 1989 to learn how to play center field . . . Hit more homers than any other center fielder in NL in 1991 . . . Born March 2, 1965, in Victoria, Tex. . . . Braves' fourth-round selection in 1983 draft . . . Earned $1,195,000 last season.

Year Club	Pos.	G	AB	R	H	2B	3B	HR	RBI	SB	Avg.
1987 Atlanta	2B	21	83	9	22	4	0	2	9	4	.265
1988 Atlanta	2B-3B	146	563	85	146	28	8	19	60	19	.259
1989 Atlanta	3B-OF	75	260	26	46	8	3	9	25	9	.177
1990 Atlanta	OF	152	575	107	174	34	3	32	84	33	.303
1991 Atlanta	OF	154	561	101	141	35	3	32	105	34	.251
Totals		548	2042	328	529	109	17	94	283	99	.259

LONNIE SMITH 36 5-9 170   Bats R Throws R

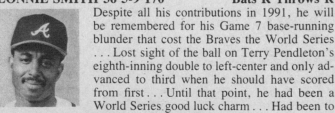

Despite all his contributions in 1991, he will be remembered for his Game 7 base-running blunder that cost the Braves the World Series . . . Lost sight of the ball on Terry Pendleton's eighth-inning double to left-center and only advanced to third when he should have scored from first . . . Until that point, he had been a World Series good luck charm . . . Had been to three previous World Series with three different teams and had come back a winner each time . . . Hit .240 in postseason . . . Replaced Otis Nixon in left after Nixon was suspended for drug use

. . . Named NL Comeback Player of the Year in 1989 after winning battle with drugs . . . . Has the weakest arm of any left fielder in baseball . . . Born Dec. 22, 1955, in Chicago . . . Earned $2,014,667 last season . . . Phils' first-round pick in 1974 draft.

Year	Club	Pos.	G	AB	R	H	2B	3B	HR	RBI	SB	Avg.
1978	Philadelphia . . .	OF	17	4	6	0	0	0	0	0	4	.000
1979	Philadelphia . . .	OF	17	30	4	5	2	0	0	3	2	.167
1980	Philadelphia . . .	OF	100	298	69	101	14	4	3	20	33	.339
1981	Philadelphia . . .	OF	62	176	40	57	14	3	2	11	21	.324
1982	St. Louis	OF	156	592	120	182	35	8	8	69	68	.307
1983	St. Louis	OF	130	492	83	158	31	5	8	45	43	.321
1984	St. Louis	OF	145	504	77	126	20	4	6	49	50	.250
1985	St. Louis	OF	28	96	15	25	2	2	0	7	12	.260
1985	Kansas City . . .	OF	120	448	77	115	23	4	6	41	40	.257
1986	Kansas City . . .	OF	134	508	80	146	25	7	8	44	26	.287
1987	Kansas City . . .	OF	48	167	26	42	7	1	3	8	9	.251
1988	Atlanta.	OF	43	114	14	27	3	0	3	9	4	.237
1989	Atlanta.	OF	134	482	89	152	34	4	21	79	25	.315
1990	Atlanta.	OF	135	466	72	142	27	9	9	42	10	.305
1991	Atlanta.	OF	122	353	58	97	19	1	7	44	9	.275
	Totals		1391	4730	830	1375	256	52	84	471	356	.291

OTIS NIXON 33 6-2 180   Bats S Throws R

Speedy outfielder was racing to best season of his career before being suspended for drug use Sept. 16 . . . Still finished second in NL in stolen bases with 72, four less than Expos' Marquis Grissom . . . Posted .297 average and .371 on-base percentage . . . Knows how to create runs with speed and that aspect of the Braves' offense was missing throughout postseason . . . Born Jan. 9, 1959, in Evergreen, N.C. . . . Brother Donell played with Mariners, Giants and Orioles . . . Signed by Expos as a free agent in 1988 . . . Originally selected by the Reds in the 21st round of the 1978 draft . . . Braves acquired him from Expos for Jimmy Kremers and Boi Rodriguez just prior to 1990 season . . . Re-signed three-year contract worth $8.1 million . . . Suspension runs through first 18 days of '92 season.

Year	Club	Pos.	G	AB	R	H	2B	3B	HR	RBI	SB	Avg.
1983	New York (AL)	OF	13	14	2	2	0	0	0	0	0	.143
1984	Cleveland	OF	49	91	16	14	0	0	0	1	12	.154
1985	Cleveland	OF	104	162	34	38	4	0	3	9	20	.235
1986	Cleveland	OF	105	95	33	25	4	1	0	8	23	.263
1987	Cleveland	OF	19	17	2	1	0	0	0	1	2	.059
1988	Montreal	OF	90	271	47	66	8	2	0	15	46	.244
1989	Montreal	OF	126	258	41	56	7	2	0	21	37	.217
1990	Montreal	OF-SS	119	231	46	58	6	2	1	20	50	.251
1991	Atlanta.	OF	124	401	81	119	10	1	0	26	72	.297
	Totals		749	1540	302	379	39	8	4	101	262	.246

GREG OLSON 31 6-0 200   Bats R Throws R

Catcher was the brains behind the young guns . . . Called for changeup that stunned Andy Van Slyke for last out of NLCS Game 6 . . . Makes up for what he lacks in talent with huge heart . . . Down the stretch, he couldn't be bulldozed away from behind the plate as he caught all but two innings over 32 consecutive games . . . Batted .373 during the season with runners in scoring position and two out . . . Accounted for seven crucial RBI in nine games from Sept. 25 through Oct. 4 . . . Charged with only four errors in 127 games . . . Threw out 22 of 108 would-be basestealers (20 percent) . . . Batted .333 in NLCS with four RBI, but only .222 with one RBI in World Series . . . Born Sept. 6, 1960, in Edina, Minn. . . . Was once a Twin . . . Earned $185,000 last year . . . After eight years in minors, he had storybook season in 1990 and was named to All-Star team . . . Last year, the fairy tale continued . . . Mets' seventh-round draft pick in 1982.

Year Club	Pos.	G	AB	R	H	2B	3B	HR	RBI	SB	Avg.
1989 Minnesota	C	3	2	0	1	0	0	0	0	0	.500
1990 Atlanta.	C–3B	100	298	36	78	12	1	7	36	1	.262
1991 Atlanta.	C	133	411	46	99	25	0	6	44	1	.241
Totals		236	711	82	178	37	1	13	80	2	.250

MARK LEMKE 26 5-9 167   Bats S Throws R

What's a Lemke? . . . After sizzling World Series, now people know . . . If Braves had pulled out Game 7, second baseman would have been named MVP, because of Series-leading .417 average, game-winning hit in Game 3 and game-winning slide in Game 4 . . . Had three career triples, then hit three in four at-bats during Series . . . Posted .708 World Series slugging percentage . . . Previous claim to fame was he wore Buddy Holly glasses and false teeth . . . During regular season, he led club in pinch-hits with 9-for-27 . . . Fanned only 27 times in 269 at-bats . . . Born Aug. 13, 1965, in Utica, N.Y. . . . Made only 49 starts at second during the season, but found a home during postseason . . . Earned $138,000 last season . . . A regular Walter Mitty story, he was Braves' 27th-round selection in 1983 draft.

Year Club	Pos.	G	AB	R	H	2B	3B	HR	RBI	SB	Avg.
1988 Atlanta.	2B	16	58	8	13	4	0	0	2	0	.224
1989 Atlanta.	2B	14	55	4	10	2	1	2	10	0	.182
1990 Atlanta.	3B-2B-SS	102	239	22	54	13	0	0	21	0	.226
1991 Atlanta.	2B-3B	136	269	36	63	11	2	2	23	1	.234
Totals		268	621	70	140	30	3	4	56	1	.225

SID BREAM 31 6-4 220   Bats L Throws L

Split first-base duties with up-and-coming Brian Hunter . . . Clubhouse leader became first Brave to belt two grand slams in a season since Dale Murphy did in 1978 . . . Hit just .125 in World Series with no RBI, stranding 16 runners in scoring position . . . Poor play may have been result of career-long knee problems . . . Underwent arthroscopic knee surgery June 18 and didn't get off DL until Aug. 28 . . . Batted just .188 after that . . . Turns the best 3-6-3 double play in the majors . . . Left Pirates as a free agent after 1990 season to sign three-year, $5.5-million contract with Braves . . . Born Aug. 3, 1960, in Carlisle, Pa. . . . Earned $1.6 million last season . . . Selected by Dodgers in second round of 1981 draft . . . Traded to Pirates with Cecil Espy and R.J. Reynolds for Bill Madlock, Sept. 9, 1985.

Year	Club	Pos.	G	AB	R	H	2B	3B	HR	RBI	SB	Avg.
1983	Los Angeles . . .	1B	15	11	0	2	0	0	0	2	0	.182
1984	Los Angeles . . .	1B	27	49	2	9	3	0	0	6	1	.184
1985	L.A.-Pitt.	1B	50	148	18	34	7	0	6	21	0	.230
1986	Pittsburgh	1B-OF	154	522	73	140	37	5	16	77	13	.268
1987	Pittsburgh	1B	149	516	64	142	25	3	13	65	9	.275
1988	Pittsburgh	1B	148	462	50	122	37	0	10	65	9	.264
1989	Pittsburgh	1B	19	36	3	8	3	0	0	4	0	.222
1990	Pittsburgh	1B	147	389	39	105	23	2	15	67	8	.270
1991	Atlanta	1B	91	265	32	67	12	0	11	45	0	.253
	Totals		800	2398	281	629	147	10	71	352	40	.262

TOM GLAVINE 26 6-0 175   Bats L Throws L

Captured NL Cy Young award with 20-win season and 2.55 ERA . . . Braves' first 20-game winner since Phil Niekro went 21-20 in 1979 . . . Notched most wins by a Brave lefty since Warren Spahn won 23 in 1963 . . . Went 6-0 in May . . . His nine complete games tied him for NL lead . . . Ranked third with 192 strikeouts, second with 246⅔ innings pitched, third in opponents' batting average at .222 and third in ERA . . . NL starter in All-Star Game, he held the AL scoreless for two innings . . . Held opponents to two earned runs or less in 23 of 34 outings . . . Worked seven-plus innings in 24 starts . . . All that work may have taken its toll in postseason . . . Was 0-2 with 3.21 ERA in NLCS and 1-1 with 2.70 mark in World Series . . . Born March 25, 1966, in Concord, Mass. . . . Braves' second-round pick in 1984 draft,

he also was fourth-round pick of NHL's Los Angeles Kings...
Earned $697,500 last season.

Year	Club	G	IP	W	L	Pct.	SO	BB	H	ERA
1987	Atlanta	9	50⅓	2	4	.333	20	33	55	5.54
1988	Atlanta	34	195⅓	7	17	.292	84	63	201	4.56
1989	Atlanta	29	186	14	8	.636	90	40	172	3.68
1990	Atlanta	33	214⅓	10	12	.455	129	78	232	4.28
1991	Atlanta	34	246⅔	20	11	.645	192	69	201	2.55
	Totals	139	892⅔	53	52	.505	515	283	861	3.81

ALEJANDRO PENA 32 6-1 203   Bats R Throws R

Saved the Braves down the stretch...After being picked up from the Mets for Tony Castillo and Joe Roa Aug. 29, he was a perfect 11-for-11 in save opportunities...Went on to save three more in NLCS against the Pirates before bubble burst in World Series...Losing pitcher in 1-0 Game 7 loss against Minnesota...Also saved four games for Mets...The third and final pitcher in Braves' no-hit victory over Padres Sept. 11, the first combined no-hitter in NL history, he kept the ball and wrote, along with the date and final score, "Save No. 8"...Born June 25, 1959, in Cambiaso, P.R....Former Dodger earned $1 million last season...Accepted arbitration in December.

Year	Club	G	IP	W	L	Pct.	SO	BB	H	ERA
1981	Los Angeles	14	25	1	1	.500	14	11	18	2.88
1982	Los Angeles	29	35⅔	0	2	.000	20	21	37	4.79
1983	Los Angeles	34	177	12	9	.571	120	51	152	2.75
1984	Los Angeles	28	199⅓	12	6	.667	135	46	186	2.48
1985	Los Angeles	2	4⅓	0	1	.000	2	3	7	8.31
1986	Los Angeles	24	70	1	2	.333	46	30	74	4.89
1987	Los Angeles	37	87⅓	2	7	.222	76	37	82	3.50
1988	Los Angeles	60	94⅓	6	7	.462	83	27	75	1.91
1989	Los Angeles	53	76	4	3	.571	75	18	62	2.13
1990	New York (NL)	52	76	3	3	.500	76	22	71	3.20
1991	NY (NL)-Atl.	59	82⅓	8	1	.889	62	22	74	2.40
	Totals	392	927⅓	49	42	.538	709	288	838	2.90

STEVE AVERY 21 6-4 190   Bats L Throws L

Best young pitcher to come along in years... His 18 wins were most by a 21-year-old in franchise history...Only Tom Glavine and John Smiley won more games in NL 1991 ...Fired back-to-back complete-game victories over Dodgers Sept. 15-20 to take the heart out of LA...Allowed only four hits and one run in first game and hurled a six-hit shutout in next . . . Went 3-0 with 0.57 ERA vs. Dodgers . . . Struck out a career-high 10 Phils Aug. 30 . . . Destroyed the Pirates in NLCS, winning two games and pitching 16⅓ shutout innings to capture MVP honors . . . Didn't get a decision in World Series . . . Left Game 3 with a 4-2 lead in the eighth and was trailing, 3-2, in Game 6 when he departed after six . . . Was Braves' first selection and third overall pick in 1988 draft . . . Earned $110,000 last season . . . Born April 14, 1970, in Trenton, Mich.

Year	Club	G	IP	W	L	Pct.	SO	BB	H	ERA
1990	Atlanta	21	99	3	11	.214	75	45	121	5.64
1991	Atlanta	35	210⅓	18	8	.692	137	65	189	3.38
	Totals.	56	309⅓	21	19	.525	212	110	310	4.10

JOHN SMOLTZ 24 6-3 185   Bats R Throws R

Turned his season around after the All-Star break . . . Staggered into break with 2-11 record and 5.16 ERA, but ripped off 12-2 record with 2.62 ERA the rest of the way . . . Sought help from a sports psychologist and that made a big difference . . . Mr. Big Game . . . Pitched NL West clincher, a complete-game, 5-2 victory Oct. 5 vs. Astros . . . Was winner in 1-0 NLCS Game 7 victory over Pirates and it was his first shutout of the year . . . Was magnificent in the World Series, too, but came away with two no-decisions and 1.26 ERA . . . Pitched 7⅓ shutout innings in Game 7, only to be beaten by Jack Morris, who went 10 shutout innings . . . Led Braves in wins in 1990 with 14 . . . Earned $355,000 last season . . . Born May 15, 1967, in Detroit . . . Signed by Tigers as a free agent in September 1985 . . . Traded to Braves by Tigers for Doyle Alexander, Aug. 12, 1987.

Year	Club	G	IP	W	L	Pct.	SO	BB	H	ERA
1988	Atlanta	12	64	2	7	.222	37	33	74	5.48
1989	Atlanta	29	208	12	11	.522	168	72	160	2.94
1990	Atlanta	34	231⅓	14	11	.560	170	90	206	3.85
1991	Atlanta	36	229⅔	14	13	.519	148	77	206	3.80
	Totals.	111	733	42	42	.500	523	272	646	3.72

TOP PROSPECTS

CHIPPER JONES 19 6-3 185   Bats S Throws R

No. 1 pick in nation in 1990 draft, he shared Braves' Minor League Player of the Year honors with first baseman Ryan Klesko by batting .323 for Macon (A) . . . Shortstop showed excellent power, slamming 15 homers, 24 doubles and 11 triples, and drove in 98 runs while scoring 104 . . . Born April 24, 1972, in Deland, Fla. . . . Definitely the Braves' shortstop of the future.

RYAN KLESKO 20 6-3 220　　　　　　**Bats L Throws L**
Big first baseman is best power-hitting prospect in organization . . . Put together solid year for Greenville (AA) by slamming 14 homers, 22 doubles and knocking in 67 runs while batting .291 . . . Posted .458 slugging percentage and .404 on-base percentage . . . Pitchers feared him . . . Was walked 75 times, 14 of those intentional . . . Born June 12, 1971, in Westminster, Cal. . . . Braves' sixth-round selection in 1989 draft.

ARMANDO REYNOSO 25 6-0 186　　　　**Bats R Throws R**
Went 10-6 with 2.61 ERA for Richmond (AAA) last season . . . Appeared in six games for the Braves and compiled a 2-1 record with 6.17 ERA . . . Winner in major-league debut vs. Astros Aug. 11, throwing six scoreless innings and allowing only two hits . . . Also won his next start vs. Padres, giving up two runs over seven innings . . . Has great pickoff move and nailed six runners over four starts . . . Signed by the Braves as a free agent from the Mexican League, Aug. 15, 1990 . . . Born May 1, 1966, in San Luis Potosi, Mexico.

VINNY CASTILLA 24 6-1 175　　　　　**Bats R Throws R**
Shortstop started the season with Greenville (AA) and batted .270 with seven homers and 44 RBI in 66 games . . . Promoted to Richmond (AAA), he hit .225 in 67 games . . . Called up in September and played in 12 games with five at-bats and one hit . . . Contract was purchased by the Braves from Saltillo of the Mexican League, March 19, 1990 . . . Born July 4, 1967, in Oaxaca, Mexico.

MANAGER BOBBY COX: Became first to win Manager of the Year awards in both leagues when he was voted NL honor after leading Atlanta to its first pennant . . . When Russ Nixon was fired during 1990 season, he was put on the hot seat . . . As GM at the time, these were his players and he was told to win with them as manager . . . That's exactly what happened last season as Braves went from worst to first, compiling

94-68 record . . . Knows how to get the most out of his players
. . . Is patient, understanding and honest . . . Joined the Braves in
October 1985 as GM, ending run of 25 years as player, coach and
manager . . . Acquired most of golden-armed pitching staff that
turned the doormat Braves into winners . . . Managed Blue Jays
from 1982-85 . . . Took team that finished seventh in 1984 to
within one game of World Series in 1985, but Toronto lost ALCS
Game 7 to eventual world champion Kansas City . . . Named AL
Manager of the Year that year . . . Third baseman spent 12 years
in baseball as a player, 10 of them in minors . . . Started managing
in the Yankee farm system in 1971 . . . Yankee first-base coach in
1977 . . . In first time around as Braves' manager, from 1978-81,
he posted a 266-323 record . . . Built foundation for Braves' Western Division championship in 1982 . . . Overall major-league managerial record is 760-745.

ALL-TIME BRAVE SEASON RECORDS

BATTING: Rogers Hornsby, .387, 1928
HRs: Eddie Mathews, 47, 1953
  Hank Aaron, 47, 1971
RBI: Eddie Mathews, 135, 1953
STEALS: Otis Nixon, 72, 1991
WINS: Vic Willis, 27, 1902
  Charles Pittinger, 27, 1902
  Dick Rudolph, 27, 1914
STRIKEOUTS: Phil Niekro, 262, 1977

CINCINNATI REDS

TEAM DIRECTORY: Principal Owner/Pres.: Marge Schott; GM: Bob Quinn; Dir. Scouting: Julian Mock; Dir. Player Development: Jim Bowden; Publicity Dir.: Jon Braude; Trav. Sec.: Joel Pieper; Mgr.: Lou Piniella. Home: Riverfront Stadium (52,952). Field distances: 330, l.f. line; 404, c.f.; 330, r.f. line. Spring training: Plant City, Fla.

SCOUTING REPORT

HITTING: The revamped Reds gave up on Eric Davis' brittle body and finally traded the outfielder to the Dodgers. The Reds led the NL in homers with 164 and Davis hit only 11 in 1991, so they figured they could live long and prosper without him. The Reds also topped the NL in slugging (.403) and total bases (2,215) and finished second in hitting (.258).

In switch-hitting Bip Roberts (.281, 66 runs, 26 steals with the Padres), the Reds added one of the top three leadoff men in the league and the acquisition of center fielder Dave Martinez (.295, 7, 42, 16 steals with the Expos) gives the Reds insurance against a flop by Reggie Sanders. First baseman Hal Morris (.318, 14, 59) came within one hit of winning the batting title. Add bangers Chris Sabo (.301, 26, 88), Paul O'Neill (.256, 28, 91) and Barry Larkin (.302, 20, 69) to the mix and you have the NL's best run-producing lineup, even if Billy Hatcher (.262, 4, 41) never regains his 1990 World Series form.

PITCHING: The biggest changes the Reds made were in a pitching staff that finished eighth in the NL with a 3.83 ERA. They stole Greg Swindell (9-16, 3.48) from the Indians for three pitchers who did not fit in their plans. Swindell is so talented that he put together a winning career record (60-55) with the toxic-waste Indians.

Belcher (10-9, 2.62 with the Dodgers) finished third in ERA and seventh in strikeouts with 156. Ace Jose Rijo (15-6, 2.51) would have won the Cy Young award, if he knew how to slide and did not miss five weeks with a chip fracture of the right ankle. Tom Browning (14-14, 4.18) has led the team in starts for four years and innings pitched for three.

In the bullpen, one day Rob Dibble (3-5, 3.17, 31 Sv) will get his head on straight and will be invincible. Newcomer Scott Ruskin (4-4, 4.24, 6 Sv with the Expos) and Norm Charlton (3-5, 2.91)

Every other NL shortstop stops short of Barry Larkin.

are the left-handed setup men following the trade of Randy Myers to the Padres.

FIELDING: When they won it all in '90, the Reds did it with pitching and defense, topping the league in fielding percentage (.983) and making the least amount of errors (102). Last season, they slipped to eighth with a .979 mark and committed 125 errors. Figure them to bounce back. Only Ozzie Smith is a better shortstop than Larkin. Catcher Joe Oliver should be over his shoulder problems following arthroscopic surgery. Martinez (.982 fielding percentage) will help make up for the loss of Davis. But Sanders, a converted shortstop, still has a long way to go in the outfield.

OUTLOOK: GM Bob Quinn and manager Lou Piniella reconstructed the Big Red Machine into the Rabbit Reds, adding speed and pitching. When you finish 20 games out with a 74-88 record one year after winning the world championship, radical changes have to be made. They have been.

CINCINNATI REDS 1992 ROSTER

MANAGER Lou Piniella
Coaches—John McLaren, Jackie Moore, Tony Perez, Sam Perlozzo,
Larry Rothschild

PITCHERS

No.	Name	1991 Club	W-L	IP	SO	ERA	B-T	Ht.	Wt.	Born
—	Ayala, Bobby	Chattanooga	3-1	91	92	4.67	R-R	6-2	190	7/8/69 Ventura, CA
—	Belcher, Tim	Los Angeles	10-9	209	156	2.62	R-R	6-3	210	10/19/61 Sparta, OH
32	Browning, Tom	Cincinnati	14-14	230	115	4.18	L-L	6-1	195	4/28/60 Casper, WY
37	Charlton, Norm	Cincinnati	3-5	108	77	2.91	S-L	6-3	200	1/6/63 Ft. Polk, LA
49	Dibble, Rob	Cincinnati	3-5	82	124	3.17	L-R	6-4	235	1/24/64 Bridgeport, CT
54	Foster, Steve	Chattanooga	0-2	16	18	1.15	R-R	6-0	180	8/16/66 Dallas, TX
		Nashville	2-3	55	52	2.14				
		Cincinnati	0-0	14	11	1.93				
—	Garcia, Victor	Chattanooga	5-3	50	51	1.98	R-R	6-2	195	9/15/69 Dominican Republic
		Nashville	2-0	24	12	2.63				
45	Hammond, Chris	Cincinnati	7-7	100	50	4.06	L-L	6-1	190	1/21/66 Atlanta, GA
—	Henry, Dwayne	Houston	3-2	68	51	3.19	R-R	6-3	205	2/16/62 Elkton, MD
39	Hill, Milton	Nashville	3-3	67	62	2.94	R-R	6-0	180	8/22/65 Atlanta, GA
		Cincinnati	1-1	33	20	3.78				
—	Hoffman, Trevor	Cedar Rapids	1-1	34	52	1.87	R-R	6-0	200	10/13/67 Bellflower, CA
		Chattanooga	1-0	14	23	1.93				
43	Layana, Tim	Nashville	3-1	47	43	3.23	R-R	6-2	190	3/2/64 Inglewood, CA
		Cincinnati	0-2	21	14	6.97				
33	Minutelli, Gino	Charleston	1-0	8	8	0.00	L-L	6-0	190	5/23/64 Wilmington, DE
		Nashville	4-7	80	64	1.90				
		Cincinnati	0-2	25	21	6.04				
60	Powell, Ross	Nashville	8-8	130	82	4.37	L-L	5-11	180	1/24/68 Grand Rapids, MI
—	Pugh, Tim	Chattanooga	3-1	38	24	1.64	R-R	6-6	225	1/26/67 Lake Tahoe, CA
		Nashville	7-11	149	89	3.81				
27	Rijo, Jose	Cincinnati	15-6	204	172	2.51	R-R	6-2	200	5/13/65 Dominican Republic
—	Ruskin, Scott	Montreal	4-4	64	46	4.24	R-L	6-1	192	6/6/63 Jacksonville, FL
52	Sanford, Mo	Chattanooga	7-4	95	124	2.74	R-R	6-6	220	12/24/66 Americus, GA
		Nashville	3-0	34	38	1.60				
		Cincinnati	1-2	28	31	3.86				
—	Satre, Jason	Cedar Rapids	8-6	133	130	2.58	R-R	6-1	180	8/24/70 Tampa, FL
		Chattanooga	1-7	44	44	5.11				
—	Swindell, Greg	Cleveland	9-16	238	169	3.48	S-L	6-3	225	1/2/65 Fort Worth, TX

CATCHERS

No.	Name	1991 Club	H	HR	RBI	Pct.	B-T	Ht.	Wt.	Born
—	Geren, Bob	New York (AL)	28	2	12	.219	R-R	6-3	228	9/22/61 San Diego, CA
9	Oliver, Joe	Cincinnati	58	11	41	.216	R-R	6-3	210	7/24/65 Memphis, TN
34	Reed, Jeff	Cincinnati	72	3	31	.267	L-R	6-2	190	11/12/62 Joliet, IL
55	Sutko, Glenn	Chattanooga	18	3	11	.286	R-R	6-3	225	5/9/68 Atlanta, GA
		Nashville	28	3	15	.209				
		Cincinnati	1	0	1	.100				

INFIELDERS

No.	Name	1991 Club	H	HR	RBI	Pct.	B-T	Ht.	Wt.	Born
57	Benavides, Freddie	Nashville	80	0	21	.242	R-R	6-2	185	4/7/66 Laredo, TX
		Cincinnati	18	0	3	.286				
—	Branson, Jeff	Chattanooga	80	2	28	.263	L-R	6-0	180	1/26/67 Waynesboro, MS
		Nashville	35	0	11	.241				
19	Doran, Bill	Cincinnati	101	6	35	.280	S-R	6-0	180	5/28/58 Cincinnati, OH
51	Lane, Brian	Cincinnati	Injured				R-R	6-3	215	6/15/69 Waco, TX
11	Larkin, Barry	Cincinnati	140	20	69	.302	R-R	6-0	185	4/28/64 Cincinnati, OH
23	Morris, Hal	Cincinnati	152	14	59	.318	L-L	6-4	215	4/9/65 Fort Rucker, AL
17	Sabo, Chris	Cincinnati	175	26	88	.301	R-R	6-0	185	1/19/62 Detroit, MI

OUTFIELDERS

No.	Name	1991 Club	H	HR	RBI	Pct.	B-T	Ht.	Wt.	Born
15	Braggs, Glenn	Cincinnati	65	11	39	.260	R-R	6-4	220	10/17/62 San Bernardino, CA
—	Brumfield, Jacob	Omaha	106	3	43	.267	R-R	6-0	170	5/27/65 Bogalusa, LA
22	Hatcher, Billy	Cincinnati	116	4	41	.262	R-R	5-9	185	10/4/60 Williams, AZ
1	Martinez, Dave	Montreal	117	7	42	.295	L-L	5-10	175	9/26/64 New York, NY
21	O'Neill, Paul	Cincinnati	136	28	91	.256	L-L	6-4	215	2/25/63 Columbus, OH
10	Roberts, Bip	San Diego	119	3	32	.281	S-R	5-7	168	10/27/63 Berkeley, CA
53	Sanders, Reggie	Chattanooga	95	8	49	.315	R-R	6-1	180	12/1/67 Florence, SC
		Cincinnati	8	1	3	.200				

RED PROFILES

BARRY LARKIN 27 6-0 185   Bats R Throws R

Established himself as the rock of the franchise ... Hit over .300 for the third year in a row, finishing at .302 ... Simply the best shortstop in baseball ... Hit career-high 20 homers to tie Leo Cardenas' team record for homers by a shortstop (1966) ... Tied major-league record with five homers in two games, June 27 vs. Padres and June 28 vs. Astros ... Quiet and efficient team leader ... Career-high 69 RBI led all NL shortstops ... Ranked fifth in NL with .506 slugging percentage ... Topped Reds with 24 steals ... Named to All-Star team for fourth straight year ... Only chink in his armor is troublesome right elbow that landed him on DL from May 18 to June 4 ... Hit .353 in 1990 World Series ... Was named Big 10 MVP twice at Michigan ... Reds drafted him fourth overall in 1985 ... Born April 28, 1964, in Cincinnati ... Earned $2.1 million last season.

Year	Club	Pos.	G	AB	R	H	2B	3B	HR	RBI	SB	Avg.
1986	Cincinnati.....	SS-2B	41	159	27	45	4	3	3	19	8	.283
1987	Cincinnati.....	SS	125	439	64	107	16	2	12	43	21	.244
1988	Cincinnati.....	SS	151	588	91	174	32	5	12	56	40	.296
1989	Cincinnati.....	SS	97	325	47	111	14	4	4	36	10	.342
1990	Cincinnati.....	SS	158	614	85	185	25	6	7	67	30	.301
1991	Cincinnati.....	SS	123	464	88	140	27	4	20	69	24	.302
	Totals		695	2589	402	762	118	24	58	290	133	.294

HAL MORRIS 26 6-4 215   Bats L Throws L

Came within one hit of winning NL batting title in first full season in majors ... Singled first three times up, but lined to center in last at-bat as his 1991 season ended with him standing in on-deck circle ... His .318 average left him one point behind Atlanta's Terry Pendleton ... One of GM Bob Quinn's sharpest deals ... Stole him from Yankees along with Rodney Imes for Tim Leary and Van Snider prior to 1990 season ... Yankees didn't know what to do with him, because they had Don Mattingly at first ... No less an authority than Tony Gwynn says this guy has one of the sweetest swings in baseball ... Hit .417 in 1990 NLCS vs. Pirates, but posted .071 mark in World Series ... Born April 9, 1965, in Fort Rucker, Ala. ... Eighth-round selection of Yankees in 1986 . . . Barry Larkin's teammate at Michigan . . . Earned just $180,000 last season.

Year	Club	Pos.	G	AB	R	H	2B	3B	HR	RBI	SB	Avg.
1988	New York (AL)	OF	15	20	1	2	0	0	0	0	0	.100
1989	New York (AL)	OF–1B	15	18	2	5	0	0	0	4	0	.278
1990	Cincinnati	1B-OF	107	309	50	105	22	3	7	36	9	.340
1991	Cincinnati	1B-OF	136	478	72	152	33	1	14	59	10	.318
	Totals		273	825	125	264	55	4	21	99	19	.320

CHRIS SABO 30 6-0 185   Bats R Throws R

Looks like he's from another world, but teammate Rob Dibble says he's from another era: "He's like a Ty Cobb" . . . Put up best numbers of his career with .301 average, 26 homers, 88 RBI, 175 hits and 19 stolen bases . . . Established career highs in average, homers, RBI and hits . . . Voted by fans as starting All-Star third baseman for second straight year . . . While teammates fell apart after the All-Star break, third baseman went into overdrive . . . Batted .331 with 22 doubles, 14 homers and 50 RBI in final 78 games . . . Hit most home runs by a Reds third baseman since Tony Perez bashed 40 in 1970 . . . Earned $1.25 million last season . . . Born Jan. 19, 1962, in Detroit . . . Reds' second-round selection in 1983 draft, out of Michigan.

Year	Club	Pos.	G	AB	R	H	2B	3B	HR	RBI	SB	Avg.
1988	Cincinnati	3B-SS	137	538	74	146	40	2	11	44	46	.271
1989	Cincinnati	3B	82	304	40	79	21	1	6	29	14	.260
1990	Cincinnati	3B	148	567	95	153	38	2	25	71	25	.270
1991	Cincinnati	3B	153	582	91	175	35	3	26	88	19	.301
	Totals		520	1991	300	553	134	8	68	232	104	.278

PAUL O'NEILL 29 6-4 210   Bats L Throws L

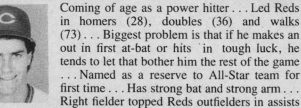

Coming of age as a power hitter . . . Led Reds in homers (28), doubles (36) and walks (73) . . . Biggest problem is that if he makes an out in first at-bat or hits in tough luck, he tends to let that bother him the rest of the game . . . Named as a reserve to All-Star team for first time . . . Has strong bat and strong arm . . . Right fielder topped Reds outfielders in assists with 13 . . . Hit two homers and drove in six runs at Chicago May 11 . . . Batted .471 in 1990 NLCS . . . Born Feb. 25, 1963, in Columbus, Ohio . . . A pitcher in high school, he became Reds' fourth selection in 1981 draft . . . Earned $975,000 last season . . . Played baseball at University of Michigan, where he was teammates with Barry Larkin and Jim Abbott.

Year	Club	Pos.	G	AB	R	H	2B	3B	HR	RBI	SB	Avg.
1985	Cincinnati	OF	5	12	1	4	1	0	0	1	0	.333
1986	Cincinnati	PH	3	2	0	0	0	0	0	0	0	.000
1987	Cincinnati	OF-1B-P	84	160	24	41	14	1	7	28	2	.256
1988	Cincinnati	OF-1B	145	485	58	122	25	3	16	73	8	.252
1989	Cincinnati	OF	117	428	49	118	24	2	15	74	20	.276
1990	Cincinnati	OF	145	503	59	136	28	0	16	78	13	.270
1991	Cincinnati	OF	152	532	71	136	36	0	28	91	12	.256
	Totals		651	2122	262	557	128	6	82	345	55	.262

BIP ROBERTS 28 5-7 168   Bats S Throws R

Reds hope switch-hitting left fielder will fill void left by departure of Eric Davis . . . Padres traded Roberts and minor leaguer to be named for Randy Myers . . . After spectacular season in 1990, he fell out of favor with Padres' management because of multiple injury problems in '91 . . . Missed a month after undergoing surgery to repair torn knee cartilage Aug. 19 and wasn't the same after returning . . . From July 15 until Aug. 16, when he injured the knee, this leadoff hitter batted .349 . . . Started season as regular second baseman, but was shifted to center and finally to left, his best position . . . Born Oct. 27, 1963, in Berkeley, Cal. . . . Signed by the Pirates in first round of secondary phase of the 1982 draft, but was left unprotected and was taken by the Padres . . . Earned $875,000 last season.

Year	Club	Pos.	G	AB	R	H	2B	3B	HR	RBI	SB	Avg.
1986	San Diego	2B	101	241	34	61	5	2	1	12	14	.253
1988	San Diego	2B-3B	5	9	1	3	0	0	0	0	0	.333
1989	San Diego	OF-3B-SS-2B	117	329	81	99	15	8	3	25	21	.301
1990	San Diego	OF-3B-SS-2B	149	556	104	172	36	3	9	44	46	.309
1991	San Diego	2B-OF	117	424	66	119	13	3	3	32	26	.281
	Totals		489	1559	286	454	69	16	16	113	107	.291

BILLY HATCHER 31 5-9 185   Bats R Throws R

Left fielder came crashing back to earth after incredible World Series success in 1990 . . . After batting .750 against the A's, bettering Babe Ruth's .625 mark in 1928 World Series, he hit .262 with only four homers and 41 RBI in 1991 . . . Injuries led to his downfall . . . Suffered left shoulder problems and left groin injury that hampered him all season . . . Still showed he was clutch by batting .340 with runners in scoring position ... Born Oct. 4, 1960, in Williams, Ariz. ... Earned $1,200,000 last year ... Pirates wanted to dump his $695,000 salary, so they traded him to the Reds for Mike Roesler and Jeff Richardson, April 3, 1990 ... Made Pirates pay by hitting .333 that year in NLCS ... Originally taken by Cubs in sixth round of 1981 draft.

Year	Club	Pos.	G	AB	R	H	2B	3B	HR	RBI	SB	Avg.
1984	Chicago (NL) ..	OF	8	9	1	1	0	0	0	0	2	.111
1985	Chicago (NL) ..	OF	53	163	24	40	12	1	2	10	2	.245
1986	Houston......	OF	127	419	55	108	15	4	6	36	38	.258
1987	Houston......	OF	141	564	96	167	28	3	11	63	53	.296
1988	Houston......	OF	145	530	79	142	25	4	7	52	32	.268
1989	Hou.-Pitt......	OF	135	481	59	111	19	3	4	51	24	.231
1990	Cincinnati.....	OF	139	504	68	139	28	5	5	25	30	.276
1991	Cincinnati.....	OF	138	442	45	116	25	3	4	41	11	.262
	Totals		886	3112	427	824	152	23	39	278	192	.265

DAVE MARTINEZ 27 5-10 175   Bats L Throws L

Enjoyed best offensive season in 1991 while starting games at all three outfield positions for Expos ... And wound up with Reds in December trade with Scott Ruskin and Willie Greene for John Wetteland and Bill Risley ... Tied career high with four hits Aug. 26 at Atlanta ... Also had four hits against Mets April 21 ... During 40-game stretch in August and September, he batted .364 with 21 runs, five doubles, three homers and six steals ... Had two outfield assists in an inning June 18 against Astros ... Collected 500th career hit June 10 against Braves' John Smoltz and hit homer in same game ... Had five straight hits from April 21-23 against Mets and Pirates ... Selected by Cubs in third round of January 1983 draft ... Traded to Expos for Mitch Webster, July 14, 1988 ... Born Sept. 26, 1964, in New York City ... Attended Valencia Junior College in Orlando, Fla. ... Earned $805,000 in 1991 ... Led Carolina League in batting (.342) and slugging percentage (.438) in 1985.

Year	Club	Pos.	G	AB	R	H	2B	3B	HR	RBI	SB	Avg.
1986	Chicago (NL) ..	OF	53	108	13	15	1	1	1	7	4	.139
1987	Chicago (NL) ..	OF	142	459	70	134	18	8	8	36	16	.292
1988	Chi.(NL)-Mont.	OF	138	447	51	114	13	6	6	46	23	.255
1989	Montreal	OF	126	361	41	99	16	7	3	27	23	.274
1990	Montreal	OF-P	118	391	60	109	13	5	11	39	13	.279
1991	Montreal	OF	124	396	47	117	18	5	7	42	16	.295
	Totals		701	2162	282	588	79	32	36	197	95	.272

JOSE RIJO 26 6-2 200   Bats R Throws R

On June 20, he tried to steal second and suffered a chip fracture of right ankle while making a Keystone Kop slide . . . Missed the next five weeks, but still managed to reach a career high in innings pitched (204⅓) and post a 15-6 record . . . Earned $2,333,333 in 1991 . . . Tied Pirates' John Smiley for first with .714 winning percentage, finished second in ERA (2.51) and opponents' batting average against (.219) . . . Tied for fourth in strikeouts (172) . . . Allowed only eight home runs . . . A terror at Riverfront, he posted 9-0 mark there . . . Surrendered three earned runs or less in 26 of 30 starts . . . Gave up only 10 earned runs in his six losses . . . Reds scored just seven runs in those games . . . Another player the Yankees let get away . . . Originally signed as free agent by New York in 1981, but was traded to A's in Rickey Henderson deal in 1984 . . . A's made huge mistake by dealing him to Reds with Tim Birtsas for Dave Parker following 1987 season . . . Born May 13, 1965, in San Cristobal, D.R.

Year	Club	G	IP	W	L	Pct.	SO	BB	H	ERA
1984	New York (AL)	24	62⅓	2	8	.200	47	33	74	4.76
1985	Oakland	12	63⅔	6	4	.600	65	28	57	3.53
1986	Oakland	39	193⅔	9	11	.450	176	108	172	4.65
1987	Oakland	21	82⅓	2	7	.222	67	41	106	5.90
1988	Cincinnati	49	162	13	8	.619	160	63	120	2.39
1989	Cincinnati	19	111	7	6	.538	86	48	101	2.84
1990	Cincinnati	29	197	14	8	.636	152	78	151	2.70
1991	Cincinnati	30	204⅓	15	6	.714	172	55	165	2.51
	Totals	223	1076⅓	68	58	.540	925	454	946	3.39

ROB DIBBLE 28 6-4 235   Bats R Throws R

Ranked second in the NL with career-high 31 saves and first in controversy as he was fined three times and suspended twice . . . Recorded the most saves by a Cincinnati right-hander since Clay Carroll posted 37 in 1972 . . . Was 23-for-23 in save opportunities at the All-Star break and pitched one scoreless inning in his second All-Star appearance . . . Was not nearly as effective the second half . . . Averaged 13.6 Ks per nine innings (124 strikeouts in 82⅓ innings), the highest rate in major-league history, breaking his own record of 12.8 in 1989 . . . Has 460 strikeouts in 338⅔ innings over major-league careeer, an average of 12.2 strikeouts per nine . . . In 1990 NLCS, he struck out 10 of 16 Pirates he faced . . . Did not allow a run in that postseason and allowed just three hits . . . Born Jan. 24, 1964, in Bridgeport, Conn. . . . First pick in January 1983 draft . . . Earned $475,000 last season.

Year	Club	G	IP	W	L	Pct.	SO	BB	H	ERA
1988	Cincinnati	37	59⅓	1	1	.500	59	21	43	1.82
1989	Cincinnati	74	99	10	5	.667	141	39	62	2.09
1990	Cincinnati	68	98	8	3	.727	136	34	62	1.74
1991	Cincinnati	67	82⅓	3	5	.375	124	25	67	3.17
	Totals	246	338⅔	22	14	.611	460	119	234	2.21

NORM CHARLTON 29 6-3 200   Bats S Throws L

Was expected to move into the rotation, but had to be shifted back to the bullpen after two stints on the disabled list with shoulder tendinitis . . . Numbers show he is best suited for pen . . . In 11 starts, he was 3-5 with 4.25 ERA . . . In 28 relief appearances, he was 0-0 with 0.84 ERA, one save and 40 strikeouts in 42⅔ innings . . . Pitched 17⅔ scoreless innings in final 13 relief appearances . . . Was suspended for admitting that he purposely hit Dodger catcher Mike Scioscia with pitch, because Scioscia had been stealing signs . . . Earned $625,000 last season . . . Born Jan. 6, 1963, in Ft. Polk, La. . . . Earned All-America honors at Rice, where he graduated with a triple major in political science, religion and physical education . . . Acquired from Montreal with Tim Barker for Wayne Krenchicki prior to the 1986 season . . . First-round pick of Expos in 1984.

Year	Club	G	IP	W	L	Pct.	SO	BB	H	ERA
1988	Cincinnati	10	61⅓	4	5	.444	39	20	60	3.96
1989	Cincinnati	69	95⅓	8	3	.727	98	40	67	2.93
1990	Cincinnati	56	154⅓	12	9	.571	117	70	131	2.74
1991	Cincinnati	39	108⅓	3	5	.375	77	34	92	2.91
	Totals	174	419⅓	27	22	.551	331	164	350	3.00

GREG SWINDELL 27 6-3 225   Bats S Throws L

Acquired from Cleveland for Scott Scudder, Jack Armstrong and Joe Turek after last season . . . Mainstay on Indian staff last year as he led them in innings pitched (238), strikeouts (169) and complete games (seven) . . . Control is outstanding . . . Averaged only one walk every 7⅔ innings, second-best mark among AL starters with at least 150 innings . . . Fashioned 2.52 ERA at home, but had just 7-9 record to show for it . . . Struggled to 2-7 record with 5.21 ERA on road... Born Jan. 2, 1965, in Fort Worth, Tex.... Chosen by Cleveland in 1986 draft as second player picked overall... Three-time All-American at University of Texas, where he boasted 43-8 career mark... Earned $2,025,000 last year.

Year	Club	G	IP	W	L	Pct.	SO	BB	H	ERA
1986	Cleveland	9	61⅔	5	2	.714	46	15	57	4.23
1987	Cleveland	16	102⅓	3	8	.273	97	37	112	5.10
1988	Cleveland	33	242	18	14	.563	180	45	234	3.20
1989	Cleveland	28	184⅓	13	6	.684	129	51	170	3.37
1990	Cleveland	34	214⅔	12	9	.571	135	47	245	4.40
1991	Cleveland	33	238	9	16	.360	169	31	241	3.48
	Totals	153	1043	60	55	.522	756	226	1059	3.79

TIM BELCHER 30 6-3 210   Bats R Throws R

Reds acquired him with John Wetteland (subsequently traded to Expos) in deal that sent Eric Davis and Kip Gross to Dodgers... Underwent arthroscopic shoulder surgery in 1990, but bounced back last season to tie Mike Morgan and Ramon Martinez for Dodger club lead in starts with 33... Considering he was fourth in NL in ERA (2.62) and seventh in strikeouts (156), you'd have expected more than 10-9 record... Has never had a lot of runs scored behind him and last year was no exception ... Earned $900,000 last season... Came to Dodgers from A's in September 1987 deal for Rick Honeycutt... Was first selection in nation in 1983 by Twins, but did not sign... Became the Yankees' first-round pick in January 1984, but was lost one week later when he was drafted by Oakland as compensation for Tom Underwood... Born Oct. 19, 1961, in Sparta, Ohio.

Year	Club	G	IP	W	L	Pct.	SO	BB	H	ERA
1987	Los Angeles	6	34	4	2	.667	23	7	30	2.38
1988	Los Angeles	36	179⅔	12	6	.667	152	51	143	2.91
1989	Los Angeles	39	230	15	12	.556	200	80	182	2.82
1990	Los Angeles	24	153	9	9	.500	102	48	136	4.00
1991	Los Angeles	33	209⅓	10	9	.526	156	75	189	2.62
	Totals	138	806	50	38	.568	633	261	680	2.99

TOP PROSPECTS

REGGIE SANDERS 24 6-1 180   Bats R Throws R

Reds' center fielder of the future... Was batting .315 for Chattanooga (AA) when he was called up to Reds Aug. 22... Collected two hits the next night in New York, but suffered right shoulder separation . . . Hit first major-league homer Sept. 26 in Atlanta, then aggravated shoulder injury two days later and did not return to action . . . Ex-shortstop needs to work on defense, because he gets a bad jump on the ball . . . Reds' seventh-round draft choice in 1987 draft . . . Born Dec. 1, 1967, in Florence, S.C.

MO SANFORD 25 6-6 220   Bats R Throws R

Began the season with Chattanooga (AA), then was promoted to Nashville (AAA) and called up to Cincinnati Aug. 4 . . . Combined Chattanooga-Nashville totals were 10-4 with 2.44 ERA and he went 1-2 with 3.88 ERA for Reds . . . Won big-league debut Aug. 9 in San Diego, allowing only two hits and one unearned run in seven innings . . . Struck out side in first and fanned six of first nine batters . . . Born Dec. 24, 1966, in Americus, Ga. . . . Drafted by Reds in 32nd round in 1988 . . . Pitched four years for the University of Alabama.

STEVE FOSTER 25 6-0 180   Bats R Throws R

Went 2-3 with 2.14 ERA, 12 saves for Chattanooga (AA) and was promoted to Nashville (AAA), where he went 0-2 with 1.15 ERA and 10 saves . . . Finished with the Reds in September, going 0-0 with 1.93 ERA . . . In his last six outings, he pitched seven innings of hitless and scoreless relief as opponents hit only .143 against him . . . Born Aug. 16, 1966, in Dallas . . . Selected in 12th round of 1988 draft.

DANNY WILSON 23 6-3 190   Bats R Throws R

Catcher hit .315 with three homers and 29 RBI for Charleston (A), then .257 with two homers and 38 RBI for Chattanooga (AA) . . . Born March 25, 1969, in Arlington Heights, Ill. . . . Taken in first round of 1990 draft as seventh pick overall . . . Selected first team All-American at the University of Minnesota.

MANAGER LOU PINIELLA: "Sweet Lou" went through  one of the most sour years of his career... Watched his team fall apart in the second half to finish 74-88 and in fourth place after winning it all in 1990... One of the most sought-after managers in baseball, but he decided to stick in Cincinnati because he was given more control over player moves at the end of the year ... After 1990 World Series sweep of A's, former Yankee star and manager had these words for Yankee owner George Steinbrenner, who fired him as manager: "George, I can manage"... Batted .295 in 11 years with the Yankees from 1974-84 and .291 lifetime... Was AL Rookie of the Year with Kansas City in 1969... Became a Yankee coach in 1985 and Yankee manager the next season, replacing Billy Martin... Posted 179-145 record in two years, but that wasn't good enough for Steinbrenner, so he was kicked upstairs as VP-GM in 1988... In 1988, he became TV color man, doing Yankee games for MSG Network, before replacing Billy Martin in dugout June 23 and leading Yanks to 45-48 finish the rest of the way... Could have wound up as manager of Blue Jays, but Steinbrenner refused to let him go without excessive compensation in summer of '89, after Jimy Williams was fired... Lifetime managerial record is 344-304... Born Aug. 28, 1943, in Tampa, he was a teammate of current A's manager Tony La Russa on local American Legion team... Some day, he might wind up managing in old hometown.

ALL-TIME RED SEASON RECORDS

BATTING: Cy Seymour, .377, 1905
HRs: George Foster, 52, 1977
RBI: George Foster, 149, 1977
STEALS: Bob Bescher, 81, 1911
WINS: Adolfo Luque, 27, 1923
       Bucky Walters, 27, 1939
STRIKEOUTS: Mario Soto, 274, 1972

HOUSTON ASTROS

TEAM DIRECTORY: Chairman: Dr. John J. McMullen; GM: Bill Wood; Asst. GM: Bob Watson; Coordinator Minor League Instruction: Jimmy Johnson; Dir. Pub. Rel.: Rob Matwick; Trav. Sec.: Barry Waters; Mgr.: Art Howe. Home: Astrodome (54,816). Field distances: 330, l.f. line; 380, l.c.; 400, c.f.; 380, r.c.; 330, r.f. line. Spring training: Kissimmee, Fla.

SCOUTING REPORT

HITTING: The Astros are moving the fences back at the Astrodome this season to help the Houston hitters. Last year, the Astros collected the most doubles (240) they've had in three years and the most triples (43) they've had in four, but they hit just 79 homers, the NL's second-lowest total. For the second straight season, the Astros set a club record for strikeouts (1,027). The only NL team that scored fewer runs than the Astros' 605 in 1991 was the Expos.

Outfielder Luis Gonzalez (.254, 13, 69) had five wall-bangers in 1991. Much will depend upon Jeff Bagwell (.294, 15, 82) duplicating his NL Rookie of the Year season and the continued emergence of Ken Caminiti (.253, 13, 80). The trade of Glenn Davis to the Orioles prior to last season paid off because the Astros landed an excellent leadoff hitter in Steve Finley (.285, 84 runs, 28 doubles, 10 triples and eight homers).

Craig Biggio compiled another solid season with a .295 average and 79 runs. Waiting for Eric Anthony (.153, 1, 7) to develop, however, is like waiting for Godot.

PITCHING: The Astros finished with a 4.00 ERA, marking the first time in 16 years the club's ERA was not under 4.00. However, Pete Harnisch (12-9, 2.70) is a pitcher to build around. Opponents hit a league-low .212 against the right-hander and his 172 strikeouts ranked fourth-best in the league and were a big reason Houston topped the NL with 1,033 strikeouts.

Darryl Kile (7-11, 3.69) was rushed and it showed. Mark Portugal (10-12, 4.49) is one of few returning veterans in the rotation, but Houston's biggest problem may be its bullpen. Left-hander Al Osuna (7-6, 3.42, 12 Sv) must cut down on his blown saves.

Rookie of the Year Jeff Bagwell filled Glenn Davis' shoes.

FIELDING: The Astros were the worst defensive team in the majors with 161 errors, their highest total since they set a club record with 174 in 1966. Even though Biggio became the first Astro catcher to be named to the All-Star team, he has been shifted to second to make room for Ed Taubensee, who was acquired from the Indians in the offseason. Third baseman Caminiti led the club with 23 errors, but he makes spectacular stops, too.

OUTLOOK: Houston's 65-97 record last year matched the highest loss total in club history. Manager Art Howe must be patient again because salary-dumping ownership did not acquire any veterans who could have blended with a core of talented youth to make the Astros more competitive.

HOUSTON ASTROS 1992 ROSTER

MANAGER Art Howe
Coaches—Bob Cluck, Matt Galante, Rudy Jaramillo, Ed Ott, Tom Spencer

PITCHERS

No.	Name	1991 Club	W-L	IP	SO	ERA	B-T	Ht.	Wt.	Born
—	Blair, Willie	Colorado Springs	9-6	114	57	4.99	R-R	6-1	185	12/18/65 Paintsville, KY
		Cleveland	2-3	36	13	6.75				
46	Bowen, Ryan	Tucson	5-5	99	78	4.38	R-R	6-0	185	2/10/68 Hanford, CA
		Houston	6-4	72	49	5.15				
35	Capel, Mike	Houston	1-3	33	23	3.03	R-R	6-1	175	10/13/61 Marshall, TX
		Tucson	4-2	56	44	2.40				
39	Gardner, Chris	Jackson	13-5	131	72	3.15	R-R	6-0	175	3/30/69 Long Beach, CA
		Houston	1-2	25	12	4.01				
60	Griffiths, Brian	Osceola	4-3	61	44	1.92	R-R	6-2	190	5/29/68 Portland, OR
27	Harnisch, Pete	Houston	12-9	217	172	2.70	R-R	6-0	195	9/23/66 Commack, NY
50	Henry, Butch	Tucson	10-11	154	97	4.80	L-L	6-1	195	10/7/68 El Paso, TX
31	Hernandez, Xavier	Houston	2-7	63	55	4.71	L-R	6-2	185	8/16/65 Port Arthur, TX
		Tucson	2-1	36	34	2.75				
37	Jones, Jimmy	Houston	6-8	135	88	4.39	R-R	6-2	190	4/20/64 Dallas, TX
59	Jones, Todd	Osceola	4-4	72	52	4.35	L-R	6-3	200	4/24/68 Marietta, GA
		Jackson	4-3	55	37	4.88				
44	Juden, Jeff	Jackson	6-3	96	75	3.10	R-R	6-7	245	1/19/71 Salem, MA
		Tucson	3-2	57	51	3.18				
		Houston	0-2	18	11	6.00				
57	Kile, Darryl	Houston	7-11	154	100	3.69	R-R	6-5	185	12/2/68 Garden Grove, CA
56	Mallicoat, Rob	Jackson	4-1	31	34	3.77	L-L	6-3	180	11/16/64 St. Helen's, OR
		Tucson	4-4	48	32	5.48				
		Houston	0-2	23	18	3.86				
29	Osuna, Al	Houston	7-6	82	68	3.42	L-L	6-3	200	8/10/65 Inglewood, CA
51	Portugal, Mark	Houston	10-12	168	120	4.49	R-R	6-0	190	10/30/62 Los Angeles, CA
38	Reynolds, Shane	Jackson	8-9	151	116	4.47	R-R	6-3	210	3/26/68 Bastrop, LA
19	Schilling, Curt	Houston	3-5	76	71	3.81	R-R	6-4	215	11/14/66 Anchorage, AK
		Tucson	0-1	24	21	3.42				
47	Simon, Richie	Jackson	4-2	70	54	2.18	R-R	6-2	200	11/29/65 Brooklyn, NY
63	Turner, Matt	Richmond	1-3	36	33	4.75	R-R	6-5	215	2/18/67 Lexington, KY
		Tucson	1-1	26	25	4.15				
53	Williams, Brian	Osceola	6-4	90	67	2.91	R-R	6-2	195	2/15/69 Lancaster, SC
		Jackson	2-1	15	15	4.20				
		Tucson	0-1	38	29	4.93				
		Houston	0-1	12	4	3.75				

CATCHERS

No.	Name	1991 Club	H	HR	RBI	Pct.	B-T	Ht.	Wt.	Born
7	Biggio, Craig	Houston	161	4	46	.295	R-R	5-11	180	12/14/65 Smithtown, NY
10	Eusebio, Tony	Jackson	58	2	31	.261	R-R	6-2	180	4/27/67 Dominican Republic
		Tucson	8	0	2	.400				
		Houston	2	0	0	.105				
9	Servais, Scott	Houston	71	2	27	.324	R-R	6-2	195	6/4/67 LaCrosse, WI
		Houston	6	0	6	.162				
—	Taubensee, Eddie	Cleveland	16	0	8	.242	L-R	6-4	205	10/31/68 Beeville, TX
		Colorado Springs	89	13	39	.310				
20	Tucker, Eddie	Shreveport	100	4	49	.284	R-R	6-2	205	11/18/66 Greenville, MS

INFIELDERS

No.	Name	1991 Club	H	HR	RBI	Pct.	B-T	Ht.	Wt.	Born
5	Bagwell, Jeff	Houston	163	15	82	.294	R-R	6-0	198	5/27/68 Boston, MA
11	Caminiti, Ken	Houston	145	13	80	.253	S-R	6-0	200	4/21/63 Hanford, CA
1	Candaele, Casey	Houston	121	4	50	.262	S-R	5-9	165	1/12/61 Lompoc, CA
17	Cedeno, Andujar	Tucson	105	7	55	.303	R-R	6-1	168	8/21/69 Dominican Republic
		Houston	61	9	36	.243				
36	Cooper, Gary	Tucson	124	14	75	.305	R-R	6-1	200	8/13/64 Lynwood, CA
		Houston	4	0	2	.250				
64	Miller, Orlando	Osceola	81	0	36	.298	R-R	6-1	180	1/13/69 Panama
		Jackson	13	1	5	.186				
23	Mota, Andy	Tucson	138	2	46	.299	R-R	5-10	180	3/4/66 Dominican Republic
		Houston	17	1	6	.189				
16	Ramirez, Rafael	Houston	55	1	20	.236	R-R	5-11	190	2/18/59 Dominican Republic
15	Yelding, Eric	Houston	67	1	20	.243	R-R	5-11	165	2/22/65 Montrose, AL
		Tucson	17	0	3	.395				

OUTFIELDERS

No.	Name	1991 Club	H	HR	RBI	Pct.	B-T	Ht.	Wt.	Born
21	Anthony, Eric	Houston	18	1	7	.153	L-L	6-2	205	11/8/67 San Diego, CA
		Tucson	107	9	63	.336				
12	Finley, Steve	Houston	170	8	54	.285	L-L	6-2	180	3/12/65 Union City, TN
26	Gonzalez, Luis	Houston	120	13	69	.254	L-R	6-2	180	9/3/67 Tampa, FL
4	Rhodes, Karl	Houston	29	1	12	.213	L-L	5-11	170	8/21/68 Cincinnati, OH
		Tucson	80	1	46	.260				
22	Simms, Mike	Tucson	73	15	59	.246	R-R	6-4	185	1/12/67 Orange, CA
		Houston	25	3	16	.203				
2	Young, Gerald	Tucson	24	0	17	.304	S-R	6-2	185	10/22/64 Honduras
		Houston	31	1	11	.218				

ASTRO PROFILES

JEFF BAGWELL 23 6-0 198   Bats R Throws R

Became first Astro to win NL Rookie of the Year honors . . . Hit .294 with team-leading 15 homers and 82 RBI in 156 games . . . First baseman came from the Red Sox for reliever Larry Andersen for 1990 stretch run and, after that season, Andersen fled back to NL as free agent and signed with Padres . . . Born May 27, 1968, in Boston and now lives in Killingworth, Conn. . . . You think the Red Sox fans might have gotten a kick watching hometown boy blast 'em over the Green Monster? . . . Chosen by Red Sox in fourth round of 1989 draft . . . Fifth in NL in on-base percentage (.387) . . . Led Astros in walks with 75 and was tied for 10th in league in that department . . . Earned $100,000 last year and is due for hefty raise . . . Astros like his power so much they will move the fences back in this season . . . Hit mammoth 457-foot home run in Pittsburgh May 5, becoming only the ninth player to reach the upper deck at Three Rivers Stadium.

Year Club	Pos.	G	AB	R	H	2B	3B	HR	RBI	SB	Avg.
1991 Houston.	1B	156	554	79	163	26	4	15	82	7	.294

CRAIG BIGGIO 26 5-11 180   Bats R Throws R

Had so much trouble throwing to second that Astros may shift him from catcher to second base, depending on progress of rookie Eddie Taubensee . . . Threw out just 46 of 172 would-be base-stealers or 27 percent . . . Nailed 17 percent three years ago and 23 percent two years ago, so inch-by-inch progress is being made . . . After driving in 60 runs in 1989, he slipped to 42 the next season and 46 last year . . . Stole 19 bases, including three in one game vs. Braves Sept. 27 . . . Made his first-ever career start at second Sept. 30 . . . Astros' first-round pick in 1987 . . . Only five other NL players had more multiple-hit games than his 48 . . . Tied his career high with four hits vs. Giants April 14 and vs. Cards July 29 . . . Earned $437,500 last year . . . Born Dec.

14, 1965, in Smithtown, N.Y. . . . Attended Seton Hall.

Year Club	Pos.	G	AB	R	H	2B	3B	HR	RBI	SB	Avg.
1988 Houston......	C	50	123	14	26	6	1	3	5	6	.211
1989 Houston......	C-OF	134	443	64	114	21	2	13	60	21	.257
1990 Houston......	C-OF	150	555	53	153	24	2	4	42	25	.276
1991 Houston......	C-3B-OF	149	546	79	161	23	4	4	46	19	.295
Totals		483	1667	210	454	74	9	24	153	71	.272

STEVE FINLEY 27 6-2 180   Bats L Throws L

Established himself as everyday center fielder and leadoff hitter after coming over from Orioles with Pete Harnisch and Curt Schilling for Glenn Davis prior to 1991 season . . . At his best leading off games, he hit .378 in that situation . . . Led club in games played with 159 . . . Only five NL players had more hits than his 170 . . . Finished third in NL in triples (10) . . . One of the best bargains around, he earned just $260,000 last season . . . Tied Jeff Bagwell for team lead in total bases with 242 . . . Improved against left-handers . . . Batted .193 vs. left-handers in 1990 and .250 last year . . . Was selected by Orioles in 14th round of 1987 draft . . . Born March 12, 1965, in Union City, Tenn.

Year Club	Pos.	G	AB	R	H	2B	3B	HR	RBI	SB	Avg.
1989 Baltimore.....	OF	81	217	35	54	5	2	2	25	17	.249
1990 Baltimore.....	OF	142	464	46	119	16	4	3	37	22	.256
1991 Houston......	OF	159	596	84	170	28	10	8	54	34	.285
Totals		382	1277	165	343	49	16	13	116	73	.269

KEN CAMINITI 28 6-0 200   Bats S Throws R

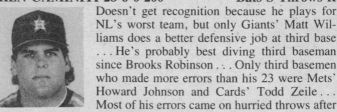

Doesn't get recognition because he plays for NL's worst team, but only Giants' Matt Williams does a better defensive job at third base . . . He's probably best diving third baseman since Brooks Robinson . . . Only third basemen who made more errors than his 23 were Mets' Howard Johnson and Cards' Todd Zeile . . . Most of his errors came on hurried throws after dazzling, diving stops . . . Has a laser for a right arm . . . For the first time in three years, he did not lead the Astros in games played, but still had 152 . . . Regained his power stroke after disappointing 1990 season . . . Established a career high in homers (13) and RBI (80) . . . On July 29 vs. Cardinals, he hit Astros' first grand slam since Kevin Bass had one Sept. 20, 1989 . . . Earned $665,000 last season . . . Born April 21, 1963, in Hanford, Cal. . . . Astros' third-round selection in 1984 draft, out of San Jose State . . . Has missed just 20 games the last three seasons.

Year	Club	Pos.	G	AB	R	H	2B	3B	HR	RBI	SB	Avg.
1987	Houston	3B	63	203	10	50	7	1	3	23	0	.246
1988	Houston	3B	30	83	5	15	2	0	1	7	0	.181
1989	Houston	3B	161	585	71	149	31	3	10	72	4	.255
1990	Houston	3B	153	541	52	131	20	2	4	51	9	.242
1991	Houston	3B	152	574	65	145	30	3	13	80	4	.253
	Totals		559	1986	203	490	90	9	31	233	17	.247

LUIS GONZALEZ 24 6-2 180   Bats L Throws R

After being first baseman and third baseman his entire career, he moved to the outfield because of shoulder problems and did a respectable job . . . Owns surprising power . . . Hit 13 homers and led Astros in doubles (28), breaking club rookie mark of 23 by Chuck Harrison in 1965 . . . Had the first four-hit game of his career July 17 at Pittsburgh . . . Knocked in a career-high and club-best five runs July 3 at San Francisco . . . On the disabled list from Aug. 29 to Sept. 12 with a partially dislocated left shoulder . . . Another John McMullen bargain at $105,000 in 1991 . . . Selected by Astros in fourth round of 1988 draft . . . Born Sept. 3, 1967, in Tampa . . . Attended South Alabama University and set school records in career hit-by-pitches . . . In 1990, he tied for Southern League lead in home runs with 24.

Year	Club	Pos.	G	AB	R	H	2B	3B	HR	RBI	SB	Avg.
1990	Houston	3B-1B	12	21	1	4	2	0	0	0	0	.190
1991	Houston	OF	137	473	51	120	28	9	13	69	10	.254
	Totals		149	494	52	124	30	9	13	69	10	.251

ERIC ANTHONY 24 6-2 205   Bats L Throws L

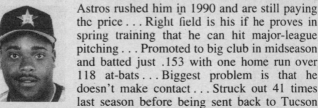

Astros rushed him in 1990 and are still paying the price . . . Right field is his if he proves in spring training that he can hit major-league pitching . . . Promoted to big club in midseason and batted just .153 with one home run over 118 at-bats . . . Biggest problem is that he doesn't make contact . . . Struck out 41 times last season before being sent back to Tucson (AAA) . . . In 1990 tryout with Astros, he hit .192 with 78 strikeouts in 239 at-bats . . . May be one of those career Triple-A stars who can't make the next step vs. major-league pitching . . . Became third Houston player to reach Astrodome upper deck, May

17, 1990 . . . Born Nov. 8, 1967, in San Diego . . . Selected in 34th round of 1986 draft . . . Earned $115,000 last year.

Year	Club	Pos.	G	AB	R	H	2B	3B	HR	RBI	SB	Avg.
1989	Houston	OF	25	61	7	11	2	0	4	7	0	.180
1990	Houston	OF	84	239	26	46	8	0	10	29	5	.192
1991	Houston	OF	39	118	11	18	6	0	1	7	1	.153
	Totals		148	418	44	75	16	0	15	43	6	.179

PETE HARNISCH 25 6-0 195   Bats R Throws R

On any other team, right-hander could have had as many as 20 wins in 1991 . . . Wins (12), innings (216⅔), strikeouts (172), starts (33), complete games (four) and shutouts (two) were all career bests . . . Opponents hit only .212 against him, best mark in NL . . . Ranked among league leaders in ERA (2.70) and strikeouts . . . Named NL All-Star his first year in the league . . . Key player in Glenn Davis deal, he was acquired from Orioles with Steve Finley and Curt Schilling for Davis prior to last season . . . Allowed two or less runs in 21 of his 33 starts and pitched six or more innings 27 times . . . Fired two-hitter at Pittsburgh May 3, but lost, 1-0, on Orlando Merced homer . . . Pitched 21 consecutive scoreless innings vs. Padres and came away with one win for his efforts . . . Astros scored 12 runs in his nine losses . . . Fanned a career-high 12 Aug. 5 vs. San Diego and matched it Sept. 6 vs. Philadelphia . . . Born Sept. 23, 1966, in Commack, N.Y. . . . Selected by the Orioles with a compensation pick between the first and second rounds of the 1987 draft . . . Earned $210,000 last year.

Year	Club	G	IP	W	L	Pct.	SO	BB	H	ERA
1988	Baltimore	2	13	0	2	.000	10	9	13	5.54
1989	Baltimore	18	103⅓	5	9	.357	70	64	97	4.62
1990	Baltimore	31	188⅔	11	11	.500	122	86	189	4.34
1991	Houston	33	216⅔	12	9	.571	172	83	169	2.70
	Totals	84	521⅔	28	31	.475	374	242	468	3.74

DARRYL KILE 23 6-5 185   Bats R Throws R

Another member of Kiddie Korps pitching staff . . . Started 22 games and relieved 15 times . . . Will be in the rotation this season . . . Needs to become more consistent . . . One day he has great stuff, the next day nothing . . . His 3.69 ERA figures to drop with more experience . . . Born Dec. 2, 1968, in Garden Grove, Cal. . . . Earned $100,000 last season . . . Selected by the Astros in the 30th round of the 1987 draft, out of Chaffey Junior College, but did not sign . . . Was 10-2 with a 2.12 ERA and 125 strikeouts in 110 innings for Chaffey before signing prior to the 1988 draft . . . Advanced to majors despite 5-10 record and 6.64 ERA for Tucson (AAA) in 1991.

Year	Club	G	IP	W	L	Pct.	SO	BB	H	ERA
1991	Houston	37	153⅔	7	11	.389	100	84	144	3.69

MARK PORTUGAL 29 6-0 190   Bats R Throws R

On Sept. 14 in Cincinnati, he surrendered three consecutive home runs, which resulted in back-to-back-to-back fireworks display . . . Pitching coach Bob Cluck trotted to the mound and said, "I just came out here to give the guy time to reload his cannon." . . . After laughing subsided, side was retired and Astros went on to win the game . . . Could wind up as a starter or in the bullpen . . . Started 27 games last season and relieved in five . . . Born Oct. 30, 1962, in Los Angeles . . . Signed with the Twins as a amateur free agent in 1980 . . . Traded to Astros before 1989 season for Todd McClure . . . Earned $705,000 in 1991.

Year	Club	G	IP	W	L	Pct.	SO	BB	H	ERA
1985	Minnesota	6	24⅓	1	3	.250	12	14	24	5.55
1986	Minnesota	27	112⅔	6	10	.375	67	50	112	4.31
1987	Minnesota	13	44	1	3	.250	28	24	58	7.77
1988	Minnesota	26	57⅔	3	3	.500	31	17	60	4.53
1989	Houston	20	108	7	1	.875	86	37	91	2.75
1990	Houston	32	196⅔	11	10	.524	136	67	187	3.62
1991	Houston	32	168⅓	10	12	.455	120	59	163	4.49
	Totals	156	711⅔	39	42	.481	480	268	695	4.20

AL OSUNA 26 6-3 200   Bats R Throws L

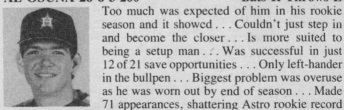

Too much was expected of him in his rookie season and it showed . . . Couldn't just step in and become the closer . . . Is more suited to being a setup man . . . Was successful in just 12 of 21 save opportunities . . . Only left-hander in the bullpen . . . Biggest problem was overuse as he was worn out by end of season . . . Made 71 appearances, shattering Astro rookie record of Charley Kerfeld (61 in 1986) . . . Only five NL pitchers made more appearances this season . . . Led Columbus (AA) with 60 appearances in 1990 before being called up by Astros for 12 more games . . . Give him a break—that's 143 appearances in two years

. . . Born Aug. 10, 1965, in Inglewood, Cal. . . . Selected by Astros in 16th round of 1987 draft . . . Pitched for Stanford and was the winner in championship game of the 1987 College World Series.

Year	Club	G	IP	W	L	Pct.	SO	BB	H	ERA
1990	Houston	12	11⅓	2	0	1.000	6	6	10	4.76
1991	Houston	71	81⅔	7	6	.538	68	46	59	3.42
	Totals	83	93	9	6	.600	74	52	69	3.58

TOP PROSPECTS

RYAN BOWEN 24 6-0 185   Bats R Throws R
Has fastball clocked in the 90s . . . Finished 5-5 with 4.38 ERA for Tucson (AAA) . . . Had two shutouts in 18 starts . . . Promoted to Astros and wound up with 6-4 record with 5.15 ERA . . . Struck out 49 and walked 36 in 71⅔ innings . . . Astros expect him to be in rotation from start of this season . . . Posted 11-1 mark with 1.30 ERA while striking out 149 in 76⅓ innings in his senior year at Hanford (Cal.) High . . . Houston's No. 1 pick and 13th overall in 1986 draft . . . Born Feb. 10, 1968, in Hanford, Cal.

JEFF JUDEN 21 6-7 245   Bats R Throws R
Like every Astro prospect, he was force-fed to big club last season, posting 0-2 record with 6.00 ERA with Astros . . . Started three games and relieved in one, struck out 11 and walked seven over 18 innings . . . Rang up 6-3 record with 3.10 ERA in 16 starts for Jackson (AA) . . . Promoted to Tucson (AAA) where he was 3-2 with 3.18 ERA . . . With Toros down 0-2 in PCL finals, he started Game 3 and allowed one run in eight innings to pick up the win and Tucson went on to win title . . . Selected by Astros in first round of 1989 draft . . . Born Jan. 19, 1971, in Salem, Mass.

BRIAN WILLIAMS 23 6-2 195   Bats R Throws R
Can really bring it . . . Made it to four levels of play last season . . . Started at Osceola (A) and was 6-4 with 2.91 ERA in 15 starts . . . Promoted to Jackson (AA), where he went 2-1 with 4.20 ERA . . . Went up to Tucson (AAA), where he was 0-1 with 4.93 ERA . . . Started two games for Astros and finished 0-1, 3.75 . . . Selected by Astros as compensation pick following first round of 1990 draft . . . Born Feb. 15, 1969, in Lancaster, S.C. . . . Starred for University of South Carolina for three years as pitcher and outfielder.

CHRIS GARDNER 23 6-0 175   Bats R Throws R
Another strong young arm . . . Posted 1-2 record with 4.01 ERA

in four starts with Astros . . . Struck out 12 in 24⅔ innings, but walked 14 . . . For Jackson (AA), he was 13-5 with 3.15 ERA, ranking second in Texas League in wins and ERA . . . Picked by Astros in sixth round of 1988 draft . . . Born March 30, 1969, in Long Beach, Cal. . . . Despite 5-10 record in Asheville in 1990, his ERA was a respectable 2.62.

EDDIE TAUBENSEE 23 6-4 205   **Bats L Throws R**
Catcher came from Indians in December with Willie Blair for Kenny Lofton and Dave Rohde . . . Hit .242 in 66 at-bats with Tribe in '91 . . . Batted .310 with 13 home runs and 39 RBI in 91 games for Colorado Springs (AAA) . . . Reds' sixth-round selection in 1986 draft . . . Born Oct. 31, 1968, in Beeville, Tex.

MANAGER ART HOWE: Likable leader was the most patient manager in baseball last season . . . Had to be more like a Boy Scout troop leader than a manager . . . How young was his team? Astros had a Family Day game, but didn't have enough sons and daughters to compete against the players . . . If not for last-day victory against Braves, 65-97 Astros would have finished with most losses in franchise's history . . . Through it all, he kept his sense of humor . . . Born Dec. 15, 1946, in Pittsburgh . . . Played on Astros' 1980 division champions . . . Came up with Pirates, but was traded to Tommy Helms in 1976 . . . The 10th manager in Houston history . . . This is his 22nd season in pro ball . . . Played baseball and football at University of Wyoming, but his football career ended with a back injury . . . Graduated with degree in business administration . . . Was a computer programmer when he attended Pirates' tryout camp . . . Served as coach for Rangers and gained managerial experience in Puerto Rican League during winters . . . Owns 226-260 major-league managerial record.

ALL-TIME ASTRO SEASON RECORDS

BATTING: Rusty Staub, .333, 1967
HRs: Jimmy Wynn, 37, 1967
RBI: Bob Watson, 110, 1977
STEALS: Gerald Young, 65, 1988
WINS: Joe Niekro, 21, 1979
STRIKEOUTS: J. R. Richard, 313, 1979

LOS ANGELES DODGERS

TEAM DIRECTORY: Pres.: Peter O'Malley; Exec. VP-Player Pers.: Fred Claire; VP-Marketing: Barry Stockhammer; VP-Communications: Tommy Hawkins; Dir. Minor League Oper.: Charlie Blaney; Dir. Scouting: Terry Reynolds; Publicity Dir.: Jay Lucas; Trav. Sec.: Billy DeLury; Mgr.: Tom Lasorda. Home: Dodger Stadium (56,000). Field distances: 330, l.f. line; 370, l.c.; 395, c.f.; 370, r.c.; 330, r.f. line. Spring training: Vero Beach, Fla.

SCOUTING REPORT

HITTING: One year after Darryl Strawberry (.265, 28, 99) celebrated his Los Angeles homecoming, it's Eric Davis' turn to bring runs home for the Dodgers.

Davis (.235, 11, 33 with the Reds) is coming off the worst year of his career and has much to prove following his trade from Cincinnati. This left fielder has tremendous potential, but a brittle body. If he remains healthy, the Dodgers could have the most explosive outfield in the majors, because Brett Butler (.296, a league-leading 112 runs, 108 walks and 38 stolen bases) is the perfect table-setter.

However, Todd Benzinger (.262, 3, 51 with the Reds and Royals) and rookie Eric Karros (.316, 22, 101 for AAA Albuquerque) will have a hard time replacing Eddie Murray at first. Juan Samuel (.271, 12, 58, 23 steals) returns to compete with Lenny Harris (.287, 3, 38) at second.

PITCHING: The Dodgers posted the majors' lowest ERA at 3.06 in 1991, then traded Tim Belcher and lost Mike Morgan to free agency during the offseason. But they picked up free agent Tom Candiotti (13-13, 2.65 with the Indians and Blue Jays) and the knuckleballer has registered double figures in wins in five of the last six seasons.

Still, the Dodgers may be counting too much on miracle man Orel Hershiser (7-2, 3.46), following the right-hander's solid return from 1990 shoulder surgery. Ramon Martinez ran out of gas the second half of last season and finished with a 17-13 record and 3.27 ERA after a Cy Young start. Bobby Ojeda (12-9, 3.18) is the only left-handed starter. Kevin Gross (10-11, 3.58) started just 10 games last season, but will be needed in the 1992 rotation.

The bullpen will be by committee, with Roger McDowell (6-3, 2.55, 7 Sv as a Dodger in 1991) leading the way if Jay

Darryl, buoyed by boyhood buddy Eric Davis, should soar.

Howell (6-5, 3.18, 16 Sv) can't stay healthy. Add Jim Gott (4-3, 2.96), John Candelaria (1-1, 3.74), Tim Crews (2-3, 3.43, 6 Sv) and ex-Indian farmhand Rudy Seanez to the mix and you've got depth.

FIELDING: Getting Kal Daniels out of left field should bring a collective smile to the Dodger pitching staff. Davis, Butler and Strawberry offer the Dodgers one of the best defensive outfields in baseball, at least potentially, although Butler has weak arm. The Dodgers turned just 126 double plays in 1991 and only four teams had less. Shortstop Jose Offerman fell apart under the pressure of his rookie season, committing 10 errors in 50 games, but should settle down. Dave Hansen will be handed the third-base job. Catcher Mike Scioscia is the best there is at blocking the plate.

OUTLOOK: GM Fred Claire took a hatchet to a team that finished one game out of first with a 93-69 record. Davis has to have a big year for Claire's gambles to pay off. There are still too many ifs in this year of transition for Tommy Lasorda's club to win this difficult division.

LOS ANGELES DODGERS 1992 ROSTER

MANAGER Tom Lasorda
Coaches—Joe Amalfitano, Mark Cresse, Joe Ferguson, Ben Hines,
Manny Mota, Ron Perranoski

PITCHERS

No.	Name	1991 Club	W-L	IP	SO	ERA	B-T	Ht.	Wt.	Born
—	Astacio, Pedro	Vero Beach	5-3	59	45	1.67	R-R	6-2	174	11/28/69 Dominican Republic
		San Antonio	4-1	113	62	4.78				
54	Candelaria, John	Los Angeles	1-1	34	38	3.74	R-L	6-6	225	11/6/53 Brooklyn, NY
49	Candiotti, Tom	Clev.-Tor.	13-13	238	167	2.65	R-R	6-2	210	8/31/57 Walnut Creek, CA
52	Crews, Tim	Los Angeles	2-3	76	53	3.43	R-R	6-0	195	4/3/61 Tampa, FL
35	Gott, Jim	Los Angeles	4-3	76	73	2.96	R-R	6-4	220	8/3/59 Hollywood, CA
45	Gross, Kevin	Los Angeles	10-11	116	95	3.58	R-R	6-5	215	6/8/61 Downey, CA
—	Gross, Kip	Nashville	5-3	48	28	2.08	R-R	6-2	190	8/24/64 Scottsbluff, NE
		Cincinnati	6-4	86	40	3.47				
55	Hershiser, Orel	Los Angeles	7-2	112	73,	3.46	R-R	6-3	192.	9/16/58 Buffalo, NY
50	Howell, Jay	Los Angeles	6-5	51	40	3.18	R-R	6-3	220	11/26/55 Miami, FL
59	James, Mike	San Antonio	9-5	89	74	4.53	R-R	6-3	180	8/15/67 Ft. Walton, FL
		Albuquerque	1-3	45	39	6.60				
—	Martinez, Pedro	Bakersfield	8-0	61	83	2.05	R-R	5-11	152	7/25/71 Dominican Republic
		San Antonio	7-5	77	74	1.76				
		Albuquerque	3-3	39	35	3.66				
48	Martinez, Ramon	Los Angeles	17-13	220	150	3.27	R-R	6-5	171	3/22/68 Dominican Republic
—	McAndrew, Jamie	Albuquerque	12-10	155	91	5.04	R-R	6-2	190	9/2/67 Williamsport, PA
31	McDowell, Roger	Phil.-LA	9-9	101	50	2.93	R-R	6-1	182	12/21/60 Cincinnati, OH
17	Ojeda, Bob	Los Angeles	12-9	189	120	3.18	L-L	6-1	195	12/17/57 Los Angeles, CA
32	Seanez, Rudy	Colorado Springs	0-0	17	19	7.27	R-R	5-10	185	10/20/68 Brawley, CA
		Cleveland	0-0	5	7	16.20				
		Canton-Akron	4-2	38	73	2.58				
38	Wilson, Steve	Iowa	3-8	114	83	3.87	L-L	6-4	195	12/13/64 Canada
		Chi. (NL)-LA	0-0	21	14	2.61				

CATCHERS

No.	Name	1991 Club	H	HR	RBI	Pct.	B-T	Ht.	Wt.	Born
—	Baar, Bryan	San Antonio	78	10	51	.224	R-R	6-3	205	4/10/68 Zeeland, MI
41	Hernandez, Carlos	Albuquerque	119	8	44	.345	R-R	5-11	185	5/24/67 Venezuela
		Los Angeles	3	0	1	.214				
—	Piazza, Mike	Bakersfield	124	29	80	.277	R-R	6-3	200	9/4/68 Norristown, PA
14	Scioscia, Mike	Los Angeles	91	8	40	.264	L-R	6-2	220	11/27/58 Upper Darby, PA
—	Wakamatsu, Don	Chicago (AL)	7	0	0	.226	R-R	6-2	200	2/22/63 Hood River, OR
		Vancouver	34	4	19	.198				

INFIELDERS

No.	Name	1991 Club	H	HR	RBI	Pct.	B-T	Ht.	Wt.	Born
—	Benzinger, Todd	Cincinnati	23	1	11	.187	S-R	6-1	190	2/11/63 Dayton, KY
		Kansas City	86	2	40	.294				
3	Hamilton, Jeff	Albuquerque	0	0	0	.000	R-R	6-3	207	3/19/64 Flint, MI
		Los Angeles	21	1	14	.223				
43	Hansen, Dave	Albuquerque	77	5	40	.303	L-R	6-0	180	11/24/68 Long Beach, CA
		Los Angeles	15	1	5	.268				
29	Harris, Lenny	Los Angeles	123	3	38	.287	L-R	5-10	205	10/28/64 Miami, FL
23	Karros, Eric	Albuquerque	154	22	101	.316	R-R	6-4	205	11/4/67 Hackensack, NJ
		Los Angeles	1	0	1	.071				
30	Offerman, Jose	Albuquerque	86	0	29	.298	S-R	6-0	160	11/8/68 Dominican Republic
		Los Angeles	22	0	3	.195				
10	Samuel, Juan	Los Angeles	161	12	58	.271	R-R	5-11	170	12/9/60 Dominican Republic
27	Sharperson, Mike	Los Angeles	60	2	20	.278	R-R	6-3	190	10/4/61 Orangeburg, SC
21	Smith, Greg	Albuquerque	35	0	17	.217	S-R	5-11	170	4/5/67 Baltimore, MD
		Los Angeles	0	0	0	.000				
—	Young, Eric	San Antonio	129	3	35	.280	R-R	5-9	180	11/26/66 Jacksonville, FL
		Albuquerque	2	0	0	.400				

OUTFIELDERS

No.	Name	1991 Club	H	HR	RBI	Pct.	B-T	Ht.	Wt.	Born
—	Ashley, Billy	Vero Beach	52	7	42	.252	R-R	6-7	220	7/11/70 Taylor, MI
22	Butler, Brett	Los Angeles	182	2	38	.296	L-L	5-10	160	6/15/67 Los Angeles, CA
28	Daniels, Kal	Los Angeles	115	17	73	.249	L-R	6-0	205	8/20/63 Vienna, GA
—	Davis, Eric	Cincinnati	67	11	33	.235	R-R	6-3	185	5/29/62 Los Angeles, CA
47	Goodwin, Tom	Albuquerque	139	1	45	.273	L-R	6-1	165	7/27/68 Fresno, CA
		Los Angeles	1	0	0	.143				
5	Javier, Stan	Los Angeles	36	1	11	.205	S-R	6-0	185	1/9/64 Dominican Republic
—	Mondesi, Raul	Bakersfield	30	3	13	.283	R-R	5-11	150	3/12/71 Dominican Republic
		San Antonio	58	5	26	.272				
		Albuquerque	3	0	0	.333				
26	Rodriguez, Henry	Albuquerque	121	10	67	.271	L-L	6-1	180	11/8/67 Dominican Republic
44	Strawberry, Darryl	Los Angeles	134	28	99	.265	L-L	6-6	200	3/12/62 Los Angeles, CA

DODGER PROFILES

DARRYL STRAWBERRY 30 6-6 200 Bats L Throws L

After eight years of feeling unwanted in New York, he came home to Dodgers as promised, but couldn't lead them to Promised Land . . . Signed five-year, $20.25-million contract as free agent following 1990 season . . . Finished seventh in NL in homers (28) and ninth in RBI (99) . . . Despite the big numbers, right fielder could have done more . . . Shoulder injury limited first-half production . . . After the All-Star break, he hit .295 with 20 homers and 60 RBI . . . His 28 homers were the most by a Dodger since Pedro Guerrero hit 33 in 1985 and 99 RBI were most since Guerrero knocked in 103 in 1983 . . . Vulnerable to high, inside heat . . . That's why he struck out 125 times last season and has averaged 122 whiffs over the last six years . . . However, Mets never should have let him get away. Without Straw holding down the fourth spot, Mets' offense collapsed . . . Left New York as Mets' all-time leader in home runs (252), RBI (733), extra-base hits (469) and runs (662) . . . Born March 12, 1962, in Los Angeles . . . First player chosen in 1980 draft.

Year	Club	Pos.	G	AB	R	H	2B	3B	HR	RBI	SB	Avg.
1983	New York (NL)	OF	122	420	63	108	15	7	26	74	19	.257
1984	New York (NL)	OF	147	522	75	131	27	4	26	97	27	.251
1985	New York (NL)	OF	111	393	78	109	15	4	29	79	26	.277
1986	New York (NL)	OF	136	475	76	123	27	5	27	93	28	.259
1987	New York (NL)	OF	154	532	108	151	32	5	39	104	36	.284
1988	New York (NL)	OF	153	543	101	146	27	3	39	101	29	.269
1989	New York (NL)	OF	134	476	69	107	26	1	29	77	11	.225
1990	New York (NL)	OF	152	542	92	150	18	1	37	108	15	.277
1991	Los Angeles . . .	OF	139	505	86	134	22	4	28	99	10	.265
	Totals		1248	4408	748	1159	209	34	280	832	201	.263

BRETT BUTLER 34 5-10 160 Bats L Throws L

This little center fielder was most valuable Dodger last season . . . Led NL in walks (108) and runs (112) . . . Second in hits with 182 and sixth in stolen bases with 38 . . . Always finds a way to get on . . . Second in NL to Barry Bonds in on-base percentage at .401 . . . Put together longest hitting streak in the majors, 23 games from June 15 to July 12 . . . Should start a singles club as 162 of his 182 hits were singles, including 61 infield hits and 21 bunt singles . . . Had at least one hit in 121 of

161 games . . . In last two seasons, he has 353 hits . . . Giants never should have let him get away . . . Has more than 150 stolen bases in each league, only fourth player in history to accomplish feat. Others are Jose Cardenal, Bill North and Dave Collins . . . Signed three-year, $10-million contract as new-look free agent prior to 1991 season . . . Earned $2,833,333 last season . . . Born June 15, 1957, in Los Angeles . . . Signed by Giants as free agent after 1987 season . . . Atlanta's 23rd-round pick in 1979 draft.

Year	Club	Pos.	G	AB	R	H	2B	3B	HR	RBI	SB	Avg.
1981	Atlanta	OF	40	126	17	32	2	3	0	4	9	.254
1982	Atlanta	OF	89	240	35	52	2	0	0	7	21	.217
1983	Atlanta	OF	151	549	84	154	21	13	5	37	39	.281
1984	Cleveland	OF	159	602	108	162	25	9	3	49	52	.269
1985	Cleveland	OF	152	591	106	184	28	14	5	50	47	.311
1986	Cleveland	OF	161	587	92	163	17	14	4	51	32	.278
1987	Cleveland	OF	137	522	91	154	25	8	9	41	33	.295
1988	San Francisco	OF	157	568	109	163	27	9	6	43	43	.287
1989	San Francisco	OF	154	594	100	168	22	4	4	36	31	.283
1990	San Francisco	OF	160	622	108	192	20	9	3	44	51	.309
1991	Los Angeles	OF	161	615	112	182	13	5	2	38	38	.296
	Totals		1521	5616	962	1606	202	88	41	400	396	.286

KAL DANIELS 28 5-11 205   Bats L Throws R

Bad knees, bad defense in left and bad attitude . . . But he did play in 137 games, three short of his career high . . . Multi-talented hitter who knocked in six runs April 24 vs. Atlanta to match career high . . . One of the very best at going with the pitch . . . Nine of his 17 homers were to the opposite field . . . Production dropped in every major category . . . Average went from .296 to .249, three points shy of his career low . . . Went into season with .402 career on-base average, second only to Wade Boggs' .436 mark, but had .337 mark last season . . . Born Aug. 20, 1963, in Vienna, Ga. . . . Earned $2,025,000 last season . . . Reds sent him to Dodgers with Lenny Harris for Tim Leary and Mariano Duncan, July 18, 1989 . . . Selected by Reds in secondary phase of 1982 draft . . . If he put his mind to it, he could do so much more.

Year	Club	Pos.	G	AB	R	H	2B	3B	HR	RBI	SB	Avg.
1986	Cincinnati	OF	74	181	34	58	10	4	6	23	15	.320
1987	Cincinnati	OF	108	368	73	123	24	1	26	64	26	.334
1988	Cincinnati	OF	140	495	95	144	29	1	18	64	27	.291
1989	Cin.-LA	OF	55	171	33	42	13	0	4	17	9	.246
1990	Los Angeles	OF	130	450	81	133	23	1	27	94	4	.296
1991	Los Angeles	OF	137	461	54	115	15	1	17	73	6	.249
	Totals		644	2126	370	615	114	8	98	335	87	.289

ERIC DAVIS 29 6-3 185   Bats R Throws R

Reds became exasperated with center fielder's injury woes and $3.6-million salary last year and now he's a Dodger, following trade with Kip Gross for Tim Belcher and John Wetteland ...Battled physical problems all year and played in just 89 games...Led club in RBI with 86 in 1990, but totaled just 33 last year ...Home runs dipped from 24 in 1990 to 11 ...Batting average dropped 25 points, too...Spent two stints on disabled list...From June 12 to June 27, he was out with strained quadricep...Missed from July 31 to Aug. 26 because of fatigue and exhaustion...Said injuries were directly related to lacerated kidney suffered in 1990 World Series...Blasted two home runs against Cubs May 11, the 13th multiple homer game of his career...Reds' eighth-round selection in 1980 draft... Born May 29, 1962, in Los Angeles.

Year	Club	Pos.	G	AB	R	H	2B	3B	HR	RBI	SB	Avg.
1984	Cincinnati	OF	57	174	33	39	10	1	10	30	10	.224
1985	Cincinnati	OF	56	122	26	30	3	3	8	18	16	.246
1986	Cincinnati	OF	132	415	97	115	15	3	27	71	80	.277
1987	Cincinnati	OF	129	474	120	139	23	4	37	100	50	.293
1988	Cincinnati	OF	135	472	81	129	18	3	26	93	35	.273
1989	Cincinnati	OF	131	462	74	130	14	2	34	101	21	.281
1990	Cincinnati	OF	127	453	84	118	26	2	24	86	21	.260
1991	Cincinnati	OF	89	285	39	67	10	0	11	33	14	.235
	Totals		856	2857	554	767	119	18	177	532	247	.268

LENNY HARRIS 27 5-10 205   Bats L Throws R

Dodgers like his style and plan on making him the regular second baseman this season... Spent most of his time at third last season, playing 91 games there, nine at second and 12 at shortstop...Committed 20 errors, second-highest total on the team...Since joining the Dodgers in 1989, he has played all three out-field positions, too...Established career highs in games (145), home runs (three), RBI (38) and walks (37)...Hit solid .287...Blasted first career grand slam June 10 at Chicago ...Broke up Mark Gardner's no-hitter July 26 with an infield single in the 10th and scored only run of the game...Born Oct. 28, 1964, in Miami...Came over from Reds with Kal Daniels for Tim Leary and Mariano Duncan, July 18, 1989...Earned

$315,000 last season . . . Selected by Reds in fifth round of 1983 draft.

Year	Club	Pos.	G	AB	R	H	2B	3B	HR	RBI	SB	Avg.
1988	Cincinnati	3B–2B	16	43	7	16	1	0	0	8	4	.372
1989	Cin.-L.A.	2B–3B–OF-SS	115	335	36	79	10	1	3	26	14	.236
1990	Los Angeles . . .	3B–2B–OF-SS	137	431	61	131	16	4	2	29	15	.304
1991	Los Angeles . . .	3B–2B–SS-OF	145	429	59	123	16	1	3	38	12	.287
	Totals		413	1238	163	349	43	6	8	101	45	.282

MIKE SCIOSCIA 33 6-2 220   Bats L Throws R

Almost any base-runner in NL can tell you a horror story about having to slide into this brick wall at the plate . . . The best in the business of keeping runners away from the dish . . . Became the franchise's all-time leader in games caught June 8 at Chicago when he was behind the plate for his 1,219th game . . . Lots of games, but not many triples . . . Hit his first since '87 on April 21 against the Padres . . . Has nine triples for his career . . . Played in over 100 games the last eight years . . . His 91 hits last year represented first time in five years he did not reach 100 . . . Earned $2,183,333 last season . . . Dodgers' No. 1 selection in 1976 draft . . . Born Nov. 27, 1958, in Upper Darby, Pa.

Year	Club	Pos.	G	AB	R	H	2B	3B	HR	RBI	SB	Avg.
1980	Los Angeles . . .	C-3B	54	134	8	34	5	1	1	8	1	.254
1981	Los Angeles . . .	C	93	290	27	80	10	0	2	29	0	.276
1982	Los Angeles . . .	C	129	365	31	80	11	1	5	38	2	.219
1983	Los Angeles . . .	C	12	35	3	11	3	0	1	7	0	.314
1984	Los Angeles . . .	C	114	341	29	93	18	0	5	38	2	.273
1985	Los Angeles . . .	C	141	429	47	127	26	3	7	53	3	.296
1986	Los Angeles . . .	C	122	374	36	94	18	1	5	26	3	.251
1987	Los Angeles . . .	C	142	461	44	122	26	1	6	38	7	.265
1988	Los Angeles . . .	C	130	408	29	105	18	0	3	35	0	.257
1989	Los Angeles . . .	C	133	408	40	102	16	0	10	44	0	.250
1990	Los Angeles . . .	C	135	435	46	115	25	0	12	66	4	.264
1991	Los Angeles . . .	C	119	345	39	91	16	2	8	40	4	.264
	Totals		1324	4025	379	1054	192	9	65	422	26	.262

RAMON MARTINEZ 24 6-5 171   Bats R Throws R

Still glitters, but is no longer the top young pitching star in NL . . . Tailed off after July, going 2-7 following 15-6 start . . . Allowed two earned runs or less in 18 of 33 starts . . . Won seven straight from April 21 to May 22 . . . After posting 15-0 record against NL West clubs, he finally came up a loser April 16 against the Giants . . . Named to All-Star team second straight year, although he could not perform because of a hip injury . . . Suffered biceps injury Aug. 20 after being hit by a line drive . . . Posted 9-4 record with 2.91 ERA at Dodger Stadium . . . Posted fourth-highest win total in NL with 17 and had six complete games . . . Opponents hit just .229 against him . . . Four shutouts left him one short of NL leader Dennis Martinez . . . On June 4, 1990, he tied Sandy Koufax' all-time Dodger single-game strikeout record with 18 . . . In 1990, he also became youngest Dodger to win 20 since Ralph Branca won 21 at 21 in 1947 . . . Born March 22, 1968, in Santo Domingo, D.R. . . . Signed as free agent at 16 . . . Earned $485,000 last year.

Year	Club	G	IP	W	L	Pct.	SO	BB	H	ERA
1988	Los Angeles	9	35⅔	1	3	.250	23	22	27	3.79
1989	Los Angeles	15	98⅔	6	4	.600	89	41	79	3.19
1990	Los Angeles	33	234⅓	20	6	.769	223	67	191	2.92
1991	Los Angeles	33	220⅓	17	13	.567	150	69	190	3.27
	Totals	90	589	44	26	.629	485	199	487	3.15

TOM CANDIOTTI 34 6-2 210   Bats R Throws R

Dodgers filled gaping hole in rotation when they signed free-agent knuckleballer to four-year contract worth $15.5 million . . . Had given Blue Jays the consistency they sought when they acquired him and Turner Ward from Cleveland for Mark Whiten, Glenallen Hill and Denis Boucher June 27 . . . Placed second in AL with 2.65 ERA . . . Ranked eighth with 167 strikeouts and tied for eighth with 238 innings pitched . . . Limited opponents to .228 average . . . Labored seven innings or more in all but 10 starts . . . Has pitched more than 200 innings in six consecutive seasons . . . Was controversial choice to open ALCS and did not pitch well in two starts, going 0-1 with 8.22 ERA and yielding seven runs in 7⅔ innings . . . Makes heavy use of curve to complement knuckler . . . Born Aug. 31, 1957, in Walnut Creek, Cal. . . . Indians' free agent find earned $2.5 million in 1991.

Year	Club	G	IP	W	L	Pct.	SO	BB	H	ERA
1983	Milwaukee	10	55⅔	4	4	.500	21	16	62	3.23
1984	Milwaukee	8	32⅓	2	2	.500	23	10	38	5.29
1986	Cleveland	36	252⅓	16	12	.571	167	106	234	3.57
1987	Cleveland	32	201⅔	7	18	.280	111	93	193	4.78
1988	Cleveland	31	216⅔	14	8	.636	137	53	225	3.28
1989	Cleveland	31	206	13	10	.565	124	55	188	3.10
1990	Cleveland	31	202	15	11	.577	128	55	207	3.65
1991	Clev.-Tor.	34	238	13	13	.500	167	73	202	2.65
	Totals	213	1404⅔	84	78	.519	878	461	1349	3.51

Ramon Martinez has 37 wins in first two full seasons.

OREL HERSHISER 33 6-3 192   **Bats R Throws R**

His greatest triumph wasn't winning Cy Young award in 1988, it was coming back from revolutionary 1990 shoulder surgery . . . By end of year, radar gun clocked him at 90 mph . . . Wound up with 7-2 record and, as free agent, signed three-year contract worth $10 million . . . First four starts of the year were in the minors during rehab . . . First Dodger start was May 29 vs. Astros and progressed to become solid starter again, winning final six decisions . . . Gave up just one homer after Aug. 11 . . . From Aug. 11 to Sept. 16, he did not walk a batter over span of 34 innings . . . Allowed two earned runs or less in 11 of 21 starts . . . Earned $3,166,667 last season . . . Was named NLCS and World Series MVP in '88 . . . Born Sept. 16, 1958, in Buffalo, N.Y. . . . Dodgers' 17th-round selection in 1979 draft.

Year	Club	G	IP	W	L	Pct.	SO	BB	H	ERA
1983	Los Angeles.........	8	8	0	0	.000	5	6	7	3.38
1984	Los Angeles.........	45	189⅔	11	8	.579	150	50	160	2.66
1985	Los Angeles.........	36	239⅔	19	3	.864	157	68	179	2.03
1986	Los Angeles.........	35	231⅓	14	14	.500	153	86	213	3.85
1987	Los Angeles.........	37	264⅔	16	16	.500	190	74	247	3.06
1988	Los Angeles.........	35	267	23	8	.742	178	73	208	2.26
1989	Los Angeles.........	35	256⅔	15	15	.500	178	77	226	2.31
1990	Los Angeles.........	4	25⅓	1	1	.500	16	4	26	4.26
1991	Los Angeles.........	21	112	7	2	.778	73	32	112	3.46
	Totals............	256	1594⅓	106	67	.613	1100	470	1378	2.77

TOP PROSPECTS

ERIC KARROS 24 6-4 205   **Bats R Throws R**
Despite terrific minor-league numbers and late-season promotion, first baseman wonders if he'll ever get a chance to play every day for Dodgers, who have a habit of burying prospects . . . Batted .316 with 22 homers for Albuquerque (AAA) . . . Got 14 at-bats for Los Angeles and collected one hit . . . Batted .352 for San Antonio (AA) in 1990 to lead Texas League . . . Dodgers' sixth-round selection in 1988 draft . . . Born Nov. 4, 1967, in Hackensack, N.J. . . . Played at UCLA, where he earned All-American honors after joining the club as a walk-on.

PEDRO MARTINEZ 20 5-11 152   **Bats R Throws R**
Ramon's little brother played on three different levels last season, compiling an 8-0 mark and 2.05 ERA for Bakersfield (A), a 7-5

Brett Butler's on-base percentage (.401) was second in NL.

record with 1.76 ERA for San Antonio (AA), and a 3-3 record with 3.66 ERA for Albuquerque (AAA)... Named to Pioneer League All-Star team in 1990... Signed as a free agent in June 1988... Born July 25, 1971, in Manoguayabo, D.R.

CARLOS HERNANDEZ 24 5-11 185   Bats R Throws R
Figures to back up Mike Scioscia this season... Led PCL in hitting with .345 mark and had eight homers and 44 RBI for Albuquerque (AAA)... Given a look late last season, he got 14 at-bats and three hits with the Dodgers... Signed as free agent

in October 1984 . . . Born May 24, 1967, in San Felix Bolivar, Venezuela . . . Signed as an infielder and switched to catcher in 1986 . . . Won prep championship in javelin throw.

JAMIE McANDREW 24 6-2 190 **Bats R Throws R**
Son of former Met right-hander Jim McAndrew, he was 12-10 with a 5.04 ERA in 155⅓ innings for Albuquerque (AAA) . . . Named the organization's Minor League Pitcher of the Year in 1990 after posting 10-3 record with 2.27 ERA for Bakersfield (A) . . . Born Sept. 2, 1967, in Williamsport, Pa. . . . Dodgers' third-round selection in 1989 draft.

MANAGER TOM LASORDA: Greatest salesman in baseball, whether hawking Dodger Blue or weight-loss products . . . Covers both ends of the scale because he also markets own pasta sauce . . . Has won six division titles, three pennants and two World Series since replacing Walter Alston 15 years ago . . . Coming to the end of the line as manager because Bill Russell is being groomed to replace him . . . Managerial record is 1,276-1,100 . . . Despite Dodgers' 93-69 record in 1991, last season was bitter disappointment because of second-place finish, one game behind Braves . . . Not only bleeds Dodger Blue, he bleeds Dodger Green, too . . . This is his 43rd year on Dodger payroll . . . Had short-lived major-league career as left-handed pitcher (1954-55 with Dodgers and 1955 with Kansas City) . . . Appeared in 26 games and had 0-4 record . . . If you get to the park early enough, you can still catch him throwing batting practice . . . Born Sept. 22, 1927, in Norristown, Pa . . . Walking into his office at Dodgers Stadium is like walking onto the set of Lifestyles of the Rich and Famous.

ALL-TIME DODGER SEASON RECORDS

BATTING: Babe Herman, .393, 1930
HRs: Duke Snider, 43, 1956
RBI: Tommy Davis, 153, 1962
STEALS: Maury Wills, 104, 1962
WINS: Joe McGinnity, 29, 1900
STRIKEOUTS: Sandy Koufax, 382, 1965

SAN DIEGO PADRES

TEAM DIRECTORY: Chairman: Tom Werner; Vice Chairmen: Russell Goldsmith, Art Engel, Art Rivkin; Pres.: Dick Freeman; Exec. VP/GM: Joe McIlvaine; Dir. Minor Leagues: Ed Lynch; Dir. Scouting: Reggie Waller; Dir. Media Rel.: Jim Ferguson; Trav. Sec.: John Mattei; Mgr.: Greg Riddoch. Home: San Diego Jack Murphy Stadium (59,254). Field distances: 327, l.f. line; 405, c.f.; 327, r.f. line. Spring training: Yuma, Ariz.

SCOUTING REPORT

HITTING: Where would the Padres' offense be if not for Tony Gwynn (.317, 4, 62) and Fred McGriff (.278, 31, 106)? Despite their contributions last year, the Padres still finished 10th in the

No-fan-do Tony Gwynn is eying fifth batting title.

league with a .244 average. GM Joe McIlvaine, who has traded two of the best table-setters in baseball in Roberto Alomar and Bip Roberts the last two winters, is gambling his team will score enough runs.

Benito Santiago (.267, 17, 87) had the best RBI year of his career. Darren Jackson (.262, 21, 49) surprised everyone, but he will have to prove that last year wasn't a fluke. McGriff will need protection in the five spot, because opposing pitchers got wise last year and walked him 105 times. Tony Fernandez (.272, 4, 38) will be moved to leadoff to take Roberts' place. The loss of Roberts also hurts the team's speed, considering the Padres finished 10th in stolen bases with his 26.

PITCHING: The Padres hope to make up for their hitting short-comings on the mound. They finished fifth in ERA with a 3.57 mark, but made opponents homer happy for the second straight year. The Padres gave up the most homers in 1990 (147) and the second-most last season (139).

The Padres are counting on Andy Benes (15-11, 3.03) to establish himself as the club's ace after Benes put together a terrific second half in 1991. Consistent Bruce Hurst (15-8, 3.29) has finished in double figures in victories for nine straight seasons. Breaking ball specialist Greg Harris overcame elbow problems and finished 9-5 with an impressive 2.23 ERA. Ed Whitson (4-6, 5.03) is coming off surgery to remove bone chips from his elbow. Young Ricky Bones (4-6, 4.83) fills out the rotation.

McIlvaine acquired his former stopper with the Mets, Randy Myers, to be the closer. Myers (6-13, 3.55, 6 Sv) shuttled between the bullpen and the rotation with the Reds in 1991 and suffered his most disappointing season in five years. The Padres are hoping Larry Andersen (3-4, 2.30 and a career-high 13 Sv) is over his neck problems and can work as Myers' setup man.

FIELDING: This club went from worst to fourth in fielding with a .982 percentage and committed the fewest number of errors in team history with 113. Fernandez solidified the shortstop slot, but Alomar was missed at second, where the Padres used six different players. McGriff gives the Padres their best defensive first baseman in years and Gwynn is a perennial Gold Glover in right. Fielding is not the Padres' problem.

OUTLOOK: Greg Riddoch's club overachieved last season to finish in third place with a 84-78 record. This year the division is too improved for the Padres to finish higher than that again.

SAN DIEGO PADRES 1992 ROSTER

MANAGER Greg Riddoch
Coaches—Bruce Kimm, Rob Picciolo, Merv Rettenmund, Mike Roarke, Jim Snyder

PITCHERS

No.	Name	1991 Club	W-L	IP	SO	ERA	B-T	Ht.	Wt.	Born
27	Andersen, Larry	San Diego	3-4	47	40	2.30	R-R	6-3	205	5/6/53 Portland, OR
40	Benes, Andy	San Diego	15-11	223	167	3.03	R-R	6-6	240	8/20/67 Evansville, IN
56	Bones, Ricky	Las Vegas	8-6	136	95	4.22	R-R	6-0	190	4/7/69 Puerto Rico
		San Diego	4-6	54	31	4.83				
49	Brocail, Doug	Wichita	10-7	146	108	3.87	L-R	6-5	220	5/16/67 Clearfield, PA
46	Harris, Greg	San Diego	9-5	133	95	2.23	R-R	6-2	187	12/1/63 Greensboro, NC
		Las Vegas	1-2	21	16	7.40				
50	Hernandez, Jeremy	Las Vegas	4-8	68	67	4.74	R-R	6-5	195	7/6/66 Burbank, CA
		San Diego	0-0	14	9	0.00				
47	Hurst, Bruce	San Diego	15-8	222	141	3.29	L-L	6-3	215	3/24/58 St. George, UT
11	Lefferts, Craig	San Diego	1-6	69	48	3.91	L-L	6-1	210	9/29/57 West Germany
39	Lewis, Jim	Wichita	0-0	3	3	0.00	R-R	6-2	215	7/20/64 Jackson, MI
		Las Vegas	6-3	85	76	3.38				
		San Diego	0-0	13	10	4.15				
37	Linskey, Mike	Hagerstown	6-5	107	71	4.46	L-L	6-5	220	6/18/66 Baltimore, MD
		Rochester	1-5	41	25	7.24				
51	Maddux, Mike	San Diego	7-2	99	57	2.46	L-R	6-2	190	8/27/61 Dayton, OH
48	Melendez, Jose	Las Vegas	7-0	59	45	3.99	R-R	6-2	175	9/2/65 Puerto Rico
		San Diego	8-5	94	60	3.27				
28	Myers, Randy	Cincinnati	6-13	132	108	3.55	L-L	6-1	208	9/19/62 Vancouver, WA
32	Peterson, Adam	Las Vegas	2-2	42	37	4.50	R-R	6-3	190	12/11/65 Long Beach, CA
		San Diego	3-4	55	37	4.45				
42	Rodriguez, Rich	San Diego	3-1	80	40	3.26	R-L	6-0	200	3/1/63 Downey, CA
44	Seminara, Frank	Wichita	15-10	176	107	3.38	R-R	6-2	195	5/16/67 Brooklyn, NY
35	Valdez, Rafael	Las Vegas	0-2	17	9	5.94	R-R	5-11	185	12/17/68 Dominican Republic
31	Whitson, Ed	San Diego	4-6	79	40	5.03	R-R	6-3	200	5/19/55 Johnson City, TN

CATCHERS

No.	Name	1991 Club	H	HR	RBI	Pct.	B-T	Ht.	Wt.	Born
7	Bilardello, Dann	Las Vegas	44	4	29	.314	R-R	6-0	190	5/26/59 Santa Cruz, CA
		San Diego	7	0	5	.269				
25	Lampkin, Tom	San Diego	11	0	3	.190	L-R	5-11	185	3/4/64 Cincinnati, OH
		Las Vegas	52	2	29	.317				
09	Santiago, Benito	San Diego	155	17	87	.267	R-R	6-1	185	3/9/65 Puerto Rico

INFIELDERS

No.	Name	1991 Club	H	HR	RBI	Pct.	B-T	Ht.	Wt.	Born
23	Faries, Paul	San Diego	23	0	7	.177	R-R	5-10	170	2/20/65 Berkeley, CA
		High Desert	13	0	5	.310				
		Las Vegas	23	1	12	.307				
1	Fernandez, Tony	San Diego	152	4	38	.272	S-R	6-2	175	6/30/62 Dominican Republic
—	Gardner, Jeff	Tidewater	147	1	56	.292	L-R	5-11	165	2/4/64 Newport Beach, CA
		New York (NL)	6	0	1	.162				
53	Holbert, Ray	High Desert	102	4	51	.264	R-R	6-0	170	9/25/70 Torrance, CA
14	Lopez, Luis	Wichita	121	1	41	.268	S-R	5-11	175	9/4/70 Puerto Rico
29	McGriff, Fred	San Diego	147	31	106	.278	L-L	6-3	215	10/31/63 Tampa, FL
—	Redington, Tom	Wichita	112	5	57	.284	R-R	6-1	200	2/13/69 Fullerton, CA
18	Shipley, Craig	Las Vegas	69	5	34	.300	R-R	6-1	185	1/7/63 Australia
		San Diego	21	1	6	.275				
—	Staton, Dave	Las Vegas	100	22	74	.267	R-R	6-5	215	4/12/68 Seattle, WA
—	Teufel, Tim	NY (NL)-SD	74	12	44	.217	R-R	6-0	175	7/7/58 Greenwich, CT
8	Valentin, Jose	Wichita	112	17	68	.251	S-R	5-10	175	10/12/69 Puerto Rico
15	Velasquez, Guillermo	Wichita	148	21	100	.295	L-R	6-3	220	4/23/68 Mexico

OUTFIELDERS

No.	Name	1991 Club	H	HR	RBI	Pct.	B-T	Ht.	Wt.	Born
22	Azocar, Oscar	Las Vegas	107	7	50	.296	L-L	6-1	195	2/21/65 Venezuela
		San Diego	14	0	9	.246				
24	Clark, Jerald	San Diego	84	10	47	.228	R-R	6-4	205	8/10/63 Crockett, TX
19	Gwynn, Tony	San Diego	168	4	62	.317	L-L	5-11	215	5/9/60 Los Angeles, CA
33	Howard, Thomas	San Diego	70	4	22	.249	S-R	6-2	205	12/11/64 Middletown, OH
		Las Vegas	29	2	16	.309				
4	Jackson, Darrin	San Diego	94	21	49	.262	R-R	6-0	187	8/22/63 Los Angeles, CA
57	Taylor, Will	Las Vegas	121	4	33	.259	R-R	6-2	170	8/19/68 Alexandria, LA
2	Vatcher, Jim	Las Vegas	105	17	67	.266	R-R	5-9	175	5/27/66 Santa Monica, CA
		San Diego	4	0	2	.200				

PADRE PROFILES

FRED McGRIFF 28 6-3 215   Bats L Throws L

Has a Will Clark-type swing . . . First baseman was acquired from Blue Jays with Tony Fernandez for Joe Carter and Roberto Alomar in blockbuster prior to 1991 season . . . Led Padres in homers with 31, tying for fourth in NL . . . Blasted the most homers by a Padre since Dave Winfield (34 in 1979) . . . Yanks' ninth-round pick in 1981 is starting to drill left-handers . . . Fourteen of his homers were hit off lefties in 1991 after he came into the season having hit just 19 of 125 career homers off left-handers . . . Drove in a career-best 106 runs, fourth-best mark in the NL . . . Earned $2,750,000 last season . . . Born Oct. 31, 1963, in Tampa . . . Hit two grand slams in 1991 . . . Ranked third in NL with 105 walks because of lack of protection in fifth spot . . . Platooned with Cecil Fielder as Toronto's DH in 1987. Considering the two sluggers had total of 75 homers last season, that's a lot of power the Blue Jays let get away.

Year	Club	Pos.	G	AB	R	H	2B	3B	HR	RBI	SB	Avg.
1986	Toronto	1B	3	5	1	1	0	0	0	0	0	.200
1987	Toronto	1B	107	295	58	73	16	0	20	43	3	.247
1988	Toronto	1B	154	536	100	151	35	4	34	82	6	.282
1989	Toronto	1B	161	551	98	148	27	3	36	92	7	.269
1990	Toronto	1B	153	557	91	167	21	1	35	88	5	.300
1991	San Diego	1B	153	528	84	147	19	1	31	106	4	.278
	Totals		731	2472	432	687	118	9	156	411	25	.278

TONY GWYNN 31 5-11 215   Bats L Throws L

Finished third in NL batting race at .317 and probably would have won fifth batting crown if not for knee problems the second half . . . Hit .358 with 48 RBI in first half, but slumped to .243 with just 14 RBI after the All-Star break . . . Right fielder underwent arthroscopic surgery on knee Sept. 18 and missed rest of the season . . . Born May 9, 1960, in Los Angeles . . . Brother Chris plays for Dodgers . . . Earned $2,350,000 in 1991 . . . Hit .380 with runners in scoring position . . . Once again, he was hardest batter in the majors to strike out with one K every 29.9 at-bats . . . Has revolutionized the use of videotape as batting tool . . . Uses the smallest bat in the majors and calls it his peashooter . . . Third-round pick in 1981 draft, out of San Diego State, where he starred in basketball . . . Sports fantasy is to beat Danny Ainge in one-on-one game . . . Won fifth Gold Glove in last six years.

Year	Club	Pos.	G	AB	R	H	2B	3B	HR	RBI	SB	Avg.
1982	San Diego	OF	54	190	33	55	12	2	1	17	8	.289
1983	San Diego	OF	86	304	34	94	12	2	1	37	7	.309
1984	San Diego	OF	158	606	88	213	21	10	5	71	33	.351
1985	San Diego	OF	154	622	90	197	29	5	6	46	14	.317
1986	San Diego	OF	160	642	107	211	33	7	14	59	37	.329
1987	San Diego	OF	157	589	119	218	36	13	7	54	56	.370
1988	San Diego	OF	133	521	64	163	22	5	7	70	26	.313
1989	San Diego	OF	158	604	82	203	27	7	4	62	40	.336
1990	San Diego	OF	141	573	79	177	29	10	4	72	17	.309
1991	San Diego	OF	134	530	69	168	27	11	4	62	8	.317
	Totals		1335	5181	765	1699	248	72	53	550	246	.328

TONY FERNANDEZ 29 6-2 175   Bats S Throws R

One of the game's top shortstops, he landed in San Diego in deal that also brought Fred McGriff from Toronto for Roberto Alomar and Joe Carter prior to 1991 . . . First season in NL was a difficult one . . . After committing just nine errors in 1990, he made a career-high 20 last season . . . Claimed there is a depth perception problem that makes it difficult to pick up the ball off the bat at Jack Murphy Stadium . . . Born June 30, 1962, in San Pedro de Macoris, D.R. . . . Because of his poverty as a youngster, he often used cardboard cut-out gloves made by his brother . . . That's probably the reason he has such soft hands . . . Plagued by injury problems last season and underwent hand surgery the day after the season . . . Dropped in nearly every major offensive category from 1990 . . . Extremely sensitive individual . . . Originally signed as free agent by Blue Jays in 1979 . . . Earned $2,100,000 in 1991.

Year	Club	Pos.	G	AB	R	H	2B	3B	HR	RBI	SB	Avg.
1983	Toronto	SS	15	34	5	9	1	1	0	2	0	.265
1984	Toronto	SS-3B	88	233	29	63	5	3	3	19	5	.270
1985	Toronto	SS	161	564	71	163	31	10	2	51	13	.289
1986	Toronto	SS	163	687	91	213	33	9	10	65	25	.310
1987	Toronto	SS	146	578	90	186	29	8	5	67	32	.322
1988	Toronto	SS	154	648	76	186	41	4	5	70	15	.287
1989	Toronto	SS	140	573	64	147	25	9	11	64	22	.257
1990	Toronto	SS	161	635	84	175	27	17	4	66	26	.276
1991	San Diego	SS	145	558	81	152	27	5	4	38	23	.272
	Totals		1173	4510	591	1294	219	66	44	442	161	.287

BENITO SANTIAGO 27 6-1 185   Bats R Throws R

Catcher figures to have huge season in 1992, because he is a free agent after this year... Embroiled in contract problems throughout most of his career... Insists he should be paid Will Clark-type numbers because he is the best at his position... Earned $1,650,000 last season... Backed up boasting by amassing career-high 87 RBI last season, at least 41 more RBI than any other NL catcher... Possesses laser arm and threw out 35 percent of would-be base-stealers, including 42 percent from his knees... Born March 9, 1965, in Ponce, P.R.... Signed as a free agent in 1982... Tied Tony Gwynn's club record with five hits in a game, Sept. 13 in San Francisco... Hit .331 in the final 40 games with 36 RBI... One of the more misunderstood players in the majors... Three-time All-Star catcher yearns to play in major media market like Los Angeles or New York... Padres may not know what they had until he's gone.

Year	Club	Pos.	G	AB	R	H	2B	3B	HR	RBI	SB	Avg.
1986	San Diego	C	17	62	10	18	2	0	3	6	0	.290
1987	San Diego	C	146	546	64	164	33	2	18	79	21	.300
1988	San Diego	C	139	492	49	122	22	2	10	46	15	.248
1989	San Diego	C	129	462	50	109	16	3	16	62	11	.236
1990	San Diego	C	100	344	42	93	8	5	11	53	5	.270
1991	San Diego	C-OF	152	580	60	155	22	3	17	87	8	.267
	Totals		683	2486	275	661	103	15	75	333	60	.266

DARRIN JACKSON 28 6-0 187   Bats R Throws R

One of the year's biggest surprises... After four years of wallowing on bench for Cubs and Padres, he broke into starting lineup in June, after Shawn Abner had flunked center field tryout... Showed amazing power, cracking homer every 17.1 at-bats and finishing season with 21... Had just 13 career homers coming into the year and was averaging a homer every 37.5 at-bats... Had only 487 career at-bats coming into 1991... Only NL center fielder to hit more home runs was Atlanta's Ron Gant... One of the best bargains in baseball, he earned $260,000 in 1991... Acquired with Calvin Schiraldi and Phil Stephenson from the Cubs for Luis Salazar and Marvell Wynne during 1989 season... Born Aug. 22, 1963, in Los Angeles... Has beaten testicular cancer to make it to the majors... Hit 23 homers for

Iowa (AAA) in 1987 . . . Cubs chose him in second round of 1981 draft.

Year	Club	Pos.	G	AB	R	H	2B	3B	HR	RBI	SB	Avg.
1985	Chicago (NL) . .	OF	5	11	0	1	0	0	0	0	0	.091
1987	Chicago (NL) . .	OF	7	5	2	4	1	0	0	0	0	.800
1988	Chicago (NL) . .	OF	100	188	29	50	11	3	6	20	4	.266
1989	Chi. (NL)-S.D.	OF	70	170	17	37	7	0	4	20	1	.218
1990	San Diego	OF	58	113	10	29	3	0	3	9	3	.257
1991	San Diego	OF	122	359	51	94	12	1	21	49	5	.262
	Totals		362	846	109	215	34	4	34	98	13	.254

GREG HARRIS 28 6-2 187   Bats R Throws R

Possesses soap-opera star good looks and one of the nastiest curves in majors . . . That's why his ERA was 2.23 and opponents hit just .233 against him in 1991 . . . Shifted from bullpen to rotation last season, he paid the price early with elbow problems that forced him to miss two months . . . Still managed to win nine games and could be a big winner this season . . . Sat out from April 23-July 4 . . . Best streak came during 12-start period in August and September when he went 7-2 with 1.88 ERA . . . Included in that span were back-to-back 1-0 shutouts, the first time a Padre pitcher had accomplished that feat and the first time it has happened in the majors since Orel Hershiser did it in 1988 . . . Born Dec. 1, 1963, in Greensboro, N.C. . . . Selected in 10th round of the 1985 draft . . . Earned $1.3 million last season.

Year	Club	G	IP	W	L	Pct.	SO	BB	H	ERA
1988	San Diego	3	18	2	0	1.000	15	3	13	1.50
1989	San Diego	56	135	8	9	.471	106	52	106	2.60
1990	San Diego	73	117⅓	8	8	.500	97	49	92	2.30
1991	San Diego	20	133	9	5	.643	95	27	116	2.23
	Totals	152	403⅓	27	22	.551	313	131	327	2.34

ANDY BENES 24 6-6 240   Bats R Throws R

Came of age last season . . . Finally took a positive outlook and did not let his emotions get the best of him . . . After going 4-10 with a 4.18 ERA in his first 18 starts, he posted 11-1 mark in final 15 starts . . . Included in that span was a 10-game winning streak, longest in the NL since Dennis Martinez won 11 straight in 1989 and best by a Padre since both LaMarr Hoyt and Andy Hawkins won a club-record 11 in a row in 1985 . . . During the streak, his ERA was astounding 0.86 . . . Threw first career shutout Aug. 29, a 1-0, two-hit gem over the Cardinals... Was only Padre starter not to miss a turn... Had 20 starts in which he allowed two runs or less... Was sixth in NL with 167 strikeouts and was ninth was career-best 3.03 ERA... Also set a career high with 13 strikeouts vs. Cincinnati April 13... Born Aug. 20, 1967, in Evansville, Ind.... First player selected in 1988 draft, two slots ahead of Atlanta's Steve Avery... Earned $235,000 last season.

Year	Club	G	IP	W	L	Pct.	SO	BB	H	ERA
1989	San Diego	10	66⅔	6	3	.667	66	31	51	3.51
1990	San Diego	32	192⅓	10	11	.476	140	69	177	3.60
1991	San Diego	33	223	15	11	.577	167	59	194	3.03
	Totals	75	482	31	25	.554	373	159	422	3.32

LARRY ANDERSEN 38 6-3 205   Bats R Throws R

Relief ace is one of the free spirits in the majors ... Played pivotal role with Padres last season, even though he was hurt most of the year and had two stints on the disabled list... Recorded a career-high 13 saves despite disc problems in his neck that forced him to pitch in pain all year ... Suffered injury of the year in July... Pulled muscle in his chest while walking into his jacuzzi and called it a "jacuzzi-tusion"... His constant joking put teammates in positive mood after bitter 1990 season... Earned $2,000,000 after signing as a free agent prior to 1991 season... Born May 6, 1953, in Portland, Ore.... Signed by Indians in 1971 as seventh-round draft selection... Has 47 career saves.

Year	Club	G	IP	W	L	Pct.	SO	BB	H	ERA
1975	Cleveland	3	6	0	0	.000	4	2	4	4.50
1977	Cleveland	11	14	0	1	.000	8	9	10	3.21
1979	Cleveland	8	17	0	0	.000	7	4	25	7.41
1981	Seattle	41	68	3	3	.500	40	18	57	2.65
1982	Seattle	40	79⅔	0	0	.000	32	23	100	5.99
1983	Philadelphia	17	26⅓	1	0	1.000	14	9	19	2.39
1984	Philadelphia	64	90⅔	3	7	.300	54	25	85	2.38
1985	Philadelphia	57	73	3	3	.500	50	26	78	4.32
1986	Phil.-Hou.	48	77⅓	2	1	.667	42	26	83	3.03
1987	Houston	67	101⅔	9	5	.643	94	41	5	3.45
1988	Houston	53	82⅔	2	4	.333	66	20	82	2.94
1989	Houston	60	87⅔	4	4	.500	85	24	63	1.54
1990	Houston	50	73⅔	5	2	.714	68	24	61	1.95
1990	Boston	15	22	0	0	.000	25	3	18	1.23
1991	San Diego	38	47	3	4	.429	40	13	39	2.30
	Totals	572	866⅔	35	34	.507	629	267	819	3.11

RANDY MYERS 29 6-1 208   Bats L Throws L

Padres sought a closer when they traded Bip Roberts and a minor leaguer to be named to the Reds for Myers in December . . . After he lost his closer's job to Rob Dibble, Reds had no idea how to use him last season . . . Pitched first half of the season out of the bullpen, then moved into starting rotation for most of second half . . . After 293 consecutive relief appearances and 93 saves, he made first major-league start July 23 at Chicago . . . Went 2-6 with 3.45 ERA in 12 starts and 4-7 with 3.65 ERA in 46 relief outings . . . Didn't get much help as a starter . . . Reds scored 11 runs in his six starts and six runs in his last five games . . . Control was a problem . . . Walked 80 in 132 innings . . . Scouts say he nibbles too much . . . Is 2-0 with four saves lifetime in postseason . . . Born Sept. 19, 1962, in Vancouver, Wash. . . . Mets' No. 1 pick in secondary phase of 1982 draft . . . Earned $2 million last year . . . Came to Reds for John Franco prior to the 1990 season . . . Saved total of 50 games for Mets in 1988 and 1989.

Year	Club	G	IP	W	L	Pct.	SO	BB	H	ERA
1985	New York (NL)	1	2	0	0	.000	2	1	0	0.00
1986	New York (NL)	10	10⅔	0	0	.000	13	9	11	4.22
1987	New York (NL)	54	75	3	6	.333	92	30	61	3.96
1988	New York (NL)	55	68	7	3	.700	69	17	45	1.72
1989	New York (NL)	65	84⅓	7	4	.636	88	40	62	2.35
1990	Cincinnati	66	86⅔	4	6	.400	98	38	59	2.08
1991	Cincinnati	58	132	6	13	.316	108	80	116	3.55
	Totals	309	458⅔	27	32	.458	470	215	354	2.85

BRUCE HURST 34 6-3 215   Bats L Throws L

Despite world of talent, he has never won 20 games . . . Finished badly, winning just one of his final eight starts . . . Did not pitch the last two weeks because of elbow tendinitis . . . Was having best season of his 12-year career, with 14-5 mark after 23 starts, then bottom fell out . . . Red Sox' first pick in 1976 draft, he recorded two wins in 1986 World Series . . . Born March 24, 1958, in St. George, Utah . . . Earned $1,883,334 in 1991 . . . Signed with Padres as free agent prior to 1989 . . . Had four complete games, but failed to record a shutout for the first time since 1982 . . . Has the best pickoff move in NL . . . Caught

six runners napping last season... Helps himself with the bunt
... Put down 12 sacrifices last season, fifth-best total in NL.

Year	Club	G	IP	W	L	Pct.	SO	BB	H	ERA
1980	Boston	12	31	2	2	.500	16	16	39	9.00
1981	Boston	5	23	2	0	1.000	11	12	23	4.30
1982	Boston	28	117	3	7	.300	53	40	161	5.77
1983	Boston	33	211⅓	12	12	.500	115	62	241	4.09
1984	Boston	33	218	12	12	.500	136	88	232	3.92
1985	Boston	35	229⅓	11	13	.458	189	70	243	4.51
1986	Boston	25	174⅓	13	8	.619	167	50	169	2.99
1987	Boston	33	238⅔	15	13	.536	190	76	239	4.41
1988	Boston	33	216⅔	18	6	.750	166	65	222	3.66
1989	San Diego	33	244⅓	15	11	.577	179	66	214	2.69
1990	San Diego	33	223⅔	11	9	.550	162	63	188	3.14
1991	San Diego	31	221⅔	15	8	.652	141	59	201	3.29
	Totals	334	2149⅓	129	101	.561	1525	667	2172	3.84

TOP PROSPECTS

JEREMY HERNANDEZ 25 6-5 195   **Bats R Throws R**
Could wind up sharing closer role with Padres... After September
promotion, he did not allow a run in 13⅓ innings and earned a
pair of saves... Got off to a rough start with Las Vegas (AAA)
and posted 4-8 record with 4.74 ERA and 13 saves... Struck out
67 in 68⅓ innings... Acquired from Cards for Randall Byers,
April 24, 1989... Born July 6, 1966, in Burbank, Cal.

RICKY BONES 22 6-0 190   **Bats R Throws R**
Made 11 late-season starts for Padres and was 4-6 with 4.83 ERA
... In his four victories, club averaged 9.75 runs... Was top
starter for Las Vegas (AAA) with 8-6 record and 4.22 ERA...
Born April 7, 1969, in Salinas, P.R.... Signed as a free agent
in May 1986... Has 53 31 mark over the last five years in the
minors... In contention for the fifth spot in the rotation.

DAVE STATON 23 6-5 215   **Bats R Throws R**
Needs to find a position where he won't hurt club defensively...
Switched from third to first last season at Las Vegas (AAA) and
made 23 errors... No problems offensively... Bashed 22 ho-
mers, tying for third in PCL... His 74 RBI led club... Born
April 12, 1968, in Seattle... Selected in fifth round of 1989 draft.

FRANK SEMINARA 24 6-2 195   **Bats R Throws R**
Led Texas League with 15 wins in first year in Padres' organization
... Lost 10 games and finished sixth in league with 3.38 ERA for

Wichita (AA). . . In 1990, he was named Pitcher of the Year in Class A following 16-8 record with 1.90 ERA . . . Drafted out of Yankees organization prior to last season . . . Born May 16, 1967, in Brooklyn, N.Y. . . . Selected in 12th round of 1988 draft by the Yankees, out of Columbia University.

MATT MIESKE 24 6-0 185   **Bats R Throws R**
This outfield standout for High Desert (A) was named California League MVP and Rookie of the Year . . . Led the league in average (.341), runs (108) and hits (168) and finished second to teammate Jay Gainer in RBI with 119 . . . Born Feb. 13, 1968, in Midland, Mich. . . . Selected in 17th round of 1990 draft . . . Topped Northwest League with 63 RBI and 12 home runs and batted .340 in 1990.

MANAGER GREG RIDDOCH: Was on hot seat in first full  season as manager because he wasn't GM Joe McIlvaine's choice, but he survived because injury-riddled club finished third at 84-78 . . . Ripped by several former players as being two-faced, he will be under pressure to get off to a good start in 1992, because McIlvaine gave him only a one-year extension . . . Former school teacher is a great believer in pregame preparation . . . Took over the reins from Jack McKeon, July 11, 1990, and finished with a 33-48 mark after starting off 1-11 . . . Has 122-122 record overall as Padres manager . . . Former first-base coach had managed on no higher level than rookie ball before taking over for McKeon . . . Born July 17, 1945, in Greeley, Col. . . . Was classmate of comedian Steve Martin at Garden Grove High in California . . . Anything but a wild and crazy guy, he approaches the game on an intellectual level.

ALL-TIME PADRE SEASON RECORDS

BATTING: Tony Gwynn, .370, 1987
HRs: Nate Colbert, 38, 1970, 1972
RBI: Dave Winfield, 118, 1979
STEALS: Alan Wiggins, 70, 1984
WINS: Randy Jones, 22, 1976
STRIKEOUTS: Clay Kirby, 231, 1971

SAN FRANCISCO GIANTS

TEAM DIRECTORY: Chairman: Bob Lurie; Pres./GM: Al Rosen; Exec. VP-Adm.: Corey Busch; VP-Baseball Oper.: Bob Kennedy; Sr. VP-Business Oper.: Pat Gallagher; VP-Asst. GM: Ralph Nelson; VP-Scouting: Bob Fontaine; Dir. Media Rel.: Matt Fischer; Trav. Sec.: Dirk Smith; Mgr.: Roger Craig. Home: Candlestick Park (58,000). Field distances: 335, l.f. line; 365, l.c.; 400, c.f.; 365, l.c.; 335, r.f. line. Spring training: Scottsdale, Ariz.

Will Clark has averaged 27 HRs and 104 RBI since '87.

SCOUTING REPORT

HITTING: The Giants got rid of a huge headache when they traded Kevin Mitchell to the Mariners, but they also lost some nuclear offense. Mitchell has hit a major league-high 109 homers the last three years. The trade broke up the fearsome threesome of Mitchell, Matt Williams and Will Clark, who combined for 90 homers last season.

While Clark (.301, 29, 116) remains the best hitter in baseball, Williams has become one of the most dangerous. The third baseman figures to do even better than last season, when he posted a .268 average, 34 homers and 98 RBI. Willie McGee (.312, 4, 43) could not make up for the loss of sparkplug Brett Butler in 1991. McGee, a much better player on artificial turf than grass, scored 45 less runs than Butler did for the Dodgers. Second baseman Robby Thompson gives the Giants one more clutch bat. Last season, he hit .313 after the sixth inning.

PITCHING: The Giants shelled out $10 million to Buddy Black prior to last season, hoping he could heal the staff infection that has plagued the rotation for years. Black led the NL in losses with a career-high 16, but did post 12 victories. The Giants tied the woeful Cubs for the NL's worst ERA at 4.03.

That's why Mitchell was sacrificed to Seattle for right-handers Bill Swift (1-2, 1.99, 17 Sv), Mike Jackson (7-7, 3.25, 14 Sv) and Dave Burba (2-2, 3.68). Opponents hit just .201 against Jackson. Swift will be in the Giants' rotation, along with Trevor Wilson (13-11, 3.56) and John Burkett (12-11, 4.18). Dave Righetti (2-7, 3.39, 24 Sv) and Jeff Brantley (5-2, 2.45, 15 Sv) will have help from Jackson in the pen.

FIELDING: Once again, this should be one of the Giants' strongest areas. They tied the Cardinals for the NL lead with a .982 fielding percentage in 1991. The best defensive infield in the NL is anchored by Clark, whose .997 fielding percentage led NL first basemen, as did his 115 double plays. Young shortstop Royce Clayton is the jewel of the Giants' system, but is he ready? Speedy Mike Felder will do better than Mitchell with the glove in left.

OUTLOOK: What's more valuable pitching or hitting? After suffering through a fourth-place, 75-87 finish, manager and former pitcher Roger Craig opted for more arms. Considering his Giants still have plenty of firepower, this team might surprise if the additions make a successful transition to a new league.

SAN FRANCISCO GIANTS 1992 ROSTER

MANAGER Roger Craig
Coaches—Carlos Alfonso, Dusty Baker, Bob Brenly, Wendell Kim, Bob Lillis

PITCHERS

No.	Name	1991 Club	W-L	IP	SO	ERA	B-T	Ht.	Wt.	Born
55	Ard, Johnny	Phoenix	3-5	62	30	5.78	R-R	6-5	220	6/1/67 Las Vegas, NV
		Shreveport	9-3	89	58	2.74				
47	Beck, Rod	Phoenix	4-3	71	35	2.02	R-R	6-1	215	8/3/68 Burbank, CA
		San Francisco	1-1	52	38	3.78				
40	Black, Bud	San Francisco	12-16	214	104	3.99	L-L	6-2	185	6/30/57 San Mateo, CA
49	Brantley, Jeff	San Francisco	5-2	95	81	2.45	R-R	5-11	180	9/5/63 Florence, AL
—	Burba, Dave	Calgary	6-4	71	42	3.53	R-R	6-4	220	7/7/66 Dayton, OH
		Seattle	2-2	37	16	3.68				
33	Burkett, John	San Francisco	12-11	207	131	4.18	R-R	6-3	205	11/28/64 New Brighton, PA
37	Downs, Kelly	San Francisco	10-4	112	62	4.19	R-R	6-4	205	10/25/60 Ogden, UT
50	Garrelts, Scott	San Francisco	1-1	20	8	6.41	R-R	6-4	210	10/30/61 Urbana, IL
53	Gunderson, Eric	San Francisco	0-0	3	2	5.40	L-L	6-0	175	3/29/66 Portland, OR
		Phoenix	7-6	107	53	6.14				
60	Hancock, Chris	San Jose	4-3	53	59	2.03	L-L	6-3	175	9/12/69 Lynwood, CA
36	Heredia, Gil	Phoenix	9-11	140	75	2.82	R-R	6-1	190	10/26/65 Nogales, AZ
		San Francisco	0-2	33	13	3.82				
41	Hickerson, Bryan	Shreveport	3-4	39	41	3.00	R-R	6-2	195	10/13/63 Bemidji, MN
		Phoenix	1-1	21	21	3.80				
		San Francisco	2-2	50	43	3.60				
—	Jackson, Mike	Seattle	7-7	89	74	3.25	R-R	6-0	200	12/22/64 Houston, TX
52	Masters, Dave	Indianapolis	4-6	70	64	6.04	R-R	6-9	225	8/13/64 San Diego, CA
		Phoenix	1-2	31	28	6.46				
48	McClellan, Paul	Shreveport	11-1	96	63	2.82	R-R	6-2	180	2/8/66 San Mateo, CA
		Phoenix	2-2	38	18	2.82				
		San Francisco	3-6	71	44	4.56				
54	Myers, Jim	Shreveport	6-4	76	51	2.48	R-R	6-1	185	4/28/69 Oklahoma City, OK
45	Oliveras, Francisco	Phoenix	2-0	18	12	2.45	R-R	5-10	180	1/31/63 Puerto Rico
		San Francisco	6-6	79	48	3.86				
19	Righetti, Dave	San Francisco	2-7	72	51	3.39	L-L	6-4	212	11/28/58 San Jose, CA
58	Rogers, Kevin	Shreveport	4-6	118	108	3.36	S-L	6-1	190	8/20/68 Cleveland, MS
—	Swift, Bill	Seattle	1-2	90	48	1.99	R-R	6-0	180	10/27/61 Portland, ME
32	Wilson, Trevor	San Francisco	13-11	202	139	3.56	L-L	6-0	195	6/7/66 Torrance, CA

CATCHERS

No.	Name	1991 Club	H	HR	RBI	Pct.	B-T	Ht.	Wt.	Born
35	Decker, Steve	San Francisco	48	5	24	.206	R-R	6-3	205	10/25/65 Rock Island, IL
		Phoenix	28	6	14	.252				
8	Manwaring, Kirt	San Francisco	40	0	19	.225	R-R	5-11	190	7/15/65 Elmira, NY
		Phoenix	18	4	14	.222				
		San Jose	0	0	0	.000				

INFIELDERS

18	Benjamin, Mike	San Francisco	13	2	8	.123	R-R	6-2	175	11/22/65 Euclid, OH
		Phoenix	46	6	31	.204				
22	Clark, Will	San Francisco	170	29	116	.301	L-L	6-1	190	3/13/64 New Orleans, LA
21	Clayton, Royce	Shreveport	136	5	68	.280	R-R	6-0	175	1/2/70 Burbank, CA
		San Francisco	3	0	2	.115				
15	Litton, Greg	San Francisco	23	1	15	.181	R-R	6-0	190	7/13/64 New Orleans, LA
		Phoenix	11	4	9	.407				
59	Patterson, John	Shreveport	137	4	56	.295	S-R	5-9	160	2/11/67 Key West, FL
56	Santana, Andres	Phoenix	144	1	35	.316	S-R	5-11	150	3/19/68 Dominican Republic
6	Thompson, Robby	San Francisco	129	19	48	.262	R-R	5-11	170	5/10/62 West Palm Beach, FL
23	Uribe, Jose	San Francisco	51	1	12	.221	S-R	5-10	170	1/21/60 Dominican Republic
		San Jose	1	0	1	.111				
		Phoenix	14	0	4	.341				
9	Williams, Matt	San Francisco	158	34	98	.268	R-R	6-2	205	11/28/65 Bishop, CA

OUTFIELDERS

17	Bass, Kevin	San Francisco	84	10	40	.233	S-R	6-0	190	5/12/59 Redwood City, CA
		San Jose	2	0	1	.105				
		Phoenix	13	2	7	.317				
25	Felder, Mike	San Francisco	92	0	18	.264	S-R	5-8	160	11/18/62 Vallejo, CA
57	Hosey, Steve	Shreveport	120	17	74	.293	R-R	6-3	215	4/2/69 Oakland, CA
1	Leonard, Mark	San Francisco	31	2	14	.240	L-R	6-0	195	8/14/64 Mountain View, CA
		Phoenix	37	8	25	.253				
2	Lewis, Darren	Phoenix	107	2	52	.340	R-R	6-0	175	8/28/67 Berkeley, CA
		San Francisco	55	0	15	.248				
51	McGee, Willie	San Francisco	155	4	43	.312	S-R	6-1	195	11/2/58 San Francisco, CA
		Phoenix	5	0	1	.500				
39	Wood, Ted	Phoenix	159	11	109	.311	L-L	6-2	178	1/4/67 Mansfield, LA
		San Francisco	3	0	1	.120				

GIANT PROFILES

WILL CLARK 28 6-1 190   Bats L Throws L

"The Thrill" did it all for the Giants in '91, leading club in hits (170), runs (84), doubles (32), triples (seven) and RBI (116) . . . Fell one RBI short of matching Mets' Howard Johnson for NL lead . . . Ranked among NL leaders in slugging percentage (.536, first) total bases (303, tied for first), home runs (29, sixth), hits (tied for sixth) and average (.301, tied for eighth) . . . Hit .332 with men on base and .336 with runners in scoring position . . . Drove in seven runs at Philadelphia July 14, matching his career high . . . Also matched his career high with five hits in that game . . . Career-high RBI total marked third time in four years he has hit the century mark . . . His .997 fielding percentage led NL first baseman and he won Gold Glove . . . Batted .489 in 1989 NLCS with 11 RBI . . . Earned $3,750,000 last year . . . Born March 13, 1964, in New Orleans . . . Giants' first selection in 1985 draft, out of Mississippi State, and second player picked overall.

Year	Club	Pos.	G	AB	R	H	2B	3B	HR	RBI	SB	Avg.
1986	San Francisco	1B	111	408	66	117	27	2	11	41	4	.287
1987	San Francisco	1B	150	529	89	163	29	5	35	91	5	.308
1988	San Francisco	1B	162	575	102	162	31	6	29	109	9	.282
1989	San Francisco	1B	159	588	104	196	38	9	23	111	8	.333
1990	San Francisco	1B	154	600	91	177	25	5	19	95	8	.295
1991	San Francisco	1B	148	565	84	170	32	7	29	116	4	.301
	Totals		884	3265	536	985	182	34	146	563	38	.302

MATT WILLIAMS 26 6-2 205   Bats R Throws R

Best two-way third baseman in NL after just two complete seasons . . . Led team in games (157), at-bats (589) and home runs (34), which was second to NL leader Howard Johnson . . . Takes a big cut and paid the price with 128 strikeouts, the fourth-highest total in NL . . . Still tends to get into mechanical ruts at the plate . . . Hit just .199 with four homers and 19 RBI in first 39 games through May 22 . . . Was hitting .238 with 12 homers and 45 RBI at the All-Star break, then went on 10-for-17 tear with two doubles, a triple, four homers and eight RBI in first four games after break . . . Hot as a firecracker rest of July, compiling 11 homers, 21 RBI and .341 average . . . Drove in runs in 10 straight games from Aug. 27 until Sept. 6 . . . Homer output marked a career high and broke the S.F. record for a third baseman . . . Ranked fourth in fielding percentage (.964) among NL third basemen and led in games and putouts . . . Earned $600,000 and Gold Glove . . . Attended Nevada-Las Vegas and Giants made him third player taken overall in 1986 draft . . . Born Nov. 28, 1965, in Bishop, Cal.

Year	Club	Pos.	G	AB	R	H	2B	3B	HR	RBI	SB	Avg.
1987	San Francisco	SS-3B	84	245	28	46	9	2	8	21	4	.188
1988	San Francisco	3B-SS	52	156	17	32	6	1	8	19	0	.205
1989	San Francisco	3B-SS	84	292	31	59	18	1	18	50	1	.202
1990	San Francisco	3B	159	617	87	171	27	2	33	122	7	.277
1991	San Francisco	3B-SS	157	589	72	158	24	5	34	98	5	.268
	Totals		536	1899	235	466	84	11	101	310	17	.245

WILLIE McGEE 33 6-1 195   Bats S Throws R

Veteran center fielder put up excellent numbers, but it didn't make up for the loss of Brett Butler on free-agent market . . . Signed as free agent prior to last season and earned $3,562,500 . . . Batted .312, fourth-best mark in league . . . Won NL batting title in 1990 while in exile with .335 mark . . . Traded to A's by Cardinals for Felix Jose, Stan Royer and Daryl Green, Aug. 29, 1990, and helped Oakland win 1990 pennant but flopped in postseason with .210 average . . . Last season, he hit .339 with men on base and .343 with runners in scoring position . . . Uses his speed by putting the ball on ground . . . Hits nearly four grounders for every flyball . . . Moved to right Aug. 1 because of rib cage injury and so Darren Lewis could play center . . . Born Nov. 2, 1958, in San Francisco . . . Yanks' first-round pick in January 1977.

Year	Club	Pos.	G	AB	R	H	2B	3B	HR	RBI	SB	Avg.
1982	St. Louis	OF	123	422	43	125	12	8	4	56	24	.296
1983	St. Louis	OF	147	601	75	172	22	8	5	75	39	.286
1984	St. Louis	OF	145	571	82	166	19	11	6	50	43	.291
1985	St. Louis	OF	152	612	114	216	26	18	10	82	56	.353
1986	St. Louis	OF	124	497	65	127	22	7	7	48	19	.256
1987	St. Louis	OF-SS	153	620	76	177	37	11	11	105	16	.285
1988	St. Louis	OF	137	562	73	164	24	6	3	50	41	.292
1989	St. Louis	OF	58	199	23	47	10	2	3	17	8	.236
1990	St. Louis	OF	125	501	76	168	32	5	3	62	28	.335
1990	Oakland	OF	29	113	23	31	3	2	0	15	3	.274
1991	San Francisco	OF	131	497	67	155	30	3	4	43	17	.312
	Totals		1324	5195	717	1548	237	81	56	603	294	.298

ROBBY THOMPSON 30 5-11 170   Bats R Throws R

Giants tried to make something out of second baseman that he's not, a leadoff man . . . Led off first 18 games and batted .238 . . . Spent the rest of the season all over the order, batting everywhere but fourth and eighth . . . Hit .313 after the sixth inning . . . Led team with career-high 63 walks . . . Strikes out too much to be at top of order . . . Whiffed 95 times last season and has 638 Ks over six seasons . . . Set S.F. record for homers by a second baseman with 19, shattering Bill Madlock's mark of 15 in 1978 . . . Overcame back and hand injuries . . Bothered by cracked bone in hand that caused him to hit .167 in last 60 at-bats of the season . . . Birthday basher, he homered on his birthday, his wife's birthday and his daughter's birthday . . . Born May 10, 1962, in West Palm Beach, Fla. . . . Giants' first-round selection in secondary phase, out of the University of Florida . . . Earned $1.5 million last season.

Year	Club	Pos.	G	AB	R	H	2B	3B	HR	RBI	SB	Avg.
1986	San Francisco	2B-SS	149	549	73	149	27	3	7	47	12	.271
1987	San Francisco	2B	132	420	62	110	26	5	10	44	16	.262
1988	San Francisco	2B	138	477	66	126	24	6	7	48	14	.264
1989	San Francisco	2B	148	547	91	132	26	11	13	50	14	.241
1990	San Francisco	2B	144	498	67	122	22	3	15	56	14	.245
1991	San Francisco	2B	144	492	74	129	24	5	19	48	14	.262
	Totals		855	2983	433	768	149	33	71	293	82	.257

TREVOR WILSON 25 6-0 195   Bats L Throws L

Pacing Giant staff in wins (13) and strikeouts (139) . . . Recorded most wins by a Giant left-hander since Vida Blue rolled 14 in 1980 and most strikeouts by Giant pitcher since Mike Krukow fanned 178 in 1986 . . . Started the season in the pen, going 0-3 with a 4.79 ERA in 13 relief appearances before getting his first start May 12 vs. Mets . . . Quickly showed he was a starter, allowing one run in five innings vs. Mets and throwing eight shutout innings in next start . . . Was 4-9 with 4.22 ERA in 28 appearances (13 starts) through July 16, but went 9-6 over final 16 starts . . . Blasted first major-league home run July 25 at Candlestick off Mets' Wally Whitehurst . . . Hurled two-hit shutout to eliminate Dodgers Oct. 5 . . . Left-handers hit just .169 off him, lowest mark in NL . . . Earned $205,000 last season . . .

Eighth-round selection in 1985 draft . . . Born June 7, 1966, in Torrance, Cal.

Year	Club	G	IP	W	L	Pct.	SO	BB	H	ERA
1988	San Francisco	4	22	0	2	.000	15	8	25	4.09
1989	San Francisco	14	39⅓	2	3	.400	22	24	28	4.35
1990	San Francisco	27	110⅓	8	7	.533	66	49	87	4.00
1991	San Francisco	44	202	13	11	.542	139	77	173	3.56
	Totals.	89	373⅔	23	23	.500	242	158	313	3.81

BILL SWIFT 30 6-0 180   Bats R Throws R

Giants acquired him with Mike Jackson and Dave Burba in December trade that made Kevin Mitchell a Mariner . . . Sinkerballer emerged as Seattle save leader with 17, three more than Mike Jackson . . . Allowed only 100 base-runners (74 hits and 26 walks) in 90⅓ innings . . . Posted career-low 1.99 ERA . . . Career mark was 4.32 going into 1991 . . . Saved seven games in final six weeks . . . Role change caused innings total to drop to lowest in six seasons . . . Versatile right-hander can start or finish games . . . Earned $850,000 in 1991 . . . Member of 1984 U.S. Olympic team . . . Had spent entire career with Mariners . . . Second player selected in 1984 draft . . . Comes from family of 15 children . . . Born Oct. 27, 1961, in South Portland, Me.

Year	Club	G	IP	W	L	Pct.	SO	BB	H	ERA
1985	Seattle	23	120⅔	6	10	.375	55	48	131	4.77
1986	Seattle	29	115⅓	2	9	.182	55	55	148	5.46
1988	Seattle	38	174⅔	8	12	.400	47	65	199	4.59
1989	Seattle	37	130	7	3	.700	45	38	140	4.43
1990	Seattle	55	128	6	4	.600	42	21	135	2.39
1991	Seattle	71	90⅓	1	2	.333	48	26	74	1.99
	Totals.	253	759	30	40	.429	292	253	827	4.04

BUD BLACK 34 6-2 185   Bats L Throws L

Caused stir by signing four-year, $10-million contract with Giants as free agent prior to last season even though his career record was under .500 . . . Led NL with a career-high 16 losses and collected 12 wins, but didn't pitch as poorly as those numbers indicate . . . Would have been fine if he could have pitched all his games in Candlestick . . . His home ERA of 2.81 was ninth-best in the NL . . . First three wins were shutouts . . . Tied for second in NL with 25 homers allowed . . . Excellent fielder, he led NL pitchers by handling 52 chances without an error . . . Born June 30, 1957, in San Mateo, Cal. . . . Selected by Mariners in 17th round of 1979 draft . . . Traded to Royals before 1982 season . . . Dealt to Indians for Pat Tabler, June 3, 1988, then moved on to Blue Jays for Mauró Gozzo, Steve Cummings and Alex Sanchez, Sept. 17, 1990 . . . Earned $2.5 million.

Year	Club	G	IP	W	L	Pct.	SO	BB	H	ERA
1981	Seattle	2	1	0	0	.000	0	3	2	0.00
1982	Kansas City	22	88⅓	4	6	.400	40	34	92	4.58
1983	Kansas City	24	161⅓	10	7	.588	58	43	159	3.79
1984	Kansas City	35	257	17	12	.586	140	64	226	3.12
1985	Kansas City	33	205⅔	10	15	.400	122	59	216	4.33
1986	Kansas City	56	121	5	10	.333	68	43	100	3.20
1987	Kansas City	29	122⅓	8	6	.571	61	35	126	3.60
1988	K.C.-Clev.	33	81	4	4	.500	63	34	82	5.00
1989	Cleveland	33	222⅓	12	11	.522	88	52	213	3.36
1990	Clev.-Tor.	32	206⅔	13	11	.542	106	61	181	3.57
1991	San Francisco	34	214⅓	12	16	.429	104	71	201	3.99
	Totals	333	1681	95	98	.492	850	499	1598	3.74

JOHN BURKETT 27 6-3 205   Bats R Throws R

Looked like he was on his way to second straight excellent season, but collapsed down the stretch, winning just three of his last 11 starts to finish 12-11 . . . His 4.18 ERA was fifth-highest among pitchers with at least 162 innings . . . Won 14 games in 1990, his rookie year after seven years in the minors and wound up being Opening Night starter in '91 . . . Fanned a career-high 10 Phils May 13 . . . Threw more than 200 innings for second straight season . . . Exceeded his rookie year totals for complete games (six), starts (34), innings pitched (206⅔) and strikeouts (131) . . . Loves to bowl and wants to become a professional when baseball career is over . . . Has bowled three perfect games, but has yet to pitch one . . . Earned $230,000 last year . . . Born Nov. 28, 1964, in New Brighton, Pa. . . . Selected in sixth round of 1983 draft.

Year	Club	G	IP	W	L	Pct.	SO	BB	H	ERA
1987	San Francisco	3	6	0	0	.000	5	3	7	4.50
1990	San Francisco	33	204	14	7	.667	118	61	201	3.79
1991	San Francisco	36	206⅔	12	11	.522	131	60	223	4.18
	Totals	72	416⅔	26	18	.591	254	124	431	4.00

DAVE RIGHETTI 33 6-4 212   Bats L Throws L

Giants gave him a huge four-year, $10-million contract as free agent prior to last season and he did respectable job...Saved 24 games, fifth-best in NL and second-best in club history behind Greg Minton's 30 in 1982...Ranks sixth on the all-time save list with 248...Ex-Yankee saved at least 20 games in each of the last eight seasons, ranking second only to Lee Smith, who has done it for nine years...Was fourth in save percentage, converting 24 of 29 attempts and had best mark in the NL for inherited runners stranded (27 of 32) and first batter average (.071)...Problem was that Giant starters couldn't give him enough chances...Had just two save opportunities in first 18 games through May...Fired no-hitter against Boston, July 4, 1983...Born Nov. 28, 1958, in San Jose, Cal....Earned $2.5 million...Rangers drafted him ninth overall in January 1977.

Year	Club	G	IP	W	L	Pct.	SO	BB	H	ERA
1979	New York (AL)	3	17	0	1	.000	13	10	10	3.71
1981	New York (AL)	15	105	8	4	.667	89	38	75	2.06
1982	New York (AL)	33	183	11	10	.524	163	108	155	3.79
1983	New York (AL)	31	217	14	8	.636	169	67	194	3.44
1984	New York (AL)	64	96⅓	5	6	.455	90	37	79	2.34
1985	New York (AL)	74	107	12	7	.632	92	45	96	2.78
1986	New York (AL)	74	106⅔	8	8	.500	83	35	88	2.45
1987	New York (AL)	60	95	8	6	.571	77	44	95	3.51
1988	New York (AL)	60	87	5	4	.556	70	37	86	3.52
1989	New York (AL)	55	69	2	6	.250	51	26	73	3.00
1990	New York (AL)	53	53	1	1	.500	43	26	48	3.57
1991	San Francisco	61	71⅔	2	7	.222	51	28	64	3.39
	Totals	583	1207⅔	76	68	.528	991	501	1063	3.13

JEFF BRANTLEY 28 5-11 180   Bats R Throws R

After collecting 19 saves in 1990, he picked up 15 last season...Already ranks eighth on Giants' all-time save list with 35, tying Craig Lefferts...Set career highs for games with staff-high 67 and strikeouts (81)...Came on strong...Was 2-0 with 1.65 ERA and six saves over final 23 appearances...Allowed 135 base-runners in 95⅓ innings, but only 27 (20 percent) of them scored...Best in clutch situations...Held opponents to .161 average with men on base and .183 mark with runners in scoring position...Was the losing pitcher in 1990 All-Star Game...Born Sept. 5, 1963, in Florence, Ala....Giants'

sixth-round selection in 1985 draft . . . Earned $166,000 last season . . . Will Clark's teammate at Mississippi State.

Year	Club	G	IP	W	L	Pct.	SO	BB	H	ERA
1988	San Francisco	9	20⅔	0	1	.000	11	6	22	5.66
1989	San Francisco	59	97⅓	7	1	.875	69	37	101	4.07
1990	San Francisco	55	86⅔	5	3	.625	61	33	77	1.56
1991	San Francisco	67	95⅓	5	2	.714	81	52	78	2.45
	Totals	190	300	17	7	.708	222	128	278	2.94

TOP PROSPECTS

ROYCE CLAYTON 22 6-0 175   Bats R Throws R
Has great range and great arm . . . Best shortstop in the organization . . . Batted .280 for Shreveport (AA) with 68 RBI and 36 steals . . . Needs to learn to control his natural talents . . . Committed 30 errors . . . Late-season promotee to Giants batted .115 in 26 at-bats and had as many errors as hits (three) . . . Born Jan. 2, 1970, in Burbank, Cal. . . . Giants' No. 1 selection in 1988 draft.

TED WOOD 25 6-2 178   Bats L Throws L
Outfielder was given brief look by Giants during fall of '91, hitting .120 in 25 at-bats . . . Struck out 11 times . . . Should be Giants' fourth outfielder this season . . . Had excellent season for Phoenix (AAA), hitting .311 with 109 RBI and 86 walks . . . Born Jan. 4, 1967, in Mansfield, La. . . . Giants' second-round selection in 1988 draft . . . Attended University of New Orleans and was member of 1988 Olympic team.

BRYAN HICKERSON 28 6-2 195   Bats L Throws L
Figures to land a spot in the rotation . . . Was 2-2 with 3.60 ERA in six late-season starts for Giants . . . Posted 3-4 mark with 3.00 ERA for Shreveport (AA) and 1-1 ledger with 3.80 ERA for Phoenix (AAA) . . . Born Oct. 13, 1963, in Bemidji, Minn. . . . Twins' seventh-round selection in 1986 draft . . . Traded to Giants with Jose Dominguez and Ray Velasquez for Dan Gladden and David Blakely prior to 1987 season.

GIL HEREDIA 26 6-1 190   Bats R Throws R
His 9-11 record wasn't outstanding, but his ERA was 2.82 for Phoenix (AAA) . . . Over last five years, he has posted 51-42 record in minor leagues . . . Born Oct. 26, 1965, in Nogales,

Ariz. . . . Graduated from University of Arizona with a degree in general business in 1990.

MANAGER ROGER CRAIG: Stress of leading a team finally  got to this mild-mannered manager when he had to undergo emergency angioplasty in September . . . A mound doctor, he knows how to keep a tattered staff together . . . Used 21 different pitchers, including 15 starters to win NL pennant in 1989 . . . No one has managed more games for San Francisco . . . Surpassed Charlie Fox in 1990 . . . After five straight winning seasons, last year was his first sub.-500 year . . . His record with Giants is 514-476 since taking over Sept. 18, 1985 . . . His pet phrase "Humm Baby"' has become a part of Bay Area vocabulary . . . Former pitcher has managed, coached or scouted for 23 years and is the guru of the split-fingered fastball . . . Stepped down as Detroit pitching coach and became scout after club won World Series in 1984 . . . Managed Padres in 1978 and '79 . . . Lifetime managerial record is 666-647 . . . Over 12 major-league seasons as pitcher, he posted 74-98 mark with 3.82 ERA . . . Lost 24 games for expansion Mets in 1962 and 22 the following year . . . Born Feb. 17, 1930, in Durham, N.C. . . . One of the classier men in the game today.

ALL-TIME GIANT SEASON RECORDS

BATTING: Bill Terry, .401, 1930
HRs: Willie Mays, 52, 1965
RBI: Mel Ott, 151, 1929
STEALS: George Burns, 62, 1914
WINS: Christy Mathewson, 37, 1908
STRIKEOUTS: Christy Mathewson, 267, 1903

MAJOR LEAGUE YEAR-BY-YEAR LEADERS

NATIONAL LEAGUE MVP

Year	Player, Club
1931	Frank Frisch, St. Louis Cardinals
1932	Chuck Klein, Philadelphia Phillies
1933	Carl Hubbell, New York Giants
1934	Dizzy Dean, St. Louis Cardinals
1935	Gabby Hartnett, Chicago Cubs
1936	Carl Hubbell, New York Giants
1937	Joe Medwick, St. Louis Cardinals
1938	Ernie Lombardi, Cincinnati Reds
1939	Bucky Walters, Cincinnati Reds
1940	Frank McCormick, Cincinnati Reds
1941	Dolph Camilli, Brooklyn Dodgers
1942	Mort Cooper, St. Louis Cardinals
1943	Stan Musial, St. Louis Cardinals
1944	Marty Marion, St. Louis Cardinals
1945	Phil Cavarretta, Chicago Cubs
1946	Stan Musial, St. Louis Cardinals
1947	Bob Elliott, Boston Braves
1948	Stan Musial, St. Louis Cardinals
1949	Jackie Robinson, Brooklyn Dodgers
1950	Jim Konstanty, Philadelphia Phillies
1951	Roy Campanella, Brooklyn Dodgers
1952	Hank Sauer, Chicago Cubs
1953	Roy Campanella, Brooklyn Dodgers
1954	Willie Mays, New York Giants
1955	Roy Campanella, Brooklyn Dodgers
1956	Don Newcombe, Brooklyn Dodgers
1957	Hank Aaron, Milwaukee Braves
1958	Ernie Banks, Chicago Cubs
1959	Ernie Banks, Chicago Cubs
1960	Dick Groat, Pittsburgh Pirates

Year	Player, Club
1961	Frank Robinson, Cincinnati Reds
1962	Maury Wills, Los Angeles Dodgers
1963	Sandy Koufax, Los Angeles Dodgers
1964	Ken Boyer, St. Louis Cardinals
1965	Willie Mays, San Francisco Giants
1966	Roberto Clemente, Pittsburgh Pirates
1967	Orlando Cepeda, St. Louis Cardinals
1968	Bob Gibson, St. Louis Cardinals
1969	Willie McCovey, San Francisco Giants
1970	Johnny Bench, Cincinnati Reds
1971	Joe Torre, St. Louis Cardinals
1972	Johnny Bench, Cincinnati Reds
1973	Pete Rose, Cincinnati Reds
1974	Steve Garvey, Los Angeles Dodgers
1975	Joe Morgan, Cincinnati Reds
1976	Joe Morgan, Cincinnati Reds
1977	George Foster, Cincinnati Reds
1978	Dave Parker, Pittsburgh Pirates
1979	Keith Hernandez, St. Louis Cardinals
	Willie Stargell, Pittsburgh Pirates
1980	Mike Schmidt, Philadelphia Phillies
1981	Mike Schmidt, Philadelphia Phillies
1982	Dale Murphy, Atlanta Braves
1983	Dale Murphy, Atlanta Braves
1984	Ryne Sandberg, Chicago Cubs
1985	Willie McGee, St. Louis Cardinals
1986	Mike Schmidt, Philadelphia Phillies
1987	Andre Dawson, Chicago Cubs
1988	Kirk Gibson, Los Angeles Dodgers
1989	Kevin Mitchell, San Francisco Giants
1990	Barry Bonds, Pittsburgh Pirates
1991	Terry Pendleton, Atlanta Braves

AMERICAN LEAGUE MVP

Year	Player, Club
1931	Lefty Grove, Philadelphia Athletics
1932	Jimmy Foxx, Philadelphia Athletics
1933	Jimmy Foxx, Philadelphia Athletics
1934	Mickey Cochrane, Detroit Tigers
1935	Hank Greenberg, Detroit Tigers
1936	Lou Gehrig, New York Yankees
1937	Charley Gehringer, Detroit Tigers

Year	Player, Club
1938	Jimmy Foxx, Boston Red Sox
1939	Joe DiMaggio, New York Yankees
1940	Hank Greenberg, Detroit Tigers
1941	Joe DiMaggio, New York Yankees
1942	Joe Gordon, New York Yankees
1943	Spud Chandler, New York Yankees
1944	Hal Newhouser, Detroit Tigers
1945	Hal Newhouser, Detroit Tigers
1946	Ted Williams, Boston Red Sox
1947	Joe DiMaggio, New York Yankees
1948	Lou Boudreau, Cleveland Indians
1949	Ted Williams, Boston Red Sox
1950	Phil Rizzuto, New York Yankees
1951	Yogi Berra, New York Yankees
1942	Bobby Shantz, Philadelphia Athletics
1953	Al Rosen, Cleveland Indians
1954	Yogi Berra, New York Yankees
1955	Yogi Berra, New York Yankees
1956	Mickey Mantle, New York Yankees
1957	Mickey Mantle, New York Yankees
1958	Jackie Jensen, Boston Red Sox
1959	Nellie Fox, Chicago White Sox
1960	Roger Maris, New York Yankees
1961	Roger Maris, New York Yankees
1962	Mickey Mantle, New York Yankees
1963	Elston Howard, New York Yankees
1964	Brooks Robinson, Baltimore Orioles
1965	Zoilo Versalles, Minnesota Twins
1966	Frank Robinson, Baltimore Orioles
1967	Carl Yastrzemski, Boston Red Sox
1968	Dennis McLain, Detroit Tigers
1969	Harmon Killebrew, Minnesota Twins
1970	Boog Powell, Baltimore Orioles
1971	Vida Blue, Oakland A's
1972	Dick Allen, Chicago White Sox
1973	Reggie Jackson, Oakland A's
1974	Jeff Burroughs, Texas Rangers
1975	Fred Lynn, Boston Red Sox
1976	Thurman Munson, New York Yankees
1977	Rod Carew, Minnesota Twins
1978	Jim Rice, Boston Red Sox
1979	Don Baylor, California Angels
1980	George Brett, Kansas City Royals

Year	Player, Club
1981	Rollie Fingers, Milwaukee Brewers
1982	Robin Yount, Milwaukee Brewers
1983	Cal Ripken Jr., Baltimore Orioles
1984	Willie Hernandez, Detroit Tigers
1985	Don Mattingly, New York Yankees
1986	Roger Clemens, Boston Red Sox
1987	George Bell, Toronto Blue Jays
1988	Jose Canseco, Oakland A's
1989	Robin Yount, Milwaukee Brewers
1990	Rickey Henderson, Oakland A's
1991	Cal Ripken Jr., Baltimore Orioles

AMERICAN LEAGUE
Batting Champions

Year	Player, Club	Avg.
1901	Napoleon Lajoie, Philadelphia Athletics	.422
1902	Ed Delahanty, Washington Senators	.376
1903	Napoleon Lajoie, Cleveland Indians	.355
1904	Napoleon Lajoie, Cleveland Indians	.381
1905	Elmer Flick, Cleveland Indians	.306
1906	George Stone, St. Louis Browns	.358
1907	Ty Cobb, Detroit Tigers	.350
1908	Ty Cobb, Detroit Tigers	.324
1909	Ty Cobb, Detroit Tigers	.377
1910	Ty Cobb, Detroit Tigers	.385
1911	Ty Cobb, Detroit Tigers	.420
1912	Ty Cobb, Detroit Tigers	.410
1913	Ty Cobb, Detroit Tigers	.390
1914	Ty Cobb, Detroit Tigers	.368
1915	Ty Cobb, Detroit Tigers	.370
1916	Tris Speaker, Cleveland Indians	.386
1917	Ty Cobb, Detroit Tigers	.383
1918	Ty Cobb, Detroit Tigers	.382
1919	Ty Cobb, Detroit Tigers	.384
1920	George Sisler, St. Louis Browns	.407
1921	Harry Heilmann, Detroit Tigers	.393
1922	George Sisler, St. Louis Browns	.420
1923	Harry Heilmann, Detroit Tigers	.398
1924	Babe Ruth, New York Yankees	.378
1925	Harry Heilmann, Detroit Tigers	.393
1926	Heinie Manush, Detroit Tigers	.377

Year	Player, Club	Avg.
1927	Harry Heilmann, Detroit Tigers	.398
1928	Goose Goslin, Washington Senators	.379
1929	Lew Fonseca, Cleveland Indians	.369
1930	Al Simmons, Philadelphia Athletics	.381
1931	Al Simmons, Philadelphia Athletics	.390
1932	David Alexander, Detroit Tigers-Boston Red Sox	.367
1933	Jimmy Foxx, Philadelphia Athletics	.356
1934	Lou Gehrig, New York Yankees	.365
1935	Buddy Myer, Washington Senators	.349
1936	Luke Appling, Chicago White Sox	.388
1937	Charlie Gehringer, Detroit Tigers	.371
1938	Jimmy Foxx, Boston Red Sox	.349
1939	Joe DiMaggio, New York Yankees	.381
1940	Joe DiMaggio, New York Yankees	.352
1941	Ted Williams, Boston Red Sox	.406
1942	Ted Williams, Boston Red Sox	.356
1943	Luke Appling, Chicago White Sox	.328
1944	Lou Boudreau, Cleveland Indians	.327
1945	Snuffy Stirnweiss, New York Yankees	.309
1946	Mickey Vernon, Washington Senators	.353
1947	Ted Williams, Boston Red Sox	.343
1948	Ted Williams, Boston Red Sox	.369
1949	George Kell, Detroit Tigers	.343
1950	Billy Goodman, Boston Red Sox	.354
1951	Ferris Fain, Philadelphia Athletics	.344
1952	Ferris Fain, Philadelphia Athletics	.327
1953	Mickey Vernon, Washington Senators	.337
1954	Bobby Avila, Cleveland Indians	.341
1955	Al Kaline, Detroit Tigers	.340
1956	Mickey Mantle, New York Yankees	.353
1957	Ted Williams, Boston Red Sox	.388
1958	Ted Williams, Boston Red Sox	.328
1959	Harvey Kuenn, Detroit Tigers	.353
1960	Pete Runnels, Boston Red Sox	.320
1961	Norm Cash, Detroit Tigers	.361
1962	Pete Runnels, Boston Red Sox	.326
1963	Carl Yastrzemski, Boston Red Sox	.321
1964	Tony Oliva, Minnesota Twins	.323
1965	Tony Oliva, Minnesota Twins	.321
1966	Frank Robinson, Baltimore Orioles	.316
1967	Carl Yastrzemski, Boston Red Sox	.326
1968	Carl Yastrzemski, Boston Red Sox	.301
1969	Rod Carew, Minnesota Twins	.332

Year	Player, Club	Avg.
1970	Alex Johnson, California Angels	.329
1971	Tony Oliva, Minnesota Twins	.337
1972	Rod Carew, Minnesota Twins	.318
1973	Rod Carew, Minnesota Twins	.350
1974	Rod Carew, Minnesota Twins	.364
1975	Rod Carew, Minnesota Twins	.359
1976	George Brett, Kansas City Royals	.333
1977	Rod Carew, Minnesota Twins	.388
1978	Rod Carew, Minnesota Twins	.333
1979	Fred Lynn, Boston Red Sox	.333
1980	George Brett, Kansas City Royals	.390
1981	Carney Lansford, Boston Red Sox	.336
1982	Willie Wilson, Kansas City Royals	.332
1983	Wade Boggs, Boston Red Sox	.361
1984	Don Mattingly, New York Yankees	.343
1985	Wade Boggs, Boston Red Sox	.368
1986	Wade Boggs, Boston Red Sox	.357
1987	Wade Boggs, Boston Red Sox	.363
1988	Wade Boggs, Boston Red Sox	.366
1989	Kirby Puckett, Minnesota Twins	.339
1990	George Brett, Kansas City Royals	.329
1991	Julio Franco, Texas Rangers	.341

NATIONAL LEAGUE
Batting Champions

Year	Player, Club	Avg.
1876	Roscoe Barnes, Chicago	.403
1877	James White, Boston	.385
1878	Abner Dalrymple, Milwaukee	.356
1879	Cap Anson, Chicago	.407
1880	George Gore, Chicago	.365
1881	Cap Anson, Chicago	.399
1882	Dan Brouthers, Buffalo	.367
1883	Dan Brouthers, Buffalo	.371
1884	Jim O'Rourke, Buffalo	.350
1885	Roger Connor, New York	.371
1886	Mike Kelly, Chicago	.388
1887	Cap Anson, Chicago	.421
1888	Cap Anson, Chicago	.343
1889	Dan Brouthers, Boston	.373
1890	Jack Glassock, New York	.336

Year	Player, Club	Avg.
1891	Billy Hamilton, Philadelphia	.338
1892	Cupid Childs, Cleveland	.335
	Dan Brouthers, Brooklyn	.335
1893	Hugh Duffy, Boston	.378
1894	Hugh Duffy, Boston	.438
1895	Jesse Burkett, Cleveland	.423
1896	Jesse Burkett, Cleveland	.410
1897	Willie Keeler, Baltimore	.432
1898	Willie Keeler, Baltimore	.379
1899	Ed Delahanty, Philadelphia	.408
1900	Honus Wagner, Pittsburgh	.380
1901	Jesse Burkett, St. Louis Cardinals	.382
1902	C.H. Beaumont, Pittsburgh Pirates	.357
1903	Honus Wagner, Pittsburgh Pirates	.355
1904	Honus Wagner, Pittsburgh Pirates	.349
1905	J. Bentley Seymour, Cincinnati Reds	.377
1906	Honus Wagner, Pittsburgh Pirates	.339
1907	Honus Wagner, Pittsburgh Pirates	.350
1908	Honus Wagner, Pittsburgh Pirates	.354
1909	Honus Wagner, Pittsburgh Pirates	.339
1910	Sherwood Magee, Philadelphia Phillies	.331
1911	Honus Wagner, Pittsburgh Pirates	.334
1912	Heinie Zimmerman, Chicago Cubs	.372
1913	Jake Daubert, Brooklyn Dodgers	.350
1914	Jake Daubert, Brooklyn Dodgers	.329
1915	Larry Doyle, New York Giants	.320
1916	Hal Chase, Cincinnati Reds	.339
1917	Edd Roush, Cincinnati Reds	.341
1918	Zack Wheat, Brooklyn Dodgers	.335
1919	Edd Roush, Cincinnati Reds	.321
1920	Rogers Hornsby, St. Louis Cardinals	.370
1921	Rogers Hornsby, St. Louis Cardinals	.397
1922	Rogers Hornsby, St. Louis Cardinals	.401
1923	Rogers Hornsby, St. Louis Cardinals	.384
1924	Rogers Hornsby, St. Louis Cardinals	.424
1925	Rogers Hornsby, St. Louis Cardinals	.403
1926	Bubbles Hargrave, Cincinnati Reds	.353
1927	Paul Waner, Pittsburgh Pirates	.380
1928	Rogers Hornsby, Boston Braves	.387
1929	Lefty O'Doul, Philadelphia Phillies	.398
1930	Bill Terry, New York Giants	.401
1931	Chick Hafey, St. Louis Cardinals	.349
1932	Lefty O'Doul, Brooklyn Dodgers	.368

Year	Player, Club	Avg.
1933	Chuck Klein, Philadelphia Phillies	.368
1934	Paul Waner, Pittsburgh Pirates	.362
1935	Arky Vaughan, Pittsburgh Pirates	.385
1936	Paul Waner, Pittsburgh Pirates	.373
1937	Joe Medwick, St. Louis Cardinals	.374
1938	Ernie Lombardi, Cincinnati Reds	.342
1939	Johnny Mize, St. Louis Cardinals	.349
1940	Debs Garms, Pittsburgh Pirates	.355
1941	Pete Reiser, Brooklyn Dodgers	.343
1942	Ernie Lombardi, Boston Braves	.330
1943	Stan Musial, St. Louis Cardinals	.330
1944	Dixie Walker, Brooklyn Dodgers	.357
1945	Phil Cavarretta, Chicago Cubs	.355
1946	Stan Musial, St. Louis Cardinals	.365
1947	Harry Walker, St. L. Cardinals-Phila. Phillies	.363
1948	Stan Musial, St. Louis Cardinals	.376
1949	Jackie Robinson, Brooklyn Dodgers	.342
1950	Stan Musial, St. Louis Cardinals	.346
1951	Stan Musial, St. Louis Cardinals	.355
1952	Stan Musial, St. Louis Cardinals	.336
1953	Carl Furillo, Brooklyn Dodgers	.344
1954	Willie Mays, New York Giants	.345
1955	Richie Ashburn, Philadelphia Phillies	.338
1956	Hank Aaron, Milwaukee Braves	.328
1957	Stan Musial, St. Louis Cardinals	.351
1958	Richie Ashburn, Philadelphia Phillies	.350
1959	Hank Aaron, Milwaukee Braves	.328
1960	Dick Groat, Pittsburgh Pirates	.325
1961	Roberto Clemente, Pittsburgh Pirates	.351
1962	Tommy Davis, Los Angeles Dodgers	.346
1963	Tommy Davis, Los Angeles Dodgers	.326
1964	Roberto Clemente, Pittsburgh Pirates	.339
1965	Roberto Clemente, Pittsburgh Pirates	.329
1966	Matty Alou, Pittsburgh Pirates	.342
1967	Roberto Clemente, Pittsburgh Pirates	.357
1968	Pete Rose, Cincinnati Reds	.335
1969	Pete Rose, Cincinnati Reds	.348
1970	Rico Carty, Atlanta Braves	.366
1971	Joe Torre, St. Louis Cardinals	.363
1972	Billy Williams, Chicago Cubs	.333
1973	Pete Rose, Cincinnati Reds	.338
1974	Ralph Garr, Atlanta Braves	.353
1975	Bill Madlock, Chicago Cubs	.354

Year	Player, Club	Avg.
1976	Bill Madlock, Chicago Cubs	.339
1977	Dave Parker, Pittsburgh Pirates	.338
1978	Dave Parker, Pittsburgh Pirates	.334
1979	Keith Hernandez, St. Louis Cardinals	.344
1980	Bill Buckner, Chicago Cubs	.324
1981	Bill Madlock, Pittsburgh Pirates	.341
1982	Al Oliver, Montreal Expos	.331
1983	Bill Madlock, Pittsburgh Pirates	.323
1984	Tony Gwynn, San Diego Padres	.351
1985	Willie McGee, St. Louis Cardinals	.353
1986	Tim Raines, Montreal Expos	.334
1987	Tony Gwynn, San Diego Padres	.370
1988	Tony Gwynn, San Diego Padres	.313
1989	Tony Gwynn, San Diego Padres	.336
1990	Willie McGee, St. Louis Cardinals	.335
1991	Terry Pendleton, Atlanta Braves	.319

NATIONAL LEAGUE
Home Run Leaders

Year	Player, Club	HRs
1900	Herman Long, Boston Nationals	12
1901	Sam Crawford, Cincinnati Reds	16
1902	Tom Leach, Pittsburgh Pirates	6
1903	Jim Sheckard, Brooklyn Dodgers	9
1904	Harry Lumley, Brooklyn Dodgers	9
1905	Fred Odwell, Cincinnati Reds	9
1906	Tim Jordan, Brooklyn Dodgers	12
1907	Dave Brain, Boston Nationals	10
1908	Tim Jordan, Brooklyn Dodgers	12
1909	Jim Murray, New York Giants	7
1910	Fred Beck, Boston Nationals	10
	Frank Schulte, Chicago Cubs	10
1911	Frank Schulte, Chicago Cubs	21
1912	Heinie Zimmerman, Chicago Cubs	14
1913	Gavvy Cravath, Philadelphia Phillies	19
1914	Gavvy Cravath, Philadelphia Phillies	19
1915	Gavvy Cravath, Philadelphia Phillies	24
1916	Dave Robertson, New York Giants	12
	Cy Williams, Chicago Cubs	12
1917	Gavvy Cravath, Philadelphia Phillies	12
	Dave Robertson, New York Giants	12
1918	Gavvy Cravath, Philadelphia Phillies	8

Year	Player, Club	HRs
1919	Gavvy Cravath, Philadelphia Phillies	12
1920	Cy Williams, Philadelphia Phillies	15
1921	George Kelly, New York Giants	23
1922	Rogers Hornsby, St. Louis Cardinals	42
1923	Cy Williams, Philadelphia Phillies	41
1924	Jack Fournier, Brooklyn Dodgers	27
1925	Rogers Hornsby, St. Louis Cardinals	39
1926	Hack Wilson, Chicago Cubs	21
1927	Cy Williams, Philadelphia Phillies	30
	Hack Wilson, Chicago Cubs	30
1928	Jim Bottomley, St. Louis Cardinals	31
	Hack Wilson, Chicago Cubs	31
1929	Chuck Klein, Philadelphia Phillies	43
1930	Hack Wilson, Chicago Cubs	56
1931	Chuck Klein, Philadelphia Phillies	31
1932	Chuck Klein, Philadelphia Phillies	38
	Mel Ott, New York Giants	38
1933	Chuck Klein, Philadelphia Phillies	28
1934	Rip Collins, St. Louis Cardinals	35
	Mel Ott, New York Giants	35
1935	Wally Berger, Boston Braves	34
1936	Mel Ott, New York Giants	33
1937	Joe Medwick, St. Louis Cardinals	31
	Mel Ott, New York Giants	31
1938	Mel Ott, New York Giants	36
1939	Johnny Mize, St. Louis Cardinals	28
1940	Johnny Mize, St. Louis Cardinals	43
1941	Dolph Camilli, Brooklyn Dodgers	34
1942	Mel Ott, New York Giants	30
1943	Bill Nicholson, Chicago Cubs	29
1944	Bill Nicholson, Chicago Cubs	33
1945	Tommy Holmes, Boston Braves	28
1946	Ralph Kiner, Pittsburgh Pirates	23
1947	Ralph Kiner, Pittsburgh Pirates	51
	Johnny Mize, New York Giants	51
1948	Ralph Kiner, Pittsburgh Pirates	40
	Johnny Mize, New York Giants	40
1949	Ralph Kiner, Pittsburgh Pirates	54
1950	Ralph Kiner, Pittsburgh Pirates	47
1951	Ralph Kiner, Pittsburgh Pirates	42
1952	Ralph Kiner, Pittsburgh Pirates	37
	Hank Sauer, Chicago Cubs	37
1953	Eddie Mathews, Milwaukee Braves	47

Year	Player, Club	HRs
1954	Ted Kluszewski, Cincinnati Reds	49
1955	Willie Mays, New York Giants	51
1956	Duke Snider, Brooklyn Dodgers	43
1957	Hank Aaron, Milwaukee Braves	44
1958	Ernie Banks, Chicago Cubs	47
1959	Eddie Mathews, Milwaukee Braves	46
1960	Ernie Banks, Chicago Cubs	41
1961	Orlando Cepeda, San Francisco Giants	46
1962	Willie Mays, San Francisco Giants	49
1963	Hank Aaron, Milwaukee Braves	44
	Willie McCovey, San Francisco Giants	44
1964	Willie Mays, San Francisco Giants	47
1965	Willie Mays, San Francisco Giants	52
1966	Hank Aaron, Atlanta Braves	44
1967	Hank Aaron, Atlanta Braves	39
1968	Willie McCovey, San Francisco Giants	36
1969	Willie McCovey, San Francisco Giants	45
1970	Johnny Bench, Cincinnati Reds	45
1971	Willie Stargell, Pittsburgh Pirates	48
1972	Johnny Bench, Cincinnati Reds	40
1973	Willie Stargell, Pittsburgh Pirates	44
1974	Mike Schmidt, Philadelphia Phillies	36
1975	Mike Schmidt, Philadelphia Phillies	38
1976	Mike Schmidt, Philadelphia Phillies	38
1977	George Foster, Cincinnati Reds	52
1978	George Foster, Cincinnati Reds	40
1979	Dave Kingman, Chicago Cubs	48
1980	Mike Schmidt, Philadelphia Phillies	48
1981	Mike Schmidt, Philadelphia Phillies	31
1982	Dave Kingman, New York Mets	37
1983	Mike Schmidt, Philadelphia Phillies	40
1984	Mike Schmidt, Philadelphia Phillies	36
1984	Dale Murphy, Atlanta Braves	36
1985	Dale Murphy, Atlanta Braves	37
1986	Mike Schmidt, Philadelphia Phillies	37
1987	Andre Dawson, Chicago Cubs	49
1988	Darryl Strawberry, New York Mets	39
1989	Kevin Mitchell, San Francisco Giants	47
1990	Ryne Sandberg, Chicago Cubs	40
1991	Howard Johnson, New York Mets	38

Howard Johnson sets sights on fourth year of 30-30.

AMERICAN LEAGUE
Home Run Leaders

Year	Player, Club	HRs
1901	Napoleon Lajoie, Philadelphia Athletics	13
1902	Ralph Seybold, Philadelphia Athletics	16
1903	John Freeman, Boston Pilgrims	13
1904	Harry Davis, Philadelphia Athletics	10
1905	Harry Davis, Philadelphia Athletics	8
1906	Harry Davis, Philadelphia Athletics	12
1907	Harry Davis, Philadelphia Athletics	8
1908	Sam Crawford, Detroit Tigers	7
1909	Ty Cobb, Detroit Tigers	9
1910	Garland Stahl, Boston Red Sox	10
1911	Frank (Home Run) Baker, Philadelphia Athletics	9
1912	Frank (Home Run) Baker, Philadelphia Athletics	10
1913	Frank (Home Run) Baker, Philadelphia Athletics	12
1914	Frank (Home Run) Baker, Philadelphia Athletics	8
	Sam Crawford, Detroit Tigers	8
1915	Bob Roth, Cleveland Indians	7
1916	Wally Pipp, New York Yankees	12
1917	Wally Pipp, New York Yankees	9
1918	Babe Ruth, Boston Red Sox	11
	Clarence Walker, Philadelphia Athletics	11
1919	Babe Ruth, Boston Red Sox	29
1920	Babe Ruth, New York Yankees	54
1921	Babe Ruth, New York Yankees	59
1922	Ken Williams, St. Louis Browns	39
1923	Babe Ruth, New York Yankees	41
1924	Babe Ruth, New York Yankees	46
1925	Bob Meusel, New York Yankees	33
1926	Babe Ruth, New York Yankees	47
1927	Babe Ruth, New York Yankees	60
1928	Babe Ruth, New York Yankees	54
1929	Babe Ruth, New York Yankees	46
1930	Babe Ruth, New York Yankees	49
1931	Babe Ruth, New York Yankees	46
	Lou Gehrig, New York Yankees	46
1932	Jimmie Foxx, Philadelphia Athletics	58
1933	Jimmie Foxx, Philadelphia Athletics	48
1934	Lou Gehrig, New York Yankees	49
1935	Hank Greenberg, Detroit Tigers	36
	Jimmie Foxx, Philadelphia Athletics	36

Year	Player, Club	HRs
1936	Lou Gehrig, New York Yankees	49
1937	Joe DiMaggio, New York Yankees	46
1938	Hank Greenberg, Detroit Tigers	58
1939	Jimmy Foxx, Boston Red Sox	35
1940	Hank Greenberg, Detroit Tigers	41
1941	Ted Williams, Boston Red Sox	37
1942	Ted Williams, Boston Red Sox	36
1943	Rudy York, Detroit Tigers	34
1944	Nick Etten, New York Yankees	22
1945	Vern Stephens, St. Louis Browns	24
1946	Hank Greenberg, Detroit Tigers	44
1947	Ted Williams, Boston Red Sox	32
1948	Joe DiMaggio, New York Yankees	39
1949	Ted Williams, Boston Red Sox	43
1950	Al Rosen, Cleveland Indians	37
1951	Gus Zernial, Philadelphia Athletics	33
1952	Larry Doby, Cleveland Indians	32
1953	Al Rosen, Cleveland Indians	43
1954	Larry Doby, Cleveland Indians	32
1955	Mickey Mantle, New York Yankees	37
1956	Mickey Mantle, New York Yankees	52
1957	Roy Sievers, Washington Senators	42
1958	Mickey Mantle, New York Yankees	42
1959	Rocky Colavito, Cleveland Indians	42
	Harmon Killebrew, Washington Senators	42
1960	Mickey Mantle, New York Yankees	40
1961	Roger Maris, New York Yankees	61
1962	Harmon Killebrew, Minnesota Twins	48
1963	Harmon Killebrew, Minnesota Twins	45
1964	Harmon Killebrew, Minnesota Twins	49
1965	Tony Conigliaro, Boston Red Sox	32
1966	Frank Robinson, Baltimore Orioles	49
1967	Carl Yastrzemski, Boston Red Sox	44
	Harmon Killebrew, Minnesota Twins	44
1968	Frank Howard, Washington Senators	44
1969	Harmon Killebrew, Minnesota Twins	49
1970	Frank Howard, Washington Senators	44
1971	Bill Melton, Chicago White Sox	33
1972	Dick Allen, Chicago White Sox	37
1973	Reggie Jackson, Oakland A's	32
1974	Dick Allen, Chicago White Sox	32
1975	George Scott, Milwaukee Brewers	36
	Reggie Jackson, Oakland A's	36

Year	Player, Club	HRs
1976	Graig Nettles, New York Yankees	32
1977	Jim Rice, Boston Red Sox	39
1978	Jim Rice, Boston Red Sox	46
1979	Gorman Thomas, Milwaukee Brewers	45
1980	Ben Oglivie, Milwaukee Brewers	41
	Reggie Jackson, New York Yankees	41
1981	Bobby Grich, California Angels	22
	Eddie Murray, Baltimore Orioles	22
	Dwight Evans, Boston Red Sox	22
	Tony Armas, Oakland A's	22
1982	Reggie Jackson, California Angels	39
	Gorman Thomas, Milwaukee Brewers	39
1983	Jim Rice, Boston Red Sox	39
1984	Tony Armas, Boston Red Sox	43
1985	Darrell Evans, Detroit Tigers	40
1986	Jesse Barfield, Toronto Blue Jays	40
1987	Mark McGwire, Oakland A's	49
1988	Jose Canseco, Oakland A's	42
1989	Fred McGriff, Toronto Blue Jays	36
1990	Cecil Fielder, Detroit Tigers	51
1991	Jose Canseco, Oakland A's	44
	Cecil Fielder, Detroit Tigers	44

CY YOUNG AWARD WINNERS

(Prior to 1967 there was a single overall major league award.)

Year Player, Club
1956 Don Newcombe, Brooklyn Dodgers
1957 Warren Spahn, Milwaukee Braves
1958 Bob Turley, New York Yankees
1959 Early Wynn, Chicago White Sox
1960 Vernon Law, Pittsburgh Pirates
1961 Whitey Ford, New York Yankees
1962 Don Drysdale, Los Angeles Dodgers
1963 Sandy Koufax, Los Angeles Dodgers
1964 Dean Chance, Los Angeles Angels
1965 Sandy Koufax, Los Angeles Dodgers
1966 Sandy Koufax, Los Angeles Dodgers

AL CY YOUNG

Year	Player, Club
1967	Jim Lonborg, Boston Red Sox
1968	Dennis McLain, Detroit Tigers
1969	Mike Cuellar, Baltimore Orioles
	Dennis McLain, Detroit Tigers
1970	Jim Perry, Minnesota Twins
1971	Vida Blue, Oakland A's
1972	Gaylord Perry, Cleveland Indians
1973	Jim Palmer, Baltimore Orioles
1974	Jim Hunter, Oakland A's
1975	Jim Palmer, Baltimore Orioles
1976	Jim Palmer, Baltimore Orioles
1977	Sparky Lyle, New York Yankees
1978	Ron Guidry, New York Yankees
1979	Mike Flanagan, Baltimore Orioles
1980	Steve Stone, Baltimore Orioles
1981	Rollie Fingers, Milwaukee Brewers
1982	Pete Vuckovich, Milwaukee Brewers
1983	LaMarr Hoyt, Chicago White Sox
1984	Willie Hernandez, Detroit Tigers
1985	Bret Saberhagen, Kansas City Royals
1986	Roger Clemens, Boston Red Sox
1987	Roger Clemens, Boston Red Sox
1988	Frank Viola, Minnesota Twins
1989	Bret Saberhagen, Kansas City Royals
1990	Bob Welch, Oakland A's
1991	Roger Clemens, Boston Red Sox

NL CY YOUNG

Year	Player, Club
1967	Mike McCormick, San Francisco Giants
1968	Bob Gibson, St. Louis Cardinals
1969	Tom Seaver, New York Mets
1970	Bob Gibson, St. Louis Cardinals
1971	Ferguson Jenkins, Chicago Cubs
1972	Steve Carlton, Philadelphia Phillies
1973	Tom Seaver, New York Mets
1974	Mike Marshall, Los Angeles Dodgers
1975	Tom Seaver, New York Mets
1976	Randy Jones, San Diego Padres

Year	Player, Club
1977	Steve Carlton, Philadelphia Phillies
1978	Gaylord Perry, San Diego Padres
1979	Bruce Sutter, Chicago Cubs
1980	Steve Carlton, Philadelphia Phillies
1981	Fernando Valenzuela, Los Angeles Dodgers
1982	Steve Carlton, Philadelphia Phillies
1983	John Denny, Philadelphia Phillies
1984	Rick Sutcliffe, Chicago Cubs
1985	Dwight Gooden, New York Mets
1986	Mike Scott, Houston Astros
1987	Steve Bedrosian, Philadelphia Phillies
1988	Orel Hershiser, Los Angeles Dodgers
1989	Mark Davis, San Diego Padres
1990	Doug Drabek, Pittsburgh Pirates
1991	Tom Glavine, Atlanta Braves

NATIONAL LEAGUE
Rookie of Year

Year	Player, Club
1947	Jackie Robinson, Brooklyn Dodgers
1948	Al Dark, Boston Braves
1949	Don Newcombe, Brooklyn Dodgers
1950	Sam Jethroe, Boston Braves
1951	Willie Mays, New York Giants
1952	Joe Black, Brooklyn Dodgers
1953	Junior Gilliam, Brooklyn Dodgers
1954	Wally Moon, St. Louis Cardinals
1955	Bill Virdon, St. Louis Cardinals
1956	Frank Robinson, Cincinnati Reds
1957	Jack Sanford, Philadelphia Phillies
1958	Orlando Cepeda, San Francisco Giants
1959	Willie McCovey, San Francisco Giants
1960	Frank Howard, Los Angeles Dodgers
1961	Billy Williams, Chicago Cubs
1962	Kenny Hubbs, Chicago Cubs
1963	Pete Rose, Cincinnati Reds
1964	Richie Allen, Philadelphia Phillies
1965	Jim Lefebvre, Los Angeles Dodgers
1966	Tommy Helms, Cincinnati Reds
1967	Tom Seaver, New York Mets
1968	Johnny Bench, Cincinnati Reds

Year	Player, Club
1969	Ted Sizemore, Los Angeles Dodgers
1970	Carl Morton, Montreal Expos
1971	Earl Williams, Atlanta Braves
1972	Jon Matlack, New York Mets
1973	Gary Matthews, San Francisco Giants
1974	Bake McBride, St. Louis Cardinals
1975	John Montefusco, San Francisco Giants
1976	Pat Zachry, Cincinnati Reds
	Butch Metzger, San Diego Padres
1977	Andre Dawson, Montreal Expos
1978	Bob Horner, Atlanta Braves
1979	Rick Sutcliffe, Los Angeles Dodgers
1980	Steve Howe, Los Angeles Dodgers
1981	Fernando Valenzuela, Los Angeles Dodgers
1982	Steve Sax, Los Angeles Dodgers
1983	Darryl Strawberry, New York Mets
1984	Dwight Gooden, New York Mets
1985	Vince Coleman, St. Louis Cardinals
1986	Todd Worrell, St. Louis Cardinals
1987	Benito Santiago, San Diego Padres
1988	Chris Sabo, Cincinnati Reds
1989	Jerome Walton, Chicago Cubs
1990	Dave Justice, Atlanta Braves
1991	Jeff Bagwell, Houston Astros

AMERICAN LEAGUE
Rookie of Year

Year	Player, Club
1949	Roy Sievers, St. Louis Browns
1950	Walt Dropo, Boston Red Sox
1951	Gil McDougald, New York Yankees
1952	Harry Byrd, Philadelphia Athletics
1953	Harvey Kuenn, Detroit Tigers
1954	Bob Grim, New York Yankees
1955	Herb Score, Cleveland Indians
1956	Luis Aparicio, Chicago White Sox
1957	Tony Kubek, New York Yankees
1958	Albie Pearson, Washington Senators
1959	Bob Allison, Washington Senators
1960	Ron Hansen, Baltimore Orioles
1961	Don Schwall, Boston Red Sox

Year Player, Club
1962 Tom Tresh, New York Yankees
1963 Gary Peters, Chicago White Sox
1964 Tony Oliva, Minnesota Twins
1965 Curt Blefary, Baltimore Orioles
1966 Tommie Agee, Chicago White Sox
1967 Rod Carew, Minnesota Twins
1968 Stan Bahnsen, New York Yankees
1969 Lou Piniella, Kansas City Royals
1970 Thurman Munson, New York Yankees
1971 Chris Chambliss, Cleveland Indians
1972 Carlton Fisk, Boston Red Sox
1973 Al Bumbry, Baltimore Orioles
1974 Mike Hargrove, Texas Rangers
1975 Fred Lynn, Boston Red Sox
1976 Mark Fidrych, Detroit Tigers
1977 Eddie Murray, Baltimore Orioles
1978 Lou Whitaker, Detroit Tigers
1979 John Castino, Minnesota Twins
        Alfredo Griffin, Toronto Blue Jays
1980 Joe Charboneau, Cleveland Indians
1981 Dave Righetti, New York Yankees
1982 Cal Ripken Jr., Baltimore Orioles
1983 Ron Kittle, Chicago White Sox
1984 Alvin Davis, Seattle Mariners
1985 Ozzie Guillen, Chicago White Sox
1986 Jose Canseco, Oakland A's
1987 Mark McGwire, Oakland A's
1988 Walt Weiss, Oakland A's
1989 Gregg Olson, Baltimore Orioles
1990 Sandy Alomar Jr., Cleveland Indians
1991 Chuck Knoblauch, Minnesota Twins

Tribe's Sandy Alomar Jr. was AL 1990 Rookie of the Year.

ALL-TIME MAJOR LEAGUE RECORDS

National	American

Batting (Season)
Average
| .438 Hugh Duffy, Boston, 1894 | .422 Napoleon Lajoie, Phila., 1901 |
| .424 Rogers Hornsby, St. Louis, 1924 | |

At Bat
| 701 Juan Samuel, Phila., 1984 | 705 Willie Wilson, Kansas City, 1980 |

Runs
| 196 William Hamilton, Phila., 1894 | 177 Babe Ruth, New York, 1921 |
| 158 Chuck Klein, Phila., 1930 | |

Hits
| 254 Frank J. O'Doul, Phila., 1929 | 257 George Sisler, St. Louis, 1920 |
| 254 Bill Terry, New York, 1930 | |

Doubles
| 64 Joseph M. Medwick, St. L., 1936 | 67 Earl W. Webb, Boston, 1931 |

Triples
| 36 J. Owen Wilson, Pitts., 1912 | 26 Joseph Jackson, Cleve., 1912 |
| | 26 Samuel Crawford, Detroit, 1914 |

Home Runs
| 56 Hack Wilson, Chicago, 1930 | 61 Roger Maris, New York, 1961 |

Runs Batted In
| 190 Hack Wilson, Chicago, 1930 | 184 Lou Gehrig, New York, 1931 |

Stolen Bases
| 118 Lou Brock, St. Louis, 1974 | 130 Rickey Henderson, Oakland, 1982 |

Bases on Balls
| 148 Eddie Stanky, Brooklyn, 1945 | 170 Babe Ruth, New York, 1923 |
| 148 Jim Wynn, Houston, 1969 | |

Strikeouts
| 189 Bobby Bonds, S.F., 1970 | 186 Rob Deer, Milwaukee, 1987 |

Pitching (Season)
Games
| 106 Mike Marshall, L.A., 1974 | 88 Wilbur Wood, Chicago, 1968 |

Innings Pitched
| 434 Joseph J. McGinnity, N.Y., 1903 | 464 Edward Walsh, Chicago, 1908 |

Victories
| 37 Christy Mathewson, N.Y., 1908 | 41 Jack Chesbro, New York, 1904 |

Losses
| 29 Victor Willis, Boston, 1905 | 26 John Townsend, Wash., 1904 |
| | 26 Robert Groom, Wash., 1909 |

Strikeouts
(Left-hander)
| 382 Sandy Koufax, Los Angeles, 1965 | 343 Rube Waddell, Phila., 1904 |

(Right-hander)
| 313 J.R. Richard, Houston, 1979 | 383 Nolan Ryan, Cal., 1973 |

Bases on Balls
| 185 Sam Jones, Chicago, 1955 | 208 Bob Feller, Cleveland, 1938 |

Earned-Run Average
(Minimum 300 Innings)
| 1.12 Bob Gibson, St. L., 1968 | 1.09 Walter Johnson, Washington, 1913 |

Shutouts
| 16 Grover C. Alexander, Phila., 1916 | 13 John W. Coombs, Phila., 1910 |

Rickey Henderson broke Lou Brock's (left) SB mark in '82.

WORLD SERIES WINNERS

Year	A. L. Champion	N. L. Champion	World Series Winner
1903	Boston Red Sox	Pittsburgh Pirates	Boston, 5-3
1905	Philadelphia Athletics	New York Giants	New York, 4-1
1906	Chicago White Sox	Chicago Cubs	Chicago (AL), 4-2
1907	Detroit Tigers	Chicago Cubs	Chicago, 4-0-1
1908	Detroit Tigers	Chicago Cubs	Chicago, 4-1
1909	Detroit Tigers	Pittsburgh Pirates	Pittsburgh, 4-3
1910	Philadelphia Athletics	Chicago Cubs	Philadelphia, 4-1
1911	Philadelphia Athletics	New York Giants	Philadelphia, 4-2
1912	Boston Red Sox	New York Giants	Boston, 4-3-1
1913	Philadelphia Athletics	New York Giants	Philadelphia, 4-1
1914	Philadelphia Athletics	Boston Braves	Boston, 4-0
1915	Boston Red Sox	Philadelphia Phillies	Boston, 4-1
1916	Boston Red Sox	Brooklyn Dodgers	Boston, 4-1
1917	Chicago White Sox	New York Giants	Chicago, 4-2
1918	Boston Red Sox	Chicago Cubs	Boston, 4-2
1919	Chicago White Sox	Cincinnati Reds	Cincinnati, 5-3
1920	Cleveland Indians	Brooklyn Dodgers	Cleveland, 5-2
1921	New York Yankees	New York Giants	New York (NL), 5-3
1922	New York Yankees	New York Giants	New York (NL), 4-0-1
1923	New York Yankees	New York Giants	New York (AL), 4-2
1924	Washington Senators	New York Giants	Washington, 4-2
1925	Washington Senators	Pittsburgh Pirates	Pittsburgh, 4-3
1926	New York Yankees	St. Louis Cardinals	St. Louis, 4-3
1927	New York Yankees	Pittsburgh Pirates	New York, 4-0
1928	New York Yankees	St. Louis Cardinals	New York, 4-0
1929	Philadelphia Athletics	Chicago Cubs	Philadelphia, 4-2
1930	Philadelphia Athletics	St. Louis Cardinals	Philadelphia, 4-2
1931	Philadelphia Athletics	St. Louis Cardinals	St. Louis, 4-3
1932	New York Yankees	Chicago Cubs	New York, 4-0
1933	Washington Senators	New York Giants	New York, 4-1
1934	Detroit Tigers	St. Louis Cardinals	St. Louis, 4-3
1935	Detroit Tigers	Chicago Cubs	Detroit, 4-2
1936	New York Yankees	New York Giants	New York (AL), 4-2
1937	New York Yankees	New York Giants	New York (AL), 4-1
1938	New York Yankees	Chicago Cubs	New York, 4-0
1939	New York Yankees	Cincinnati Reds	New York, 4-0
1940	Detroit Tigers	Cincinnati Reds	Cincinnati, 4-3
1941	New York Yankees	Brooklyn Dodgers	New York, 4-1
1942	New York Yankees	St. Louis Cardinals	St. Louis, 4-1
1943	New York Yankees	St. Louis Cardinals	New York, 4-1
1944	St. Louis Browns	St. Louis Cardinals	St. Louis (NL), 4-2
1945	Detroit Tigers	Chicago Cubs	Detroit, 4-3
1946	Boston Red Sox	St. Louis Cardinals	St. Louis, 4-3
1947	New York Yankees	Brooklyn Dodgers	New York, 4-3
1948	Cleveland Indians	Boston Braves	Cleveland, 4-2
1949	New York Yankees	Brooklyn Dodgers	New York, 4-1
1950	New York Yankees	Philadelphia Phillies	New York, 4-0
1951	New York Yankees	New York Giants	New York (AL), 4-2
1952	New York Yankees	Brooklyn Dodgers	New York, 4-3
1953	New York Yankees	Brooklyn Dodgers	New York, 4-2

Year	A. L. Champion	N. L. Champion	World Series Winner
1954	Cleveland Indians	New York Giants	New York, 4-0
1955	New York Yankees	Brooklyn Dodgers	Brooklyn, 4-3
1956	New York Yankees	Brooklyn Dodgers	New York, 4-3
1957	New York Yankees	Milwaukee Braves	Milwaukee, 4-3
1958	New York Yankees	Milwaukee Braves	New York, 4-3
1959	Chicago White Sox	Los Angeles Dodgers	Los Angeles, 4-2
1960	New York Yankees	Pittsburgh Pirates	Pittsburgh, 4-3
1961	New York Yankees	Cincinnati Reds	New York, 4-1
1962	New York Yankees	San Francisco Giants	New York, 4-3
1963	New York Yankees	Los Angeles Dodgers	Los Angeles, 4-0
1964	New York Yankees	St. Louis Cardinals	St. Louis, 4-3
1965	Minnesota Twins	Los Angeles Dodgers	Los Angeles, 4-3
1966	Baltimore Orioles	Los Angeles Dodgers	Baltimore, 4-0
1967	Boston Red Sox	St. Louis Cardinals	St. Louis, 4-3
1968	Detroit Tigers	St. Louis Cardinals	Detroit, 4-3
1969	Baltimore Orioles	New York Mets	New York, 4-1
1970	Baltimore Orioles	Cincinnati Reds	Baltimore, 4-1
1971	Baltimore Orioles	Pittsburgh Pirates	Pittsburgh, 4-3
1972	Oakland A's	Cincinnati Reds	Oakland, 4-3
1973	Oakland A's	New York Mets	Oakland, 4-3
1974	Oakland A's	Los Angeles Dodgers	Oakland, 4-1
1975	Boston Red Sox	Cincinnati Reds	Cincinnati, 4-3
1976	New York Yankees	Cincinnati Reds	Cincinnati, 4-0
1977	New York Yankees	Los Angeles Dodgers	New York, 4-2
1978	New York Yankees	Los Angeles Dodgers	New York, 4-2
1979	Baltimore Orioles	Pittsburgh Pirates	Pittsburgh, 4-3
1980	Kansas City Royals	Philadelphia Phillies	Philadelphia, 4-2
1981	New York Yankees	Los Angeles Dodgers	Los Angeles, 4-2
1982	Milwaukee Brewers	St. Louis Cardinals	St. Louis, 4-3
1983	Baltimore Orioles	Philadelphia Phillies	Baltimore, 4-1
1984	Detroit Tigers	San Diego Padres	Detroit, 4-1
1985	Kansas City Royals	St. Louis Cardinals	Kansas City, 4-3
1986	Boston Red Sox	New York Mets	New York, 4-3
1987	Minnesota Twins	St. Louis Cardinals	Minnesota, 4-3
1988	Oakland A's	Los Angeles Dodgers	Los Angeles, 4-1
1989	Oakland A's	San Francisco Giants	Oakland, 4-0
1990	Oakland A's	Cincinnati Reds	Cincinnati, 4-0
1991	Minnesota Twins	Atlanta Braves	Minnesota, 4-3

1991 WORLD SERIES

Game 1
At MINNESOTA
Saturday, October 19 (night)

```
Atlanta ..........  000 001 010   2 6 1
Minnesota .......  001 031 00x   5 9 1
```
LEIBRANDT, Clancy (5), Wohlers (7) and Stanton (8)
MORRIS, Guthrie (8) and Aguilera (S) (8)
HR: Minnesota (1)-Gagne, Hrbek
Time: 3:00
Att: 55,108

Game 2
At MINNESOTA
Sunday, October 20 (night)

```
Atlanta ..........  010 010 000   2 8 1
Minnesota .......  200 000 01x   3 4 1
```
GLAVINE and
TAPANI and Aguilera (S) (9)
HR: Minnesota (2)-Davis, Leius
Time: 2:37
Att: 55,145

Game 3
At ATLANTA
Tuesday, October 22 (night)

```
Minnesota .......  100 000 120 000   4 10 1
Atlanta ..........  010 120 000 001   5 8 2
```
Erickson, West (5), Leach (5), Bedrosian (6), Willis (8), Guthrie (10) and AGUILERA (12)
Avery, Pena (8), Stanton (10), Wohlers (12), Mercker (12) and CLANCY (12)
HR: Atlanta (2)-Justice, Smith; Minnesota (2)-Puckett, Davis
Time: 4:04
Att: 50,878

MINNESOTA TWINS

PLAYER	AVG	G	AB	R	H	2B	3B	HR	RBI	SH	SF	HB	BB	SO	SB	CS	E
Brown, J.	.000	3	3	0	0	0	0	0	0	0	0	0	0	1	0	0	0
Bush, R.	.250	3	4	0	1	0	0	0	0	0	0	0	0	0	0	0	0
Davis, C.	.222	6	18	4	4	0	0	2	4	0	0	0	2	3	0	0	0
RIGHT	.167		12		2												
Gagne, G.	.333	7	6	1	2	0	0	1	3	0	0	0	2	2	0	0	0
Gladden, D.	.167	7	30	5	5	1	2	0	0	1	0	0	1	4	2	0	0
Harper, B.	.233	7	21	2	8	2	0	0	1	0	0	0	2	0	0	1	0
Hrbek, K.	.381	7	26	2	5	2	0	1	0	0	0	0	4	6	0	0	0
Knoblauch, C.	.115	7	26	3	8	1	0	0	0	0	0	0	2	2	4	0	0
LEFT	.308		2		1												
Larkin, G.	.500	4	2	0	1	0	0	0	2	0	0	0	0	0	0	0	0
RIGHT	.500		2		1												
LEFT	.500		2		1												
Leius, S.	.357	7	14	2	5	1	0	1	2	0	0	0	2	2	0	0	0
Mack, S.	.130	6	23	4	3	0	0	0	1	0	0	0	2	7	0	1	0
Newman, A.	.000	4	2	2	0	0	0	0	0	0	0	0	0	0	0	0	0
RIGHT	.000		1														
LEFT	1.000		1		1												
Ortiz, J.	.200	3	5	0	1	0	0	0	1	0	0	0	0	2	0	0	0
Pagliarulo, M.	.273	6	11	1	3	1	0	1	3	0	0	0	0	2	0	0	0
Puckett, K.	.250	7	24	4	6	0	0	1	3	0	0	0	5	7	1	0	0
Sorrento, P.	.000	3	2	0	0	0	0	0	0	0	0	0	1	2	0	0	0
Aguilera, R.	.000	4	1	0	0	0	0	0	0	1	0	0	0	0	0	0	0
Erickson, S.	.000	3	2	0	0	0	0	0	0	0	0	0	0	1	0	0	0
Morris, J.	.000	3	2	1	0	0	0	0	0	3	0	0	0	3	0	0	0
Tapani, K.	.000	2	1	0	0	0	0	0	0	1	0	0	0	0	0	0	0
DH	.200	7	15	1	3	0	0	0	3	0	0	0	2	2	2	0	0
PITCHERS	.000	7	5	1	0	0	0	0	0	6	0	0	0	3	0	0	0
TWINS	.232	7	241	24	56	8	4	8	24	2	3	1	21	48	7	3	4
BRAVES	.253	7	249	29	63	10	4	8	29	4	1	2	26	39	5	1	6

PITCHER		W	L	ERA	G	GS	CG	SHO	SV	IP	H	R	ER	HR	HB	BB	SO	WP
Aguilera, R.	R	1	1	1.80	4	0	0	0	2	5.0	6	1	1	0	0	1	3	0
Bedrosian, S.	R	0	0	5.40	4	0	0	0	0	3.1	6	2	2	1	0	0	3	1
Erickson, S.	R	1	0	5.06	2	2	0	0	0	10.2	10	7	6	3	0	4	5	1
Guthrie, M.	L	0	1	2.25	4	0	0	0	0	4.0	3	1	1	0	1	1	3	1
Leach, T.	R	0	0	3.86	2	0	0	0	0	2.1	3	1	1	0	0	2	1	0
Morris, J.	R	2	0	1.17	3	3	1	1	0	23.0	18	3	3	1	0	9	15	2
Tapani, K.	R	0	1	4.50	2	2	0	0	0	12.0	13	6	6	1	0	2	7	0
West, D.	L	0	0	—	1	0	0	0	0	0.0	2	4	4	0	0	2	0	0
Willis, C.	R	0	0	5.14	2	0	0	0	0	7.0	6	4	4	2	1	0	2	0
TWINS		4	3	3.74	7	7	1	1	2	67.1	63	29	28	8	1	26	39	5
BRAVES		3	4	2.89	7	7	1	0	0	65.1	56	24	21	8	1	21	48	1

Game 4
At ATLANTA
Wednesday, October 23 (night)

```
Minnesota........ 010 000 100   2 7 0
Atlanta.......... 001 000 101   3 8 0
```
Morris, Willis (7), GUTHRIE (8) and Bedrosian (9)
Smoltz, Wohlers (8) and STANTON (8)
HR: Atlanta (2)-Pendleton, Smith; Minnesota (1)-Pagliarulo
Time: 2:57
Att: 50,878

Game 5
At ATLANTA
Thursday, October 24 (night)

```
Minnesota........ 000 003 011    5  7 1
Atlanta.......... 000 410 63 x  14 17 1
```
TAPANI, Leach (6), West (7), Bedrosian (7) and Willis (8)
GLAVINE, Mercker (6), Clancy (7) and St. Claire (9)
HR: Atlanta (3)-Justice, Smith, Hunter
Time: 2:59
Att: 50,878

Game 6
At MINNESOTA
Saturday, October 26 (night)

```
Atlanta.......... 0 0 0 020 100 00   3 9 1
Minnesota........ 200 010 000 01    4 9 0
```
Avery, Stanton (7), Pena (9) and LEIBRANDT (11)
Erickson, Guthrie (7), Willis (7) and AGUILERA (10)
HR: Atlanta (1)-Pendleton; Minnesota (1)-Puckett
Time: 3:36
Att: 55,155

Game 7
At MINNESOTA
Sunday, October 27 (night)

```
Atlanta.......... 000 000 000 0   0  7 0
Minnesota........ 000 000 000 1   1 10 0
```
Smoltz, Stanton (8) and PENA (9)
MORRIS
Time: 3:23
Att: 55,118

ATLANTA BRAVES

PLAYER	AVG	G	AB	R	H	2B	3B	HR	RBI	SH	SF	HB	BB	SO	SB	CS	E
Belliard, R.	.375	7	16	0	6	1	0	0	4	2	-	1	-	2	0	0	0
Blauser, J.	.167	5	6	0	1	0	0	0	0	-	-	-	3	4	0	0	0
Bream, S.	.125	7	24	0	3	2	0	0	4	-	-	-	4	3	0	0	0
Cabrera, F.	.000	3	1	0	0	0	0	0	0	-	-	-	0	0	0	0	0
Gant, R.	.267	7	30	3	8	0	1	0	4	-	-	-	3	7	1	0	0
Gregg, T.	.000	4	3	0	0	0	0	0	0	-	-	-	0	2	0	0	0
Hunter, B.	.190	5	21	2	4	1	0	2	6	-	1	-	2	5	0	0	1
Justice, D.	.259	7	27	5	7	1	0	2	6	-	-	-	5	4	2	0	0
Lemke, M.	.417	6	24	4	10	1	3	0	4	1	-	-	2	1	0	1	0
RIGHT	1.000	-	1	-	1	-	-	-	-	-	-	-	-	-	-	-	-
LEFT	.391	-	23	-	9	-	-	-	-	-	-	-	-	-	-	-	-
Mitchell, K.	.000	3	23	1	9	-	-	-	-	5	-	1	4	0	0	0	1
Olson, G.	.222	7	27	3	6	3	0	0	3	-	-	-	5	4	0	0	0
Pendleton, T.	.367	7	30	6	11	3	0	2	6	-	-	-	1	3	1	0	2
RIGHT	.333	-	3	-	1	-	-	-	-	-	-	-	-	-	-	-	-
LEFT	.370	-	27	-	10	-	-	-	-	-	-	-	-	-	-	-	-
Smith, L.	.231	7	26	5	6	0	0	3	3	-	-	-	1	0	0	0	0
Treadway, J.	.250	3	4	1	1	0	0	0	0	-	-	-	0	1	0	0	0
Willard, J.	.000	3	3	0	0	0	0	0	0	-	-	-	0	0	0	0	1
Avery, S.	.000	2	2	0	0	0	0	0	0	2	-	-	0	2	0	0	0
Clancy, J.	.000	2	3	0	0	0	0	0	0	-	-	-	0	2	0	0	0
Glavine, T.	.000	2	2	0	0	0	0	0	0	-	-	-	0	0	0	0	0
Smoltz, J.	.154	7	13	2	2	0	0	0	0	1	-	-	0	1	0	0	0
DH																	
BRAVES	.253	7	249	29	63	10	4	8	29	4	3	1	26	39	5	1	6
TWINS	.232	7	241	24	56	8	4	8	24	2	2	1	21	48	7	3	4

PITCHER		W	L	ERA	G	GS	CG	SHO	SV	IP	H	R	ER	HR	HB	BB	SO	WP
Avery, S.	L	0	0	3.46	2	2	0	0	0	13.0	10	6	5	1	0	4	8	0
Clancy, J.	R	1	0	4.15	2	0	0	0	0	4.1	3	2	2	0	0	1	0	0
Glavine, T.	L	1	1	2.70	2	2	1	0	0	13.1	13	8	4	2	1	2	5	0
Lebrandt, C.	L	0	2	11.25	2	1	0	0	0	4.0	8	5	5	2	0	2	3	0
Mercker, K.	L	0	0	0.00	2	0	0	0	0	1.0	1	0	0	0	0	0	1	0
Pena, A.	R	0	0	3.38	3	0	0	0	0	5.1	6	2	2	0	0	3	7	1
Smoltz, J.	R	0	0	1.26	2	2	0	0	0	14.1	11	3	1	1	0	4	11	0
St. Claire, R.	R	0	0	9.00	1	0	0	0	0	1.0	2	1	1	0	0	0	0	0
Stanton, M.	L	1	0	0.00	5	0	0	0	0	7.1	5	0	0	0	0	2	7	0
Wohlers, M.	R	0	0	0.00	3	0	0	0	0	1.2	2	0	0	0	0	2	1	0
BRAVES		3	4	2.89	7	7	1	0	0	65.1	56	24	21	8	1	21	48	2
TWINS		4	3	3.74	7	7	1	0	1	67.1	63	29	28	8	0	26	39	2

OFFICIAL 1991
NATIONAL LEAGUE RECORDS

COMPILED BY MLB-IBM BASEBALL INFORMATION SYSTEM
Official Statistician: ELIAS SPORTS BUREAU

FINAL STANDINGS

EASTERN DIVISION	W	L	PCT.	GB	WESTERN DIVISION	W	L	PCT.	GB
PITTSBURGH	98	64	.605		ATLANTA	94	68	.580	-
ST. LOUIS	84	78	.519	14.0	LOS ANGELES	93	69	.574	1.0
PHILADELPHIA	78	84	.481	20.0	SAN DIEGO	84	78	.519	10.0
CHICAGO	77	83	.481	20.0	SAN FRANCISCO	75	87	.463	19.0
NEW YORK	77	84	.478	20.5	CINCINNATI	74	88	.457	20.0
MONTREAL	71	90	.441	26.5	HOUSTON	65	97	.401	29.0

Championship Series: Atlanta defeated Pittsburgh, 4 games to 3

Batting

Individual Batting Leaders

Batting Average	.319	Pendleton	Atl.
Games	161	Butler	L.A.
At Bats	619	Grace	Chi.
Runs	112	Butler	L.A.
Hits	187	Pendleton	Atl.
Total Bases	303	Clark	S.F.
		Pendleton	Atl.
Singles	162	Butler	L.A.
Doubles	44	Bonilla	Pit.
Triples	15	Lankford	St.L.
Home Runs	38	Johnson	N.Y.
Runs Batted In	117	Johnson	N.Y.
Sacrifice Hits	30	Bell	Pit.
Sacrifice Flies	15	Johnson	N.Y.
Hit by Pitch	13	Bagwell	Hou.
Bases on Balls	108	Butler	L.A.
Intentional Bases on Balls	26	McGriff	S.D.
Strikeouts	151	DeShields	Mon.
Stolen Bases	76	Grissom	Mon.
Caught Stealing	28	Butler	L.A.
Grounded Into Double Play	21	Santiago	S.D.
Slugging Percentage	.536	Clark	S.F.
On-Base Percentage	.410	Bonds	Pit.
Longest Batting Streak	23	Butler	L.A. (June 15-July 12)

TOP 15 QUALIFIERS FOR BATTING CHAMPIONSHIP

BATTER	TEAM	B	AVG	G	AB	R	H	TB	2B	3B	HR	RBI	SH	SF	HP	BB	IBB	SO	SB	CS	GI DP	SLG	OBP	E
Pendleton, T	ATL	S	.319	153	586	94	187	303	34	8	22	86	7	7	1	43	8	70	10	4	16	.517	.363	24
Morris, H	CIN	L	.318	136	478	72	152	229	33	1	14	59	7	5	1	46	8	61	10	2	4	.479	.374	9
Gwynn, T	SD	L	.317	134	530	69	168	229	27	11	4	62	5	5	0	34	8	19	8	8	11	.432	.355	3
McGee, W.	SF	L	.312	131	497	67	155	203	30	3	4	43	8	5	2	34	2	74	17	8	11	.408	.357	6
Jose, F	STL	S	.305	154	568	69	173	249	40	6	8	77	0	5	2	50	8	113	20	9	12	.438	.360	6
Larkin, B	CIN	R	.302	123	464	88	140	235	27	4	20	69	3	2	3	55	1	64	24	6	7	.506	.378	15
Bonilla, B	PIT	S	.302	157	577	102	174	284	44	6	18	100	3	11	3	90	8	67	2	6	14	.492	.391	15
Clark, W	SF	L	.301	148	565	84	170	303	32	7	29	116	2	4	2	51	12	91	4	2	5	.536	.359	4
Sabo, C	CIN	R	.301	153	582	91	175	294	35	3	26	88	5	3	6	44	3	79	19	4	13	.505	.354	12
Calderon, I	MON	L	.300	134	470	69	141	226	22	3	19	75	1	10	4	53	4	64	31	6	7	.481	.368	7
Butler, B	LA	L	.296	161	615	112	182	211	13	5	2	38	5	5	2	108	4	79	38	28	3	.343	.401	0
Biggio, C	HOU	R	.295	149	546	79	161	204	23	4	4	46	5	3	2	53	3	71	19	6	2	.374	.358	11
Bagwell, J	HOU	R	.294	156	554	79	163	242	26	4	15	82	1	13	13	75	3	116	7	4	12	.437	.387	12
Kruk, J	PHI	L	.294	152	538	84	158	260	27	6	21	92	0	9	1	67	16	100	7	0	11	.483	.367	3
Bonds, B	PIT	L	.292	153	510	95	149	262	28	5	25	116	0	13	4	107	25	73	43	13	8	.514	.410	3

INDIVIDUAL BATTING

BATTER	TEAM	B	AVG	G	AB	R	H	TB	2B	3B	HR	RBI	SH	SF	HP	BB	IBB	SO	SB	CS	GI DP	SLG	OBP	E
Abner, S	SD	R	.165	53	115	15	19	28	4	1	1	5	1		1	7	4	25	0	0	3	.243	.218	0
Agosto, J	STL	L	.333	72	3	0	1	1	0	0	0	0						2	0	0	0	.333	.500	2
Akerfelds, D	PHI	R	.000	30	3	0	0	0	0	0	0	0						3	0	1	0	.000	.000	1
Aldrete, M	SD	L	.000	12	15	2	0	0	0	0	0	0				3		4	0	0	0	.000	.167	0
Alicea, L	STL	S	.191	56	68	5	13	16	3	0	0	0				8		19	0	1	0	.235	.276	0
Andersen, L	SD	R	.000	38	2	0	0	0	0	0	0	0						1	0	0	0	.000	.000	0
Anderson, D	SF	R	.248	100	226	24	56	71	5	2	2	13	2	2		12	1	35	2	4	8	.314	.286	1
Anthony, E	HOU	L	.153	39	118	11	18	27	6	0	1	7		2		12	1	41	1	0	2	.229	.227	11
Armstrong, J	CIN,	R	.093	27	43	3	4	5	1	0	0	2	5			1		18	0	0	1	.116	.114	2
Ashby, A	PHI	R	.083	8	12	0	1	1	0	0	0	0	1					9	0	0	0	.083	.083	0

BATTER	TEAM	B	AVG	G	AB	R	H	TB	2B	3B	HR	RBI	SH	SF	HP	BB	IBB	SO	SB	CS	GI DP	SLG	OBP	E
Assenmacher, P ... CHI		L	.250	75	4	1	1	1	0	0	0	0	0	0	0	1	0	1	1	0	0	.250	.400	1
Avery, S	ATL	L	.215	37	79	17	17	20	1	1	0	2	5	0	0	4	0	31	0	1	1	.253	.253	1
Azocar, O	SD	L	.246	38	57	5	14	16	2	0	0	9	0	1	1	1	0	9	2	2	0	.281	.267	2
Backman, W	PHI	S	.243	94	185	20	45	57	12	0	0	15	2	3	0	30	1	30	3	0	2	.308	.344	4
Bagwell, J	HOU	R	.294	156	554	79	163	242	26	4	15	82	1	7	13	75	5	116	7	4	12	.437	.387	12
Banister, J	PIT	R	1.000	1	1	0	1	1	0	0	0	0	0	0	0	0	0	0	0	0	0	1.000	1.000	0
Barberie, B	MON	S	.353	57	136	16	48	70	12	1	2	18	1	3	2	20	2	22	0	0	4	.515	.435	5
Barnes, B	MON	L	.082	28	49	1	4	4	0	0	0	1	3	0	0	7	0	19	0	0	0	.082	.196	2
Barrett, M	MON	R	.188	12	16	1	3	7	1	0	1	3	0	0	0	0	0	3	0	0	0	.438	.235	0
Bass, K	SF	S	.233	124	361	43	84	132	10	4	10	40	1	2	1	36	8	56	7	4	12	.366	.307	4
Batiste, K	PHI	R	.222	10	27	2	6	6	0	0	0	0	0	0	0	1	0	8	0	1	0	.222	.250	1
Beck, R	SF	R	.500	31	2	0	1	1	0	0	0	1	7	0	0	0	0	0	0	0	0	.500	.500	0
Belcher, T	LA	R	.119	33	67	3	8	10	2	0	0	3	2	0	0	2	0	26	0	0	1	.149	.119	2
Belinda, S	PIT	R	.000	60	7	0	0	0	0	0	0	0	0	0	0	0	0	5	0	0	0	.000	.000	10
Bell, G	CHI	R	.285	149	558	63	159	261	27	0	25	86	0	9	4	32	6	62	2	0	10	.468	.323	10
Bell, J	PIT	R	.270	157	608	96	164	260	32	8	16	67	30	3	4	52	2	99	10	6	15	.428	.330	24
Bell, M	ATL	L	.133	17	30	4	4	7	0	0	1	1	0	1	0	2	0	7	1	0	2	.233	.188	2
Belliard, R	ATL	R	.249	149	353	36	88	101	9	2	0	27	7	1	1	22	2	63	3	6	4	.286	.296	18
Benavides, F	CIN	R	.286	24	63	11	18	19	1	0	0	3	1	0	1	1	0	15	1	3	1	.302	.303	2
Benes, A	SD	R	.032	33	62	4	2	5	0	0	1	1	7	0	2	2	0	29	0	0	0	.081	.143	0
Benjamin, M	SF	R	.123	54	106	12	13	22	3	0	2	8	3	0	2	6	1	26	3	2	2	.208	.188	3
Benzinger, T	CIN	S	.187	51	123	7	23	33	3	2	1	11	1	2	0	7	2	20	0	0	0	.268	.244	2
Berenguer, J	ATL	R	.000	49	5	0	0	0	0	0	0	0	4	0	0	0	0	3	0	0	0	.000	.000	0
Berryhill, D	CHI-ATL	R	.188	63	160	13	30	52	7	0	5	14	0	1	0	11	0	42	0	2	2	.325	.243	8
Bielecki, M	CHI-ATL	R	.065	41	46	1	3	3	0	0	0	7	4	0	0	3	0	21	0	0	0	.065	.122	0
Biggio, C	HOU	R	.295	149	546	79	161	204	23	4	4	46	5	3	2	53	0	71	19	6	5	.374	.358	11
Bilardello, D	SD	R	.269	15	26	4	7	11	2	1	0	5	0	0	0	3	0	4	0	0	1	.423	.345	0
Black, B	SF	L	.183	35	71	3	13	16	3	0	0	6	9	0	0	3	0	20	0	0	0	.225	.183	0
Blauser, J	ATL	R	.259	129	352	49	91	144	14	3	11	54	4	3	2	54	0	59	5	6	4	.409	.358	17
Boever, J	PHI	R	.333	68	3	0	1	1	0	0	0	1	4	0	0	0	0	0	0	0	0	.333	.333	0
Bonds, B	PHI	L	.292	153	510	95	149	262	28	5	25	116	0	13	4	107	25	73	43	13	8	.514	.410	3
Bones, R	SD	R	.077	11	13	1	1	1	0	0	0	1	4	0	0	2	0	5	0	0	0	.077	.200	0
Bonilla, B	PIT	S	.302	157	577	102	174	284	44	6	18	100	0	11	2	90	8	67	2	4	14	.492	.391	15

Player	B	AVG	G	AB	R	H	2B	3B	HR	RBI	BB	SO	SB	CS	SLG	OBP	GDP
Booker, R ....PHI	L	.226	28	53	3	12	1	0	0	0	1	7	0	0	.245	.236	0
Boskie, S ....CHI	R	.171	30	41	3	7	2	0	1	1	3	15	0	0	.293	.227	2
Boston, D ....NY	L	.275	137	255	40	70	16	2	4	21	30	42	8	3	.416	.350	3
Bowen, R ....HOU	R	.182	17	22	2	4	1	0	0	0	3	11	0	0	.227	.280	2
Boyd, D ....MON	R	.083	19	36	1	3	0	0	0	2	0	19	0	0	.083	.154	0
Braggs, G ....CIN	R	.260	85	250	36	65	10	0	11	39	23	46	3	1	.432	.323	5
Brantley, C ....PHI	R	.000	6	8	0	0	0	0	0	0	0	4	0	0	.000	.000	1
Brantley, J ....SF	R	.000	67	0	0	0	0	0	0	0	0	1	0	0	.000	.313	0
Bream, S ....ATL	L	.253	91	265	32	67	12	0	11	45	25	31	0	0	.423	.077	3
Brewer, R ....STL	L	.077	19	13	0	1	0	0	0	1	0	5	0	0	.077	.077	1
Brooks, H ....NY	R	.238	103	357	48	85	11	1	16	50	44	62	3	1	.409	.324	5
Browning, T ....CIN	L	.171	36	70	3	12	3	0	1	5	3	19	0	0	.257	.205	5
Buechele, S ....PIT	R	.246	31	114	16	28	7	0	4	19	10	28	1	0	.412	.315	4
Bullett, S ....PIT	L	.000	11	4	2	0	0	0	0	0	1	3	1	0	.000	.200	0
Bullock, E ....MON	L	.222	73	72	6	16	4	0	1	6	9	13	0	0	.319	.305	2
Burke, T ....MON-NY	R	.000	36	6	0	0	0	0	0	0	0	4	0	0	.000	.000	1
Burkett, J ....SF	R	.091	36	55	6	5	1	0	0	1	3	26	0	0	.109	.138	2
Butler, B ....LA	L	.296	161	615	112	182	13	5	2	38	108	79	38	13	.343	.401	1
Cabrera, F ....ATL	R	.242	44	112	23	27	6	0	5	23	20	20	0	0	.432	.284	0
Calderon, I ....MON	R	.300	134	470	69	141	22	1	19	75	53	64	31	3	.481	.368	3
Caminiti, K ....HOU	S	.253	152	574	65	145	30	3	13	80	46	85	4	5	.383	.312	7
Campusano, S ....PHI	R	.114	15	35	2	4	0	0	1	2	2	10	0	0	.200	.139	23
Candaele, C ....HOU	S	.262	151	461	44	121	20	7	4	50	40	49	9	2	.362	.319	0
Carman, D ....CIN	L	.000	28	5	0	0	0	0	0	0	0	3	0	0	.000	.000	0
Carpenter, C ....STL	R	.333	59	3	1	1	0	0	0	1	0	0	0	0	.333	.333	0
Carr, C ....NY	S	.182	12	11	1	2	0	0	0	0	0	2	1	0	.182	.182	0
Carreno, A ....PHI	R	.000	3	0	0	0	0	0	0	0	0	1	0	0	.000	.000	0
Carreon, M ....NY	R	.260	106	254	18	66	14	0	4	21	12	26	2	1	.331	.297	3
Carter, G ....LA	R	.246	101	248	22	61	14	0	6	26	22	26	2	3	.375	.323	5
Castilla, V ....ATL	R	.200	12	5	1	1	0	0	0	0	2	2	0	0	.200	.200	0
Castillo, F ....PHI	R	.173	28	52	3	9	3	0	0	2	7	15	1	0	.231	.189	1
Castillo, B ....CHI	R	.143	18	35	0	5	0	0	0	0	0	13	0	0	.143	.189	0
Castillo, T ....ATL-NY	L	.000	17	4	0	0	0	0	0	0	2	0	0	0	.000	.000	0
Cedeno, A ....HOU	R	.243	67	251	27	61	13	2	9	36	9	74	4	2	.418	.270	18
Cerone, R ....NY	R	.273	90	227	18	62	13	0	2	16	30	24	1	0	.357	.360	6

BATTER	TEAM	B	AVG	G	AB	R	H	TB	2B	3B	HR	RBI	SH	SF	HP	BB	IBB	SO	SB	CS	GI DP	SLG	OBP	E
Chamberlain, W ... PHI		R	.240	101	383	51	92	153	16	3	13	50	1	4	0	2	31	0	73	9	4	8	.399	.300	3
Charlton, N ... CIN		S	.043	41	23	1	1	1	0	0	0	0	4	0	0	2	0	0	10	0	0	0	.087	.043	1
Clancy, J ... HOU-ATL		R	.000	54	6	0	0	0	0	0	0	0	1	0	0	0	0	0	2	0	1	0	.000	.000	1
Clark, J ... SD		R	.228	118	369	26	84	130	16	0	10	47	1	4	6	31	12	90	2	0	10	.352	.295	2
Clark, M ... STL		R	.000	7	7	0	0	0	0	0	0	0	1	0	0	0	0	0	2	0	0	0	.000	.000	0
Clark, W ... SF		L	.301	148	565	84	170	303	32	7	29	116	0	4	2	51	12	91	4	2	5	.536	.359	4
Clayton, R ... SF		R	.115	9	26	0	3	4	1	0	0	2	0	0	0	0	0	6	0	0	0	.154	.148	3
Clements, P ... SD		R	.000	12	1	0	0	0	0	0	0	0	1	0	0	0	0	0	1	0	0	0	.000	.000	0
Coleman, V ... NY		S	.255	72	278	45	71	91	7	5	1	17	1	0	0	39	0	47	37	14	3	.327	.347	3
Coles, D ... SF		R	.214	11	14	1	3	3	0	0	0	0	0	0	1	2	0	2	0	0	1	.214	.214	0
Combs, P ... PHI		L	.133	14	15	1	2	2	0	0	0	0	2	0	0	2	0	7	0	0	0	.133	.278	0
Cone, D ... NY		L	.125	34	72	3	9	9	0	0	0	5	6	1	2	3	0	14	0	0	3	.125	.179	4
Cook, D ... LA		L	.000	20	1	0	0	0	0	0	0	0	1	0	0	0	0	1	0	0	0	.000	.000	0
Coolbaugh, S ... SD		R	.217	60	180	12	39	55	8	1	2	15	4	1	1	19	2	45	0	3	8	.306	.294	7
Cooper, G ... HOU		R	.250	9	16	1	4	5	1	0	0	2	0	0	0	3	0	6	0	0	0	.313	.368	1
Cormier, R ... STL		L	.238	11	21	2	5	5	0	0	0	1	1	0	0	0	0	5	0	0	0	.238	.238	0
Corsi, J ... HOU		R	.000	47	1	0	0	0	0	0	0	0	1	0	1	0	0	1	0	0	0	.000	.000	1
Costello, J ... SD		R	.000	27	1	0	0	0	0	0	0	0	1	0	0	0	0	1	0	0	0	.000	.000	0
Cox, D ... PHI		R	.103	23	29	4	3	3	0	0	0	1	4	0	0	2	0	16	0	0	0	.103	.161	0
Crews, T ... LA		R	.000	60	1	0	0	0	0	0	0	0	0	0	0	1	0	1	0	0	0	.000	.500	1
Daniels, K ... LA		L	.249	137	461	54	115	183	15	1	17	73	0	6	1	63	6	116	6	1	9	.397	.337	5
Darling, R ... NY-MON		R	.125	20	40	1	5	9	4	0	0	3	6	0	0	2	0	16	0	0	0	.225	.125	6
Dascenzo, D ... CHI		S	.255	118	239	40	61	75	11	0	1	18	6	2	2	24	2	26	14	7	3	.314	.327	2
Daulton, D ... PHI		L	.196	89	285	36	56	104	12	0	12	42	2	5	2	41	4	66	5	0	4	.365	.297	8
Davidson, M ... HOU		R	.190	85	142	10	27	39	6	0	2	15	2	2	2	12	0	28	0	0	2	.275	.263	0
Davis, B ... LA		R	.000	1	1	0	0	0	0	0	0	0	0	0	0	0	0	0	0	0	0	.000	.000	0
Davis, E ... CIN		R	.235	89	285	39	67	110	10	0	11	33	0	6	2	48	5	92	14	4	4	.386	.353	3
Dawson, A ... CHI		R	.272	149	563	69	153	275	21	4	31	104	0	5	5	22	3	80	4	5	10	.488	.302	3
DeJesus, J ... PHI		R	.129	31	62	3	8	8	0	0	0	4	4	0	0	3	0	39	0	0	0	.129	.156	1
DeLeon, J ... STL		R	.043	28	46	0	2	2	0	0	0	0	5	0	0	0	0	17	0	0	0	.043	.043	0
Decker, S ... SF		R	.206	79	233	11	48	72	7	1	5	24	8	4	3	16	0	44	0	1	7	.309	.262	7
Deshaies, J ... HOU		L	.098	28	41	1	4	4	0	0	0	0	8	0	0	0	0	16	0	0	1	.098	.178	3
DeShields, D ... MON		L	.238	151	563	83	134	187	15	4	10	51	8	5	2	95	2	151	56	23	6	.332	.347	27

Player	Team	B	AVG	G	AB	R	H	TB	2B	3B	HR	RBI	BB	SO	SB	CS	GDP	OBP	SLG
Dibble, R.	CIN	L	.000	67	2	0	0	0	0	0	0	0	0	0	0	0	1	.000	.000
Donnels, C.	NY	L	.225	37	89	7	20	22	2	0	0	5	14	19	1	0	2	.330	.247
Doran, B.	CIN	S	.280	111	361	51	101	135	12	2	6	35	—	39	4	4	7	.359	.374
Dorsett, B.	SD	R	.083	11	12	0	1	1	0	0	0	1	0	3	0	0	0	.083	.083
Downs, K.	SF	R	.087	45	23	6	2	2	0	0	0	0	1	5	0	0	1	.125	.087
Drabek, D.	PIT	R	.179	36	84	46	15	16	1	0	0	2	1	28	0	0	5	.188	.190
Duncan, M.	CIN	R	.258	100	333	59	86	137	7	0	12	40	12	57	4	0	9	.288	.411
Dunston, S.	CHI	R	.260	142	492	73	128	200	22	3	12	50	23	64	6	9	21	.292	.407
Dykstra, L.	PHI	L	.297	63	246	48	73	105	13	3	3	12	37	20	4	1	4	.391	.427
Elster, K.	NY	R	.241	115	348	33	84	122	16	1	6	36	40	53	3	4	14	.318	.351
Espy, C.	PIT	S	.244	43	82	7	20	27	4	2	1	11	5	17	0	0	2	.281	.329
Eusebio, H.	HOU	R	.105	10	19	4	2	3	0	0	0	0	6	8	0	1	1	.320	.158
Fajardo, H.	PIT	R	.000	2	3	0	0	0	0	0	0	0	0	0	0	0	0	.000	.000
Faries, P.	SD	R	.177	57	130	13	23	28	3	1	0	7	14	21	1	1	2	.262	.215
Fassero, J.	MON	L	.000	51	3	0	0	0	0	0	0	0	1	2	0	0	1	.250	.000
Felder, M.	SF	S	.264	132	348	51	92	114	10	3	0	18	30	31	6	5	4	.325	.328
Fernandez, S.	NY	L	.154	8	13	5	2	3	0	0	0	0	0	7	0	0	0	.154	.231
Fernandez, T.	SD	S	.272	145	558	81	152	201	27	10	4	38	55	74	9	12	20	.337	.360
Finley, S.	HOU	L	.285	159	596	84	170	242	28	10	8	54	42	65	18	8	5	.331	.406
Fitzgerald, M.	MON	R	.202	71	198	17	40	61	5	2	4	28	22	35	2	5	5	.278	.308
Fletcher, D.	PHI	L	.228	46	136	31	31	42	8	0	1	12	5	15	1	2	2	.255	.309
Foley, T.	MON	L	.208	86	168	12	35	48	11	1	0	15	14	30	0	4	6	.269	.286
Franco, J.	NY	L	.000	52	1	0	0	0	0	0	0	0	0	1	0	0	1	.000	.000
Fraser, W.	STL	R	.000	35	2	0	0	0	0	0	0	0	0	2	0	0	0	.000	.000
Freeman, M.	ATL	R	.000	34	7	0	0	0	0	0	0	0	0	5	0	0	0	.000	.000
Frey, S.	MON	L	.000	31	2	0	0	0	0	0	0	0	1	2	0	0	0	.000	.000
Galarraga, A.	MON	R	.219	107	375	34	82	126	13	2	9	33	23	86	0	0	9	.268	.336
Gant, R.	ATL	R	.251	154	561	101	141	278	35	2	32	105	71	104	6	6	6	.338	.496
Garcia, C.	PIT	R	.250	12	24	2	6	10	0	0	0	1	1	8	15	6	1	.280	.417
Gardner, C.	HOU	R	.000	5	5	0	0	0	0	0	0	0	0	0	0	0	1	.167	.000
Gardner, J.	NY	L	.162	13	37	3	6	6	0	0	1	1	4	6	0	0	6	.238	.162
Gardner, M.	MON	R	.091	27	55	5	5	5	0	0	0	4	1	18	0	0	1	.107	.091
Gardner, W.	SD	R	.000	14	4	1	0	0	0	0	0	0	0	2	0	0	0	.000	.000
Garrelts, S.	SF	R	.000	11	4	1	0	0	0	0	0	0	0	1	0	0	0	.000	.000
Gedman, R.	STL	L	.106	46	94	7	10	20	1	1	3	8	4	15	1	2	5	.140	.213

BATTER	TEAM	B	AVG	G	AB	R	H	TB	2B	3B	HR	RBI	SH	SF	HP	BB	IBB	SO	SB	CS	GI DP	SLG	OBP	E
Gilkey, B ....STL		R	.216	81	268	28	58	84	7	2	5	20	1	2	0	39	0	33	14	8	14	.313	.316	1
Girardi, J ....CHI		R	.191	21	47	3	9	11	2	0	0	6	1	0	0	6	0	6	0	0	1	.234	.283	3
Glavine, T ....ATL		L	.230	36	74	1	17	18	1	0	0	6	15	0	0	6	0	19	1	0	1	.243	.288	0
Gonzalez, J ....LA-PIT		R	.042	58	48	5	2	5	0	0	1	6	3	0	0	2	0	15	0	0	0	.104	.078	0
Gonzalez, L ....HOU		R	.254	137	473	51	120	205	28	9	13	69	2	4	8	40	4	101	10	7	9	.433	.320	5
Gooden, D ....NY		R	.238	27	63	7	15	21	3	0	1	6	8	0	0	2	0	9	1	1	0	.333	.238	2
Goodwin, T ....LA		L	.143	16	7	3	1	1	0	0	0	0	1	0	0	0	0	0	1	1	0	.143	.143	0
Gott, J ....LA		R	.500	55	2	0	1	1	0	0	0	0	0	0	0	0	0	1	0	0	0	.500	.500	0
Grace, M ....CHI		L	.273	160	619	87	169	231	28	5	8	58	0	7	3	70	7	53	3	4	6	.373	.346	8
Greene, T ....PHI		R	.268	38	71	4	19	27	8	0	0	7	4	0	1	4	0	15	0	0	0	.380	.307	1
Gregg, T ....ATL		L	.187	72	107	13	20	33	2	1	2	7	0	0	0	12	2	24	0	2	1	.308	.275	0
Griffin, A ....LA		S	.243	109	350	27	85	95	8	1	0	27	7	5	0	22	5	49	5	4	5	.271	.286	22
Grimsley, J ....PHI		R	.059	12	17	1	1	1	0	0	0	0	1	0	0	2	0	6	0	0	0	.059	.158	1
Grissom, M ....MON		R	.267	148	558	73	149	208	23	9	6	39	4	1	2	34	0	89	76	17	8	.373	.310	6
Gross, K ....LA		R	.280	48	25	2	7	8	1	0	0	3	2	0	0	2	0	14	0	0	0	.320	.333	1
Gross, K ....CIN		R	.091	29	22	1	2	2	0	0	0	0	3	0	0	0	0	6	0	0	0	.091	.091	2
Guerrero, P ....STL		R	.272	115	427	41	116	154	12	1	8	70	0	7	1	37	2	46	1	2	12	.361	.326	16
Gwynn, C ....LA		L	.252	94	139	18	35	57	5	1	5	22	1	3	0	10	8	23	1	8	5	.410	.301	0
Gwynn, T ....SD		L	.317	134	530	69	168	229	27	11	4	62	0	5	0	34	8	19	8	8	11	.432	.355	3
Hamilton, J ....LA		L	.223	41	94	4	21	28	4	0	1	14	1	0	2	4	0	21	0	0	0	.298	.255	5
Hammaker, A ....SD		S	.000	1	1	0	0	0	0	0	0	0	0	0	0	0	0	1	0	0	0	.000	.000	0
Hammond, C ....CIN		L	.353	20	34	1	12	15	3	0	0	1	2	0	0	2	0	10	0	0	1	.441	.389	2
Haney, C ....MON		L	.074	16	27	1	2	2	0	0	0	0	7	0	0	0	0	3	0	0	0	.074	.074	0
Hansen, D ....LA		L	.268	53	56	3	15	22	4	0	1	5	0	1	1	4	1	12	0	1	2	.393	.293	0
Harkey, M ....CHI		R	.400	4	5	2	2	2	0	0	0	0	1	0	0	0	0	0	0	0	0	.400	.500	1
Harnisch, P ....HOU		R	.097	33	62	4	6	7	1	0	0	4	7	1	0	4	0	21	0	0	1	.113	.132	0
Harris, G ....SD		R	.083	20	36	0	3	3	0	0	0	2	2	0	1	1	0	13	0	0	0	.083	.149	1
Harris, L ....LA		L	.287	145	429	59	123	150	16	1	3	38	12	2	5	37	5	32	12	3	16	.350	.349	20
Hartley, M ....LA-PHI		L	.000	58	5	0	0	0	0	0	0	0	1	0	0	0	0	1	0	0	0	.000	.000	0
Hassey, R ....MON		L	.227	52	119	5	27	38	8	0	1	14	2	1	0	13	1	16	1	1	5	.319	.301	1
Hatcher, B ....CIN		R	.262	138	442	45	116	159	25	3	4	41	4	3	1	26	4	55	11	9	13	.360	.312	2
Hayes, C ....PHI		R	.230	142	460	34	106	167	23	1	12	53	2	5	1	16	3	75	3	2	13	.363	.257	15
Hayes, V ....PHI		L	.225	77	284	43	64	81	15	1	0	21	0	5	3	31	0	42	9	2	6	.285	.303	2

Player	Team	B	AVG	G	AB	R	H	TB	2B	3B	HR	RBI	SLG	OBP	E
Heath, M	ATL	R	.209	49	139	4	29	37	3	1	1	12	.266	.250	2
Heaton, N	PIT	L	.286	44	14	0	4	5	1	0	0	1	.357	.333	1
Heep, D	ATL	L	.417	14	12	4	5	6	1	0	0	3	.500	.462	0
Henry, D	HOU	R	.000	52	1	0	0	0	0	0	0	0	.000	.000	0
Heredia, G.	SF	R	.429	7	7	0	3	3	0	0	0	0	.429	.500	0
Hernandez, C.	LA	R	.214	15	14	1	3	4	1	0	0	0	.286	.250	0
Hernandez, J.	SD	R	.000	9	2	0	0	0	0	0	0	0	.000	.000	1
Hernandez, X	HOU	R	.000	32	10	0	0	0	0	0	0	0	.000	.167	0
Herr, T	NY-SF	L	.209	102	215	23	45	58	8	0	0	21	.270	.344	0
Hershiser, O.	LA	S	.258	21	31	6	8	10	2	0	0	2	.323	.324	0
Hickerson, B	SF	R	.000	17	12	0	0	0	0	0	0	0	.000	.000	1
Hill, K.	STL	L	.100	30	50	2	5	5	0	0	0	3	.100	.000	0
Hill, M.	CIN	R	.000	22	1	0	0	0	0	0	0	0	.000	.167	2
Hollins, D.	PHI	R	.298	56	151	18	45	77	10	2	6	21	.510	.378	8
Howard, T.	SD	S	.249	106	281	30	70	100	12	3	4	22	.356	.309	1
Howell, J.	SD	L	.206	58	160	24	33	56	3	1	6	16	.350	.287	2
Hudler, R.	STL	S	.227	101	207	21	47	64	10	2	1	15	.309	.260	2
Hundley, T.	NY	R	.133	21	60	5	8	13	1	1	1	7	.217	.221	0
Hunter, B	ATL	S	.251	97	271	32	68	122	16	0	12	50	.450	.296	8
Hurst, B.	SD	L	.134	31	67	3	9	10	1	1	0	6	.149	.183	2
Innis, J.	NY	R	.000	69	2	0	0	2	0	0	0	0	.000	.000	1
Jackson, D.	CHI	R	.087	17	23	1	2	2	0	0	0	1	.087	.087	1
Jackson, D.	SD	R	.262	122	359	51	94	171	12	2	21	49	.476	.315	2
Javier, S.	LA	S	.205	121	176	21	36	50	5	3	2	11	.284	.268	3
Jefferies, G.	NY	S	.272	136	486	59	132	182	19	2	9	62	.374	.336	17
Jefferson, R	CIN	S	.143	5	7	1	1	1	0	0	0	1	.571	.250	0
Jefferson, S.	CIN	R	.053	13	19	1	1	1	0	0	0	0	.053	.100	0
Johnson, H.	NY	S	.259	156	564	108	146	302	34	4	38	117	.535	.342	31
Jones, B.	MON	R	.000	77	1	0	0	0	0	0	0	0	.000	.000	3
Jones, C.	CIN	R	.252	52	89	14	26	37	1	2	2	6	.416	.304	0
Jones, J.	HOU	R	.184	26	38	7	7	8	0	0	0	0	.211	.244	2
Jones, R.	PHI	L	.154	28	26	0	4	6	2	0	0	3	.231	.214	0
Jones, T.	STL	L	.167	16	24	1	4	6	2	0	0	0	.250	.222	0
Jordan, R.	PHI	R	.272	101	301	38	82	136	21	3	9	49	.452	.304	9
Jose, F.	STL	S	.305	154	568	69	173	249	40	6	8	77	.438	.360	3

BATTER	TEAM	B	AVG	G	AB	R	H	TB	2B	3B	HR	RBI	SH	SF	HP	BB	IBB	SO	SB	CS	GI DP	SLG	OBP	E
Juden, J	HOU	R	.000	4	5	0	0	0	0	0	0	0	0	0	0	0	0	4	0	0	0	.000	.000	3
Justice, D	ATL	L	.275	109	396	67	109	199	25	1	21	87	0	5	3	65	9	81	8	8	4	.503	.377	7
Karros, E	LA	R	.071	14	14	0	1	2	1	0	0	1	0	0	0	1	0	6	0	0	0	.143	.133	0
Kennedy, T	SF	L	.234	69	171	12	40	58	7	1	3	13	0	1	1	11	4	31	0	0	1	.339	.283	6
Kile, D	HOU	R	.000	37	38	2	0	0	0	0	0	1	4	0	0	0	0	23	0	0	0	.000	.073	3
King, J	PIT	R	.239	33	109	16	26	41	4	0	4	18	0	1	1	14	3	15	3	1	3	.376	.328	2
Kingery, M	SF	L	.182	91	110	13	20	26	2	2	0	8	1	0	0	15	1	21	1	0	3	.236	.280	1
Kipper, B	PIT	R	.000	52	2	0	0	0	0	0	0	0	0	0	0	0	0	1	0	0	0	.000	.000	2
Kruk, J	PHI	L	.294	152	538	84	158	260	27	6	21	92	0	9	1	67	16	100	7	0	11	.483	.367	3
LaCoss, M	SF	R	.222	18	9	2	2	2	0	0	0	0	1	0	0	0	0	6	0	0	0	.222	.300	1
LaPoint, D	PHI	L	.000	2	2	0	0	0	0	0	0	0	0	0	0	1	0	1	0	0	0	.000	.000	1
LaValliere, M	PIT	L	.289	108	336	25	97	121	11	0	3	41	1	5	2	33	4	27	0	1	10	.360	.351	2
Lake, S	PHI	R	.228	58	158	12	36	45	4	1	1	11	4	0	0	3	0	26	2	0	5	.285	.238	0
Lampkin, T	SD	L	.190	38	58	4	11	16	3	1	0	3	6	0	3	0	0	9	0	0	0	.276	.230	0
Lancaster, L	CHI	R	.179	64	28	4	5	7	2	0	0	2	2	0	0	0	0	13	0	0	0	.250	.179	0
Landrum, B	PIT	R	.000	61	4	0	0	0	0	0	0	0	0	0	0	0	0	0	0	0	0	.000	.000	2
Landrum, C	CHI	L	.233	56	86	28	20	24	2	1	0	6	3	0	0	10	0	18	27	5	2	.279	.301	6
Lankford, R	STL	L	.251	151	566	83	142	222	23	15	9	69	4	3	1	41	1	114	44	20	4	.392	.301	15
Larkin, B	CIN	R	.302	123	464	88	140	235	27	4	20	69	3	2	3	55	1	64	24	6	7	.506	.378	1
Layana, T	CIN	R	.000	23	1	0	0	0	0	0	0	0	0	0	0	0	0	1	0	0	0	.000	.000	0
Lee, T	CIN	R	.000	3	6	0	0	0	0	0	0	0	0	0	0	0	0	2	0	0	0	.000	.000	1
Lefferts, C	SD	L	.000	54	6	1	0	0	0	0	0	0	0	1	0	0	0	0	4	0	0	0	.000	.000	0
Leibrandt, C	ATL	R	.043	36	70	1	3	7	2	1	0	2	12	0	0	3	0	18	0	1	9	.100	.082	2
Lemke, M	ATL	S	.234	136	269	36	63	84	11	2	2	23	6	4	2	29	2	27	1	0	3	.312	.305	10
Leonard, M	SF	R	.240	64	129	14	31	46	7	1	2	14	1	2	0	12	1	25	1	2	9	.357	.306	0
Lewis, D	SF	L	.248	72	222	41	55	69	5	3	1	15	7	0	0	36	0	30	13	7	3	.311	.358	0
Lewis, J	SD	R	.000	2	2	0	0	0	0	0	0	0	0	0	0	0	0	1	0	0	0	.000	.000	1
Lilliquist, D	SD	L	.000	6	2	0	0	0	0	0	0	0	0	0	0	0	0	0	0	0	0	.000	.000	0
Lind, J	PIT	R	.265	150	502	53	133	170	16	6	3	54	6	6	2	30	10	56	7	4	20	.339	.306	9
Lindeman, J	PHI	R	.337	65	95	13	32	37	5	0	0	12	2	0	0	13	0	14	0	1	1	.389	.413	0
Lindsey, D	PHI	R	.000	1	3	0	0	0	0	0	0	0	0	0	0	0	0	0	0	0	0	.000	.000	0
Litton, G	SF	R	.181	59	127	13	23	35	7	1	1	15	3	1	0	11	0	25	0	2	2	.276	.250	2
Lofton, K	HOU	L	.203	20	74	9	15	16	1	0	0	0	0	0	0	5	0	19	2	0	0	.216	.253	1

Name	Team	B	AVG	G	AB	R	H	TB	2B	3B	HR	RBI	BB	SLG	OBP
Lyons, B	LA	R	.000	9	9	0	0	0	0	0	0	0	0	.000	.000
Maddux, G	CHI	R	.205	39	88	8	18	23	2	0	1	7	2	.261	.222
Maddux, M	SD	L	.077	64	13	1	1	1	0	0	0	0	2	.077	.200
Magadan, D	NY	L	.258	124	418	58	108	143	23	0	4	51	83	.342	.378
Mahler, R	MON-ATL	R	.143	23	14	0	2	3	1	0	0	0	0	.214	.143
Mallicoat, R	HOU	L	.000	24	1	0	0	0	0	0	0	0	0	.000	.000
Manwaring, K	SF	R	.225	67	178	16	40	49	9	0	0	19	9	.275	.271
Martinez, C	PIT-CIN	R	.224	64	154	13	36	59	5	0	6	19	16	.383	.301
Martinez, Da	MON	L	.255	124	396	47	117	166	18	5	7	42	20	.419	.332
Martinez, De	MON	R	.153	32	72	8	11	15	1	0	1	2	1	.208	.164
Martinez, R	LA	R	.117	33	77	6	9	13	0	2	0	9	1	.169	.128
Mason, R	PIT	R	.000	24	0	0	0	0	0	0	0	0	0	.000	.000
Mauser, T	PHI	R	.000	3	0	0	0	0	0	0	0	0	0	.000	1.000
May, D	CHI	L	.227	15	22	4	5	10	2	0	1	3	1	.455	.280
McClellan, P	SF	R	.143	13	21	5	3	3	0	0	0	1	1	.143	.182
McClendon, L	PIT	R	.288	85	163	24	47	75	7	0	7	24	18	.460	.366
McClure, B	STL	L	1.000	32	1	1	1	1	0	0	0	0	0	1.000	1.000
McDaniel, T	NY	R	.207	23	29	1	6	7	0	0	0	2	1	.241	.233
McDowell, R	PHI-LA	R	.000	72	2	0	0	0	0	0	0	0	0	.000	.000
McElroy, C	CHI	L	.300	71	10	1	3	4	1	0	0	2	0	.400	.300
McGee, W	SF	S	.312	131	497	67	155	203	30	3	4	43	34	.408	.357
McGriff, F	SD	L	.278	153	528	84	147	261	19	1	31	106	105	.494	.396
McLemore, M	HOU	S	.148	61	61	6	9	10	1	0	0	2	6	.164	.221
McReynolds, K	NY	R	.259	143	522	65	135	217	32	1	16	74	49	.416	.322
Melendez, J	SD	R	.100	31	20	1	2	3	0	0	0	0	1	.150	.143
Merced, O	PIT	S	.275	120	411	83	113	164	17	2	10	50	64	.399	.373
Mercker, K	ATL	L	.100	50	10	1	1	1	0	0	0	2	1	.100	.182
Miller, K	NY	R	.280	98	275	41	77	113	22	1	4	23	23	.411	.345
Miller, P	PIT	R	.000	3	3	0	0	0	0	0	0	0	0	.000	.000
Minutelli, G	CIN	L	.000	16	0	0	0	0	0	0	0	0	0	.000	.000
Mitchell, K	SF	R	.256	113	371	52	95	191	13	1	27	69	43	.515	.338
Mitchell, K	ATL	R	.318	48	66	11	21	27	0	0	2	5	8	.409	.392
Morandini, M	PHI	L	.249	98	325	38	81	103	11	4	1	20	29	.317	.313
Morgan, M	LA	R	.092	34	76	7	7	7	0	0	0	3	1	.092	.101
Morris, H	CIN	L	.318	136	478	72	152	229	33	1	14	59	46	.479	.374

BATTER	TEAM	B	AVG	G	AB	R	H	TB	2B	3B	HR	RBI	SH	SF	HP	BB	IBB	SO	SB	CS	GI DP	SLG	OBP	E
Morris, J	PHI	L	.220	85	127	15	28	35	2	1	1	6	0	0	1	12	4	25	2	0	1	.276	.293	2
Mota, A	HOU	R	.189	27	90	4	17	22	2	0	1	6	0	0	0	2	0	17	2	0	0	.244	.198	3
Mota, J	SD	S	.222	17	36	4	8	8	0	0	0	2	2	0	1	2	0	7	0	0	0	.222	.282	3
Moyer, J	STL	L	.000	8	8	0	0	0	0	0	0	0	5	0	0	0	0	4	0	0	0	.000	.111	0
Mulholland, T	PHI	R	.088	35	80	3	7	7	0	0	0	0	0	0	1	1	0	32	0	0	2	.088	.110	5
Murphy, D	PHI	R	.252	153	544	66	137	226	33	1	18	81	0	7	1	48	3	93	1	0	20	.415	.309	5
Murray, E	LA	S	.260	153	576	69	150	232	23	1	19	96	0	8	0	55	17	74	10	3	17	.403	.321	7
Myers, R	CIN	L	.172	58	29	3	5	6	1	0	0	2	3	0	0	0	0	16	0	0	0	.207	.200	2
Nabholz, C	MON	L	.115	24	52	5	6	6	0	0	0	1	9	0	0	3	0	14	1	0	0	.115	.164	1
Nichols, C	HOU	R	.196	20	51	3	10	13	3	0	0	1	3	0	0	5	1	17	0	0	2	.255	.268	3
Nixon, O	ATL	S	.297	124	401	81	119	131	10	0	0	26	7	3	2	47	3	40	72	21	5	.327	.371	3
Noboa, O	MON	R	.242	67	95	5	23	29	3	0	1	2	0	3	0	3	1	8	2	3	1	.305	.250	1
Nolte, E	SD	L	.111	6	9	2	1	1	0	0	0	0	2	0	0	0	0	6	0	0	0	.111	.111	0
O'Brien, C	NY	R	.185	69	168	16	31	43	6	0	2	14	0	2	4	17	1	25	0	1	5	.256	.272	4
O'Neill, P	CIN	L	.256	152	532	71	136	256	36	0	28	91	0	7	1	73	14	107	12	7	8	.481	.346	2
Oberkfell, K	HOU	L	.229	53	70	7	16	20	4	0	0	14	0	0	0	14	4	8	0	0	5	.286	.357	2
Offerman, J	LA	S	.195	52	113	10	22	24	2	0	0	3	1	0	0	25	2	32	3	0	0	.212	.200	0
Ojeda, B	LA	L	.161	31	56	2	9	12	0	0	1	3	6	0	0	2	0	10	0	0	0	.214	.200	0
Olivares, O	STL	R	.226	28	53	4	12	15	3	0	0	6	4	0	0	2	0	16	0	0	1	.283	.255	2
Oliver, J	STL	R	.216	94	269	21	58	102	11	0	11	41	4	4	0	18	5	53	0	0	14	.379	.265	11
Oliveras, F	SF	R	.200	55	10	0	2	2	0	0	0	0	4	0	0	0	0	4	0	0	0	.200	.200	1
Olson, G	ATL	R	.241	133	411	46	99	142	25	0	6	44	2	3	3	44	3	48	1	1	13	.345	.316	4
Oquendo, J	STL	S	.240	127	366	37	88	110	11	4	1	26	4	4	0	67	13	48	1	2	5	.301	.357	9
Ortiz, J	HOU	R	.277	47	83	7	23	32	4	1	1	5	3	0	14	0	0	14	1	0	3	.386	.381	0
Osuna, A	HOU	R	.000	71	2	0	0	0	0	0	0	0	1	0	0	0	0	0	0	0	0	.000	.000	0
Owen, S	MON	S	.255	139	424	39	108	155	22	3	3	26	8	4	1	42	6	61	9	6	11	.366	.321	8
Pagnozzi, T	STL	R	.264	140	459	38	121	161	24	5	2	57	5	5	4	36	6	63	9	13	10	.351	.319	7
Palacios, V	PIT	R	.071	36	14	0	1	1	0	0	0	0	5	0	0	0	0	7	0	0	0	.071	.071	0
Pappas, E	CHI	R	.176	7	17	1	3	3	0	0	0	2	0	0	0	1	0	5	0	0	0	.176	.222	0
Parker, R	SF	R	.071	13	14	0	1	1	0	0	0	0	0	0	0	0	0	5	0	0	0	.071	.133	1
Parrett, J	ATL	R	.000	18	0	0	0	0	0	0	0	0	0	0	0	0	0	0	0	0	0	.000	.000	0
Patterson, B	PIT	R	.250	54	4	0	1	1	0	0	0	0	0	0	0	1	0	2	0	0	0	.250	1.000	0
Pena, A	NY-ATL	R	.000	59	1	1	0	0	0	0	0	0	0	0	0	0	0	1	0	0	0	.000	.000	1

Player	Team	B	AVG	G	AB	R	H	2B	3B	HR	RBI	BB	SO	SB	CS	GDP	SLG	OBP	E
Pena, G	STL	S	.243	104	185	38	45	8	3	5	17		45	15	5	0	.400	.322	6
Pendleton, T	ATL	R	.319	153	586	94	187	34	8	22	86		70	10	2	16	.517	.363	24
Perezchica, T	SF	R	.229	23	48	11	11	4	0	0	1		12	0	1	0	.354	.260	2
Perry, G	STL	L	.240	109	242	29	58	8	4	6	36		34	15	8	2	.380	.300	5
Peterson, A	SD	R	.000	13	13	0	0	0	0	0	0		9	0	0	0	.000	.133	0
Petry, D	ATL	R	.200	10	5	1	1	0	0	0	0		0	0	0	0	.200	.200	0
Platt, D	MON	L	.000	21		0	0	0	0	0	0		0	0	0	0	.000	.000	3
Portugal, M	HOU	R	.136	33	46	9	10	0	0	1	3		4	0	0	2	.217	.269	0
Power, T	CIN	R	.000	68	3	0	0	0	0	0	1		3	0	0	3	.000	.250	3
Presley, J	SD	R	.136	20	59	8	8	3	0	1	5		16	1	0	3	.186	.200	7
Prince, T	PIT	S	.285	26	34	3	11	3	0		7		3	0	2	3	.441	.405	7
Quinones, L	CIN	R	.222	97	212	31	69	10			20		31		3	0	.325	.297	8
Ramirez, R	HOU	L	.236	101	233	40	68	7	1		20		40	0	0	5	.292	.274	1
Rasmussen, D	SD	R	.136	25	44	12	6	1	0				12		1	0	.159	.224	3
Ready, R	PHI	R	.249	76	205	25	51	10	1				25	3	3	6	.322	.385	1
Redfield, J	PIT	R	.111	11	18	1	2	0					1	0	0	0	.111	.273	3
Redus, G	PIT	R	.246	98	252	45	62	12	2				39	17	1		.393	.324	6
Reed, J	CIN	L	.267	91	270	20	72	15	1				38		3		.370	.321	5
Reed, R	PIT	R	.500	8	7	1	2	1					0	0	1		1.000	.500	0
Remlinger, M	SF	L	.000	4	2	0	0						2				.000	.125	1
Renfroe, L	CHI	S	.000	4	8	1	0						0				.000	.000	0
Reuschel, R	SF	R	.000	4	7	1	0						0				.000	.000	11
Reyes, G	MON	R	.217	83	207	11	45	9	0		13		51	2	2	1	.261	.285	0
Reynoso, A	ATL	L	.000	6	7	0	0						5				.000	.125	4
Rhodes, K	HOU	L	.213	44	136	7	29	3	1		12		26	2	2		.272	.289	0
Richardson, J	PIT	R	.250	6	4	0	1						3				.250	.250	2
Riesgo, D	MON	L	.143	7	7	1	1	0	0				1				.143	.400	0
Righetti, D	SF	R	.000	117	3	0	0						2		1		.000	.000	3
Rijo, J	CIN	L	.209	35	67	7	14	2	0				13				.209	.232	10
Ritchie, W	PHI	R	.000	18	3	0	0						0				.000	.000	0
Roberts, L	SD	S	.281	65	424	66	119	13			32		71	26			.347	.342	0
Robinson, D	SF	R	.150	29	117	35	18	6			4		13				.175	.171	0
Rodriguez, R	PIT	L	.000		3	1	0	1					0				.000	.000	0
Rodriguez, R	SD	L	.000		5	0	0	0					2				.000	.000	0
Rohde, D	HOU	S	.122		41	3	5	0			5		8				.122	.217	0

BATTER	TEAM	B	AVG	G	AB	R	H	TB	2B	3B	HR	RBI	SH	SF	HP	BB	IBB	SO	SB	CS	GI DP	SLG	OBP	E
Rojas, M.	MON	R	.000	37	4	0	0	0	0	0	0	0	1	0	0	0	0	3	0	0	0	.000	.000	0
Rosenberg, S.	SD	L	.000	10	1	0	0	0	0	0	0	0	0	0	0	0	0	1	0	0	0	.000	.000	0
Rossy, R.	ATL	R	.000	5	1	1	0	0	0	0	0	0	0	0	0	0	0	1	0	0	0	.000	.000	0
Royer, S.	STL	R	.286	9	21	0	6	7	1	0	0	0	6	0	1	0	0	2	0	0	0	.333	.318	2
Ruffin, B.	PHI	S	.000	31	24	1	0	0	0	0	0	0	6	4	0	0	0	18	0	0	0	.000	.143	1
Ruskin, S.	MON	R	.000	64	2	1	0	0	0	0	0	0	0	0	0	1	0	1	0	0	0	.000	.333	0
Sabo, C.	CIN	R	.301	153	582	91	175	294	35	3	26	88	5	3	6	44	3	79	19	6	13	.505	.354	12
Salazar, L.	CHI	R	.258	103	333	34	86	144	14	1	14	38	2	5	1	15	1	45	0	3	8	.432	.292	10
Sampen, B.	MON	R	.231	43	13	3	3	3	0	0	0	1	2	0	0	0	0	6	0	0	0	.231	.231	1
Samuel, J.	LA	R	.271	153	594	74	161	231	22	6	12	58	10	3	3	49	4	133	23	8	8	.389	.328	17
Sanchez, R.	CHI	R	.261	13	23	1	6	6	0	0	0	2	1	0	0	0	0	3	1	0	0	.261	.370	0
Sandberg, R.	CHI	R	.291	158	585	104	170	284	32	2	26	100	0	9	2	87	4	89	22	3	9	.485	.379	4
Sanders, D.	ATL	L	.191	54	110	16	21	38	1	2	4	13	0	0	0	12	0	23	11	1	1	.345	.270	3
Sanders, R.	CIN	R	.200	9	40	6	8	11	0	0	1	3	0	0	2	0	0	9	0	1	0	.275	.200	0
Sanford, M.	CIN	R	.000	5	8	0	0	0	0	0	0	0	0	0	0	0	0	5	0	0	0	.000	.000	0
Santiago, B.	SD	R	.267	152	580	60	155	234	22	3	17	87	0	7	4	23	5	114	8	10	21	.403	.296	14
Santovenia, N.	MON	R	.250	41	96	7	24	35	5	0	2	14	0	2	2	2	2	18	0	0	6	.365	.255	3
Sasser, M.	NY	L	.272	96	228	18	62	95	14	2	5	35	1	4	1	9	2	19	0	2	4	.417	.298	3
Scanlan, B.	CHI	R	.042	40	24	0	1	1	0	0	0	1	2	0	0	0	0	10	0	0	3	.042	.080	2
Schilling, C.	HOU	R	.333	56	3	0	1	1	0	0	0	0	0	0	0	0	0	0	0	0	0	.333	.333	1
Schourek, P.	NY	L	.136	35	22	3	3	4	1	0	0	3	1	0	0	2	0	9	0	0	0	.182	.208	0
Schu, R.	PHI	R	.091	17	22	1	2	2	0	0	0	2	0	0	0	0	0	7	0	0	1	.091	.125	0
Schulz, J.	PIT	L	.000	3	3	0	0	0	0	0	0	0	0	0	0	0	0	2	0	0	0	.000	.000	0
Scioscia, M.	LA	L	.264	119	345	39	91	135	16	0	8	40	5	4	3	47	3	32	4	3	5	.391	.353	7
Scott, D.	CIN	S	.158	10	19	0	3	3	0	0	0	0	0	0	0	2	0	2	0	1	0	.158	.158	0
Scott, G.	CHI	R	.165	31	79	8	13	19	3	0	1	5	1	0	3	13	0	14	0	0	2	.241	.305	2
Scott, M.	HOU	R	.000	2	1	0	0	0	0	0	0	0	2	0	0	0	0	0	0	0	0	.000	.000	0
Scudder, S.	CIN	R	.103	27	29	2	3	6	0	0	0	1	2	0	0	0	0	11	0	0	0	.207	.103	0
Searcy, S.	PHI	L	.000	18	4	0	0	0	0	0	0	0	1	0	0	0	0	3	0	0	0	.000	.000	0
Servais, S.	HOU	R	.162	16	37	0	6	9	3	0	0	6	1	0	0	4	0	8	0	0	1	.243	.244	1
Sharperson, M.	LA	R	.278	105	216	24	60	81	11	2	2	20	10	0	1	25	0	24	3	3	1	.375	.355	4
Shipley, C.	SD	R	.275	37	91	6	25	31	3	0	1	6	1	0	1	2	0	14	1	1	2	.341	.298	7
Simms, M.	HOU	R	.203	49	123	18	25	39	5	0	3	16	0	2	0	18	0	38	1	0	2	.317	.301	6

Player	Team	B	AVG	G	AB	R	H	2B	HR	RBI	SO	OBP	SLG
Simons, D.	NY	L	.000	42	3	0	0	0	0	0	0	.000	.000
Slaught, D.	PIT	R	.285	77	220	19	65	17	1	21	32	.395	.363
Slocumb, H.	CHI	R	.000	52	0	0	0	0	0	0	0	.000	.000
Smiley, J.	PIT	L	.110	33	70	3	7	0	0	3	24	.100	.137
Smith, B.	STL	R	.246	31	65	6	17	1	1	8	11	.262	.254
Smith, Da.	CHI	R	.000	35	1	0	0	0	0	0	0	.000	.000
Smith, Dw.	CHI	L	.228	90	167	16	38	7	6	21	32	.347	.279
Smith, G.	LA	S	.000	5	3	0	0	0	0	0	2	.000	.000
Smith, L.	ATL	R	.275	122	353	58	97	19	9	44	64	.394	.377
Smith, O.	STL	S	.285	150	550	96	157	30	1	50	36	.367	.380
Smith, P.	ATL	R	.167	14	12	1	2	1	0	1	5	.167	.231
Smith, Z.	PIT	L	.183	36	71	3	13	3	0	3	8	.225	.224
Smoltz, J.	ATL	R	.108	38	65	7	7	3	0	5	28	.154	.171
St. Claire, R.	ATL	R	.500	19	2	0	1	0	0	0	1	.500	.500
Stanton, M.	ATL	L	.500	74	6	0	3	0	0	1	0	.667	.571
Stephens, R.	STL	R	.286	6	7	0	2	0	0	0	3	.286	.375
Stephenson, P.	SD	L	.286	11	7	0	2	0	0	0	3	.286	.444
Strange, D.	CHI	S	.444	9	9	0	4	1	0	0	1	.556	.455
Strawberry, D.	LA	L	.265	139	505	86	134	22	28	99	125	.491	.361
Sutcliffe, R.	CHI	L	.094	20	32	2	3	1	0	2	9	.125	.121
Sutko, G.	CIN	R	.100	10	10	3	1	0	0	0	6	.100	.250
Templeton, G.	SD-NY	S	.221	112	276	25	61	10	2	26	38	.304	.246
Terry, S.	STL	R	.143	65	7	1	1	0	0	1	2	.143	.143
Teufel, T.	NY-SD	R	.217	117	341	41	74	16	10	44	77	.370	.319
Tewksbury, B.	STL	R	.155	30	58	5	9	1	0	4	16	.172	.210
Thompson, M.	STL	L	.307	115	326	55	100	16	6	34	53	.442	.368
Thompson, R.	SF	R	.262	144	492	74	129	24	19	48	95	.447	.352
Thon, D.	PHI	R	.252	146	539	136	136	18	9	44	84	.351	.283
Tolentino, J.	HOU	L	.259	44	54	6	14	4	1	6	9	.389	.305
Tomlin, R.	PIT	L	.192	32	52	5	10	1	0	2	18	.212	.222
Torve, K.	NY	L	.000	10	8	0	0	0	0	0	1	.000	.000
Treadway, J.	ATL	L	.320	106	306	41	98	17	3	32	19	.418	.368
Uribe, J.	SF	S	.221	90	231	23	51	8	1	12	33	.303	.283
Van Slyke, A.	PIT	L	.265	138	491	87	130	24	17	83	85	.446	.355
Vanderwal, J.	MON	L	.213	21	61	4	13	4	1	8	18	.361	.222

BATTER	TEAM	B	AVG	G	AB	R	H	TB	2B	3B	HR	RBI	SH	SF	HP	BB	IBB	SO	SB	CS	GIDP	SLG	OBP	E
Varsho, G	PIT	L	.273	99	187	23	51	78	11	2	4	23	1	1	2	19		34	9	2	2	.417	.344	1
Vatcher, J	SD	R	.200	17	20	3	4	4	1	0	0	2	1	0	0	4		6	1	0	0	.200	.333	1
Villanueva, H	CHI	R	.276	71	192	23	53	104	10	1	13	32	0	0		21	1	30	0	0	3	.542	.346	6
Viola, F	NY	L	.127	35	71	2	9	11	2	0	0	1	10	0	0	2		13	0	1	1	.155	.151	4
Vizcaino, J	CHI	S	.262	93	145	7	38	43	5	2	0	10	2	2	0	5	1	18	2	0	1	.297	.283	7
Walk, B	PIT	R	.205	25	39	2	8	12	1	0	1	5	2	0	0	1		12	0	0	1	.308	.225	2
Walker, C	CHI	S	.257	124	374	51	96	126	10	1	6	34	1	3	0	33	3	57	13	5	3	.337	.315	8
Walker, L	MON	L	.290	137	487	59	141	223	30	2	16	64	0	4	5	42	5	102	14	9	6	.458	.349	6
Wallach, T	MON	R	.225	151	577	60	130	193	22	1	13	73	0	4	6	50	8	100	2	1	12	.334	.292	14
Walton, J	CHI	R	.219	123	270	42	59	89	13	1	5	17	3	3	1	19	0	55	14	7	7	.330	.275	3
Ward, K	CHI	R	.243	44	107	13	26	43	7	2	2	8	1	1	0	6	0	27	2	4	3	.402	.308	1
Webster, M	PIT-LA	S	.222	94	171	21	38	62	8	5	2	19	1	0		18	0	52	1	1	0	.363	.296	2
Wehner, J	PIT	R	.340	37	106	15	36	43	7	0	0	7	1	0	0	7	0	17	3	1	3	.406	.381	6
Whitehurst, W	NY	R	.182	36	33	2	6	7	1	0	0	0	5	1	0	1	0	6	0	0	0	.212	.229	0
Whitson, E	SD	R	.125	13	24	1	3	3	0	0	0	0	2	0	0	0	0	6	0	0	0	.125	.160	2
Wilkerson, C	PIT	S	.188	85	191	20	36	53	9	1	0	18	7	0	0	15	2	40	4	3	2	.277	.243	0
Wilkins, D	HOU	R	.000	2	3	0	0	0	0	0	0	0	0	0	0	0			0	0	0	.000	.000	3
Wilkins, R	CHI	R	.222	86	203	21	45	72	9	0	6	22	0	6	0	19	2	56	3	3	3	.355	.307	0
Willard, J	ATL	L	.214	17	14	1	3	6	0	0	1	4	0	0	0	2		5	0	0	0	.429	.313	0
Williams, B	HOU	R	.000	2	3	0	0	0	0	0	0	0	0	0	0	0		0	0	0	0	.000	.000	2
Williams, K	MON	R	.271	34	70	11	19	28	5	2	0	1	0	1	1	3	0	22	2	1	0	.400	.311	3
Williams, M	PHI	L	.000	69	1	0	0	0	0	0	0	0	0	0	0	1	0	1	0	0	0	.000	.500	
Williams, M	SF	R	.268	157	589	72	158	294	24	5	34	98	0	7	6	33	6	128	5	5	11	.499	.310	16
Wilson, C	STL	R	.171	60	82	5	14	16	2	0	0	13	2	2	2	6	2	10	0	0	2	.195	.222	2
Wilson, S	CHI-LA	L	.000	20	5	0	0	0	0	0	0	0	3	0	0	0		1	0	0	0	.000	.000	0
Wilson, T	SF	L	.235	48	51	7	12	16	1	0	1	5	8	0	1	11	0	16	0	4	2	.314	.304	1
Winningham, H	CIN	L	.225	98	169	17	38	49	6	1	1	4	0	1	1	11	2	40	4	4	2	.290	.272	5
Wohlers, M	ATL	R	.000	17	1	0	0	0	0	0	0	0	1	0	0	0		1	0	0	0	.000	.000	0
Wood, T	SF	L	.120	10	25	0	3	3	0	0	0	1	3	0	0	2	0	11	0	0	4	.120	.185	0
Yelding, E	HOU	R	.243	78	276	19	67	83	11	1	0	20	3	1	0	13	3	46	11	9	4	.301	.276	20
Young, A	NY	R	.143	10	14	0	2	3	1	0	0	0	1	0	0	4		4	0	0	0	.214	.143	1
Young, G	HOU	S	.218	108	142	26	31	39	3	1	1	11	1	2	0	24	0	17	16	5	3	.275	.327	0
Zeile, T	STL	R	.280	155	565	76	158	233	36	3	11	81	0	6	5	62	3	94	17	11	15	.412	.353	25

CLUB BATTING

CLUB	AVG	G	AB	R	OR	H	TB	2B	3B	HR	GS	RBI	SH	SF	HP	BB	IBB	SO	SB	CS	GI DP	LOB	SHO	SLG	OBP
PITTSBURGH	.263	162	5449	768	632	1433	2170	259	50	126	5	725	99	66	35	620	62	901	124	46	111	1188	6	.398	.338
CINCINNATI	.258	162	5501	689	691	1419	2215	250	27	164	2	654	72	41	32	488	54	1006	124	56	85	1110	9	.403	.320
ATLANTA	.258	162	5456	749	644	1407	2145	255	30	141	3	704	86	45	32	563	55	906	165	76	104	1111	9	.393	.328
ST. LOUIS	.255	162	5362	651	648	1366	1915	239	53	68	0	599	58	47	21	532	48	857	202	110	94	1072	14	.357	.322
CHICAGO	.253	160	5522	695	734	1395	2156	232	26	159	4	654	75	55	36	442	41	879	123	64	87	1074	4	.390	.309
LOS ANGELES	.253	162	5408	665	565	1366	1939	191	29	108	3	605	94	46	28	583	50	957	126	68	109	1151	8	.359	.326
SAN FRANCISCO	.246	162	5463	649	697	1345	2079	215	48	141	2	605	90	33	40	471	59	973	95	57	91	1110	13	.381	.309
MONTREAL	.246	161	5412	579	655	1329	1934	236	42	95	1	536	64	47	28	484	51	1056	221	100	97	1074	10	.357	.308
HOUSTON	.244	162	5504	605	717	1345	1908	240	43	79	1	570	78	43	35	502	45	1027	125	68	87	1131	16	.347	.309
SAN DIEGO	.244	162	5408	636	646	1321	1960	204	36	121	4	591	60	38	32	501	60	1069	101	64	122	1080	12	.362	.310
NEW YORK	.244	161	5359	640	646	1305	1954	250	24	117	4	605	52	52	27	578	53	789	153	70	97	1114	9	.365	.317
PHILADELPHIA	.241	162	5521	629	680	1332	1979	248	33	111	6	590	52	49	21	490	48	1026	92	30	114	1108	12	.358	.303
TOTALS	.250	970	65365	7955	7955	16363	24354	2819	441	1430	35	7438	891	562	367	6254	626	11446	1651	809	1198	13323	122	.373	.317

Cubs' Ryne Sandberg joined 200 Home Run Club.

Braves' Tom Glavine was the NL Cy Young winner.

Pitching

Individual Pitching Leaders

Games Won	20	Glavine	Atl.
		Smiley	Pit.
Games Lost	16	Black	S.F.
Won-Lost Percentage	.714	Smiley	Pit. (20-8)
Earned Run Average	2.39	Martinez	Mon.
Games	77	Jones	Mon.
Games Started	37	Maddux	Chi.
Complete Games	9	Glavine	Atl.
		Martinez	Mon.
Games Finished	61	L. Smith	St.L.
Shutouts	5	Martinez	Mon.
Saves	47	L. Smith	St.L.
Innings	263.0	Maddux	Chi.
Hits	259	Viola	N.Y.
Batsmen Faced	1070	Maddux	Chi.
Runs	124	Browning	Cin.
Earned Runs	107	Browning	Cin.
Home Runs	32	Browning	Cin.
Sacrifice Hits	19	Leibrandt	Atl.
Sacrifice Flies	11	Greene	Phi.
Hit Batsmen	10	Burkett	S.F.
Bases on Balls	128	DeJesus	Phi.
Intentional Bases on Balls	20	McDowell	Phi.-L.A.
Strikeouts	241	Cone	N.Y.
Wild Pitches	20	Smoltz	Atl.
Balks	6	Black	S.F.
Games Won, Consecutive	10	Benes	S.D. (July 28-Sept. 25)
Games Lost, Consecutive	9	Rasmussen	S.D. (June 26-Aug. 9)

TOP 15 QUALIFIERS FOR EARNED RUN AVERAGE CHAMPIONSHIP

PITCHER	TEAM	T	W	L	ERA	G	GS	CG	SHO	GF	SV	IP	H	TBF	R	ER	HR	SH	SF	HB	BB	IBB	SO	WP	BK	OPP AVG
Martinez, De	MON	R	14	11	2.39	31	31	9	5	0	0	222.0	187	905	70	59	9	7	3	4	62	3	123	3	0	.226
Rijo, J	CIN	R	15	6	2.51	30	30	3	1	0	0	204.1	165	825	69	57	8	4	3	4	55	4	172	6	2	.219
Glavine, T	ATL	L	20	11	2.55	34	34	9	1	0	0	246.2	201	989	83	70	17	7	6	2	69	6	192	10	2	.222
Belcher, T	LA	R	10	9	2.62	33	33	2	1	0	0	209.1	189	880	76	61	10	11	3	2	75	3	156	7	0	.240
Harnisch, P	HOU	R	12	9	2.70	33	33	4	2	0	0	216.2	169	900	71	65	14	9	7	5	83	1	172	5	2	.212
DeLeon, J	STL	R	5	9	2.71	28	28	1	0	0	0	162.2	144	679	57	49	15	4	6	6	61	1	118	1	1	.239
Morgan, M	LA	R	14	10	2.78	34	33	5	1	0	0	236.1	197	949	85	73	12	10	4	3	61	10	140	6	0	.226
Tomlin, R	PIT	L	8	7	2.98	31	27	4	2	0	1	175.0	170	736	75	58	9	5	2	6	54	7	104	2	3	.254
Benes, A	SD	R	15	11	3.03	33	33	4	1	0	0	223.0	194	908	76	75	23	5	6	3	59	4	167	3	4	.232
Drabek, D	PIT	R	15	14	3.07	35	35	5	2	0	0	234.2	245	977	92	80	16	12	3	3	62	6	142	5	0	.274
Smiley, J	PIT	L	20	8	3.08	33	32	2	1	0	0	207.2	194	836	78	71	17	11	6	3	44	0	129	3	1	.251
Ojeda, B	LA	R	12	9	3.19	31	31	2	0	0	0	189.1	181	802	78	67	15	15	4	2	70	9	120	4	2	.257
Smith, Z	PIT	L	16	10	3.20	35	35	6	3	0	0	228.0	234	916	95	81	15	7	5	2	29	3	120	1	0	.268
Tewksbury, B	STL	R	11	12	3.25	30	30	3	0	0	0	191.0	206	798	86	69	13	12	10	5	38	2	75	0	0	.281
Martinez, R	LA	R	17	13	3.27	33	33	6	4	0	0	220.1	190	916	89	80	18	8	4	7	69	4	150	6	0	.229

INDIVIDUAL PITCHING

PITCHER	TEAM	T	W	L	ERA	G	GS	CG	SHO	GF	SV	IP	H	TBF	R	ER	HR	SH	SF	HB	BB	IBB	SO	WP	BK	OPP AVG
Agosto, J	STL	L	5	3	4.81	72	0	0	0	22	2	86.0	92	377	52	46	4	11	3	8	39	4	34	6	0	.291
Akerfelds, D	PHI	R	2	1	5.26	30	0	0	0	11	0	49.2	49	229	30	29	5	6	2	3	27	4	31	4	0	.257
Andersen, L	SD	R	3	4	2.30	38	0	0	0	24	13	47.0	39	188	13	12	0	4	2	0	13	3	40	1	0	.232
Armstrong, J	CIN	R	7	13	5.48	27	24	1	0	1	0	139.2	158	611	90	85	25	6	9	2	54	2	93	2	1	.293

PITCHER TEAM	T	W	L	ERA	G	GS	CG	SHO	GF	SV	IP	H	TBF	R	ER	HR	SH	SF	HB	BB	IBB	SO	WP	BK	OPP AVG
Ashby, A........PHI	R	1	5	6.00	8	8	0	0	0	0	42.0	41	186	28	28	5	1	3	3	19	0	26	6	0	.256
Assenmacher, P..CHI	L	8	8	3.24	75	0	0	0	31	15	102.2	85	427	41	37	10	8	4	3	31	6	117	4	0	.223
Avery, S.......ATL	L	18	8	3.38	35	35	3	1	0	0	210.1	189	868	89	79	21	8	4	3	65	0	137	1	1	.240
Barnes, B......MON	L	5	8	4.22	28	27	0	0	0	0	160.0	135	684	82	75	16	9	5	6	84	2	117	5	1	.233
Beatty, B.......NY	L	0	0	2.79	5	0	0	0	1	0	9.2	9	42	3	3	0	1	1	0	4	0	7	1	0	.250
Beck, R.........SF	R	1	2	3.78	31	0	0	0	10	1	52.1	53	214	22	22	4	4	2	3	13	2	38	0	0	.273
Belcher, T......LA	R	10	9	2.62	33	33	2	0	1	0	209.1	189	880	76	61	10	11	2	4	75	3	156	7	0	.240
Belinda, S.....PIT	R	7	5	3.45	60	0	0	0	37	16	78.1	50	318	30	30	10	4	3	4	35	4	71	2	0	.184
Benes, A........SD	R	15	11	3.03	33	33	4	1	0	0	223.0	194	908	76	75	23	5	4	4	59	7	167	3	4	.232
Berenguer, J....ATL	R	0	3	2.24	49	0	0	0	35	17	64.1	43	255	18	16	5	3	4	3	20	2	53	6	0	.189
Bielecki, M....CHI-ATL	R	13	11	4.46	41	25	0	0	9	0	173.2	171	727	91	86	18	10	2	2	56	6	75	0	0	.262
Black, B.........SF	L	12	16	3.99	34	34	3	0	3	0	214.1	201	893	104	95	25	11	4	4	71	8	104	6	6	.251
Boever, J......PHI	R	3	5	3.84	68	0	0	0	27	0	98.1	90	431	45	42	10	3	6	4	54	11	89	6	1	.245
Bones, R........SD	R	4	9	4.83	11	11	0	0	0	0	54.0	57	234	33	29	3	0	6	0	18	0	31	4	0	.269
Boskie, S......CHI	R	4	9	5.23	28	20	0	0	2	0	129.0	150	582	78	75	14	8	6	5	52	4	62	1	1	.294
Bowen, R.......HOU	R	6	8	5.15	14	13	0	0	0	0	71.2	73	319	43	41	4	2	6	3	36	4	49	8	0	.268
Boyd, D........MON	R	6	8	3.52	19	19	1	0	0	0	120.1	115	496	49	47	9	2	3	3	40	2	82	2	3	.256
Brantley, C....PHI	R	2	2	3.41	6	5	0	0	0	0	31.2	26	140	12	12	0	2	2	1	19	0	25	2	2	.228
Brantley, J.....SF	R	5	2	2.45	67	0	0	0	39	15	95.1	78	411	27	26	4	5	4	5	52	10	81	6	2	.225
Bross, T........NY	R	0	0	1.80	8	0	0	0	4	0	10.0	7	39	2	2	0	1	0	0	3	0	5	0	0	.200
Brown, K.......CIN	R	0	0	2.25	11	0	0	0	3	0	12.0	15	56	4	3	1	0	0	0	6	4	4	1	1	.306
Browning, T.....CIN	L	14	14	4.18	36	36	1	0	0	0	230.1	241	983	124	107	32	8	9	4	56	4	115	3	1	.266
Burke, T......MON-NY	R	6	7	3.36	72	0	0	0	31	6	101.2	96	421	46	38	8	3	3	4	26	8	59	5	1	.249
Burkett, J......SF	R	12	11	4.18	36	34	3	0	0	0	206.2	223	890	103	96	19	8	8	10	60	2	131	3	0	.277
Candelaria, J...LA	L	1	1	3.74	59	0	0	0	10	2	33.2	31	138	16	14	3	1	3	0	11	2	38	5	1	.252
Capel, M.......HOU	R	3	3	3.03	25	0	0	0	13	0	32.2	33	143	14	11	3	3	1	0	15	1	23	0	0	.266
Carman, D......CIN	L	0	0	5.25	28	0	0	0	10	0	36.0	40	164	23	21	8	3	1	0	19	9	15	2	1	.286
Carpenter, C...STL	R	10	4	4.23	59	0	0	0	19	0	66.0	53	266	31	31	6	3	2	2	20	7	47	1	0	.220
Carreno, A......PHI	R	0	0	16.20	3	0	0	0	0	0	3.1	5	20	6	6	1	0	0	0	3	0	2	0	0	.333
Castillo, F......CHI	R	6	7	4.35	18	18	4	0	0	0	111.2	107	467	56	54	5	6	3	2	33	2	73	5	0	.252
Castillo, T...ATL-NY	L	2	1	3.34	17	3	0	0	6	0	32.1	40	148	16	12	4	2	1	0	11	1	18	0	0	.299

Player	T	W	L	ERA	G	GS	CG	SV	IP	H	R	ER	HR	BB	SO	WP	BK	AVG
Charlton, N.......CIN	L	3	5	2.91	39	11	0	0	108.1	92	37	35	7	34	77	11	0	.236
Christopher, M....LA	R	0	0	0.00	3	0	0	0	4.0	2	0	0	0	3	2	0	0	.167
Clancy, J.......HOU-ATL	R	3	5	3.91	54	0	0	0	89.2	73	42	39	8	34	50	10	0	.223
Clark, M.......STL	R	1	1	4.03	12	2	0	0	22.1	17	10	10	3	11	13	2	0	.215
Clements, P.......SD	L	2	0	3.77	14	0	0	0	14.1	13	8	6	0	9	8	0	0	.255
Combs, P.......PHI	L	2	6	4.90	13	13	0	0	64.1	64	41	35	7	43	41	7	1	.254
Cone, D.......NY	R	14	14	3.29	34	34	5	0	232.2	204	95	85	13	73	241	17	0	.235
Cook, D.......LA	L	1	0	0.51	20	1	0	0	17.2	12	3	1	1	8	8	0	1	.203
Cormier, R.......STL	L	4	5	4.12	11	10	0	0	67.2	74	35	31	3	23	38	2	0	.277
Corsi, J.......HOU	R	0	5	3.71	47	0	0	2	77.2	76	37	32	4	17	53	1	1	.259
Costello, J.......SD	R	0	0	3.09	27	0	0	0	35.0	37	15	12	6	39	24	2	1	.276
Cox, D.......PHI	R	4	6	4.57	23	17	0	0	102.1	98	52	52	4	19	46	7	1	.258
Crews, T.......LA	R	2	3	3.43	60	0	0	6	76.0	75	30	29	7	33	53	3	0	.256
Darling, R.......NY-MON	R	5	8	4.37	20	20	0	0	119.1	121	66	58	7	44	69	13	4	.265
Dascenzo, D.......CHI	R	0	0	0.00	3	0	0	0	4.0	2	0	0	0	0	0	0	0	.154
DeJesus, J.......PHI	R	10	9	3.42	31	29	1	0	181.2	147	74	69	11	73	118	10	0	.224
DeLeon, J.......STL	R	5	9	2.71	28	28	2	0	162.2	144	57	49	5	61	118	1	0	.239
Deshaies, J.......HOU	L	5	12	4.98	28	28	2	0	161.0	156	89	89	5	72	98	0	0	.259
Dibble, R.......CIN	R	3	5	3.17	67	0	0	31	82.1	67	32	29	4	25	124	5	0	.223
Downs, K.......SF	R	10	4	4.19	45	11	0	0	111.2	99	59	52	12	53	62	4	1	.239
Drabek, D.......PIT	R	15	14	3.07	35	35	5	0	234.2	245	92	80	16	62	142	5	1	.274
Fajardo, H.......PIT	R	0	0	9.95	2	0	0	0	6.1	7	7	7	0	7	8	3	0	.357
Fassero, J.......MON	L	2	5	2.44	51	0	0	0	55.1	39	15	15	6	17	42	4	0	.196
Fernandez, S.......NY	L	1	3	2.86	8	8	2	0	44.0	36	18	14	5	9	31	0	0	.222
Foster, S.......CIN	R	0	1	1.93	11	0	0	0	14.0	5	5	3	0	4	11	0	0	.143
Franco, J.......NY	L	5	9	2.93	52	0	0	30	55.1	61	28	18	2	18	45	6	1	.271
Fraser, W.......STL	R	3	3	4.93	35	0	0	0	49.1	44	28	27	3	21	25	4	0	.242
Freeman, M.......ATL	R	1	0	3.00	34	0	0	0	48.0	37	19	16	3	13	34	3	0	.214
Frey, S.......MON	L	0	1	4.99	31	0	0	6	39.2	43	22	22	2	23	21	3	1	.281
Gardner, C.......HOU	R	1	2	4.01	5	4	0	0	24.2	19	12	11	7	14	12	0	0	.218
Gardner, M.......MON	R	9	11	3.85	27	27	1	0	168.1	139	78	72	17	75	107	2	0	.230
Gardner, W.......SD	R	0	0	7.08	14	0	0	0	20.1	27	16	16	0	12	9	1	0	.310
Garrelts, S.......SF	R	1	1	6.41	8	3	0	2	19.2	25	14	14	5	9	8	0	0	.313

PITCHER TEAM	T	W	L	ERA	G	GS	CG	SHO	GF	SV	IP	H	TBF	R	ER	HR	SH	SF	HB	BB	IBB	SO	WP	BK	OPP AVG
Glavine, T ......ATL	L	20	11	2.55	34	34	9	3	0	1	246.2	201	989	83	70	17	7	6	2	69	6	192	10	2	.222
Gooden, D ......NY	R	13	7	3.60	27	27	3	1	0	0	190.0	185	789	80	76	12	5	4	3	56	2	150	5	2	.257
Gott, J ......LA	R	4	3	2.96	55	0	0	0	26	2	76.0	63	322	28	25	5	6	1	1	32	7	73	6	3	.223
Grater, M ......STL	R	0	0	0.00	3	0	0	0	3	0	3.0	5	15	0	0	0	0	0	0	2	0	0	0	1	.385
Greene, T ......PHI	R	13	7	3.38	36	27	3	2	0	0	207.2	177	857	85	78	19	9	3	3	66	4	154	9	0	.230
Grimsley, J ......PHI	R	1	7	4.87	12	12	0	0	0	0	61.0	54	272	34	33	4	3	2	3	41	3	42	14	0	.242
Gross, K ......LA	R	10	11	3.58	46	10	0	0	16	3	115.2	123	509	55	46	10	6	4	0	50	6	95	3	1	.275
Gross, K ......CIN	R	6	6	3.47	29	9	0	0	6	1	85.2	93	381	43	33	8	6	2	0	40	2	40	5	1	.279
Gunderson, E ......SF	L	0	0	5.40	1	0	0	0	1	0	3.1	6	18	4	2	0	0	0	0	1	0	2	0	0	.353
Hammaker, A ......SD	L	0	1	5.79	1	1	0	0	0	0	4.2	8	27	7	3	0	2	0	0	3	0	2	1	0	.364
Hammond, C ......CIN	L	7	7	4.06	20	18	0	0	0	0	99.2	92	425	51	45	4	6	1	1	48	3	50	3	0	.250
Haney, C. ......MON	L	3	3	4.04	16	16	0	0	0	0	84.2	94	387	49	38	6	6	1	0	43	1	51	9	0	.280
Harkey, M. ......CHI	R	0	2	5.30	4	4	0	0	0	0	18.2	21	84	11	11	3	0	1	0	6	0	15	1	0	.273
Harnisch, P ......HOU	R	12	9	2.70	33	33	3	4	0	0	216.2	169	900	71	65	14	9	5	7	83	5	172	5	2	.212
Harris, G ......SD	R	9	5	2.23	20	20	0	0	0	0	133.0	111	537	42	33	16	2	7	5	27	6	95	2	2	.233
Hartley, M. ......LA-PHI	R	4	1	4.21	58	0	0	0	16	2	83.1	74	368	40	39	11	9	1	6	47	8	63	10	0	.237
Heaton, N ......PIT	L	3	3	4.33	42	1	0	0	5	1	68.2	72	293	37	33	6	3	6	4	21	7	34	2	2	.275
Henry, D ......HOU	R	3	2	3.19	52	0	0	0	25	0	67.2	51	282	25	24	7	6	2	1	39	2	51	5	1	.219
Heredia, G. ......SF	R	0	2	3.82	7	4	0	0	1	0	33.0	27	126	14	14	4	3	2	0	7	1	13	0	0	.233
Hernandez, J ......SD	R	0	0	0.00	9	0	0	0	7	2	14.1	8	56	1	0	0	1	0	0	5	2	9	2	0	.157
Hernandez, X ......HOU	R	2	7	4.71	32	6	0	0	8	3	63.0	66	285	34	33	6	1	1	2	32	7	55	2	4	.263
Hershiser, O ......LA	R	7	2	3.46	21	21	0	0	0	0	112.0	112	473	43	43	3	2	3	2	32	6	73	2	2	.259
Hickerson, B ......SF	L	2	2	3.60	17	6	0	0	4	0	50.0	53	212	20	20	3	3	2	1	17	3	43	2	1	.275
Hill, K ......STL	R	11	10	3.57	30	30	0	0	0	0	181.1	147	743	76	72	15	7	6	6	67	4	121	7	1	.224
Hill, M. ......CIN	R	1	1	3.78	22	0	0	0	8	0	33.1	36	137	14	14	1	3	1	1	8	2	20	1	0	.295
Howell, J ......LA	R	6	6	3.18	44	0	0	0	35	16	51.0	39	202	19	18	3	5	1	0	11	3	40	0	0	.213
Huismann, M. ......PIT	R	0	0	7.20	5	0	0	0	4	0	5.0	7	25	6	4	0	0	0	0	2	1	5	0	0	.304
Hurst, B ......SD	L	15	8	3.29	31	31	4	0	0	0	221.2	201	909	89	81	17	8	3	3	59	6	141	5	1	.241
Innis, J ......NY	R	0	2	2.66	69	0	0	0	29	0	84.2	66	336	30	25	2	8	4	0	23	6	47	4	1	.219
Jackson, D ......CHI	L	1	5	6.75	17	14	0	0	0	0	70.2	89	347	59	53	8	6	2	1	48	4	31	1	0	.309
Jackson, D ......SD	R	0	0	9.00	1	0	0	0	1	0	2.0	3	10	2	2	0	0	0	0	2	0	0	1	0	.375

Name/Team	T	W	L	ERA	G	GS	CG	GF	SV	IP	H	BFP	R	ER	HR	BB	SO	AVG
Jones, B ....MON	R	4	9	3.35	77	0	0	46	13	88.2	76	353	35	33	8	33	46	.246
Jones, J ....HOU	R	6	8	4.39	26	22	1	0	0	135.1	143	593	73	66	9	51	88	.270
Juden, J ....HOU	R	2	2	6.00	4	3	0	0	0	18.0	19	81	14	12		7	11	.275
Kile, D ....HOU	R	7	11	3.69	37	22	1	5	0	153.2	144	689	84	63		84	100	.246
Kipper, B ....PIT	L	2	2	4.65	52	0	0	18	0	60.0	66	264	34	31		22	38	.276
LaCoss, M ....SF	R	1	5	7.23	18	5	0	6	0	47.1	61	225	39	38		24	30	.314
LaPoint, D ....PHI	L	0	2	16.20	5	2	0	0	0	5.0	10	32	10	9		6	3	.435
Lancaster, L ....CHI	R	9	7	3.52	64	0	0	21	3	156.0	150	653	68	61	13	49	102	.256
Landrum, B ....PIT	R	4	4	3.18	61	0	0	43	17	76.1	76	322	32	27	4	19	45	.252
Layana, T ....CIN	R	1	6	6.97	22	0	0	9	0	20.2	23	95	18	16		11	14	.277
Lefferts, C ....SD	L	1	6	3.91	54	0	0	40	23	69.0	74	290	35	30	5	14	48	.285
Leibrandt, C ....ATL	L	15	13	3.49	36	36	5	0	0	229.2	212	949	105	89	18	56	128	.245
Lewis, J ....SD	R	0	0	4.15	12	0	0	0	0	13.0	14	64	7	6		4	10	.275
Lilliquist, D ....SD	L	0	2	8.79	6	2	0	2	0	14.1	25	70	14	14		3	7	.379
Litton, G ....SF	R	0	0	9.00	1	0	0	0	0	1.0	7	7	2	1		4	0	.250
Long, B ....MON	R	0	0	10.80	3	0	0	1	0	1.2	4	12	2	2		3	0	.500
Maddux, G ....CHI	R	15	11	3.35	37	37	7	0	0	263.0	232	1070	113	98	18	66	198	.237
Maddux, M ....SD	R	7	2	2.46	64	8	0	27	5	98.2	78	388	37	27	4	27	57	.221
Mahler, R ....MON-ATL	R	2	4	4.50	23	3	0	2	0	66.0	70	291	33	33	2	28	27	.275
Mallicoat, R ....HOU	L	1	1	3.86	24	0	0	4	0	23.1	22	103	10	10	2	13	18	.259
Martinez, De ....MON	R	14	11	2.39	31	31	9	0	0	220.1	187	905	70	59	9	62	123	.226
Martinez, R ....LA	R	17	13	3.27	33	33	6	0	0	220.0	190	916	89	80	18	69	150	.229
Mason, R ....PIT	R	3	2	3.03	24	0	0	6	3	29.2	21	114	10	10	3	6	21	.200
Mauser, T ....PHI	R	0	0	7.59	3	0	0	0	0	10.2	18	53	9	9		3	6	.367
May, S ....CHI	R	0	0	18.00	1	0	0	1	0	2.0	6	12	4	4		1	1	.545
McClellan, P ....SF	R	3	6	4.56	13	13	0	0	0	71.0	68	300	41	36	12	25	44	.252
McClure, B ....STL	L	1	1	3.13	32	0	0	9	0	23.0	24	98	8	8	0	8	15	.282
McDowell, R ....PHI-LA	R	9	9	2.93	71	0	0	34	10	101.1	100	445	40	33	4	48	50	.262
McElroy, C ....CHI	L	6	2	1.95	71	0	0	12	3	101.1	92	419	24	22		57	92	.210
Melendez, J ....SD	R	8	5	3.27	31	9	1	0	0	93.2	77	381	35	34	11	24	92	.211
Mercker, K ....ATL	L	5	3	2.58	50	4	0	28	6	73.1	56	306	23	21	5	35	62	.222
Miller, P ....PIT	R	0	0	5.40	1	1	0	0	0	5.0	4	21	3	3	0	2	2	.222
Minutelli, G ....CIN	L	0	2	6.04	16	3	0	2	0	25.1	30	124	17	17	5	18	21	.288

PITCHER	TEAM	T	W	L	ERA	G	GS	CG	SHO	GF	SV	IP	H	TBF	R	ER	HR	SH	SF	HB	BB	IBB	SO	WP	BK	OPP AVG
Morgan, M	LA	R	14	10	2.78	34	33	5	1	0	1	236.1	197	949	85	73	12	10	4	3	61	10	140	6	0	.226
Moyer, J	STL	L	0	5	5.74	8	7	0	0	1	0	31.1	38	142	21	20	5	4	2	1	16	0	20	2	1	.319
Mulholland, T	PHI	L	16	13	3.61	34	34	8	3	0	0	232.0	231	956	100	93	15	11	6	3	49	2	142	3	1	.260
Myers, R	CIN	L	6	13	3.55	58	12	0	0	18	6	132.0	116	575	61	52	8	8	6	1	80	5	108	2	1	.242
Nabholz, C	MON	L	8	7	3.63	24	24	1	0	0	0	153.2	134	631	66	62	6	8	4	2	57	4	99	3	1	.237
Nolte, E	SD	L	3	2	11.05	6	6	0	0	0	0	22.0	37	111	27	27	6	0	4	9	10	0	15	1	1	.378
Ojeda, B	LA	L	12	9	3.18	31	31	2	2	0	2	189.1	181	802	78	67	15	15	3	3	70	9	120	4	2	.257
Olivares, O	STL	R	11	7	3.71	28	24	1	0	0	1	167.1	148	688	78	69	13	11	5	5	61	1	91	3	1	.243
Oliveras, F	SF	R	6	6	3.86	55	0	0	0	17	3	79.1	69	316	36	34	12	5	3	1	22	4	48	1	2	.242
Oquendo, J	STL	R	0	0	27.00	1	0	0	0	0	0	1.0	7	7	3	3	0	2	0	0	2	0	0	1	0	.400
Osuna, A	HOU	L	7	6	3.42	71	0	0	0	32	12	81.2	59	353	39	31	5	6	5	0	46	5	68	0	3	.201
Palacios, V	PIT	R	6	3	3.75	36	7	1	0	8	3	81.2	69	347	34	34	12	4	5	1	38	2	64	6	2	.228
Parrett, J	ATL	R	1	2	6.33	18	0	0	0	9	1	21.1	31	109	18	15	2	2	0	0	12	2	14	4	0	.326
Patterson, B	PIT	L	4	3	4.11	54	0	0	0	19	0	65.2	67	270	32	30	7	2	2	0	15	1	57	0	0	.267
Pavlas, D	CHI	R	0	0	18.00	1	0	0	0	1	0	1.0	3	5	2	2	1	2	0	0	2	0	0	0	0	.750
Pena, A	NY-ATL	R	8	1	2.40	59	0	0	0	36	15	82.1	74	331	23	22	6	3	4	1	22	4	62	1	0	.245
Perez, M	STL	R	0	2	5.82	14	0	0	0	2	0	17.0	19	75	11	11	0	7	0	2	7	0	7	0	1	.288
Perez, Y	CHI	L	1	0	2.08	3	0	0	0	1	0	4.1	16	1	0	0	2	0	0	2	0	3	0	0	.167
Peterson, A	SD	R	3	4	4.45	13	11	0	0	0	0	54.2	50	241	33	27	10	4	2	0	28	2	37	7	1	.242
Petry, D	ATL	R	0	0	5.55	10	0	0	0	4	0	24.1	29	116	17	15	2	3	0	0	14	1	9	2	0	.296
Piatt, D	MON	R	0	3	2.60	21	0	0	0	3	1	34.2	29	145	11	10	3	6	0	0	17	5	29	1	0	.230
Portugal, M	HOU	R	10	12	4.49	32	27	0	0	0	1	168.1	163	710	91	84	19	9	6	2	59	5	120	1	1	.256
Power, T	CIN	R	5	3	3.62	68	0	0	0	22	3	87.0	87	371	37	35	6	6	4	2	31	5	51	6	1	.265
Rasmussen, D	SD	L	6	13	3.74	24	24	1	0	0	0	146.2	155	633	74	61	12	4	6	0	49	3	75	3	0	.271
Reed, R	PIT	R	0	0	10.38	1	0	0	0	0	0	4.1	8	21	6	5	1	0	2	0	1	0	2	0	0	.400
Remlinger, M	SF	L	2	1	4.37	8	6	1	0	1	0	35.0	36	155	17	17	5	4	0	1	20	1	19	4	0	.271
Renfroe, L	CHI	R	0	1	13.50	4	0	0	0	2	0	4.2	11	27	7	7	1	0	0	0	7	0	4	0	0	.440
Reuschel, R	SF	R	0	2	4.22	4	4	0	0	0	0	10.2	11	54	5	5	0	0	0	0	2	0	1	0	0	.370
Reynoso, A	ATL	R	2	1	6.17	6	5	0	0	0	0	23.1	26	103	18	16	4	3	3	0	10	2	10	2	0	.299
Righetti, D	SF	L	2	7	3.39	61	0	0	0	49	24	71.2	64	304	29	27	4	4	4	2	28	6	51	1	1	.240
Rijo, J	CIN	R	15	6	2.51	30	30	3	1	0	0	204.1	165	825	69	57	8	4	8	4	55	4	172	2	4	.219

Pitcher	Tm	T	W	L	ERA	G	GS	CG	IP	SO	AVG
Ritchie, W	PHI	L	1	2	2.50	39	0	0	50.1	26	.234
Robinson, D	SF	R	5	9	4.38	34	16	0	121.1	78	.265
Rodriguez, R	PIT	L	1	1	4.11	18	0	0	15.1	10	.246
Rodriguez, R	SD	L	1	1	3.26	64	0	0	80.0	40	.234
Rojas, M	MON	R	3	3	3.75	37	0	0	48.0	37	.228
Rosenberg, S	SD	L	1	1	6.94	10	0	0	11.2	6	.250
Ruffin, B	PHI	L	4	7	3.78	31	15	0	119.0	85	.272
Ruskin, S	MON	L	4	4	4.24	64	0	0	63.2	46	.241
Sampen, M	MON	R	9	5	4.00	43	8	0	92.1	52	.273
Sanford, M	CIN	R	1	1	3.86	5	0	0	28.0	31	.186
Sauveur, R	NY	L	0	0	10.80	6	0	0	3.1	4	.467
Scanlan, B	CHI	R	7	8	3.89	40	13	0	111.0	44	.269
Schilling, C	HOU	R	3	5	3.81	56	0	0	75.2	71	.271
Schmidt, D	MON	R	1	1	10.38	4	0	0	4.1	1	.429
Schourek, P	NY	L	5	4	4.27	35	8	0	86.1	67	.248
Scott, M	HOU	R	0	2	12.86	2	0	0	7.0	3	.367
Scott, T	SD	R	0	0	9.00	2	0	0	1.0	1	.400
Scudder, S	CIN	R	6	9	4.35	27	14	0	101.1	51	.246
Searcy, S	PHI	L	2	1	4.15	18	0	0	30.1	21	.252
Segura, J	SF	R	1	1	4.41	11	0	0	16.1	10	.303
Sherrill, T	STL	L	0	0	8.16	10	0	0	14.1	4	.339
Simons, D	NY	L	2	3	5.19	42	0	0	60.2	38	.246
Sisk, D	ATL	L	2	1	5.02	14	0	0	14.1	5	.333
Slocumb, H	CHI	R	1	2	3.45	52	0	0	62.2	34	.231
Smiley, J	PIT	L	20	8	3.08	33	32	2	207.2	129	.251
Smith, B	STL	R	12	9	3.85	31	31	3	198.2	94	.251
Smith, Da	CHI	R	0	6	6.00	35	0	0	33.0	16	.302
Smith, L	STL	R	6	6	2.34	67	0	0	73.0	67	.249
Smith, P	ATL	R	1	3	5.06	14	0	0	48.0	29	.262
Smith, Z	PIT	L	16	10	3.20	35	35	6	228.0	120	.268
Smoltz, J	ATL	R	14	13	3.80	36	36	5	229.2	148	.243
St. Claire, R	ATL	R	0	0	4.08	19	0	0	28.2	30	.282
Stanton, M	ATL	L	0	5	2.88	74	0	0	78.0	54	.217

PITCHER TEAM	T	W	L	ERA	G	GS	CG	SHO	GF	SV	IP	H	TBF	R	ER	HR	SH	SF	HB	BB	IBB	SO	WP	BK	OPP AVG
Sutcliffe, R........CHI	R	6	5	4.10	19	18	0	0	0	0	96.2	96	422	52	44	4	5	8	0	45	0	52	2	2	.264
Terry, S............STL	R	4	4	2.80	65	0	0	0	13	1	80.1	76	339	31	25	1	2	0	0	32	14	52	0	0	.249
Tewksbury, B......STL	R	11	12	3.25	30	30	3	2	0	0	191.0	206	798	86	69	13	12	10	5	38	2	75	0	3	.281
Tomlin, R..........PIT	L	8	7	2.98	31	27	4	2	0	0	175.0	170	736	75	58	9	5	2	6	54	4	104	1	3	.254
Valera, J ....NY	R	0	0	0.00	2	0	0	0	1	0	2.0	1	11	0	0	0	0	0	1	4	0	1	0	0	.143
Viola, F ....NY	L	13	15	3.97	35	35	3	0	0	0	231.1	259	980	112	102	25	15	5	1	54	1	132	6	1	.286
Wainhouse, D .....MON	R	0	2	6.75	2	0	0	0	1	0	2.2	2	14	2	2	0	0	1	0	4	0	1	2	1	.222
Walk, B.............PIT	R	9	2	3.60	25	20	0	0	3	0	115.0	104	484	53	46	10	7	4	5	35	0	67	2	2	.240
Wetteland, J ......LA	R	1	0	0.00	6	0	0	0	3	0	9.0	5	36	2	0	0	0	1	1	3	0	9	1	0	.161
Whitehurst, W ....NY	R	7	12	4.19	36	20	0	0	6	0	133.1	142	556	67	62	12	6	3	4	25	3	87	3	4	.274
Whitson, E..........SD	R	4	6	5.03	13	12	2	0	0	1	78.2	93	337	47	44	13	6	3	0	17	3	40	1	0	.299
Wilkins, D ....HOU	R	2	1	11.25	7	0	0	0	3	0	8.0	16	51	14	10	0	2	0	0	10	2	4	1	1	.410
Williams, B........HOU	R	0	1	3.75	2	2	0	0	0	0	12.0	11	49	5	5	2	0	0	0	4	0	4	0	0	.250
Williams, M........PHI	L	12	5	2.34	69	0	0	0	60	30	88.1	56	386	24	23	4	4	4	8	62	5	84	4	1	.182
Wilson, S ....CHI-LA	L	0	1	2.61	19	0	0	0	5	0	20.2	14	81	7	6	1	2	5	0	9	1	14	0	1	.197
Wilson, T...........SF	L	13	11	3.56	44	29	2	1	6	0	202.0	173	841	87	80	13	14	5	5	77	4	139	5	3	.234
Wohlers, M.........ATL	R	3	1	3.20	17	0	0	0	4	2	19.2	17	89	7	7	0	2	2	2	13	3	13	0	0	.239
Young, A...........NY	R	2	5	3.10	10	8	0	0	2	0	49.1	48	202	20	17	4	1	1	1	12	1	20	1	0	.257

CLUB PITCHING

CLUB	W	L	ERA	G	CG	SHO	REL	SV	IP	H	R	ER	HR	HB	BB	IBB	SO	WP	BK	OPP AVG
LOS ANGELES..	93	69	3.06	162	15	14	367	40	1458.0	1312	565	496	96	28	500	77	1028	48	12	.241
PITTSBURGH....	98	64	3.44	162	18	11	353	51	1456.2	1411	632	557	117	30	401	34	919	40	12	.256
ATLANTA........	94	68	3.49	162	18	7	345	48	1452.2	1304	644	563	118	28	481	39	969	66	13	.240
NEW YORK	77	84	3.56	161	12	11	314	39	1437.1	1403	646	568	108	25	410	41	1028	59	14	.257
SAN DIEGO	84	78	3.57	162	14	11	334	47	1452.2	1385	646	577	139	13	457	56	921	49	13	.252
MONTREAL	71	90	3.64	161	12	14	367	39	1440.1	1304	655	583	111	32	584	42	909	51	9	.244
ST. LOUIS	84	78	3.69	162	9	5	369	51	1435.1	1367	648	588	114	47	454	52	822	33	7	.255
CINCINNATI	74	88	3.83	162	7	11	354	43	1440.0	1372	691	613	127	28	560	41	997	60	9	.253
PHILADELPHIA..	78	84	3.86	162	16	13	321	35	1463.0	1346	680	628	111	43	670	58	988	81	6	.246
HOUSTON	65	97	4.00	162	7	13	365	36	1453.0	1347	717	646	129	29	651	62	1033	46	17	.247
SAN FRANCISCO.	75	87	4.03	162	10	10	334	45	1442.0	1397	697	646	143	36	544	60	905	44	14	.257
CHICAGO	77	83	4.03	160	12	4	360	40	1456.2	1415	734	653	117	28	542	64	927	48	12	.257
TOTALS	970	970	3.68	970	150	122	4183	514	17387.2	16363	7955	7118	1430	367	6254	626	11446	625	138	.250

OFFICIAL 1991 AMERICAN LEAGUE RECORDS

COMPILED BY MLB-IBM BASEBALL INFORMATION SYSTEM
Official Statistician: ELIAS SPORTS BUREAU

FINAL STANDINGS

AMERICAN LEAGUE EAST					AMERICAN LEAGUE WEST				
CLUB	WON	LOST	PCT.	GB	CLUB	WON	LOST	PCT.	GB
TORONTO	91	71	.562	-	MINNESOTA	95	67	.586	-
DETROIT	84	78	.519	7.0	CHICAGO	87	75	.537	8.0
BOSTON	84	78	.519	7.0	TEXAS	85	77	.525	10.0
MILWAUKEE	83	79	.512	8.0	OAKLAND	84	78	.519	11.0
NEW YORK	71	91	.438	20.0	SEATTLE	83	79	.512	12.0
BALTIMORE	67	95	.414	24.0	KANSAS CITY	82	80	.506	13.0
CLEVELAND	57	105	.352	34.0	CALIFORNIA	81	81	.500	14.0

Championship Series: Minnesota defeated Toronto, 4 games to 1

Batting

INDIVIDUAL BATTING LEADERS

Batting Average	.341	Franco	Tex.
Games	162	Carter	Tor.
		Fielder	Det.
		C. Ripken	Bal.
At Bats	665	Molitor	Mil.
Runs	133	Molitor	Mil.
Hits	216	Molitor	Mil.
Total Bases	368	C. Ripken	Bal.
Singles	156	Franco	Tex.
Doubles	49	Palmeiro	Tex.
Triples	13	L. Johnson	Chi.
		Molitor	Mil.
Home Runs	44	Canseco	Oak.
		Fielder	Det.
Runs Batted In	133	Fielder	Det.
Sacrifice Hits	19	Sojo	Cal.
Sacrifice Flies	10	A. Davis	Sea.
		Olerud	Tor.
Hit by Pitch	10	Carter	Tor.
Bases on Balls	138	F. Thomas	Chi.
Intentional Bases on Balls	25	Boggs	Bos.
Strikeouts	175	Deer	Det.
Stolen Bases	58	R. Henderson	Oak.
Caught Stealing	23	Polonia	Cal.
Grounded Into Double Play	27	Puckett	Min.
Slugging Percentage	.593	Tartabull	K.C.
On-Base Percentage	.453	F. Thomas	Chi.
Longest Batting Streak	22	B. McRae	K.C. (July 20-Aug. 13)

TOP 15 QUALIFIERS FOR BATTING CHAMPIONSHIP

BATTER	TEAM	B	AVG	G	AB	R	H	TB	2B	3B	HR	RBI	SH	SF	HP	BB	IBB	SO	SB	CS	GI DP	SLG	OBP	E
Franco, J	TEX	R	.341	146	589	108	201	279	27	3	15	78	0	2	3	65	8	78	36	9	13	.474	.408	14
Boggs, W	BOS	L	.332	144	546	93	181	251	42	2	8	51	0	6	0	89	25	32	1	2	16	.460	.421	12
Randolph, W	MIL	R	.327	124	431	60	141	161	14	3	0	54	3	3	3	75	3	38	4	2	14	.374	.424	20
Griffey Jr, K	SEA	L	.327	154	548	76	179	289	42	1	22	100	4	9	1	71	21	82	18	6	10	.527	.399	4
Molitor, P	MIL	R	.325	158	665	133	216	325	32	13	17	75	0	1	6	77	16	62	19	8	11	.489	.399	6
Ripken, C	BAL	R	.323	162	650	99	210	368	46	5	34	114	0	9	5	53	15	46	6	1	19	.566	.374	11
Palmeiro, R	TEX	L	.322	159	631	115	203	336	49	3	26	88	2	7	6	68	10	72	4	3	17	.532	.389	12
Puckett, K	MIN	R	.319	152	611	92	195	281	29	6	15	89	8	7	4	31	4	78	11	5	27	.460	.352	6
Thomas, F	CHI	R	.318	158	559	104	178	309	31	2	32	109	0	2	1	138	13	112	1	2	20	.553	.453	2
Tartabull, D	KC	R	.316	132	484	78	153	287	35	3	31	100	0	5	3	65	6	121	6	3	9	.593	.397	7
Sierra, R	TEX	S	.307	161	661	110	203	332	44	5	25	116	0	5	0	56	7	91	16	4	17	.502	.357	7
Martinez, E	SEA	R	.307	150	544	98	167	246	35	1	14	52	2	4	8	84	9	72	0	3	19	.452	.405	15
Sax, S	NY	R	.304	158	652	85	198	270	38	2	10	56	5	6	3	41	2	38	31	11	15	.414	.345	10
Joyner, W	CAL	L	.301	143	551	79	166	269	34	3	21	96	2	5	1	52	4	66	2	0	11	.488	.360	8
Greenwell, M	BOS	L	.300	147	544	76	163	228	26	6	9	83	1	7	3	43	6	35	15	5	11	.419	.350	3

INDIVIDUAL BATTING

BATTER	TEAM	B	AVG	G	AB	R	H	TB	2B	3B	HR	RBI	SH	SF	HP	BB	IBB	SO	SB	CS	GI DP	SLG	OBP	E
Abner, S	CAL	R	.228	41	101	12	23	37	6	1	2	9	0	0	0	4	0	18	1	2	3	.366	.257	0
Afenir, T	OAK	R	.091	5	11	0	1	1	0	0	0	0	0	0	0	0	0	2	0	1	1	.091	.091	0
Aldrete, M	CLE	L	.262	85	183	22	48	59	6	1	1	19	0	2	0	36	1	37	0	2	0	.322	.380	4
Allanson, A	DET	R	.232	60	151	10	35	48	10	0	1	16	2	0	0	7	0	31	0	1	3	.318	.266	5
Allred, B	CLE	L	.232	48	125	17	29	41	3	0	3	12	3	2	1	25	0	35	2	2	1	.328	.359	3
Alomar, R	TOR	S	.295	161	637	88	188	278	41	11	9	69	16	5	4	57	3	86	53	11	5	.436	.354	15

BATTER	TEAM	B	AVG	G	AB	R	H	TB	2B	3B	HR	RBI	SH	SF	HP	BB	IBB	SO	SB	CS	GI DP	SLG	OBP	E
Alomar, S	CLE	R	.217	51	184	10	40	49	9	0	0	7	2	1	4	8	1	24	0	4	4	.266	.264	4
Amaral, R	SEA	S	.063	14	16	2	1	1	0	0	0	0	0	0	1	1	0	5	0	0	1	.063	.167	2
Amaro, R	CAL	S	.217	10	23	0	5	6	1	0	0	2	0	0	0	3	0	3	0	0	0	.261	.308	1
Anderson, B	BAL	L	.230	113	256	40	59	83	12	3	2	27	11	3	5	38	1	44	12	5	1	.324	.338	3
Baerga, C	CLE	S	.288	158	593	80	171	236	28	2	11	69	4	3	6	48	0	74	3	2	12	.398	.346	27
Baines, H	OAK	L	.295	141	488	76	144	231	25	1	20	90	0	5	4	72	5	67	1	1	12	.473	.383	1
Barfield, J	NY	R	.225	84	284	37	64	127	13	1	17	48	0	1	0	36	22	80	0	0	11	.447	.312	0
Barnes, S	DET	R	.289	75	159	28	46	78	13	2	5	17	4	1	2	9	6	24	10	7	1	.491	.325	2
Bell, D	TOR	R	.143	18	28	5	4	4	0	0	0	1	0	0	0	1	0	5	1	0	0	.143	.314	0
Bell, J	BAL	S	.172	100	209	26	36	52	9	2	1	15	4	2	0	6	1	51	3	2	2	.249	.201	2
Belle, A	CLE	R	.282	123	461	60	130	249	31	2	28	95	0	5	0	25	0	99	3	1	24	.540	.323	9
Beltre, E	CHI	R	.167	8	6	1	1	1	0	0	0	0	0	0	0	1	0	1	0	0	0	.167	.286	9
Benzinger, T	KC	S	.294	78	293	29	86	113	15	0	4	40	0	1	3	17	2	46	2	6	5	.386	.338	0
Bergman, D	DET	L	.237	86	194	23	46	79	10	1	7	29	0	2	0	35	2	40	1	0	5	.407	.351	3
Bernazard, T	DET	R	.167	6	12	0	2	2	0	0	0	0	0	0	0	0	0	4	0	0	0	.167	.167	1
Berry, S	KC	R	.133	31	60	5	8	11	3	0	0	1	0	0	0	5	0	23	0	0	1	.183	.212	2
Bichette, D	MIL	R	.238	134	445	53	106	175	18	0	15	59	1	6	1	22	4	107	14	8	9	.393	.272	7
Blankenship, L	OAK	R	.249	90	185	33	46	63	8	0	3	21	2	0	3	23	0	42	12	3	2	.341	.336	3
Blowers, M	NY	R	.200	15	35	4	7	10	0	0	1	3	1	0	0	4	0	5	0	0	1	.286	.282	3
Boggs, W	BOS	L	.332	144	546	93	181	251	42	2	8	51	0	6	0	89	25	32	1	2	16	.460	.421	12
Borders, P	TOR	R	.244	105	291	22	71	103	17	0	5	36	6	3	1	11	1	45	0	4	8	.354	.271	4
Bordick, M	OAK	R	.238	90	235	21	56	63	7	0	0	21	12	2	1	14	0	37	3	4	3	.268	.289	11
Bradley, S	SEA	L	.203	83	172	10	35	42	5	1	0	11	5	2	3	19	2	19	0	0	2	.244	.280	4
Brett, G	KC	L	.255	131	505	77	129	203	40	2	10	61	1	8	0	58	10	75	3	0	20	.402	.327	1
Briley, G	SEA	L	.260	139	381	39	99	128	17	3	2	26	1	3	0	27	1	51	23	11	7	.336	.307	4
Brock, G	MIL	L	.283	31	60	9	17	24	4	0	1	6	1	0	0	14	0	9	1	1	1	.400	.419	0
Brosius, S	OAK	R	.235	36	68	9	16	27	5	0	2	4	0	0	2	3	0	11	3	1	2	.397	.268	0
Browne, J	MIN	R	.216	38	37	3	8	8	0	0	0	4	1	0	0	2	0	8	7	1	0	.216	.256	1
Browne, J	CLE	S	.228	107	290	28	66	78	5	2	1	29	12	4	1	27	0	29	2	4	5	.269	.292	14
Brumley, M	BOS	S	.212	63	118	16	25	30	5	0	0	5	4	0	0	10	0	22	2	2	0	.254	.273	7
Brunansky, T	BOS	R	.229	142	459	54	105	179	24	1	16	70	0	8	3	49	2	72	1	2	8	.390	.303	3
Buechele, S	TEX	R	.267	121	416	58	111	186	17	2	18	66	10	5	5	39	4	69	0	4	11	.447	.335	3
Buhner, J	SEA	R	.244	137	406	64	99	202	14	4	27	77	2	4	6	53	5	117	0	1	10	.498	.337	5

Name	Team	B	AVG	G	AB	R	H	TB	2B	3B	HR	RBI	SF	HP	GW	BB	IBB	SO	SB	CS	GDP	SLG	OBP	SH
Burks, E	BOS	R	.251	130	474	56	119	200	33	3	14	56	2	3	6	39	2	81	6	11	7	.422	.314	2
Bush, R	MIL	L	.303	93	165	21	50	80	10	1	6	23	0	0	3	24	3	25	0	2	5	.485	.401	2
Canale, G	MIL	L	.176	21	34	6	6	17	2	0	3	10	0	2	0	8	0	6	0	0	5	.500	.318	2
Canseco, J	OAK	R	.266	154	572	115	152	318	32	2	44	122	6	6	9	78	8	152	26	6	16	.556	.359	9
Capra, N	TEX	R	.000	2	0	0	0	2	0	0	0	0	0	0	0	1	0	2	0	0	0	.000	1.000	0
Carter, J	TOR	R	.273	162	638	89	174	321	42	3	33	108	9	9	10	49	12	112	20	9	6	.503	.330	8
Castillo, C	MIN	L	.167	11	12	0	2	4	0	0	0	1	0	0	0	0	0	2	0	0	0	.333	.231	0
Clark, D	KC	L	.200	10	10	1	2	2	0	1	0	1	0	0	1	1	0	1	0	0	0	.200	.273	0
Clark, J	BOS	S	.249	140	481	75	120	224	18	1	28	87	0	5	3	96	3	133	0	2	17	.466	.374	0
Cochrane, D	SEA	R	.247	65	178	16	44	63	13	2	2	22	1	1	1	9	0	38	0	0	3	.354	.286	7
Cole, A	CLE	R	.295	122	387	58	114	137	17	3	0	21	4	2	0	58	2	47	27	17	8	.354	.386	8
Cole, S	KC	L	.143	14	35	1	1	1	1	0	0	7	0	0	0	0	0	2	0	0	0	.143	.333	0
Cooper, S	BOS	R	.457	14	35	6	16	24	4	2	3	18	0	0	2	2	0	2	0	0	1	.686	.486	2
Cora, J	CHI	S	.241	100	228	37	55	63	6	2	1	18	8	3	5	20	0	21	11	6	7	.276	.313	10
Cotto, H	SEA	R	.305	66	177	35	54	82	6	3	0	23	1	1	3	10	0	27	16	3	3	.463	.347	2
Cromartie, W	KC	L	.313	69	131	13	41	55	7	2	0	20	0	1	1	15	0	18	3	3	7	.420	.381	1
Cron, C	CAL	S	.133	6	15	2	2	2	0	0	1	7	12	0	0	2	0	5	0	0	0	.133	.235	0
Cuyler, M	DET	S	.257	154	475	77	122	160	15	7	12	33	4	2	5	52	0	92	41	10	4	.337	.335	6
Daugherty, J	TEX	S	.194	58	144	8	28	38	3	1	2	11	3	3	3	16	0	23	1	0	2	.264	.270	1
Davis, A	SEA	L	.221	145	462	39	102	155	15	2	29	69	10	10	10	56	9	78	0	9	8	.335	.299	0
Davis, C	MIN	S	.277	153	534	84	148	271	34	1	10	93	0	4	0	95	13	117	5	0	9	.507	.385	0
Davis, G	BAL	R	.227	49	176	29	40	81	9	1	10	28	4	2	5	16	0	29	4	0	2	.460	.307	8
Davis, M	CAL	R	.000	3	2	2	0	0	0	0	0	0	0	0	0	0	1	0	0	3	0	.000	.000	1
Deer, R	DET	R	.179	134	448	64	80	173	14	2	25	64	0	2	5	89	0	175	16	2	3	.386	.314	7
de los Santos, L	DET	R	.167	16	30	1	5	7	0	0	0	2	0	0	0	2	1	4	0	9	2	.233	.219	1
Dempsey, R	MIL	R	.231	61	147	15	34	51	5	2	4	23	3	3	3	23	2	20	0	1	13	.347	.329	2
Devereaux, M	BAL	R	.260	149	608	82	158	262	27	2	19	59	7	4	4	47	2	115	2	0	5	.431	.313	3
Diaz, M	TEX	R	.264	96	182	24	48	58	7	1	1	27	1	1	1	15	0	18	5	1	0	.319	.318	7
Disarcina, G	CAL	R	.211	18	57	5	12	14	2	0	0	3	0	0	0	2	7	4	4	0	7	.246	.274	4
Downing, B	TEX	R	.278	123	407	76	113	185	17	2	17	49	2	2	2	58	0	70	2	2	0	.455	.377	0
Ducey, R	TOR	L	.235	39	68	8	16	25	2	2	1	6	1	0	5	6	1	26	0	3	1	.368	.297	4
Eisenreich, J	KC	L	.301	135	375	47	113	147	22	3	2	47	3	6	6	20	0	35	1	0	10	.392	.333	5
Escobar, J	CLE	R	.200	39	15	0	3	3	0	0	1	1	0	0	0	1	0	4	0	1	1	.200	.250	0
Espinoza, A	NY	R	.256	148	480	51	123	165	23	2	2	33	9	2	2	16	2	57	4	3	10	.344	.282	21
Evans, D	BAL	R	.270	101	270	35	73	102	9	1	6	38	1	2	2	54	0	54	2	7	7	.378	.393	2

BATTER	TEAM	B	AVG	G	AB	R	H	TB	2B	3B	HR	RBI	SH	SF	HP	BB	IBB	SO	SB	CS	GI DP	SLG	OBP	E
Fariss, M.	TEX	R	.258	19	31	6	8	12	1	0	1	6	0	0	0	7	0	11	1	0	0	.387	.395	0
Felix, J.	CAL	S	.283	66	230	32	65	85	10	2	2	26	0	2	3	11	0	55	7	5	5	.370	.321	3
Fermin, F.	CLE	R	.262	129	424	30	111	128	13	2	0	31	13	3	6	26	0	27	5	4	17	.302	.307	12
Fielder, C.	DET	R	.261	162	624	102	163	320	25	1	44	133	0	4	7	78	12	151	0	1	17	.513	.347	8
Fisk, C.	CHI	R	.241	134	460	42	111	190	25	0	18	74	0	2	3	32	4	86	1	0	19	.413	.299	6
Fletcher, S.	CHI	R	.206	90	248	14	51	66	10	1	1	28	6	3	1	17	0	26	1	2	3	.266	.262	3
Flora, K.	CAL	R	.125	8	8	1	1	1	0	0	0	0	0	0	0	1	0	5	0	0	1	.125	.222	1
Franco, J.	TEX	R	.341	146	589	108	201	279	27	3	15	78	0	2	3	65	8	78	36	9	13	.474	.408	14
Fryman, T.	DET	R	.259	149	557	65	144	249	36	3	21	91	6	6	3	40	0	149	12	5	13	.447	.309	23
Gaetti, G.	CAL	R	.246	152	586	58	144	222	22	1	18	66	6	5	8	33	3	104	5	9	15	.379	.293	17
Gagne, G.	MIN	R	.265	139	408	52	108	161	22	3	8	42	2	5	2	26	0	72	11	9	15	.395	.310	9
Gallagher, D.	CAL	R	.293	90	270	32	79	99	17	0	1	30	5	0	2	24	0	43	2	4	6	.367	.355	0
Gallego, M.	OAK	R	.247	159	482	67	119	178	15	4	12	49	10	3	3	67	3	84	6	6	6	.369	.343	12
Gantner, J.	MIL	L	.283	140	526	63	149	190	27	4	2	47	7	4	5	27	5	34	6	9	13	.361	.320	12
Geren, R.	NY	R	.219	64	128	7	28	37	3	1	2	12	3	0	0	9	0	31	0	1	5	.289	.270	3
Giannelli, R.	TOR	L	.167	9	24	2	4	5	1	0	0	0	3	0	0	5	0	9	1	0	0	.208	.310	1
Gibson, K.	KC	L	.236	132	462	81	109	186	17	4	16	55	1	4	6	69	3	103	18	4	9	.403	.341	4
Gladden, D.	MIN	R	.247	126	461	65	114	164	14	6	6	52	5	5	5	36	1	60	15	9	13	.356	.306	3
Gomez, L.	BAL	R	.233	118	391	40	91	160	17	2	16	45	6	7	2	40	0	82	1	1	11	.409	.302	7
Gonzales, R.	TOR	R	.195	71	118	16	23	29	3	0	1	4	5	4	1	12	0	22	0	0	5	.246	.289	7
Gonzalez, J.	CLE	R	.159	33	69	10	11	18	3	0	1	4	0	3	1	11	0	27	0	0	2	.261	.284	1
Gonzalez, J.	TEX	R	.264	142	545	78	144	261	34	1	27	102	0	3	5	42	7	118	4	10	10	.479	.321	6
Grebeck, C.	CHI	R	.281	107	224	37	63	103	16	4	1	31	4	0	1	38	0	40	1	3	0	.460	.386	10
Green, G.	TEX	R	.150	8	20	0	3	4	1	0	0	0	0	0	0	1	0	6	0	0	0	.200	.190	1
Greenwell, M.	BOS	L	.300	147	544	76	163	228	26	6	9	83	1	7	3	43	6	35	15	5	11	.419	.350	3
Griffey Jr, K.	SEA	L	.327	154	548	76	179	289	42	1	22	100	0	9	1	71	21	82	18	6	10	.527	.399	4
Griffey Sr, K.	SEA	L	.282	30	85	10	24	34	7	1	1	9	0	2	1	13	0	13	0	2	2	.400	.380	0
Gruber, K.	TOR	R	.252	113	429	58	108	190	18	2	20	65	3	5	6	31	5	70	12	7	7	.443	.308	13
Guillen, O.	CHI	L	.273	154	524	52	143	178	20	3	0	49	13	7	0	11	1	38	21	15	7	.340	.284	21
Gullickson, B.	DET	R	.000	35	0	0	0	0	0	0	0	0	0	0	0	0	0	0	0	0	0	.000	.000	0
Hall, M.	NY	L	.285	141	492	67	140	224	23	2	19	80	0	6	3	26	6	40	0	1	6	.455	.321	3
Hamilton, D.	MIL	L	.311	122	405	64	126	156	15	6	1	57	0	3	0	33	2	38	16	6	3	.385	.361	1
Hare, S.	DET	L	.053	9	19	0	1	2	1	0	0	0	0	0	0	0	0	1	0	0	0	.105	.143	0

Player	Team	B	AVG	G	AB	R	H	2B	3B	HR	RBI	BB	SO	SB	CS	SLG	OBP	GDP
Harper, B	MIN	R	.311	123	441	54	137	28	1	10	69	14	22	0	2	.447	.336	8
Harris, D	TEX	R	.375	18	8	4	3	0	0	1	2	1	3	0	0	.750	.444	0
Hemond, S	OAK	R	.217	23	23	5	5	0	0	0	0	3	7	6	2	.217	.250	1
Henderson, S	OAK	R	.276	150	572	86	158	33	1	25	85	58	113	2	6	.465	.346	
Henderson, R	OAK	R	.268	134	470	105	126	17	1	18	57	98	73	58	18	.423	.400	1
Hernandez, J	TEX	S	.184	45	98	18	18	2	0	0	4	3	31	0	0	.224	.208	8
Hill, D	CAL	R	.239	77	209	36	50	8	2	1	20	0	21	1	0	.301	.335	4
Hill, G	TOR-CLE	R	.258	72	221	29	57	8	1	8	25	16	54	6	4	.421	.324	8
Hoiles, C	BAL	R	.243	107	341	36	83	15	0	11	31	29	61	0	0	.384	.304	3
Horn, S	BAL	L	.233	121	317	45	74	16	0	23	61	41	99	0	0	.502	.326	1
Housie, W	BOS	S	.250	11	8	2	2	2	0	0	0	0	3	1	0	.375	.333	
Howard, C	SEA	R	.167	8	6	1	1	1	0	0	0	1	2	0	2	.333	.286	0
Howard, D	KC	S	.216	94	236	20	51	7	3	0	17	16	45	3	1	.258	.267	0
Howell, J	CAL	L	.210	32	81	11	17	0	0	1	7	11	11	1	0	.309	.304	12
Howitt, D	OAK	L	.167	45	42	5	7	2	0	4	3	1	12	0	4	.262	.182	2
Hrbek, K	MIN	L	.284	132	462	72	131	20	0	20	89	67	48	4	4	.461	.373	0
Huff, M	CLE-CHI	R	.251	102	243	42	61	10	0	3	25	37	48	14	1	.346	.361	8
Hulett, T	BAL	R	.204	79	206	29	42	9	1	7	18	13	49	1	0	.350	.255	2
Humphreys, M	NY	S	.200	25	40	9	8	8	0	0	0	9	7	0	3	.200	.347	4
Huson, J	TEX	L	.213	119	268	36	57	12	3	2	26	39	32	2	3	.287	.312	1
Incaviglia, P	DET	R	.214	97	337	38	72	3	0	11	38	36	92	8	2	.353	.290	15
Jackson, B	CHI	R	.225	23	71	16	16	1	0	4	14	12	25	0	1	.408	.333	3
Jacoby, B	CLE-OAK	R	.224	129	419	28	94	21	0	5	14	27	54	2	4	.308	.274	0
James, C	CLE	R	.238	115	437	31	104	16	1	2	41	18	61	3	0	.318	.273	7
Jeffcoat, M	TEX	L	1.000	70	1	0	1	0	0	0	1	0	0	0	1	2.000	1.000	0
Jefferson, R	CLE	L	.198	26	101	10	20	3	0	2	12	3	22	0	0	.297	.219	0
Jennings, D	OAK	L	.111	8	9	1	1	0	0	0	0	1	2	0	0	.111	.273	2
Johnson, L	CHI	L	.274	159	588	72	161	14	13	0	49	26	58	26	7	.342	.304	0
Jones, T	SEA	R	.251	79	175	30	44	3	0	3	24	15	22	2	1	.354	.321	2
Joyner, W	CAL	L	.301	143	551	79	166	34	3	21	96	52	66	2	9	.488	.360	0
Karkovice, R	CHI	R	.246	75	167	25	41	13	0	5	22	15	42	0	2	.341	.310	8
Kelly, P	NY	R	.242	96	298	35	72	6	3	3	23	15	52	12	1	.339	.288	4
Kelly, R	NY	R	.267	126	486	77	130	22	4	20	69	45	77	32	11	.444	.333	18
Kirby, W	CLE	L	.209	21	43	4	9	2	0	0	5	2	6	1	0	.256	.239	4
Kittle, R	CHI	R	.191	17	47	7	9	0	0	2	7	5	9	0	0	.319	.291	2

Danny Tartabull's .593 slugging at KC led the majors.

Beloved Bosox Boggs has hit .345 for a decade.

BATTER	TEAM	B	AVG	G	AB	R	H	TB	2B	3B	HR	RBI	SH	SF	HP	BB	IBB	SO	SB	CS	GI DP	SLG	OBP	E
Knoblauch, C.	MIN	R	.281	151	565	78	159	198	24	6	0	50	1	5	4	59	0	40	25	5	8	.350	.351	18
Knorr, R.	TOR	R	.000	3	1	0	0	0	0	0	0	0	0	0	0	1	0	1	0	0	0	.000	.500	0
Komminsk, B.	OAK		.120	24	25	1	3	4	0	0	0	2	0	0	0	2	0	9	1	0	0	.160	.185	0
Kreuter, C.	TEX	S	.000	3	4	0	0	0	0	0	0	0	0	0	0	0	0	1	0	0	0	.000	.000	0
Lansford, C.	OAK	R	.063	5	16	0	1	1	0	0	0	0	0	0	2	0	0	2	0	0	0	.063	.063	0
Larkin, G.	MIN	S	.286	98	255	34	73	95	14	1	2	19	3	2	0	30	0	21	2	3	9	.373	.361	3
Law, V.	OAK	R	.209	74	134	11	28	37	7	1	0	9	5	0	0	18	0	27	2	2	4	.276	.303	5
Lee, M.	TOR	S	.234	138	445	41	104	128	18	3	0	29	10	4	0	24	1	107	7	5	11	.288	.274	19
Leius, S.	MIN	R	.286	109	199	35	57	83	7	2	5	20	5	4	0	30	1	35	5	2	4	.417	.378	7
Lennon, P.	SEA	R	.125	9	8	2	1	2	1	0	0	1	0	0	0	3	0	1	0	0	0	.250	.293	0
Lewis, M.	CLE	R	.264	84	314	29	83	100	15	1	0	30	2	5	0	15	0	45	2	1	12	.318	.300	9
Leyritz, J.	NY	R	.182	32	77	8	14	17	3	0	0	4	0	2	0	13	0	15	0	1	0	.221	.300	3
Liriano, N.	KC	S	.409	10	22	5	9	9	0	0	0	1	0	0	0	2	0	2	0	1	0	.409	.409	0
Livingston, S.	DET	L	.291	44	127	19	37	48	5	0	2	11	2	0	0	10	1	25	2	1	0	.378	.341	2
Lopez, L.	CLE	S	.220	35	82	7	18	24	4	1	0	7	3	0	0	4	0	7	0	0	0	.293	.261	2
Lovullo, T.	NY	R	.176	22	51	0	9	11	2	0	0	2	0	5	0	5	0	7	0	0	0	.216	.250	3
Lusader, S.	NY	L	.143	11	7	1	1	1	0	0	0	0	0	1	0	0	0	3	0	0	0	.143	.250	0
Lyons, B.	CAL	L	.200	2	5	1	1	1	0	0	0	1	0	0	0	0	0	2	0	0	0	.200	.200	0
Lyons, S.	BOS	L	.241	87	212	15	51	75	10	1	4	17	3	1	1	11	2	35	10	3	1	.354	.277	3
Maas, K.	NY	L	.220	148	500	69	110	195	14	1	23	63	0	5	4	83	3	128	5	1	4	.390	.333	6
Macfarlane, M.	KC	R	.277	84	267	34	74	135	18	2	13	41	1	5	6	17	1	52	5	9	4	.506	.330	3
Mack, S.	MIN	R	.310	143	442	79	137	234	27	8	18	74	2	5	6	34	1	79	13	9	11	.529	.363	7
Magallanes, E.	CLE	L	.000	3	2	0	0	0	0	0	0	0	0	0	0	1	0	1	0	0	0	.000	.000	2
Maldonado, C.	MIL-TOR	R	.250	86	288	37	72	123	15	0	12	48	0	3	6	36	0	76	4	0	8	.427	.342	1
Manrique, F.	OAK	R	.143	9	21	2	3	3	1	0	0	0	0	0	0	2	0	1	0	0	0	.143	.217	0
Manto, J.	CLE	R	.211	47	128	15	27	40	7	0	2	13	0	4	4	14	0	22	2	2	3	.313	.306	8
Marshall, M.	BOS-CAL	R	.261	64	69	4	18	25	6	0	1	7	0	0	0	0	0	20	0	0	1	.362	.261	1
Martinez, C.	KC	R	.207	44	121	17	25	43	4	0	6	10	1	4	0	11	3	25	0	0	3	.355	.351	3
Martinez, C.	BAL	L	.269	67	216	32	58	111	12	1	13	33	0	0	0	10	0	51	1	1	2	.514	.303	2
Martinez, C.	CLE	R	.284	72	257	22	73	102	14	5	5	30	1	2	2	10	2	43	3	1	10	.397	.310	8
Martinez, E.	SEA	R	.307	150	544	98	167	246	35	1	14	52	0	8	8	84	9	72	0	3	19	.452	.405	15
Martinez, T.	SEA	L	.205	36	112	11	23	37	2	3	4	9	2	0	1	11	0	24	0	2	2	.330	.272	2
Marzano, J.	BOS	R	.263	49	114	10	30	38	8	0	0	9	1	2	1	1	0	16	0	0	5	.333	.271	3

Player	Team	B	AVG	G	AB	R	H	TB	2B	3B	HR	RBI	SH	SF	HP	BB	IB	SO	SB	CS	DP	SLG	OBP	E
Mattingly, D	NY	L	.288	152	587	64	169	231	35	0	9	68	0	9	4	46	11	42	2	0	21	.394	.339	5
Maurer, R	TEX	L	.063	13	16	2	1	2	1	0	0	1	0	0	0	2	0	8	0	0	0	.125	.211	0
Mayne, B	KC	L	.251	85	231	22	58	75	8	0	3	23	3	2	2	23	0	10	0	1	6	.325	.315	6
McCray, R	CHI	R	.286	17	7	2	2	2	0	0	0	0	0	0	0	0	0	8	5	1	0	.286	.286	0
McGwire, M	OAK	R	.201	154	483	62	97	185	22	0	22	75	0	3	5	93	1	116	2	0	13	.383	.330	4
McIntosh, T	MIL	R	.364	7	11	2	4	8	1	0	1	1	0	0	0	1	0	1	0	0	0	.727	.417	0
McKnight, J	BAL	S	.171	16	41	2	7	8	1	0	0	1	0	0	0	9	0	8	0	0	0	.195	.320	0
McRae, B	KC	R	.261	152	629	86	164	234	24	6	8	64	9	3	5	24	0	99	20	8	9	.372	.288	3
Medina, L	CLE	R	.063	5	16	0	1	1	0	0	0	0	0	0	0	0	0	8	0	0	0	.063	.118	0
Melvin, B	BAL	R	.250	79	228	11	57	70	11	1	0	24	2	1	1	11	0	23	0	0	11	.307	.279	1
Mercedes, L	BAL	R	.204	10	54	10	11	13	1	0	0	2	1	0	0	2	0	10	0	0	0	.241	.259	0
Merullo, M	CHI	L	.229	80	140	8	32	48	8	1	2	21	0	1	0	9	0	18	0	0	2	.343	.268	2
Meulens, H	NY	R	.222	96	288	37	64	92	17	1	6	29	0	0	1	18	0	97	0	0	5	.319	.276	6
Milligan, R	BAL	R	.263	141	483	57	127	196	17	2	16	70	2	6	2	84	4	108	0	2	17	.406	.373	0
Molitor, P	MIL	R	.325	158	665	133	216	325	32	13	17	75	0	1	7	77	0	62	19	3	11	.489	.399	6
Moore, B	KC	R	.357	18	14	3	5	6	1	0	0	0	0	0	0	2	0	2	0	0	0	.429	.400	0
Morman, R	KC	R	.261	12	23	3	6	6	0	0	0	1	0	0	0	1	0	5	0	0	0	.261	.292	0
Moseby, L	DET	L	.262	74	260	37	68	103	15	1	6	35	1	3	2	44	0	44	8	3	3	.396	.321	6
Moses, J	DET	S	.048	13	21	5	1	1	0	0	0	1	0	0	0	2	0	7	1	0	0	.048	.130	0
Mulliniks, R	TOR	L	.250	97	240	27	60	80	12	1	2	24	0	2	1	44	0	26	0	0	9	.333	.364	1
Munoz, P	MIN	R	.283	51	138	15	39	69	9	0	7	26	2	2	2	7	0	36	2	1	3	.500	.327	1
Myers, G	TOR	L	.262	107	309	25	81	127	22	0	8	36	0	4	1	21	0	45	0	2	6	.411	.306	3
Naehring, T	BOS	R	.109	18	55	6	6	7	1	0	0	3	0	0	0	6	0	15	0	0	3	.127	.197	4
Newman, A	MIN	S	.191	118	246	25	47	52	5	0	0	19	5	1	0	21	0	21	5	2	5	.211	.260	2
Newson, W	CHI	L	.295	71	132	20	39	56	5	0	4	25	2	5	0	34	0	25	5	2	2	.424	.419	6
Nokes, M	NY	L	.268	135	456	52	122	214	20	0	24	77	0	9	0	25	3	49	3	0	6	.469	.308	5
O'Brien, P	SEA	L	.248	152	560	58	139	225	29	3	17	88	0	9	0	44	3	61	0	0	14	.402	.300	5
Olander, J	MIL	R	.000	12	9	2	0	0	0	0	0	0	0	0	0	0	0	5	0	0	0	.000	.182	0
Olerud, J	TOR	L	.256	139	454	64	116	199	30	1	17	68	0	3	2	68	6	84	0	2	12	.438	.353	5
Orsulak, J	BAL	L	.278	143	486	57	135	174	22	1	5	43	1	4	1	28	2	45	6	2	15	.358	.321	1
Ortiz, J	MIN	R	.209	61	134	9	28	35	4	0	1	11	0	0	1	10	0	17	0	0	10	.261	.293	1
Orton, J	CAL	R	.203	29	69	7	14	18	4	0	0	4	2	1	0	6	0	21	1	0	3	.261	.313	1
Pagliarulo, M	MIN	L	.279	121	365	38	102	140	20	0	6	36	2	3	2	21	1	55	1	3	10	.384	.322	11
Palmeiro, R	TEX	L	.322	159	631	115	203	336	49	3	26	88	0	7	2	68	6	72	4	2	19	.532	.389	12
Palmer, D	TEX	R	.187	81	268	38	50	108	9	2	15	37	0	2	1	32	0	98	0	1	9	.403	.281	9

BATTER	TEAM	B	AVG	G	AB	R	H	TB	2B	3B	HR	RBI	SH	SF	HP	BB	IBB	SO	SB	CS	GI DP	SLG	OBP	E
Paredes, J	DET	R	.333	16	18	4	6	6	0	0	0	0	0	0	0	0	0	1	1	1	0	.333	.333	1
Parent, M	TEX	R	.000	3	1	0	0	0	0	0	0	0	0	0	0	0	0	1	0	0	0	.000	.000	0
Parker, D	CAL-TOR	L	.239	132	502	47	120	183	26	2	11	59	0	3	0	33	3	98	1	1	7	.365	.288	0
Parrish, L	CAL	R	.216	119	402	38	87	156	12	1	18	51	0	5	5	35	3	117	3	0	9	.388	.285	2
Pasqua, D	CHI	L	.259	134	417	71	108	194	23	5	18	66	1	3	3	62	4	86	0	2	9	.465	.358	6
Pecota, B	KC	R	.286	125	398	53	114	159	23	4	6	45	7	2	2	41	0	45	16	7	12	.399	.356	4
Pedre, J	KC	R	.263	10	19	0	5	8	1	0	0	3	0	0	0	3	0	5	0	0	0	.421	.364	1
Pena, T	BOS	R	.231	141	464	45	107	149	23	1	5	48	4	3	4	37	1	53	8	3	23	.321	.291	5
Perezchica, T	CLE	R	.364	17	22	4	8	10	2	0	0	3	0	0	0	3	0	5	0	0	0	.455	.440	0
Petralli, G	TEX	L	.271	87	199	21	54	70	8	1	2	20	7	1	0	21	1	25	2	1	4	.352	.339	11
Pettis, G	TEX	S	.216	137	282	37	61	78	5	5	0	19	6	6	3	54	0	91	29	13	4	.277	.341	6
Phillips, T	DET	S	.284	146	564	87	160	247	28	4	17	72	3	1	6	79	1	95	10	5	8	.438	.371	8
Plantier, P	BOS	L	.331	53	148	27	49	91	7	1	11	35	0	2	3	23	5	38	1	0	2	.615	.420	2
Polonia, L	CAL	L	.296	150	604	92	179	229	28	8	2	50	3	1	1	52	4	74	48	23	11	.379	.352	5
Powell, A	SEA	R	.216	57	111	16	24	41	6	1	3	12	0	2	1	11	0	24	2	1	1	.369	.288	2
Puckett, K	MIN	R	.319	152	611	92	195	281	29	6	15	89	0	8	4	31	4	78	11	5	27	.460	.352	6
Puhl, T	MIN	L	.222	15	18	4	4	4	0	0	0	4	0	0	0	3	1	2	0	0	0	.222	.333	0
Pulliam, H	KC	R	.273	18	33	4	9	19	1	0	3	4	0	0	0	1	0	9	1	0	0	.576	.333	2
Quintana, C	BOS	L	.295	149	478	69	141	197	21	1	11	71	3	6	2	61	2	66	1	0	17	.412	.375	9
Quirk, J	OAK	L	.261	76	203	16	53	60	7	0	0	17	3	3	2	16	1	28	0	3	7	.296	.321	6
Raines, T	CHI	S	.268	155	609	102	163	210	20	6	5	50	9	3	5	83	9	68	51	15	7	.345	.359	3
Ramos, J	NY	R	.308	10	26	4	8	9	1	0	0	3	0	0	0	3	0	3	0	0	1	.346	.310	0
Randolph, W	MIL	R	.327	124	431	60	141	161	14	3	0	54	3	3	1	75	3	38	4	2	14	.374	.424	20
Reed, J	BOS	R	.283	153	618	87	175	236	42	4	5	60	11	3	4	60	2	53	6	5	15	.382	.349	14
Reimer, K	TEX	L	.269	136	394	46	106	188	22	2	20	69	0	7	6	33	6	93	0	3	11	.477	.332	6
Reynolds, H	SEA	S	.254	161	631	95	160	215	34	6	3	57	14	6	7	72	3	63	28	8	11	.341	.332	18
Riles, E	OAK	L	.214	108	281	30	60	91	11	4	4	32	1	4	1	31	2	42	3	2	11	.324	.290	11
Ripken, B	BAL	R	.216	104	287	24	62	75	11	0	0	14	11	4	0	15	0	31	0	1	14	.261	.253	7
Ripken, C	BAL	R	.323	162	650	99	210	368	46	5	34	114	0	9	5	53	15	46	6	1	19	.566	.374	11
Rivera, L	BOS	R	.258	129	414	64	107	159	22	3	8	40	12	4	3	35	0	86	4	4	10	.384	.318	24
Rodriguez, C	NY	S	.189	15	37	1	7	7	0	0	0	2	1	0	0	2	0	2	0	0	3	.189	.211	2
Rodriguez, I	TEX	R	.264	88	280	24	74	99	16	0	3	27	2	2	5	5	0	42	0	1	1	.354	.276	10
Romine, K	BOS	R	.164	44	55	7	9	14	2	0	1	7	0	0	0	3	0	10	1	1	1	.255	.207	1

Player	Team	B	AVG	G	AB	R	H	2B	3B	HR	RBI	SO	SB	SLG	OBP	GDP
Rose, B.	CAL	R	.277	22	65	5	18	5	1	0	8	13	0	.431	.304	0
Rowland, R.	DET	R	.250	4	4	0	1	0	0	0	0	2	0	.250	.333	0
Russell, J.	TEX	L	.111	22	27	3	3	0	0	0	1	7	1	.111	.138	0
Salas, M.	DET	R	.088	33	57	2	5	1	1	0	7	10	0	.158	.117	0
Sax, S.	NY	R	.304	158	652	85	198	38	2	10	56	38	5	.414	.345	10
Schaefer, J.	SEA	R	.250	84	164	19	41	7	3	0	11	25	6	.323	.272	6
Schofield, D.	CAL	R	.225	134	427	44	96	9	3	1	31	69	7	.260	.310	15
Scruggs, T.	TEX	S	.000	5	6	1	0	0	0	0	0	1	0	.000	.000	0
Segui, D.	BAL	S	.278	86	212	15	59	11	0	2	22	19	3	.340	.316	3
Seitzer, K.	KC	R	.265	85	234	28	62	12	3	1	25	21	1	.350	.350	11
Sheffield, G.	MIL	R	.194	50	175	25	34	8	1	3	22	15	5	.320	.277	8
Shelby, J.	DET	S	.154	53	143	19	22	8	0	1	8	23	1	.287	.204	2
Sheridan, P.	NY	L	.204	62	113	13	23	8	1	3	7	30	1	.336	.286	0
Shumpert, T.	KC	S	.217	144	369	45	80	16	4	1	34	75	10	.322	.283	16
Sierra, R.	TEX	S	.307	161	661	110	203	44	5	29	116	91	9	.502	.357	7
Sinatro, M.	SEA	R	.250	5	8	0	2	0	0	0	1	1	0	.250	.333	0
Skinner, J.	CLE	R	.243	99	284	23	69	14	0	3	24	67	4	.303	.279	5
Snyder, C.	CHI-TOR	R	.175	71	166	14	29	4	1	3	17	60	4	.265	.216	3
Sojo, L.	CAL	R	.258	113	364	44	94	13	1	3	20	26	19	.327	.295	11
Sorrento, P.	MIN	L	.255	26	47	6	12	2	0	4	13	11	0	.553	.314	0
Sosa, S.	CHI	R	.203	116	316	39	64	10	3	10	33	98	5	.335	.240	6
Spehr, T.	KC	R	.189	37	74	7	14	5	1	2	14	18	3	.378	.282	3
Spiers, B.	MIL	L	.283	133	414	71	117	13	6	2	54	55	10	.401	.337	17
Sprague, E.	TOR	R	.275	61	160	17	44	7	0	4	20	43	5	.394	.361	14
Stanley, M.	TEX	R	.249	95	181	25	45	13	1	2	25	44	5	.381	.372	6
Steinbach, T.	OAK	R	.274	129	456	50	125	31	7	6	57	70	1	.386	.312	15
Stevens, L.	CAL	L	.293	18	58	8	17	7	1	6	9	12	1	.414	.354	1
Stillwell, K.	KC	S	.265	122	385	44	102	17	2	2	51	56	5	.361	.322	18
Stubbs, F.	MIL	L	.213	103	362	48	77	16	4	8	38	71	0	.359	.282	9
Surhoff, B.	MIL	L	.289	143	505	57	146	19	4	5	68	33	13	.372	.319	4
Sveum, D.	MIL	S	.241	90	266	33	64	19	1	2	43	78	5	.365	.320	10
Tabler, P.	TOR	R	.216	82	185	20	40	5	0	1	21	21	2	.270	.318	3
Tackett, J.	BAL	R	.125	6	8	0	1	0	0	0	0	2	1	.125	.300	0
Tanana, F.	DET	L	.000	33	1	0	0	0	0	0	0	0	0	.000	.000	1
Tartabull, D.	KC	R	.316	132	484	78	153	35	3	31	100	121	6	.593	.397	7

BATTER	TEAM	B	AVG	G	AB	R	H	TB	2B	3B	HR	RBI	SH	SF	HP	BB	IBB	SO	SB	CS	GI DP	SLG	OBP	E
Taubensee, E.	CLE	L	.242	26	66	5	16	20	2	1	0	8	0	2	0	5	1	16	0	3	1	.303	.288	2
Tettleton, M.	DET	S	.263	154	501	85	132	246	17	2	31	89	0	4	2	101	9	131	0	3	12	.491	.387	6
Thomas, F.	CHI	R	.318	158	559	104	178	309	31	2	32	109	0	2	1	138	13	112	1	1	20	.553	.453	8
Thome, J.	CLE	L	.255	27	98	7	25	36	4	2	1	9	0	1	0	5	0	16	1	0	0	.367	.298	4
Thurman, G.	KC	R	.277	80	184	24	51	66	9	0	2	13	3	1	1	11	0	42	15	5	4	.359	.320	3
Tingley, R.	CAL	R	.200	45	115	11	23	33	7	1	1	13	4	1	1	8	0	34	1	1	4	.287	.258	9
Trammell, A.	DET	R	.248	101	375	57	93	140	20	0	9	55	5	3	0	37	0	39	11	2	7	.373	.320	0
Turner, S.	BAL	L	.000	4	1	0	0	0	0	0	0	0	0	0	0	0	0	0	0	0	0	.000	.000	0
Valle, D.	SEA	R	.194	132	324	38	63	97	8	1	8	32	6	3	9	34	0	49	0	2	19	.299	.286	6
Vaughn, G.	MIL	R	.244	145	542	81	132	247	24	5	27	98	0	7	6	62	2	125	2	2	5	.456	.319	2
Vaughn, M.	BOS	L	.260	74	219	21	57	81	12	1	4	32	2	2	2	26	2	43	2	1	7	.370	.339	6
Velarde, R.	NY	R	.245	80	184	19	45	61	11	1	1	15	5	3	2	18	0	43	3	1	6	.332	.322	15
Venable, M.	CAL	L	.246	82	187	24	46	67	8	2	3	21	4	2	1	11	2	30	3	4	5	.358	.292	3
Ventura, R.	CHI	L	.284	157	606	92	172	268	25	1	23	100	8	7	4	80	3	67	2	2	22	.442	.367	18
Vizquel, O.	SEA	S	.230	142	426	42	98	125	16	4	1	41	8	0	0	45	0	37	12	4	8	.293	.302	13
Wakamatsu, D.	CHI	R	.226	18	31	2	7	7	0	0	0	2	0	0	1	1	0	6	0	0	0	.226	.250	0
Walling, D.	TEX	L	.091	24	44	1	4	5	1	0	0	0	0	2	0	3	0	8	0	0	3	.114	.184	1
Ward, T.	CLE-TOR	S	.239	48	113	12	27	34	7	0	0	7	4	0	0	11	0	18	0	0	2	.301	.306	0
Webster, L.	MIN	S	.294	18	34	7	10	20	1	0	3	8	1	0	0	6	0	10	0	0	2	.588	.390	1
Webster, M.	CLE	S	.125	13	32	2	4	4	0	0	0	0	0	0	0	3	0	9	2	0	0	.125	.200	0
Wedge, E.	BOS	R	1.000	1	1	0	1	1	0	0	0	0	0	0	0	0	0	0	0	0	0	1.000	1.000	0
Weiss, W.	OAK	S	.226	40	133	15	30	38	6	1	0	13	2	2	0	12	0	14	6	6	3	.286	.286	5
Whitaker, L.	DET	L	.279	138	470	94	131	230	26	2	23	78	1	8	2	90	6	45	4	2	3	.489	.391	4
White, D.	TOR	S	.282	156	642	110	181	292	40	10	17	60	5	6	7	55	0	135	33	10	7	.455	.342	1
Whiten, M.	TOR-CLE	S	.243	116	407	46	99	158	18	7	9	45	0	6	3	30	1	85	4	0	13	.388	.297	7
Whitt, E.	BAL	L	.242	35	62	2	15	17	2	0	0	3	0	3	0	8	1	12	0	0	3	.274	.329	0
Williams, B.	NY	S	.238	85	320	43	76	112	19	1	3	34	2	1	1	48	0	57	10	5	4	.350	.336	5
Williams, K.	TOR	R	.207	13	29	5	6	11	2	0	1	3	0	0	1	4	0	5	2	1	2	.379	.314	0
Wilson, M.	TOR	S	.241	86	241	26	58	84	12	4	2	28	2	2	0	35	1	35	11	3	4	.349	.277	2
Wilson, W.	OAK	S	.238	113	294	38	70	92	14	4	0	28	1	1	0	18	1	43	20	5	11	.313	.290	3
Winfield, D.	CAL	R	.262	150	568	75	149	268	27	4	28	86	0	2	1	56	4	109	0	2	21	.472	.326	2
Witmeyer, R.	OAK	L	.053	11	19	0	1	1	0	0	0	0	0	0	0	0	0	5	0	0	1	.053	.053	0

BATTER	TEAM	B	AVG	G	AB	R	H	TB	2B	3B	HR	RBI	SH	SF	HP	BB	IBB	SO	SB	CS	GIDP	SLG	OBP	
Worthington, C.......BAL		R	.225	31	102	11	23	38	3	0	4	12	1	0	1	12	0	14	0	0	3	.373	.313	2
Yount, R.......MIL		R	.260	130	503	66	131	189	20	4	10	77	1	9	4	54	8	79	6	4	13	.376	.332	2
Zosky, E.......TOR		R	.148	18	27	2	4	7	1	1	0	2	1	0	0	0	0	8	0	0	1	.259	.148	0
Zupcic, R.......BOS		R	.160	18	25	3	4	7	0	0	1	3	1	0	1	1	0	6	0	0	0	.280	.192	2

TOP 15 DESIGNATED HITTERS
(Minimum: 100 At-Bats)

BATTER	TEAM	B	AVG	G	AB	R	H	TB	2B	3B	HR	RBI	SH	SF	HP	BB	IBB	SO	SB	CS	GIDP	SLG	OBP
Thomas, F.......CHI		R	.325	101	363	71	118	207	21	1	22	68	0	1	1	94	8	79	1	1	13	.570	.464
Molitor, P.......MIL		R	.321	112	476	88	153	226	23	10	10	45	0	0	4	50	11	50	10	3	6	.475	.391
Baines, H.......OAK		L	.299	125	447	69	133	211	22	1	18	81	0	5	1	68	22	60	0	1	10	.472	.388
Belle, A.......CLE		R	.287	32	129	18	37	66	12	1	5	24	0	2	0	4	0	22	2	1	12	.512	.304
Martinez, C.......CLE		R	.282	41	156	11	44	61	8	0	3	16	0	1	1	6	1	19	3	2	8	.391	.311
Davis, C.......MIN		S	.277	150	531	84	147	269	33	1	29	93	0	4	1	94	13	116	5	1	9	.507	.384
Downing, B.......TEX		R	.272	109	393	75	107	178	16	2	17	45	1	2	8	58	7	69	5	6	4	.453	.375
Brett, G.......KC		L	.251	118	463	73	121	195	40	2	10	60	1	8	0	56	10	66	1	0	20	.421	.336
Reimer, K.......TEX		L	.258	56	178	23	46	83	10	1	9	27	0	5	3	13	3	45	2	0	4	.466	.312
Mulliniks, R.......TEX		L	.258	81	217	25	56	76	12	0	2	20	0	2	0	43	2	40	0	0	8	.350	.379
Winfield, D.......CAL		R	.256	34	125	14	32	52	5	0	5	16	1	1	0	16	1	31	3	1	6	.416	.338
Fielder, C.......DET		R	.254	42	169	21	43	88	9	0	12	33	0	1	0	19	3	40	0	0	6	.521	.326
Clark, J.......BOS		R	.252	135	476	75	120	224	18	1	28	87	0	5	3	96	3	130	0	2	17	.471	.378
Tabler, P.......TOR		R	.250	57	116	13	29	34	5	0	0	12	2	4	1	18	5	14	0	0	0	.293	.345
Incaviglia, P.......DET		R	.248	41	145	23	36	61	5	1	6	14	1	0	1	18	0	35	1	0	3	.421	.335

CLUB BATTING

CLUB	AVG	G	AB	R	OR	H	TB	2B	3B	HR	GS	RBI	SH	SF	HP	BB	IBB	SO	SB	CS	GI DP	LOB	SHO	SLG	OBP
MINNESOTA	.280	162	5556	776	652	1557	2331	270	42	140	4	733	44	49	40	526	38	747	107	68	157	1137	8	.420	.344
MILWAUKEE	.271	162	5611	799	744	1523	2224	247	53	116	4	750	52	66	23	556	48	802	106	68	137	1122	11	.396	.336
TEXAS	.270	162	5703	829	814	1539	2420	288	31	177	2	774	59	41	42	596	51	1039	102	50	128	1187	9	.424	.341
BOSTON	.269	162	5530	731	712	1486	2219	305	25	126	5	691	50	51	32	593	49	820	59	39	143	1216	12	.401	.340
KANSAS CITY	.264	162	5584	727	722	1475	2198	290	41	117	7	689	53	47	35	523	47	969	119	68	126	1117	9	.394	.328
CHICAGO	.262	162	5594	758	681	1464	2185	226	39	139	6	722	76	41	37	610	45	896	134	74	132	1183	12	.391	.336
TORONTO	.257	162	5489	684	622	1412	2196	295	45	133	0	649	56	65	58	499	49	1043	148	53	108	1134	9	.400	.322
NEW YORK	.256	162	5541	674	777	1418	2146	249	19	147	3	630	37	50	39	473	38	861	109	36	125	1101	10	.387	.316
CALIFORNIA	.255	162	5470	653	649	1396	2044	245	29	115	3	607	63	38	38	448	28	928	94	56	114	1073	15	.374	.314
SEATTLE	.255	162	5494	702	674	1400	2104	268	29	126	4	665	55	62	37	588	57	811	97	44	139	1150	10	.383	.328
CLEVELAND	.254	162	5470	576	759	1390	1915	236	26	79	1	546	62	46	43	449	24	888	84	58	146	1106	18	.350	.313
BALTIMORE	.254	162	5604	686	796	1421	2245	256	26	170	5	660	47	45	33	528	33	974	50	33	147	1162	6	.401	.319
OAKLAND	.248	162	5410	760	776	1342	2103	246	19	159	7	716	41	49	50	642	56	981	151	64	131	1105	14	.389	.331
DETROIT	.247	162	5547	817	794	1372	2310	259	26	209	5	778	38	44	31	699	40	1185	109	47	90	1194	7	.416	.333
TOTALS	.260	1134	77603	10172	10172	20195	30640	3680	453	1953	54	9610	733	687	538	7730	603	12944	1469	758	1823	15987	150	.395	.329

Pitching

Individual Pitching Leaders

Games Won	20	Erickson	Min.
		Gullickson	Det.
Games Lost	19	McCaskill	Cal.
Won-Lost Percentage	.750	Hesketh	Bos. (12-4)
Earned Run Average	2.62	Clemens	Bos.
Games	81	D. Ward	Tor.
Games Started	35	Clemens	Bos.
		Gullickson	Det.
		J. McDowell	Chi.
		Morris	Min.
		Stewart	Oak.
		Welch	Oak.
Complete Games	15	J. McDowell	Chi.
Games Finished	63	B. Harvey	Cal.
Shutouts	4	Clemens	Bos.
Saves	46	B. Harvey	Cal.
Innings	271.1	Clemens	Bos.
Hits	257	Terrell	Det.
Batsmen Faced	1077	Clemens	Bos.
Runs	135	Stewart	Oak.
Earned Runs	130	Stewart	Oak.
Home Runs	31	DeLucia	Sea.
Sacrifice Hits	13	Swindell	Cle.
Sacrifice Flies	16	Hough	Chi.
Hit Batsmen	13	Boddicker	K.C.
		K. Brown	Tex.
Bases on Balls	152	R. Johnson	Sea.
Intentional Bases on Balls	13	Gullickson	Det.
Strikeouts	241	Clemens	Bos.
Wild Pitches	15	Morris	Min.
Balks	4	J. Abbott	Cal.
		D. Boucher	Tor.-Cle.
Games Won, Consecutive	12	Erickson	Min. (April 21-June 24)
Games Lost, Consecutive	8	Nichols	Cle. (May 14-July 12)

TOP 15 QUALIFIERS FOR EARNED RUN AVERAGE CHAMPIONSHIP

PITCHER	TEAM	T	W	L	ERA	G	GS	CG	SHO	GF	SV	IP	H	TBF	R	ER	HR	SH	SF	HB	BB	IBB	SO	WP	BK	OPP AVG
Clemens, R.	BOS	R	18	10	2.62	35	35	13	4	0	0	271.1	219	1077	93	79	15	6	8	5	65	12	241	6	0	.221
Candiotti, T	CLE-TOR	R	13	13	2.65	34	34	6	0	0	0	237.3	202	981	82	70	12	4	11	6	73	1	167	11	0	.228
Wegman, B.	MIL	R	15	7	2.84	28	28	7	2	0	0	193.1	176	785	76	61	16	6	4	7	40	0	89	6	0	.242
Abbott, J	CAL	L	18	11	2.89	34	34	5	1	0	0	243.0	222	1002	85	78	14	6	7	5	73	6	158	6	4	.244
Ryan, N.	TEX	R	12	6	2.91	27	27	2	2	0	0	173.0	102	683	58	56	12	3	9	5	72	0	203	8	0	.172
Moore, M.	OAK	R	17	8	2.96	33	33	3	1	0	0	210.0	176	887	75	69	11	5	9	4	105	1	153	14	0	.229
Tapani, K	MIN	R	16	9	2.99	34	34	4	1	0	0	244.0	225	974	84	81	23	9	6	5	40	0	135	3	3	.245
Langston, M	CAL	L	19	8	3.00	34	34	7	0	0	0	246.1	190	992	89	82	30	4	2	6	96	3	183	6	3	.215
Key, J.	TOR	L	16	12	3.05	33	33	2	2	0	0	209.1	207	877	84	71	12	10	5	3	44	3	125	1	0	.254
Saberhagen, B.	KC	R	13	8	3.07	28	28	7	2	0	0	196.1	165	789	76	67	12	8	9	5	45	5	136	8	1	.228
Guzman, J.	TEX	R	13	7	3.08	25	25	1	0	0	0	169.2	152	730	67	58	10	5	3	4	84	1	125	8	0	.239
Erickson, S.	MIN	R	20	8	3.18	32	32	5	3	0	0	204.0	189	851	80	72	13	5	7	6	71	3	108	4	0	.248
Bosio, C.	MIL	R	14	10	3.25	32	32	5	1	0	0	204.2	187	840	80	74	15	2	6	8	58	0	117	5	0	.244
McDowell, J	CHI	R	17	10	3.41	35	35	15	3	0	0	253.2	212	1028	97	96	19	8	4	4	82	2	191	10	1	.228
Appier, K.	KC	R	13	10	3.42	34	31	6	3	0	1	207.2	205	881	97	79	13	8	2	6	61	3	158	7	1	.255

INDIVIDUAL PITCHING

PITCHER	TEAM	T	W	L	ERA	G	GS	CG	SHO	GF	SV	IP	H	TBF	R	ER	HR	SH	SF	HB	BB	IBB	SO	WP	BK	OPP AVG
Abbott, J	CAL	L	18	11	2.89	34	34	5	1	0	0	243.0	222	1002	85	78	14	7	5	5	73	6	158	1	4	.244
Abbott, K	CAL	L	1	2	4.58	5	3	0	0	0	0	19.2	22	90	11	10	2	3	0	1	13	0	12	1	1	.301
Abbott, P	MIN	R	3	1	4.75	15	3	0	0	1	0	47.1	38	210	27	25	5	7	3	2	36	1	43	5	0	.232
Acker, J	TOR	R	3	5	5.20	54	4	0	0	11	1	88.1	77	374	53	51	16	8	5	2	36	5	44	7	0	.238
Aguilera, R.	MIN	R	4	5	2.35	63	0	0	0	60	42	69.0	44	275	20	18	3	1	3	1	30	6	61	3	0	.183
Aldred, S	DET	L	2	4	5.18	11	11	1	0	0	0	57.1	58	253	37	33	9	3	2	0	30	2	35	3	1	.266

Player	T	W	L	ERA	G	GS	CG	ShO	SV	IP	H	R	ER	HR	HB	BB	IBB	SO	WP	BK	AVG
Alexander, G. ......TEX	R	5	3	5.24	30	9	0	0	4	89.1	93	56	52	11	6	48	3	50	7	3	.272
Allison, D. ......OAK	L	1	1	7.36	10	0	0	0	0	11.0	16	9	9	0	0	5	0	9	1	0	.381
Alvarez, W. ......CHI	L	3	2	3.51	10	9	2	0	1	56.1	47	26	22	9	1	29	0	32	0	2	.230
Anderson, A. ......MIN	L	13	10	4.96	29	22	6	0	1	134.1	148	82	74	24	6	42	5	51	4	3	.281
Appier, K. ......KC	R	8	4	3.42	34	31	6	0	0	207.2	205	97	79	13	8	61	5	158	3	7	.255
Aquino, L. ......KC	R	0	0	3.44	38	18	0	0	9	157.0	152	87	60	10	6	47	0	80	5	1	.253
Arnsberg, B. ......TEX	R	9	0	8.38	9	0	0	0	0	9.2	10	9	9	5	0	5	0	8	0	1	.256
August, D. ......MIL	R	0	8	5.47	28	23	0	0	3	138.1	166	87	84	18	9	47	3	62	2	5	.301
Austin, J. ......MIL	R	9	0	8.31	5	0	0	0	0	8.2	8	8	6	1	3	11	1	5	1	1	.276
Bailes, S. ......CAL	L	1	2	4.18	42	0	0	0	14	51.2	41	26	24	5	1	22	4	41	5	2	.218
Ballard, J. ......BAL	L	6	12	5.60	26	22	0	0	1	123.2	153	91	77	16	2	28	2	37	2	3	.302
Bankhead, S. ......SEA	R	3	1	4.90	17	9	0	0	0	60.2	73	35	33	8	3	21	2	28	0	0	.297
Banks, W. ......MIN	R	1	0	5.71	5	3	0	0	2	17.1	21	15	11	1	2	12	0	16	1	3	.288
Bannister, F. ......CAL	L	0	0	3.96	16	9	0	0	2	25.0	25	12	11	5	0	10	0	16	0	0	.266
Barfield, J. ......TEX	L	4	1	4.54	28	9	0	0	4	83.1	96	51	42	11	0	22	0	27	1	0	.289
Bautista, C. ......BAL	R	0	1	16.88	5	0	0	0	0	5.1	13	10	10	1	3	5	0	3	0	2	.464
Beasley, C. ......CAL	R	0	0	3.38	22	0	0	0	8	26.2	26	13	10	2	0	10	1	14	1	2	.257
Bedrosian, S. ......MIN	R	5	3	4.42	56	0	0	0	22	77.1	70	42	38	11	2	38	3	44	4	1	.243
Bell, E. ......CLE	R	1	0	0.50	10	0	0	0	3	18.0	5	5	1	1	0	11	0	2	0	0	.091
Bitker, J. ......TEX	R	0	0	6.75	9	0	0	0	2	14.2	17	11	11	4	2	4	0	16	0	0	.274
Blair, W. ......CLE	R	2	3	6.75	11	5	0	0	1	36.0	58	27	27	7	1	27	2	13	2	1	.377
Boddicker, M. ......KC	R	12	3	4.08	30	29	1	0	0	180.2	188	89	82	13	10	82	13	79	5	3	.272
Bohanon, B. ......TEX	L	4	3	4.84	11	11	1	0	0	61.1	66	35	33	4	2	33	2	34	4	3	.274
Bolton, T. ......BOS	L	9	5	5.24	25	19	2	0	0	110.0	136	72	64	16	6	64	4	51	6	3	.308
Bosio, C. ......MIL	R	14	10	3.25	32	32	5	0	0	204.2	187	80	74	15	1	74	6	117	2	5	.244
Boucher, D. ......TOR-CLE	L	1	2	6.05	12	12	0	0	0	58.0	74	41	39	12	3	39	1	29	3	0	.308
Boyd, D. ......TEX	R	2	7	6.68	12	12	0	0	0	62.0	81	47	46	12	0	46	0	33	0	3	.314
Briscoe, J. ......OAK	R	0	0	7.07	11	0	0	0	0	14.0	12	12	11	3	1	13	1	10	0	0	.235
Brown, K. ......TEX	R	9	12	4.40	33	33	9	0	0	210.2	233	116	103	17	6	103	13	96	5	12	.284
Brown, K. ......MIL	L	2	2	5.51	15	10	0	0	0	63.2	66	39	39	6	5	39	0	30	2	6	.270
Burba, D. ......SEA	R	2	2	3.68	22	0	0	0	11	36.2	34	15	15	6	0	15	0	16	2	1	.245
Burns, T. ......OAK	R	1	0	3.38	9	0	0	0	5	13.1	10	5	5	2	2	5	2	3	1	1	.217
Cadaret, G. ......NY	L	8	6	3.62	68	5	0	0	17	121.2	110	52	49	8	6	49	2	105	6	3	.246

PITCHER	TEAM	T	W	L	ERA	G	GS	CG	SHO	GF	SV	IP	H	TBF	R	ER	HR	SH	SF	HB	BB	IBB	SO	WP	BK	OPP AVG
Campbell, K ......OAK	R	1	0	2.74	14	0	0	0	2	0	23.0	13	94	7	7	4	1	0	1	14	0	16	0	0	.167
Candiotti, T ......CLE-TOR	R	13	13	2.65	34	34	6	0	0	0	238.0	202	981	82	70	12	4	11	6	73	1	167	11	0	.228
Carter, J ......CHI	R	1	0	5.25	5	2	0	0	1	0	12.0	8	49	8	7	1	0	0	0	5	0	2	0	0	.182
Cary, C ......NY	L	0	6	5.91	10	9	0	0	0	0	53.1	61	247	35	35	6	4	1	1	32	2	34	2	1	.285
Casian, L ......MIN	L	1	0	7.36	15	0	0	0	4	0	18.1	28	87	16	15	4	0	0	1	7	2	6	2	0	.354
Cerutti, J ......DET	L	3	6	4.57	38	8	1	0	10	2	88.2	94	389	49	45	9	7	3	2	37	9	29	4	1	.276
Chapin, D ......NY	R	0	0	5.06	8	0	0	0	2	0	5.1	3	25	3	3	0	0	0	0	6	0	5	0	0	.158
Chiamparino, S...TEX	R	1	0	4.03	5	5	0	0	0	0	22.1	26	101	11	10	1	0	1	0	12	0	8	2	0	.295
Chitren, S ......OAK	R	1	4	4.33	56	0	0	0	20	4	60.1	59	271	31	29	8	4	2	2	32	4	47	2	0	.258
Clemens, R ......BOS	R	18	10	2.62	35	35	13	4	0	0	271.1	219	1077	93	79	15	6	8	5	65	12	241	6	1	.221
Comstock, K ......SEA	L	0	0	54.00	1	0	0	0	0	0	0.1	3	4	2	2	0	0	0	0	1	0	0	0	0	.667
Corbin, A ......KC	R	0	0	3.86	2	0	0	0	1	0	2.1	3	12	1	1	0	0	0	0	2	0	1	0	1	.300
Crawford, S ......KC	R	3	0	5.98	33	0	0	0	17	1	46.2	60	216	31	31	9	3	1	3	18	5	38	5	3	.311
Crim, C ......MIL	R	8	5	4.63	66	0	0	0	29	3	91.1	115	408	52	47	9	3	2	1	25	5	39	3	3	.305
Dalton, M ......DET	L	0	0	3.38	4	0	0	0	1	0	8.0	12	38	3	3	2	0	1	2	2	0	4	0	0	.333
Darling, R ......OAK	R	3	7	4.08	12	12	0	0	0	0	75.0	64	319	34	34	7	5	4	2	38	1	60	3	1	.237
Darwin, D ......BOS	R	3	6	5.16	12	12	0	0	0	0	68.0	71	292	39	39	15	3	0	5	15	1	42	2	0	.263
Davis, M ......KC	L	6	3	4.45	29	5	0	0	8	1	62.2	55	276	36	31	6	2	2	1	39	0	47	1	0	.240
Davis, S ......KC	R	3	9	4.96	51	9	0	0	22	2	114.1	140	515	69	63	11	6	4	4	46	9	53	1	0	.306
Dayley, K ......TOR	L	0	0	6.23	8	0	0	0	3	0	4.1	7	26	3	3	0	1	0	1	5	1	3	2	0	.368
de la Rosa, F ......BAL	R	0	0	4.50	8	0	0	0	1	0	6.0	6	20	3	3	0	0	0	0	2	0	1	0	0	.353
Dempsey, R ......MIL	R	0	0	4.50	2	0	0	0	2	0	2.0	3	10	1	1	0	0	0	0	1	0	0	0	0	.333
DeLucia, R ......SEA	R	12	13	5.09	32	31	0	0	0	0	182.0	176	779	107	103	31	5	14	4	78	4	98	10	0	.260
Dopson, J ......BOS	R	0	0	18.00	1	0	0	0	0	0	1.0	2	6	2	2	0	0	0	0	0	0	0	0	0	.500
Drahman, B ......CHI	R	3	2	3.23	28	0	0	0	8	0	30.2	21	125	12	11	4	2	1	1	13	0	18	0	0	.193
Drees, T ......CHI	L	0	0	12.27	4	0	0	0	1	0	7.1	10	37	10	10	4	1	0	0	6	0	2	2	0	.345
Dressendorfer, K OAK	R	3	3	5.45	7	7	0	0	0	0	34.2	33	159	28	21	5	2	1	1	21	0	17	3	0	.244
Eckersley, D ......OAK	R	5	4	2.96	67	0	0	0	59	43	76.0	60	299	26	25	11	2	0	3	9	3	87	1	0	.208
Edens, T ......MIN	R	2	2	4.09	8	0	0	0	6	0	33.0	34	143	15	15	2	0	0	1	10	1	19	1	0	.256
Edwards, W ......CHI	L	0	2	3.86	13	0	0	0	3	0	23.1	22	106	14	10	2	2	0	0	17	3	12	2	0	.259
Egloff, B ......CLE	R	0	0	4.76	6	0	0	0	2	0	5.2	8	28	3	3	1	0	0	0	4	1	8	2	0	.333

Pitcher	Club	T	W	L	ERA	G	IP	H	R	ER	BB	SO	AVG
Eichhorn, M.	CAL	R	3	3	1.98	70	81.2	63	21	18	13	49	.219
Eiland, D.	NY	R	2	5	5.33	18	72.2	87	51	43	23	18	.302
Eldred, C.	MIL	R	2	0	4.50	3	16.0	20	9	8	6	10	.299
Erickson, S.	MIN	R	20	8	3.18	32	204.0	189	80	72	71	108	.248
Espinoza, A.	NY	R	0	0	0.00	1	0.2	0	0	0	0	0	.000
Fajardo, H.	TEX	R	0	0	5.68	3	19.0	25	13	12	4	15	.329
Farr, S.	NY	R	5	5	2.19	60	70.0	57	19	17	20	60	.219
Fernandez, A.	CHI	R	9	13	4.51	34	191.2	186	109	96	88	145	.259
Fetters, M.	CAL	R	2	5	4.84	19	44.2	53	29	24	28	24	.305
Finley, C.	CAL	L	18	9	3.80	34	227.1	205	102	96	101	171	.244
Flanagan, M.	BAL	L	2	7	2.38	64	98.1	84	27	26	25	55	.236
Fleming, D.	SEA	L	1	0	6.62	9	17.2	19	13	13	3	11	.284
Fossas, T.	BOS	L	3	2	3.47	64	57.0	49	27	22	28	29	.236
Fraser, W.	TOR	R	0	3	6.15	13	26.1	33	24	18	11	12	.303
Frohwirth, T.	BAL	R	7	3	1.87	51	96.1	64	24	20	29	77	.190
Gakeler, D.	DET	R	1	4	5.74	31	73.2	73	52	47	39	43	.256
Garcia, R.	CHI	R	4	4	5.40	16	78.1	79	37	31	31	40	.269
Gardiner, M.	BOS	R	9	10	4.85	22	130.0	140	79	70	47	91	.274
Gardner, W.	KC	R	0	0	4.59	3	5.2	5	4	3	0	3	.217
George, C.	MIL	L	0	1	3.00	2	6.0	6	2	2	1	3	.333
Gibson, P.	DET	L	5	7	4.59	68	96.0	112	51	49	48	52	.297
Gleaton, J.	DET	L	3	2	4.06	47	75.1	74	37	34	39	47	.269
Gordon, T.	KC	R	9	14	3.87	45	158.0	129	76	68	87	167	.221
Gossage, R.	TEX	R	4	2	3.57	44	40.1	33	16	16	16	28	.228
Gozzo, M.	CLE	R	0	0	19.29	2	4.2	9	10	4	7	4	.450
Grahe, J.	CAL	R	3	7	4.81	18	73.0	84	43	39	33	40	.288
Gray, J.	BOS	R	2	3	2.34	50	61.2	39	17	16	10	41	.181
Gubicza, M.	KC	R	9	12	5.68	26	133.0	168	42	84	42	89	.308
Guetterman, L.	NY	L	3	4	3.68	64	88.0	93	41	36	25	35	.268
Gullickson, B.	DET	R	20	9	3.90	35	226.1	256	109	98	44	91	.288
Guthrie, M.	MIN	L	7	5	4.32	41	98.0	116	52	47	41	72	.303
Guzman, J.	TEX	R	13	7	3.08	25	169.2	152	67	58	84	125	.239
Guzman, J.	TOR	R	10	3	2.99	23	138.2	98	53	46	66	123	.197

PITCHER	TEAM	T	W	L	ERA	G	GS	CG	SHO	GF	SV	IP	H	TBF	R	ER	HR	SH	SF	HB	BB	IBB	SO	WP	BK	OPP AVG
Guzman, J	OAK	L	1	1	9.00	5	0	0	0	0	0	5.0	11	24	5	5	0	0	2	1	2	0	3	0	0	.500
Haas, D	DET	R	0	1	6.75	11	0	0	0	1	0	10.2	8	50	8	8	1	2	0	0	12	3	6	1	0	.242
Habyan, J	NY	R	4	2	2.30	66	0	0	0	16	2	90.0	73	349	28	23	8	2	1	0	20	2	70	1	2	.225
Hanson, E	SEA	R	8	8	3.81	27	27	2	1	0	0	174.2	182	744	82	74	16	2	2	2	56	5	143	14	1	.269
Harris, G	BOS	R	11	12	3.85	53	21	1	0	15	2	173.0	157	731	79	74	13	4	8	5	69	5	127	6	2	.243
Harris, G	SEA	R	0	0	4.05	8	0	0	0	3	1	13.1	15	66	8	6	1	1	0	0	10	3	6	1	0	.273
Harris, R	OAK	R	0	0	12.00	2	0	0	0	1	0	3.0	5	15	4	4	0	1	0	0	0	1	2	2	0	.455
Harvey, B	CAL	R	2	4	1.60	67	0	0	0	63	46	78.2	51	309	20	14	6	3	1	2	17	3	101	2	1	.178
Hawkins, A	NY-OAK	R	4	6	5.52	19	17	0	0	2	0	89.2	91	399	56	55	10	0	3	5	42	2	45	1	0	.262
Henke, T	TOR	R	0	2	2.32	49	0	0	0	43	32	50.1	33	190	13	13	2	0	3	0	11	2	53	1	0	.184
Henneman, M	DET	R	10	2	2.88	60	0	0	0	50	21	84.1	81	358	29	27	2	5	2	0	34	8	61	0	0	.258
Henry, D	MIL	R	2	1	1.00	32	0	0	0	25	15	36.0	16	137	5	4	2	0	2	0	14	0	28	1	0	.133
Hentgen, P	TOR	R	0	0	2.45	9	3	0	0	1	0	7.1	5	30	2	2	1	0	0	0	3	0	6	1	0	.208
Hernandez, R	CHI	R	1	0	7.80	9	3	0	0	5	0	15.0	18	69	15	13	1	0	1	2	6	0	3	1	0	.290
Hesketh, J	BOS	L	12	4	3.29	39	17	0	0	5	0	153.1	142	631	59	56	19	7	3	0	53	3	104	8	1	.250
Hibbard, G	CHI	L	11	11	4.31	32	29	3	0	0	0	194.0	196	806	107	93	23	8	2	0	57	1	71	1	0	.266
Hickey, K	BAL	L	1	1	9.00	19	0	0	0	6	0	14.0	15	62	14	14	2	2	0	0	10	0	6	0	0	.278
Higuera, T	MIL	L	3	2	4.46	7	6	0	0	1	0	36.1	37	153	18	18	2	0	1	1	10	0	33	0	0	.262
Hillegas, S	CLE	R	3	6	4.34	51	3	0	0	31	7	83.0	90	359	42	40	16	6	3	0	46	7	66	5	0	.268
Holman, B	SEA	R	13	14	3.69	30	30	5	2	0	0	195.1	199	839	88	80	16	6	3	7	77	0	108	6	0	.268
Holmes, D	MIL	R	1	4	4.72	40	0	0	0	9	3	76.1	37	344	43	40	6	8	3	1	27	1	59	8	0	.295
Honeycutt, R	OAK	L	2	4	3.58	43	0	0	0	7	0	37.2	37	167	16	15	3	2	1	2	20	3	26	0	1	.261
Horsman, V	TOR	L	1	0	0.00	4	0	0	0	2	0	4.0	2	16	0	0	0	2	0	0	3	1	2	0	0	.167
Hough, C	CHI	R	9	10	4.02	31	29	2	0	1	0	199.1	167	858	98	89	21	8	1	11	94	0	107	5	1	.229
Howe, S	NY	L	3	1	1.68	37	0	0	0	10	3	48.1	39	189	12	9	1	2	1	3	7	2	34	2	0	.222
Hunter, J	MIL	R	0	5	7.26	8	6	0	0	0	0	31.0	45	152	26	25	3	1	1	4	17	0	14	3	0	.349
Ignasiak, M	MIL	R	2	0	5.68	6	1	0	0	0	0	12.2	7	50	13	8	2	3	0	0	8	0	10	1	0	.163
Irvine, D	BOS	R	0	0	6.00	9	0	0	0	5	0	18.0	25	91	13	12	2	1	0	0	9	0	8	3	0	.321
Jackson, M	SEA	R	7	7	3.25	72	0	0	0	35	14	88.2	64	363	35	32	5	4	6	6	34	11	74	3	3	.201
Jeffcoat, M	TEX	L	5	3	4.63	70	0	0	0	21	1	79.2	104	363	46	41	8	5	4	4	25	3	43	3	3	.321
Johnson, D	BAL	R	4	8	7.07	22	14	2	0	4	0	84.0	127	393	68	66	18	5	1	4	24	3	38	0	0	.349

Pitcher	T	W	L	ERA	G	GS	CG	GF	ShO	Sv	IP	H	R	ER	HR	SH	SF	HB	BB	SO	WP	BK	AVG
Johnson, J. ...NY	L	6	11	5.95	23	23	0	0	0	0	127.0	156	89	84	15	7	4	6	33	62	5	1	.305
Johnson, R. ...SEA	L	13	10	3.98	33	33	2	0	0	0	201.1	151	96	89	15	9	8	12	152	228	12	2	.213
Johnston, J. ...KC	R	1	0	0.40	13	0	0	6	0	1	22.1	9	1	1	0	0	0	3	9	21	0	0	.120
Jones, C. ...SEA	R	2	2	2.53	27	4	0	6	0	2	46.1	33	14	13	2	1	5	5	29	42	1	0	.209
Jones, D. ...CLE	R	4	8	5.54	36	0	0	29	0	7	63.1	87	42	39	6	0	5	2	17	48	0	0	.320
Jones, S. ...BAL	R	0	1	4.09	4	1	0	0	0	0	11.0	11	6	5	2	2	0	0	5	10	0	0	.256
Kaiser, J. ...DET	L	0	1	9.00	1	0	0	1	0	0	5.0	6	5	5	0	0	0	0	5	4	0	0	.256
Kamieniecki, S. ...NY	R	4	4	3.90	9	9	0	0	0	0	55.1	54	24	24	5	3	2	3	22	34	3	1	.286
Key, J. ...TOR	L	16	12	3.05	33	33	2	0	0	0	209.1	207	84	71	12	10	5	2	44	125	1	3	.256
Kiecker, D. ...BOS	R	2	3	7.36	18	5	0	3	0	0	40.1	56	34	33	6	5	2	4	23	21	3	1	.344
Kiely, J. ...DET	R	0	0	14.85	7	0	0	2	0	0	6.2	13	11	11	2	1	1	2	9	1	0	0	.448
Kilgus, P. ...BAL	L	0	2	5.08	38	0	0	14	0	0	62.0	60	38	35	7	4	7	2	24	32	2	0	.256
King, E. ...CLE	L	6	11	4.60	25	24	1	0	0	0	150.2	166	83	77	8	3	4	7	44	59	2	2	.279
Kiser, G. ...CLE	R	0	0	9.64	7	0	0	4	0	0	4.2	7	5	5	1	0	0	0	4	3	0	0	.368
Klink, J. ...OAK	L	10	3	4.35	62	0	0	10	0	2	62.0	66	30	30	8	5	3	1	21	34	0	0	.260
Knudson, M. ...MIL	R	0	1	7.97	12	7	0	2	0	0	35.0	54	33	31	8	3	0	4	15	23	4	0	.355
Kramer, T. ...CLE	R	0	0	7.36	9	0	0	1	0	0	4.2	10	9	9	3	0	0	0	6	9	1	0	.476
Krueger, B. ...SEA	L	11	8	3.60	35	25	1	2	0	0	175.0	194	82	70	15	6	9	6	60	91	4	0	.289
Lamp, D. ...BOS	R	6	3	4.70	51	0	0	8	0	0	92.0	100	54	48	8	3	3	2	31	57	7	0	.275
Langston, M. ...CAL	L	19	8	3.00	34	34	7	0	0	0	246.1	190	89	82	30	4	6	3	96	183	3	0	.215
Law, V. ...OAK	R	0	0	0.00	1	0	0	1	0	0	0.2	1	0	0	0	0	0	0	0	0	0	0	.333
Leach, T. ...MIN	R	1	2	3.61	50	0	0	22	0	0	67.1	82	28	27	3	2	4	5	14	32	0	1	.299
Leary, T. ...NY	R	4	10	6.49	28	18	1	4	0	0	120.2	150	89	87	20	7	3	2	57	83	4	0	.312
Lee, M. ...MIL	L	2	0	3.86	62	0	0	9	0	0	67.2	72	33	29	4	5	2	3	31	43	2	1	.283
Leiter, A. ...TOR	L	0	0	27.00	3	1	0	0	0	0	1.2	3	5	5	1	0	0	0	5	1	1	0	.429
Leiter, M. ...DET	R	9	7	4.21	38	15	1	7	0	1	134.2	125	66	63	16	6	2	6	50	103	9	2	.245
Lewis, S. ...CAL	R	3	5	6.27	16	11	0	0	0	0	60.1	81	43	42	9	3	0	2	21	37	0	0	.316
Lyons, S. ...BOS	R	0	0	0.00	1	0	0	1	0	0	1.0	2	0	0	0	0	0	0	0	0	0	0	.400
Machado, J. ...MIL	R	3	3	3.45	54	0	0	13	0	3	88.2	65	36	34	3	2	3	3	55	98	0	1	.211
MacDonald, B. ...TOR	L	3	3	2.85	45	0	0	18	0	0	53.2	51	19	17	5	2	2	2	25	24	0	0	.252
Magnante, M. ...KC	L	0	1	2.45	38	0	0	10	0	0	55.0	55	19	15	5	1	3	1	23	42	0	0	.262
Maldonado, C. ...KC	R	0	0	8.22	5	0	0	2	0	0	7.2	11	7	7	0	0	1	0	9	7	0	0	.333
Manuel, B. ...TEX	R	1	0	1.13	8	0	0	5	0	0	16.0	7	2	2	0	0	3	0	6	5	2	0	.143

PITCHER	TEAM	T	W	L	ERA	G	GS	CG	SHO	GF	SV	IP	H	TBF	R	ER	HR	SH	SF	HB	BB	IBB	SO	WP	BK	OPP AVG
Manzanillo, J ......BOS	R	0	0	18.00	1	0	0	0	0	0	1.0	2	8	2	2	0	0	0	0	3	0	1	0	0	.400
Mathews, T ....TEX	R	4	2	3.61	34	2	0	0	8	1	57.1	54	236	24	23	5	0	6	0	18	3	51	5	0	.251
McCaskill, K ......CAL	R	10	19	4.26	30	30	0	0	0	0	177.2	193	762	93	84	19	6	6	3	66	1	71	6	0	.283
McClure, B ....CAL	L	0	8	9.31	13	0	0	0	2	0	9.2	13	48	11	10	3	6	1	0	5	0	5	2	1	.317
McDonald, B ......BAL	R	6	8	4.84	21	21	4	0	0	0	126.1	126	532	71	68	16	1	3	4	43	0	85	3	1	.261
McDowell, J ....CHI	R	17	10	3.41	35	35	15	3	0	0	253.2	212	1028	97	96	19	8	4	2	82	2	191	10	0	.228
McGaffigan, A ....KC	R	0	0	4.50	4	0	0	0	1	0	8.0	14	39	5	4	0	0	4	0	2	0	3	0	0	.389
Meacham, R ......DET	R	2	1	5.20	10	0	0	0	4	0	27.2	35	126	17	16	4	1	3	0	11	0	14	0	1	.315
Mesa, J ....BAL	R	6	11	5.97	23	23	2	1	0	0	123.2	151	566	86	82	11	5	4	3	62	0	64	3	1	.307
Milacki, B ....BAL	R	10	9	4.01	31	26	3	0	1	0	184.0	175	758	86	82	17	7	5	1	53	3	108	1	2	.253
Mills, A ....NY	R	1	1	4.41	6	0	0	0	3	0	16.1	16	72	9	8	1	0	0	0	8	0	11	2	0	.254
Monteleone, R ......NY	R	3	1	3.64	26	0	0	0	10	0	47.0	42	201	27	19	5	2	2	1	19	3	34	1	1	.236
Montgomery, J...KC	R	4	4	2.90	67	0	0	0	55	33	90.0	83	376	32	29	6	6	4	0	28	2	77	0	0	.246
Moore, M........OAK	R	17	8	2.96	33	33	3	1	0	0	210.0	176	887	75	69	11	5	4	3	105	1	153	14	1	.229
Morris, J ....MIN	R	18	12	3.43	35	35	10	2	0	0	246.2	226	1032	107	94	18	5	8	5	92	5	163	15	1	.245
Morton, K ......BOS	R	6	5	4.59	16	15	0	0	0	0	86.1	93	379	49	44	9	3	7	5	40	0	45	1	1	.284
Munoz, M ....DET	L	0	0	9.64	6	0	0	0	4	0	9.1	14	46	11	10	4	3	0	1	10	0	3	1	0	.350
Murphy, R ......SEA	L	0	1	3.00	57	0	0	0	26	4	48.0	47	211	17	16	4	3	1	0	19	4	34	4	0	.250
Mussina, M ......BAL	R	4	5	2.87	12	12	2	0	0	0	87.2	77	349	31	28	7	4	3	1	21	7	52	3	1	.239
Mutis, J ....CLE	L	0	3	11.68	3	3	0	0	1	0	12.1	23	68	16	16	1	1	2	0	6	7	6	1	2	.397
Nagy, C ....CLE	R	10	15	4.13	33	33	6	2	0	0	211.1	228	914	103	97	15	5	9	6	66	7	109	6	2	.275
Navarro, J ......MIL	R	15	12	3.92	34	34	10	2	0	0	234.0	237	1002	117	102	18	7	8	0	73	3	114	10	0	.261
Neagle, D ....MIN	L	0	1	4.05	7	3	0	0	2	0	20.0	28	92	9	9	3	2	0	0	7	1	14	1	0	.329
Nelson, G ....OAK	R	1	5	6.84	44	0	0	0	11	0	48.2	60	229	38	37	12	6	4	3	23	1	23	0	0	.306
Nichols, R ....TEX	R	2	11	3.54	31	16	3	1	4	0	137.1	145	578	63	54	6	6	0	6	30	3	76	3	3	.273
Nolte, E ....TEX	L	0	0	3.38	3	0	0	0	2	0	2.2	3	14	1	1	0	0	0	0	3	0	1	0	0	.273
Nunez, E ....MIL	R	2	1	6.04	23	0	0	0	18	2	25.1	28	119	20	17	6	2	0	0	13	2	24	0	0	.277
Olin, S ....CLE	R	3	6	3.36	48	0	0	0	32	17	56.1	61	249	26	21	2	2	1	1	23	7	38	0	0	.274
Olson, G ....BAL	R	4	6	3.18	72	0	0	0	62	31	73.2	74	319	28	26	4	5	3	1	29	5	72	8	1	.262
Orosco, J ....CLE	L	2	0	3.74	47	0	0	0	20	0	45.2	52	202	20	19	7	8	3	1	15	8	36	1	0	.286
Otto, D ....CLE	L	2	8	4.23	18	14	1	0	0	0	100.0	108	425	52	47	7	8	4	4	27	6	47	3	0	.283

Pitcher	T	W	L	ERA	G	IP	H	R	ER	BB	SO	BA
Pall, D. ....CHI	R	7	2	2.41	51	71.0	59	22	19	24	40	.231
Patterson, K. ......CHI	L	3	0	2.83	43	63.2	48	22	20	35	32	.214
Pecota, B. ....KC	R	0	0	4.50	1	2.0	4	1	1	1	1	.444
Perez, M. ....CHI	R	8	7	3.12	49	135.2	111	49	47	52	128	.224
Perez, P. ....NY	R	2	4	3.18	14	73.2	68	26	26	16	41	.250
Petkovsek, M. .....TEX	R	0	1	14.46	4	9.1	21	15	15	7	6	.438
Petry, D. ....DET-BOS	R	2	3	4.79	30	77.0	87	41	41	30	30	.286
Plesac, D. ....MIL	L	2	7	4.29	45	92.1	92	49	44	39	61	.263
Plunk, E. ....NY	R	2	5	4.76	43	111.2	128	69	59	62	103	.286
Plympton, J. ....BOS	R	0	0	0.00	4	5.1	5	0	0	6	2	.263
Poole, J. ....TEX-BAL	L	3	2	2.36	29	42.0	29	14	11	12	38	.196
Radinsky, S. ....CHI	L	5	5	2.02	67	71.1	53	18	16	23	49	.206
Reardon, J. ....BOS	R	1	4	3.03	57	59.1	54	21	20	16	44	.236
Rhodes, A. ....BAL	L	0	3	8.00	8	36.0	47	35	32	23	23	.320
Rice, P. ....SEA	R	0	1	3.00	7	21.0	18	10	7	10	12	.234
Ritz, K. ....DET	R	0	3	11.74	11	15.1	17	22	20	22	10	.288
Robinson, J. ....CAL	R	0	3	5.37	39	57.0	56	34	34	29	57	.259
Robinson, J. ....BAL	R	4	9	5.18	21	104.1	119	62	60	51	62	.289
Robinson, R. ....MIL	R	0	0	6.23	1	4.1	6	3	3	3	3	.353
Rogers, K. ....TEX	L	10	10	5.42	63	109.2	121	72	66	61	73	.281
Rosenthal, W. ......TEX	R	1	4	5.25	36	70.1	72	43	41	36	61	.257
Russell, J. ....TEX	R	6	4	3.29	68	79.1	71	36	29	26	52	.236
Ryan, N. ....TEX	R	12	6	2.91	27	173.0	102	58	56	72	203	.172
Saberhagen, B. ......KC	R	13	8	3.07	28	196.1	165	79	67	45	136	.228
Sanderson, S. ....NY	R	16	10	3.81	34	208.0	200	95	88	29	130	.252
Schatzeder, D. ......KC	L	0	0	9.45	8	6.2	11	9	7	7	4	.367
Schiraldi, C. ....TEX	R	0	0	11.57	3	4.2	9	6	6	5	7	.263
Schooler, M. ....SEA	R	3	8	3.67	34	34.1	25	17	14	10	31	.198
Seanez, R. ....CLE	R	0	1	16.20	5	5.0	10	10	9	7	7	.385
Searcy, S. ....DET	L	2	3	8.41	16	40.2	33	40	38	30	30	.313
Shaw, J. ....CLE	R	0	5	3.36	29	72.1	72	34	27	27	31	.262
Show, E. ....OAK	R	1	2	5.92	23	51.2	62	34	34	17	20	.300
Slusarski, J. ....OAK	R	5	7	5.27	20	109.1	121	64	64	52	60	.283

PITCHER	TEAM	T	W	L	ERA	G	GS	CG	SHO	GF	SV	IP	H	TBF	R	ER	HR	SH	SF	HB	BB	IBB	SO	WP	BK	OPP AVG
Smith, R	BAL	R	5	4	5.60	17	14	0	0	0	0	80.1	99	348	52	50	9	2	3	1	24	0	25	3	1	.311
Stewart, D	OAK	R	11	11	5.18	35	35	2	1	0	0	226.0	245	1014	135	130	24	5	15	9	105	2	144	13	0	.278
Stieb, D	TOR	R	4	3	3.17	9	9	1	0	0	0	59.2	52	244	22	21	4	4	2	0	23	0	29	0	0	.243
Stottlemyre, T	TOR	R	15	8	3.78	34	34	0	0	0	0	219.0	194	921	97	92	21	4	8	12	75	3	116	4	0	.235
Swan, R	SEA	L	6	2	3.43	63	0	0	0	11	0	78.2	81	336	35	30	8	6	1	0	28	3	33	8	0	.269
Swift, B	SEA	R	1	2	1.99	71	0	0	0	30	17	90.1	74	359	22	20	3	2	1	0	26	7	48	6	0	.224
Swindell, G	CLE	L	9	16	3.48	33	33	7	0	0	0	238.0	241	971	112	92	21	13	8	3	31	4	169	2	1	.263
Tanana, F	DET	L	13	12	3.77	33	33	3	2	0	0	217.1	217	920	98	91	26	12	9	3	78	9	107	3	1	.265
Tapani, K	MIN	R	16	9	2.99	34	34	4	1	0	0	244.0	225	974	84	81	23	9	6	2	40	0	135	3	1	.245
Taylor, W	NY	R	7	12	6.27	23	22	0	0	0	0	116.1	144	528	85	81	13	2	7	7	53	0	72	3	3	.314
Telford, A	BAL	R	0	0	4.05	9	1	0	0	4	0	26.2	27	109	12	12	3	1	0	0	6	0	24	1	0	.265
Terrell, W	DET	R	12	14	4.24	35	33	8	0	2	0	218.2	257	954	115	103	16	10	9	2	79	10	80	8	0	.301
Thigpen, B	CHI	R	7	5	3.49	67	0	0	0	58	30	69.2	63	309	32	27	10	7	3	4	38	8	47	2	0	.245
Timlin, M	TOR	R	11	6	3.16	63	3	0	0	17	3	108.1	94	463	43	38	6	6	2	1	50	11	85	5	2	.233
Valdez, E	CLE	L	0	0	1.50	7	0	0	0	1	0	6.0	5	27	1	1	0	1	1	0	3	1	11	0	0	.238
Valdez, S	CLE	R	1	0	5.51	6	2	0	0	0	0	16.1	15	70	11	10	3	1	1	0	5	0	11	1	0	.238
Valenzuela, F	CAL	L	0	2	12.15	2	1	0	0	0	0	6.2	14	36	10	9	0	1	0	0	3	0	5	0	0	.452
Van Poppel, T	OAK	R	0	0	9.64	1	1	0	0	0	0	4.2	7	21	5	5	1	1	0	0	2	0	6	0	0	.368
Wagner, H	KC	R	1	1	7.20	2	2	0	0	0	0	10.0	16	49	10	8	2	0	0	0	3	0	5	0	0	.348
Walker, M	CLE	R	0	1	2.08	5	0	0	0	3	0	4.1	6	22	1	1	0	1	0	0	2	1	2	0	0	.316
Walton, B	OAK	R	1	0	6.23	12	0	0	0	5	0	13.0	11	56	9	9	3	0	0	0	6	0	10	3	0	.229
Wapnick, S	CHI	R	0	1	1.80	6	0	0	0	4	0	5.0	2	22	1	1	1	0	0	0	4	0	1	0	0	.111
Ward, D	TOR	R	7	6	2.77	81	0	0	0	46	23	107.1	80	428	36	33	3	3	4	2	33	3	132	6	0	.207
Wayne, G	MIN	L	1	1	5.11	38	0	0	0	2	2	12.1	11	52	9	7	1	1	2	1	4	1	4	0	0	.244
Weathers, D	TOR	R	1	0	4.91	15	0	0	0	4	0	14.2	15	79	9	8	1	2	1	2	17	3	13	0	0	.263
Wegman, B	MIL	R	15	7	2.84	28	28	7	2	0	0	193.1	176	785	76	61	16	6	4	7	40	6	89	6	2	.242
Welch, B	OAK	R	12	13	4.58	35	35	7	1	0	0	220.0	220	950	124	112	25	6	6	11	91	3	101	3	2	.263
Wells, D	TOR	L	15	10	3.72	40	28	0	0	3	1	198.1	188	811	88	82	24	6	6	2	49	1	106	10	3	.252
West, D	MIN	L	4	4	4.54	15	12	0	0	2	0	71.1	66	305	37	36	13	6	3	1	28	0	52	3	0	.244
Weston, M	TOR	R	0	0	0.00	2	0	0	0	0	0	2.0	1	8	0	0	0	1	0	0	1	0	1	0	0	.143
Williamson, M	BAL	R	5	5	4.48	65	0	0	0	21	4	80.1	87	357	42	40	9	1	5	0	35	7	53	0	0	.275

Pitcher	T	W	L	ERA	G	GS	CG	GF	SV	IP	H	TBF	R	ER	HR	SH	HB	BB	IBB	SO	WP	BK	AVG
Willis, C ......MIN	R	8	3	2.63	40	0	0	9	2	89.0	76	355	31	26	3	4	1	19	2	53	4	1	.232
Willis, F ......TOR	R	0	1	16.62	4	0	0	3	0	4.1	8	27	8	8	2	0	1	5	0	2	0	0	.421
Witt, B ......TEX	R	3	7	6.09	17	16	1	0	0	88.2	84	413	66	60	3	4	1	74	1	82	8	0	.254
Witt, M ......NY	R	1	1	10.13	2	2	0	0	0	5.1	8	26	7	6	0	0	1	1	0	0	1	0	.320
York, M ......CLE	R	1	4	6.75	14	4	0	3	0	34.2	45	163	29	26	3	4	0	19	3	19	2	0	.333
Young, C ......OAK	L	4	2	5.00	41	0	0	6	6	68.1	74	306	38	38	3	1	2	34	2	27	0	0	.278
Young, C ......CAL	L	1	0	4.26	11	1	0	1	0	12.2	12	49	6	6	0	0	0	3	1	6	0	0	.261
Young, M ......BOS	L	3	7	5.18	19	16	0	1	0	88.2	92	404	55	51	1	2	2	53	2	69	5	0	.266

CLUB PITCHING

CLUB	W	L	ERA	G	CG	SHO	REL	SV	IP	H	R	ER	HR	HB	BB	IBB	SO	WP	BK	OPP AVG
TORONTO	91	71	3.50	162	10	16	347	60	1462.2	1301	622	569	121	43	523	41	971	55	8	.238
CALIFORNIA	81	81	3.69	162	18	10	310	50	1441.2	1351	649	591	141	38	543	29	990	49	11	.250
MINNESOTA	95	67	3.69	162	21	12	291	53	1449.1	1402	652	595	139	27	488	39	876	57	5	.255
SEATTLE	83	79	3.79	162	10	13	383	48	1464.1	1387	674	616	136	47	628	50	1003	82	7	.253
CHICAGO	87	75	3.79	162	28	8	338	40	1478.0	1302	681	622	154	31	601	25	923	44	6	.239
KANSAS CITY ..	82	80	3.92	162	17	12	295	41	1466.0	1473	722	639	105	43	529	44	1004	47	5	.261
BOSTON	84	78	4.01	162	15	13	328	45	1439.2	1405	712	642	147	31	530	59	999	42	5	.257
MILWAUKEE	83	79	4.14	162	23	11	341	41	1463.2	1498	744	674	147	45	527	31	859	53	4	.266
CLEVELAND	57	105	4.23	162	22	8	289	33	1441.1	1551	759	678	110	39	441	61	862	48	5	.276
NEW YORK	71	91	4.42	162	3	11	377	37	1444.0	1510	777	709	152	42	506	29	936	53	6	.271
TEXAS	85	77	4.47	162	9	10	386	41	1479.0	1486	814	734	151	45	662	37	1022	77	14	.262
DETROIT	84	78	4.51	162	18	8	326	38	1450.1	1570	794	726	148	24	593	88	739	50	12	.281
OAKLAND	84	78	4.57	162	14	10	397	49	1444.1	1425	776	734	155	55	655	30	892	60	5	.260
BALTIMORE	67	95	4.59	162	8	8	372	42	1457.2	1534	796	743	147	28	504	40	868	49	7	.273
TOTALS	1134	1134	4.09		216	150	4780	618	20382.0	20195	10172	9272	1953	538	7730	603	12944	766	103	.260

OFFICIAL 1992 AMERICAN LEAGUE SCHEDULE

BOLD = SUNDAY   ( ) = HOLIDAY   * = NIGHT GAME   (2) DOUBLEHEADER

	AT SEATTLE	AT OAKLAND	AT CALIFORNIA	AT TEXAS	AT KANSAS CITY	AT MINNESOTA	AT CHICAGO
SEATTLE		June 22*,23*,24 Sept. 10*,11*,12,13	April 24*,25*,26 July 27*,28*,29,30	June 8*,9*,10* Sept. 25*,26*,27	June 5*,6*,7 Sept. 21*,22*,23*,24*	June 19*,20*,21 Sept. (7),8*,9	April 13,15*,16* July 31* Aug. 1*,2
OAKLAND	June 29*,30* July 1 Sept. 18*,19*,20		June 19* 20,21 Sept. (7),8*,9	April 17*,18,19 Aug. 3*,4*,5*,6*	April 13,14*,15*,16* July 31* Aug. 1,2*	April 24*,25,26 July 27*,28*,29*	June 5*,6*,7 Sept. 21*,22*,23*,24*
CALIFORNIA	June 25*,26*,27*,**28** Sept. 15*,16	April 20*,21*,22 Aug. 13,14*,15,16		April 13*,14*,15*,16* July 31* Aug. 1*,2*	April 17*,18,19 Aug. 4*,5*,6	June 22*,23*,24 Sept. 11*,12,13	June 8*,9*,10*,11 Sept. 25*,26*,27
TEXAS	April 6*,7*,8*,9* Aug. 7*,8*,9	June 12*,13,14 Sept. 29*,30* Oct. 1*	June 15*,16*,17* Oct. 2*,3*,4		May 29*,30*,31 Aug. 31* Sept. 1*,2*	April 10*,11*,12* Aug. 10*,11*,12*,13	Apri. 30* May 1*,2,3 Aug. 18*,19*,20
KANSAS CITY	April 10*,11*,12 Aug. 10*,11*,12	April 6*,8*,9 Aug. 7*,8,9	June 12*,13*,14 Sept. 28*,29*,30* Oct. 1	May 21*,22*,23*,24 Aug. 25*,26*,27*		June 15*,16*,17*,18 Sept. 25*,26*,27	May 18*,19*,20* Aug. 21*,22*,23
MINNESOTA	April 20*,21*,22,23 Aug. 14*,15*,16	June 25,26*,27,28 Sept. 14*,15*,16	June 29*,30* July 1 Sept. 17*,18*,19*,20	June 4*,5*,6*,7* Sept. 22*,23*	June 8*,9*,10* Oct. 2*,3*,4		April 17*,18*,19 Aug. 4*,5,6
CHICAGO	June 15*,16*,17*,18 Oct. 2*,3*,4	April 10*,11,12 Aug. 10*,11*,12	April 7*,8*,9* Aug. 7*,8,9	May 26*,27*,28* Aug. 28*,29*,30*	June 1*,2*,3* Sept. 3*,4*,5*,6	June 12*,13,14 Sept. 28*,29*,30* Oct. 1	

MILWAUKEE	June 12*,13*,14 Sept. 29*,30* Oct. 1*	April 10*,11*,12 Aug. 10*,11*,12	May 8*,9,10 July 6*,7*,8*	May 6*,7* July 2*,3*,(4),5	April 14*,15* July 30*,31* Aug. 1*,2	May 4*,5* July 16*,17*,18*,19
DETROIT	May 8*,9,10 July 20*,21*,22*	May 12*,13 July 23*,24*,25,26	April 21*,22*,23* Aug. 14*,15*,16*	May 15*,16*,17 Aug. 17*,18*,19*	May 29,30*,31 Aug. 24*,25*,26*	June 19*,20*,21 Sept. 8*,9*,10*
CLEVELAND	May 22*,23*,24 Aug. 25*,26*,27*	May 29*,30*,31 Aug. 31* Sept. 1*,2	May 6*,7* July 9*,10*,11*,12*	May 12*,13* July 16*,17*,18*,19	May 8*,9,10 July 20*,21*,22	June 22*,23*,24* Sept. 11*,12*,13
TORONTO	May 6*,7* July 16*,17*,18*,19	May 4*,5* July 23*,24*,25,26	June 22*,23*,24* Sept. 11*,12*,13	June 19*,20*,21 Sept. (7*),8*,9*	June 1*,2*,3* Aug. 21*,22*,23	May 22*,23*,24 Aug. 24*,25*,26*
BALTIMORE	May 29,30,31 Aug. 31* Sept. 1*,2	June 1*,2*,3 July 4*,5,6	May 12*,13* July 16*,17*,18*,19*	April 21*,22*,23* Aug. 14*,15*,16	April 27*,28*,29 July 3*,(4),5	May 15*,16*,17 July 20*,21*,22
NEW YORK	May 26,26*,27 Aug. 28*,29*,30	May 6*,7* July 16*,17*,18*,19	June 1*,2*,3* July 3*,(4*),5*	June 23*,24*,25 Sept. 18*,19*,20	May 26*,27 Aug. 27*,28*,20*,30	April 21*,22* Aug. 14*,15*,16*,17*
BOSTON	May 29*,30*,31 Aug. 31* Sept. 1*,2	May 26*,27*,28* Aug. 28*,29,30	June 19*,20*,21* Sept. (7*),8*,9*	May 8*,9,10 July 20*,21*,22*	May 12*,13* July 16*,17*,18,19	May 6*,7 July 2*,3*,(4*),5

JULY 14 - ALL - STAR GAME AT SAN DIEGO.

OFFICIAL 1992 AMERICAN LEAGUE SCHEDULE

BOLD = SUNDAY ( ) = HOLIDAY * = NIGHT GAME (2) DOUBLEHEADER

	AT MILWAUKEE	AT DETROIT	AT CLEVELAND	AT TORONTO	AT BALTIMORE	AT NEW YORK	AT BOSTON
SEATTLE	April 17*,18,19 Aug. 4*,5,6	April 28*,29* July 3*(4*),5,6	June 2,3,4* Sept. 4*,5,6	May 14*,15*,16,17 July 7*,8*	May 1*,2,3 Aug. 18*,19*,20	May 12*,13* July 9*,10*,11,12	May 18*,19*,20* Aug. 21*,22,23
OAKLAND	June 8*,9*,10 Sept. 25*,26,27	April 30* May 1*,2,3 July 7*,8*	April 28*,29* July 3*,(4),5*,6*	May 12*,13* July 9*,10*,11,12	May 18*,19*,20* Aug. 21*,22,23	May 15,16,17 Aug. 18*,19*,20*	May 22*,23,24 Aug. 24*,25*,26
CALIFORNIA	June 5*,6*,7 Sept. 22*,23*,24*	May 4*,5 July 9*,10*,11,12	April 30 May 1*,2,3 July 7*,8*	April 28*,29* July 3*,4,5,6*	May 22*,23*,24 Aug. 24*,25*,26*	May 18*,19*,20* Aug. 21*,22,23	May 15,16,17 Aug. 18*,19*,20*
TEXAS	May 15*,16,17* July 20*,21*,22	June 25*,26*,27,28 Sept. 15*,16*	May 18*,19*,20* Aug. 21*,22,23	June 29*,30* July (1) Sept. 18*,19,20	May 4*,5 July 23*,24*,25,26	April 27*,28*,29* Sept. 4*,5,6	April 24*,25,26 July 27*,28*,29*
KANSAS CITY	April 28*,29 July 9*,10*,11,12	May 26*,27*,28* Aug. 28,29,30	May 4*,5* July 23*,24*,25,26	April 24*,25,26* July 28*,29*,30*	June 26*,27*,28 Sept. 14*,15*,16*	June 29*,30* July 1 Sept. 11*,12,13	May 1*,2,3 July 6*,7*,8*
MINNESOTA	April 6,8*,9 Aug. 7,8*,9	May 22*,23,24* Aug. 31* Sept. 1,2	May 15,16,17 Aug. 18*,19*,20*	May (18),19*,20* Sept. 4,5,6	May 6*,7* July 9*,10*,11,12	May 1*,2,3 July 6*,7*,8*	May 4*,5* July 23*,24*,25,26*
CHICAGO	May 12*,13 July 23*,24*,25*,26	April 24*,25*,26 July 28*,29*,30	June 29*,30* July 1* Sept. 18*,19,20	May 29*,30,31 Aug. 31* Sept. 1*,2	May 8*,9*,10 July 6*,7*,8*	June 26*,27,28* Sept. 14*,15*,16*	April 28*,29* July 9*,10*,11,12

	vs MILWAUKEE	vs DETROIT	vs CLEVELAND	vs TORONTO	vs BALTIMORE	vs NEW YORK	vs BOSTON
MILWAUKEE		May 18*,19*,20*,21* / Sept. 4*,5*,6	April 24*,25,26 / July 27*,28*,29	May 26*,27* / Aug. 27,28* 29,30	June 29*,30* / July 1 / Sept. 11*,12*,13	May 22*,23,24,(25) / Aug. 24*,25*,26*	June 26*,27,28 / Sept. 14*,15*,16*,17*
DETROIT	June 1*,2*,3 / Aug. 21*,22*,23		April 13,14*,15*,16 / July 31* / Aug. 1,2	June 16*,17*,18 / Oct. 2,3,4	April 17*,18,19,20* / Aug. 3*,4*,5*	June 4*,5,6*,7 / Sept. 22*,23*,24*	June 29*,30* / July 1* / Sept. 11*,12,13
CLEVELAND	June 18*,19*,20*,21 / Sept. (7),8*,9*	June 8*,9*,10* / Sept. 25,26,27		April 21,22*,23* / Sept. 14*,15*,16*,17*	April 6,8,9* / Aug. 7,8,9	April 17*,18,19,20 / Aug. 3*,4*,5*	June 5*,6,7 / Sept. 22*,23*,24*
TORONTO	April 30* / May 1*,2,3 / Aug. 18*,19*,20	April 6,8,9 / Aug. 6*,7,8* 9	June 26*,27*,28 / Aug. 14*,15*,16		April 10,11,12 / Aug. 10*,11*,12,13	June 8*,9*,10* / Sept. 25,26,27	April 17*,18,19,20 / Aug. 3*,4*,5
BALTIMORE	June 23*,24*,25 / Sept. 18*,19*,20,21*	June 11*,12*,13*,14 / Sept. 29*,30*	June 15*,16*,17 / Oct. 1*,2*,3,4	April 10,11,12 / Aug. 10*,11*,12,13		April 24*,25,26 / July 28*,29*,30	April 13,15,16* / July 31* / Aug. 1,2
NEW YORK	May 29*,30*,31 / Aug. 31* / Sept. 1*,2	April 10*,11,12 / Aug. 10*,11*,12	June 12*,13,14 / Sept. 28*,29*,30*	April 13*,14*,15*,16 / July 31* / Aug. 1,2	June 19*,20*,21*,22* / Sept. (7*),8*,9*		June 15*,16*,17*,18* / Oct. 2*,3,4
BOSTON	April 21*,22*,23 / Sept. 24	April 22*,23,24 / Sept. 18*,19,20,21*	April 11,12(2) / Aug. 10*,11*,12*,13*	June 11*,12*,13,14 / Sept. 29*,30*	April 13*,14*,15*,16 / July 31* / Aug. 1,2	April 7,9* / Aug. 6,7,8,9	

JULY 14 - ALL - STAR GAME AT SAN DIEGO

OFFICIAL 1992

EAST

	AT CHICAGO	AT MONTREAL	AT NEW YORK
Chicago		June 5*(tn),7 Aug. 3*,4*,5* Sept. 25*,26*,27	June 22*,23*,24*,25 July 31*, Aug. 1*,2 Sept. 21*,22*
Montreal	June 12,13*,14 Aug. 10,11,12 Oct. 2,3,4		April 10,11,12 June 15*,16*,17* Sept. 18*,19,20
New York	June 29,30*,July 1 Aug. 6*,7,8,9* Sept. 14*,15	April 17*,18,19 June 8*,9*,10* Sept. 11*,12*,13*	
Philadelphia	April 20*,21,22,23 June 26,27,28 Sept. 16,17	June 22*,23*,24 July 30*,31*, Aug. 1*,2 Sept. 21*,22*	April 13*,14*,15* Aug. 14*,15*,16 Sept. 28*,29*,30*
Pittsburgh	April 24,25,26 July 27*,28,29 Sept. 28,29*,30	April 20,21*,22*,23 June 26*,27*,28 Sept. 23*,24*	June 12*,13*,14 Aug. 10*,11*,12 Oct. 2*,3,4
St. Louis	April 10,11,12 June 15*,16,17 Sept. 18,19,20	April 13,14*,15* Aug. 14*,15*,16 Sept. 7,8*,9*	April 21*,22*,23 June 18*,19*,20*,21 Sept. 16*,17*
Atlanta	May 4*,5 July 9*,10,11*,12	May 22*,23,24 Aug. 18*,19*,20*	May 29*,30,31 Aug. 31*, Sept. 1*,2
Cincinnati	May 8,9,10 July 6*,7,8	May 18,19*,20* Aug. 21*,22*,23	May 25*,26*,27* Aug. 28*,29,30*
Houston	May 6,7* Aug. 13*,14,15,16	May 25,26*,27 Sept. 4*,5*,6	April 28*,29*,30* July 3*,4*,5
Los Angeles	May 29,30,31 Aug. 31*,Sept. 1,2	May 11*,12*,13* July 24*,25*,26	May 8*,9,10 July 20*,21*,22
San Diego	June 1*,2,3 Sept. 4,5,6	May 5*,6* July 16*,17*,18*,19	May 11*,12*,13* July 24*,25*,26
San Francisco	May 26*,27,28 Aug. 28,29,30	May 8*,9,10 July 20*,21*,22*	June 1*,2* July 16*,17*,18*,19

* NIGHT GAME   (tn) Twi-Night Doubleheader
HEAVY BLACK FIGURES DENOTE SUNDAYS
NIGHT GAMES: ANY GAME STARTING AFTER 5:00 P.M.

NATIONAL LEAGUE SCHEDULE

EAST

	AT PHILADELPHIA	AT PITTSBURGH	AT ST. LOUIS
Chicago	April 7,8*,9* June 18*,19*,20*,21 Sept. 23*,24*	April 14*,15* July 16*,17*,18*,19* Sept. 7,8*,9*	April 17*,18,19 June 8*,9*,10* Sept. 11*,12*,13*
Montreal	June 29*,30*, July 1* Aug. 6*,7*,8*,9 Sept. 14*,15*	April 6*,8*,9 June 18*,19*,20*,21 Sept. 16*,17*	April 24*,25*,26 July 27*,28*,29* Sept. 28*,29*,30*
New York	April 24*,25*,26 July 27*,28*,29 Sept. 7*,8*,9*	June 4*,5*,6*,7 Aug. 4*,5* Sept. 25*,26*,27	April 6*,7*,8*,9 June 26*,27,28 Sept. 23*,24*
Philadelphia		April 17*,18,19 June 15*,16*,17* Sept. 18*,19*,20	June 12*,13*,14 Aug. 3*,4*,5 Oct. 2*,3,4
Pittsburgh	April 10*,11*,12 June 8*,9*,10* Sept. 11*,12*,13		June 29*,30*,July 1 Aug. 6*,7*,8*,9 Sept. 14*,15*
St. Louis	June 5*,6*,7* Aug. 11*,12*,13* Sept. 25*,26*,27	June 22*,23*,24* July 30*,31*, Aug. 1,2 Sept. 21*,22*	
Atlanta	May 25*,26*27* Aug, 28*,29*,30	May 6*,7* Aug. 14*,15*,16*,17*	May 8*,9*,10,11* July 21*,22*
Cincinnati	May 22*,23*,24 Aug.17*,18*,19	May 4*,5* July 2*,3*,4,5	May 12*,13* July 23*,24*,25*,26
Houston	May 18*,19*,20* Aug. 21*,22*,23	May 8*,9*,10 July 6*,7*,8*	May 22*,23*,24 Aug. 18*,19*,20*
Los Angeles	May 5*,6* July 16,17*,18*,19	June 1*,2*,3 Sept. 4*,5*,6	May 25,26*,27* Aug. 28*,29*,30
San Diego	May 8*,9*,10 July 20*,21*,22*	May 15*,16*,17 Aug. 18*,19*,20	May 29*,30*,31 Aug. 31*, Sept. 1*,2*
San Francisco	May 11*,12*,13* July 24*,25*,26	May 29*,30*,31 Sept. 1*,2*,3*	May 5*,6*,7 Sept. 4*,5*,6

July 14 - All-Star Game at San Diego

OFFICIAL 1992

WEST

	AT ATLANTA	AT CINCINNATI	AT HOUSTON
Chicago	April 27*,28*,29 July 3*,4,**5**	May 1*,**2,3** July 20*,21*,22*	May 11*,12*,13* July 24*,25*,**26**
Montreal	May 15*,16*,**17** Aug. 25*,26*,27*	May 29*,30*,**31** Aug. 31*, Sept. 1*,2*	June 1*,2*,3* Aug. 28*,29*,**30**
New York	May 1*,2,**3** July 6*,7*,8*	May 6*,7 Sept. 3*,4*,5*,**6**	May 4*,5 July 9*,10*,11*,**12**
Philadelphia	June 1*,2*,3 Sept. 4*,5*,**6**	May 15*,16*,**17** Aug. 24*,25*,26*	May 29*,30*,**31** Aug. 31*,Sept. 1*,2*
Pittsburgh	May 12*,13*,14* July 24*,25*,**26**	April 28*,29* July 9*,10*,11*,**12**	May 1*,2*,**3*** July 20*,21*,22*
St. Louis	May 18*,19*,20* Aug. 21*,22*,**23***	June 2*,3 July 16*,17*,18*,**19**	May 15*,16*,**17** Aug. 25*,26*,27*
Atlanta		April 13*,14*,15 June 26*,27,**28** Sept. 15*,16*,17*	April 7*,8* July 16*,17*,18,**19** Sept. 11*,12*,**13**
Cincinnati	June 18*,19*,20*,**21** Aug. 4*,5*,6* Sept. 9*,10*		April 9*,10*,11*,**12** June 29*,30*,July 1 Sept. 7,8*
Houston	April 24*,25*,**26** July 27*,28*,29 Sept. 18*,19*,**20**	June 22*,23*,24* July 31*,Aug. 1*,**2,3** Sept. 21*,22	
Los Angeles	June 15*,16*,17* Aug. 7*,8,9,10* Sept. 7,8*	June 12*,13,**14*** Aug. 11*,12*,13 Sept. 29*,30*,Oct. 1*	April 13*,14*,15 June 19*,20,**21** Oct. 2*,3*,**4**
San Diego	June 12*,13*,**14** Aug. 11*,12*,13* Oct. 2*,3*,**4**	April 6,7*,8 Aug. 14*,15*,**16** Sept. 18*,19,**20**	April 17*,18*,**19** June 15*,16*,17 Sept. 29*,30*,Oct. 1*
San Francisco	April 9*,10*,11*,**12** June 23*,24* Sept. 29*,30*,Oct.1*	June 15*,16*,17 Aug. 7*,8*,**9** Oct. 2*,3,4	April 20*,21*,22* June 12*,13*,**14** Sept. 14*,15*,16*

* NIGHT GAME (tn) Twi-Night Doubleheader
HEAVY BLACK FIGURES DENOTE SUNDAYS
NIGHT GAMES: ANY GAME STARTING AFTER 5:00 P.M.

NATIONAL LEAGUE SCHEDULE

WEST

	AT LOS ANGELES	AT SAN DIEGO	AT SAN FRANCISCO
Chicago	May 18*,19*,20* Aug. 21*,22*,23	May 22*,23*,24 Aug. 24*,25*,26*	May 15*,16,17 Aug. 18*,19,20
Montreal	May 1*,2*,3 July 6*,7*,8	April 29*,30 July 2*,3*,4*,5	April 27*,28* July 9,10*,11,12
New York	May 15*,16*,17 Aug. 18*,19*,20*	May 18*,19*,20*,21 Aug. 22*,23	May 22*,23,24 Aug. 24*,25*,26
Philadelphia	April 29*,30* July 2*,3*,4*,5	April 27*,28* July 9,10*,11,12*	May 1*,2,3 July 6*,7*,8
Pittsburgh	May 22*,23*,24 Aug. 24*,25*,26*	May 25*,26*,27 Aug. 27,29*,30	May 19*,20,21 Aug. 21*,22,23
St. Louis	April 27*,28* July 9*,10*,11,12	May 1*,2*,3 July 6*,7*,8*	April 29,30 July 2*,3*,4*,5
Atlanta	April 16*,17*,18*,19* June 8*,9*,10 Sept. 21*,22*	April 20*,21*,22 June 5*,6*,7 Sept. 25*,26*,27	June 29*,30,July 1 July 30*,31*,Aug. 1,2 Sept. 23*,24
Cincinnati	April 20*,21*,22* June 4*,5*,6*,7 Sept. 23*,24*	April 24*,25*,26 July 27*,28*,29 Sept. 11*,12*,13	April 17*,18,19 June 8*,9*,10 Sept. 25*,26,27
Houston	June 25*,26*,27*,28 Aug. 4*,5* Sept. 25*,26,27	June 8*,9*,10 Aug. 6*,7*,8*,9 Sept. 23*,24	June 4*,5*,6,7 Aug. 10*,11,12 Sept. 9*,10
Los Angeles		April 9*,10*,11*,12 June 22*,23 Sept. 14*,15*,16*	April 24*,25,26 July 27*,28*,29 Sept. 18*,19,20*
San Diego	June 29*,30*, July 1 July 30*,31*,Aug. 1*,2 Sept. 9*,10*		April 14*,15*,16 June 18*,19*,20,21 Sept. 7*,8*
San Francisco	April 6,7* Aug. 14*,15*,16,17* Sept. 11*,12*,13	June 25*,26*,27*,28 Aug. 3*,4*,5* Sept. 21*,22	

July 14 - All-Star Game at San Diego

Roberto Alomar is dad Sandy Sr.'s superior at second.

Nolan Ryan: 314 Ws, 5,511 Ks . . . and counting.

Newly revised and updated third edition!

THE ILLUSTRATED SPORTS RECORD BOOK
Zander Hollander and David Schulz

Here, in a single book, are more than 400 all-time—and current—sports records with 50 new stories and 125 action photos so vivid, it's like "being there." Featured is an all-star cast that includes Martina Navratilova, Joe DiMaggio, Joe Montana, Michael Jordan, Jack Nicklaus, Mark Spitz, Wayne Gretzky, Nolan Ryan, Muhammad Ali, Greg LeMond, Hank Aaron, Carl Lewis and Magic Johnson. This is *the* authoritative book that sets the record straight and recreates the feats at the time of achievement!